W9-CAH-251

Frommer's®

Barcelona

3rd Edition

by Peter Stone

Here's what the critics say about Frommer's:

"Amazingly easy to use. Very portable, very complete."
—**BOOKLIST**

"Detailed, accurate, and easy-to-read information for all price ranges."
—**GLAMOUR MAGAZINE**

"Hotel information is close to encyclopedic."
—**DES MOINES SUNDAY REGISTER**

"Frommer's Guides have a way of giving you a real feel for a place."
—**KNIGHT RIDDER NEWSPAPERS**

WILEY
Wiley Publishing, Inc.

Published by:

WILEY PUBLISHING, INC.

111 River St.
Hoboken, NJ 07030-5774

ISBN 978-0-470-38747-4

Editor: Jennifer Polland
Production Editor: Michael Brumitt
Cartographer: Andrew Murphy
Photo Editor: Richard Fox
Production by Wiley Indianapolis Composition Services

Front cover photo: Interior detail of Els Quatre Gats Restaurant, waiter in foreground
Back cover photo: Barcelona, April Fair, women seen from behind, next to picture of flamenco dancers painted on wall

For information on our other products and services or to obtain technical support, please contact our Customer Care Department within the U.S. at 877/762-2974, outside the U.S. at 317/572-3993 or fax 317/572-4002.

Wiley also publishes its books in a variety of electronic formats. Some content that appears in print may not be available in electronic formats.

Manufactured in the United States of America

5   4   3   2   1

CONTENTS

4 SUGGESTED BARCELONA ITINERARIES 71

5 WHERE TO STAY 90

6 WHERE TO DINE 128

7 WHAT TO SEE & DO 169

8 STROLLING AROUND BARCELONA 207

9 SHOPPING 221

10 BARCELONA AFTER DARK 240

11 SIDE TRIPS IN CATALONIA 260

LIST OF MAPS

AN INVITATION TO THE READER

In researching this book, we discovered many wonderful places—hotels, restaurants, shops, and more. We're sure you'll find others. Please tell us about them, so we can share the information with your fellow travelers in upcoming editions. If you were disappointed with a recommendation, we'd love to know that, too. Please write to:

Frommer's Barcelona, 3rd Edition
Wiley Publishing, Inc. • 111 River St. • Hoboken, NJ 07030-5774

AN ADDITIONAL NOTE

Please be advised that travel information is subject to change at any time—and this is especially true of prices. We therefore suggest that you write or call ahead for confirmation when making your travel plans. The authors, editors, and publisher cannot be held responsible for the experiences of readers while traveling. Your safety is important to us, however, so we encourage you to stay alert and be aware of your surroundings. Keep a close eye on cameras, purses, and wallets, all favorite targets of thieves and pickpockets.

ABOUT THE AUTHOR

Born in London England, **Peter Stone** started his working life in the Foreign Office in Downing Street before moving on to translating and journalism. Over the last 29 years he has resided in different areas of Spain, including Málaga, Barcelona, Alicante, Palma de Mallorca, and Las Palmas de Gran Canaria, and also lived in Greece and North Africa. A lifelong lover of Spanish culture, history and language, he made Madrid his home in 1998, and his publications on the Spanish capital include *Madrid Escapes* and *Frommer's Madrid*. He has also contributed to a wide variety of international magazines and guidebooks, including *Time Out, Insight, Intelliguide, Spain Gourmetour,* and *Pauline Frommer's Spain.*

Other Great Guides for Your Trip:

Frommer's Spain 2009
Frommer's Madrid
Frommer's Europe
Spain For Dummies

FROMMER'S STAR RATINGS, ICONS & ABBREVIATIONS

Every hotel, restaurant, and attraction listing in this guide has been ranked for quality, value, service, amenities, and special features using a **star-rating system.** In country, state, and regional guides, we also rate towns and regions to help you narrow down your choices and budget your time accordingly. Hotels and restaurants are rated on a scale of zero (recommended) to three stars (exceptional). Attractions, shopping, nightlife, towns, and regions are rated according to the following scale: zero stars (recommended), one star (highly recommended), two stars (very highly recommended), and three stars (must-see).

In addition to the star-rating system, we also use **seven feature icons** that point you to the great deals, in-the-know advice, and unique experiences that separate travelers from tourists. Throughout the book, look for:

Finds	Special finds—those places only insiders know about
Fun Facts	Fun facts—details that make travelers more informed and their trips more fun
Kids	Best bets for kids, and advice for the whole family
Moments	Special moments—those experiences that memories are made of
Overrated	Places or experiences not worth your time or money
Tips	Insider tips—great ways to save time and money
Value	Great values—where to get the best deals

The following **abbreviations** are used for credit cards:

AE	American Express	DISC	Discover	V	Visa
DC	Diners Club	MC	MasterCard		

FROMMERS.COM

Now that you have this guidebook to help you plan a great trip, visit our website at **www.frommers.com** for additional travel information on more than 4,000 destinations. We update features regularly to give you instant access to the most current trip-planning information available. At Frommers.com, you'll find scoops on the best airfares, lodging rates, and car rental bargains. You can even book your travel online through our reliable travel booking partners. Other popular features include:

- Online updates of our most popular guidebooks
- Vacation sweepstakes and contest giveaways
- Newsletters highlighting the hottest travel trends
- Podcasts, interactive maps, and up-to-the-minute events listings
- Opinionated blog entries by Arthur Frommer himself
- Online travel message boards with featured travel discussions

What's New in Barcelona

Ever inventive and dynamic, Barcelona is a city that is constantly changing and advancing deeper into the 21st century. In Barceloneta, the city's harborfront region, the huge horseshoe-shaped Brullet-Pineda–designed **Barcelona Biomedical Research Park** (**PRBB;** www.prbb.org), between the Hospital del Mars and Arts Hotel, was finished in 2008. It features state-of-the-art laboratories, as well as an impressive auditorium and sports center. Around Port Olympic, just past Barceloneta, nearly 3,000 new apartments and houses are due for completion by 2009, and more renovations to the **Forum**—which hosted the city's 2004 exhibition—were carried out to prepare it for the Euro Science Open Forum in 2008. Meanwhile, west of the city center, just 3.2km (2 miles) from Montjuïc, work is continuing on the **Fira of Barcelona** (www.firabcn.es), which currently hosts 80 trade fairs a year. When construction is finished, it will be one of the largest business centers in Europe.

PLANNING YOUR TRIP TO BARCELONA Barcelona's El Prat airport, the second-largest airport in Spain, is undergoing an expansion that will add a fourth terminal in 2009 which will cover long-haul flights to distant destinations, especially Asia. It's calculated that the airport's annual number of passengers will mushroom from 33 million in 2008 to 55 million by 2010.

More passengers are choosing to fly the economy airline **Clickair** (www.clickair.com), which is based in Barcelona, rather than larger airlines, like **Iberia** (www.iberia.com). However, Iberia's "Air Bridge" to Madrid still remains the busiest flight route in the country.

High-speed **AVE trains** from Barcelona to Madrid started operating in 2008. This new service carries passengers between the two cities in just over $2^1/_2$ hours. The service has been incredibly popular, and as an added bonus, if any AVE train arrives more than 10 minutes late, the passenger gets a full reimbursement for the cost of the ticket. In the future, there are plans to extend this line as far as Perpignan, France, where TGV connections will make Barcelona just $4^1/_2$ hours from Paris. For more information, visit the Spanish rail website, www.renfe.es.

GETTING AROUND The city recently implemented a bike-rental plan which encourages visitors and residents alike to use bicycles as a means of transportation. Around 3,000 new red bikes are now available for short rentals at a weekly fee of just 1€ ($1.30) from over a hundred different stops. At press time, bike rentals were limited to 30 minutes, but the numerous pickup stations and the increasing proliferation of cycle trails in Barcelona offer many possibilities for the short period. For more information or to download a map marking pickup points, visit www.bicing.com.

WHERE TO STAY   The **Mandarin Oriental Hotel,** Passeig de Gràcia 18 (*C* **93-481-54-42;** www.mandarinoriental.com), a 98-room luxury hotel in a magnificently refurbished mid-20th-century building, is due to open in 2009. It'll have 52 spacious and exquisitely designed suites, several first-class restaurants and bars including one with alfresco dining on a large outdoor terrace, plus a rooftop pool and an innovative spa featuring "holistic rejuvenation."

WHERE TO DINE   Emu (*C* **93-218-45-02;** p. 158) is a new adventurous restaurant run by a young Aussie couple in chic Gràcia. It serves what are probably the best and most pungent curries in town and even provides Antipodean wines to go with them. The real specialty is Thai and Malaysian grub, so look out for the spicy yellow chicken curry.

MARKETS   The **Mercat El Born** at the eastern end of the Ciutat Vella, designed by *moderniste* architect Antoni Rovira i Trias, is one of the most beautiful 19th-century industrial revolution structures in Barcelona. It closed for renovation several years back with the aim of being converted into the city's main provincial library. But during excavations it was discovered that beneath the market were the remarkably well-preserved remains of the original medieval city. Work has since ceased while the authorities deliberate on whether they should continue with the library project or build a whole new museum with a basement re-creation of Barcelona in the Middle Ages, on the lines of Museu de l'Historia de la Ciutat's subterranean Roman city. The decision should be made in 2009, so watch out for what could be yet another fascinating contribution to the city's historic attractions.

Another traditional covered market earmarked for a face-lift is **Sant Antoni** (also designed by Rovira i Trias), which lies just beyond the western boundaries of El Raval. No ruins have been discovered here, so it will follow in the footsteps of the already renovated and still flourishing **Mercat Barceloneta** and La Ribera's **Mercat Santa Caterina,** both of which have undergone some nifty surgery in recent years that's left them looking immaculate without shedding their original character. Work on Sant Antoni will start at the end of 2009 or beginning of 2010.

PARKS   In 2008 the finishing touches were made to the long rambling **Parc Central de Poble Nou,** which runs into the **Parc Diagonal Mar** at its far eastern end. This latest leisure area is the work of Jean Nouvel, who designed the controversial Agbar tower, and it is very much a cool, 21st-century creation rather than a traditional stroll-and-picnic place. Its virtual lunar landscape, interspersed with a few huge plants and surrealistic statues, is slightly softened by a central perfumed garden and its flanking bougainvillea-covered walls. Further up the coast in the still-burgeoning zone beyond the Forum, the 11-hectare (27-acre) **Parc de la Pau** (Park of Peace)—finished in 2006—has helped brighten up the unlovely industrial suburb of Sant Adrià de Besòs.

The Best of Barcelona

With its agricultural wealth, excellent harbor, and industrious population, Barcelona has always managed to flourish through both good times and bad. When Madrid was still a dusty Castilian hamlet, the *Ciudad Condal* (as it's popularly known) was a powerful, diverse capital with a Mediterranean empire that extended as far as Athens. Influenced over the centuries by Romans, Visigoths, Franks, and even Castilians, it absorbed a little of each of their influences to become the fascinatingly complete city it is today.

Landmark Gothic buildings and world-class museums fill the historic center, and the whimsical creations of the *modernisme* movement and cutting-edge contemporary architecture line the wide boulevards of the newer city. An array of nightlife (Barcelona is a *big* party town) and shopping possibilities, plus nearby wineries, ensure that you'll be entertained 'round the clock. It makes for some serious sightseeing; you'll need plenty of time to take them all in and just as much to appreciate the city's unique, hidden charm.

The surrounding green and fertile countryside is equally enticing and the cove-indented Costa Brava coastline to the north boasts some of the loveliest scenery in all the Mediterranean. Inland, the towering Pyrénées mountain range that separates the province from France is a paradise for walkers and skiers. In all it's a stimulating and rewarding region to savor and appreciate to the full, and one of the most richly varied in the country.

1 THE MOST UNFORGETTABLE BARCELONA EXPERIENCES

- **Strolling Along La Rambla:** Barcelona's most famous promenade pulses with life. The array of living statues, street musicians, performers, hustlers, and eccentrics ensure there is never a dull moment during your kilometer-long stroll. See p. 71.

- **Having a Drink at Sunset on the Beach:** The Catalan capital's 4-mile stretch of new city beaches, whose promenade, jetties, and marinas are lapped by inviting Mediterranean waters, have been transformed from a once-neglected area into a round-the-clock international playground. Their atmospheric *chiringuitos* (waterside bars and eating spots specializing in seafood dishes) are perfect spots either for lunch or a relaxing end-of-day drink, often accompanied by the music of an in-house DJ. See p. 252.

- **Exploring the El Born Neighborhood:** This compact medieval quarter just inland from Barceloneta was once a labyrinth of earthy artisan workshops. Now the "in" crowds converge on its narrow tangle of streets lined by renovated old mansions: by day to check out top museums like the Picasso and smart shops exhibiting the latest in cutting-edge fashion and design; at night to enjoy the plethora of bars and restaurants offering the ultimate in New Catalan cuisine. See p. 211.

- **Attending a Concert at the Palau de la Música Catalana:** This masterpiece of *modernista* (Art Nouveau) architecture must be one of the most lavish concert halls in the world. All strains of classical and jazz are played, but even the most finicky music lover will be moved by the Palau's onslaught of decorative detail. See p. 179.

- **Eating Breakfast at the Boqueria:** There are about a dozen bars and restaurants in the city's main food market, one of the largest and most colorful in Spain. It's become fashionable these days and you can now rub shoulders with Barcelona's top chefs and gourmands over a coffee and croissant as you watch the day's deliveries coming in. See p. 255.

- **Bar-Hopping in the Barri Gòtic:** Whether it's an iconic, smoke-filled tapas bar, an Irish pub frequented by expats, or a cocktail lounge filled with minimalist furniture and minimally clad patrons, Barcelona's Old City is a watering-hole mecca, bar none. One of the best locales is **Ginger,** a comfy, classy tapas and wine bar with the feel of a private club. See p. 249.

- **Spending a Sunday on Montjuïc:** The sharply rising hill of Montjuïc is the first sight that greets visitors arriving at the port. Behind its rocky seaside face are acres of pine-dotted parkland beloved by cyclists, joggers, and strollers on the weekend. Topped by a castle museum with stunning city views, it provides a tranquil alternative to the hustle of the city below and offers some welcome breathing space. See p. 191.

- **Taking a Trip to Tibidabo by Tram and Funicular:** The summit of the city's distinctive inland backdrop is reached in two stages: first by a "blue tram" *(tramvia blau),* which winds past Sarrià district's elegant houses, and then by a creaky Art Deco funicular lift, which rattles its way up the mountainside to reveal increasingly breathtaking views of the city below. Both of these vintage forms of transport were built over a century ago to transport people to the church and amusement park on the mountain's peak. The exhilarating journey they provide is part of the fun. See p. 203.

- **Dining at Els Quatre Gats:** The original acted as a fraternity house for late-18th-century dandies. It later became a preferred hangout for the young Picasso and his Bohemian contemporaries. While most of the art adorning the walls is now reproductions, this classic Catalan restaurant is still alive with history. The resident pianist and general formality only add to the atmosphere. See p. 134.

- **Taking Your First Glance at the Sagrada Família:** Nothing quite prepares you for the first glimpse of Gaudí's most famous work, which erupts from the center of a suburban city block like some retro-futurist grotto. Draw your eyes skyward from a facade rich in religious symbolism to the temple's four towers. Then step over the threshold to the unfinished interior. See p. 184.

- **People-Watching at the Museu d'Art Contemporari de Barcelona (MACBA):** The forecourt of the Museum of Contemporary Art is a snapshot of the new multicultural Barcelona. Spend some time at one of its outside bars watching Pakistani cricket players, local kids playing soccer, and Northern European skateboarders in a fascinating melting pot of recreational activity. See p. 181.

- **Staying Up Until Dawn:** A long dinner, a few drinks at a bar, on to a club, and then before you know it the sun is rising over the Mediterranean's party capital, throwing a warm glow over the city's palm-filled plazas and streets. Nothing beats a slow walk home at this magical hour (preferably through the Old City). If you manage to catch up on your sleep during the day, chances are you will repeat the experience that night.

- **Looking Up at the Torre Agbar:** Even more controversial than the Sagrada Família when it first appeared, this 470-foot multi-hued phallic-shaped tower erupts surrealistically from the otherwise bland cityscape around the Plaça de Glòries. The tower was built by architect Jean Nouvel in honor of the city's 2004 Forum. It has over 4,000 multiform light-reflecting windows and currently houses the offices of the Barcelona Water Board. You get a great view of it from the top of Montjuïc. See p. 11.

2 THE BEST SPLURGE HOTELS

- **Hotel 1898,** La Rambla 109 (© **93-552-95-52**): This deluxe hideaway in the Barri Gòtic is a 19th-century building that's been updated with some ultra-sharp interior decor that includes lavish colors on each floor. See p. 99.
- **Hotel Casa Fuster,** Passeig de Gràcia 132 (© **93-225-30-00**): This *modernista* masterpiece was an emblematic building *before* it was recently converted into this luxury five-star. The rooms have been restored to turn-of-the-20th-century opulence, but now have all the modern conveniences. See p. 106.
- **Hotel Arts,** Marina 19–21 (© **93-221-10-00**): The preferred choice of top models and temperamental rock stars, the Hotel Arts has remained a jet-set playground and symbol of "cool Barcelona" for well over a decade. See p. 122.
- **Hotel España,** Sant Pau 11 (© **93-318-17-58**): This hotel combines comfort and luxury with the evocation of a bygone age. Designed by a contemporary of Gaudí's, the street-level dining room, filled with florid motif and brass fixtures, will whisk you back to the early 1900s, when it was filled with chattering patrons taking supper after a trip to the opera house next door. See p. 104.

3 THE BEST MODERATELY PRICED HOTELS

- **Hotel Peninsular,** Sant Pau 34–36 (© **93-302-31-38**): Serenity and character abound in this nunnery-turned-hotel. Located on a colorful street just off La Rambla, it features an Art Nouveau elevator and a lush inner courtyard that make it feel like a refuge from the hustle and bustle outside. It's understandably popular, so book ahead. See p. 104.
- **Hostal D'Uxelles,** Gran Vía 688 and 667 (© **93-265-25-60**): This *hostal* looks like it has stepped straight off the pages of one of those rustic-interiors magazines. Located on the first floor of two adjacent buildings, each of the 14 rooms has a distinct character, but all include canopied beds, antique furniture, and Andalusian-style ceramic bathrooms. See p. 115.
- **Marina Folch,** Carrer del Mar 16, principal (© **93-310-37-09**): This small family-run hotel is your best low-cost option in the beachside neighborhood of Barceloneta, where there are plenty of outdoor bars and open spaces for the kids to run wild. Ask for a room at the front for a balcony with a view of the port. See p. 124.

4 THE MOST UNFORGETTABLE DINING EXPERIENCES

- **Having a Paella at the Beach:** This is one of the quintessential Barcelona experiences, and there is no place better to do it than **Can Majó,** Almirall Aixada 23 (✆ **93-221-54-55**). Right on the seafront, this restaurant prides itself on its paellas and *fideuàs* (which replace noodles for rice) and is an established favorite among the city's well-heeled families. See p. 164.

- **Tasting the Cuisine of Catalonia's Top Chef:** Carles Abellán has been hailed as one of the most innovative chefs of nouvelle Catalan cuisine. His restaurant, **Comerç 24,** Comerç 24 (✆ **93-319-21-02**), was conceived as a playful take on all that's hot in the tapas world. Delights such as "kinder egg surprise" (a soft-boiled egg with truffle-infused yolk) and an intensely flavored mini *suquet* (fish stew) will tempt you. See p. 140.

- **Partaking in a Sunday Dining Tradition:** The lines say it all: **7 Portes,** Passeig Isabel II 14 (✆ **93-319-30-33**), one of the oldest restaurants in Barcelona, is a Sunday institution. Extended families dine on their excellent meat and fish dishes in the turn-of-the-20th-century atmosphere. See p. 162.

- **Sampling the Finest Regional Dishes:** In spite of its Italian name, the **Via Veneto,** Ganduxer 10 (✆ **93-200-72-44**), is traditional to the core, serving up some of the finest Catalan cooking in the land. The restaurant exudes old-fashioned class. One of the serving methods, such as the sterling silver duck press, seems to belong to another century (as do some of the clients). See p. 167.

- **Eating the Freshest Seafood in Barcelona:** You'll find it at **Els Pescadors,** Plaça Prim 1 (✆ **93-225-20-18**), in the atmospheric working-class beachside suburb of Poble Nou. People come here for the food—not the view—to sample prawns, whitebait, or *dorada* (bream). They serve whatever has been caught that day. Book ahead on weekends (p. 161).

- **Trying a Tasting Menu:** Tasting menus, a series of small gourmet dishes resembling deluxe tapas, are all the rage. They can be expensive, though, so if you want the best value head to **Coure,** Pasaje Marimón 20 (✆ **93-200-75-32**), in Gràcia and sample chef Albert Ventura's offerings, which include such exquisite delights as lime-flavored tuna and eucalyptus *helado* (ice cream). See p. 156.

5 THE BEST THINGS TO DO FOR FREE

- **Enjoying the Freebie Cultural Treats:** Top visits here are the **Foment de les Arts i del Disseny (FAD)** cultural center, where you can view exhibitions and sometimes buy bargain paintings by promising young unknowns (p. 181); and **Caixaforum** art gallery, which has an ever-changing trio of stimulating exhibitions (p. 191). Around the city you'll find an impressive variety of open-air **public art** displays: Antoni Llena's bizarre metal **David i Goliat,** Frank Gehry's copper **Peix** (Fish) in the Olimpic Port, and Colombian sculptor Fernando Botero's rather chubby **Gat** (Cat) in El Raval. There's also Roy Lichtenstein's trademark comic strip-style **Barcelona Head,** near the Columbus statue down by the harbor, and Joan Miró's **Dona i Ocell** (Woman and

Bird), finished in 1981 just before his death, and located in the park named after him in Sants.

- **Strolling in the Parks:** Despite its densely urban appearance, Barcelona is actually filled with parks where you can relax, stroll, and in many cases enjoy fun amenities. (Visit the website www.bcn. es/parcsijardins for the full list.) **Parc de la Ciutadella,** just to the east of the Old City, with its fountains and statues is a relaxing respite from the adjoining claustrophobic medieval labyrinth (p. 179), while **Parc Güell,** higher up in Gràcia district, delights visitors of all ages with its fairy-tale Gaudí structures (p. 189). In Montbau, the **Parc de la Crueta del Coll** has a playground and public summer pool (which in winter reverts to being an artificial lake). To the west, rambling hilltop **Montjuïc**—with its marvelous harbor views, jogging paths, the **Fundació Joan Miró Museum, Botanical Gardens,** and illuminated **Font Màgica** (magic fountain)—is a spacious kaleidoscope of greenery and cultural and sporting attractions. Less well known and more "countrified" is the **Parc d'en Castell de l'Oreneta,** just above the Pedralbes Monastery, where you can enjoy marvelous panoramic city and coastal views as you wander along signposted trails among meadows.

- **Taking in the Ecclesiastical Gems:** The city is full of amazing historical and religious monuments, and many of them are free. For example, unlike in most of Spain's major cities, there is no charge for visiting the **Catedral** (p. 172), though there is a fee for its museum. Other monumental treats are the **Capella de Sant Jordi** (p. 175), and churches of **La Mercé** (p. 174) and **Santa María del Pi** (p. 175), each of which makes its own unique contribution to the spiritual and architectural beauty of the city and shows you another aspect of its rich history. Another marvel is the **Santa Maria del Mar** church in the Born section of La Ribera (p. 212).

6 THE BEST STUFF TO BRING HOME

- **Leather:** Leather has long been one of Spain's most highly valued products, and best buys range from stylish belts and handbags to handmade shoes and fine jackets. The top spot for such purchases in Barcelona is **Loewe,** which mails its goods throughout the world (p. 233).

- **Ceramics and Pottery:** Though this is not a Barcelona specialty, you'll find a wide selection of ceramic vases, dishes, and jugs from Valencia, some of which have the style and finesse of fine art. There's also plenty of choices from areas such as Toledo and Seville. **Artesania i Coses** near the Picasso Museum is a good place to browse (p. 236).

- **Porcelain:** Most popular and widely available ornaments in this field are made by the Valencian company Lladró, similar in style to the Italian Capodimonte. Though considered rather twee by some, they're extremely popular with the majority of visitors. **Kastoria,** at Avinguda Catedral, is the place to check out statuettes and friezes (p. 236).

- **Antiques:** If you're looking for some interesting traditional engravings, carvings, or just simple bric-a-brac to take home, you have plenty of options. The best (and most expensive) locale is the three-story **Sala d'Art Artur Ramón** in the Ciutat Vella (p. 223).

- **Hats:** If you yearn to stroll around at home in a genuine wide-brimmed Spanish *sombrero* or a traditional low-key *campesino*'s beret, the place to look is **Sombrería Obach** in the old Jewish quarter of El Call (p. 232).

7 THE BEST ACTIVITIES FOR FAMILIES

- **In the City:** Anything by Antoni Gaudí, the city's most famous architect, immediately appeals to young eyes and imaginations. His whimsical **Parc Güell** (p. 189), with its imagery from the animal kingdom and hidden grottoes, is a particular favorite. Speaking of animals, the city's world-class **Aquarium** (p. 197), with its walk-through tunnels and superb collection of Mediterranean marine life, is also a good bet. The somewhat older and less-funded **Parc Zoológic** (p. 180) has a fantastic primate collection and is located in the **Parc de la Ciutadella** (p. 179), which also boasts a lake with rowboats for hire, swings, and other assorted kiddie attractions. Museum-wise, a trip to the **Maritime Museum** (p. 198), with its 16th-century galley and early submarine, could be combined with a jaunt on **Las Golondrinas** (p. 206), quaint, double-decker pleasure boats that take you from the port to the breakwater. The **Museu de la Cera** (**Wax Museum;** p. 174) may not be up to the standard of its counterpart in London, but is interesting enough to make it worth a visit. Older children will also find the **Chocolate Museum** (p. 177) enticing, and the **Science Museum** (p. 199) has excellent hands-on exhibits for all ages. Then, of course, there are the beaches—most with showers, toilets, bars, and hammocks for hire. **Happy Park** (p. 205) in L'Eixample, just off the Passeig de Gràcia, is a vast indoor all-weather fun park where teenies can enjoy twister slides, ball pools, and other fun activities. There's also a day care center for tots.

- **On the Outskirts:** An all-time favorite is the **Parc d'Atraccions Tibidabo** (p. 203). This veteran amusement park, perched on top of the city's highest peak, provides death-defying attractions and a few gentler ones from bygone days. The **Parc del Laberint d' Horta** (p. 204), meanwhile, is a neoclassical park on the outskirts of the city; and up in the Zona Alta above Pedralbes, the **Parc del Castell de l'Oreneta** has miniature train rides, weekend pony canters, and playgrounds with games for kids.

- **Further Afield:** In Torrelles de Llobregat, just 5 miles out of town, you'll find **Catalunya en Miniatura,** a Lilliputian mock-up of Barcelona and its province that includes a tiny Sagrada Família and Girona cathedral. A suitably dwarf-size train transports young passengers, and there are daily shows by clowns. At Vilassar de Dalt, 15 miles north of Barcelona, is the **Illa Fantasia** (Fantasy Island), a lively and spacious aquatic park with water slides, picnic areas, and a host of children's games and competitions. Visit www.illafantasia.com for more information. **Montserrat** (p. 260), Catalonia's "spiritual heart," offers plenty of walking tracks amid its phantasmagoric terrain of huge rocks and outcrops, caves, and, of course, the monumental monastery.

- **Museu Nacional d'Art de Catalunya (MNAC):** Located in the imposing Palau Nacional on the northern edge of Montjuïc, this museum overlooks the Font Màgica and is arguably one of the greatest repositories of Romanesque religious works in the world. Many of the icons and frescoes have been moved here from tiny churches high up in the Pyrénées where replicas now fill the spaces they originally occupied. Gothic styles are also well represented, and more recently there have been *moderniste* additions—many taken from the Manzana de la Discordia (p. 194).

- **Fundació Joan Miró:** This museum contains Spain's best collection of the famed Catalan contemporary artist's works (all donated by the great man himself). The museum is tucked away on Montjuïc Hill in a location that enjoys marvelous vistas of port and city from its roof terrace, where there's an attractive sculpture garden. Concerts take place here in summer. Highlights are the **Foundation Tapestry** and **Mercury Fountain,** by his American sculptor friend Alexander Calder (p. 192).

- **Museu d'Art Contemporani de Barcelona (MACBA):** This is Catalonia's answer to Paris' Pompidou Center, and it's right in the heart of the earthy yet partially gentrified Raval district, beside a lively square filled with students, passersby, and noisy skateboard fans. It has one of the best collections of modern art in Spain, featuring works by Tàpies and Barceló; there's also a library, bookshop, and cafeteria (p. 181).

- The **Picasso Museum:** One of the most visited cultural spots in the city, this museum is mainly dedicated to works by the younger Picasso which have been collected and assembled by his friend Jaume Sabartés y Gual. It spreads through a quintet of medieval palaces in La Ribera's atmospheric Calle Montcada. The artist donated many of the works himself, and highlights include the famed *Las Meninas* and *The Harlequin* (p. 178).

- **Museu Frederic Marés:** This charming old palace of secret patios and high ceilings houses one of the most richly varied collections of medieval sculptures in the world, all donated by Marés—a talented sculptor himself. Exhibits can be viewed on two floors—which open on alternative days—and range from polychromatic Roman crucifixes and Gothic statues to a "Ladies' Room" filled with Victorian knickknacks, and "Museu Sentimental" dedicated to Barcelona over the past 2 centuries (p. 174).

Barcelona in Depth

Barcelona is unlike any other Spanish city. It's dynamic, restlessly creative, constantly changing, and always looking outward and away from Spain for inspiration.

Barcelona is the vibrant city it is today because of two major events. The first was in 1975 when General Francisco Franco—who had systematically and often brutally tried to eradicate the treasured Catalan language and culture for 4 long decades—died, and the city and province started to live and breathe again independently. The second came with the 1992 Summer Olympics, which brought a fever of renovation work that radically transformed Barcelona from a drab, gray industrial city to a gleaming new metropolis. The medieval facades of the Barri Gòtic, which for centuries had been coated under a thick layer of grime, were sand-blasted, cleaned, and restored to their pristine glory. The city swung with intoxicating speed from being ignored to being awesomely revered. Word had spread and suddenly Barcelona was "in." The media baptized Barcelona the coolest rendezvous in Europe, saying that the city boasted some of the most inventive cutting-edge restaurants, bars, shops, and hotels in Europe. Such is the city's fame, and today no fewer than eight million visitors arrive annually to explore this relatively new-found wonder.

1 BARCELONA TODAY

Today multitudes of tourists flock to Barcelona for a number of very good reasons: to view the Picassos, Dalís, Tàpies, and Mirós; to marvel at its historic UNESCO-awarded sites (10 in all), and at the *moderniste* extravaganzas of Antoni Gaudí and the modern eccentricities of Frank Gehry and Jean Nouvel; to sample Ferran Adria's "New Catalan Cuisine," spearheading a culinary revival that's resulted in half a dozen Michelin-rated restaurants; and to spend money in some of Europe's most sophisticated shops and stores, especially in L'Eixample's Passeig de Gràcia—Barcelona's riposte to Paris's Champs Elysées.

There are so many tourists that they cram the narrow streets of the Ciutat Vella, almost clogging its central walkway, Les Ramblas, the former sacred territory of locals who now have to wait to resume their old habits until the quieter winters. Some critics have expressed the concern that the city is currently more interested in its surface image and in packaging itself as a sellable commodity than in dealing with practical matters, such as more judicious city planning. Heavyweight luminaries like art critic Robert Hughes—who wrote the definitive in-depth portrait of the city at the time of the 1992 Olympics (see "Barcelona in Popular Culture," later)—have been particularly disappointed, and many fear that in the quest for media approval, the city will become a virtual theme park for tourists.

Regardless, the Catalan metropolis has certainly experienced many changes for the better—starting with the fact that today it's even easier to get to and get around the city. By train, visitors can travel

(Fun Facts) How Tibidabo Got Its Name

Only in author Dan Brown's wildest imagination would Jesus Christ and the Devil have found themselves chatting to each other on top of the great hill behind the city. But locals love to tell you it was here that the Devil tried to tempt Christ by offering him all he could see—in this case, the lovely coastline all the way north toward the Costa Brava and (on a clear day) the Pyrénées mountains—if he would renounce God's ways and follow him. "Ti dabo" means "I give to you" in Latin and represents the Devil making his offer. The story may be an unlikely myth, but try telling that to the Catalans.

from Madrid to Barcelona's main Sants station in just over 3 hours, thanks to a high-speed (300kmph/186 mph) AVE train service, which started in 2007. The lightweight tram, TGV, and Metro services that can get you around the city quickly and efficiently also continue to expand and improve.

Like many forward-thinking cities, Barcelona is becoming more eco-friendly. Following Amsterdam's model, the city implemented a bike-rental plan in 2007, which encourages residents and visitors alike to use a **bike-sharing system** in which red *bicicletas* (3,000 in all) are available for free from a variety of bus and Metro stations for up to 30 minutes to those who want to make short trips along some of the city's new cycle lanes. (See "What's New in Barcelona" for more information.)

Barcelona is home to some beautiful parks, ranging from the much-loved veteran **Parc de la Ciutadella** to the sprawling pine-covered **Parc de Collserola** to the eccentric fairyland **Parc Güell.** There are expansive grassy areas on **Montjuïc,** above the port. But there are also newcomers, like **Parc Diagonal Mar** and Poble Nou's **Parc Central,** both of which opened in 2008 and which filled in wastelands left by departing industries. However, these parks tend to be more designer-conscious, resembling modern works of art rather than places to relax amid soothing greenery.

In the past a wealth of architectural styles, from medieval Gothic to 19th-century *moderniste,* made Barcelona famous. Today, ultra-modern, mold-breaking buildings also dominate the skyline, from Jean Nouvel's **Torre Agbar** on the eastern edge of L'Eixample to Norman Foster's **"Needle"** tower high on the wooded hills near Tibidabo. Even a traditional market like La Ribera's **Santa Caterina** now has an avant-garde roof designed by Enric Miralles (who was responsible for the Parc Diagonal Mar, mentioned above), giving truth to writer V. S. Prithcett's saying that Catalans "live artwardly" even when it comes down to workaday matters.

With the increase in tourism, traditional industries such as car and textile production have declined in the city and relocated out of town where many continue to flourish. High-tech businesses like Intel have sprung up in areas such as the Llobregat Delta, near the airport. Within the city, old working-class areas are definitely changing, mostly for the better. Neighborhoods like **Poble Sec,** where girls used to work on assembly lines in calico factories, and **Poble Nou,** where the old chimneys of the former textile works still stand beside warehouses converted into trendy pads for "yuppies," are exchanging their gritty proletarian look for stylish gentrification. Call it a theme park if you want, but it sure looks better.

Today Barcelona is a multicultural polyglot city which is home to various international communities. There is a large and industrious Chinese community, who ironically flourish around the mis-named Barri Xino (Chinese Quarter), even though few Asians lived there for decades in the past. (The name was inspired by a lurid crime book called *Sangre en las Atarazanas [Blood in the Dockyards]*, which was written by Francisco Madrid in 1926 and set in an imaginary version of Los Angeles's Chinatown.) There are also thriving Arab, Eastern European, South American, and African communities, some of whom live in the once seedy but now up-and-coming Raval quarter.

Despite all these changes, the native Barcelonans remain what they have always been: practical, businesslike, proletarian, nonconformist, rebellious, artistic, and hedonistic. Barcelonans embody a complex and contradictory blend of traits that at least partly explain how the city perpetually manages to experiment, adapt, and use its amazing natural energy and creativity to constantly reinvent itself.

2 LOOKING BACK AT BARCELONA

EARLY DAYS: IBERIANS, GREEKS, & ROMANS (5TH C. B.C.–4TH C. A.D.)

Long before any conquerors arrived, the plains surrounding the spot where Barcelona now stands were populated by peaceful, agrarian people known as the **Laetani,** while other parts of Catalonia were settled by the **Iberians.** The **Greeks** were the region's first real immigrants, setting up a sizable trading colony on the northern coast at Empúries, whose remains can still be seen today. Empúries was also the entry point for the Romans, who were at war with Carthage, a northern African power, for dominance over the western Mediterranean. Their base on the Peninsula was down the coast at New Carthage (Cartagena), a city rich in silver and bronze mines that the Romans saw as prime booty. In response to an attack on Rome by Hannibal, the Romans set about subjugating the Peninsula using Tarraco (Tarragona) as a base. Barcino (Barcelona) at that time had no harbor and served merely as port of call between Tarraco and Narbonne in France. But a sizable town quickly mushroomed out from Mons Taber, the highest point of today's city, where the cathedral now stands. You can still see traces of Roman civilization in Barcelona today, though they're eclipsed by smaller Tarragona's surprising wealth of monuments.

Down Among the Romans

A big surprise for many visitors to Barcelona is the remarkably intact layout of Julia Faventia Agusta Pia Barcino (or Barcino for short), the old Roman city that lies directly under the **City History Museum** in the heart of the Barri Gòtic. Descend a few steps and all around you are the foundations of its villas, temples, and squares, clearly marked and evocative enough for you to imagine life as it was then. This spot puts you within reach of three worlds: beside you are the Roman remains, on the surface is medieval architecture, and large modern constructions and stores are nearby.

> **Fun Facts**   **Was Count Wilfred Actually Hairy?**
>
> Almost everyone in those days had a substantial beard, so what made Wilfred so different? The answer is that he's said to have had hair on a part of his body that no other mortal was known to have. There are no hard facts to support this, but it's tacitly assumed that Wilfred sported hair on the soles of his feet. (If true, this would have reduced the need for him to wear sandals.) Hair was said to be a sign of virility and Wilfred was clearly macho, as his actions prove.

VISIGOTHS & MOORS

When Rome was crushed by the Barbarians in the 5th century, the Visigoths pounced on this northeastern corner of Spain, taking a broad swath stretching from the eastern Pyrénées to Barcelona. The chaotic rule of the Visigoth kings, who imposed their sophisticated set of laws on existing Roman ones, lasted about 300 years. They were prolific church builders, and Visigothic fragments still survive in Barcelona and, again more vividly, in Tarragona's cathedral.

In A.D. 711, Moorish warriors led by Tarik crossed over into Spain and conquered the country. Three years later they controlled most of it, except for a few mountain regions around Asturias. Their occupation of Barcelona was short-lived, though, which explains why the city has virtually no vestiges of Moorish architecture compared with *al-Andalús,* or Andalusia, where their culture flourished.

CHRISTIAN COUNT WILFRED (THE HAIRY) TAKES OVER

Up in the Pyrénées, Catalonia's heartland, the Moors clashed head-on with the Franks, who, led by Charlemagne, drove them back south. In 801, Louis the Pious, son of Charlemagne, took Barcelona and set up a buffer state, marking the territorial boundaries (known as the Marcha Hispánica) of what was to become medieval Catalonia and endowing the local language with elements of his own (Provençal). Local counts were awarded various territories. **Guifré el Pilós (Wilfred the Hairy;** 878–97) acquired several (including Barcelona) and managed to unite the area through a bloody battle that history has earmarked as the birth of Catalonia. In the 9th century, mortally wounded from a battle against the Moors, the Frankish emperor managed to dip the fingers of the hairy warrior in his own blood and trace them down the count's shield, creating the Quatre Barres, the future flag of Catalonia. What followed was a 500-year-long dynasty of Catalan count-kings with the freedom to forge a nation.

THE GOLDEN AGE & DECLINE

Catalonia entered the next millennium as a series of counties operating under the feudal system. It was growing stronger politically, and artistic and artisan disciplines were beginning to flourish. Under Ramón Berenguer III (1096–1131) and his son, the region annexed the southern Tarragonese territories and neighboring Aragon as well. Then came Jaume I (1213–76), whose powerful navy conquered Sicily and the Balearic Islands and established Catalonia as the principal maritime power of the Mediterranean. Under his long reign, the second city walls (more extensive than the old Roman ones) and the massive *drassanes* (shipyards) were

Santa María del Mar: From Jousting to Hobnobbing

The short, broad *paseo* that leads from the magnificent Santa María del Mar cathedral to the currently closed market of El Born is a trendy passage, lined with chic cafes and bars. Today, it seems difficult to imagine that a few centuries ago these cafes would have been in the path of a heavily armored *caballero* charging, with a lance, at his opponent. But jousting was commonplace in this area during the Middle Ages. In fact, the word *born* is Catalan for *joust*.

built, and a code of sea trade and local parliament were established. Local merchants grew rich and contributed toward the building of Gothic edifices, such as the church of **Santa María del Mar** and its surrounding mansions, the **Saló del Tinell** at the Royal Palace, and the **Saló del Cent.** Catalan literature and language flourished alongside the city's continuing prosperity.

In 1479, however, this was interrupted by the most far-reaching of all royal unions, that of Fernando II of Catalonia-Aragon to Isabel of Castile. Spain was united, but Catalonia lost its autonomy in the shift. The pious "Catholic Kings" roughly expelled all the Muslims and Jews, including those living in Barcelona's tiny El Call quarter. And even though Columbus was received in Barcelona upon his return from the discovery of America, Catalans were not allowed to trade with the New World. In the early 17th century, under the rule of **Felipe IV** (1605–55), anti-centralist feeling was further agitated by Spain's "Thirty Year War" with France, Catalonia's neighbor, with which Catalonia soon allied. The most emotive of all uprisings, the so-called Guerra dels Segadors (Harvesters' War), was squashed by Spanish troops, and as a final blow, in 1650 the king ceded Catalan lands north of the Pyrénées to France.

In 1700, a Bourbon prince, **Philip V** (1683–1746), became king, and the country fell under French influence. A Hapsburg archduke of Austria then challenged Philip

V's right to the throne, precipitating the War of the Spanish Succession. Catalonia gambled on his victory by supporting him, and they lost. Philip V, after taking the city on September 11, 1714 (still celebrated as the Diada, the Catalan national day), punished the province by outlawing the Catalan language, closing all universities, and building a citadel (on the site of the Ciutadella Park) to keep an eye on the rowdy population.

THE RENAIXENÇA & MODERNISM

Backed by a hardworking populace, Barcelona was the first Spanish city to embrace the industrial revolution. Textiles, with raw materials being brought in from the New World, suddenly became big business, and Barcelona gained the reputation as the "Manchester of the South." This newfound wealth led to the 19th-century *renaixença* (renaissance), a heady time of artistic and economic growth that returned the city to its great medieval levels of prosperity.

Catalonia rejoiced in this resurgence in a variety of ways. It revived the Jocs Florals, a poetry competition that celebrated the Catalan language, demolished the city walls, built L'Eixample (*extension,* or "new city"), and launched the landmark *moderniste* movement, where Antoni Gaudí and his architectural contemporaries held sway. The **Universal Exhibition** of 1888, a showcase for the glories of the new, cashed-up Catalonia, drew over two million visitors. Politically speaking, the Lliga de Catalunya, the province's first pro-independence party, was founded. Anarchist and communist groups were convening underground and acting out above ground; in 1893 a guerrilla extremist threw bombs into the audience at the Liceu Opera House, to the horror of the rest of Europe, creating widespread panic and disarray. As in most periods of rapid growth, the gap between rich and poor was becoming increasingly evident, and a subculture grew, planting the seeds of the city's reputation for excess, seediness, and political action.

In 1876 Spain became a constitutional monarchy. But labor unrest, disputes with the Catholic Church, and war in Morocco combined to create further political chaos throughout the country. The political polarization of Barcelona and Madrid erupted in 1909. Furious that the national government had lost the colonies in America (and therefore valuable trade) and was conscripting Catalans for an unwanted war in Morocco, rabble-rousers set fire to dozens of religious institutions in the city. Known as the Setmana Tràgica (Tragic Week), it caused the deaths of over 100 people and injured many more. All suspected culprits, even some who had not been in Barcelona at the time, were executed.

THE 20TH CENTURY: REPUBLICAN STRIFE & CIVIL WAR

On April 14, 1931, a revolution occurred, the second Spanish Republic was proclaimed, and **King Alfonso XIII** (1886–1941) and his family were forced to flee. Initially, the liberal constitutionalists took control, but they were swiftly pushed aside by the socialists and anarchists, who adopted a constitution separating church and state, secularizing education, and containing several other radical provisions, including autonomous rule for Catalonia. In 1931 **Francesc Macià** (1859–1933) declared himself president of the Catalan republic.

But the extreme nature of these reforms fostered the growth of the conservative Falange party (*Falange española,* or "Spanish Phalanx"), modeled after Italy and Germany's fascist parties. By the time of the 1936 elections, the country was split politically, with Catalonia firmly to the left. In Barcelona, attacks on bourgeois symbols (and people) and the occupation of public buildings by collectives were common. On July 18, 1936, the army, supported by Mussolini and Hitler, tried to seize power, igniting the **Spanish Civil War.** General **Francisco Franco** flew from Morocco to Spain in a tiny Dragon Rapide aircraft and led the Nationalist (rightist)

Parc de la Ciutadella: From Prison to Playground

Few corners of the city are as serene and relaxing as **Ciutadella Park.** Lakes, fountains, shrubs, flowers, palms, and quaint statues greet people as they wander through its winding paths. Yet for the best part of 2 centuries, these were the grounds of a hated citadel which housed many prisoners who never again saw the light of day. The fortress was presided over by the formidable General Prim during its demolition in 1888 when it was decided to hold the city's first Universal Exhibition here. Its huge grounds were accordingly turned into the spacious park you see today. Quite a change from the horrors of its past.

Impressions

We are the yanquis of Europe.
—Francesc de Paula Rius i Taulet, mayor of Barcelona, 1888, comparing the
city's energy and business sense with that of the United States

forces in fighting that instantly ravaged the country. By October 1, Franco was clearly in charge of the leadership of nationalist Spain, abolishing popular suffrage and regional autonomy—in effect, establishing totalitarian rule. Over the next 3 years, Barcelona and the Catalan coast were bombed by German and Italian fighter planes, untold numbers of citizens were executed, and thousands fled across the Pyrénées into France. Then Franco's forces marched into Barcelona under the banner "Spain is here." The Catalan language and culture were once again forced underground, and Francesc Macià was sentenced to 30 years in prison.

Spurred on by even worse conditions in the south, where hunger and poverty were an everyday threat, millions of immigrants arrived in Barcelona in the midcentury. The 1960s saw another economic boom, this time led by tourism, which grew into an important industry on the Costa Brava and Costa Daurada. Communists formed militant trade unions, and a working class was embittered by decades of repression. Before his death, General Franco selected as his successor Juan Carlos de Borbón y Borbón, son of the pretender to the Spanish throne.

The electorate eagerly approved a new constitution and the king, Juan Carlos de Borbón y Borbón. This guaranteed human and civil rights, as well as free enterprise, and ended the status of the Roman Catholic Church as the church of Spain. It also granted limited autonomy to several regions, including Catalonia and the Basque provinces. In 1980 the conservative **Convergènica i Unio** party, with

Jordi Pujol (b. 1930) at the helm, was voted in, initiating a series of negotiations for greater self-rule that still continue today.

In 1981 a group of right-wing military officers seized the Cortés (parliament) in Madrid and called upon King Juan Carlos to establish a Francoist state. The king, however, refused, and the conspirators were arrested. The fledgling democracy had overcome its first test, and Catalonia's morale and optimism were boosted even further when the socialists won the national elections a year later. Catalanista liberals, such as the Gauche Divine (Divine Left) party, dominated the city's counterculture for the rest of the decade, as engineers and town planners at the socialist-led city hall prepared Barcelona for the 1992 Olympic Games and its new, modern era. In 1998 Catalan became the official language of education and the judiciary, with quotas imposed on the media as well. The following year more than 43,000 adults enrolled for the free Catalan language courses supplied by the **Generalitat (Catalan Regional Government).**

THE 21ST CENTURY

In 2003, after 20 years as head of the Generalitat, the conservative Jordi Pujol lost to the socialist Pasqual Maragall (who served as mayor of Barcelona during the Olympic years). In coalition with the left-wing ERC (Esquerra Republicana de Catalunya, meaning Republican Left of Catalan) party (whose aim is *total* independence for Catalonia), Maragall has been accused of placing more emotive issues of a nationalist nature before policymaking. But the fact remains that Catalonia contributes more to the central government's tax coffers than any other region—and receives less in paybacks. The following year, in 2004, the Spanish Socialist government in Madrid, led by the pragmatic José Luis Zapatero, gave the official seal of approval for Catalan to be a written and spoken language within the European Union, and in 2006 helped pass a new *estatut*—or statute—granting the province more autonomy. The region's central goal is to have an independent, self-governing Catalonia, but they're playing it cool.

Socially, Barcelona is facing a relatively new issue. Today, immigrants make up 5% of the city's total population of just over four million, rocketing to 50% in some inner-Barcelona pockets. The government now recognizes the need to provide education for immigrants, emphasize religious and cultural tolerance, regulate the foreign workforce, and implement the immersion of Catalan language and culture, despite cries from the right that the Catalan culture and language will be lost if Catalonia absorbs any more foreigners. Immigrants are essential, however, for the region's primary industry. South Americans and North Africans are now employed in the vast acres of vineyards, olive groves, and other agrarian pursuits. Secondary industry sectors include chemical, car, and textile manufacturing, with a growing Internet and technology sector. Tourism employs a huge number of temporary workers during the summer, but unemployment still hovers, as it does in the rest of the country, at around 10%.

3 BARCELONA'S ART & ARCHITECTURE

BARCELONA'S ART THROUGH THE AGES

From the cave paintings discovered at Lleida to several true giants of the 20th century—**Picasso, Dalí,** and **Miró**—Catalonia has had a long and significant artistic tradition. Today it is the Spanish center of the plastic arts and design culture.

The first art movement to attract attention in Barcelona was **Catalan Gothic sculpture,** which held sway from the 13th to the 15th centuries and produced such renowned masters as Mestre Bartomeu and Pere Johan. Sculptors working with Italian masters brought the Renaissance to Barcelona, but few great Catalonian legacies remain from this period. The rise of baroque art in the 17th and 18th centuries saw Catalonia filled with several impressive examples, but nothing worth a special pilgrimage; the great masters such as El Greco and Velázquez worked in other parts of Spain (El Toledo and Madrid, respectively).

In the neoclassical period of the 18th century, Catalonia—and, particularly, Barcelona—arose from an artistic slumber. Art schools opened and foreign painters arrived, exerting considerable influence. The 19th century produced many Catalan artists who followed the general European trends of the time without forging any major creative breakthroughs.

The 20th century brought renewed artistic ferment to Barcelona, as reflected by the arrival of Málaga-born **Pablo Picasso.** (The Catalan capital today is the site of a major Picasso museum.) The great surrealist painters of the Spanish school, **Joan Miró** (who also has an eponymous museum in Barcelona) and **Salvador Dalí** (whose fantastical museum is along the Costa Brava, north of Barcelona), also came to the Catalan capital.

Many Catalan sculptors achieved acclaim in this century, including Casanovas, Llimon, and Blay. The Spanish Civil War brought cultural stagnation, yet against all odds many Catalan artists continued to make bold statements. **Antoni Tàpies** was one of the principal artists of this period (the Fundació Tàpies in Barcelona is devoted to his work). Among the various schools formed in Spain at the time was the **neofigurative band,** which included such artists as Vásquez Díaz and Pancho Cossio. The Museum of Modern Art in the neighborhood of El Raval (p. 181) illustrates the various 20th-century Catalan artistic movements, including the Dau al Set, the surrealist movement started in the 1940s by the "visual poet" Joan Brossa. His art and many other works by leading sculptors dot the streets of Barcelona, making it a vibrant outdoor museum. Watch out for Roy Lichtenstein's *Barcelona Head* opposite the main post office in the Plaça d' Antoni López, Joan Miró's phallic *Dona i Cell* in the park of the same name, and Fernando Botero's giant cat on the Rambla del Raval.

Today many Barcelona artists are making major names for themselves, and their works are sold in the most prestigious galleries of the Western world. Outstanding among these is sculptor **Susana Solano,** who ranks among the most renowned names in Spanish contemporary art, and the neo-expressionist Miguel Barceló. Design and the graphic arts have thrived in Barcelona since the heady days of *modernisme.* It seems that nothing in Barcelona, from a park bench to a mailbox, escapes the "designer touch." Leading names include the architect and interior and object designer Oscar Tusquets, and the quirky graphic artist Javier Mariscal,

whose work can be seen in many of the city's designer housewares stores. The most important plastic arts schools in Spain are located in Barcelona, and the city acts as a magnet for young, European creatives who flock here to set up shop.

BARCELONA'S ARCHITECTURE

Like many other cities in Spain, Barcelona claims its share of Neolithic dolmens and ruins from the Roman periods. Relics of the Roman colony of Barcino can be seen (and more are being found all the time), as can monuments surviving from the Middle Ages, when the Romanesque solidity of no-nonsense barrel vaults, narrow windows, and fortified design were widely used.

In the 11th and 12th centuries, religious fervor swept through Europe, and pilgrims began to flock to Barcelona on their way west to Santiago de Compostela, bringing with them French building styles and the need for new and larger churches. The style that emerged, called Catalan Gothic, had harsher lines and more austere ornamentation than traditional Gothic. Appropriate for both civic and religious buildings, it used massive ogival (pointed) vaults; heavy columns; gigantic sheets of sheer stone, clifflike walls; and vast rose windows set with colored glass. One of Barcelona's purest and most-loved examples of this style is the **Basilica of Santa María del Mar,** northeast of the city's harbor. Built over a period of only 54 years, it is the purest example of Catalan Gothic in the city. Other examples include the Church of Santa María del Pi, the Saló del Tinell (part of the Museu de la Ciutat), and, of course, the mesmerizing Barri Gòtic itself.

In 1858 the expansion of Barcelona into the northern **L'Eixample** district provided a blank canvas for *moderniste* architects. The gridlike pattern of streets was intersected with broad diagonals. Although it was never endowed with the more radical details of its original design, it provided a carefully planned, elegant path in which a growing city could showcase its finest buildings. Today L'Eixample boasts the highest concentration of *moderniste* architecture in the world.

Modernisme is a confusing term, as "modernism" generally denotes 20th-century functionality. It is best known as Art Nouveau, a movement that took hold of Europe in the late 1800s in the arts. In Barcelona, it shone in architecture and its star was **Antoni Gaudí.**

The *modernistas* were obsessed with detail. They hailed the past in their architectural forms (from Arabic to Catalan Gothic) and then sublimely sprinkled them with nature-inspired features employing iron, glass, and florid ceramic motif, all of which are seen in dazzling abundance in the city. Other *moderniste* giants were **Domènech i Montaner** and **Puig i Cadafalch,** whose elegant mansions and concert halls seemed perfectly suited to the enlightened, sophisticated prosperity of the 19th-century Catalonian bourgeoisie. A 19th-century economic boom coincided with the profusion of geniuses that emerged in the building business. Entrepreneurs who had made their fortunes in the fields and mines of the New World commissioned some of the beautiful and elaborate villas in Barcelona and nearby Sitges. There are also lesser-known designers, such as **Pere Falqués,** whose wrought-iron lampposts line parts of the Passeig de Gràcia, and **José María Jujol i Gibert,** who was responsible for the

beautiful *trencadis* (colorful broken mosaic patterns) that adorn Parc Güell.

Consistent with the general artistic stagnation in Spain during the Franco era (1939–75), the 1950s and 1960s saw a tremendous increase in the number of anonymous housing projects around the periphery of Barcelona and, in the inner city, eyesore-ridden decay. But as the last tears were being shed over the death of General Franco elsewhere in the country, Barcelona's left-field intelligentsia were envisioning how to regenerate their city after decades of physical degradation under the dictator.

When Barcelona won its Olympic bid to host the Summer Games in 1992, work on their vision of "New Barcelona" accelerated. City planners made possible the creation of smart new urban beaches, a glitzy port and marina, city traffic-reducing ring roads, daring public sculptures and parks, and promenades and squares weaving through the Old City. The planners shunned a master plan and instead employed smaller, more benign projects, the sum of which made up this grand vision. The objective was to rejuvenate the *barri,* the distinct village-neighborhoods of Barcelona that often denote one's income or political stance (sometimes even the language or football team) and make up the city's peculiar territoriality. This radical and ingenious approach did not go unnoticed by the rest of the world. In 1999 the Royal Institute of British Architects presented Barcelona's City Council with their Gold Medal, the first time a city (as opposed to an architect, such as previous winners Le Corbusier and Frank Lloyd Wright) had received the accolade. Barcelona is now used as a model across Europe for town planners wishing to overhaul their own downtrodden cities.

Over 15 years after the city's Olympic Year, the physical face of Barcelona is still changing in leaps and bounds. With an engaged local government still at the helm, broad swaths of industrial wasteland have

Gaudí: "My Place Is Here, with the Poor"

June 7, 1926, started as normally as any other day in the life of the architect **Antoni Gaudí i Cornet.** Leaving his humble studio at his work in progress, the Temple of the Sagrada Família, the old man shuffled through the L'Eixample district with the help of his cane on his way to evening vespers. He did not hear the bells of the no. 30 tram as it came pelting down the Gran Vía. While waiting for an ambulance, people searched the pockets of his threadbare suit for some clue as to his identity but none was to be found. Mistaking the great architect for a vagrant, he was taken to the nearby public hospital of Santa Creu.

For the next 3 days, Gaudí lay in agony. Apart from occasionally opening his mouth to utter the words, "Jesus, my God!" his only other communication was to protest a suggestion that he be moved to a private clinic. "My place is here, with the poor," he is reported to have said.

Gaudí was born in 1852 in the rural township of Reus. The son of a metal-worker, he spent long hours studying the forms of flora, fauna, and topography of the typically Mediterranean agrarian terrain. "Nature is a great book, always open, that we should make ourselves read," he once said. As well as using organic forms for his lavish decorations (over 30 species of plant are seen on the famous Nativity Facade of the Sagrada Família), he was captivated by the structure of plants and trees. As far as he was concerned, there was no shape or form that could be devised on an architect's drawing table that did not already exist in nature. "All styles are organisms related to nature," he claimed.

Apart from Mother Nature, Gaudí's two other guiding lights were religion and Catalan nationalism. When the *moderniste* movement was in full swing, architects such as Luis Domènech i Montaner and Josep Puig i Cadafalch were designing buildings taking florid decoration and detail to the point of delirium.

been reclaimed north of the city for parkland, a new marina, and the emergence of dot-com and ritzy residential neighborhoods. A new city nucleus in the north has been created around the new AVE high-speed train terminal that now links Madrid to Barcelona in a 3-hour journey. Still a city that's not afraid to take risks with its architecture, Barcelona's skyline has been enhanced by French architect Jean Nouvel's daring and controversial **Torre Agbar** (in the outer suburb of Glòries), which has become the towering symbol of a city embracing the future with bravado.

4 BARCELONA IN POPULAR CULTURE

LITERATURE

NON-FICTION For a firsthand account of the civil war and its devastating effects on Barcelona and Catalonia, George Orwell's *Homage to Catalonia* remains a classic. Irish writer Colm Tóibin takes a more light-hearted look at post-Orwell Barcelona, with plenty of anecdotes and colors through the eyes of a *güiri* (foreigner) in *Homage to Barcelona* (Penguin, 1992).

Gaudí, in the latter half of his life, disapproved of their excess and their capricious, outward-reaching (that is, European) notions. He even formed a counterculture, the Artistic Circle of Saint Luke, a collective of pious creatives with a love of God and the fatherland equal to his own.

He never married and, when he was close to 50, moved into a house in the Parc Güell, the planned "garden city" above Barcelona, with his ailing niece and housekeeper. After they both died, his dietary habits, always seen as somewhat eccentric by the carnivorous Catalans (Gaudí was a strict vegetarian), became so erratic that a group of Carmelite nuns who lived in the park took it upon themselves to make sure that he was properly nourished. His appearance was also starting to take on a bizarre twist. He would let his beard and hair grow for months, forget to put on underwear, and wear old slippers both indoors and out.

What became apparent by the end of his life, and long after, was that Gaudí was one of the greatest architects the world has known, whose revolutionary techniques are still the subject of theory and investigation and whose vision was an inspiration for some of today's top architects, including Spain's own Santiago Calatrava. In 2003, **Año Gaudí,** the celebration of the 150th anniversary of his birth, saw an equal number of tourists flock to Barcelona as Paris for the first time ever. In 2010 the construction of the roof, which will be a new structure built in a style that will blend with the rest of the edifice, is scheduled to take place. Expect even greater crowds if the temple of the Sagrada Família is finished, as predicted, for the centenary of his death in 2026.

Palafrugell-based writer **Josep Pla** produced a number of first-rate travel books on the whole region, but his masterpiece is generally acknowledged to be the *Cuadern Gris* (Gray Book), about his experiences as a very young man launching a local newspaper and dividing life and work between his hometown and Barcelona in the 1920s. *Twelve Walks Through Barcelona's Past* by James Amelang covers a dozen walks with historical themes and is a good companion to chapter 8, "Strolling Around Barcelona."

Strictly for soccer enthusiasts, *Barça: A People's Passion,* by Jimmy Burns (Bloomsbury, 2000), is a dramatic history of the city's soccer team, the richest and possibly most politically charged soccer club in the world.

Barcelona (Knopf, 1992) by art critic Robert Hughes is a well-versed and witty articulation of the city's architectural and cultural legacy. According to the *New York Times,* the book is probably destined to become "a classic in the genre of urban history." To prepare for a visit to Barcelona's Picasso Museum, read *Picasso, Creator and Destroyer* by Arianna Stassinopoulos Huffington (Simon & Schuster, 1988) and *Picasso: A Biography* by Patrick O'Brian, which is the most comprehensive examination yet of the artist and his work. In *Salvador Dalí: A Biography* (Dutton,

1986), author Meryle Secrest asks: Was he a mad genius or a cunning manipulator? Spanish resident-chronicler Ian Gibson scrutinized Dalí from a racier angle in his book, *The Shameful Life of Salvador Dalí* (W.W. Norton & Company, 1998). In *Gaudí: A Biography,* by Gijs van Hensbergen (Perennial, 2003), the author claims that Gaudí was "drunk on form," and that the architect still has not lost his power to astonish with his idiosyncratic and innovative designs.

FICTION   An important classic novel is Joanot Martorell's *Tirant lo Blanc,* the Catalan language's lesser-known 15th-century equivalent of *Don Quijote,* a knights-and-fair-damsels saga.

For a realistic account of what it was like to grow up in the austere days of post–Civil War Barcelona, read *La Plaça del Diamant* (Diamond Square) by Merce Rodoreda, set in the formerly working-class and now trendy area of Gràcia, and *Nada* by Carmen Laforet, which describes the hardships of growing up in a tyrannical household in L'Eixample.

Eduardo Mendoza's *The City of Marvels* tells a rags-to-riches story of a young farmer who arrives in Barcelona at the time of the 1888 exhibition and becomes one of the city's richest and most influential businessmen. Juan Marsé's *Shanghai Nights,* in contrast, depicts the disillusioned existences of failed anarchists after the Civil War in the grittier corners of Barcelona and Toulouse, and of their children who dream of a more glamorous world in an imaginary Shanghai.

The city's most prolific writer, poet, and essayist was **Manuel Vázquez Montalbán,** who died in 2003. He wrote *The Angst-Ridden Executive, Murder in the Central Committee,* and other popular works featuring the food-loving Barcelonan private eye Pepe Carvalho. In between describing Carvalho's unorthodox methods of solving his fictional cases, Vázquez Montalbán inserts an enticing number of (real-life) gourmet spots that make the reader's mouth water. Vázquez Montalbán also wrote the *Barcelonas,* an in-depth insider guidebook which combines lively accounts of Catalan history, character, and culture with scathing wit and insight.

FILM

Many film directors have been enamored with Barcelona, and as a result the city seems to play a major role in several films. *Barcelona* (1994), directed by American Whit Stillman, is based on the director's own experiences in the city during the final stages of the Cold War. Susan Seidelman's mystery-comedy *Gaudí Afternoons* (2001) made less of an impact, in spite of some more colorful location work around the city and a star cast, including Marcia Gay Harden and Juliette Lewis. *All About My Mother* (1999), a 1999 Oscar Award–winning film directed by Pedro Almodóvar, set many scenes in a surrealistically marginal Barcelona which was in reality the seedy Camp Nou area. The latest film in which the city virtually plays a main character is Woody Allen's *Vicky Cristina Barcelona* (2008), featuring Scarlett Johansson, Penélope Cruz, and Javier Bardem; this film depicts a highly romanticized version of the Ciudad Condal and should be seen as a typical Woody Allen film, rather than a realistic view of the place.

The picturesque Costa Brava has also found its place in film history. British heartthrob James Mason and screen goddess Ava Gardner starred in *Pandora and the Flying Dutchman* (1951), which was filmed along the Costa Brava, focusing on Tossa de Mar (see p. 287 in chapter 11, "Side Trips in Catalonia"). *Los Pianos Mecánicos* (1965) recounts the intrigues and affairs of a small idyllic Spanish village. It was filmed in Cadaqués (known in the movie as Caldeya) by Spanish director J. A. Bardem (Javier's uncle), and several colorful scenes were also shot in Barcelona.

CATALAN MUSIC

The two most famous Catalan **composers** were Camprodón-born **Isaac Albéniz**—a child prodigy who played in piano concerts at the age of 4—who is known for his *Iberia* suite, and **Enrique Granados** from Lleida, who is best known for the lively *Goyescas*. **Federico Mompou** was an unassuming composer whose works include *Charmes* and *Impressions Intimes.*

The region's greatest creator of operas was the 19th-century composer **Felipe Pedrell;** his two prime achievements, *Los Pirineos* and *La Celestina,* are occasionally performed in the Palau de la Musica. Barcelona's leading **opera singer** is **Josep Carreras,** who successfully survived leukemia in the late 1980s to become, alongside Placido Domingo, Spain's greatest tenor.

Pablo (Pau) Casals was one of Spain's most talented cellists (he died in 1973). You can visit his house museum at El Vendrell near Tarragona (see p. 268 in chapter 11, "Side Trips in Catalonia"). **Joan Manuel Serrat** is the region's most noted *cantautor* (singer-songwriter), and a champion for the region's rights. He sings many of his songs in Catalan.

5 EATING & DRINKING IN BARCELONA

Meals are an extremely important social activity in Catalonia; eating out remains a major pastime, whether in the evening with friends, at lunch in a local bar with workmates, or with the traditional Sunday family feast. Although Barcelona is a fast-paced city, mealtimes, especially lunchtime, are still respected, with the whole city shifting into first gear between the hours of 2 and 4pm. Many people either head home or crowd into a local eatery for a three-course *menú del día* (lunch of the day).

Catalan grub is quite different from the food of the rest of the Spain. In Barcelona, the mainstay diet is typically Mediterranean, with an abundance of fish, legumes, and vegetables, the latter often served simply boiled with a drizzle of olive oil. Pork, in all its forms, is widely eaten, whether as grilled filets, the famous Serrano ham, or delicious *embutidos* (cold cuts) from inland Catalonia. In more contemporary restaurants, portions tend to be smaller than in the U.S. Another local characteristic is the lack of tapas bars. Very good ones do exist but not in the same abundance as in the rest of Spain. Instead Catalans tend to go for *raciones* (plates of cheese, pâtés, and cured meats) if they want something to pick at.

Many restaurants in Barcelona close on Sunday and Monday, so check ahead of time before heading out. Hotel dining rooms are generally open 7 days a week, and there's always something open in the touristy areas. If you really want to get a true taste of Catalan cuisine, stay away from places in La Rambla, ask your hotel concierge for recommendations, or check chapter 6, "Where to Dine." Dining in Barcelona can range from memorable to miserable (or memorable for all the wrong reasons!), so it pays to do a bit of research. If possible, always book ahead for reputable restaurants, especially on the weekends.

BREAKFAST In Catalonia, as in the rest of Spain, the day starts with a light continental breakfast, usually in a bar. Most Spaniards have coffee, usually strong, served with hot milk—either a *café con leche* (half coffee, half milk) or a *cortado* (a shot of espresso "cut" with a dash of milk). If you find these too strong or bitter for your taste, you might ask for a more diluted *café americano.* Most people just have a croissant *(cruasan),* doughnut, or *ensaimada* (a light, sugar-sprinkled pastry). If you want something more substantial, you can always ask for a *bocadillo*

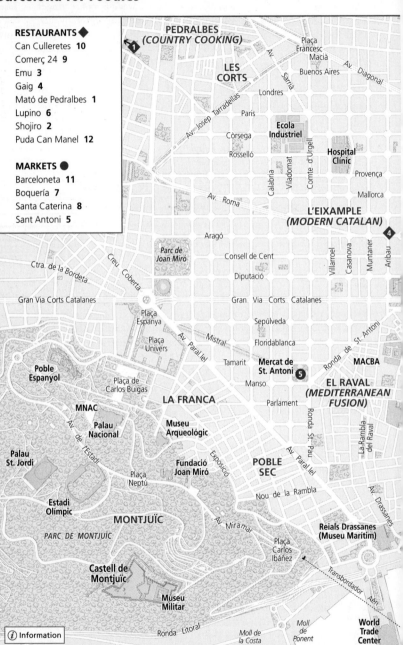

RESTAURANTS ◆
Can Culleretes **10**
Comerç 24 **9**
Emu **3**
Gaig **4**
Mató de Pedralbes **1**
Lupino **6**
Shojiro **2**
Puda Can Manel **12**

MARKETS ●
Barceloneta **11**
Boquería **7**
Santa Caterina **8**
Sant Antoni **5**

PEDRALBES
(COUNTRY COOKING)

LES CORTS

Plaça Francesc Macià
Buenos Aires
Av. Diagonal

Av. Sarrià

Av. Josep Tarradellas

Londres
Paris
Còrsega
Rosselló

Ecola Industriel

Hospital Clinic

Provença
Mallorca

Comte d'Urgell
Viladomat
Calàbria

L'EIXAMPLE
(MODERN CATALAN)

Av. Roma

Aragó
Consell de Cent
Diputació

Parc de Joan Miró

Ctra. de la Bordeta

Creu Coberta

Gran Via Corts Catalanes

Gran Via Corts Catalanes

Villarroel
Casanova
Muntaner
Aribau

Sepúlveda
Floridablanca

Plaça Espanya

Av. Paral·lel

Mistral

Tamarit
Plaça Univers

Mercat de St. Antoni

Manso

Ronda de St. Antoni

MACBA

EL RAVAL
(MEDITERRANEAN FUSION)

Poble Espanyol

Plaça de Carlos Buigas

LA FRANCA

Museu Arqueológic

Parlament

Ronda St. Pau

MNAC

Palau Nacional

Av. de l'Estadi

Exposició

Fundació Joan Miró

POBLE SEC

Av. Paral·lel

La Rambla del Raval

Palau St. Jordi

Plaça Neptú

Nou de la Rambla

Av. Drassanes

Estadi Olímpic

MONTJUÏC

PARC DE MONTJUÏC

Av. Miramar

Reials Drassanes
(Museu Marítim)

Castell de Montjuïc

Plaça Carlos Ibáñez

Transbordador Aeri

Museu Militar

ⓘ Information

Ronda Litoral

Moll de la Costa

Moll de Ponent

World Trade Center

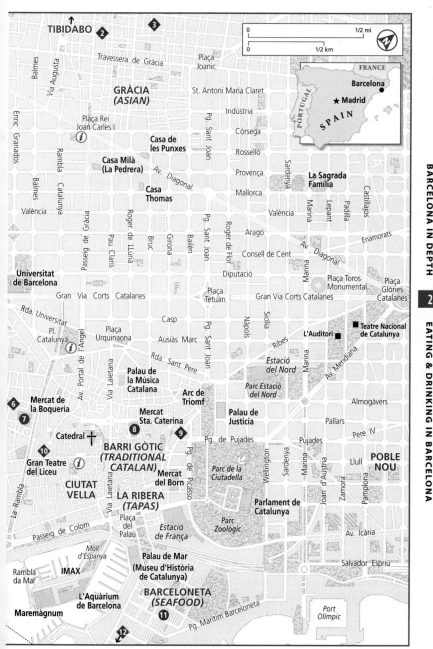

Tips **Barcelona for Foodies**

Though foodie frontiers in the city are not absolute, there are certain areas that are known for certain types of food. The heart of the Barri Gòtic quarter is, for example, one of the best spots to sample good old-fashioned **Catalan cooking** (as at **Can Culleretes;** p. 134), while Barceloneta is an unrivaled location for gorging on Mediterranean **seafood.** In sophisticated L'Eixample, the food is as richly inventive and innovative as the *moderniste* architecture it touts. Eat lunch at a key spot like **Gaig** (p. 151) and you'll get the picture.

Cozy village-like Gràcia, just above L'Eixample, is, alternatively, home to some nifty new **Asian** eateries, from **Emu's** Malaysian curries to **Shojiro's** top-notch Japanese delights. In polyglot El Raval you'll not only find cheap and cheerful Middle Eastern, Mexican, and Filipino joints, but also some stunningly stylish **Mediterranean "Fusion"** establishments (check out the delectable **Lupino,** p. 144). Though Barcelona is not traditionally known for its tapas, you'll find some highly imaginative versions all over, but especially in a chic La Ribera bar like **Comerç 24** (p. 140).

You can find excellent country cooking (without heading too far out into the lovely Catalan countryside) in the Upper City's **Pedralbes** district, where beside a serenely beautiful monastery, the homey **Mató de Pedralbes** (p. 166) offers rustic *venta-* (country inn) style dishes like *anclas de ranas* (frog's legs) and *cargols a la llauna* (snails).

The traditional covered markets are a must-see for foodies. They were built in the city's *moderniste* heyday and are worth visiting as historic monuments as much as exotic food emporiums. Top markets are the famed **Boqueria, Santa Caterina, Sant Antoni,** and **Barceloneta.** Feast your eyes on their curving arches and high ceilings before savoring the colorful cornucopia of local produce that fills the stalls.

(roll) with cheese or grilled meat or cold cuts, or ask to see the list of *platos combinados* (combination plates). These consist of a fried egg, french fries, bacon, and a steak or a hamburger. A *bikini* is an old-fashioned, toasted ham-and-cheese sandwich.

LUNCH The most important meal of the day in Barcelona, lunch is comparable to the farm-style midday "dinner" in the United States. It usually includes three or four courses, although some smarter eateries in the Old Town are now offering just one course with dessert for lighter eaters. It begins with a choice of soup, salad, or vegetables. Then follows the meat, chicken,

or fish dish, simply grilled or in a rich stew or casserole. At some point, meat eaters should definitely try *botifarras,* the locally made sausages. Desserts are (thankfully) light: fruit, yogurt, or a *crema catalana* (crème brûlée). Wine and bread is always part of the meal. Lunch is served from 1:30 to 4pm, with "rush hour" at 2pm.

DINNER If you had a heavy or late lunch, you may want to simply go for tapas or a few *raciones* in a wine bar; this is the perfect time to try the quintessential Catalan snack *pa amb tomàquet* (rustic bread rubbed with olive oil and tomato pulp, served with cheese, pâté, or cold cuts). If you choose a restaurant, expect a slightly finer version of what you had at lunch but with a larger bill, as the set-menu deal is a lunchtime-only thing. The chic dining hour is 10 or 10:30pm. (In well-touristed regions and hardworking Catalonia, you can usually dine at 8pm, but you still may find yourself alone in the restaurant.)

WHAT TO EAT

As well as producing many dishes that are uniquely its own, Barcelona looks toward France and central Spain for some of its culinary inspiration. Its *bullabesa* (bouillabaisse), *cargols* (snails), and *anclas de ranas* (frog's legs) are clearly Gallic-influenced, while a classic stew like *escudella i carn d'olla*—viewed by singer-songwriter Lluis Llach as "reflecting all the wisdom of Catalan people"—is really a blend of the French *pot au feu* and Madrileño *cocido*, and the ubiquitous *lechona* (suckling pig) is an import from central Castile. In countryside inns (or *ventas*) you'll often find hunting fare like hare and pheasant, which again show influences from the rest of Spain. But the real traditional cuisine throughout Barcelona and its inland areas is rather like the inhabitants: solid and gutsy. Meaty dishes such as veal and blood sausage are accompanied by hearty garbanzos (chickpeas), *lentejas* (lentils), *mongetes* (white beans), or *judias blancas y negras* (white and black-eyed beans), rather than fresh vegetables (though these are sometimes available). And the traditional fishy paella of southerly neighbor Valencia is often transformed into noodle-based *fideuà* containing rabbit, chicken, and rich regional *botifarra* sausage.

Since Barcelona is right beside the Mediterranean, conventional seafood and rice paellas also abound. The long Catalan coast shelters over 30 fishing ports and fish is a supreme passion with local gourmets, and the choice highly varied. A popular local dish is *suquet de peix,* a rich fish-and-potato stew that was once a favorite

breakfast of fisherman who'd been out on the water with their nets all night. Another masterpiece is *zarzuela,* a stew that combines an extraordinarily wide range of Mediterranean fish, from *salmonetes* (red mullet) and *besugo* (bream) to *mejillones* (mussels) and *gambas* (prawns). *Sardinas* (sardines) are particularly scrumptious—and inexpensive—when grilled over a pine-wood fire. Squid, octopus, and *sepia* (cuttlefish) feature heavily, from *calamares romana* (deep-fried squid) to *chipirones* (bite-size baby octopus, also fried) to squid cooked in its own ink. Basque-style *bacallà* (salted cod), originating from chillier Northern Atlantic waters, is another favorite, whether it's simply baked *(a la llauna)* or forms the base of a cold garlicky hors d'oeuvre called *esqueixada.* (Don't confuse this, by the way, with the similar-sounding *escalivada,* which consists of strips of char-grilled sweet peppers and eggplant, and is also served cold.)

Catalans are particularly inventive with their tortillas (egg, not corn variety), and these can include white beans, asparagus, and garlic shoots, often served with *pa amb tomàquet,* that Catalan gem of simplicity consisting of bread, garlic, crushed tomato, and generously applied olive oil. (Some of Spain's very best oil comes from Catalonia's Lleida province.) A pungent white sauce that adds an extra dimension to any meal is *allioli,* made from garlic, salt, and mayonnaise. Vegetables are uncommon accompaniments to main courses, but an *ensalada catalana*—a salad of lettuce, tomato, onions, and olives—is invariably available, with the added bonus (for some) of local cold cuts like *mortadella* or mountain ham. (Vegetarians and vegans should always check that no meat is included in what appears to be a vegetable dish or salad on the menu.) Desserts are more modest and include the nifty milk-and egg-based flan (caramel custard) and *crema catalana* (crème brûlée).

Frommer's Favorite Local Spots

Mercè Vins (Calle Amargos 1; ☎ **93-302-60-56**) is a colorful little spot that is essentially a breakfast bar serving great coffee and huge *ensaimadas* (cholesterol-charged Majorcan buns). It's especially good for bargain set lunches (8.50€/$11) that may include generous salads, *sopa de calabaza* (pumpkin soup), and *longaniza picante* (spicy local sausage). Its coup de grâces are the criminally rich sweets (try the chocolate flan or rich fig pudding).

Don't be put off by the cutesy faux-rustic decor that features pitchforks, wagon wheels, and gingham tablecloths at **Mesón Jesús** (Cecs de la Boqueria 4; ☎ **93-317-46-98**). The staff is so friendly and the delicious, simple food is so cheap that it's a must. Try the bargain *gambas* (prawns) or *suquet* (fish stew) and we guarantee you'll be back.

If huge menus don't terrify you head for **Fil Manila** (Carrer Ramelleres 2; ☎ **93-318-64-87**), a nifty Philippine-run spot in the heart of multiethnic Raval. When you are tired of reading the menu, just stab your finger at random and trust luck. You're unlikely to go wrong and could end up with anything from sour fish soup to pork with noodles, all good and inexpensive.

WHAT TO DRINK

Catalan wines, though less world-renowned than the northerly Riojas, are in fact among Spain's best—particularly in the southerly Penedès wine region where oenologist Miguel Torres produces rich Corona reds and Viña Sol whites. Penedès also accounts for about 75% of all the *cava* (sparkling wine) made in Spain, and the infinitely different varieties range from small family-made "garage" bodega wines to international brands like Freixenet and Codorníu, produced in *cava* capital Sant Sadurni d'Anoia. Codorníu is housed in a spectacular *moderniste* building that is part of the Spanish heritage trust, with 15km (9²/₃ miles) of underground tunnels to explore while you learn about the *cava*-making process. The jewel in Catalonia's winemaking crown, however, is Tarragona province's deep, dark red—and impressively expensive—Priorat. Its most notable promoter was Carles Pastrana of Clos L'Obac, who set about establishing a set of D.O. *(denominación de origen)* standard rules and regulations.

The famed *sangria,* a red-wine punch that combines wine with oranges, lemons, *gaseosa* (seltzer), and sugar, was originally conceived as a refreshing summer drink blending cheap wine with *gaseosa* or lemonade, though today's spirit- and additive-boosted touristy versions tend to be artificially stronger, so take care.

If you prefer something lighter, there's the lager-like San Miguel *cerveza* (beer), which, though originally from the Philippines, has been produced for decades in inland Lleida. This is by far the province's most popular beer. All beer tends to be lighter, more like the U.S. version than the British. A *clara* is a glass of beer mixed with lemon soda. A small bottle of beer is called a *mediana*, and a glass is a *caña*.

Although water is safe to drink, many find the taste of Barcelona's tap water unpleasant. Mineral water, in bottles of .5 to 5 liters, is available everywhere. Bubbly water is *agua con gas;* noncarbonated is *agua sin gas.* Vichy Catalan, rather salty carbonated water that many people believe acts as a digestive aid, is very popular. Soft drinks are also popular, and standard, nationally produced versions of Fanta and Coca-Cola are also widely available.

The coffee you have with your breakfast or after your meal is invariably first-class, richer and stronger than in the U.S., and if you've waded through a particularly large lunch or dinner, a *carajillo,* coffee containing a dash of cognac (Catalonia's top cognac brand is Mascaró), will either finish you off or help it go down.

Planning Your Trip to Barcelona

Although Barcelona, with its three million inhabitants, muggy climate, congested streets, and inevitable rush-hour traffic jams, is no longer the laid-back (and relatively little-known) Mediterranean port it once was, there's plenty to make your visit here much easier than you might imagine.

For one thing, you don't have to bother with the hassle of arranging visas before you set off, and once you arrive, there's an abundance of helpful *oficinas de turismo* (tourist information offices) to ensure you're briefed on what to see and do. A very good local transportation system includes **Metro** (subway), **tramvías** (streamlined tram), and *rodalíes* (suburban train services), and the cost of travel is extremely low—particularly if you purchase the 10-tickets-in-one deal (p. 45). Additionally, there's an increasing number of amenities for travelers with disabilities.

The benign Mediterranean climate ensures it's rarely uncomfortably cold, even in winter. Summers can be hot and humid, though, and this may restrict mobility for older visitors when they're touring the sights. But you can always take a break and relish verdant shady areas like Ciutadella Park, Montjuïc, and Tibidabo, which have panoramic Mediterranean and city vistas.

Violent **crime** is fairly uncommon, but you should definitely watch out for potential bag snatchers and muggers in the narrow lanes around La Rambla and around the Plaça Reial—especially late at night.

If you decide to take your own computer along you'll find a wide choice of places where you can connect to the **Internet.** The number of hotels equipped with Wi-Fi is mushrooming, and cybercafes are opening up continuously throughout the city.

For additional help in planning your trip, and for more on-the-ground resources in Barcelona, please turn to Appendix A: Fast Facts, Toll-Free Numbers & Websites on p. 320.

1 VISITOR INFORMATION

TOURIST OFFICES You can begin your info search with Spain's tourist offices located in the following places:

In the United States For information before you go, contact the **Tourist Office of Spain,** 666 Fifth Ave., Fifth Floor, New York, NY 10103 (© 212/265-8822). It can provide sightseeing information,

events calendars, train and ferry schedules, and more. Elsewhere in the United States, branches of the Tourist Office of Spain are located at 8383 Wilshire Blvd., Suite 956, Beverly Hills, CA 90211 (© 323/658-7188); 845 N. Michigan Ave., Suite 915E, Chicago, IL 60611 (© 312/642-1992);

Destination Barcelona: Pre-Departure Checklist

- If you're flying, are you carrying a current, government-issued ID? The citizens of E.U. countries can cross into Spain for as long as they wish, but citizens of other countries, including the United States, must have a passport.
- If you're driving, did you pack your driver's license and some detailed road maps?
- Do you have the address and phone number of your country's embassy or consulate with you?
- Did you find out your daily ATM withdrawal limit?
- Do you have your credit card PINs? If you have a five- or six-digit PIN, did you obtain a four-digit number from your bank? (Five- and six-digit numbers do not work in Spain.)
- To check in at a kiosk with an e-ticket, do you have the credit card you bought your ticket with or a frequent-flier card?
- If you purchased traveler's checks, have you recorded the check numbers and stored the documentation separately from the checks?
- Did you bring your ID cards that could entitle you to discounts, such as AAA and AARP cards, student IDs, and so on?
- Did you leave a copy of your itinerary with someone at home?
- Do any theater, restaurant, or travel reservations need to be booked in advance?
- Did you make sure your favorite attraction is open? Call ahead for opening and closing times. (Bear in mind, for example, that most museums close on Monday in Spain.)

and 1221 Brickell Ave., Suite 1850, Miami, FL 33131 (© **305/358-1992**).

In Canada Contact the **Tourist Office of Spain,** 102 Bloor St. W., Suite 3402, Toronto, Ontario M5S 1M9, Canada (© **416/961-3131**).

In Great Britain Write to the **Spanish National Tourist Office,** 22–23 Manchester Sq., London W1M 5AP (© **020/ 7486-8077**).

WEBSITES You can find lots of great information at the following sites: **Tourist Office of Spain** (www.okspain.org), **All About Spain** (www.red2000.com), and **CyberSp@in** (www.cyberspain.com).

More Catalonia-specific information can be found on **www.barcelonaturisme. com**. The official site of city hall, **www. bcn.es**, is slow to load, but useful for things such as opening times and upcoming events (in English). The *Barcelona Metropolitan,* the local magazine in English (**www.barcelona-metropolitan.com**), is mainly aimed at expats, but will appeal to the visitor who wants more of an insider look at the city. For one-stop tour, hotel, and activity booking try **www.barcelona. com**. If you want to pre-book train tickets, **www.renfe.es** is the official site of Spain's rail network.

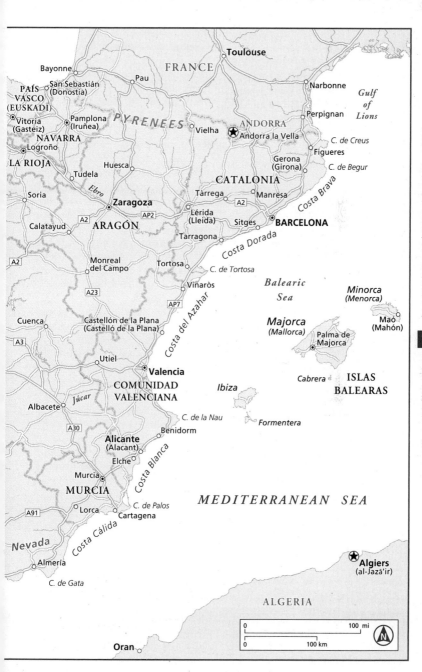

3

2 ENTRY REQUIREMENTS

PASSPORTS

A valid **passport** is all that an American, British, Canadian, or New Zealand citizen needs to enter Spain. Australians, however, need a visa—see below. For information on how to obtain a passport, go to "Passports" in Appendix A: Fast Facts, Toll-Free Numbers & Websites (p. 320).

VISAS

No visas are required for U.S. visitors to Spain, providing your stay does not exceed 90 days. Australian visitors need a visa. For specifics on how to get a visa, go to "Visas" in Appendix A: Fast Facts, Toll-Free Numbers & Websites (p. 320).

MEDICAL REQUIRE-MENTS

For information on medical requirements and recommendations, see "Health," p. 52.

CUSTOMS
What You Can Bring into Spain

You can bring most personal effects and the following items duty-free: two still cameras and 10 rolls of film per camera, tobacco for personal use, 1 liter each of liquor and wine, a portable radio, a cassette digital recorder, a laptop computer, a bicycle, sports equipment, and fishing gear.

What You Can Take Home from Spain

U.S. Citizens: For specifics on what you can bring back and the corresponding fees, download the invaluable free pamphlet *Know Before You Go* online at www.cbp. gov. (Click on "Travel," and then click on "Know Before You Go.") Or contact the **U.S. Customs & Border Protection (CBP),** 1300 Pennsylvania Ave., NW, Washington, DC 20229 (© **877/287-8667**), and request the pamphlet.

Canadian Citizens: For a clear summary of Canadian rules, write for the booklet *I Declare,* issued by the Canada Border Services Agency (© **800/461-9999** in Canada, or 204/983-3500; **www.cbsa-asfc.gc.ca**).

U.K. Citizens: For information, contact **HM Revenue & Customs** at © **0845/010-9000** (from outside the U.K., 020/8929-0152), or consult their website at **www.hmce.gov.uk**.

Australian Citizens: A helpful brochure available from Australian consulates or Customs offices is *Know Before You Go.* For more information, call the **Australian Customs Service** at © **1300/363-263,** or log on to **www.customs.gov.au**.

New Zealand Citizens: Most questions are answered in a free pamphlet available at New Zealand consulates and Customs offices: *New Zealand Customs Guide for Travellers, Notice no. 4.* For more information, contact **New Zealand Customs,** The Customhouse, 17–21 Whitmore St., Box 2218, Wellington (© **04/473-6099** or 0800/428-786; **www.customs.govt.nz**).

3 WHEN TO GO

CLIMATE

Barcelona is blessed with a benign, Mediterranean climate. Spring and fall are ideal times to visit, especially May to June and September to October. Even in the winter, days are crisp to cold (due to its proximity to the mountains) but often sunny. Snow is rare and never lasts more than a day or

Cut to the Front of the Airport Security Line as a Registered Traveler

In 2003, the **Transportation Security Administration** (**TSA;** www.tsa.gov) approved a pilot program to help ease the time spent in line for airport security screenings. In exchange for information and a fee, persons can be prescreened as registered travelers, granting them a front-of-the-line position when they fly. The program is run through private firms—the largest and most well-known is Steven Brill's **Clear** (www.flyclear.com)—and it works like this: Travelers complete an online application providing specific points of personal information, including name, addresses for the previous 5 years, birth date, social security number, driver's license number, and a valid credit card (you're not charged the **$99 fee** until your application is approved). Print out the completed form and take it, along with proper ID, to an "enrollment station" (this can be found in over 20 participating airports and in a growing number of American Express offices around the country, for example). It's at this point where it gets seemingly sci-fi. At the enrollment station, a Clear representative will record your biometrics necessary for clearance; in this case, your fingerprints and your irises will be digitally recorded.

Once your application has been screened against no-fly lists, outstanding warrants, and other security measures, you'll be issued a clear plastic card that holds a chip containing your information. Each time you fly through participating airports (and the numbers are steadily growing), go to the Clear Pass station located next to the standard TSA screening line. Here you'll insert your card into a slot and place your finger on a scanner to read your print—when the information matches up, you're cleared to cut to the front of the security line. You'll still have to follow all the procedures of the day, like removing your shoes and walking through the X-ray machine, but Clear promises to cut 30 minutes off your wait time at the airport.

On a personal note: Each time I've used my Clear Pass, my travel companions are still waiting to go through security while I'm already sitting down, reading the paper, and sipping my overpriced smoothie. Granted, registered traveler programs are not for the infrequent traveler, but for those of us who fly on a regular basis, it's a perk I'm willing to pay for.

—David A. Lytle

two. Most of the rainfall occurs in April, but some quite spectacular storms, as is typical of the Mediterranean, can occur all year round. July and August are hot and humid, even at night, as the temperature often only drops minimally. The surrounding sea is warm enough to swim in from the end of June to early October. Inland, the temperatures drop slightly, as does the humidity. North on the Costa Brava, a strong wind known as the *tramontana* often blows.

August is the major vacation month in Europe. The traffic from France, the Netherlands, and Germany to Spain becomes a veritable migration, and low-cost hotels along the coastal areas are virtually impossible to find unless booked well in advance. To compound the problem, many restaurants and shops also decide it's time for a vacation, thereby limiting the visitors' selections for both dining and shopping. That said, Barcelonese also head out of town for cooler climes, leaving tourists to enjoy the city for themselves. Barcelona is also a major international trade fair and conference destination. These happen throughout the year, so if you plan to stay in a mid- to high-range hotel it should be booked well in advance. Barcelona is officially Spain's most popular destination, and tourism is now year-round. The only time you may not be rubbing shoulders with fellow travelers is Christmas!

Barcelona's Average Daytime Temperatures & Rainfall

	Jan	Feb	Mar	Apr	May	June	July	Aug	Sept	Oct	Nov	Dec
Temp. (°F)	48	49	52	55	61	68	73	73	70	63	55	50
Temp. (°C)	9	9	11	13	16	20	23	23	21	17	13	10
Rainfall (in.)	1.7	1.4	1.9	2	2.2	1.5	.9	1.6	3.1	3.7	2.9	2

CATALAN & NATIONAL HOLIDAYS

Holidays observed are January 1 (New Year's Day), January 6 (Feast of the Epiphany), March/April (Good Friday and Easter Monday), May 1 (May Day), May/June (Whit Monday), June 24 (Feast of St. John), August 15 (Feast of the Assumption), September 11 (National Day of Catalonia), September 24 (Feast of Our Lady of Mercy), October 12 (Spain's National Day), November 1 (All Saints' Day), December 8 (Feast of the Immaculate Conception), December 25 (Christmas), and December 26 (Feast of St. Stephen).

If a holiday falls on a Thursday or Tuesday, many people also take off the weekday in between, creating an extra-long weekend. While this only really affects those doing business in the city, you should book hotels well ahead of time on these popular *puentes* (bridges).

BARCELONA CALENDAR OF EVENTS

Barcelona—like Seville and Madrid—is a big fiesta city; whether it's a rip-roaring street carnival or a culture fest, the year's calendar is sprinkled with events to keep in mind when planning your trip. Note that on official holidays (see above) shops, banks, and some restaurants and museums close for the day.

The dates for festivals and events given below may not be precise. Sometimes the exact days are not announced until 6 weeks before the actual festival. Also, days allotted to celebrate Easter Carnival and some other religious days change each year. Check with the Barcelona Tourist Office (see "Visitor Information," earlier in this chapter) if you're planning to attend a specific event.

JANUARY

Día de los Reyes (Three Kings Day). Parades are held around the country on the eve of the Festival of the Epiphany, which is traditionally when Christmas gift-giving is done (the concept of "Santa Claus" has crept into the culture in the past years, meaning that people now also exchange gifts on Christmas). In Barcelona, the three "kings" arrive by boat at the port in the evening to dispense candy to all the incredibly excited children. January 5.

FEBRUARY

Carnaval. Compared to other parts of Spain, particularly Seville in the south,

(Fun Facts) Saint George Conquers the World

In 1995, taking a cue from Catalonia, UNESCO declared April 23 "World Book Day" to encourage people to buy books, to think about books, and to simply read more. In the U.K., children receive a book token and online chat rooms are set up with well-known authors. The idea seems to be catching on, with as many as 30 countries participating.

Carnaval in Barcelona is a low-key event. The most dressing up you are likely to see is done by groups of children or stall owners in the local markets who organize a competition between themselves for "best costume" (buying fresh fish off a woman dressed in full Louis VI regalia is one of those "only in Barcelona" experiences you will treasure), as well as the city's main Carnaval parade. Just south of the city, however, in the seaside town of Sitges, locals, especially the local gay community, go all out and many Barcelonese take the short train ride to celebrate along with them. Just before Lent.

MARCH/APRIL

Semana Santa (Holy Week). Catalonia has some Easter traditions not found in the rest of the country. The Mona is a whimsical chocolate and pastry creation given in the same way we give Easter eggs. On Palm Sunday, palm leaves are blessed in Gaudí's Sagrada Família and the city's main cathedral has the curious *L'ou com balla*—a hollowed-out egg shell that is placed on top of a fountain in the city's cathedral's cloister to bob around and "dance." Out of town, the ominously named Dansa de la Mort (Dance of Death) sees men dressed as skeletons performing a "death" dance in the village of Verges near Girona, and various Passion Plays are also performed, the most famous in the village of Esparraguera, 40km (25 miles) outside of Barcelona. One week before Easter.

La Diada de St. Jordi. Saint George (St. Jordi in Catalan) is the patron saint of Catalonia, and his name day coincides with the deaths of *Don Quixote* writer Miguel Cervantes and William Shakespeare. On this day men give a single red rose to the significant women in their lives (mother, girlfriend, sister, and so on), and women give a book in return (although, in the interest of gender equality, many men now give women a book). This is one of the most colorful days in Catalonia, as thousands of rose-sellers take to the streets and bookshops set up open-air stalls along the major thoroughfares. April 23.

MAY

May Day. Also known as Labor Day, this day sees a huge march by the city's trade union members. On this day, dozens of herbs, natural remedies, and wholesome goodies are sold along the Carrer de l'Hospital in the Fira de Sant Ponç. May 1.

Corpus Christi. During this festival, the streets of Sitges are carpeted in flowers. Can fall in May or June.

JUNE

Verbena de Sant Juan. Catalonia celebrates the Twelfth Night with fiery activities that can keep even grannies up till dawn. Families stock up on fireworks a week in advance before setting them off in streets and squares and even off balconies. Bonfires are lit along the beachfront, and the sky is ablaze with smoke and light. Lots of *cava* is consumed, and it is traditional to have the first dip in the sea of the year at dawn (officially the first day of summer). Madcap fun. June 23.

Sónar. This dance-music and multimedia festival has gained the reputation of being one of the best on the world circuit. Thousands from all over Europe descend on the city for the DJs, live concerts, and other related events. During the day events are held at the Museum of Contemporary Art; at night, they move to the enormous trade fair buildings. Purchase tickets to this wildly popular festival well in advance at www.sonar.es. Early to mid-June.

JULY

El Grec. International names in all genres of music and theater come to the city to perform in various open-air venues, including the mock-Greek theater, namesake of the city's main culture fest. Beginning of July.

AUGUST

Festa Major de Gràcia. This charming weeklong fiesta is held in the village-like neighborhood of Gràcia. All year long, the residents of Gràcia work on elaborate decorations with themes such as marine life, the solar system, or even local politics to hang in the streets. By day, long trestle tables are set up for communal lunches and board games; at night, thousands invade the tiny streets for outdoor concerts, balls, and general revelry. Early to mid-August.

SEPTEMBER

La Diada de Catalunya. This is the most politically and historically significant holiday in Catalonia. Although it celebrates the region's autonomy, the date actually marks the day the city was besieged by Spanish and French troops in 1714 during the War of Succession. Demonstrations calling for greater independence are everywhere; wreath-laying ceremonies take place at tombs of past *politicos;* and the *senyera,* the flag of Catalonia, is hung from balconies. Not your typical tourist fare, but interesting for anyone who wishes to understand Catalan nationalism. September 11.

La Mercè. This celebration honors Our Lady of Mercy (La Mercè), the city's patron saint. Legend has it she rid Barcelona of a plague of locusts, and the Barcelonese give thanks in rip-roaring style. Free concerts, from traditional to contemporary music, are held in the plazas (particularly Plaça de Catalunya and Plaça Sant Jaume), and folkloric figures such as the *gigants* (giants) and *cap grosses* (fatheads) take to the streets. People come out to perform the *sardana* (the traditional Catalan dance) and to watch the nail-biting *castellers* (human towers). Firework displays light up the night, and the hair-raising *correfoc,* a parade of firework-brandishing "devils" and dragons, is the grand finale. One of the best times to be in Barcelona, especially for children. September 24.

OCTOBER

Dia de la Hispanitat. Spain's national day (which commemorates Columbus' "discovery" of the New World) is met with mixed receptions in Catalonia, due to the region's overriding sense of independence. The only street events you are likely to see are demonstrations calling for exactly that, or low-key celebrations from groups of people from other regions of Spain. October 12.

NOVEMBER

All Saints' Day. This public holiday is reverently celebrated, as relatives and friends lay flowers on the graves (or *nichos*—in Spain, people are buried one on top of another in tiny compartments) of the dead. The night before, some of the bars in the city hold Halloween parties, another imported custom that seems to be catching on. November 1.

The Pooping Catalan

When you go to the Fira d' Santa Lucia, look out for one unique personage among the Magi, farm animals, and other *pessebre* figurines. The *caganer* is a small fellow, usually dressed in the garb of a peasant farmer (but also seen in anything from formal attire to the Barcelona Football Club attire). He is squatting, has his pants down, and a stream of excrement connects his bare buttocks to the earth. His origins are lost in folklore, but it is generally believed that he sprang from the Catalan philosophy of "giving back to the earth what one takes from it." The artist Joan Miró placed him in *La Granja* (The Farm), one of his most famous works that is on display at Barcelona's Miró Foundation.

DECEMBER

Nadal (Christmas). In mid-December stall holders set up Fira d' Santa Lucia, a huge open-air market held in the streets around the main cathedral. Thousands come to buy handicrafts, Christmas decorations, trees, and the figurines for their *pessebres* (nativity dioramas) that are hugely popular here. The Betlem Church on La Rambla holds an exhibition of them throughout the month, and a life-size one is constructed outside the city hall in the Plaça Sant Jaume. December 25.

4 GETTING THERE & GETTING AROUND

GETTING TO BARCELONA
By Plane

FROM NORTH AMERICA Flights from the U.S. east coast to Spain take 6 to 7 hours. The national carrier of Spain, **Iberia Airlines** (✆ 800/772-4642; www. iberia.com), has more routes into and within Spain than any other airline. It offers almost daily services from most major U.S. cites (New York, Washington, Chicago, Atlanta) either direct to Barcelona or via Madrid. Also available are attractive rates on fly/drive packages within Iberia and Europe; they can substantially reduce the cost of both the air ticket and the car rental.

A good money-saver to consider is **Iberia's SpainPass.** Available only to passengers who simultaneously arrange for transatlantic passage on Iberia, the SpainPass consists of coupons equivalent to a one-way/one-person ticket to destinations on mainland Spain and the Balearic Islands. Travelers must purchase a three-coupon minimum (228€/$296), and extra coupons can be bought at 60€ ($78) each. The **Europass** services European destinations and can only be purchased as a part of an Iberian Airlines itinerary from your home country.

Iberia's main Spain-based competitor is **Air Europa** (✆ 888/238-7672; www. air-europa.com), which offers daily service from Newark Airport using Continental Airlines to Madrid, with connecting flights to Barcelona. Fares are usually lower than Iberia's.

Delta (✆ 800/241-4141; www.delta. com) runs daily nonstop service from Atlanta (its worldwide hub) and New York (JFK) to Barcelona. Delta's Dream Vacation department offers independent fly/

drive packages, land packages, and escorted bus tours.

FROM THE U.K. British Airways (© 0845/773-3377; www.britishairways.com), **Iberia** (© 020/7830-0011 in London), and **easyJet** (www.easyjet.com) are the three major carriers flying between England and Spain. More than a dozen daily flights, on either British Airways or Iberia, depart from London's Heathrow and Gatwick airports. About the same number of easyJet flights depart daily from Stansted, Luton, and Gatwick airports. easyJet also has direct flights from Liverpool and Newcastle. Another Internet service, **Thomas Cook** (www.flythomascook.com), offers daily service from a variety of airports in the U.K., including Bournemouth, Birmingham, Bristol, and Cardiff. **Ryanair** (www.ryanair.com), which uses Girona (Gerona) Airport, located about an hour outside of Barcelona, flies in from Bournemouth, Dublin, and the East Midlands, as well as London. (There is a connecting bus service from Girona Airport to central Barcelona.) The best air deals on scheduled flights from England are those requiring a Saturday-night stopover.

Budget airlines are giving the major carriers a run for their money and many have now had to slash their fares to compete.

The efficiency of these services has been proven (both easyJet and Ryanair have excellent "on time" records), and most travelers seem happy to forgo the frills and arrive in Barcelona with a few more euros in their pocket.

Charter flights to the regional Catalan airports of Reus and Girona leave from many British regional airports. Girona serves those heading to the Costa Brava north of Barcelona, while Reus is mainly used by those holidaying on the resorts on the Costa Daurada in the south. **Trailfinders** (© 020/7937-5400 in London; www.trailfinders.com) operates charters to both destinations.

In London, there are many bucket shops around Victoria Station and Earls Court that offer cheap fares. Make sure the company you deal with is a member of the IATA, ABTA, or ATOL. These umbrella organizations will help you if anything goes wrong.

CEEFAX, the British television information service, runs details of package holidays and flights to Europe and beyond. Just switch to your CEEFAX channel and you'll find travel information.

FROM AUSTRALIA From Australia, there are a number of options to fly to Spain. The most popular is **Qantas** (www.qantas.com)/**British Airways** (www.ba.com),

---

(Tips) **Europass: A Cost-Cutting Technique**

A noteworthy cost-cutting option is Iberia's Europass. Available only to passengers who simultaneously arrange for transatlantic passage on Iberia and a minimum of two additional flights, it allows passage on any flight within Iberia's European or Mediterranean dominion for $250 for the first two flights and $133 for each additional flight. This is especially attractive for passengers wishing to combine trips to Spain with, for example, visits to such far-flung destinations as Cairo, Tel Aviv, Istanbul, Moscow, and Munich. For details, ask Iberia's phone representative. Iberia's main Spain-based competitor is **Air Europa** (© 888/238-7672; www.air-europa.es), which offers nonstop service from New York's JFK Airport to Barcelona, with continuing service to major cities within Spain. Fares are competitive.

> ## (i) Tips   On Time in Spain
>
> In Spain, a time change occurs the first weekend of spring. Check your watch. Many unsuspecting visitors have arrived at the airport too late and missed their planes.

which flies daily via Asia and London. Other popular and cheaper options are Qantas/**Lufthansa** (www.lufthansa.com) via Asia and Frankfurt, Qantas/**Air France** (www.airfrance.com) via Asia and Paris, and **Alitalia** (www.alitalia.com) via Bangkok and Rome. The most direct option is on **Singapore Airlines** (www.singaporeair. com), with just one stop in Singapore. Alternatively, there are flights on **Thai Airways** (www.thaiair.com) via Bangkok and Rome, but the connections are not always good.

Getting into Town from the Airport

El Prat, Barcelona's airport, is 13km (8 miles) from the city center and there are several options you can use to get into town. One is the **Aerobús,** which leaves just outside all three terminals every 15 minutes from 6am to midnight and stops at Plaça Espanya, Gran Vía Corts Catalanes, Plaça Universitat, and Plaça de Catalunya (taking about 40 min. to reach the last stop). Another is by half-hourly **rail service** that departs between 6:15am and 11:15pm from the El Prat **train station** to Sants (25 min.), which has connections with the Metro or subway. The third is by **taxi** from ranks outside all terminals.

If you've rented a car and are driving into the city yourself, be sure to familiarize yourself with the road signs beforehand.

Long-Haul Flights: How to Stay Comfortable

- Your choice of airline and airplane will definitely affect your legroom. Find more details about U.S. airlines at

www.seatguru.com. For international airlines, the research firm Skytrax has posted a list of average seat pitches at **www.airlinequality.com**.

- Emergency exit seats and bulkhead seats typically have the most legroom. Emergency exit seats are usually left unassigned until the day of a flight (to ensure that someone able-bodied fills the seats); it's worth getting to the ticket counter early to snag one of these spots for a long flight. Many passengers find that bulkhead seating (the row facing the wall at the front of the cabin) offers more legroom, but keep in mind that bulkheads are where airlines often put baby bassinets, so you may be sitting next to an infant.

- To have two seats for yourself in a three-seat row, try for an aisle seat in a center section toward the back of coach. If you're traveling with a companion, book an aisle and a window seat. Middle seats are usually booked last, so chances are good you'll end up with three seats to yourselves.

- Ask about entertainment options. Many airlines offer seatback video systems where you get to choose your movies or play video games—but only on some of their planes. (Boeing 777s are your best bet.)

- To sleep, avoid the last row of any section or the row in front of an emergency exit, as these seats are the least likely to recline. Avoid seats near highly trafficked toilet areas. Avoid seats in the back of many jets—these can be narrower than those in the rest of coach. You also may want to reserve a window

ⓘ Tips   Coping with Jet Lag

Jet lag is a pitfall of traveling across time zones. If you're flying north-south and you feel sluggish when you touch down, your symptoms will be the result of dehydration and the general stress of air travel. When you travel east-west or vice versa, however, your body becomes thoroughly confused about what time it is, and everything from your digestive system to your brain is knocked for a loop. Traveling east, say from Chicago to Barcelona, is more difficult on your internal clock than traveling west, say from London to Hawaii, because most people's bodies are more inclined to stay up late than fall asleep early.

Here are some tips for combating jet lag:

- **Reset your watch** to your destination time before you board the plane.
- **Drink lots of water** before, during, and after your flight. Avoid alcohol.
- **Exercise and sleep well** for a few days before your trip.
- If you have trouble sleeping on planes, **fly eastward on morning flights.**
- **Daylight** is the key to resetting your body clock. At the website for **Outside In** (www.bodyclock.com), you can get a customized plan of when to seek and avoid light.

seat so you can rest your head and avoid being bumped in the aisle.

- Get up, walk around, and stretch every 60 to 90 minutes to keep your blood flowing. See the box "Avoiding 'Economy-Class Syndrome,'" under "Health," p. 53.
- Drink water before, during, and after your flight to combat the lack of humidity in airplane cabins. Avoid alcohol, which will dehydrate you.
- If you're flying with kids, don't forget to carry on toys, books, pacifiers, and chewing gum to help them relieve ear pressure buildup during ascent and descent.

By Car

If you're touring the rest of Europe in a rented car, you might, for an added cost, be allowed to drop off your vehicle in Barcelona.

Highway approaches to Spain are across France on expressways. The most popular border crossing is near Biarritz, but there are 17 other border stations between Spain and France. If you're going to Barcelona or

Catalonia and along the Levante coast (Valencia), take the expressway in France to Toulouse, then the A-61 to Narbonne, and then the A-9 toward the border crossing at La Junquera. You can also take the RN-20, with a border station at Puigcerdà.

Barcelona is tucked away in the northeast corner of Spain, just below the Pyrénées. Main highways within Spain from the city run west and south and the best connections are with Madrid (NII) and Valencia (E15). To get to northern cities such as Pamplona, Burgos, and Bilbao take the A2 highway first to Zaragoza and look for the appropriate connection.

If you're driving from Britain, make sure you have a cross-Channel reservation, as traffic tends to be very heavy, especially in summer.

The major ferry crossings between Britain and France connect Dover and Folkestone with Dunkirk, Calais, or Boulogne. Newhaven is connected with Dieppe and Plymouth with Roscoff. Crossing from Dover to Calais on **P & O Ferries** (ⓒ **800/677-8585** in North America or

08705/20-20-20; www.poferries.com) costs £40 ($64) one-way for a car and two passengers and takes 1¼ hours.

There is one other option for crossing the English Channel. **Norfolkline** (℗ **020/8127-8303;** www.norfolkline.com) operates a ferry service from Dover to Dunkirk that takes 1 hour and 45 minutes and costs £20 to £40 ($32–$64) one-way for a car and two passengers. The drive from Calais to the border would take about 15 hours.

You can take the Chunnel, the underwater Channel Tunnel linking Britain (Folkestone) and France (Calais), by road and rail. **Eurostar** tickets, for train service between London and Paris or Brussels, are available through Rail Europe (℗ **800/EUROSTAR** [3876-7827]; www.eurostar.com for information). In London, make reservations for Eurostar at ℗ **0870/530-00-03.** The tunnel also accommodates passenger cars, charter buses, taxis, and motorcycles, transporting them under the English Channel from Folkestone, England, to Calais, France. It operates 24 hours a day, 365 days a year, running every 15 minutes during peak travel times, and at least once an hour at night. Tickets may be purchased at the tollbooth at the tunnel's entrance. With "Le Shuttle," gone are the days of weather-related delays, seasickness, and advance reservations.

Once you land, you'll have about an 18-hour drive to Barcelona.

If you plan to transport a rental car between England and France, check in advance with the rental company about license and insurance requirements and additional drop-off charges. And be aware that many car-rental companies, for insurance reasons, forbid transport of one of their vehicles over the water between England and France.

CAR RENTALS Many of North America's biggest car-rental companies, including Avis, Budget, and Hertz, maintain offices throughout Spain. Although several Spanish car-rental companies exist, we've received lots of letters from readers of previous editions telling us they've had hard times resolving billing irregularities and insurance claims, so you might want to stick with the U.S.-based rental firms.

Note that tax on car rentals is a whopping 15%, so don't forget to factor that into your travel budget. Usually, prepaid rates do not include taxes, which will be collected at the rental kiosk itself. Be sure to ask explicitly what's included when you're quoted a rate.

Avis (℗ **800/331-1212;** www.avis.com) maintains about 100 branches throughout Spain. If you reserve and pay for your rental by telephone at least 2 weeks before your departure from North America, you'll qualify for the company's best rate, with unlimited kilometers included.

You can usually get competitive rates from **Hertz** (℗ **800/654-3131;** www.hertz.com) and **Budget** (℗ **800/472-3325;** www.budget.com); it always pays to comparison shop. Budget doesn't have a drop-off charge if you pick up a car in one Spanish city and return it to another. All three companies require that drivers be at least 21 years of age and, in some cases, not older than 72. To be able to rent a car, you must have a passport and a valid driver's license; you must also have a valid credit card or a prepaid voucher. An international driver's license is not essential, but you might want to present it if you have one; it's available from any North American office of the American Automobile Association (AAA).

Two other agencies of note include **Kemwel** (℗ **877/820-0668;** www.kemwel.com) and **Auto Europe** (℗ **800/223-5555;** www.autoeurope.com).

Many packages include airfare, accommodations, and a rental car with unlimited mileage. Compare these prices with the cost of booking airline tickets and renting a car separately, in order to see if these offers are good deals. Internet resources can make comparison shopping easier. **Expedia** (www.expedia.com) and **Travelocity** (www.travelocity.com) help you compare prices and locate car-rental bargains from various companies nationwide. They will even make your reservation for you once you've found the best deal.

Most cars hired in Spain are stick shift, not automatic. Most are air-conditioned and nearly all use unleaded gas.

Usual minimum-age limit for rentals is 21 for compact or intermediate size cars, but some van or larger car rentals require that drivers be 25 years of age (or even older). Upper-age requirements reach 70 to 75 for certain vehicles.

For listings of the major car-rental agencies in Barcelona, please see Appendix A: Fast Facts, Toll-Free Numbers & Websites (p. 320).

DRIVING RULES Spaniards drive on the right side of the road. Drivers should pass on the left; local drivers sound their horns when passing another car and flash their lights at you if you're driving slowly (slowly for high-speed Spain) in the left lane. Autos coming from the right have the right-of-way.

Spain's express highways are known as *autopistas,* which charge a toll, and *autovías,* which don't. To exit in Spain, follow the SALIDA (exit) sign, except in Catalonia, where the exit sign says SORTIDA. On most express highways, the speed limit is 120kmph (75 mph). On other roads, speed limits range from 90kmph (56 mph) to 100kmph (62 mph). You will see many drivers far exceeding these limits.

If you must drive through Barcelona try to avoid morning and evening rush hours. Never park your car facing oncoming traffic, as that is against the law. If you are fined by the highway patrol *(Guardia Civil de Tráfico),* you must pay on the spot. Penalties for drinking and driving are very stiff (**breathalyzers** are now being far more strictly used than in the past).

MAPS For one of the best overviews of the Iberian Peninsula (Spain and Portugal), get Michelin map no. 990 (folded version) or map no. 460 (spiral-bound version). For more detailed looks at Spain, Michelin has a series of six maps (nos. 441–446) showing specific regions, complete with many minor roads.

For extensive touring, purchase *Mapas de Carreteras—España y Portugal,* published by Almax Editores and available at most leading bookstores in Spain. This cartographic compendium of Spain provides an overview of the country and includes road and street maps of some of its major cities.

The American Automobile Association (AAA; www.aaa.com) publishes a regional map of Spain that's available free to members at most AAA offices in the United States. Incidentally, the AAA is associated with the **Real Automóvil Club de España (RACE; ✆ 90-240-45-45;** www.race.es). This organization can supply helpful information about road conditions in Spain, including tourist and travel advice. It will also provide limited road service, in an emergency, if your car breaks down.

BREAKDOWNS These can be a serious problem. If you're driving a Spanish-made vehicle that needs parts, you'll probably be able to find them. But if you are driving a foreign-made vehicle, you may be stranded. Have the car checked before setting out on a long trek through Spain. On a major motorway you'll find strategically placed emergency phone boxes. On secondary roads, call for help by asking the operator to locate the nearest Guardia Civil, which will put you in touch with a garage that can tow you to a repair shop.

As noted above, the Spanish affiliate of AAA can provide limited assistance in the event of a breakdown.

By Bus

Bus travel to Spain is possible but not popular—it's quite slow. But coach services

Rapidíssimo!

The Spanish railway system is getting faster and more efficient by the year. A new **AVE high-speed train service,** launched in 2007, connects Barcelona with Madrid in merely 3¹/₄ hours, stopping en route at Lleida and Zaragoza. The train travels at a speed of up to 300km (186 miles) per hour. Quite a reduction from the previous 5-hour-long Talgo service trip, and an astounding improvement from the 7-and-a-half-hour trek a decade ago. The times are indeed changing. Who knows what another decade will bring?

do operate regularly from major capitals of Western Europe to Barcelona, from which bus connections can be made to Madrid. The busiest routes are from London and are run by **Eurolines Limited,** 52 Grosvenor Gardens, London SW1W 0AU (© **0990/ 143-219** or 020/7730-8235). The journey from London's Victoria Station to Barcelona takes 27 hours and 15 minutes, departing from Victoria Station at 3:30pm and arriving at Barcelona Nord at 6:45pm the following day. There is a 30-minute wait in Lyon, France, en route.

By Train

Catalonia has a comprehensive network of rail lines. Hundreds of trains depart every day for points around the region or to more far-flung destinations such as Paris, Madrid, Southern Spain, or even Milan.

If you're already in Europe, you may want to go to Spain by train, especially if you have a Eurailpass. Even if you don't, the cost is moderate. Rail passengers who visit from Britain or France should make *couchette* (bunk beds in a sleeper car) and sleeper reservations as far in advance as possible, especially during the peak summer season.

Since Spain's rail tracks are of a wider gauge than those used for French trains (except for the TALGO and Trans-Europe-Express trains), you'll probably have to change trains at the border unless you're on an express train. For long journeys on Spanish rails, seat and sleeper reservations are mandatory.

The most comfortable and the fastest trains in Spain are the AVE, ALTARIA, TER, TALGO, and Electrotren. However, you pay a supplement to ride on these fast trains. Both first- and second-class fares are sold on Spanish trains. Tickets can be purchased in the United States or Canada at the nearest office of French Rail or from any reputable travel agent. Confirmation of your reservation will take about a week.

All trains in Catalonia are operated by **Spanish State Railways (RENFE).** For day and overnight trips, the comfortable high-speed trains of the TALGO, TER, and Electrotren types are the ones you will be likely to catch.

If you want your car carried, you must travel Auto-Expreso in Spain. This type of auto transport can be booked only through travel agents or rail offices once you arrive in Europe.

To go from London to Barcelona by rail, you'll need to change not only the train but also the rail terminus in Paris. Trip time from London to Paris is about 6 hours; from Paris to Barcelona, about 12 hours, which includes 2 hours spent in Paris changing trains and stations. Many rail passes are available in the United Kingdom for travel in Europe.

GETTING AROUND BARCELONA
By Subway (Metro)

Barcelona has an excellent underground public transport system. The **Metro** goes

(Tips) **All Aboard!**

The most convenient way to see all of Barcelona, especially if your time is limited, is to hop on (and off) the **Bus Turístic** (© 93-318-70-74; www.tmb.net/en_US/ turistes/busturistic/busturistic.jsp). This double-decker, open-top tourist bus travels to all the major areas and sights; you can either choose to disembark or stay on and continue your journey. There are two routes—the red or Nord (North) route, which covers L'Eixample and Tibidabo with Gaudí's main works (including the Sagrada Família) as the highlights, or the blue or Sur (South) route, which allows you to see the Old Town and Montjuïc, both with multilingual commentary along the way. The main point of embarkation is Plaça de Catalunya, outside the El Corte Ingles department store. Cost is 18€ ($23) for the 1-day pass (10€/$13 children 4–12) and 21€ ($27) for the 2-day pass (14€/$18 children 4–12). Tickets can be purchased onboard or at the Tourist Information Office at the Plaça de Catalunya. The service operates daily from 9am to 9:30pm. There is no service on Christmas or New Year's Day.

pretty much any place in the city you will need to get to. It is run by the **TMB** (Transports Metropolitans de Barcelona), who also manage the bus network and the FGC (Ferrocarrils de la Generalitat), a pre-Metro, part underground, part overground system.

It is the efficient Metro system, however, that most visitors to the city are likely to use. There are five color-coded and numbered lines that fan out from the center of the city. Stations are recognizable by a red diamond-shaped sign with the letter M in the center. Maps are available from the stations themselves and tourist information offices. The stations Plaça de Catalunya, Sants, and Passeig de Gràcia connect with RENFE or over-ground trains. When you purchase a ticket for another part of Spain or Catalonia (which you can do from RENFE offices at Sants and Passeig de Gràcia stations) make sure you ask which station it leaves from.

All Metro tickets can be bought on the day of journey or beforehand inside the station, either from the ticket office or a touch-screen vending machine. Various options are available. A single (*senzill* or *sencillo*) ticket costs 1.25€ ($1.65). More

economic options include a T-10 at 6.90€ ($8.95), which offers 10 journeys that can be shared by two or more people, or a T-Día for unlimited 24-hour transport in central Barcelona for 5.25€ ($6.85). Travel Cards valid for 2 or 3 days are also available for 9.60€ to 13.70€ ($12–$18). You can also get reduced tickets for longer periods, but for most short visits the T-10 is your best bet, with the T-Día in reserve for extra-busy days. All these tickets are valid for the FGC and bus systems as well as the Metro.

Note that even with a *sencillo* ticket, once it is activated, it is valid for up to 75 minutes on a different form of transport if you need to do a combined Metro/bus journey. The Metro runs 5am to midnight Sunday to Thursday and 5am to 2am Friday and Saturday. TMB's easy-to-navigate website (www.tmb.net) has lots of information on the city's transport system in English, including which Metro stations and buses are equipped to take wheelchairs. The customer service number is © **93-318-70-74**; there are also customer service centers at Universitat, Sagrada Família, Sants, and Diagonal stations. While it's tempting to hop on and off the

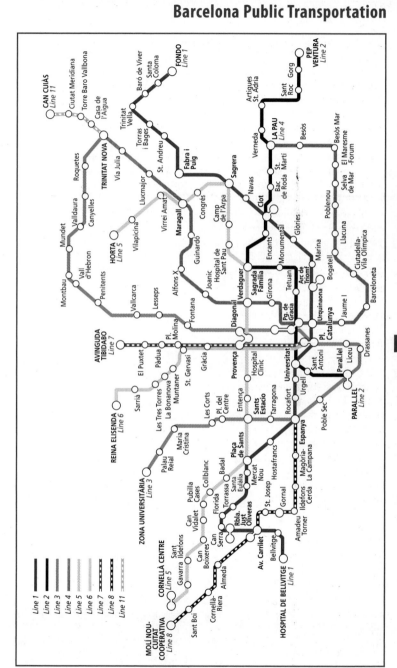

Metro when seeing the sights remember that Metro stations are often only about a 5- to 10-minute walk apart; a good pair of shoes is the best way around central Barcelona!

By Bus

Buses are plentiful, but less convenient, as they lie at the mercy of the city's infamous traffic snarls. Most bus routes stop at the Plaça de Catalunya, also the stop-off point for the Aerobús (see "Getting into Town from the Airport," earlier) and the Bus Turístic (see below). Routes are clearly marked on each stop as are timetables—but most buses stop running well before the Metro closes. One bus service that is particularly useful is the Nitbus, which runs from 11pm to 4am and is often the only alternative to the 2 to 3am taxi drought. These are bright yellow, clearly marked with an N, and most leave from Plaça de Catalunya. Note that while Travel Cards and other TMB passes are valid for daytime buses they're not valid on Nitbuses. Tickets for the latter (1.25€/$1.65 one-way) are bought directly from the driver.

By Taxi

Taxis are plentiful and still reasonably priced. Most of the time you simply hail one in the street (a green light denotes their availability). Taxis have meters, but don't make the mistake of confusing the cheaper day rate (Tariff 2, starting at 1.75€/$2.30) with the slightly more expensive post-8pm night rate (Tariff 1, starting at 1.85€/$2.40). A list of prices and surcharges is (by law) on display on the back passenger window. There have been recent reports of some unscrupulous taxi drivers charging exorbitant fares for short distances, but this seems to mainly be confined to the Ryanair bus drop-off point (see "Getting into Town from the Airport," earlier). Do make sure that the meter is turned on when you start your journey. If you wish to book a cab, either

for the next available or the next day, call the **Institut Metropolità del Taxi** at ℂ **93-223-51-51.** They can also give you information about booking wheelchair-adapted taxis.

By Bicycle

One growing form of transport in the city is the bicycle. There are a number of bicycle lanes in the center of the city and a few firms that rent them, including **Un Coxte Menys,** Esparteria 3 (ℂ **93-268-21-05**), and **Biciclot,** Verneda 16 (ℂ **93-307-74-75**). You are not required by law to wear a helmet.

Other Forms of Transport

At some point in your journey, you may want to visit the mountain of Tibidabo for the views and fun-fair. A century-old tram called the **Tramvía Blau (Blue Streetcar)** goes from Plaça Kennedy to the bottom of the funicular to Tibidabo. It operates daily from 10am to 8pm from mid-June to mid-September and 10am to 6pm on weekends only the rest of the year.

At the end of the run, you can go the rest of the way by funicular to the top, at 503m (1,650 ft.), for a stunning panoramic view of Barcelona. The funicular operates only when the fun-fair at Tibidabo is open (p. 203). Opening times vary according to the time of year and the weather conditions. As a rule, the funicular starts operating 20 minutes before the fun-fair opens and then every half-hour. During peak visiting hours, it runs every 15 minutes. The fare is 2.10€ ($2.75) one-way, and 3.10€ ($4.05) round-trip.

The **Tibibus** goes from the Plaça de Catalunya, in the center of the city, to Tibidabo at limited times, again depending on when the park opens and closes. The one-way fare is 2.10€ ($2.75). Call city hall's information hot line (ℂ **010**) for times.

Barcelona's newest form of public transport is the sleek and comfortable Tramvía Baix, a modern cable car that mainly services the outer suburbs. It is handy, however, for reaching the outer limits of the Diagonal and the Palau de Pedralbes (p. 79). Hop on at Plaça Francesc Macià.

By Car
A car offers the greatest flexibility while you're touring, even if you're just doing day trips from Barcelona. Don't, however, plan to drive *in* Barcelona; it's too congested, street parking is a nightmare, and garage or lot parking is expensive. Theoretically, rush hour is Monday through Saturday from 8 to 10am and 4 to 7:30pm. In reality, it's always busy.

On the other hand, if you're touring Catalonia province, a car can be useful if you want to really get off the beaten track—although bus and train transport to all the main places of interest, such as Tarragona, Montserrat, Girona, and the Costa Brava, is extremely efficient and economical (see chapter 11, "Side Trips in Catalonia").

5 MONEY & COSTS

CURRENCY
The **euro** (€), the single European currency, became the official currency in Spain and 11 other participating countries on January 1, 1999. After an overlapping period of just over 3 years, the old currency, the Spanish peseta, disappeared into history on March 1, 2002, and the euro became the sole currency in use. Exchange rates of participating countries were subsequently locked into a common currency fluctuating against the dollar. Unfortunately for U.S. visitors, in the last couple of years, the euro has gone from basically a one-to-one exchange rate with the dollar to a much stronger position. However, in today's unpredictable economy, exchange rates fluctuate often, so it is best to check the current exchange rate before you go to Spain.

Spain is, therefore, no longer a budget destination and Barcelona itself is often quoted as being the most expensive city in the country (in studies based on everything from the cost of renting an apartment to the price of a loaf of bread). Everything is relative, however, and compared to other major European cities such as London or Paris, it can still be a bargain. If you're from an expensive city in the U.S., you will probably find a lot of the prices comparable, but if you're not used to big-city prices, you could have a bit of sticker shock.

The old adage "You get what you pay for" is as true here as any other European city, up to a point. Reflecting a modern, cosmopolitan city that has to cater to all budgets, you can choose to go either up- or down-market in your choice of dining and accommodations. Often you will find that the most memorable experience is not wholly dependent on the price tag. Staying away from the tourist traps and seeking out family-run restaurants will generally make you more inclined to hand over your credit card with a smile when the check comes. In a climate of stiff competition (especially from the holiday apartment sector), hotels are usually clean and comfortable. Trains are very reasonably priced, fast, and on time, and most service personnel treat you with respect. And, of course, once you move beyond Barcelona and into the rural areas you will find that the price of things (particularly hotels and restaurants) drops noticeably.

In Spain, many prices for children—generally defined as ages 6 to 17—are lower than for adults. Fees for children under 6 are generally waived.

For up-to-the-minute conversion rates, check the **Universal Currency Converter** website: **www.xe.com/ucc**.

The Euro, the U.S. Dollar & the British Pound

Euro €	U.S. $	U.K. £	Euro €	U.S. $	U.K. £
1.00	1.30	0.80	75.00	97.50	61.00
2.00	2.60	1.65	100.00	130.00	81.00
3.00	3.90	2.45	125.00	162.50	102.00
4.00	5.20	3.25	150.00	195.00	122.00
5.00	6.50	4.05	175.00	227.50	142.00
6.00	7.80	4.90	200.00	260.00	163.00
7.00	9.10	5.70	225.00	292.50	183.00
8.00	10.40	6.50	250.00	325.00	203.00
9.00	11.70	7.30	275.00	357.50	224.00
10.00	13.00	8.15	300.00	390.00	244.00
15.00	19.50	12.20	350.00	455.00	285.00
20.00	26.00	16.25	400.00	520.00	325.00
25.00	32.50	20.35	500.00	650.00	407.00
50.00	65.00	40.65	1,000.00	1,300.00	813.00

FOR AMERICAN READERS At the euro's inception, the U.S. dollar and the euro traded on par (that is, $1 approximately equaled 1€). But in recent years the euro has gained considerable strength against the dollar and in converting prices to U.S. dollars, we used the current conversion rate of 1€ = $1.30. However, conversion rates fluctuate often, so double-check the exchange rate before you go.

FOR BRITISH READERS At this writing, £1 equals approximately US$1.60 and trades at 1.23 euros. These were the rates of exchange used to calculate the values in the table "The Euro, the U.S. Dollar & the British Pound."

Exchange rates are more favorable at the point of arrival. Nevertheless, it's often helpful to exchange at least some money before going abroad. Currency and traveler's checks (for which you'll receive a better rate than cash) can be changed at all principal airports, though standing in line at the *cambio* (exchange bureau) at Barcelona airport could make you miss the next bus leaving for downtown.

Before leaving, therefore, check with any of your local American Express or Thomas Cook offices or major banks. Or, order euros in advance from the following: **American Express** (© **800/221-7282**; www.americanexpress.com), **Thomas Cook** (© **800/223-7373**; www.thomascook.com), or **Capital for Foreign Exchange** (© **888/ 842-0880**).

When you get to Barcelona, it's best to exchange currency or traveler's checks at a bank, not a *cambio,* hotel, or shop. Note the rates and ask about commission fees; it can sometimes pay to shop around and ask the right questions.

Many Barcelona hotels don't accept dollar- or pound-denominated checks; those that do will almost certainly charge for the conversion. In some cases, they'll accept countersigned traveler's checks or a credit card, but if you're prepaying a deposit on hotel reservations, it's cheaper and easier to pay with a check drawn on a Spanish bank.

This can be arranged by a large commercial bank or by a specialist such as

Ruesch International, 700 11th St. NW, 4th Floor, Washington, DC 20001-4507 (☎ 800/424-2923; www.ruesch.com), which performs a wide variety of conversion-related tasks, usually for only $5 to $15 per transaction.

If you need a check payable in euros, call Ruesch's toll-free number, describe what you need, and note the transaction number given to you. Mail your dollar-denominated personal check (payable to Ruesch International) to the address above. Upon receiving this, the company will mail a check denominated in euros for the financial equivalent, minus the $2 charge. The company can also help you with many different kinds of wire transfers and conversions of VAT (value-added tax, known as IVA in Spain), refund checks, and also will mail brochures and information packets on request. Brits can contact Ruesch International Ltd., Marble Arch Tower, 14 Floor, 55 Bryanston St., London W14 7AA, England (☎ 0207/563-3300).

ATMS

The easiest and best way to get cash away from home is from an ATM (automated teller machine), sometimes referred to as a "cash machine" or a "cashpoint." In Spain only four-digit numbers are valid so be sure to change any five- or six-digit personal identification number (PIN) you may have to a four-digit number before you go.

The Cirrus (☎ 800/424-7787; www.mastercard.com) and PLUS (☎ 800/843-7587; www.visa.com) networks span the globe; look at the back of your bank card to see which network you're on and then call or check online for ATM locations at your destination. Be sure you know your PIN and daily withdrawal limit before you depart. *Note:* Remember that many banks impose a fee every time you use a card at another bank's ATM, and that fee can be higher for international transactions (up to $5 or more) than for domestic ones (where they're rarely more than $2.50). In addition, the bank from which you withdraw cash may charge its own fee. For international withdrawal fees, ask your bank.

CREDIT CARDS

Credit cards are another safe way to carry money. They also provide a convenient record of all your expenses, and they generally offer relatively good exchange rates. You can withdraw cash advances from your credit cards at banks or ATMs, provided you know your PIN. Keep in mind that you'll pay interest from the moment of your withdrawal, even if you pay your monthly bills on time. Also, note that many banks now assess a 1% to 3% "transaction fee" on *all* charges you incur abroad (whether you're using the local currency or your native currency).

What Things Cost in Barcelona	Euro€	US$	UK£
Cup of coffee	1.30€–1.75€	$1.70–$2.30	1.05£–1.40£
Glass of beer (half pint)	2.50€	$3.25	2.05£
Movie ticket	7.50€	$9.75	6.10£
Taxi from airport to center	25€–30€	$33–$39	20£–24£
Three-course meal for one with wine	25€–30€	$33–$39	20£–24£

Tips **Easy Money**

You'll avoid lines at airport ATMs by exchanging at least some money—just enough to cover airport incidentals and transportation to your hotel—before you leave home.

When you change money, ask for some small bills or loose change. Petty cash will come in handy for tipping and public transportation. Consider keeping the change separate from your larger bills, so that it's readily accessible and you'll be less of a target for theft.

American Express, Visa, MasterCard, and Diners Club credit cards are all widely accepted in Spain.

TRAVELER'S CHECKS

Traveler's checks are accepted in Spain at banks, travel agencies, hotels, and some shops, and you can buy them at most banks before you leave.

They are offered in denominations of $20, $50, $100, $500, and sometimes $1,000. Generally, you'll pay a service charge ranging from 1% to 4%.

The most popular traveler's checks are offered by **American Express** (② **800/807-6233** or 800/221-7282 for cardholders)—this number accepts collect calls, offers service in several foreign languages, and exempts Amex gold and platinum cardholders from the 1% fee; **Visa** (② **800/732-1322**)—AAA members can obtain Visa checks for up to $1,500 at most AAA offices or by calling ② **866/339-3378;** and **MasterCard** (② **800/223-9920**).

American Express, Thomas Cook, Visa, and **MasterCard** offer **foreign currency traveler's checks,** which are useful if you're traveling to one country, or to the Euro zone; they're accepted at locations where dollar checks may not be.

If you carry traveler's checks, keep a record of their serial numbers separate from your checks in the event that they are stolen or lost. You'll get a refund faster if you know the numbers.

6 HEALTH

STAYING HEALTHY

Spain should not pose any major health hazards. The rich cuisine—garlic, olive oil, and wine—may give some travelers mild diarrhea, so take along some anti-diarrhea medicine, moderate your eating habits, and even though the water is generally safe, drink mineral water only. Fish and shellfish from the polluted Mediterranean should only be eaten cooked; however, a lot of the fish and shellfish you see in markets and restaurants actually come from the cleaner Atlantic-washed northern provinces, and you might risk the odd raw *percebe* (goose barnacle) if you can afford it.

If you are traveling around Spain (particularly southern Spain) over the summer, limit your exposure to the sun, especially during the first few days of your trip and, thereafter, from 11am to 2pm. Use a sunscreen with a high protection factor and apply it liberally. Remember that children need more protection than adults do.

The water is safe to drink throughout Spain; however, do not drink the water in

Avoiding "Economy-Class Syndrome"

Deep vein thrombosis, or, as it's known in the world of flying, "economy-class syndrome," is a blood clot that develops in a deep vein. It's a potentially deadly condition that can be caused by sitting in cramped conditions—such as an airplane cabin—for too long. During a flight (especially a long-haul flight), get up, walk around, and stretch your legs every 60 to 90 minutes to keep your blood flowing. Other preventive measures include frequent flexing of the legs while sitting, drinking lots of water, and avoiding alcohol and sleeping pills. If you have a history of deep vein thrombosis, heart disease, or another condition that puts you at high risk, some experts recommend wearing compression stockings or taking anticoagulants when you fly; always ask your physician about the best course for you. Symptoms of deep vein thrombosis include leg pain or swelling, or even shortness of breath.

mountain streams, regardless of how clear and pure it looks.

General Availability of Health Care

No shots of any sort are required before traveling to Spain. Once there, medicines for a wide variety of common ailments, from colds to diarrhea, can be obtained over the counter at local pharmacies or *farmacias.* Generic equivalents of common prescription drugs are also usually available in Spain. (However, it does no harm to bring OTC medicines with you to be on the safe side.)

Contact the **International Association for Medical Assistance to Travellers (IAMAT;** ✆ **716/754-4883** or, in Canada, 416/652-0137; www.iamat.org) for specific tips on travel and health concerns in Spain and for lists of local, English-speaking doctors. The United States **Centers for Disease Control and Prevention** (✆ **800/311-3435;** www.cdc.gov) provides up-to-date information on health hazards by region or country and offers tips on food safety. The website **www.trip prep.com,** sponsored by a consortium of travel medicine practitioners, may also offer helpful advice on traveling abroad. You can find listings of reliable clinics overseas at the **International Society of Travel Medicine** (www.istm.org).

COMMON AILMENTS

CHANGE OF DIET No need to go on a tempting cholesterol binge if you really don't want to. Vegetarians can follow their usual diet pattern in Barcelona, as there is an increasing number of vegetarian eating spots available (p. 60) as well as a multitude of *herbolarios,* or health food shops.

SUN EXPOSURE In the hot weather, do as the locals do and avoid the sun between noon and 4pm. Use a sunscreen with a high protection factor and apply it liberally. Remember that children need more protection than adults do.

SEA HAZARDS Urban beaches in Barcelona have lifeguards on duty and are marked by flags; green is safe, yellow means you should take caution, and red means stay out. Where there are no guards on duty use your common sense and note that, particularly north of Barcelona along the Costa Brava, the seabed is rocky. Over the past years much has been done to improve the standard of Spain's beaches in terms of water pollution, leading to a consistently high rating in terms of cleanliness. At the onset of summer, jellyfish can

Healthy Travels to You

The following government websites offer up-to-date health-related travel advice.
* **Australia:** www.smartraveller.gov.au
* **Canada:** www.hc-sc.gc.ca/index_e.html
* **U.K.:** www.nhs.uk/Healthcareabroad
* **U.S.:** www.cdc.gov/travel

be a problem. They are not poisonous but do have a nasty sting. If you do get stung, seek assistance from the nearest *farmacia* (drugstore).

RESPIRATORY ILLNESSES Lodged between the mountains and the sea, Barcelona can often trap smog from its nearby industrial belt. While the quality of the air is monitored, local media do not publish "high risk" days. Although the problem is nowhere near the level of, say, Beijing, common sense is required for people with respiratory illnesses.

WHAT TO DO IF YOU GET SICK AWAY FROM HOME

Spanish medical facilities are among the best in the world. If a medical emergency arises, your hotel staff can usually put you in touch with a reliable doctor. If not, contact the American embassy or a consulate; each one maintains a list of English-speaking doctors. Medical and hospital services aren't free, so be sure that you have

appropriate insurance coverage before you travel. For travel abroad, you may have to pay all medical costs upfront and be reimbursed later.

Pack prescription medications in your carry-on luggage. Carry written prescriptions in generic, not brand-name, form, and dispense all prescription medications from their original vials. Also bring along copies of your prescriptions in case you lose your pills or run out.

If you suffer from a chronic illness, consult your doctor before your departure. Pack **prescription medications** in your carry-on luggage, and carry them in their original containers, with pharmacy labels—otherwise they won't make it through airport security. Carry the generic name of prescription medicines, in case a local pharmacist is unfamiliar with the brand name.

We list **additional emergency numbers** and insurance information in Appendix A, p. 321.

7 SAFETY

TERRORISM The bomb attacks on three suburban trains in Madrid on March 11, 2004, resulted in the deaths of 200 people; since then political and public attention throughout Spain has been strongly focused on the threat of terrorism.

A direct or indirect consequence of the massacre was that after a massive protest

demonstration of two million people in the streets of the city, voters unexpectedly returned the Socialist party to power in the 2004 general elections. (The policy of the prime minister, Rodríguez Zapatero, had always been to oppose the war in Iraq, and one of his first acts was to authorize the full withdrawal of Spanish troops from that country just over 3 months later.)

To date there is nothing to suggest that Islamic terrorism constitutes a more serious threat in Barcelona than in any other major world city. U.S. tourists traveling to Spain should, however, exercise caution and refer to the guidance offered in the Worldwide Caution Public Announcements issued in the wake of the September 11, 2001, terrorist attacks in the U.S.

The more local threat comes from **ETA,** the Basque separatist-terrorist organization. Negotiations between the PSOE government, helmed by Zapatero, and the outlawed Herri Batasuna party—the front for ETA—led at first to cautious optimism for a peaceful settlement. After 4 decades of deadly bomb attacks, ETA announced a "permanent" ceasefire in 2006—but broke that ceasefire less than 1 year later, with the bombing of the parking garage at Madrid Barajas International Airport in 2006, killing two Ecuadorian immigrants who were sleeping in their cars.

Since then there have been more fatal ETA attacks, including a car bomb that killed a Spanish police officer and the murder of a businessman responsible for building the projected high-speed train route that will pass through the Basque Country to Northern Europe, both in 2008. In light of ETA's continuing intransigence, all direct negotiations with them are currently on hold. Thanks to combined Spanish and French intelligence efforts several leading terrorists were captured and arrested on both sides of the Pyrénées in 2008, and now many people view the ETA as a weakened force whose days are numbered. This may still be just wishful thinking, though.

CONVENTIONAL CRIME While most of Spain has a moderate rate of conventional crime, and most tourists have trouble-free visits to Spain each year, the principal tourist areas have been experiencing an increase in violent crime.

Barcelona has reported a growing incidence of muggings and violent attacks, and older tourists and Asian Americans seem to be particularly at risk. Criminals frequent tourist areas and major attractions such as museums, monuments, restaurants, hotels, beach resorts, trains, train stations, airports, subways, and ATMs.

Reported incidents have occurred in key tourist areas such as La Rambla and the narrow lanes of the Barri Gòtic. Travelers should exercise caution, carry limited cash and credit cards, and leave extra cash, credit cards, passports, and personal documents in a safe location. Crimes have occurred at all times of day and night, though visitors— and residents—are more vulnerable in the early hours of the morning.

Thieves often work in teams or pairs. In most cases, one person distracts a victim while the accomplice performs the robbery. For example, a stranger might wave a map in your face and ask for directions or "inadvertently" spill something on you. While your attention is diverted, an accomplice makes off with the valuables. Attacks can also be initiated from behind, with the victim being grabbed around the neck and choked by one assailant while others rifle through the belongings. A group of assailants may surround the victim, maybe in a crowded popular tourist area or on public transportation, and only after the group has departed does the person discover he/she has been robbed. Some attacks have been so violent that victims have needed to seek medical attention afterward.

Theft from parked cars is also common. Small items like luggage, cameras, or briefcases are often stolen from parked cars. Travelers are advised not to leave valuables in parked cars and to keep doors locked, windows rolled up, and valuables out of sight when driving. "Good Samaritan" scams are unfortunately common. A passing car will attempt to divert the driver's attention by indicating there is a mechanical problem. If the driver stops to check the vehicle, accomplices steal from the car while the driver is looking elsewhere. Drivers should be cautious about accepting help from anyone other than a uniformed Spanish police officer or Civil Guard.

The loss or theft abroad of a U.S. passport should be reported immediately to the local police and the nearest U.S. embassy or consulate. U.s. citizens may refer to the Department of State's pamphlet, *A Safe Trip Abroad,* for ways to promote a more trouble-free journey. The pamphlet is available by mail from the Superintendent of Documents, U.S. Government Printing Office, 732 North Capitol St. NW, Washington, DC 20402; via the Internet at www.gpoaccess.gov/index.html; or via the Bureau of Consular Affairs home page at http://travel.state.gov.

DEALING WITH DISCRIMINATION

As Barcelona's population slowly becomes more international, overt racial prejudice appears to be diminishing. Still, as in other places, there is a small fringe of hard-core racists.

Since the Madrid bombings of 2004, there has been a slight hardening of attitudes toward Arabs by certain members of the community; and some residents' attitudes toward Latin Americans have been soured by the appearance (in relatively small numbers) of young criminal gangs such as the "Latin Kings" and "Dominicans Don't Play" in the outer areas of the city.

Barcelona is as liberal as any other city in its acceptance of gays and lesbians, including homosexual marriages (see "Gay & Lesbian Travelers," below).

Solo female travelers can expect a reasonably hassle-free trip (see "Women Travelers," below).

8 SPECIALIZED TRAVEL RESOURCES

TRAVELERS WITH DISABILITIES

Most disabilities shouldn't stop anyone from traveling. There are more options and resources out there than ever before.

Because of the endless flights of stairs in most buildings in Barcelona, visitors with disabilities may have difficulty getting around the city, but conditions are slowly improving: Newer hotels are more sensitive to the needs of persons with disabilities, and the more expensive restaurants are generally wheelchair-accessible. However, since most places have very limited, if any, facilities for people with disabilities, you might consider taking an organized tour specifically designed to accommodate such travelers.

For the names and addresses of such tour operators as well as other related information, contact the **Society for**

Accessible Travel and Hospitality (SATH), 347 Fifth Ave., New York, NY 10016 (© **212/447-7284;** www.sath.org). Annual membership dues are $49, or $29 for seniors and students. **AirAmbulance-Card.com** is now partnered with SATH and allows you to preselect top-notch hospitals in case of an emergency. Another organization that offers assistance to travelers with disabilities is **MossRehab** (www.mossresourcenet.org).

For the blind or visually impaired, the best source is the **American Foundation for the Blind (AFB),** 15 W. 16th St., New York, NY 10011 (© **800/232-5463** to order information kits and supplies, or 212/502-7600; www.afb.org). It offers information on travel and various requirements for the transport and border formalities for Seeing Eye dogs. It also issues identification cards to those who are legally blind.

Many travel agencies offer customized tours and itineraries for travelers with disabilities. One of the best organizations serving the needs of persons with disabilities (wheelchairs and walkers) is **Flying Wheels Travel,** 143 W. Bridge, P.O. Box 382, Owatonna, MN 55060 (✆ **800/535-6790** or 507/451-5005; www.flyingwheels travel.com), which offers various escorted tours and cruises internationally. Others include **Access-Able Travel Source** (✆ **303/232-2979;** www.access-able.com) and **Accessible Journeys** (✆ **800/846-4537** or 610/521-0339; www.disabilitytravel. com).

If you're flying around Spain, the airline and ground staff will help you on and off planes and reserve seats for you with sufficient legroom, but it is essential to arrange for this assistance *in advance* by contacting your airline.

Avis Rent a Car has an "Avis Access" program that offers such services as a dedicated 24-hour toll-free number (✆ **888/879-4273**) for customers with special travel needs; special car features such as swivel seats, spinner knobs, and hand controls; and accessible bus service.

Check out the quarterly magazine *Emerging Horizons* (www.emerging horizons.com), and *Open World* magazine, published by SATH.

FOR BRITISH TRAVELERS WITH DISABILITIES The annual vacation guide *Holidays and Travel Abroad* costs £5 from **Royal Association for Disability and Rehabilitation (RADAR),** Unit 12, City Forum, 250 City Rd., London EC1V 8AF (✆ **020/7250-3222;** www.radar.org.uk). RADAR also provides a number of information packets on such subjects as sports and outdoor vacations, insurance, financial arrangements for persons with disabilities, and accommodations in nursing care units for groups or for the elderly. Each of these fact sheets is available for £2. Both the fact sheets and the holiday guides can be mailed outside the United Kingdom for a nominal postage fee.

Another good service is the **Holiday Care,** 2nd Floor Imperial Buildings, Victoria Road, Horley, Surrey RH6 7PZ (✆ **01293/774-535;** fax 01293/784-647; www.holidaycare.org.uk), a national charity that advises on accessible accommodations for elderly people or those with disabilities. Annual membership costs £15 (U.K. residents) and £30 (abroad). Once you're a member, you can receive a newsletter and access to a free reservations network for hotels throughout Britain and, to a lesser degree, Europe and the rest of the world.

For more on organizations that offer resources to travelers with disabilities, go to www.frommers.com/planning.

GAY & LESBIAN TRAVELERS

In 1978, Spain legalized homosexuality among consenting adults. In April 1995, the parliament of Spain banned discrimination based on sexual orientation, and marriage between same-sex couples became legal in 2005. Catalonia has helped pave the way in rights for gay couples, preempting national laws by granting same-sex couples the same official status and conjugal rights as heterosexual ones, and has given the green light for changes in the law that would facilitate same-sex couples adopting. Barcelona is one of the major centers of gay life in Spain, and two of the most popular resorts for gay travelers, Sitges (south of Barcelona) and the island of Ibiza, are within close proximity.

To learn about gay and lesbian travel in Spain, you can secure publications or join data-dispensing organizations before you go. Both lesbians and gay men might want to pick up a copy of *Gay Travel A to Z,* which provides general information as well as listings for bars, hotels, restaurants, and places of interest for gay travelers throughout the world.

The **International Gay & Lesbian Travel Association (IGLTA),** 4331 N. Federal, Suite 304, Ft. Lauderdale, FL 33308 (✆ **800/448-8550** or 954/776-2626; www.iglta.com), specializes in connecting travelers with the appropriate gay-friendly service organization or tour specialist. It offers a quarterly newsletter, marketing mailings, and a membership directory that is updated four times a year. For an online directory of gay- and lesbian-friendly travel businesses, go to their website and click on "Members."

Many agencies offer tours and travel itineraries specifically for gay and lesbian travelers. Among them are **Above and Beyond Tours** (✆ **800/397-2681;** www. abovebeyondtours.com); **Now, Voyager** (✆ **800/255-6951;** www.nowvoyager. com); and **Olivia** (✆ **800/631-6277;** www.olivia.com).

Gay.com Travel (✆ **800/929-2268** or 415/644-8044; www.gay.com/travel or www.outandabout.com) provides regularly updated information about gay-owned, gay-oriented, and gay-friendly lodging, dining, sightseeing, nightlife, and shopping establishments in every important destination worldwide.

The following travel guides are available at many bookstores, or you can order them from any online bookseller: *Spartacus International Gay Guide* (Bruno Gmünder Verlag; www.spartacusworld. com/gayguide); *Odysseus: The International Gay Travel Planner* (Odysseus Enterprises Ltd.); and the *Damron* guides (www.damron.com), with separate, annual books for gay men and lesbians.

For more gay and lesbian travel resources visit www.frommers.com/planning.

SENIOR TRAVEL

Many discounts are available for seniors traveling to Barcelona, but often you need to be a member of an association to obtain them.

For information before you go, write for the free booklet, *101 Tips for the Mature Traveler,* available from **Grand Circle Travel,** 347 Congress St., Suite 3A, Boston, MA 02210 (✆ **800/221-2610** or 617/350-7500; www.gct.com).

One of the most dynamic travel organizations for seniors is **Elderhostel,** 11 Avenue de Lafayette, Boston, MA 02111 (✆ **877/426-8056;** www.elderhostel.org). Established in 1975, it operates an array of programs throughout Europe, including Spain. Most courses last around 3 weeks and are a good value, since they include airfare, accommodations in student dormitories or modest inns, all meals, and tuition. Courses involve no homework, are not graded, and are often liberal arts oriented. These are not luxury vacations, but they are fun and fulfilling. Participants must be at least 55 years old. A companion must be at least 50 years old; spouses may participate regardless of age. **ElderTreks** (✆ **800/741-7956;** www.eldertreks.com) offers small-group tours to off-the-beaten-path or adventure-travel locations, restricted again to travelers 50 and older.

In the United States, the best organization to join is the **AARP,** 601 E St. NW, Washington, DC 20049 (✆ **800/424-3410** or 202/434-AARP [2277]; www. aarp.org). Members get discounts on hotels, airfares, and car rentals. AARP offers members a wide range of benefits, including *AARP: The Magazine* and a monthly newsletter. Anyone over 50 can join.

Recommended publications offering travel resources and discounts for seniors include the quarterly magazine *Travel 50 & Beyond* (www.travel50andbeyond. com); *Travel Unlimited: Uncommon Adventures for the Mature Traveler* (Avalon); *101 Tips for Mature Travelers,* available from Grand Circle Travel (✆ **800/221-2610** or 617/350-7500; www.gct.com); and *Unbelievably Good Deals and Great Adventures That You Absolutely Can't Get Unless You're Over 50* (McGraw-Hill), by Joan Rattner Heilman.

For more information and resources on travel for seniors, see www.frommers.com/planning.

FAMILY TRAVEL

Barcelona is a lively and very crowded city that also happens to be a very good destination for families with **children.** From the peaceful **Parc Güell** to the **Parque Zoológico,** as well as fun spots like **Happy Park Port Aventura** and **Cataluña en Miniatura,** there's plenty to choose from.

To locate accommodations, restaurants, and attractions that are particularly kid-friendly, refer to the "Kids" icon throughout this guide.

For some general tips on family travel check our very own *Frommer's 500 Places to Take Your Kids Before They Grow Up,* which can be purchased via www.amazon.com.

Note that children traveling to Spain with companions other than their own parents should have a notarized letter from their parents to this effect. For full entry requirements to Spain check www. travel.state.gov.

For a list of more family-friendly travel resources, visit www.frommers.com/planning.

WOMEN TRAVELERS

In Barcelona women are as emancipated as in any other main European city. If a degree of machismo still exists it is minimal today, and women are increasingly reaching high positions in all walks of life. Women who explore the city on their own should not expect any hassle.

For general advice to female travelers check out the award-winning website **Journeywoman** (www.journeywoman.com), a women's travel-information network where you can sign up for a free e-mail newsletter and get advice on everything from etiquette and dress to safety; or the travel guide *Safety and Security for Women Who Travel* by Sheila Swan and Peter Laufer (Travelers' Tales, Inc.), offering common-sense tips on safe travel.

For general travel resources for women, go to www.frommers.com/planning.

MULTICULTURAL TRAVELERS

As Barcelona becomes increasingly multicultural, particularly in areas of the Old Town such as El Raval, visitors and residents of all nationalities are naturally accepted by what is in effect a fairly open-minded society. A person of a different race or skin color rarely draws more than a second glance, unlike a few decades back when Barcelona was a 99% *castizo* city.

That said, instances of racial conflict are not unknown, though these tend to be with African, Arabic, and Latin American locals rather than foreign visitors. (See "Dealing with Discrimination," above.)

FOR AFRICAN-AMERICAN TRAVELERS Black Travel Online (www.blacktravelonline.com) posts news on upcoming events and includes links to articles and travel-booking sites. **Soul of America** (www.soulofamerica.com) is a comprehensive website, with travel tips, event and family-reunion postings, and sections on historically black beach resorts and active vacations.

STUDENT TRAVEL

Check out the **International Student Travel Confederation (ISTC;** www.istc.org) website for comprehensive travel services information and details on how to get an **International Student Identity Card (ISIC),** which qualifies students for substantial savings on rail passes, plane tickets, entrance fees, and more. It also provides students with basic health and life insurance and a 24-hour help line. The card is valid for a maximum of 18 months. You can apply for the card online or in person at **STA Travel** (© **800/781-4040** in North America; 132-782 in Australia;

PLANNING YOUR TRIP TO BARCELONA

3

SPECIALIZED TRAVEL RESOURCES

Tips **Barcelona's Vegetarian Scene**

Being a "veggie" no longer means being an outsider in the Catalan capital. In the past decade the traditional dominance of carnivore-oriented establishments has been challenged by a small but growing number of vegetarian restaurants.

You don't have to confine yourself to 100% green establishments to get the goods, though, as many standard Catalan eating spots offer a large choice of noncarnivorous *platos.*

Apart from the ubiquitous tortilla (made, *naturalmente,* with eggs Spanish-style and not from cornmeal Mexican-style), look for dishes like *escalivada* (grilled red and green pepper salad), *berengenas al horno* (eggplant baked in the oven), *calabaza guisada* (stewed pumpkin), *setas al jerez* (mushrooms cooked in sherry), and *pisto* (Spain's answer to ratatouille with tomatoes, peppers, eggplant, zucchini, and onions all cooked in oil and garlic—avoid the Manchego version, though, as this has bits of ham in it). *Jamón* (Mountain or cooked, Serrano or York) is scarcely regarded as "real" meat in Spain and can even appear in apparently innocuous dishes such as *caldo* (broth), so confirm with the waiter before you order.

Arabic, Indian, and Italian restaurants may also provide what you're looking for, with their inventive range of couscous, rice, and pasta-based dishes. If fish is an acceptable option, there are, of course, plenty of seafood restaurants to choose from, though these tend to be expensive.

087/1230-0040 in the U.K.; www.sta travel.com), the biggest student travel agency in the world; check out the website to locate STA Travel offices worldwide. If you're no longer a student but are still under 26, you can get an **International Youth Travel Card (IYTC)** from the same people, which entitles you to some discounts. **Travel CUTS** (© **800/592-2887;** www.travelcuts.com) offers similar services for both Canadians and U.S. residents. Irish students may prefer to turn to **USIT** (© **01/602-1904;** www.usit.ie), an Ireland-based specialist in student, youth, and independent travel.

SINGLE TRAVELERS

On package vacations, single travelers are often hit with a "single supplement" to the base price. To avoid it, you can agree to room with other single travelers or find a compatible roommate before you go, from one of the many roommate-locator agencies.

For more information on traveling single, go to www.frommers.com/planning.

FOR VEGETARIAN VISITORS

There is an increasing choice of vegetarian restaurants in Barcelona. Check chapter 6, "Where to Dine," or visit the website **www.vegdining.com.**

9 SUSTAINABLE TOURISM

Sustainable tourism is conscientious travel. It means being careful with the environments you explore, and respecting the communities you visit. Two overlapping components of sustainable travel are **ecotourism** and **ethical tourism.** The

International Ecotourism Society (TIES) defines ecotourism as responsible travel to natural areas that conserves the environment and improves the well-being of local people. TIES suggests that ecotourists follow these principles:

- Minimize environmental impact.
- Build environmental and cultural awareness and respect.
- Provide positive experiences for both visitors and hosts.
- Provide direct financial benefits for conservation and for local people.
- Raise sensitivity to host countries' political, environmental, and social climates.
- Support international human rights and labor agreements.

You can find some eco-friendly travel tips and statistics, as well as touring companies and associations—listed by destination under "Travel Choice"—at the **TIES** website, www.ecotourism.org.

There are a surprising number of beautiful and untouched eco-friendly regions near Barcelona. If you don't want to rent a car, you can easily get there by bus or local train *(cercanías)*. The **Illes Medes** is a group of seven miniscule islets close to the fishing port/resort of Estartit; the clear waters here are ideal for boating and scuba-diving excursions to see the water's rich variety of plant and marine life. The **Parc Natural del Delta del Ebre,** near Tortosa, is a salty and fertile region of marshes, dunes, and rice paddies that is great for bird-watching, sailing, and cycling along reed-lined waterside paths.

While much of the focus of ecotourism is about reducing impacts on the natural environment, ethical tourism concentrates on ways to preserve and enhance local economies and communities, regardless of location. You can embrace ethical tourism by staying at a locally owned hotel or shopping at a store that employs local workers and sells locally produced goods.

Responsible Travel (www.responsible travel.com) is a great source of sustainable travel ideas; the site is run by a spokesperson for ethical tourism in the travel industry. **Sustainable Travel International** (www.sustainabletravelinternational.org) promotes ethical tourism practices, and manages an extensive directory of sustainable properties and tour operators around the world.

In the U.K., **Tourism Concern** (www.tourismconcern.org.uk) works to reduce social and environmental problems connected to tourism. The **Association of Independent Tour Operators** (AITO; www.aito.co.uk) is a group of specialist operators leading the field in making holidays sustainable.

Volunteer travel has become increasingly popular among those who want to venture beyond the standard group-tour experience to learn languages, interact with locals, and make a positive difference while on vacation. Volunteer travel usually doesn't require special skills—just a willingness to work hard—and programs vary in length from a few days to a number of weeks. Some programs provide free housing and food, but many require volunteers to pay for travel expenses, which can add up quickly.

For general info on volunteer travel, visit **www.volunteerabroad.org** and **www.idealist.org**. Before you commit to a volunteer program, it's important to make sure any money you're giving is truly going back to the local community, and that the work you'll be doing will be a good fit for you. **International Volunteer Programs Association** (www.volunteerinternational.org) has a helpful list of questions to ask to determine the intentions and the nature of a volunteer program.

Animal-Rights Issues
A Load of Bull

Spain is not a country that has been particularly noted for its kindness to animals in the past. Fiestas which include torturing bulls by attacking them with lances in the Castilian town of Tordesillas still prevail

It's Easy Being Green

Here are a few simple ways you can help conserve fuel and energy when you travel:

- Each time you take a flight or drive a car greenhouse gases release into the atmosphere. You can help neutralize this danger to the planet through "carbon offsetting"—paying someone to invest your money in programs that reduce your greenhouse gas emissions by the same amount you've added. Before buying carbon offset credits, just make sure that you're using a reputable company, one with a proven program that invests in renewable energy. Reliable carbon offset companies include **Carbonfund** (www.carbonfund.org), **TerraPass** (www.terrapass.org), and **Cool Climate** (http://coolclimate.berkeley.edu).

- Whenever possible, choose nonstop flights; they generally require less fuel than indirect flights that stop and take off again. Try to fly during the day—some scientists estimate that nighttime flights are twice as harmful to the environment. And pack light—each 15 pounds of luggage on a 5,000-mile flight adds up to 50 pounds of carbon dioxide emitted.

- Where you stay during your travels can have a major environmental impact. To determine the green credentials of a property, ask about trash disposal and recycling, water conservation, and energy use; also question if sustainable materials were used in the construction of the property. The website **www.greenhotels.com** recommends green-rated member hotels around the world that fulfill the company's stringent environmental requirements. Also consult **www.environmentallyfriendlyhotels.com** for more green accommodations ratings.

- At hotels, request that your sheets and towels not be changed daily. (Many hotels already have programs like this in place.) Turn off the lights and air-conditioner (or heater) when you leave your room.

- Use public transport where possible—trains, buses, and even taxis are more energy-efficient forms of transport than driving. Even better is to walk or cycle; you'll produce zero emissions and stay fit and healthy on your travels.

- If renting a car is necessary, ask the rental agent for a hybrid, or rent the most fuel-efficient car available. You'll use less gas and save money at the tank.

- Eat at locally owned and operated restaurants that use produce grown in the area. This contributes to the local economy and cuts down on greenhouse gas emissions by supporting restaurants where the food is not flown or trucked in across long distances. Visit **SustainLane** (www.sustainlane.org) to find sustainable eating and drinking choices around the U.S.; also check out **www.eatwellguide.org** for tips on eating sustainably in the U.S. and Canada.

(though the notorious throwing-a-donkey-off-a-tower shebang that took place annually in an Extremaduran village has happily disappeared).

The main bone of contention is, of course, the **bullfight,** which is one traditional Spanish activity that has never been as popular in Catalonia as it has in more stalwart bastions like Andalusia and Madrid. It's a national event unique in Europe (in Portugal and Southern France they have bullfights but don't kill the bull), and a big moneymaker. For purely financial reasons, it's not likely to be dropped yet.

In general, Catalans have always had a gentler attitude toward animals than most other Spaniards, and today even more Barcelonans are proud owners of *perros* (dogs), despite impractically cramped or congested grass-free urban surroundings. Throughout Spain people who mistreat any animal will be punished by law, even if it is only with comparatively small fines.

Spain's socialist government—which is more attentive to humane issues than any ruling party before—declared its support for the Great Ape Project in June 2008, which proposes to grant life, liberty, and protection to chimpanzees, gorillas, and their kin, ensuring their protection from mistreatment in circuses, scientific experiments, and even advertising campaigns. That's one small step for animalkind. Maybe there's still hope for the bull.

For information on animal-friendly issues throughout the world, visit **Tread Lightly** (www.treadlightly.org).

10 PACKAGES FOR THE INDEPENDENT TRAVELER

Package tours are not the same thing as escorted tours. With a package tour, you travel independently but pay a group rate. Packages usually include airfare, a choice of hotels, and car rentals, and packagers often offer several options at different prices. In many cases, a package that includes airfare, hotel, and transportation to and from the airport will cost you less than just the hotel alone would have, had you booked it yourself. That's because packages are sold in bulk to tour operators—who resell them to the public at a cost that drastically undercuts standard rates.

RECOMMENDED PACKAGE TOUR OPERATORS

One good source of package deals is the airlines themselves. Most major airlines offer air/land packages. See "By Plane," earlier in this chapter; most airlines offer packages that may include car rentals and accommodations in addition to your airfare.

The best place to start your search is the travel section of your local Sunday newspaper. Also check the ads in the back of national travel magazines like *Travel + Leisure, National Geographic Traveler,* and *Condé Nast Traveler.* One of the biggest packagers in the Northeast, **Liberty Travel** (© 888/271-1584; www.libertytravel. com), usually boasts a full-page ad in Sunday papers. **American Express Travel** (© 800/941-2639; www.americanexpress. com/travel) is another option.

Among the airline packagers, **Iberia Airlines** (© 800/772-4642 or 90-240-05-00 in Spain; www.iberia.com) leads the way. Other packages for travel in Spain are offered by **United Airlines** (© 800/241-6522; www.united.com), **American Airlines Vacations** (© 800/321-2121;

Tips Ask Before You Go

Before you invest in a package deal or an escorted tour:

- Always ask about the **cancellation policy.** Can you get your money back? Is there a deposit required?
- Ask about the **accommodations choices and prices** for each. Then look up the hotels' reviews in a Frommer's guide and check their rates online for your specific dates of travel. Also find out what types of rooms are offered.
- Request a complete **schedule.** (Escorted tours only)
- Ask about the **size** and demographics of the group. (Escorted tours only)
- Discuss what is included in the **price** (transportation, meals, tips, airport transfers, etc.; escorted tours only).
- Finally, look for **hidden expenses.** Ask whether airport departure fees and taxes, for example, are included in the total cost—they rarely are.

www.aavacations.com), and **Delta Vacations** (© 800/872-7786; www.deltavacations.com). **Continental Airlines Vacations** (© 800/301-3800; www.co vacations.com) is also worth a look. Several big **online travel agencies**—Expedia, Travelocity, Orbitz, Site59, and Last minute.com—also do a brisk business in packages.

Travel packages are also listed in the travel section of your local Sunday newspaper. Or check ads in the national travel magazines such as *Arthur Frommer's Budget Travel Magazine, Travel + Leisure, National Geographic Traveler,* and *Condé Nast Traveler.*

11 ESCORTED GENERAL-INTEREST TOURS

Escorted tours are structured group tours, with a group leader. The price usually includes everything from airfare to hotels, meals, tours, admission costs, and local transportation. Many people derive security and peace of mind from the structure they offer, as they take you to the maximum number of sights in the minimum amount of time with the least amount of hassle. They're particularly convenient for people with limited mobility and they can be a great way to make new friends. On the downside, you'll have little opportunity for serendipitous interactions with locals. The tours can be jam-packed with

activities, leaving little room for individual sightseeing, whim, or adventure—plus they often focus on the heavily touristed sites, so you miss out on many a lesser-known gem.

RECOMMENDED ESCORTED TOUR OPERATORS

There are many escorted tour companies to choose from, each offering transportation to and within Spain, prearranged hotel space, and such extras as bilingual tour guides and lectures. Some of the most expensive and luxurious tours are run by

Frommers.com: The Complete Travel Resource

Planning a trip or just returned? Head to **Frommers.com,** voted Best Travel Site by *PC Magazine.* We think you'll find our site indispensable before, during, and after your travels—with expert advice and tips; independent reviews of hotels, restaurants, attractions, and preferred shopping and nightlife venues; vacation giveaways; and an online booking tool. We publish the complete contents of over 135 travel guides in our **Destinations** section, covering over 4,000 places worldwide. Each weekday, we publish original articles that report on **Deals and News** via our free **Frommers.com Newsletters.** What's more, **Arthur Frommer** himself blogs 5 days a week, with cutting opinions about the state of travel in the modern world. We're betting you'll find our **Events** listings an invaluable resource; it's an up-to-the-minute roster of what's happening in cities everywhere—including concerts, festivals, lectures, and more. We've also added weekly **podcasts, interactive maps,** and hundreds of new images across the site. Finally, don't forget to visit our **Message Boards,** where you can join in conversations with thousands of fellow Frommer's travelers and post your trip report once you return.

Abercrombie & Kent International (© 800/323-7308 or 630/954-2944; www.abercrombiekent.com), including a deluxe 11-day "Highlights of Spain" tour that spends 4 days in Barcelona. **Trafalgar Tours** (© 800/854-0103 or 212/689-8977; www.trafalgartours.com) offers a number of tours of Spain. **Insight Vacations** (© 800/582-8380; www.insight vacations.com) offers a "Highlights of Spain" tour that is an 11-day tour that begins in Madrid and sweeps along the southern and eastern coasts, stopping in Barcelona; prices for this tour start at $2,000 (1,538€). **Petrabax Tours** (© 800/634-1188; www.petrabax.com) attracts those who prefer to see Spain by bus, although fly/drive packages are also offered, featuring stays in *paradors* (high-standard, state-run hotels—some modern, some in historic buildings).

12 SPECIAL-INTEREST TRIPS

The **Barcelona Information Office** (www.barcelonaturisme.com) provides several detailed walks covering different architectural and aesthetic aspects of the city (Gothic, *modernisme,* gourmet and Picasso). They depart from the Plaça de Catalunya, last between 1¹/₂ and 2 hours, and cost between 10€ ($13) and 15€ ($20) per adult.

More personal and expensive walking trips are arranged by **My Favourite Things** (© 63-726-54-05; www.myft.net). These cover more offbeat and idiosyncratic aspects of Barcelona and cost from 30€ ($39) per adult.

For food and wine lovers there's **Saboroso** (© 66-777-04-92; www.saboroso.com), which arranges gourmet tapas tours and visits to top Catalan vineyards such as Priorat and Penedés.

13 STAYING CONNECTED

TELEPHONES

If you don't speak Spanish, you'll find it easier to telephone from your hotel, but remember that this is often very expensive because hotels impose a surcharge on every operator-assisted call. In some cases it can be as high as 40% or more. On the street, phone booths (known as *cabinas*) have dialing instructions in English, although very few actually take coins. Instead, purchase a *tarjeta telefónica* from a newsstand or tobacconist. If you need to make a lengthy overseas call, a *locutorio* (call center) is the best bet. Located throughout the Old Town, these call centers offer the best rates and booths are provided for privacy. *Locutorios* also sell phone cards supplied by private operators. You can purchase as much as 3 hours of call time to the U.S. for as little as 6€ ($7.80), although you will pay the connection fee (the cost of a local call) on top. These cards can be used from both fixed and mobile phones and must be used within a month of the first call.

In Barcelona some smaller establishments, especially bars, discos, and a few informal restaurants, don't have phones. Further, many summer-only bars and discos secure a phone for the season only and then get a new number the next season. Many attractions, such as small churches or even minor museums, have no staff to receive inquiries from the public.

In 1998, all telephone numbers in Spain changed to a nine-digit system instead of the six- or seven-digit method used previously. Each number is now preceded by its provincial code for local, national, and international calls. For example, when calling to Barcelona from Barcelona or another province within Spain, telephone customers must dial 91-123-4567. Similarly, when calling Girona from within or outside the province, dial 972-123-4567.

To call Barcelona: If you're calling Barcelona from the United States:

1. Dial the international access code: **011.**
2. Dial the country code for Spain: **34.**
3. Dial **91** for Barcelona and then the number. So the whole number you'd dial would be 011-34-1-000-0000. (***Note:*** If you are dialing a Barcelona number from within Spain the prefix code is **93.**)

To make international calls from Barcelona: Dial 00 and then the country code (U.S. or Canada 1, U.K. 44, Ireland 353, Australia 61, New Zealand 64). Dial the area code and number. For example, if you wanted to call the British Embassy in Washington, D.C., you would dial 00-1-202-588-7800.

For directory assistance: Dial ✆ **11818** if you're looking for a number inside Spain, and dial ✆ **11825** for numbers to all other countries.

For operator assistance: If you need operator assistance in making an international call, dial ✆ **1008** (for Europe, Morocco, Tunisia, Libya, and Turkey) or **1005** (for the U.S.A. and all other countries), and ✆ **1009** if you want to call a number in Spain.

Rechargeable online phone cards: Planet Phone Cards (www.planetphonecards.com) offers a wide range of phone cards online.

Toll-free numbers: Numbers beginning with **900** in Spain are toll-free, but calling a 1-800 number in the States from Spain is not toll-free. In fact, it costs the same as an overseas call.

When in Spain, the access number for an **AT&T** calling card is ✆ **800/CALL-ATT** (225-5288). The access number for **Sprint** is ✆ **800/888-0013.**

More information is also available on the Telefónica website at www.telefonica.es.

CELLPHONES

The three letters that define much of the world's **wireless capabilities** are GSM (Global System for Mobiles), a big, seamless network that makes for easy cross-border cellphone use throughout Europe and dozens of other countries worldwide. In the U.S., T-Mobile, AT&T Wireless, and Cingular use this quasi-universal system; in Canada, Microcell and some Rogers customers are GSM, and all Europeans and most Australians use GSM.

If your cellphone is on a GSM system, and you have a world-capable multiband phone such as many Sony Ericsson, Motorola, or Samsung models, you can make and receive calls across civilized areas on much of the globe, from Andorra to Uganda. Just call your wireless operator and ask for "international roaming" to be activated on your account. Unfortunately, per-minute charges can be high—usually $1 to $1.50 in Western Europe. That's why it's important to buy an "unlocked" world phone from the get-go. Many cellphone operators sell "locked" phones that restrict you from using any other removable computer memory phone chip (called a **SIM card**) card other than the ones they supply. Having an unlocked phone allows you to install a cheap, prepaid SIM card (found at a local retailer) in your destination country. (Show your phone to the salesperson; not all phones work on all networks.) You'll get a local phone number—and much, much lower calling rates. Getting an already locked phone unlocked can be a complicated process, but it can be done; just call your cellular operator and say you'll be going abroad for several months and want to use the phone with a local provider.

For many, **renting** a phone is a good idea. While you can rent a phone from any number of overseas sites, including kiosks at airports and at car-rental agencies, I suggest renting the phone before you leave home. Phone rental isn't cheap. You'll usually pay $40 to $50 per week, plus airtime fees of at least a dollar a minute.

In Barcelona, however, there is only one company that offers this service: You can rent a cellphone from **Rent A Phone,** Carrer Numància 212 (✆ **93-280-21-31**). Rent A Phone charges by *pasos,* which translates into units of a call. A call to another cellphone in Spain is likely to cost 80¢ (.60€) per minute, and up to 1.50€ ($1.95) per minute for calls to the States. A deposit of 1.50€ ($1.95) is also required.

North Americans can rent from **InTouch USA** (✆ **800/872-7626;** www.intouchglobal.com) or **Roadpost** (✆ **888/290-1606** or 905/272-5665; www.roadpost.com). Give them your itinerary, and they'll tell you what wireless products you need. InTouch will advise you, for free, on whether your existing phone will work overseas.

Buying a phone can be economically attractive, as many nations have cheap, no-questions-asked prepaid phone systems. Once you arrive at your destination, stop by a local cellphone shop and get the cheapest package; you'll probably pay less than $100 for a phone and a starter calling card. Local calls may be as low as 10¢ per minute, and in many countries incoming calls are free. Note that in Spain you must show your passport when you buy a phone and/or phone card.

Wilderness adventurers, or those heading to less-developed countries, might consider renting a **satellite phone ("satphone").** It's different from a cellphone in that it connects to satellites and works where there's no cellular signal or ground-based tower. You can rent satellite phones from Roadpost (see above). InTouch USA (see above) also offers a wider range of satphones but at higher rates. Per-minute call charges can be even cheaper than

Online Traveler's Toolbox

Veteran travelers usually carry some essential items to make their trips easier. Following is a selection of handy online tools to bookmark and use.

- **Airplane Food** (www.airlinemeals.net)
- **Airplane Seating** (www.seatguru.com and www.airlinequality.com)
- **Foreign Languages for Travelers** (www.travlang.com)
- **Maps** (www.mapquest.com)
- **Time and Date** (www.timeanddate.com)
- **Travel Warnings** (http://travel.state.gov, www.fco.gov.uk/travel, www. voyage.gc.ca, www.smartraveller.gov.au)
- **Universal Currency Converter** (www.oanda.com)
- **Weather** (www.intellicast.com and www.weather.com)
- **Tickets** to events in Barcelona (www.telentrada.com)
- **Event Guide** to Barcelona (www.bcn.es and www.barcelona-online.com)
- **Tourist Information** (www.barcelonaturisme.com and www.spain.info)

roaming charges with a regular cellphone, but the phone itself is more expensive. As of this writing, satphones were outrageously expensive to buy, so don't even think about it.

VOICE-OVER INTERNET PROTOCOL (VOIP)

If you have Web access while traveling, consider a broadband-based telephone service (in technical terms, **Voice-over Internet protocol,** or **VoIP**) such as Skype (www.skype.com) or Vonage (www.vonage. com), which allow you to make free international calls from your laptop or in a cybercafe. Neither service requires the people you're calling to also have that service (though there are fees if they do not). Check the websites for details.

INTERNET & E-MAIL

Travelers in Barcelona have a number of ways to check their e-mail and access the Internet on the road. Of course, using your own laptop—or even a PDA (personal digital assistant)—gives you the most flexibility. But even if you don't have a computer, you can still access the Internet from cybercafes.

With Your Own Computer

More and more hotels, cafes, and retailers are signing on as Wi-Fi (wireless fidelity) "hotspots." Mac owners have their own networking technology: Apple AirPort. **Boingo** (www.boingo.com) has set up Wi-Fi hotspots in airports and high-class hotel lobbies around the world, including Spain. iPass providers (see below) also give you access to a few hundred wireless hotel lobby setups. To locate other hotspots that provide free wireless networks in cities around the world, including in Barcelona, go to **www.personaltelco.net/index.cgi/ WirelessCommunities**.

Major Internet Service Providers (ISPs) have **local access numbers** around the world, allowing you to go online by placing a local call. The **iPass** network has dial-up numbers around the world. You'll have to sign up with an iPass provider, who will then tell you how to set up your computer for your destination. For a list of iPass providers, go to www.ipass.com and click on "Individuals Buy Now." One solid provider is **i2roam** (ℭ **866/811-6209** or 920/235-0475; www.i2roam.com).

Most business-class hotels in Barcelona offer high-speed Internet service, and many now offer free Wi-Fi connections. The Catalan-run **Petit Palace** hotel, for example, provides free Wi-Fi connections in all rooms. **Call your hotel in advance** to see what your options are.

Wherever you go, bring a **connection kit** of the right power and phone adapters, and a spare Ethernet network cable if you do not have Wi-Fi—or find out whether your hotel supplies them to guests.

In Spain the electricity connection is 220 volts, though it may occasionally be 125 volts. A two-prong plug is needed to connect appliances.

Without Your Own Computer

It's hard nowadays to find a city that *doesn't* have a few cybercafes, and Barcelona is no exception. To find Internet cafes in Barcelona, check **www.cybercaptive.com** and **www.cybercafe.com**.

Aside from these formal cybercafes, most **youth hostels** have at least one computer you can get to the Internet on. And most **public libraries** across the world offer Internet access free or for a small charge. Avoid **hotel business centers** unless you're willing to pay exorbitant rates.

Most major airports now have **Internet kiosks** scattered throughout their gates. These kiosks give you basic Web access for a per-minute fee that's usually higher than cybercafe prices. The kiosks' clunkiness and high price mean they should be avoided whenever possible.

For help locating cybercafes and other establishments where you can go for Internet access, please see "Internet Access" in Appendix A: Fast Facts, Toll-Free Numbers & Websites (p. 320).

14 TIPS ON ACCOMMODATIONS

Barcelona is one of the most popular destinations in Europe and has hotels to suit every taste, from the most deluxe hotels on La Rambla to budget *hostales* in the Ciutat Vella. There are cutting-edge chic hotels that lure the young and hip, and quaint traditional hotels with panoramic mountain and sea views. In Barcelona, you are spoiled for choice.

Safety is an important factor when choosing accommodations, and a former deterring factor with cheaper hotels was

House-Swapping

House-swapping is becoming a more popular and viable means of travel; you stay in their place, they stay in yours, and you both get an authentic and personal view of the area, the opposite of the escapist retreat that many hotels offer. Try **HomeLink International** (www.homelink.org), the largest and oldest home-swapping organization, founded in 1952, with over 11,000 listings worldwide ($75 for a yearly membership). It has a number of apartments available for exchange in Barcelona. You can also check the corresponding Spanish website, www.spainlink.net. **HomeExchange.com** and **Intervac.com** are also reliable. Many travelers find great housing swaps on **Craigslist** (www.craigslist.org), too, though the offerings cannot be vetted or vouched for. Swap at your own risk.

that they tended to be in less desirable parts of town. Today, however, those neighborhoods aren't quite what they used to be and budget *hostales* are often found alongside luxury hotels in *barris* once regarded as distinctly un-chic—such as El Raval.

For more detailed information on all types of accommodations and tips on how to save on your hotel room, see chapter 5. For tips on surfing for hotel deals online, visit www.frommers.com/planning.

There's no shortage of properties you can rent; two agencies that offer rentals in Barcelona are **Visit Barcelona** (www.

visit-bcn.com), which has many Barri Gòtic properties for rent, and **Friendly Rentals** (www.friendlyrentals.com), which is a bit pricier. Check out the box "Barcelona's Self-Catering Scene" in chapter 5, "Where to Stay," for information.

You can also rent a **casa rural** (country cottage) in the mountains or wooded valleys of the Catalan countryside that surrounds Barcelona. This provides a relaxing break from the pressures and stimulations of the big city and gives you an idea of what life is like in the real Catalonia. Check the website **www.casasrurales barcelona.com** for more information.

4

Suggested Barcelona Itineraries

You can cover quite a few of central Barcelona's monuments and architectural highlights in just a day. But the more time you have available, the more justice you can do to the wealth of sights in and near the city. Here are some recommendations on how to spend your time.

1 CITY LAYOUT

Plaça de Catalunya (**Plaza de Cataluña** in Spanish) is the city's heart, the world-famous **La Rambla**—also known as Les Ramblas—its main artery. La Rambla begins at the Plaça Portal de la Pau, with its 49m-high (161-ft.) monument to Columbus opposite the port, and stretches north to the Plaça de Catalunya. Along this wide promenade you'll find newsstands, stalls selling birds and flowers, portrait painters, and cafe tables and chairs, where you can sit and watch the passing parade. Moving northward along La Rambla, the area on your left is **El Raval,** the largest neighborhood in Barcelona, and to your right is the **Barri Gòtic (Gothic Quarter).** These two neighborhoods, plus the area of **La Ribera,** which lies further to your right across another main artery, the Vía Laietana, make up the sizable **Ciutat Vella (Old City).** Within these three neighborhoods are two subregions. One is the infamous *Barri Xinès* or **Barrio Chino** (literally, **Chinese Quarter,** though this is no Chinatown; see below) near the eastern end of El Raval bordering La Rambla. The other is El Born—prosperous in the Middle Ages and today Barcelona's bastion of cool—in the lower, port-side pocket of La Ribera. As this whole condensed, character-filled area is large—though not as large as sprawling but amorphous L'Eixample (see below)—I have subdivided all its attractions into El Raval, Barri Gòtic, and La Ribera.

Across the **Plaça de Catalunya,** La Rambla becomes **Rambla Catalunya,** with the elegant **Passeig de Gràcia** running parallel to the immediate right. These are the two main arteries of **L'Eixample,** or the *extension.* This is where most of the jewels of the *modernisme* period, including key works by Antoni Gaudí, dot the harsh grids of this graceful, middle-class neighborhood. Both end at the **Diagonal,** a major cross-town artery that also serves as the city's business and commercial hub. Northward across the Diagonal is the suburb of **Gràcia.** Once a separate village, it makes up in sheer atmosphere for what it lacks in notable monuments.

The other areas of interest for the visitor are **Montjuïc,** the bluff to the southwest of the city, and the maritime area of **Barceloneta** and the beaches. The first is the largest green zone in the city, contains some of its top museums, and was the setting for the principal events of the 1992 Summer Olympic Games. The second is a peninsula that has long been the city's populist playground, with dozens of fish restaurants, some facing the beaches that sprawl northward along the coast. Behind the city to the northwest, higher than Montjuïc, is **Tibidabo,** looming like a sentinel and enjoying great views of

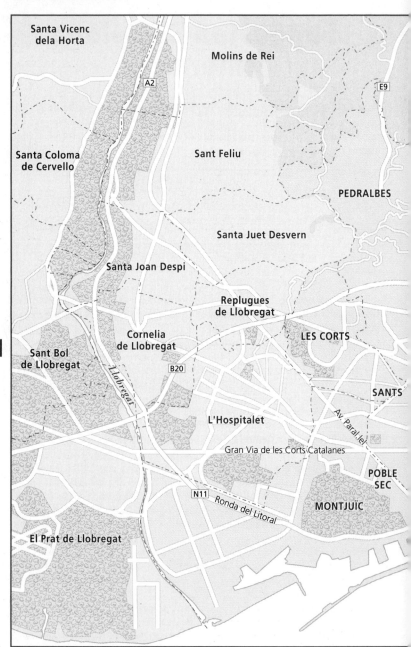

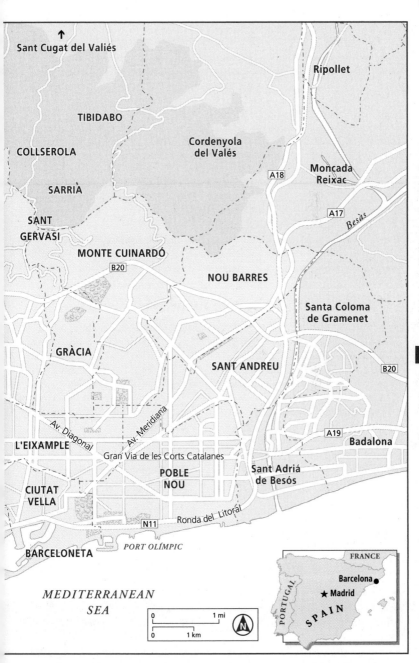

the city and the Mediterranean. It also has a veteran amusement park and a kitsch pseudo-Gothic church which aspires to emulate Paris's Sacré Coeur.

FINDING AN ADDRESS/MAPS Finding a Barcelona address doesn't generally pose too many problems. The Eixample district is built on a grid system, so by learning the cross street you can easily find the place you are looking for. Barcelona is hemmed in on one side by the sea *(mar)* and the mountain of Tibidabo *(montaña)* on the other, so often people just describe a place as being on the *mar* or *montaña* side of the street in L'Eixample. The Ciutat Vella, or Old City, is a little more confusing, and you will need a good map (available in the news kiosks along La Rambla) to find specific places. However, the city abounds with long boulevards and spacious squares, making it easier to navigate. The designation s/n *(sin número)* means that the building has no number; however, this is mainly limited to large buildings and monuments, so it's pretty obvious once you get there where it is. In built-up Barcelona, the symbol "o" designates the floor (for example, the first floor is 1o). Street names are in Catalan. Some people still refer to them in Spanish, but there is very little difference between the two so it shouldn't cause any confusion. The word for "street" *(carrer* in Catalan and *calle* in Spanish) is nearly always dropped; that is, Carrer Ferran is simply referred to as Ferran. *Passeig* (or *paseo* in Spanish) and *avinguda* (or *avenida* in Spanish), meaning respectively "boulevard" and "avenue," are nearly always kept, as in Passeig de Gràcia and Avinguda de Tibidabo. *Rambla* means a long, pedestrianized avenue and *plaça* (or *plaza* in Spanish), a square.

THE NEIGHBORHOODS IN BRIEF

CIUTAT VELLA (OLD TOWN)

Barri Gòtic Next to the excesses of the 19th-century *moderniste* period, Barcelona's golden age was between the 13th and 15th centuries, the Gothic period. The city expanded rapidly in medieval times, so much so that it could no longer be contained within the old Roman walls. So new ones were built. They originally ran from the port northward along what was to become La Rambla, down the Ronda Sant Pere to Calle Rec Comtal, and back to the sea again. Except for a few remaining sections along the Vía Laietana, most of them have now been destroyed. But the ensemble of 13th- to 15th-century buildings (or parts of) that remain make up the most complete Barri Gòtic (Gothic Quarter) on the continent. These include government buildings, churches (including the main cathedral), and guild houses.

Guilds *(gremis)* were a forerunner to the trade unions and the backbone of Barcelona medieval life. Many of their shields can be seen on buildings dotted around the Barri Gòtic, which would have denoted the headquarters of each particular trade. Tiny workshops were also enclosed in the area, and even now many street names bear the name of the activity that went on there for centuries—such as Escudellers (shield makers), Assaonadors (tanners), Carders (wool combers), and Brocaters (brocade makers), to name a few. El Call, the original Jewish ghetto, is also located within the Barri Gòtic. A tiny area around the Carrer del Call and L'Arc de Sant Ramon del Call was the scene of the sacking of the Jews by Christian mobs in the late 1400s.

Apart from the big attractions such as the **Cathedral de la Seu,** the **Plaça Sant Jaume** (which contains the two organs of Catalan politics, the Ajuntament and the Generalitat), and the medieval palace of the **Plaça del Rei,** where Columbus was received after returning from the New World, the Barri Gòtic's charm lies in its details. Smaller squares, such as the **Plaça Felip Neri** with its central fountain, the oasis-like courtyard of the **Frederic Marès Museum,** gargoyles peering down from ancient towers, and small chapels set into the sides of medieval buildings—this is what makes the area so fascinating. Most of them can only be discovered on foot, ideally at sunset when the fading Mediterranean light lends the stone buildings a warm hue, and musicians, mainly of the classical nature, jostle for performance spaces around the Cathedral.

Some of the sites in the Barri Gòtic are not medieval at all (architecture and history purists argue that the name has remained simply for the sake of tourism) but of no less merit. The most famous of these is the so-called Bridge of Sighs (nothing like the Venetian original) in Carrer del Bisbe, built during the city's Gothic Revival in the 1920s. But even modern additions do nothing to diminish the character of the Barri Gòtic. The abundance of specialist shops, from old fan and espadrille makers to more cutting-edge designer ware, is another attraction, as are the dozens of outdoor eateries where you can enjoy a coffee or two looking out onto an ancient edifice.

The sizable Barri Gòtic is hemmed in on one side by the ugly, ever-busy Vía Laietana and on the other by **La Rambla.**

The most famous promenade in Spain, ranking with Madrid's Paseo del Prado, was once a sewer. These days, street entertainers, flower vendors, news vendors, cafe patrons, and strollers flow along its length. The gradual 1.5km (1-mile) descent toward the sea has often been called a metaphor for life because its bustling action combines cosmopolitanism and crude vitality.

La Rambla actually consists of five sections, each a particular *rambla*—Rambla de Canaletes, Rambla dels Estudis, Rambla de Sant Josep, Rambla dels Caputxins, and Rambla de Santa Mónica. The shaded pedestrian esplanade runs from the Plaça de Catalunya to the port—all the way to the Columbus Monument. Along the way you'll pass the **Gran Teatre del Liceu,** on Rambla dels Caputxins, one of the most magnificent opera houses in the world, restored to its former glory after a devastating fire in 1994. Watch out for the giant sidewalk mosaic by Miró halfway down at the Plaça de la Boqueria.

El Raval On the opposite side of La Rambla lies El Raval, Barcelona's largest inner-city neighborhood. This is where the ambitious plans for the post-Olympic "New Barcelona" are at their most evident as entire blocks of dank apartment buildings were bulldozed to make way for cutting-edge new edifices, squares, and boulevards. El Raval has recently been cited as the neighborhood with the greatest multicultural mix in Europe, and a quick stroll around its maze of streets, where Pakistani fabric merchants and South American spice sellers stand side by side with traditional establishments selling dried cod and local wine, seems to confirm the fact. The *Adhan* (the Muslim call to prayer) wafts from mosques located in ground-floor locales located next to neo-hippie bars, yoga schools, and contemporary art galleries. The largest of these is the **MACBA (Museum of Contemporary Art),** a luminous white behemoth designed by the American architect Richard Meir. It resides on a huge concrete square that has, since its opening in 1995, become the neighborhood's most popular playground. At any time of the day, the space will be inundated by kids playing cricket and soccer, skateboarders cruising the ramps of the museum's forecourt, and housewives on their way to the nearby **Boqueria** market. Another favorite stomping ground is the Rambla del Raval—a wide, airy pedestrianized avenue dating from 2000 and lined with cafes and multinational (mainly Asian) eating spots.

The signs of gentrification are everywhere, and while this still attracts its fair share of criticism, no one can deny the life-enhancing benefits of the above-mentioned developments for a neighborhood that has been historically deprived of light and breathing space. The neighborhood's former reputation as a seedy inner-city slum is gradually receding, though the area still has its rough edges.

Change is slower to come to the so-called **Barri Xinès** or **Barrio Chino,** the lower half of El Raval between the waterfront and Carrer de l'Hospital. Despite the name ("Chinese Quarter"), this isn't Chinatown. In fact, most attribute its nickname to an imaginative writer by the name of Francisco Madrid who, influenced by a fellow journalist who'd just returned from a visit to the States where he felt New York's Chinatown reminded him of this area, published a 1926 book on these lines called *Sangre en las Atarazanas* ("Blood on the Dockyards"). A decade later the French writer Jean Genet wrote *A Thief's Journal* during a stint in one if its peseta-a-night whorehouses. In some pockets of the Chino, you would be forgiven for thinking that little has changed; while drug dealing has been largely shipped out to the outer suburbs, prostitution still openly exists, as does the general seediness of many of the streets. But, as with all of the Old City, the times they are a-changin' and you may find yourself wandering down here at night to attend the opening of a new bar or club. Petty thieves, prostitutes, drug dealers,

and purse-snatchers are just some of the neighborhood "characters," so exercise caution. Although Barri Xinès has a long way to go, an urban renewal program has led to the destruction of some of the rougher parts of the barrio.

La Ribera Another neighborhood that stagnated for years but is now well into a renaissance is La Ribera. Across the noisy artery Vía Laietana and southward of Calle Princesa, this small neighborhood is bordered by the **Port Vell (Old Port)** and the **Parc de la Ciutadella.** Like the Barrio Chino (see above), **El Born** is La Ribera's "neighborhood within a neighborhood." But far from being a rough diamond, El Born is a polished pastiche of the Old Town where designer clothing and housewares showcases occupy medieval buildings and workshops. The centerpiece is the imposing **Santa María del Mar,** a stunningly complete Gothic basilica that was built with funds from the cashed-up merchants that once inhabited the area. Many of them lived in the mansions and palaces along the Carrer de Montcada, today home to a trio of top museums including the **Museu Picasso.** Most of the mansions in this area were built during one of Barcelona's major maritime expansions, principally in the 1200s and 1300s. During this time, El Born was the city's principal trade area. The recently refurbished **La Llotja,** the city's first stock exchange, lies on its outer edge on the Plaça Palau; although the facade dates from 1802, the interior is pure Catalan Gothic. The central **Passeig del Born** got its name from the medieval jousts that used to occur here. At the northern end, the wrought-iron Mercat del Born was the city's principal wholesale market until the mid-1970s. Recent excavation work has revealed entire streets and homes dating back to the 18th century, sealing the edifice's fate as a new museum where these ruins can be viewed via glass flooring and walkways. Behind the Mercat del Born, the Parc de la Ciutadella is a tranquil oasis replete with a man-made lake; wide, leafy walkways; and yet more museums.

THE PORT AND WATERFRONT

Barceloneta, the Beaches & the Harbor Although Barcelona has a long seagoing tradition, its waterfront stood in decay for years. Today, the waterfront promenade, **Passeig del Moll de la Fusta,** bursts with activity. The best way to get a bird's-eye view of the area is to take an elevator to the top of the Columbus Monument in Plaça Portal de la Pau at the port end of La Rambla.

Near the monument are the **Reials Drassanes,** or royal shipyards, a booming place during the Middle Ages. Years before Columbus landed in the New World, ships sailed around the world from here, flying the yellow-and-red flag of Catalonia. These days, they are home to the excellent Museu Marítim. Across the road, the wooden swing bridge known as the Rambla del Mar takes you across the water to the Maremagnum entertainment and shopping complex.

To the east, the glitzy **Port Vell (Old Port)** was one of the main projects for the city's Olympic renewal scheme. Its chic yachting marina is similar to those of other great Mediterranean ports like Marseilles and Piraeus, and there are large expanses of open recreational areas where people get out and enjoy the sun. It is also home to the city's Aquarium. On one side it is flanked by the **Passeig Joan de Borbón,** the main street of **La Barceloneta (Little Barcelona).** Formerly a fishing district dating from the 18th century, the neighborhood is full of character and is still one of the best places to eat seafood in the city. The blocks here are long and narrow—architects planned them that way so that each room in every building fronted a street. The streets end at Barceloneta beach. Like all of the city's beaches, this was neglected to the point of nonexistence pre-1992. The harbor front was clogged with industrial buildings—many of them abandoned—and tatty but well-patronized *chiringuitos* (beach bars). Today they are some of the finest urban beaches in Europe. From Barceloneta, separated by breakwaters, no fewer than seven of them sprawl northward. The **Port Olimpic,** dominated by a pair of landmark, sea-facing skyscrapers (one accommodating the five-star Hotel Arts and the city's casino), boasts yet another marina and a host of restaurants and bars. Take them all in at your leisure as you stroll along the Passeig Marítim (seafront promenade).

MORE CENTRAL BARCELONA

L'Eixample To the north of the Plaça de Catalunya is the massive section of Barcelona (known as the *Ensanche* in Spanish) that grew beyond the old medieval walls. In the mid-1800s, Barcelona, as was the case with many European cities, was simply bursting at the seams. The dank, serpentine streets of the old-walled city were not only breeding grounds for cholera and typhoid, but habitual mass rioting. Rather than leveling the Old Town, the city's authorities had a sloping sweep of land just outside the walls at their disposal and contracted the socialist engineer Idelfons Cerdà to offer a solution. His subsequent 1856 work, *Monograph on the Working Class of Barcelona,* became the first-ever attempt to study the living, breathing landscape of a city: urbanization to you and me, a term Cerdà himself coined in the process.

Cerdà actually visited hundreds of Old City hovels before he drew up plans for Barcelona's New City. Needless to say, his fact checking led him to the bowels of human suffering; he found out that life expectancy for the proletariat was half that of the bourgeoisie (while paying double per square meter for their decaying hovels) and mortality rates were lower in the narrower streets. Above all, he concluded that air and sunshine were vital to basic well-being.

Today little remains of Cerdà's most radical plans for L'Eixample, apart from the rigorous regularity of its 20m-wide (66-ft.) streets and famous chamfered pavements. The *modernistas* were the neighborhood's earliest architects, filling the blocks with their labored fantasies, such as Gaudí's La Sagrada Família, Casa Mila, and Casa Batlló. His works aside, L'Eixample is a living, breathing museum piece with an abundance of Art Nouveau architecture and details unfound anywhere in Europe. **La Ruta del Modernismo** is a specially designed walking tour that will guide you to the best of them. See also walk 4 in chapter 8, "Strolling Around Barcelona."

In accordance with Cerdà's basic plans, avenues form a grid of perpendicular streets, cut across by a majestic boulevard—**Passeig de Gràcia,** a posh shopping street ideal for leisurely promenades. L'Eixample's northern boundary is the **Avinguda Diagonal** (or simply the Diagonal), which links the expressway and the heart of the city and acts as Barcelona's business and banking hub.

Gràcia This charming neighborhood sprawls out northward of the intersection of the **Passeig de Gràcia** and **Diagonal.** Its contained, village-like ambience stems from the fact that it was once a separate town, only connected to central Barcelona in 1897 with the construction of the Passeig de Gràcia. It has a strong industrial and artisan history, and many street-level workshops can still be seen. Rather than in monuments or museums, Gràcia's charm lies in its low-level housing and series of squares—the Plaça del Sol and Plaça Ruis i Taulet are two of the prettiest. The residents themselves have a strong sense of neighborhood pride and a marked independent spirit, and their annual fiestas (p. 36) are some of the liveliest in the city. For the casual visitor, Gràcia is a place to wander through for a slice of authentic *barri* life.

Montjuïc & Tibidabo Locals call them "mountains," and while northerly Tibidabo does actually rise to over 488m (1,600 ft.), the port-side bluff of Montjuïc is somewhat lower. Both are great places to go for fine views and cleaner air. The most accessible, Montjuïc (named the "Hill of the Jews" after a Jewish necropolis that once stood there), gained prominence in 1929 as the site of the World's Fair and again in 1992 as the site of the Summer Olympic Games. Its major attractions are the **Joan Miró museum,** the Olympic installations, and the **Poble Espanyol (Spanish Village),** a 2-hectare (5-acre) site constructed for the World's Fair. Examples of Spanish art and architecture are on display against the backdrop of a traditional Spanish village. Opposite the village lies the **CaixaForum,** one of the city's newer contemporary art showcases housed in a converted *moderniste* textile factory. In a recent push to raise Montjuïc's status even further, new parks and gardens (such as the Jardí Botanic) have been laid out. At the base of Montjuïc is the working-class neighborhood of Poble Sec and the Ciutat del Teatre, location of the city's theatrical school and a conglomeration of performing arts spaces. Tibidabo (503m/1,650 ft.) is where you should go for your final look at Barcelona. On a clear day you can see the mountains of Majorca, some 209km (130 miles) away. Reached by train, tram, and cable car, Tibidabo is a popular Sunday excursion in Barcelona, when whole families head to the fun-fair of the same name.

Outer Barcelona

Pedralbes At the western edge of El Diagonal, next to the elite districts of Sant Gervasí and Putxet, is the equally posh residential area where wealthy Barcelonans live in either stylish blocks of apartment houses, 19th-century villas behind ornamental fences, or stunning *modernista* structures. Set in a park, the **Palau de Pedralbes,** Av. Diagonal 686, was constructed in the 1920s as a gift from the city to Alfonso XIII, the grandfather of King Juan Carlos. Today it has a new life, housing the Ceramic and Decorative Arts Museums. The Finca Güell is also part of the estate, the country home of Gaudí's main patron, Eusebi Güell. Although not open to the public, the main gate and gatehouse, both designed by Gaudí, are visible from the street. The pride of this zone is the 14th-century Gothic church-cum-convent of **Monestir de Pedralbes,** where you can view lovely cloisters and well-preserved kitchens.

2 THE BEST OF BARCELONA IN 1 DAY

This is going to be a very full day, so make an early start at the **Plaça de Catalunya.** Spend the morning wandering down **La Rambla** to the **Mirador de Colón** beside the port. Return via the **Placa Reial** and explore the neighboring **Barri Gòtic** with its central **Catedral.** In the afternoon visit Antoni Gaudí's unfinished masterpiece, **La Sagrada Família,** and the **Parc Güell** before returning to the **Raval** and **Poble Sec** districts on the western side of **La Rambla.** From there, take the funicular to the top of **Montjuïc** for a fine view of Barcelona and its harbor. Explore the gardens and castle museum, and if there's time, pop into the Museu Nacional d'Art de Catalunya for a glimpse of the finest collection of Romanesque relics in Spain.

❶ Plaça de Catalunya

Located at the top end of La Rambla and midway between the medieval Old City and the 19th-century L'Eixample, this circular plaça with its fountains and sculptures, is the cultural hub of the city. Surrounded by large stores, open-air cafes, and hotels, it's a place to watch passersby, listen to the Latino buskers, feed the pigeons, and even try to join in and dance the *sardana* on festive occasions. As the afternoon proceeds it gets increasingly crowded and colorful (p. 71).

❷ La Rambla ★★★

Also known as Les Ramblas, this mile-long avenue is divided into five distinct sections named, successively, Canaletes, Estudis, Sant Josep, Caputxins, and Santa Mónica. It's a stage set of human statues, jugglers, singers, eccentrics, misfits, transvestites, caged small animals, kiosks, cafes, and radiant flower stalls, all shaded by a leafy canopy of huge plane trees. Originally called *ramla* (riverbed) by the Arabs, it's the favorite stroll for Barcelonans and visitors alike. For year-round atmosphere, there's nowhere else like it in Spain (p. 71).

1 Plaça de Catalunya
2 La Rambla
3 Mirador de Colón
4 Café de l'Opera
5 Plaça Reial
6 Barri Gòtic
7 Catedral
8 Can Culleretes
9 Montjuïc
10 Montjuic Castle Café
11 Sagrada Família
12 Parc Güell

LES CORTS

Plaça Francesc Macià
Buenos Aires
Av. Diagonal
Av. Sarrià
Av. Josep Tarradellas
Londres
Paris
Còrsega
Rosselló
Ecola Industriel
Hospital Clínic
Provença
Mallorca
València
Calàbria
Viladomat
Comte d'Urgell
Aragó
Consell de Cent
Diputació
Gran Via Corts Catalanes
Sepúlveda
Floridablanca
Villarroel
Casanova
Muntaner
Aribau
Parc de Joan Miró
Creu Coberta
Ctra. de la Bordeta
Gran Via Corts Catalanes
Plaça Espanya
Plaça Univers
Av. Paral.lel
Mistral
Tamarit
Manso
Mercat de St. Antoni
MACBA
Ronda de St. Antoni
EL RAVAL
Poble Espanyol
Plaça de Carlos Buigas
MNAC
Palau Nacional
LA FRANCA
Museu Arqueológic
Parlament
Ronda St. Pau
La Rambla del Raval
Palau St. Jordi
Av. de l'Estadi
Fundació Joan Miró
Exposició
POBLE SEC
Av. Paral.lel
10 Estadi Olímpic
Plaça Neptú
9 MONTJUÏC
PARC DE MONTJUÏC
Av. Miramar
Nou de la Rambla
Reials Drassanes (Museu Marítim)
Av. Drassanes
Castell de Montjuïc
Museu Militar
Plaça Carlos Ibáñez
Transbordador Aeri
Ronda Litoral
Moll de la Costa
Moll de Ponent
World Trade Center

☕ Take a Break
ⓘ Information

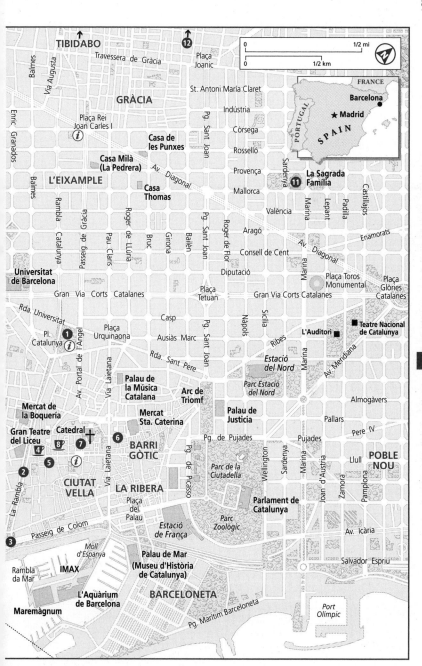

❸ Mirador de Colón

Situated at the port end of La Rambla, this ornate bronze statue in honor of the Genovese sailor who discovered you-know-where was built during Barcelona's 19th-century industrial boom. After 10am you can get to the top by elevator and enjoy marvellous views of the harbor and Ciutat Vella. Spot the deliberate mistake: He's pointing out east across the Mediterranean to Mallorca instead of west toward the Atlantic (p. 174).

---

❹ CAFÉ DE L'OPERA

Halfway down La Rambla, **Café de l'Opera,** La Rambla 74 (✆ **93-317-75-85**), is a 19th-century Parisian-style cafe. Its murals, iron columns, and wall mirrors with etchings evoke a more elegant age, when waiters with bowties serve you with commendable indifference. It's the ideal spot to sit back, enjoy a quality coffee, and watch the nonstop activity outside.

---

❺ Plaça Reial ★

This is one of the city's great old squares, with neoclassical pillars and archways, 19th-century lampposts, slender aging palm trees, and enough semi-resident marginals—from drug addicts to transsexuals—to do justice to any Almodóvar movie worth its salt. More ominous in the past, today it is virtually a tourist attraction. Watch out for pickpockets, though.

❻ Barri Gòtic ★★★

Said to be the largest inhabited (and probably most densely populated) medieval quarter in Europe, the narrow-alleyed Barri Gòtic really needs a minimum of a half a day's leisurely exploration, so if you're in town for more than 3 days, come back again (and again) to remotely do it full justice. At night its illuminated streets and buildings give it a magical touch. If you're only here a day, then the **Catedral** (see below) is an absolute must. Also not

to be missed are the central **Plaça del Rei** with its two key monuments, and the **Museu d'Historia de la Ciutat,** built over a complete subterranean Roman township. Another must-see is the **Palau del Rei,** where Columbus introduced American Indians to Spain's monarchs for the first time in its **Saló del Tinell** (p. 14).

❼ Catedral ★★★

Originally built on the site of the old Roman town, this monumental place of worship has seen many changes over the centuries, though it was mercifully one of the few to be spared the destructive fury of the Civil War. Here the young Santa Eulalia—cruelly martyred for protesting her Christianity during Dacian's repressive rule—is buried. Don't miss the 14th-century choir stalls and chapter house and roof (extra fee); or the unexpectedly delightful cloister which bucolically harbors tall palms, a cluster of orange trees, and a pond with geese amid the surrounding Gothic and Renaissance splendor (p. 172).

---

❽ CAN CULLERETES

For an atmospheric lunch, you can't do better than Barcelona's oldest restaurant (est. 1786), **Can Culleretes,** Quintana 5 (✆ **93-317-64-85**). It's tucked away in a secretive lane in the heart of the Barri Gòtic. You won't be the only non-Catalan visitor—the place is in too many guidebooks—but the restaurant is a monument, the service and decor from another age, and the traditional food and wine pretty good. See p. 134.

---

❾ Montjuïc ★★

Topped by an imposing castle, which is now a military museum, this distinctive hill on the city's west flank offers some of the best vistas of the Catalan capital. After the radical improvements prior to the 1992 Olympics (don't forget to take an outside peep at the stadium), it's now also the city's greatest green zone, with a wealth of walkways, parklands, leisure areas, and cultural attractions to explore. Get there by the funicular from Poble Sec or by the more vertiginous Telefèric de Montjuïc, which carries you high above the harbor (p. 191).

> **☕ MONTJUÏC CASTLE CAFÉ**
> This unpretentious self-service cafe, tucked away inside the castle with a patio section where you can sit outside in good weather, is a great spot for relaxing and savoring the old *"castell"* ambience.

In the evening cross the city to:

⓫ Sagrada Família ★★

Abandoned for decades, this still-unfinished cathedral finally saw restoration and expansion work carried out when its hermit-like architect Antoni Gaudí (who was killed by a tram in 1926 and whose tomb can be viewed in the crypt) came back into fashion in the 1990s. The four original spires—by the master himself—are generally acknowledged to be far superior to the additional quartet designed by modern architects. You can now take a ride up to the top of one of the towers and enjoy the fine view. Loved and reviled in equal measure, the building remains unique. Current construction progress is slow, however, and even the most optimistic forecaster doesn't see the whole thing reaching completion for at least another decade (p. 184).

⓬ Parc Güell ★★

You can imagine gremlins living in this unique fairy-tale park located high up in the city and loved by children and adults alike. Look out for its mosaic serpent and Hansel and Gretel houses at the entrance (one of which is a tiny museum, the Centre d'Interpretació i Acollida, devoted to describing creator Gaudí's building methods). At its center, up some steps, the Banc de Trencadís—a multi-colored ceramic bench—curves around a spacious esplanade, while behind it footpaths climb into the pine woods of Vallcarca and Monte Carmel, offering scenic views through the trees of the city below (p. 132).

3 THE BEST OF BARCELONA IN 2 DAYS

On the first day follow the itinerary described above. On the second day stroll through the pond- and garden-filled **Parc de la Ciutadella** and visit the Zoo, time permitting. Then explore the narrow-laned *barrio* of **La Ribera,** with its **Picasso Museum** and imposing **Santa María del Mar** church, and walk down to the old (but gentrified) maritime quarter and beachfront of **La Barceloneta** with its modern adjoining Port Olimpic area. It's the ideal spot for an atmospheric seafood lunch. In the afternoon wander around **Port Vell** and explore the regenerated **El Raval** district.

❶ Parc de la Ciutadella ★★

Once the site of a fort ("Ciutadella" is Catalan for "citadel"), the verdant park is the most attractive and popular spot in Lower Barcelona, complete with two lush but small botanical gardens, a Gaudí-designed fountain (La Cascada) with a huge statue of a primeval elephant, and a quiet lake where you can go rowing. Other attractions include the Castell dels Tres Dragons (Castle of the Three Dragons) and Parlement de Catalunya (Catalan Parliament), which you can visit for free if you have time to make an appointment. The zoo's well worth a look, whatever your age (p. 179).

❷ La Ribera ★★

The western part of La Ciutat Vella is really two districts, El Born and Sant Pere (referring to the area's oldest square and church, respectively). Its name, La Ribera, actually means "the shore," as the sea once reached its southern edge. The central Carrer Montcada is lined with museums and the whole former medieval merchants' quarter is packed with traditional shops, tiny squares, and narrow streets named after various local trades that were carried out here—such as Carrer Carders (wool combers), Carrer Assaonadors (tanners), and Carrer Flassaders (blanket weavers).

❸ Museu Picasso ★★★

By far the most popular art museum in town, the Picasso is tastefully spread throughout a quintet of fine old mansions in the heart of La Ribera. Be prepared for long queues, but if you do manage to squeeze it into your time-challenged schedule, don't miss the Malagueño artist's version of Velazquez' La Meninas. The museum concentrates mainly on more conventional works and etchings of the adolescent artist, who arrived in town with his family in 1895 and wasted no time in opening his very first (and very modest) studio in Carrer de la Plata (p. 178).

> ### ❹ TEXTIL CAFÉ
>
> **Textil Café**, Carrer Montcada 12 (☏ **93-268-25-98**), is a charming spot nestled in the patio of the 14th-century mansion containing the Textile Museum, just a few steps away from the Picasso Museum. Enjoy your coffee and pastries in an elegant year-round setting. Even in winter—notwithstanding rare rainy days—you can still sit outside, under gas heaters.

❺ Santa María del Mar Church ★

Once upon a time this magnificent church, with its soaring vaults and wonderful stained-glass windows, stood right on the shore of the Mediterranean (as the district's name, La Ribera, implies). It was the focal point of a then-vibrant seafaring and trading quarter which eventually receded, as did the sea. Today it's one of the best-preserved Gothic monuments in the city, most evocative for being less crowded than some of the better-known sights (p. 212).

❻ La Barceloneta (and Port Olimpic) ★

Built on the compact triangle of land (reclaimed from marshes) between the Port Vell and the first of the city beaches (Sant Sebastiá), this 18th-century working-class zone—which is built in a formal grid system of lanes around a central market—has today become more "gentrified" and sought after by visitors and residents alike. Its once-neglected beach is now well cared for and has a palm-lined promenade where folks walk their pooches. The original, tatty, much-loved *chiringuitos* (shacks) that bordered the shore serving delicious seafood dishes were demolished pre-1992 to make way for today's more acceptably salubrious establishments (still known as *chiringuitos*), which sell exactly the same food at increased prices. Moving with the times, it remains a great location and a fun spot for a paella, as is the vibrant adjoining Port Olimpic with its long promenade, beaches, yachting marinas, and even trendier eating spots and nightclubs.

> ### ❼ CAN COSTA
>
> You can't pass though Barceloneta without sampling one of its finest—and definitely oldest—seafood eating spots, **Can Costa**, Passeig de Joan de Borbón (☏ **93-221-59-03**). It's located a block back from the waterfront, as all the genuine locales are. This is the real McCoy, with excellent *fideuà de paella* (made with noodles, not rice) and baby *calamares* that are worth leaving home for. It can get busy for lunch, so arrive early—and that's anytime before 2pm in Spain (p. 160).

Map legend:
1. Parc de la Ciutadella
2. La Ribera
3. Museu Picasso
4. Textil Cafe
5. Santa María del Mar
6. La Barceloneta (& Port Olímpic)
7. Can Costa
8. Marina Port Vell
9. Museu Maritim
10. El Raval
11. Bar Marsella

8 Marina Port Vell ★

The main port is the most visibly changed part of Barcelona's waterfront, which for decades notoriously "turned its back on the sea." Today the once-drab industrial zone, where piles of containers brooded under sad-looking palms, has been cleansed, revitalized, and transformed. At its northern end, the large yachting marina beside the older Moll de Barceloneta is lined with international vessels of all shapes and sizes. A smart promenade with public seats runs southward around the harbor past two large, modern jetties: the Moll d'Espanya, whose exclusive Club Maritim, aquarium, IMAX cinema, and Maremagnum zone of trendy shops and

nightspots are all linked to the promenade by the curving Rambla de Mar footbridge; and the Moll de Barcelona, with its high, modern World Trade Center and Torre de Jaume 1 tower, opposite the 14th-century Reials Drassanes (Royal Shipyards) museum (p. 198).

9 Museu Maritim

The Gothic arches inside the Royal Shipyards building loom impressively over what's probably the best nautical museum in the Mediterranean: a superb testament to Barcelona's great naval past. Check out the marvelous "Great Adventure of the Sea" collection, with its full-scale replica of Don Juan of Austria's Royal Galley from the decisive 16th-century Battle of Lepanto, when Spain defeated the Ottomans. There are smaller models of Magellan's world-navigating *Santa María,* and one of the earliest submarines, the *Ictíneo;* and just outside you can go on board the old *Santa Eulalia* sailing ship moored in Moll de la Fusta (p. 198).

⑩ El Raval

Once largely a seedy run-down district, with red-light sections (some of which still exist) and many buildings little more than slums, this is another rejuvenated corner of the city, more polyglot than most due to the large number of immigrant residents. In 2000 the center was bulldozed to provide much-needed breathing space in the form of a brand-new Rambla complete with trees, benches, and kiddies' play areas—part of an ambitious "Ravall obert al cel" (Ravall open to the sky) project. Around it some of the city's most stimulating new art galleries sprang up, spearheaded

by the **MACBA** (Museum of Contemporary Art of Barcelona). The continuing proliferation of rough edges enhances the *barrio's* appeal for some, giving it more "street cred," if you like. And a few classic local buildings like Gaudí's **Palau Güell** (p. 182) and the Romanesque **Sant Pau del Camp** (p. 183) retain a real sense of history in this atmospheric western corner of the Ciutat Vella.

> **⑪ BAR MARSELLA**
> It's the end of your second day, so why not treat yourself to a well-earned snifter of cloudy anis-favored pastis at **Bar Marsella,** Carrer Sant Pau 65 (ⓒ **93-442-72-63**)? A Provençal-cum-Catalan landmark to hedonism, it's a 19th-century oasis of huge mirrors, heavy drapes, creaky rafters, and high chandeliers. The place has been run by the same family for five generations. Among its first customers was a young Jean Genet, reveling in the degeneracy of those early Raval days.

4 THE BEST OF BARCELONA IN 3 DAYS

Spend the first 2 days as described in the above two itineraries. On Day 3 make a leisurely morning exploration of **L'Eixample,** the 19th-century district that expanded the city away from the congested Barric Gòtic and Ciutat Vella in general. This is where you'll find Barcelona's widest avenue, the **Passeig de Gràcia,** and greatest concentration of *moderniste* (Art Nouveau) architecture, highlighted by the **Manzana de Discordia** zone, where Gaudí's **Casa Batlló,** Puig i Cadafalch's **Casa Amatller,** and Domenech i Muntaner's **Casa Lleo Morera** are all so close they virtually shake hands with each other. Most famous of all is another Gaudí gem, **Casa Mila** (popularly known as **La Pedrera**) further along the *paseo.* Pop into Vinçon, the city's famed design emporium, for a descent to relative normality, and then continue up to the village-like district of **Gràcia** at the northern edge of L'Eixample. Return to have lunch in **Casa Calvet,** a restaurant housed in an early work of the omnipresent Gaudí. (This whole area is also covered by Walking Tour 4 in chapter 8, "Strolling Around Barcelona.")

In the afternoon catch the Metro up to **Pedralbes** and visit its monastery and palace. Then continue up to **Tibidabo** by funicular for the best overall panoramic views of the city and coast stretching north toward the Costa Brava. In the evening wander into the adjoining **Collserola Park,** still high above the city.

❶ Passeig de Gràcia
❷ Manzana de la Discordia
❸ Casa Alfonso
❹ Casa Milà (La Pedrera)
❺ Gràcia
❻ Casa Calvet
❼ Monestir de Pedralbes
❽ Tibidabo
❾ Merbeyé
❿ Collserola Park

❶ Passeig de Gràcia

Compared with the color and life of La Rambla, this 60m-wide (197-ft.) avenue, with its traffic-filled center, two pedestrian mini-*paseos,* and four rows of trees, is both more urban and more cosmopolitan. Known locally as the "Queen of Paseos" and lined with elegant buildings, trendy shops, and sought-after eating spots, it rises gently from Plaça de Catalunya through the heart of the 19th-century Eixample to the village-like district of Gràcia.

❷ Manzana de Discordia

A short way up the *paseo* you'll find this remarkable block, with its trio of architectural standouts designed by maestros of the *moderniste* movement: the inimitable Gaudí's frilly and curvaceous **Casa Batlló,** Puig i Cadafalch's staid Flemish-style **Casa Amatller,** and Domenech i Muntaner's decidedly eccentric **Casa Lleo Morera,** compared by some to a collapsed wedding cake. Manzana means both "block" and "apple" in Spanish, so the double meaning could also refer to the mythical golden

Apple of Discord, which was to be given to the winner of a beauty contest judged by Paris. Here you can decide for yourself which building comes out on top.

☕ **CASA ALFONSO**

Casa Alfonso, Roger de Lluria 6 ((📞 **93-301-97-83**), is a great tapas bar that serves a wide enough variety of mouth-watering snacks and raciones to satisfy anyone with an early morning appetite. Their Jabugo ham from the Huelva province is considered by many to be Spain's best. At this hour, though, you may simply prefer to settle for a café con leche and admire the aromatic rows of hanging pork (p. 155).

❹ Casa Mila (La Pedrera)

You've not finished with *moderniste* architecture by a long shot. On its own some 457m (1500 ft.) further up the avenue is what many feel to be the most striking building of all: Casa Mila (by Gaudí again), also known as "La Pedrera" or the Rock Quarry, since its twisted verandas and frivolous chimneys are all made of bizarrely sculptured limestone from Montjuïc hill. It's really a block of apartments, the most original in the entire city, and the high point of any visit comes when you get onto the roof and enjoy the Mary Poppins cityscape visible past those astonishing chimneys (p. 184).

❺ Gràcia

This intimate district at the northern end of the Passeig de Gràcia, just past the Avinguda Diagonal, started life as a small village built around an 18th-century convent; then, during Barcelona's Industrial Revolution, it became a working-class zone where a famed revolt over the reintroduction of military drafting is commemorated by a tall bell tower that stands in Plaça Ruis i Taulet. Today it's a sought-after and slightly gentrified corner of the city in which many traditional features, such as vintage *herbolarios* (nature cure shops) and

fortune-telling palm readers, have attractively lingered on amid the abundance of tiny squares and narrow lanes. Its mood is vaguely Bohemian, and many artists have chosen to establish their homes and workshops here. The August festival is a riot of street fun that lasts a week. Don't miss it if you're here then (p. 189).

☕ **CASA CALVET**

Head back down into the lower Eixample for an indulgent (but not too indulgent if you want to get through the afternoon) lunch at **Casa Calvet,** Carrer Casp 48 ((📞 **93-412-40-12**), a Gaudí-designed ground-floor restaurant. The *moderniste* setting is complemented by a new and old blend of top Catalan cuisine (p. 150).

❼ Monestir de Pedralbes

Situated high up in one of the city's classiest suburbs alongside a Catalan Gothic church, this 14th-century gem founded by Queen Elisenda is one of Barcelona's oldest and most attractive religious buildings. Once inside you take a peep at its secluded garden and fountain; explore the beautiful three-floored cloister; and visit the pharmacy, kitchen, and high-vaulted refectory with restored artifacts of daily convent life. An added attraction since 1993 is the superb Thyssen-Bornemisza art collection of European masters highlighted by Fra Angelico's moving *Madonna of Humility* and Ferrer Bassa's murals in the tiny Sant Miguel chapel (p. 200).

❽ Tibidabo

You can arrive at this strange mixture of the ecclesiastic and the brassy either by Tramvia Blau (Blue Tram; weekends only in winter) and funicular lift, or by taking a bus all the way up from Plaça Doctor Andreu. At the top, 488m (1,600 ft.) above the sea and enjoying sensational views of the city and coast, is one of the few places in the world you'll find a church next to a fun-fair. The church, named

Sagrat Cor (or Holy Heart), is built in an unattractive gray neo-Gothic, and its silhouette can be seen from so many miles away that it's become one of the city's most familiar landmarks. The fun-fair's been in operation for over 80 years and its truly vintage attractions include the wheezy Aeromàgic mountain ride and a 1928 flight simulator. The name is said to come from the Devil's words to Christ, *"ti dabo,"* meaning "I give to you," signifying when Satan offered Jesus all he could see if he would follow him. Tempting enough when you consider the panorama below.

> ### ☕9 MERBEYÉ
> **Merbeyé,** Plaça Doctor Andreu, Tibidabo (✆ **93-417-92-79**), is a showy and colorful cocktail bar cum cafe. It has a plush jazz-oriented lounge, with cool background music, plus a more tranquil open-air terrace where you can sit and unwind after the day's sightseeing over a daiquiri or *café con leche* and enjoy the great view.

❿ Collserola Park

To the southwest of Tibidabo, on the same high massif, is this splendid 8,000-hectare (19,768-acre) area of wild countryside where footpaths meander amid the oak forests and offer occasional spectacular vistas. Within the park are farmhouses, chapels, and springs, including the charming Font de la Budellera. Along the way you'll also see plaques with verses by the Catalan poet Jacint Verdaguer. (See the small museum dedicated to him inside the 18th-century Villa Joana.) A far more recent eye-catcher is the 15-year-old Norman Foster–designed Torre de Collserola, shaped like a giant syringe, which is just 5 minutes' stroll away from Tibidabo (see above). There's an unbeatable view from the top, accessible by a vertigo-inducing elevator. At night you can see its lights flashing from way below.

Where to Stay

Barcelona is now the number-one short city break destination in Europe, and though hotels are mushrooming annually to meet the demand—90,000 at the last count—it's still often a struggle to find a room here. At the top end of the market are first-class and deluxe hotels, which are reasonably priced compared to similar lodgings in Paris or London, giving you a chance to splurge—especially over weekends—on bargains. (It's a good idea to scour the Internet for package deals and ask about any special offers when you call to reserve.)

But even visitors on a budget will have ample choice. Attractive changes have taken place in many of the older establishments in Barcelona. Traditionally—and especially in the heart of the Ciutat Vella quarter—these old *hostales* are centered around a well or patio and may have seemed dark, gloomy, and almost claustrophobic in the past. Today, however, many of these hotels have been renovated and transformed into bright, appealing places to sleep. Some even have gardens and patios to look out on. One thing that has not changed, however, is the noise (especially from weekend revelers), though mercifully more rooms are soundproof these days. Modernized facades and original tiled floors have also been retained in many hotels, and the city's increasing number of attractive "boutique" establishments are decorated with all the stylistic inventiveness you'd expect to find in such a famously avant-garde metropolis.

Keeping pace with the times, nearly all hotels—even the most budget-oriented ones—offer Internet services, such as high-speed ADSL and Wi-Fi connections.

Our newer inclusions cover most tastes and pockets. They range from the traditionally deluxe **Hotel Palace** (p. 108), which occupies the prestigious premises of the former Ritz, to the down-to-earth **Hostal HMB** (p. 116); from the state-of-the-art, cutting-edge **ME Barcelona** (p. 110) and hip **Chic & Basic** (p. 98) to the panoramic delights of Montjuïc's hillside **Hotel Miramar** (p. 119).

SAVING ON YOUR HOTEL ROOM

The **rack rate** is the maximum rate that a hotel charges for a room. The truth is, *hardly anybody pays rack rates* and, with the exception of smaller B&Bs, you can usually pay quite a bit less than the rates shown below. If you decide to come to Barcelona during the very hot months of July and August (in reality, the capital's "low season") you'll usually pick up some bargains in the higher-priced hotels at lower rates than those we officially list here. Check directly with the hotel, or visit the regularly updated website **www. venere.com**, which, by cutting out booking agents, is able to get some of the most competitive rates available. High-price times are Easter and Christmas, so avoid those periods if you can.

Here's how I've organized the price categories:

- **Very Expensive,** $400 and up
- **Expensive,** $275 to $399
- **Moderate,** $150 to $274
- **Inexpensive,** under $150

These are all high-season prices, with no discounts applied. But *always* peruse the category above your target price—you might just find the perfect match, especially if you follow the advice below. ***Note to single travelers:*** Rates for singles may be available in some of the accommodations listed in this chapter—call the hotel directly for specific rates. To lower the cost of your room:

- **Ask about special rates or other discounts.** Always ask whether a room less expensive than the first one quoted is available, or whether any special rates apply to you. You may qualify for corporate, student, military, senior, or other discounts. Mention membership in AAA, AARP, frequent-flier programs, or trade unions, which may entitle you to special deals as well. Find out the hotel policy on children—do kids stay free in the room or is there a special rate?
- **Dial direct.** When booking a room in a chain hotel, you'll often get a better deal by calling the individual hotel's reservation desk rather than the chain's main number.
- **Book online.** Many hotels offer Internet-only discounts, or supply rooms to Priceline, Hotwire, or Expedia at rates much lower than the ones you can get through the hotel itself. Shop around. And if you have special needs—a quiet room, a room with a view— call the hotel directly and make your needs known after you've booked online.
- **Remember the law of supply and demand.** Resort hotels are most crowded and therefore most expensive on weekends, so discounts are usually available for midweek stays. Business hotels in downtown locations are busiest during the week, so you can expect big discounts over the weekend. Many hotels have high-season and low-season prices, and booking the day after "high season" ends can mean big discounts.
- **Look into group or long-stay discounts.** If you come as part of a large group, you should be able to negotiate a bargain rate, since the hotel can then guarantee occupancy in a number of rooms. Likewise, if you're planning a long stay (at least 5 days), you might qualify for a discount. As a general rule, expect 1 night free after a 7-night stay.
- **Avoid excess charges and hidden costs.** When you book a room, ask whether the hotel charges for parking. Use your own cellphone, pay phones, or prepaid phone cards instead of dialing direct from hotel phones, which usually have exorbitant rates. And don't be tempted by the room's minibar offerings: Most hotels charge through the nose for water, soda, and snacks. Finally, ask about local taxes and service charges, which can increase the cost of a room by 15% or more. If a hotel insists upon tacking on a surprise "energy surcharge" that wasn't mentioned at check-in or a "resort fee" for amenities you didn't use, you can often make a case for getting it removed.
- **Book an efficiency.** A room with a kitchenette allows you to shop for groceries and cook your own meals. This is a big money saver, especially for families on long stays.
- Carefully consider your hotel's meal plan. If you enjoy eating out and sampling the local cuisine, it makes sense to choose a **Continental Plan (CP),** which includes breakfast only, or a **European Plan (EP),** which doesn't include any meals and allows you maximum flexibility. If you're more interested in saving money, opt for a **Modified American Plan (MAP),** which includes breakfast and one meal, or the **American Plan (AP),** which includes three meals. If you must choose a MAP, see if you can get a free lunch at your hotel if you decide to do dinner out.
- **Consider enrolling in hotel "frequent-stay" programs,** which are upping the ante lately to win the loyalty of repeat customers. Frequent guests can now accumulate points or credits to earn free hotel nights, airline miles, in-room amenities, merchandise, tickets to concerts and events, and discounts on sporting facilities. Perks are awarded not only

by many chain hotels and motels (Hilton HHonors, Marriott Rewards, Wyndham ByRequest, to name a few), but also by individual inns and B&Bs. Many chain hotels partner with other hotel chains, car-rental firms, airlines, and credit card companies to give consumers additional incentive to do repeat business.

HOW TO GET THE BEST ROOM

Somebody has to get the best room in the house. It might as well be you. If you choose to stay at a chain hotel, you can start by joining the hotel's frequent-guest program, which may make you eligible for upgrades. A hotel-branded credit card usually gives its owner "silver" or "gold" status in frequent-guest programs for free. Always ask about a corner room. They're often larger and quieter, with more windows and light, and they often cost the same as standard rooms. When you make your reservation, ask if the hotel is renovating; if it is, request a room away from the construction. Ask about nonsmoking rooms; rooms with views; and rooms with twin, queen-, or king-size beds. If you're a light sleeper, request a quiet room away from vending machines, elevators, restaurants, bars, and discos. Ask for a room that has been most recently renovated or redecorated. If you aren't happy with your room when you arrive, ask for another one. Most lodgings will be willing to accommodate you.

WHICH QUARTER FOR FULL SATISFACTION?

The **Barri Gòtic (Gothic Quarter)** is good for *hostales* (not to be confused with hostels) and cheaper guesthouses, and you can live and eat less expensively here than in any other part of Barcelona and save money on transport, as most sights are within walking distance. Hold on to your belongings, however, as bag-snatching is rife here, in the gentrified El Born area, and in the still-edgy El Raval. While you are unlikely to suffer any bodily harm, be careful when returning to your hotel late at night.

More modern, but more expensive, accommodations can be found north of the Barri Gòtic in the **Eixample district,** centered on the Metro stops Plaça de Catalunya and Universitat. Many buildings are in the *modernista* style, from the last decades of the 19th century. Be aware that sometimes the elevators and plumbing are of the same vintage. However, the Eixample is a desirable and safe neighborhood, especially along its wide boulevards, and is excellent for good restaurants. Traffic noise is the only problem you might encounter.

The area around **Sants** and **Plaça Espanya** is the main hub of business hotels and convenient for conferences, meetings, and trade shows. It's also convenient for the airport (just 20 min. away by taxi) and the hotels here tend to be quite good if family-size rooms are needed. However, most leisure travelers will probably find it too far away from the city center.

Farther north, above the Avinguda Diagonal, you'll enter the **Gràcia** area, where you can enjoy distinctively Catalan neighborhood life. It has a villagey feel, low-rise buildings, and plenty of sunny plazas populated by students. The main attractions are a bit distant but easily reached by public transportation; still, the neighborhood does have a uniquely eclectic feel that makes the barrio worth exploring. Above this the neighborhoods of **Sarrià** and **Sant Gervasi** are mainly upper-class residential areas, with plenty of top-end bars and restaurants.

Barcelona's seafront has never been much of a hotspot for hotels, though after decades of practically ignoring its shoreline, the last few years have seen the area transform into a bustling seaside promenade. The few hotels that do exist tend to be four- or five-star and expensive, although the area of **Poble Nou** is becoming increasingly popular among new developers and is a good choice for anyone looking to get away from the tourist crowds while staying close to the beach.

Another option is to look at **aparthotels** and short-term rented **apartments** (self-catering accommodations), which are becoming increasingly popular. They give you independence, a kitchen to cook for yourself, and the sensation of a home-away-from-home. Finally, there is a new wave in **bed-and-breakfast** accommodations. Virtually unheard of until 2 or 3 years ago, these family-run guesthouses (often no more than two or three rooms) offer a highly personal and cheap alternative.

But whichever option you choose, you *must* book well ahead to secure something on your list of first choices. Don't even think of rolling up into town without a booking in hand or you may find yourself sculling to the outer suburbs or out of Barcelona altogether. This is not just true of the summer months: Tourism here is nonstop year-round.

Many of Barcelona's hotels were built before the invention of the automobile, and even the more modern ones rarely have garages. When parking is available at the hotel, the price is indicated; otherwise, the hotel staff will direct you to a garage. Expect to pay upward of 15€ ($20) for 24 hours, and if you do have a car, you might as well park it and leave it there, because driving around the city can be excruciating. If you don't plan to leave the city, then there is little point in hiring a car at all.

1 THE BEST HOTEL BETS

- **Best for a Romantic Getaway:** Lovebirds have good reasons not to leave the confines of **Gran Hotel La Florida,** Carretera de Tibidabo s/n (© **93-259-30-00**), a fabulous historic hotel—and not all of those reasons are to be found in the bedrooms. The stainless-steel lap pool, spa, and gardens offering sweeping views of the city are enticement enough to keep you holed up for days. See p. 125.

- **Best for Art Lovers:** As stylish as anywhere in the city, the **Hotel Claris,** Pau Claris 150 (© **93-487-62-62**), has rooms and foyers dotted with early Egyptian art and artifacts, 19th-century Turkish kilims, and even some Roman mosaics, a fruit of the owner's passion for collecting. See p. 106.

- **Best for Business Travelers:** In the heart of the business district, the **AC Diplomatic,** Pau Claris 122 (© **93-272-38-10**), exudes efficiency. The highly tasteful interior and amenities have just the right balance of detail and function, allowing those with a job to do to get on with it in comfort. See p. 111.

- **Best for Celebrity Spotting:** Preferred choice of top models and temperamental rock stars, the **Hotel Arts,** Marina 19–21 (© **93-221-10-00**), has remained a jet-set playground and symbol of "cool Barcelona" for over a decade. See p. 122.

- **Best for Service:** As well as being a highly regarded hotel, the **Prestige,** Passeig de Gràcia 62 (© **93-272-41-80**), offers a unique service to its clients. The role of the concierge is replaced with "Ask Me," specially trained information officers on call to find the answers to the most challenging queries, from how to score soccer tickets to where to find halal restaurants. See p. 109.

- **Best In-House Restaurant:** When celebrated chef Fermin Puig took over the food department of the highly regarded **Majestic,** Passeig de Gràcia 70 (© **93-488-17-17**), he not only revolutionized what clients receive on their breakfast tray but also created

Drolma, one of the country's most celebrated haute cuisine restaurants. Puig's take on traditional Catalan and Southern French cooking has impressed even the most demanding gourmand. See p. 148.

- **Best Historic Hotel:** The *modernista* masterpiece **Hotel Casa Fuster,** Passeig de Gràcia 132 (© **93-225-30-00**), was an emblematic building *before* it was converted into a luxury residence. The rooms have been restored to turn-of-the-20th-century opulence, but with all the mod-cons expected by today's high society. See p. 106.

- **Best Modern Design:** Local talent joined forces to create the **Hotel Omm,** Rosselló 265 (© **93-445-40-00**), which was conceived as homage to the city's vibrant design culture. Daring concepts prevail, from the metal facade to the sleek open-plan suites and private terraces. On the ground floor, the Omm's restaurant, Moo, is fast becoming the place to see and be seen among Barcelona's arts elite. See p. 108.

- **Best for Sheer Atmosphere:** If faded glory is your thing, then look no further than the **Hotel España,** Sant Pau 11 (© **93-318-17-58**). Designed by a contemporary of Gaudí's, the street-level dining room, filled with florid motif and brass fixtures, will whisk you back to the early 1900s, when it was filled with chattering patrons taking supper after a trip to the opera house next door. See p. 104.

- **Best for Architecture Buffs:** Hailing from the early '50s, the **Park Hotel,** Av. Marquès de L'Argenteria 11 (© **93-319-60-00**), was the first example of post-war *modernista* architecture in the city. The renovation carried out 4 decades later only enhances its singular style. Among its highlights is one of the most striking staircases in existence. See p. 102.

- **Best Boutique Hotel:** The boutique concept took its time coming to Barcelona. Forefront of the movement was **Banys Orientals,** Argenteria 37 (© **93-268-84-60**), and it remains the best. It's perfectly located in the middle of El Born district, Barcelona's bastion of urban chic. See p. 104.

- **Best Small Hotel: Hostal D'Uxelles,** Gran Vía 688 and 667 (© **93-265-25-60**), looks like it has stepped straight off the pages of one of those rustic-interiors magazines. Located on the first floor of two adjacent buildings, each of the 30 rooms has a character all of its own, but all include canopied beds, antique furniture, and Andalusian-style ceramic bathrooms. See p. 115.

- **Best for Sea Views:** Imagine stepping off a luxury cruise liner and straight into a top-class hotel. That is pretty much possible at **Hotel Grand Marina,** World Trade Centre, Moll de Barcelona (© **93-603-90-00**). It's housed in the western wing of the city's World Trade Center, on a wide jetty which is, in effect, a man-made island in the port. From its windows and terraces you can enjoy some splendid Mediterranean vistas. See p. 121.

- **Best for City Views:** The **Hotel Miramar,** Plaça Carlos Ibañez 3 (© **93-281-16-00**), perched on the northeasterly flank of Montjuïc hill and surrounded by attractive gardens, enjoys magnificent bird's-eye views of the city, inland hills, and coastline below. See p. 119.

- **Best Inexpensive Hotel:** Serenity and character abound in **Hotel Peninsular,** Sant Pau 34–36 (© **93-302-31-38**), a nunnery-turned-hotel. Located on a colorful street just off La Rambla, the hotel—with its Art Nouveau elevator, long hallways in tones of green and white, and lush inner courtyard—is an oasis from the hustle and bustle outside. Book ahead. See p. 104.

- **Best for Families Who Don't Want to Break the Bank:** The family-run **Marina Folch,** Carrer del Mar 16, principal (© **93-310-37-09**), is the only hotel in the beachside neighborhood of Barceloneta, with plenty of open spaces for the kids to run wild. Ask for a room at the front for a balcony with a view of the port. See p. 124.

- **Best Hostal:** Forget faded curtains and floral wallpaper. **Gat Raval,** Joaquín Costa 44 (𝒞 **93-481-66-70**), is a streamlined *hostal* fitted out in acid green and black that has been conceived for the modern world traveler on a budget. On-demand Internet access and touches of abstract art add to its contemporary ambience and the foyer is always abuzz with travelers exchanging information. See p. 103.

2 CIUTAT VELLA (BARRI GÒTIC, EL RAVAL & LA RIBERA)

The **Ciutat Vella (Old City)** forms the monumental center of Barcelona, taking in Les Ramblas, Plaça de Sant Jaume, Vía Laietana, Passeig Nacional, the Passeig de Colom, and the full-of-character Raval and La Ribera neighborhoods. It contains some of the city's best hotel bargains. Most of the glamorous, and more expensive, hotels are located in the Eixample and beyond.

VERY EXPENSIVE

Le Méridien Barcelona ★★★   Totally renovated in 2007, this is the finest hotel in the Old Town, as the long roster of internationally famous guests testifies. It's even superior in comfort to its two closest—and highly regarded—rivals in the area, the Colón and the Rivoli Ramblas. Its impeccable suites are, understandably, the most expensive in town. Guest rooms are spacious and comfortable, with extra-large beds and heated bathroom floors with tub/shower combos. There is an attentive and hospitable staff. An added bonus for working travelers is the well-equipped Renaissance Club, an executive floor providing a wide range of business facilities.

Les Ramblas 111, 08002 Barcelona. 𝒞 **888/250-8577** in the U.S., or 93-318-62-00. Fax 93-301-77-76. www.lemeridien-barcelona.com. 233 units. 400€–475€ ($520–$618) double; 550€–2,000€ ($715–$2,600) suite. AE, DC, MC, V. Parking 20€ ($26). Metro: Liceu or Plaça de Catalunya. **Amenities:** Restaurant; bar; health club; limited room service; babysitting; laundry service; dry cleaning. *In room:* A/C, TV, minibar, hair dryer, safe.

EXPENSIVE

Duquesa de Cardona ★★★ (Moments)   This small boutique hotel—popular with honeymooners—is across the road from the harbor of Port Vell, and the rooftop terrace and small plunge pool with Jacuzzi have splendid views of the pleasure and party boats that dock here year-round. The hotel occupies what was once a 19th-century palace, and many of its original Art Deco features have been preserved and mixed with elements of modern style to ensure maximum comfort. Communal areas include a stylish living room with deep, cream-colored sofas and a smart Mediterranean restaurant with original marble tiles. The bedrooms have an intimate, romantic feel and all have well-equipped bathrooms with tub/shower combos. If you're used to American-style bedrooms, however, they might seem a little cramped (especially those at the back), and it is worth paying the extra money to get a front-facing room with views of the harbor.

Passeig Colom 12, Barri Gòtic, 08002 Barcelona. 𝒞 **866/376-7831** in the U.S. and Canada or 93-268-90-90. Fax 93-268-29-31. www.hduquesadecardona.com. 44 units. 275€ ($358) double; 375€ ($488) junior suite; 50€ ($65) sea-view supplement. AE, DC, MC, V. Public parking nearby 20€ ($26). Metro: Jaume I or

Drassanes. **Amenities:** Restaurant; 2 lounges; outdoor swimming pool; solarium; business center; room service; babysitting; laundry service; dry cleaning; nonsmoking rooms. *In room:* A/C, TV, Wi-Fi, minibar, hair dryer, safe.

Grand Hotel Central

Avant-garde and with an astute blend of hedonistic and practical amenities, this dazzling 1920s office conversion—located between Santa Caterina market and the cathedral—is one of the latest fashionable hostelries to hit town. Rooms, designed by the prestigious local Sandra Tarruella and Isabel López design team, are spacious and coolly furnished in subtle grays, light browns, and creams, with shiny pinewood flooring and pristine tiled en-suite bathrooms. The executive rooms and suites are even more spectacularly comfortable, and there are also floors devoted to nonsmoking and visitors with disabilities. A big draw is the rooftop "vertiginous infinity" swimming pool and adjoining solarium. Generous buffet breakfasts are served in the mornings and at night you can dine in the **Ávalon** restaurant, presided over by top chef Ramón Freixa.

Via Laietana 30, 08003 Barcelona. ✆ **93-295-79-00.** Fax 93-268-12-15. www.grandhotelcentral.com. 147 units. 185€–200€ ($241–$260) double; 255€–575€ ($332–$748) suite. AE, MC, V. Parking 25€ ($33). Metro: Jaume I. **Amenities:** Restaurant; bar; infinity pool; room service; babysitting; laundry service; dry cleaning. *In room:* A/C, flatscreen TV, DVD player, Wi-Fi, minibar, hair dryer, safe.

Hotel Colón ★★ (Kids)

The long-established Colón, with its dignified neoclassical facade, is located in the heart of Barcelona's Ciutat Vella, right opposite the main entrance to the cathedral (the best rooms on the sixth floor have small terraces with splendid views). Inside, you'll find comfortingly traditional public lounges, a helpful staff, and good-size guest rooms filled with cozy furnishings. Despite recent renovations, the decor remains strongly focused on sturdy Catalan-patterned drapes and upholstery. Sixth-floor rooms with balconies overlooking the square are the most desirable, while back rooms are quieter and lower rooms are rather dark. Upon request, families can often be given more spacious rooms, and the hotel regularly offers attractive Christmas, New Year, and summer-season deals.

Av. de la Catedral 7, 08002 Barcelona. ✆ **800/845-0636** in the U.S., or 93-301-14-04. Fax 93-317-29-15. www.hotelcolon.es. 145 units. 275€ ($358) double; from 440€ ($572) suite. AE, DC, MC, V. Bus: 16, 17, 19, or 45. **Amenities:** Restaurant; bar; room service; babysitting; laundry service; dry cleaning. *In room:* A/C, TV, high-speed Internet, minibar, hair dryer, safe.

Hotel NH Calderón ★★

Efficiently maintained and well staffed with a multilingual corps of employees, this hotel delivers exactly what it promises: comfortable accommodations in a well-conceived, standardized format that's akin to many other modern hotels around the world. Originally built in the 1960s, this 10-story hotel wasn't particularly imaginative then, but was greatly improved in the early 1990s after its acquisition by the NH Hotel Group and has been renovated at regular intervals since then. Accommodations have comfortable, contemporary-looking furnishings with hints of high-tech design, good lighting, lots of varnished hardwood, and colorful fabrics. All units have bathrooms with tub/shower combos.

Rambla de Catalunya 26, 08007 Barcelona. ✆ **93-301-00-00.** Fax 93-412-41-93. www.nh-hoteles.es. 253 units. Mon–Thurs 275€ ($358) double; Fri–Sun 195€ ($254) double. AE, DC, MC, V. Parking 16€ ($21). Metro: Passeig de Gràcia. **Amenities:** Restaurant; bar; indoor and outdoor pool; health club; sauna; business center; limited room service; laundry service; dry cleaning; nonsmoking rooms. *In room:* A/C, TV, high speed Internet, minibar, hair dryer, safe.

Rivoli Ramblas ★

Behind a dignified Art Deco town house on the upper section of La Rambla a block south of the Plaça de Catalunya, this well-renovated hotel incorporates

L'EIXAMPLE

Gran Via Corts Catalanes

1

Rda. Universitat

2

3

Pl. Catalunya

BARCELONA
Map Area

35

4 MACBA

Ronda de St. Antoni

Tallers

Pelai

Plaça Urquinaona

Plaça Catalunya

Rda. Sant Pere

Mercat de St. Antoni

EL RAVAL

6

7

8

Sta. Anna

14

13

12

10

Palau de la Música Catalana

P. Fortuny

9

11

Av. Portal de l'Angel

Via Laietana

St. Pere Més Baix

Ronda St. Pau

Cera

Hospital

Carmes

Mercat de la Boqueria

16

Portaferrissa

15

La Rambla

33

Plaça Antoni Maura

Mercat Sta. Caterina

Reina Amalia

Carretes

Rierata

La Rambla del Raval

17

18

20

21

22

23

19

27

24 **25**

Catedral

Plaça St. Jaume

26

36

Bòria

Princesa

Corders

Comerç

34

St. Pau del Camp

Gran Teatre del Liceu

Ferran

BARRI GÒTIC

37

Av. Paral·lel

Nou de la Rambla

CIUTAT VELLA

28

29

Via Laietana

Pg. de Picasso

POBLE SEC

Av. Drassanes

La Rambla

LA RIBERA

30

Mercat del Born

Plaça del Palau

31 **32** Av. Marquès de l'Argentera

Estació de França

Reials Drassanes (Museu Marítim)

Passeig de Colom

Monument á Colom

Moll d'Espanya

Palau de Mar (Museu d'Història de Catalunya)

Catalonia Albioni **10**	Hotel Barcino **26**	HUSA Oriente **7**
Chic & Basic **37**	Hotel Colón **25**	Jardí **16**
Duques de Bergara **12**	Hotel 1898 **9**	La Ciudadela Hotel **34**
Duquesa de Cardona **30**	Hotel España **18**	Le Meridien Barcelona **6**
Gat Raval **4**	Hotel Gravina **2**	Market Hotel **35**
Gat Xino **5**	Hotel Neri **22**	Mesón Castilla **3**
Grand Hotel Central **36**	Hotel NH Calderón **1**	Montecarlo **13**
H10 Raco del Pi **24**	Hotel Nouvel **8**	NH Duc de la Victoria **23**
Hostal Operaramblas **19**	Hotel Peninsular **17**	Park Hotel **31**
Hostal Orleans **32**	Hotel Regencia Colón **11**	Petit Palace Opera
Hotel Banys Orientals **29**	Hotel Roma Reial **21**	Gardens Ramblas **27**
Hotel Barcelona	Hotel Royal Ramblas **15**	Rivoli Ramblas **14**
Catedral **33**	Hotel Sant Agustí **20**	7 Balconies **28**

WHERE TO STAY

5

CIUTAT VELLA (BARRI GÒTIC, EL RAVAL & LA RIBERA)

many fine examples of avant-garde Catalan design in its stylish interior. The communal areas have acres of polished marble and it's a popular choice for guests in town on business. One of the Rivoli's highlights is the handsome wood-decked roof terrace—a pleasant place to start the day. Guest rooms are carpeted, soundproofed, and elegant, and range from cozy and compact to large and quite spacious. All have immaculately kept bathrooms with tub/shower combos.

La Rambla 128, 08002 Barcelona. ☎ **93-302-66-43.** Fax 93-317-50-53. www.hotelriviloramblas.com. 129 units. 275€ ($358) double; 300€–750€ ($390–$975) suite. AE, DC, MC, V. Metro: Plaça de Catalunya or Liceu. **Amenities:** Restaurant; bar; health spa; sauna; solarium; car rental; limited room service; babysitting; laundry service; dry cleaning; nonsmoking rooms. *In room:* A/C, TV, Wi-Fi, minibar, hair dryer, safe.

MODERATE

Catalonia Albinoni ★★   An ideal choice for shopaholics, the Albinoni is situated halfway up the Portal de l'Angel, where you'll find shoulder-to-shoulder Spanish fashion stores like Zara and Mango and El Corte Inglés (Spain's major department store) at one end, and boutiques and trinket shops at the other. Housed in a former palace dating back to 1876, it was converted into a hotel in 1998 and totally refurbished—while carefully retaining all its traditional highlights—in 2007. It remains on Barcelona's artistic heritage list and many of the original romantic and baroque features have been beautifully preserved. Not least impressive is the elegant marble lobby and stately interior courtyard where the bar and reception area are located. All 74 of the plush bedrooms have polished wood floors, comfortable beds, and en-suite marble bathrooms with tub/shower combos. Breakfast (though overpriced) is served in a wedding-style tent.

Av. Portal de l'Angel 17, Barri Gòtic, 08002 Barcelona. 🕐 **93-318-41-41.** Fax 93-301-26-31. www.hoteles-catalonia.es. 74 units. 140€–185€ ($182–$241) double. AE, DC, MC, V. Public parking nearby 20€ ($26). Metro: Plaça de Catalunya. **Amenities:** Cafeteria; car rental; computers w/Internet; room service; babysitting; laundry service; dry cleaning. *In room:* A/C, TV, minibar, hair dryer, safe.

Chic & Basic ★   Set in an old Born district building that's retained its grand old stairway and lounge furnishings, this modern hotel-apartment concept (the coolest and most self-contained of the five now spread throughout the city) offers dazzling self-contained units that are anything but traditional in design and decor. Each hotel room is ravishingly colored in a different monochromatic hue, from suave gray to virgin white, and has its own small relaxing lounge area complete with fridge, microwave, and coffee-making facilities. The one- or two-bedroom apartments have fully equipped kitchens and access to a small terrace. No smoking is permitted anywhere in the hotel, except the restaurant, and some rooms are equipped for travelers with disabilities.

Calle Princesa 50. 🕐 **93-295-46-52.** www.chicandbasic.com. 31 units. 175€ ($228) double; 200€–240€ ($260–$312) apartment. AE, DC, MC. Metro: Arc de Triomf or Jaume I. **Amenities:** Restaurant; gym. *In room:* TV, Wi-Fi.

Duques de Bergara ★★   This upscale hotel occupies an 1898 town house built for the Duke of Bergara by the architect Emilio Salas y Cortés (a protégée of Gaudí). Lots of elegant *modernista* touches remain, including the original wood-molded ceiling with a rose dome on the first floor, and a handful of original artworks from the era. In the reception area, look for stained-glass panels displaying the heraldic coat of arms of the building's original occupant and namesake, the Duke of Bergara. In 1998 the original five-story structure more than doubled in size with the addition of a seven-story tower. Guest rooms throughout have the same conservative, traditional comforts. Each unit has large, comfortable beds with first-rate mattresses, elegant fabrics, and good lighting. The roomy marble bathrooms are equipped with tub/shower combos.

Bergara 11, 08002 Barcelona. 🕐 **93-301-51-51.** Fax 93-317-34-42. www.hoteles-catalonia.es. 149 units. 180€–245€ ($234–$319) double; 275€–305€ ($358–$397) triple. AE, DC, MC, V. Public parking nearby 20€ ($26). Metro: Plaça de Catalunya. **Amenities:** Restaurant; cafe/bar; outdoor pool; Internet access; room service; laundry service; dry cleaning. *In room:* A/C, TV, minibar, hair dryer, safe.

Gran Hotel Barcino ★ (Finds)   Still one of the city's undiscovered four-star gems, the hospitable Barcino is located right in the heart of the Old Quarter close to a wealth of stylish eating spots and key historic monuments. Its rooms are classically decorated and all have en-suite bathrooms with tub/shower combos. The best rooms have whirlpool baths (big enough for sharing) and private terraces with views over the rooftops and the cathedral, perfect for a predinner drink. The hotel's buffet breakfast may be a bit pricey at 16€ ($21), but it's comprehensive and filling enough to satisfy all tastes. If you want something less extravagant, there are plenty of local cafes serving coffee and croissants or *ensaimadas* (local pastries) a stone's throw from the front door.

Jaume I no. 6, Barri Gòtic, 08002 Barcelona. ℂ 93-302-20-12. Fax 93-301-42-42. www.hotelbarcino.com. 53 units. 250€ ($325) double. AE, DC, MC, V. Public parking nearby 18€ ($23). Metro: Jaume I or Plaça de Catalunya. **Amenities:** Restaurant; cafe/bar; room service; babysitting; laundry service. *In room:* A/C, TV, high-speed Internet, minibar, hair dryer, safe.

Hotel Barcelona Catedral   Ideally located in a narrow street close to the cathedral and all Ciutat Vella sights, the stylish but well-priced Barcelona Catedral aims to provide quality accommodations at affordable prices. On-site amenities range from a pool and "chill out" terrace area to full Internet access and rooms for clients with disabilities. Special services include cooking lessons, wine tastings, and Sunday guided tours around the neighboring Barri Gòtic. All rooms have private bathrooms with bath/shower combo.

Capellans 4, Ciutat Vella, 08002 Barcelona. ℂ 93-304-22-55. www.barcelonacatedral.com. 80 units. 150€–180€ ($195–$234) double. AE, DC, MC, V. Public parking lot nearby. Metro: Jaume 1. **Amenities:** Restaurant; bar/terrace; fitness center; business center; room service; laundry service; dry cleaning. *In room:* AC, TV, radio, free Wi-Fi, minibar, safe.

Hotel 1898 ★   Located right beside the upper stretch of La Rambla in an emblematic 19th-century building that was the former headquarters of the Philippine Tobacco Company, this is one of the city's most deluxe new hotels. Vintage *moderniste* outside, it's lively and abrasive 21st century inside, with each floor decorated in different arrays of dazzling striped colors. There are also ceiling fans, brick walkways, and jet-black leather couches filling the communal areas. The rooms are stylishly and comfortably furnished, and pricier units have terraces with wooden floorboards. Accommodations are also available for nonsmokers and visitors with disabilities.

La Rambla 109, 08002 Barcelona. ℂ 93-552-95-52. www.nnhotels.es. 169 units. 185€–495€ ($241–$644) double. Parking: 24€ ($31). AE, DC, MC, V. Metro: Liceu. **Amenities:** Restaurant; bar; outdoor and indoor pools w/solarium; fitness center; spa; business center w/5 conference rooms; library. *In room:* A/C, TV, Wi-Fi, minibar, hair dryer, safe.

Hotel Gravina Ⓥalue   Part of the reliable H10 chain, the Gravina is a three-star hotel on a quiet street close to the university. This means it's handy for public transport, sights, and shopping, but far enough removed from the main tourist drag to offer some breathing space from the bustle of the Ciutat Vella. The 19th-century facade promises great things to come, but don't get too excited. The interior is essentially modern and functional with the focus more on practical facilities than atmosphere. That said, it's good value with friendly, accommodating staff and comfortable, fully equipped bedrooms complete with TV and Wi-Fi connection. It's worth specifying that you want a larger room. All rooms have soundproofed windows and en-suite bathrooms with tub/shower combos. This is a good choice for business travelers on a budget.

Gravina 12, 08001 Barcelona. ℂ 93-301-68-68. Fax 93-317-28-38. www.hotel-gravina.com. 82 units. 150€–225€ ($195–$293) double; 250€–375€ ($325–$488) suite. AE, DC, MC, V. Public parking nearby 25€ ($33). Metro: Universitat or Plaça de Catalunya. **Amenities:** Restaurant; cafe/bar; room service; laundry service; dry cleaning; nonsmoking rooms. *In room:* A/C, TV, Wi-Fi, minibar, hair dryer, safe.

Hotel Neri ★★★ (Moments) The captivating Neri is located in a former Gothic palace close to the cathedral and the charming little Plaça Felip Neri. Its interior features gold leaf decor, red velvet drapes, and soft-lit, echoing hallways, and the bedrooms are plush with high-thread-count cotton sheets, shot-silk pillowcases, throws, and rugs. The minibar has all the usual tipples plus exotic extras like incense and candles. Some rooms have a tub as well as a shower, and there are also two spacious suites (which have in the past attracted illustrious visitors such as John Malkovich). Relaxing bonuses are a coffee and cocktail terrace right on the plaza and a rooftop garden resplendent with jasmine plants and creepers. The Neri's "Aromatic Mediterranean cuisine" restaurant is another favored rendezvous for followers of the—trendily expensive—Catalan gourmet scene.

Sant Sever 5, Barri Gòtic, 08002 Barcelona. ✆ **93-304-06-55**. Fax 93-304-03-37. www.hotelneri.com. 22 units. 180€–200€ ($234–$260) double; 220€–275€ ($286–$358) suite. AE, DC, MC, V. Public parking nearby 24€ ($31). Metro: Jaume I or Liceu. **Amenities:** Restaurant; cafe/bar; book/CD library; room service; babysitting; laundry service; dry cleaning; nonsmoking rooms. *In room:* A/C, TV, Wi-Fi, minibar, hair dryer, safe.

Hotel Nouvel (Moments) A smartly renovated hotel that dates back to 1917 and retains plenty of its original atmospheric *modernista* flourishes, the Nouvel is a charming retreat right in the heart of the Old City. It's wonderful for lovers of the Art Deco style, with many of the original carved wood panels, smoked-glass partitions, and elaborate floor tiles. The bedrooms offer a mix of newly renovated accommodations, though the rooms with the most character are the more old-fashioned kind with the original tiles. All have modernized bathrooms with tub/shower combos. The best have balconies, and it's worth asking for a room at the rear if street noise bothers you.

Santa Ana 20, Barri Gòtic, 08002 Barcelona. ✆ **93-301-82-74**. Fax 93-301-83-70. www.hotelnouvel.com. 54 units. 160€–220€ ($208–$286) double. Rate includes breakfast. MC, V. Public parking nearby 24€ ($31). Metro: Plaça de Catalunya. **Amenities:** Restaurant (lunch daily, dinner Thurs–Sat); Wi-Fi; babysitting; laundry service; dry cleaning; nonsmoking rooms. *In room:* A/C, TV, minibar, safe in some rooms.

Hotel Regencia Colón (Value) The Regencia Colón is conveniently located in a narrow central street behind the pricier Hotel Colón, right in the shadow of the imposing cathedral. This stately six-story stone building attracts a number of major international tour groups thanks to its excellent value and location. The formal lobby may be a bit featureless and downbeat, but the staff is very welcoming and the well-maintained rooms are comfortable, quite spacious, and feature modern conveniences such as satellite TV. Rooms are fully soundproof, and 40 have full bathrooms with tubs (the remainder have showers only). All have comfortable beds and piped-in music.

Sagristans 13–17, 08002 Barcelona. ✆ **93-318-98-58**. Fax 93-317-28-22. www.hotelregenciacolon.com. 50 units. 175€ ($228) double; 195€ ($254) triple. AE, DC, MC, V. Public parking 20€ ($26). Metro: Plaça de Catalunya or Urquinaona. **Amenities:** Restaurant; bar; car rental; babysitting; laundry service; dry cleaning. *In room:* A/C, TV, high-speed Internet, minibar, hair dryer, safe.

Hotel Royal Ramblas (Value) The flat-packed office block look of this hotel—all concrete and glassed-in balconies—doesn't compare too well with the striking period architecture in many other parts of the city, but don't let that put you off. Tastefully stylish refurbishments have resulted in a decidedly more attractive interior, which offers spacious rooms with comfortable beds and furnishings and modern facilities. All have en-suite bathrooms with tub/shower combos and the better bedrooms have balconies offering fabulous views over Barcelona's real-life street theater: La Rambla.

La Rambla 117, Barri Gòtic, 08002 Barcelona. ✆ **93-301-94-94**. Fax 93-317-31-79. www.royalramblas hotel.com. 108 units. 160€–225€ ($208–$293) double. AE, DC, MC, V. Parking 20€ ($26). Metro: Plaça de

Catalunya. **Amenities:** Restaurant; cafe/bar; business center; room service; babysitting; laundry service; dry cleaning; nonsmoking rooms. *In room:* A/C, TV, Wi-Fi, minibar, hair dryer, safe.

Hotel Sant Agustí   Dating from the 1840s—when it was a convent—this tastefully renovated five-story hotel stands in the center of the Old City on a pretty square near the Boqueria market, overlooking the brick walls of an unfinished Romanesque church. Its sandstone facade is dominated by large curving windows while the interior hall and lounge feature a lush blend of emerald-hued furnishings and rose pink decor. The small guest rooms are comfortable and modern with tiled bathrooms with tub/shower combos. The outdoor cafe is a good place to chill on a hot afternoon and the immediate vicinity is full of the funky character that has made El Raval the city's grittiest bohemian retreat. Some units are equipped for travelers with disabilities.

Plaça de Sant Agustí 3, El Raval, 08001 Barcelona. ℂ **93-318-16-58.** Fax 93-317-29-28. www.hotelsa. com. 76 units. 110€–160€ ($143–$208) double; 175€–190€ ($228–$247) triple; 185€–195€ ($241–$254) quad; 225€–250€ ($293–$325) 2-bedroom family unit. Rates include breakfast. AE, DC, MC, V. Metro: Liceu. **Amenities:** Restaurant; lounge; high-speed Internet; room service; laundry service. *In room:* A/C, TV, hair dryer, safe.

H10 Racó del Pi ★   Locations don't get much better than this one, right next to the Old City's prettiest plaza, which is bustling most days with pavement cafes, weekend produce markets, street performers, and artists. The hotel itself has plenty of character; it's small and intimate with a helpful staff who provide some nice touches like offering a glass of *cava* (sparkling wine) to guests on arrival. They also serve a good breakfast buffet offering a range of homemade products. The rooms tend to be compact and dark (one disadvantage of staying in the Barri Gòtic), but this seems a small price to pay for staying in such a cozy place and in such a desirable corner of the town center. All have en-suite mosaic tiled bathrooms with tub/shower combos.

Del Pi 7, Barri Gòtic, 08002 Barcelona. ℂ **93-342-61-90.** Fax 93-342-61-91. www.hotelracodelpi.com. 37 units. 195€ ($254) double. AE, DC, MC, V. Public parking nearby 20€ ($26). Metro: Liceu. **Amenities:** Restaurant; cafe/bar; car rental; business center; limited room service; laundry service; dry cleaning; nonsmoking rooms. *In room:* A/C, TV, high-speed Internet, minibar, hair dryer, safe.

HUSA Oriente   Situated on the site of a Franciscan monastery right beside the bustling Rambla, the Oriente was one of the original "grand hotels" of Barcelona and dates back to 1842. Such was its prominence by the 1950s that it attracted the likes of Toscanini, Maria Callas, and Errol Flynn (who once passed out drunk and was put on public display in his room—unconscious and in the nude—by a somewhat unscrupulous manager). Renovations have improved the hotel's amenities but it lacks the style and charisma of its former glory days, today attracting mainly frugal travelers. The arched ballroom of yesterday has been turned into an atmospheric lounge, and the dining room still has a certain grandeur. The simple but comfortable rooms all have tiled bathrooms with shower.

La Rambla 45, 08002 Barcelona. ℂ **93-302-25-58.** Fax 93-412-38-19. www.husa.es. 142 units. 195€ ($254) double; 210€ ($273) triple. AE, DC, MC, V. Metro: Liceu. **Amenities:** Restaurant (summer only); bar; laundry service. *In room:* A/C, TV, safe.

Market Hotel   Located on the western side of the Old Town close to the city's lesser-known Sant Antoni market, this chic new hotel deftly combines style and economy. Run by the owners of the Quinze Nits chain of attractively priced hotels and eateries, it provides small but comfortable rooms coolly decorated in minimalist blacks and grays and all fully equipped with en-suite bathrooms. Two of the rooms have been adapted for guests with disabilities.

Passatge Sant Antoni Abat 10. ✆ **93-325-12-05.** www.markethotel.com.es. 47 units. 100€–150€ ($130–$195) double. AE, MC, V. Metro: Sant Antoni. **Amenities:** Restaurant; Wi-Fi. *In room:* A/C, flatscreen TV.

Mesón Castilla ★ ⓥalue

This government-rated two-star hotel, a former apartment building now owned and operated by the Spanish hotel chain HUSA, has a Castilian facade with a wealth of Art Nouveau detailing on the interior. Filled with antiques and quirky trinkets, it's one of the most atmospheric spots to stay in town. It's also handily located close to the hip secondhand stores and record shops of the upper Raval, the MACBA, and the CCCB. The midsize rooms are comfortable—beds have ornate Catalan-style headboards—and some open onto large terraces. The tiled bathrooms are equipped with tub/shower combos.

Valldoncella 5, 08001 Barcelona. ✆ **93-318-21-82.** Fax 93-412-40-20. www.mesoncastilla.com. 57 units. 150€ ($195) double; 190€ ($247) triple. Rates include breakfast. AE, DC, MC, V. Parking 20€ ($26). Metro: Plaça de Catalunya or Universitat. **Amenities:** Breakfast room; lounge; room service; babysitting; laundry service; dry cleaning; safe. *In room:* A/C, TV, minibar, hair dryer.

Montecarlo ★★★

The fabulously ornate facade of this La Rambla hotel dates back 200 years to the days when it was an opulent private home and the headquarters of the Royal Artistic Circle of Barcelona. Public areas include some of the building's original accessories, with carved doors, a baronial fireplace, and crystal chandeliers. In the 1930s, it was transformed into the comfortably unpretentious hotel you'll find today. A legend in its own lifetime, the Montecarlo today combines traditional comforts with modern amenities like free Internet connection. Each of the midsize guest rooms is smartly decorated, with extras that make all the difference, such as adjustable beds, large marble bathrooms with Jacuzzi tubs, bathrobes, and slippers. The service is exemplary and nothing is too much trouble, whether you want to book a winery excursion or simply park your car.

La Rambla 124, 08002 Barcelona. ✆ **93-412-04-04.** Fax 93-318-73-23. www.montecarlobcn.com. 55 units. 175€–360€ ($228–$468) double; 450€ ($585) suite. AE, DC, MC, V. Parking 18€ ($23). Metro: Plaça de Catalunya. **Amenities:** Lounge; bar; room service; babysitting; laundry service; dry cleaning; terrace solarium. *In room:* A/C, TV, free Wi-Fi, minibar, hair dryer, safe.

NH Duc de la Victoria ⓥalue

Part of the NH Hotel Chain which aims to provide smooth, seamless comfort in midprice accommodations, this smart hotel is well situated on a quiet street in the heart of the Barri Gòtic. It's of a somewhat higher standard than most *hostales* in the area and makes a great base for discerning visitors who want to have all central amenities, from shops and restaurants to historical monuments, right on their doorstep. Spotlessly clean throughout, it provides continental breakfasts but no main meals. Bedrooms are of a decent size with cool parquet floors and all have compact bathrooms with tub/shower combos. Fifth-floor rooms with private balconies are the best.

Duc de la Victoria 15, Barri Gòtic, 08002 Barcelona. ✆ **93-270-34-10.** Fax 93-412-77-47. www.hotelnh ducdelavictoria.com. 156 units. 180€ ($234) double; 250€ ($325) suite. AE, DC, MC, V. Public parking nearby 18€ ($23). Metro: Plaça de Catalunya. **Amenities:** Restaurant; cafe/bar; Wi-Fi; room service; babysitting; laundry service; dry cleaning; nonsmoking rooms. *In room:* A/C, TV, minibar, hair dryer, safe.

Park Hotel ★

This laid-back hotel is a unique example of mid-20th-century rationalist architecture and its standout interior features include a stunning, spiral staircase and a sleek, mosaic tiled bar. Bedrooms are stylish (though slightly small) and comfortably decorated in warm colors with tasteful furnishings. All have en-suite bathrooms with tub/shower combos. ***Note:*** Some visitors have reported having their luggage stolen on their way in, so keep an eye on your things while transferring them from the taxi to the hotel entrance doorway. The Estació de Franca is close by, the Parc de la Ciutadella (central Barcelona's greenest area) lies just across the road, and the Barceloneta beach is a 10-minute walk away.

Av. Marquès de l'Argentera 11, Born, 08003 Barcelona. © **93-319-60-00.** Fax 93-319-45-19. www.park hotelbarcelona.com. 91 units. 110€–190€ ($143–$247) double. AE, DC, MC, V. Parking 12€ ($16). Metro: Barceloneta or Jaume I. **Amenities:** Restaurant; lounge; room service; laundry service; dry cleaning; nonsmoking rooms. *In room:* A/C, TV, high-speed Internet, minibar, hair dryer, safe.

Petit Palace Opera Garden Ramblas ★ (Finds)   This well-appointed member of the Petit Palace high-tech hotel chain is conveniently located in the heart of the Rambla, close to two famous Barcelona landmarks: the Liceu Theater and the Boqueria covered market. It's an ideal choice both for business and leisure travelers who want to keep in touch, as the neatly furnished modern rooms all have laptop computers with free high-speed Internet access and Wi-Fi connections. Accommodations cover everyone from single executives to families of four (with king-size beds) and all have hydromassage showers (larger rooms also have saunas). General facilities include a business center in the main hall, a bar/cafeteria, and a gourmet dining room.

Carrer La Boqueria 10, Ramblas 78, 08002 Barcelona. © **93-302-00-92.** Fax 93-302-15-66. www.opera garden.barcelonahotels.it. 70 units. 200€ ($260) single; 240€–280€ ($312–$364) double; 280€–320€ ($364–$416) quad. Metro: Liceu. **Amenities:** Restaurant; cafeteria; lounge; business center; meeting room; laundry service; all nonsmoking rooms. *In room:* A/C, TV, Wi-Fi, minibar, safe.

INEXPENSIVE

Gat Raval ★★ (Value)   From grim and grungy to green and groovy, the Gat Raval is the first in this extraordinary little chain's mini-empire and has been pioneering in giving *hostal* accommodations a much-needed face-lift. The Gats (Catalan for "cats") are notably both cool and economical, though guests may find it a bit noisy when that coolness occasionally yields to unrestrained hedonistic exuberance. Decorated in bright acid greens with black trim, the neat bedrooms are decorated with original works from the local art school that give it an upbeat bohemian vibe. Only some of the bedrooms have en-suite bathrooms (stipulate when booking) and communal arrangements are so clean you could eat your dinner off the floor.

Joaquín Costa 44, 2ª, 08001 Barcelona. © **93-481-66-70.** Fax 93-342-66-97. www.gataccommodation. com. 24 units. 70€ ($91) double w/sink; 85€ ($111) double w/bathroom. MC, V. Metro: Universitat. **Amenities:** High-speed Internet; safe. *In room:* TV.

Gat Xino ★★ (Finds)   Those wishing to experience the same Gat über-coolness with a dash more luxury can opt instead for the Gat Xino, which caters to a slightly more grown-up and affluent visitor. This hip guesthouse has a sleek breakfast room, and there's a wood-decked terrace and a roof terrace for soaking up the rays. All of the rooms have their own apple-green bathrooms with showers, and there are a few added extras like flatscreen TVs and light boxes above the beds giving abstract photographic views of the city.

Hospital 149–155, 08001 Barcelona. © **93-324-88-33.** Fax 93-324-88-34. www.gatrooms.es/en. 35 units. 90€–100€ ($117–$130) double. Rate includes breakfast. MC, V. Metro: Liceu. **Amenities:** High-speed Internet; safe (2€/$2.60 per day). *In room:* A/C, TV.

Hostal Operaramblas (Value)   Cheap and cheerful, this safe, well-maintained *hostal,* located almost next to the famed Opera House, is good for those traveling on a tight budget or alone. Be warned, though: This is basic, no-frills accommodations, with notably thin walls (light sleepers might do well to travel with earplugs) and no luxuries. Plus

104 factors are its friendly and obliging staff and upbeat personality. Some rooms are better than others, however, and if you arrive without a reservation, ask to look around first. Otherwise, opt for something at the back with a private bathroom (shower only), as the street outside—just off La Rambla—can be noisy until the early hours.

Sant Pau 20, El Raval, 08001 Barcelona. ✆ **93-318-82-01.** www.operaramblas.com. 69 units. 70€ ($91) double. MC, V. Metro: Liceu. **Amenities:** High-speed Internet; safe. *In room:* A/C.

Hostal Orleans ⟨**Value**⟩ Located just across the street from one of Barcelona's oldest and most imposing churches, Santa María del Mar is a modest hotel that combines a desirable location in El Born with highly affordable rates. Rooms are spotlessly clean and the hotel is filled with objects and color schemes that take you back to the 1970s. Bedrooms are mainly compact, with comfortable beds and private bathrooms with a half-size bath and shower. Some have balconies overlooking the street, which are great for people-watching, though often noisy at night as revelers wend their way between the lively local bars. The communal sitting room is well-stocked with English-language magazines, and a good place to meet other guests. Other pluses are the friendly service and a genuinely Catalan vibe.

Av. Marquès de l´Argentera 13, 1st floor, El Born, 08003 Barcelona. ✆ **93-319-73-82.** Fax 93-319-22-19. www.hostalorleans.com. 27 units. 70€ ($91) double. MC, V. Metro: Barceloneta or Jaume I. **Amenities:** TV lounge. *In room:* 8€ ($10) supplement for A/C, TV.

Hotel Banys Orientals ★★ ⟨**Finds**⟩ Set in a 19th-century mansion adjoining the chic **Senyor Parellada** eatery (which partly acts as the hotel's own restaurant), this hip haven lies in the heart of the lively—and often noisy—Born district. The variably sized minimalist-style rooms have been very tastefully renovated and all have either a spacious walk-in shower or full bathroom (the latter must be pre-booked.) A buffet breakfast is served on its mezzanine and guests can run up a tab for lunch/evening meals as well. A wealth of cool shops and bars is right on your doorstep, but be sure to ask for a room at the back if you want to enjoy a relatively peaceful night's sleep.

Argenteria 37, La Ribera, 08003 Barcelona. ✆ **93-268-84-60.** Fax 93-268-84-61. www.hotelbanysorientals. com. 43 units. 100€ ($130) double. AE, DC, MC, V. Public parking nearby 18€ ($23). Metro: Jaume I. **Amenities:** Restaurant; limited room service; laundry service; nonsmoking rooms; free minibar for refreshments. *In room:* A/C, TV, high-speed Internet, hair dryer, safe.

Hotel España ⟨**Value**⟩ Set just off the Lower Rambla in a historic building constructed in 1902 by fabled architect Doménech i Montaner (designer and architect of the Palau de la Música), the España still boasts a classically styled foyer and highly elegant dining room that also evokes the heyday of Barcelonan *modernisme*. The renovated rooms, while less classical, are quite spacious, with neat but functional furnishings, comfortable beds, attractive tiled floors, and mellow drapes over the high windows. All have en-suite marble tiled tub/shower combos. Some rooms are equipped for travelers with disabilities. An old elevator serves the building's four floors, and the genial hardworking staff is always eager to converse with non-Spanish-speaking visitors.

Carrer Sant Pau 9-11, El Raval, 08001 Barcelona. ✆ **93-318-17-58.** Fax 93-317-11-34. www.hotelespanya. com. 80 units. 110€ ($143) double; 135€ ($176) triple. AE, DC, MC, V. Metro: Liceu or Drassanes. **Amenities:** 3 restaurants. *In room:* A/C, TV, hair dryer, safe.

Hotel Peninsular ⟨**Value**⟩ Further along the same street as the España, this Art Nouveau–style hotel is a welcoming haven for the budget traveler. Constructed within the shell of a monastery that used to have a passageway connection with Sant Agustí church, the hotel was thoroughly modernized in the early 1990s. Its use of wicker

left margin: WHERE TO STAY

5

CIUTAT VELLA (BARRI GÒTIC, EL RAVAL & LA RIBERA)

furnishings gives it a colonial air, and its inner courtyard, lined with plants, is its most charming feature. In the typical *modernista* style of its era, the Peninsular has long hallways and high doorways and ceilings. The bedrooms are basic but clean, and the better ones have en-suite bathrooms with shower.

Carrer Sant Pau 34–36, El Raval, 08001 Barcelona. (C) **93-302-31-38.** Fax 93-412-36-99. www.hotel peninsular.net. 70 units. 78€ ($101) double; 95€ ($124) triple. Rates include breakfast. MC, V. Metro: Liceu. **Amenities:** Breakfast bar; safe. *In room:* A/C.

Hotel Roma Reial

This is a good choice for youngsters who want to be out barhopping and clubbing long into the night and who don't mind a bit of background noise (the Plaça Reial is a magnet for budding songsters and partygoers unwilling to go home). Located in an attractive traditional building that blends perfectly with its historic neighbors around the plaza, it's a friendly and well-located bargain. The compact and comfortable rooms come with additional facilities such as air-conditioning and TV, and all have their own tiled bathrooms. Some have good views of the lively square itself.

Plaça Reial 11, Barri Gòtic, 08002 Barcelona. (C) **93-302-03-66.** Fax 93-301-18-39. www.hotel-romareial. com. 61 units. 75€–85€ ($98–$111) double. Rates include breakfast, depending on season. MC, V. Metro: Liceu. **Amenities:** Cafeteria; safe. *In room:* A/C, TV.

Jardí (Value)

Enjoying one of Barcelona's most favored locations, this friendly five-story hotel opens onto the tree-shaded Plaça Sant Josep Oriol, whose cafes huddle around the Gothic medieval church of Santa María del Pi in the heart of the Ciutat Vella. More recent touches include a modern elevator and some rather over-enthusiastic lighting (which for some dissipates the historic charm of the building), but much of the original architectural charm still remains. The rooms themselves are austerely atmospheric with comfortable beds and en-suite bathrooms with tub and shower. The quieter units are at the top and five of the accommodations have private terraces, while 26 have small balconies. Under separate management, **Bar del Pi,** on the ground floor, is a favorite of artists and students who live nearby.

Plaça Sant Josep Oriol 1, 08002 Barcelona. (C) **93-301-59-00.** Fax 93-342-57-33. www.hoteljardi-barcelona. com. 40 units. 90€–106€ ($117–$138) double. MC, V. Metro: Liceu. *In room:* A/C, TV, safe.

La Ciudadela Hotel ★ (Finds)

This small, homey, family-run pension provides goodvalue accommodations in a quiet zone on the northern edge of the Ciutatela (Ciudadela) Park. From here you can simply cross the road into the park or wander 5 minutes west into the popular La Ribera district. Beside the hotel's own restaurant (which precedes it by 30 years) there's a cafe terrace where you can relax in the sun in summer. The unpretentious but cozy rooms are all equipped with private bathrooms and tub/shower combinations. This genial spot is a remarkable value.

Paseo Lluis Companys 2 (corner of Paseo Pujades), 08018 Barcelona. 13 units. (C) **93-309-95-57.** Fax 93-528-63-35. www.ciudadelaparc.com. 75€–85€ ($98–$111). MC, V. Public parking. Metro: Arc de Triomf. **Amenities:** Restaurant; café w/terrace. *In room:* A/C, TV, free Wi-Fi, safe.

7 Balconies ★ (Finds)

This charmingly old-fashioned three-room guesthouse has been in the same family for over a century and has a snug and inviting ambience that makes you feel instantly at home. Don't expect any modern conveniences; instead you'll find a cozy retreat filled with heavy antique furniture, faded Art Deco tiling, black-andwhite family photos, and crisp, cotton bed linens. The suite has two rooms (one of which has a sofa bed) and the other two rooms share a bathroom. Few places beat it when it comes to creating a simple homey ambience.

Cervantes 7, Barri Gòtic, 08002 Barcelona. ℭ 65-423-81-61. Fax 93-302-07-52. 3 units. 90€–125€ ($117–$163). MC, V for room deposit only. Room payment in cash only. Parking nearby 20€ ($26). Metro: Liceu or Jaume I. **Amenities:** Tearoom. *In room:* TV, fridge, safe.

3 L'EIXAMPLE

If *moderniste* architecture, designer shopping, and high-class restaurants are your bag, then the Eixample (*extension* in Catalan) is the place to be. The area was built in the mid–19th century to cope with the overflow of the Ciutat Vella and has retained its middle-class, residential flavor.

VERY EXPENSIVE

Hotel Casa Fuster ★★★ (**Moments**) Located in one of the city's most emblematic buildings, the meticulously renovated Casa Fuster blends sheer luxury with first-rate state-of-the-art amenities. Traditional highlights from its great *moderniste* era include the elegant foyer and downstairs Vienna cafe—once a well-known meeting spot for the city's intelligentsia—while many of the Belle Epoque–style rooms—all lavishly decorated in mauve, magenta, and mellow gray-brown decor—have balconies overlooking the wide cosmopolitan Passeig de Gràcia. Marble structures, drapery, cushions, and padding generously abound while other luxuries range from Loewe toiletries to hydromassage bathtubs and an extremely high staff-to-guest ratio. If you can tear yourself away from all these pampering comforts, some of L'Eixample's very best shops and historical monuments are virtually on your doorstep.

Passeig de Gràcia 132, 08008 Barcelona. ℭ **90-220-23-45** for reservations, or 93-255-30-00. Fax 93-255-30-02. www.hotelcasafuster.com. 105 units. 380€–525€ ($494–$683) double; 575€–2,050€ ($748–$2,665) suite. AE, DC, MC, V. Valet parking 25€ ($33). Metro: Diagonal. **Amenities:** Restaurant; bar; 11 lounges; pool; health center; Jacuzzi; sauna; solarium, business center; room service; babysitting; laundry service; dry cleaning; nonsmoking rooms; free newspaper service; audiovisual equipment service. *In room:* A/C, TV, high-speed Internet, minibar, hair dryer, safe.

Hotel Claris ★★★ Formerly known as the Vedruna Palace, this landmark seven-story 19th-century building is a genuine luxurious treat. Furnishings and decor throughout are a lavish amalgam of teak, marble, steel, and glass while the opulent blue-violet guest rooms feature wood marquetry and paneling, custom furnishings, safes, and some of the city's most sumptuous beds. State-of-the-art electronic accessories are in turn complemented by exotically unusual art objects ranging from Turkish kilims to Hindu sculptures, and the immaculate marble tiled bathrooms are roomy and filled with deluxe toiletries and tub/shower combos. If money is no object, book one of the 20 individually designed duplex units. Other pluses include a small second-floor museum of Egyptian antiquities (from the owner's personal collection) and a rooftop swimming pool and garden with panoramic city views.

Pau Claris 150, 08009 Barcelona. ℭ **93-487-62-62.** Fax 93-215-79-70. www.derbyhotels.com. 120 units. 325€–415€ ($423–$540) double; 495€ ($644) suite. AE, DC, MC, V. Self/valet parking 20€ ($26). Metro: Passeig de Gràcia. **Amenities:** 2 restaurants; 2 bars; outdoor pool; fitness center; sauna; business center; room service; babysitting; laundry service; dry cleaning; nonsmoking rooms; private museum. *In room:* A/C, TV, Wi-Fi, minibar, hair dryer, safe.

Hotel Condes de Barcelona ★ Situated on the wide shop-filled Passeig de Gràcia, this former private villa (1895) is one of Barcelona's most popular and glamorous quality hotels. It boasts a unique neo-medieval facade that shows strong Gaudí influences and

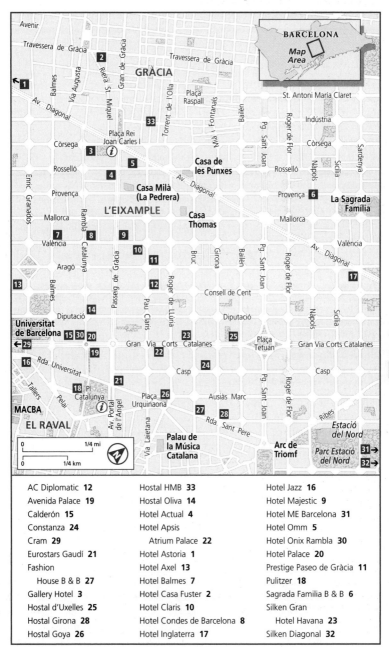

AC Diplomatic **12**	Hostal HMB **33**	Hotel Jazz **16**
Avenida Palace **19**	Hostal Oliva **14**	Hotel Majestic **9**
Calderón **15**	Hotel Actual **4**	Hotel ME Barcelona **31**
Constanza **24**	Hotel Apsis	Hotel Omm **5**
Cram **29**	Atrium Palace **22**	Hotel Onix Rambla **30**
Eurostars Gaudí **21**	Hotel Astoria **1**	Hotel Palace **20**
Fashion	Hotel Axel **13**	Prestige Paseo de Gràcia **11**
House B & B **27**	Hotel Balmes **7**	Pulitzer **18**
Gallery Hotel **3**	Hotel Casa Fuster **2**	Sagrada Familia B & B **6**
Hostal d'Uxelles **25**	Hotel Claris **10**	Silken Gran
Hostal Girona **28**	Hotel Condes de Barcelona **8**	Hotel Havana **23**
Hostal Goya **26**	Hotel Inglaterra **17**	Silken Diagonal **32**

has modern attractions that include having supper on the roof with a live jazz accompaniment. The comfortable midsize guest rooms all contain marble bathrooms, with tub/shower combos, reproductions of Spanish paintings, and soundproof windows. Unfortunately, the 74-room extension across the street (**Carrer Majorca**)—though comfortable and well equipped—doesn't quite capture the uniquely exotic flair of the original, so make sure you get a room in the main hotel.

Passeig de Gràcia 73–75, 08008 Barcelona. ✆ **93-488-22-00.** Fax 93-467-47-81. www.condesde barcelona.com. 183 units. 185€–375€ ($241–$488) double; 525€ ($683) suite. AE, DC, MC, V. Parking 20€ ($26). Metro: Passeig de Gràcia. **Amenities:** Restaurant; cafe; bar; outdoor pool; business center; room service; babysitting; laundry service; dry cleaning; nonsmoking rooms. *In room:* A/C, TV, Wi-Fi, minibar, hair dryer, safe.

Hotel Majestic ★★ This hotel is one of Barcelona's most visible landmarks and has been since the 1920s, when it was built in this sought-after location that lies within a 10-minute walk from Plaça de Catalunya. In the early 1990s it was radically renovated and upgraded into deluxe status while retaining the dignified stateliness of the public areas, but with an added sense of color and contemporary drama in the bedrooms. Today, each is outfitted in a different, mainly monochromatic color scheme, with carpets, artwork, and upholsteries. All units come equipped with bathrooms containing tub/shower combos. Staff is hardworking and conscientious, albeit sometimes swamped with tour buses containing dozens of clients arriving all at once. Its **Drolma** restaurant (p. 148) has a Michelin star.

Passeig de Gràcia 68, 08007 Barcelona. ✆ **93-488-17-17.** Fax 93-488-18-80. www.hotelmajestic.es. 303 units. 220€–395€ ($286–$514) double; 475€–650€ ($618–$845) suite. AE, DC, MC, V. Parking 16€ ($21). Metro: Passeig de Gràcia. **Amenities:** 2 restaurants; 2 bars; outdoor pool; fitness center; sauna; courtesy car for guests in suites and apts; business center; room service; laundry service; dry cleaning. *In room:* A/C, TV, Wi-Fi, minibar, hair dryer, safe.

Hotel Omm ★★★ Chic, intelligent, and strikingly executed, the hyper-trendy Omm has become a modern city landmark thanks to its "wafers of stone" facade. Inside, the dark atmospheric communal halls and lounges are skillfully contrasted with bright, naturally lit bedrooms. All rooms feature ample but nonintrusive cupboard and wardrobe space and a variety of state-of-the-art modern conveniences, including flatscreen TVs, DVDs, and stereos. From the rooftop lap pool, you can see the roof of Gaudí's La Pedrera, and the chic sun deck is a privileged spot where you can laze away languid Barcelonese evenings. The Omm is owned by Tragaluz, one of Barcelona's most famous restaurateurs, and the in-house restaurant **Moo** (p. 152) is an "in" spot for a predinner drink.

Rosselló 265, 08008 Barcelona. ✆ **93-445-40-00.** Fax 93-445-40-04. www.hotelomm.es. 59 units. 325€– 425€ ($423–$553) double; 525€ ($683) suite. AE, DC, MC, V. Parking 22€ ($29). Metro: Diagonal. **Amenities:** Restaurant; cocktail bar; health center; business center; room service; babysitting; laundry service; dry cleaning; nonsmoking rooms. *In room:* A/C, TV, DVD player, Wi-Fi, minibar, hair dryer, safe.

Hotel Palace ★★★ Formerly the legendary Ritz, and now a member of Spain's top HUSA chain, this Art Deco hotel—which dates back nearly a century—is currently in the throes of total refurbishment, which should be finished by mid-2009. Throughout this period, its service will continue as usual with more rooms gradually reopening as the updating continues. The character of the hotel will be retained, and original features such as the cream-and-gilt neoclassical lobby will remain unchanged, as will the elegant decor and furnishings of the spacious, high-ceilinged rooms and their mosaic and marble-accented bathrooms. The superb restaurant also continues in the hands of the Michelin-awarded chef Romain Fornell.

Gran Vía de les Corts Catalanes 668, 08010 Barcelona. ☎ **93-510-11-30.** Fax 93-318-01-48. www.hotel palacebarcelona.com. 120 units. 380€ ($494) double; from 525€ ($683) junior suite; 1,200€ ($1,560) suite. AE, DC, MC, V. Parking 22€ ($29). Metro: Passeig de Gràcia. **Amenities:** Restaurant; 2 bars; fitness center; car rental; room service; babysitting. In room: A/C, TV.

Prestige Paseo de Gràcia ★★★   Restyled by top Catalan architect Josep Santpere from a 1930s building, the Prestige is one of the most fashionable hotels in town. It has some nice touches, such as the **Zeroom** breakfast bar and library where you can enjoy laid-back mornings, and the Oriental garden where you can also sip coffee amid ivory sun loungers and bamboo planters. There's an "Ask Me" service—really a kind of human-genie-in-a-bottle who vows to hunt down any sort of information on the city you need to know, whether it's the opening hours of a museum or the nearest kosher restaurant. And the Japanese-inspired bedrooms are sleek and spacious with all the added extras one could possibly need for a good night's sleep. All that's missing is a fancy restaurant with a celebrity chef at the helm.

Passeig de Gràcia 62, 08007 Barcelona. ☎ **93-272-41-80.** Fax 93-272-41-81. 45 units. 245€–350€ ($319–$455) double; from 450€ ($585) suite. AE, DC, MC, V. Valet parking 2€ ($2.60) per hr. Metro: Diagonal. **Amenities:** Cafe/bar; lounge; health and beauty center; Jacuzzi; sauna; business center; room service; babysitting; laundry service; dry cleaning; nonsmoking rooms; shoeshine; free newspaper service; private garden; Barcelona and music library; "Ask Me service." In room: A/C, TV, high-speed Internet, minibar, hair dryer, safe.

Pulitzer ★★ Finds   Another stalwart addition to Barcelona's designer hotel scene, the super-trendy Pulitzer is a mere stone's throw from the Plaça de Catalunya. Its stylish lounge area is a comfortable oasis of white leather sofas, black marble trim, and floor-to-ceiling bookshelves lined with tomes such as *California Homes, Moroccan Interiors,* and *The World's Greatest Hotels.* There's also a smart restaurant and a candle-lit roof terrace furnished with loungers where you can relax over a coffee or cocktail as you admire the fabulous day and night city vistas. The variably sized bedrooms are decorated in inky-black and charcoal-gray hues and are big on sumptuous fabrics—leather, silk, and down pillows—while the showy bathrooms have tub and shower combos that are generous with the toiletries.

Bergara 8, Eixample Esquerra, 08002 Barcelona. ☎ **93-481-67-67.** Fax 93-481-64-64. www.hotelpulitzer. es. 91 units. 175€–255€ ($228–$332) double. AE, DC, MC, V. Public parking nearby 25€ ($33). Metro: Plaça de Catalunya. **Amenities:** Restaurant; cocktail bar; lounge; external health center; solarium; business center; library; room service; babysitting; laundry service; dry cleaning; nonsmoking rooms. In room: A/C, TV, Wi-Fi, minibar, hair dryer, safe.

Silken Gran Hotel Havana ★   The Havana occupies a 19th-century building which was tastefully refurbished in 2007 but still retains much of its original *moderniste* architecture and design. Rooms here are spacious and well equipped and the vast en-suite Italian marble bathrooms have both walk-in shower and tub, plus toiletries that are restocked on a daily basis. The best and priciest rooms are the executive suites on the sixth floor, which have private terraces with stunning views. Though all rooms are sound-proof, those facing the ever-busy Gran Vía avenue still suffer from a certain amount of traffic noise. (If you're a light sleeper it's best to ask for a room at the rear.) The rooftop pool and sun terrace are an added bonus.

Gran Vía de les Corts Catalanes 647, Eixample Dreta, 08010 Barcelona. ☎ **93-412-11-15.** Fax 93-412-26-11. www.silken-granhavana.com. 145 units. 205€ ($267) double; 220€–380€ ($286–$494) suite. AE, DC, MC, V. Parking 18€ ($23). Metro: Passeig de Gràcia, Tetuan, or Girona. **Amenities:** Restaurant; bar; pool; business center; room service; babysitting; laundry service; dry cleaning; nonsmoking rooms. In room: A/C, TV, Wi-Fi, minibar, hair dryer, safe.

Family-Friendly Hotels

Hotel Colón (p. 96)   Opposite the cathedral in the Gothic Quarter. Here families ask for, and often get, spacious rooms.

Hotel Fira Palace (p. 118)   At the base of the city's most expansive green zone, Montjuïc. Areas where the kids can run wild are only a short distance away.

Citadines (p. 127)   An in-house kitchen and maid service take some of the hassle out of catering to little ones.

EXPENSIVE

Avenida Palace ★★   This superb hotel stands behind a pair of mock-fortified towers in an enviable 19th-century neighborhood filled with elegant shops and apartment buildings. Despite its relative modernity (it dates from 1952), it evokes an old-world sense of charm, partly because of the attentive staff, and partly because of the flowers, antiques, and 1950s-era accessories that fill the public rooms. Celebrity guests have been coming for decades, and the Beatles stayed in the master suite after their summer concert in 1965. The soundproof rooms range from midsize to spacious and have comfortable beds, solidly traditional decor, and mainly dark wood furnishings. Some are set aside for nonsmokers. Bathrooms are well equipped, with dual basins, tub/shower combos, and heat lamps.

Gran Vía de les Corts Catalanes 605 (at Passeig de Gràcia), 08007 Barcelona. ☎ **93-301-96-00.** Fax 93-318-12-34. www.avenidapalace.com. 160 units. 235€–275€ ($306–$358) double; 350€ ($455) suite. AE, DC, MC, V. Parking 18€ ($23). Metro: Passeig de Gràcia. **Amenities:** 2 restaurants; bar; business center; salon; room service; babysitting; laundry service; dry cleaning; currency exchange. *In room:* A/C, TV, Wi-Fi, minibar, hair dryer, safe.

Calderón   As business hotels go, the Calderón has two things in its favor. One: location—it is situated right on the leafy promenade of Rambla de Catalunya and is just minutes from the Barri Gòtic, so when you're not working, leisure time is never far away. Two: size—it is huge, with plenty of amenities for those who need stay-at-home comforts with gargantuan, bright, airy bedrooms with all the modern conveniences and spacious en-suite bathrooms. It offers good value for your money.

Rambla de Catalunya 26, 08007 Barcelona. ☎ **93-301-00-00.** Fax 93-412-41-93. www.nh-hotels.com. 252 units. 250€ ($325) double; 550€ ($715) suite. AE, DC, MC, V. Parking 18€ ($23). Metro: Plaça de Catalunya. **Amenities:** Restaurant; cafeteria; bar; lounge; indoor/outdoor pool; health center; sauna; solarium; business center; room service; babysitting; laundry service; dry cleaning; nonsmoking rooms. *In room:* A/C, TV, Wi-Fi, minibar, hair dryer, safe.

Hotel ME Barcelona   Located at the eastern end of L'Eixample, close to the landmark Agbar Tower and junction of Diagonal and Pere IV avs., this cutting-edge 24-story hotel—opened in 2007—is one of the best equipped for both leisure and business travelers in town. Accommodations vary from standard rooms to lofts and suites, all immaculately furnished in minimalistic style with state-of-the-art communications facilities and en-suite bathrooms. There are also top-quality conference salons and health facilities that include hydrotherapy and aromatherapy, and stylish eating spots highlighted by the top-floor Dos Cielos dining room, which has adjoining terraces that offer some of the most stunning panoramic views in the city.

Diagonal-Pere IV 272–286, 08005 Barcelona. ✆ **93-367-20-50.** www.me-barcelona.com. 259 units. 250€–320€ ($325–$416) double. AE, DC, MC, V. Metro: Poble Nou. **Amenities:** 3 restaurants; bars; rooftop terrace; penthouse pool lounge; YHI spa and heath center; business center; meeting and conference areas; room service; babysitting; laundry service. *In room:* A/C, TV, free Wi-Fi, minibar.

MODERATE

AC Diplomatic ★   This top-end, glass-fronted, four-star hotel oozes style even though it's predominantly a business hotel. If you keep one eye on its pleasing Zen-like design focus and another on the small details that make a difference, such as 24-hour laundry service, free minibar, and nonsmoking rooms, you'll realize that these features alone make it a cut above most chain hotels. The restaurant, with its avant-garde aura, offers a "Sanísimo" (low-fat) menu, instead of the usual steak and potatoes. Bedrooms are a good size and are warmly decorated with wood paneling, parquet floors, and a small sitting area. All have en-suite bathrooms with shower and/or tub.

Pau Claris 122, 08009 Barcelona. ✆ **93-272-38-10.** Fax 93-272-38-11. www.achoteldiplomatic.com. 211 units. 175€ ($228) double; 300€ ($390) suite. AE, DC, MC, V. Parking 20€ ($26). Metro: Passeig de Gràcia. **Amenities:** Restaurant; bar; lounge; outdoor pool; health center; sauna; room service; massage service; babysitting; laundry service; dry cleaning; nonsmoking rooms; safe. *In room:* A/C, TV, Wi-Fi, minibar, hair dryer.

Constanza ★★★ (Finds)   A smart boutique hotel located within easy walking distance of La Ribera's shopping, cultural, and culinary attractions, the Constanza combines style and comfort with a young vibe and an upbeat, trendy ambience. The lobby is filled with white boxy couches and red trim, and beyond it there's a minimalist breakfast room decorated with a continually changing routine of flower prints. The first-floor bedrooms are bright and fresh with clean lines, leather-trimmed furniture, and white cotton sheets. All have en-suite bathrooms with showers. Some are rather small, and those at the front can be noisy, but if you can book a room with its own private terrace the place offers very good value.

Bruc 33, 08010 Barcelona. ✆ **93-270-19-10.** Fax 93-317-40-24. www.hotelconstanza.com. 20 units. 150€ ($195) double. AE, MC, V. Public parking nearby 20€ ($26). Metro: Urquinaona. **Amenities:** Health center; room service; laundry service; dry cleaning; safe. *In room:* A/C, TV, high-speed Internet, minibar, hair dryer.

Cram ★★ (Finds)   This eminently stylish addition to the hip Barcelona scene (not as crowded as its name implies, incidentally, and with a special appeal to cool thirty-somethings) is located in a 19th-century building in the heart of L'Eixample. While the original rose-pink facade has been retained, the interior lounges have been tastefully refurbished with dark red cushions, gleaming black surfaces, and futuristic disc-shaped chairs. The elegant bedrooms have mirrored walls, amber-wood floors, mellow gold and burgundy decor, and en-suite bathrooms (some with showers, others with Jacuzzis). The cosmopolitan shops and cafes of the Passeig de Gràcia can be reached on foot in 5 to 10 minutes, and gourmets will delight in the on-site presence of the long-established Gaig restaurant.

Aribau 54, 08011 Barcelona. ✆ **93-216-77-00.** Fax 93-216-77-07. www.hotelcram.com. 67 units. 175€–290€ ($228–$377) double; 250€–450€ ($325–$585) executive and privilege units; 290€–525€ ($377–$683) suite. AE, MC, V. Parking 16€ ($21). Metro: Universitat. **Amenities:** Restaurant; bar; outdoor pool; spa; solarium; room service; laundry service; dry cleaning; nonsmoking rooms; rooms for those w/limited mobility. *In room:* A/C, TV, Wi-Fi, hair dryer, safe.

Eurostars Gaudí   Not to be confused with the Gaudí hotel in the lower Gothic Quarter, this sleek member of the highly regarded Eurostars group is located in the heart of the Eixample just northwest of the city's Monumental main bullring. It's a highly contemporary hotel with a relaxing decor of richly textured color schemes. The staff are friendly and attentive, and the bright spacious dining room provides quality international cuisine and buffet breakfasts. Couples staying in the romantic double rooms receive a complimentary bottle of *cava* on arrival. From the rooftop sun terrace you get great city views that take in the nearby Sagrada Família church. The stylish rooms all have en-suite bathrooms with shower/tub combos.

Consell de Cent. 498–500, 08013 Barcelona. ✆ **93-232-02-88.** Fax 93-232-02-87. www.eurostarshotels. com/gaudi. 45 units. 150€–240€ ($195–$312) double. AE, DC, MC, V. Metro: Monumental. **Amenities:** Restaurant; bar; lounge; sun terrace w/panoramic view; laundry service; dry cleaning; nonsmoking rooms; facilities for visitors w/disabilities. *In room:* A/C, flatscreen TV, free Wi-Fi, minibar, hair dryer, safe.

Gallery Hotel ★ (Finds   Named after a nearby district of major art galleries, this stylishly decorated modern hotel lies between the Passeig de Gràcia and Rambla de Catalunya, just below the wide Diagonal avenue in the upper district of the Eixample. It's a long-established choice for both business and leisure visitors and its guest rooms are mainly midsize and tastefully furnished with pleasing touches such as fresh flowers and crisp bed linens. All have a small en-suite bathroom with tub and shower. The on-site restaurant is renowned for its savory Mediterranean cuisine.

Calle Rosello 249, 08008 Barcelona. ✆ **93-415-99-11.** Fax 93-415-91-84. www.galleryhotel.com. 110 units. Mon–Thurs 200€ ($260) double, 350€ ($455) suite; Fri–Sun 150€ ($195) double, 175€ ($228) suite. AE, DC, MC, V. Parking 18€ ($23). Metro: Diagonal. **Amenities:** Restaurant; bar; fitness center; sauna; solarium; business center; room service; babysitting; laundry service; dry cleaning; nonsmoking rooms. *In room:* A/C, TV, high-speed Internet, minibar, hair dryer, safe.

Hotel Acta Atrium Palace ★★★ (Finds   This high-tech designer hotel, with its sleek lines and oatmeal marble decor, stylishly combines business and pleasure, with facilities ranging from a library-cum-business center with complimentary Internet access, photocopiers, and printers to a softly lit restaurant and a climatized indoor swimming pool with an adjoining Jacuzzi. The spacious bedrooms have comfortable beds with quilted throws and small sitting areas, and the well-equipped adjoining bathrooms are marble-tiled with tub/shower combos. There are also nice touches that include a free daily quota of mineral water and fruit juice. Top-floor suites offer maximum comfort; they feature a separate living room, two TVs, and a private terrace with deck chairs, a temperature-controlled hot tub, and great views.

Gran Vía de les Corts Catalanes 656, Eixample Esquerra, 08010 Barcelona. ✆ **93-342-80-00.** Fax 93-342-80-01. www.hotel-atriumpalace.com. 71 units. 175€–260€ ($228–$338) double; 275€–350€ ($358–$455) suite. AE, DC, MC, V. Parking 22€ ($29). Metro: Passeig de Gràcia or Plaça de Catalunya. **Amenities:** Restaurant; bar; pool; health center; business center; library; room service; babysitting; laundry service; dry cleaning; nonsmoking rooms. *In room:* A/C, TV, free Wi-Fi, minibar, hair dryer, safe.

Hotel Actual (Value   Situated across the road from the ultra-hip Hotel Omm (see earlier), the nifty contemporary Actual nevertheless manages to hold its own, offering a smart and highly respectable money-saving alternative. (And of course you can still make use of the Omm's wonderful bar and restaurant.) Small but perfectly formed wood paneling, brushed steel, and large windows give the hotel a light, airy feel with a designer edge. Bedrooms are simply but elegantly decorated with chocolate-brown soft furnishings and plain white walls and bed linens, and all have compact bathrooms with tub/

shower combos. The staff is helpful and obliging and on-site amenities include a pool for
relaxed summertime swimming.

Rosselló 238, Eixample Esquerra, 08008 Barcelona. ☏ **93-552-05-50.** Fax 93-552-05-55. www.hotel actual.com. 29 units. 200€ ($260) double. AE, DC, MC, V. Public parking 22€ ($29). Metro: Diagonal. **Amenities:** Cafeteria; lounge; outdoor pool; room service; babysitting; laundry service; dry cleaning; nonsmoking rooms. *In room:* A/C, TV, Wi-Fi, minibar, hair dryer, safe.

Hotel Astoria ★ ⟨**Value**⟩   This renovated 1950s member of the distinguished Derby Hotel chain is located high up in the Eixample, close to the junction of Carrer Enric Granados and the wide shop- and restaurant-filled Avenida Diagonal. Retained features include the Art Deco facade, high ceilings, glossy tiled floors, marble pillars, geometric designs, and brass-studded detail in the public rooms—all strongly influenced by Moorish and Andalusian styles. The guest rooms are comfortable, midsize, and soundproof, with slick louvered closets and gleaming white walls. All rooms have private bathrooms containing showers. Older units have warm textures of exposed cedar, and pristine modern accessories. Recent welcome additions are the rooftop pool and sauna.

París 203, 08036 Barcelona. ☏ **93-209-83-11.** Fax 93-202-30-08. www.derbyhotels.es. 115 units. 160€–205€ ($208–$267) double; 255€ ($332) suite. AE, DC, MC, V. Parking nearby 18€ ($23). Metro: Diagonal. **Amenities:** Restaurant; bar; lounge; rooftop swimming pool and sauna; fitness center; business center; room service; laundry service; dry cleaning. *In room:* A/C, TV, Wi-Fi, minibar, hair dryer, safe.

Hotel Axel ★★★ ⟨**Moments**⟩   Located in a fine *moderniste* building in a zone known as "Gaixample," this boutique hotel has widened its original single-sex net to embrace heteros and gays alike. The staff is hip, and amenities range from a cool, scarlet-colored cocktail bar and restaurant in the lobby to an "in" rooftop pool, bar, sauna, and sun deck. For dress-conscious visitors there's a men's designer clothing store next door (run by the Axel). All bedrooms have soundproof windows, king-size beds covered with large soft pillows, a subtly erotic decor, and smart en-suite bathrooms—designed for two—with tub/shower combos (or Jacuzzis in the superior rooms). A nice extra touch is the provision of free bottled mineral water in refrigerators on every floor. There are also a few rooms for visitors with disabilities and nonsmokers.

Aribau 33, Eixample Esquerra, 08011 Barcelona. ☏ **93-323-93-93.** Fax 93-323-93-94. www.axelhotels. com. 66 units. 180€–250€ ($234–$325) double; from 320€ ($416) suite. AE, DC, MC, V. Parking 16€ ($21). Metro: Universitat. **Amenities:** Restaurant; bar; lounge; outdoor pool; health center; Jacuzzi; sauna; solarium; *hammam* (Arab-style bathhouse); library; room service; massage service; laundry service; dry cleaning; nonsmoking rooms; safe. *In room:* A/C, TV, Wi-Fi, minibar, hair dryer.

Hotel Balmes   Set in a seven-story structure built in the late 1980s, this chain hotel successfully combines conservative decor with modern accessories. It has a well-trained and friendly staff. Bedrooms have a warm color scheme of rich terra cottas and sunset yellows that brighten an otherwise white interior, allowing residents—many of whom are in town on business—to live and work comfortably. Marble-trimmed bathrooms are equipped with tub/shower combinations. If you're looking for peace and quiet, rooms at the back of the hotel overlook a small garden and swimming pool and are calmer and more relaxing than those facing the busy street.

Majorca 216, 08008 Barcelona. ☏ **93-451-19-14.** Fax 93-451-00-49. www.derbyhotels.es. 100 units. 150€–220€ ($195–$286) double; 205€–275€ ($267–$358) triple. AE, DC, MC, V. Parking 16€ ($21). Metro: Diagonal. **Amenities:** Restaurant; bar; outdoor pool; business center; room service; laundry service; dry cleaning. *In room:* A/C, TV, Wi-Fi, minibar, hair dryer, safe.

Hotel Inglaterra (Value) Despite the name, this quietly elegant hotel features mainly exotic Japanese-inspired decor. One of the very first boutique hotels in town, it provides spacious communal areas that include comfortable lounges, a snazzy breakfast room and bar, and a well-equipped roof terrace for sunbathing and reading. The spacious minimalist rooms have private bathrooms with tub/shower combos. All in all, this quality, chilled-out hotel provides amazingly good value for your money.

Pelai 14, Eixample Esquerra, 08001 Barcelona. ⓒ 93-505-11-00. Fax 93-505-11-09. www.hotel-inglaterra. com. 55 units. 200€ ($260) double. AE, DC, MC, V. Public parking nearby 24€ ($31). Metro: Plaça de Catalunya or Universitat. **Amenities:** Restaurant; lounge; room service; laundry service; dry cleaning; safe. *In room:* A/C, TV, Wi-Fi, minibar, hair dryer.

Hotel Jazz Just around the corner from Plaça de Catalunya, the Jazz is located in an enclave of design-led hotels. It has a low-key and downbeat decor that includes bleached wood floors and oatmeal paintwork which blends with a cool mix of gray and beige, and is interspersed with odd splashes of brighter colors. The spacious soundproof rooms all have immaculate en-suite black tiled bathrooms. The big plus comes on the roof, where you'll find a swimming pool and a wood deck terrace, and some impressive views over the urban rooftops. If you're here on a working trip there's also a well-equipped business center and free high-speed Internet access.

Pelai 3, 08001 Barcelona. ⓒ 93-552-96-96, 0870/120-1521 (U.K.), or 207/580-2663 (U.S.) Fax 93-552-96-97. www.hoteljazz.com. 180 units. 180€–210€ ($234–$273) double; 280€–320€ ($364–$416) suite. AE, DC, MC, V. Parking 20€ ($26) per day. Metro: Plaça de Catalunya or Universitat. **Amenities:** Cafeteria; lounge; outdoor pool; solarium; business center; room service; babysitting; laundry service; dry cleaning; nonsmoking rooms. *In room:* A/C, TV, Wi-Fi, minibar, hair dryer, safe.

Hotel Onix Rambla ★ (Value) An oasis of modernity in the midst of Gothic Quarter mansions, the elegantly minimalist Onix Rambla is an excellent choice for anyone who wants to stay in a designer hotel without paying designer prices. The hotel is filled with discreetly tasteful works of modern art, and communal amenities include a pleasant breakfast room and an on-site new-wave snack bar. There are also bonuses such as the large rooftop sun terrace and plunge pool. Bedrooms are tastefully decorated with natural materials, like wood, leather, and tiles, and all have en-suite bathrooms with tub/shower combos.

Rambla Catalunya 24, Eixample Esquerra, 08007 Barcelona. ⓒ 93-342-79-80. Fax 93-342-51-52. www. hotelonixrambla.com. 40 units. 175€ ($228) double. AE, DC, MC, V. Metro: Passeig de Gràcia or Universitat. **Amenities:** Cafeteria; lounge; outdoor pool; health center; solarium; business center; Wi-Fi; room service; babysitting; laundry service; dry cleaning; nonsmoking rooms. *In room:* A/C, TV, high-speed Internet, minibar, hair dryer, safe.

Silken Diagonal Located next to the extraordinary Torre Agbar building (p. 5), in the southeast corner of L'Eixample, the Silken Diagonal was designed by distinguished local architect Juli Capella. It features a striking black-and-white facade that conceals an unexpectedly bright and naturally lit interior. Its spacious public areas include four lounges, a designer cuisine restaurant (Piano) providing top Catalan and Basque specialties, and a cozy cafe (the Tecla) where full buffet breakfasts are served. There is a small but popular rooftop swimming pool and surrounding wooden-floored solarium which offers splendid city views. The stylish and comfortable rooms and suites, decorated in luminous whites and grays, all have private bathrooms with shower/tub combos, and some have facilities for nonsmokers and guests with disabilities.

Av. Diagonal 205, 08018 Barcelona. ☏ **93-489-53-09.** Fax 93-489-53-09. www.hoteldiagonalbarcelona.
com. 240 units. 220€–275€ ($286–$358) double. AE, DC, MC, V. Metro: Glòries. **Amenities:** Restaurant; cafeteria/bar; lounges; rooftop pool and solarium w/snack bar; laundry service; dry cleaning; nonsmoking areas. *In room:* A/C, TV, high-speed Internet, minibar, hair dryer, iron, safe.

INEXPENSIVE

Fashion House B&B ★ Finds   One of the increasing number of hostelries in the center of Barcelona offering quality bed-and-breakfast accommodations, the Fashion House is located in an elegantly restored 19th-century town house decorated with stylish stuccoes and friezes. Two bedrooms share a bathroom, and all are bright and nicely decorated with pastel colors. The best have verandas. La Suite, which doubles as a self-catering apartment, is an ideal choice for families who need more space and independence; it has private access to the communal terrace, which is well supplied with shaded tables and chairs and plenty of greenery. Breakfast is served here in the summer.

Bruc 13 principal, 08010 Barcelona. ☏ **63-790-40-44.** Fax 93-301-09-38. www.bcn-fashionhouse.com. 8 units. 80€ ($104) double; 95€ ($124) double w/balcony; 90€ ($117) triple; 115€ ($150) triple w/balcony; 125€ ($163) suite. Rates include breakfast. 12€ ($16) supplement in high season. MC, V. Metro: Urquinaona. **Amenities:** Breakfast room. *In room:* A/C, TV (suite only), kitchenette (suite only).

Hostal d'Uxelles ★ Finds   A picture-postcard hotel with helpful staff, the genteel Hostal d'Uxelles is well located in the busy heart of L'Eixample. Pastel hues, lush drapes, and beatific models of angels enhance the *hostal's* rustic charm, and all rooms are individually decorated with ornate Art Deco wood paneling and romantic flourishes such as cupid's-bow drapes above the bed. Each comes with its own individual bathroom complete with Andalusian tiling and tub/shower combo, and the best have private plant-filled balconies big enough to hold a table and two chairs.

Gran Vía de les Corts Catalanes 667 (Hostal 2) and 668 (Hostal 1), Eixample Dreta, 08010 Barcelona. ☏ **93-265-25-60.** Fax 93-232-85-67. www.hotelduxelles.com. 30 units. 80€–90€ ($104–$117) double; 100€–125€ ($130–$163) triple; 150€–190€ ($195–$247) quadruple. AE, DC, MC, V. Parking nearby 18€ ($23). Metro: Tetuan or Girona. **Amenities:** TV lounge; room service; laundry service; safe. *In room:* TV.

Hostal Girona ★★ Value   Designed in the 1860s by leading *moderniste* architect Ildefons Cerda, this is one of the most character-filled *hostales* in town. Its wall hangings, rugs, gilded picture frames, and teardrop chandeliers offset the period decor to perfection, creating a nostalgia-invoking ambience that's transformed it into a highly sought-after city center retreat. It offers a variety of bedrooms, from singles without bathrooms to more plush doubles with en-suite bathrooms with tub/shower combos. Some have balconies which either overlook the street or a quiet rear patio. All are comfortable and freshly painted with plain white linen bedspreads. It's an individual gem and a bargain at that.

Girona 24 1–1, Eixample Dreta, 08010 Barcelona. ☏ **93-265-02-59.** Fax 93-265-85-32. www.hostal girona.com. 19 units. 60€–80€ ($78–$104) double. MC, V. Metro: Girona or Urquinaona. **Amenities:** Safe. *In room:* A/C, TV.

Hostal Goya ★★ Finds   A superior *hostal* largely patronized by a young and lively clientele, the traditional yet tastefully refurbished Goya is noted for its friendly service and colorful *moderniste* decor—that includes original magnificent tiled floors. It offers a range of warmly furnished doubles, some with large, sunny balconies, and all complete with renovated immaculate private bathrooms. Bonuses include a Scandinavian-looking comfortable sitting room where free tea, coffee, and hot chocolate are available throughout the day. Its homey character and convenient central location have made it a popular choice, so book early if you want to stay here.

Barcelona's Self-Catering Scene

If you've ever been curious about the cute-looking apartments in the Old City with their curved-beamed ceilings and balconies brimming with ferns, or the tiled-entrance apartments with Art Nouveau facades in L'Eixample, now's your chance to get up close and personal. Wander around the Barri Gòtic these days, and many of the residential apartments you see are available for rent at reasonable prices by the day (normally a 3-day minimum), week, or month, enabling visitors to get a taste of what it's really like to live in the city, shop in its markets, cook its food, and make merry over glasses of wine around the dinner table.

Google "self-catering accommodations Barcelona" and you'll come up with pages of options, with something to suit every whim and budget. The array of apartments on offer ranges from small, practical studios to luxury apartments and penthouses for families or groups of friends.

If you're looking for something cultural and unconventional, one of the most interesting of these is **La Casa de les Lletres (House of Letters; ⓒ 93-226-37-30;** www.cru2001.com)—a thematic collection of apartments that pay homage to writers like George Orwell and the Catalan journalist and food writer Josep Pla, who had a special relationship with the city. Accommodations mix state-of-the-art facilities with an intellectual bohemian vibe. Poetry and prose are literally written on the walls. Situated in an elegant town house on the handsome Plaça Antonio López, the location couldn't be better, just minutes from Barceloneta and the Barri Gòtic.

More basic accommodations can be found at **www.nivellmar.net**, which offers seaside apartments—or at least those that are no more than 200m (656

Pau Claris 74, Eixample Dreta, 08010 Barcelona. ⓒ **93-302-25-65.** Fax 93-412-04-35. www.hostalgoya. com. 19 units. 100€–120€ ($130–$156) double; 125€ ($163) suite w/bathroom and private terrace. MC, V. Metro: Urquinaona or Plaça de Catalunya. **Amenities:** TV lounge. *In room:* A/C in some units.

Hostal HMB One of the more recent, welcome additions to Barcelona's low-cost hotel scene is this nifty and stylish little establishment which offers just 13 compact but high-ceilinged rooms decorated in bright blues and greens and with polished bare-wood floors. All rooms have flatscreen TVs and en-suite bathrooms. Furnishings are modestly comfortable throughout and the public areas and corridors feature contemporary works of art. The location in the northern end of L'Eixample ensures that a wide variety of shops and city monuments—especially the *moderniste* gems—are in easy reach.

Calle Bonavista 21–1º, 08012 Barcelona. ⓒ **93-368-20-13.** Fax 93-368-19-96. www.hostalhmb.com. 13 units. 75€–90€ ($98–$117) double. MC, V. Metro: Diagonal. **Amenities:** TV, free Wi-Fi.

Hostal Oliva (Value) This unpretentious yet character-filled hotel is a genuine Eixample original dating from the 1930s, and its vintage attractions include high ceilings, tiled floors, and a period wooden elevator with bench-style seats and a mirror. The neatly refurnished rooms are simple and rather basic, but the best ones overlook Barcelona's smartest shopping street and have their own bathrooms. All are well priced, and if you're ft.) from the beach—all the way from Barceloneta to Poble Nou. The places on their books tend to go after function rather than form, but are reasonably decorated, clean, and fairly priced. They are ideal for young travelers, or those with young children, who just want to be close to the sea.

For character apartments that won't break the bank, check out **www.visit-bcn.com**, which offers a wide range of different apartments, from classic Barri Gòtic town houses—such as the lovely Dos Amigos in the heart of the Old City with its gorgeous tiles, warm paint work, and small terrace—to minimalist loft-style apartments.

If it's luxury you're after, try **www.friendlyrentals.com**, which offers chic, design-led properties at surprisingly good prices. Every place is categorized for its artistic personality (for instance, Rembrandt, *moderniste,* Impressionist, Romantic, or Art Deco) and is described and photographed in detail. Many have private terraces and/or swimming pools and work out considerably cheaper than a hotel in the same class.

Most self-catering apartments, whether booked through an agency or directly through the owner, require a deposit of 1 night and possibly a security deposit, both of which are paid via credit card or PayPal. Things to be on the lookout for include "hidden" costs such as cleaning and extra-person charges, although compared to hotels, these apartments are extremely cost-effective, especially for longer stays. Don't forget that you are on your own—there is no concierge to help you find a drugstore in the middle of the night, or direct you to the Picasso Museum.

on a strict budget the cheapest of all are the darker interior rooms which share bathroom amenities with others on the same floor. The downside is that it can get noisy at times—especially over weekends, when revelers return late.

Passeig de Gràcia 32, Eixample, 08007 Barcelona. ✆ **93-488-01-62.** Fax 93-487-04-97. www.lasguias. com/hostaloliva/homepageingles.htm. 16 units. 70€ ($91) double without bathroom; 80€ ($104) double w/bathroom. No credit cards. Metro: Passeig de Gràcia. **Amenities:** Lounge. *In room:* TV.

Sagrada Família B&B ★★ (Finds)   This small bed-and-breakfast, located in a reno-vated building that dates back to 1900, is run by a hospitable duo, Eduardo and Nacho, who deftly manage to make you feel you're staying in an apartment with friends. The three pleasantly decorated rooms all have queen-size beds and private balconies; all rooms share a communal bathroom. The large living room has an open fireplace and comfort-able sofa and chairs that add to the relaxing atmosphere. Breakfasts (5€/$6.50) are taken in the cozy kitchen-lounge area. It's an ideal choice for travelers looking for home-style comforts. The whole place can also be rented as a private apartment for six people. The eponymous Gaudí-built cathedral is just a few minutes' stroll away.

Nàpols 266, Eixample Dreta, 08025 Barcelona. ✆ **65-189-14-13.** www.sagradafamilia-bedandbreakfast. com. 3 units. 60€–80€ ($78–$104) double; 125€–185€ ($163–$241) as a self-contained 3-bedroom apt. No credit cards. Metro: Diagonal. **Amenities:** Lounge; kitchen.

4 SANTS, PARAL.LEL & MONTJUÏC

The place to be for business travelers, this is the hub of Barcelona's out-of-towner meeting district with practical four-star accommodations galore, the Fira (exhibition centers of Plaça Espanya), and the World Trade Center at the bottom of Paral.lel. There are leisure amenities in the immediate vicinity, but the art galleries, museums, and scenic parklands of Montjuïc are 10 minutes' walk away.

EXPENSIVE

Catalonia Barcelona Plaza ★ Located on a busy plaza overlooking a shopping mall converted from the former Arenas bullring, this large hotel caters mainly to business travelers attending the various conference and convention halls across the street, and its standard amenities include meeting rooms, an in-house travel agency, and bank. It's very convenient for the airport (about 20 min. by cab) and can host meetings of up to 700 people. The comfortable rooms are smartly furnished and decorated, and all have en-suite bathrooms with tub/shower combos. (Be warned, though, that lower units get a certain amount of traffic noise.) The rooftop swimming pool (covered in winter) and its adjoining sun terraces offer some fine panoramic views that take in nearby Montjuïc and distant Tibidabo.

Plaça Espanya 6–8, 08014 Barcelona. ℂ **93-426-26-00.** Fax 93-426-04-00. www.cataloniabarcelonaplaza. com. 347 rooms. 185€–300€ ($241–$390) double; 310€–390€ ($403–$507) suite. AE, DC, MC, V. Parking 16€ ($21). Metro: Plaça Espanya. **Amenities:** Restaurant; bar; lounge; rooftop pool; health center; solarium; business center; room service; babysitting; laundry service; dry cleaning; nonsmoking rooms. *In room:* A/C, TV, high-speed Internet, minibar, hair dryer, safe.

Gran Hotel Torre Catalunya ★★ A vast skyscraper-style hotel close to Sants railway station and the Plaça Espanya, this modern four-star hotel is far and away the most deluxe in the area, offering American-style facilities in terms of the size of the bedrooms, excellent service, and modern amenities. Added extras include turndown service, chocolates on the pillows, and huge marble bathrooms with walk-in showers and deep bathtubs. Ciudad Condal, the restaurant on the 23rd floor, has awesome views over the city and is worth the visit for these alone. There are also excellent spa facilities with massage cabins, Jacuzzi, Turkish bath, and a climatized indoor pool.

Av. De Roma 2–4, Sants, 08014 Barcelona. ℂ **93-325-81-00.** Fax 93-325-51-78. www.torrecatalunya. com. 272 units. 120€–250€ ($156–$325) double; 180€–300€ ($234–$390) suite. AE, DC, MC, V. Free parking. Metro: Sants Estació. **Amenities:** Restaurant; bar; indoor swimming pool; gymnasium; health spa w/ massage cabins, snow shower, and sauna; Turkish bath; business center w/7 conference rooms; room service; laundry service; dry cleaning; nonsmoking rooms. *In room:* A/C, TV, CD player, high-speed Internet, minibar, hair dryer, safe.

Hotel Fira Palace ★★ (Kids) Popular among business travelers for its plush conference facilities and easy access to the exhibition centers of Plaça Espanya, this well-equipped hotel is another reliable all-around choice. If you are traveling with kids, the Fira offers some of the best family accommodations around, including huge comfortable rooms with separate Italian marble bathrooms and massage shower facilities. Communal facilities include a relaxing piano bar and two first-rate—but rather expensive—restaurants, a selection of health and fitness facilities, and an indoor swimming pool (closed Sun). Montjuïc hill's gardens, parks, and rambling footpaths are within easy strolling

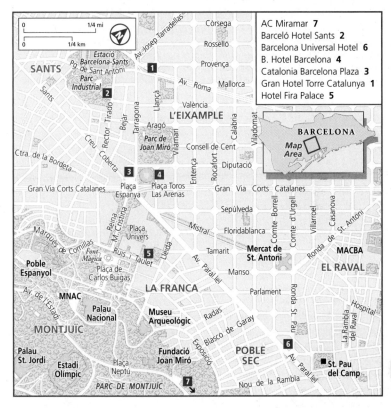

AC Miramar **7**
Barceló Hotel Sants **2**
Barcelona Universal Hotel **6**
B. Hotel Barcelona **4**
Catalonia Barcelona Plaza **3**
Gran Hotel Torre Catalunya **1**
Hotel Fira Palace **5**

distance, and the main central historic sights can be easily reached by frequent bus and Metro service in about 10 minutes.

Av. Ruis I Taulet 1–3, 08004 Barcelona. (*℃* **93-426-22-23.** Fax 93-425-50-47. www.fira-palace.com. 276 units. 250€–300€ ($325–$390) double; 350€–400€ ($455–$520) suite. AE, DC, MC, V. Parking 18€ ($23). Metro: Plaça Espanya. **Amenities:** 2 restaurants; piano bar; indoor pool; health center; sauna; business center; room service; massage; babysitting; laundry service; dry cleaning; nonsmoking rooms; patio garden. *In room:* A/C, TV, Wi-Fi, minibar, hair dryer, safe.

Hotel Miramar ★★   One of the most prestigious members of the SLH (Small Luxury Hotels of the World), the Miramar is attractively located right next to the Montjuïc i Llobera Botanical Gardens, overlooking both the city and port. Built by distinguished architect Oscar Tusquets for the 1929 World's Fair, it was recently restored and converted into a hotel, retaining the privacy, style, and charm of the original while introducing bright avant-garde decor and state-of-the-art amenities that include well-equipped conference salons (one of which is integrated into the hotel's gardens). The comfortable and tastefully furnished rooms all have en-suite bathrooms and terraces and enjoy garden or panoramic sea views. Some have wheelchair accessibility. At mealtimes the Forestier restaurant, adjoining the former palace's Patio de los Naranjos (Orange Tree Courtyard), provides a creative blend of Catalan and international dishes.

Plaça Carlos Ibañez 3, 08068 Barcelona. ℂ **93-281-16-00.** Fax 93-281-66-01. www.hotelmiramar barcelona.com. 75 units. 280€ ($364) double; 750€ ($975) suite. Extra beds available. 150€ ($195). Cots free. AE, DC, MC, V. Nearby parking 20€ ($26). Metro: Paral.lel. **Amenities:** Restaurant; bar; lounge; indoor and outdoor swimming pools; spa w/massage cabins, sauna, and Turkish bath; concierge; conference rooms; room service. *In room:* A/C, flatscreen TV, CD/DVD player, iPod docking station, Wi-Fi, minibar.

MODERATE

Barcelona Universal Hotel   Predominantly catering to business travelers attending company meetings, the well-appointed Universal offers stylish, modern facilities within easy reach of the World Trade Center and the Exhibition sites at Plaça Espanya. Bonuses include a small rooftop terrace with raised wood decking and a sunken pool. Bedrooms are spacious and comfortable and all have en-suite bathrooms with tub/shower combos. Although the rooms are soundproof, noise from the busy street can still be a problem for many guests, so if you do stay here ask for something at the rear, where you're less likely to be disturbed.

Av. Paral.lel 76–78, 08001 Barcelona. ℂ **93-567-74-47.** Fax 93-567-74-40. www.hotelbarcelonauniversal. com. 169 units. 140€–210€ ($182–$273) double; 240€–300€ ($312–$390) suite. AE, DC, MC, V. Parking 20€ ($26). Metro: Paral.lel. **Amenities:** Restaurant; bar; pool; fitness center; solarium; business center; room service; babysitting; laundry service; dry cleaning; nonsmoking rooms. *In room:* A/C, TV, Wi-Fi, minibar, hair dryer, safe.

Barceló Sants   The main reasons for staying at this well-run, solidly equipped hotel are practical. It's located right on top of Estació de Sants—Barcelona's main train station—and couldn't be more convenient if you're arriving late at night or have an early morning departure. Unequivocally commercial, the Barceló Sants makes no attempt to dazzle guests with either history or culture, but instead provides big, comfortable beds; well-equipped rooms; and clean and functional bathrooms with tub/shower combos.

Plaça dels Països Catalans s/n, 08014 Barcelona. ℂ **93-503-53-00.** Fax 93-490-60-45. www.barcelosants. com. 377 units. 95€–200€ ($124–$260) double; 145€–250€ ($189–$325) suite. AE, DC, MC, V. Parking 14€ ($18). Metro: Sants Estació. **Amenities:** 2 restaurants; bar; pool; health center; sauna; business center; room service; massage; babysitting; laundry service; dry cleaning; nonsmoking rooms. *In room:* A/C, TV, high-speed Internet, minibar, hair dryer, safe.

B-Hotel Barcelona   Owned by the same innovative group that created the stylish Hotel Jazz, this modern low-key hotel is a comfortable and affordable alternative to the big high-priced business hotels that tend to proliferate in the Sants area. The decor is modern minimalistic with polished bare floorboards and a cool blue-gray color scheme, and all rooms have en-suite bathrooms with shower. Those at the front have particularly good views of the Plaça Espanya. On-site communal facilities include a bar/cafeteria serving snacks and full buffet breakfasts. There's also an outdoor rooftop swimming pool and gym. For families with children, Montjuïc hill has ample gardens and parks, and is just a quick walk away.

Gran Via de les Corts Catalanes 389, 08015 Barcelona. ℂ **93-552-95-00.** Fax 93-552-95-01. www.b-hotel-barcelona.com. 84 units. 140€–185€ ($182–$241). AE, DC, MC, V. Metro: Plaça Espanya. **Amenities:** Bar/cafeteria serving snacks and buffet breakfasts; rooftop pool; fitness center; solarium; conference rooms; laundry service; dry cleaning. *In room:* A/C, satellite TV, Wi-Fi, minibar, hair dryer, safe.

5 BARRIO ALTO & GRÀCIA

The Alto represents the *pijo* (posh) part of town with swanky restaurants and cocktail bars, millionaire's mansions, and Mercedes, contrasting with the more eclectic, villagey atmosphere of Gràcia with its two-story houses, sunny plazas, and student/bohemian vibe.

EXPENSIVE

Meliá Barcelona ★ One block from the junction of the Avinguda Sarrià and the Avinguda Diagonal in the heart of the business district, this long-established member of the illustrious Meliá chain offers a wide range of leisure and business amenities. The comfortably upholstered, carpeted guest rooms and suites are done in neutral international modern style, and all have wide beds with firm mattresses and bathrooms with tub/shower combos. The best accommodations are in the first-floor section known simply as "The Level," which was totally renovated in 2007 and offers a personalized and highly organized private service. Another big new attraction is the Espai Sarrià conference center, which houses up to 700 visitors in seven individual salons equipped with state-of-the-art communications technology.

Av. Sarrià 50, 08029 Barcelona. ✆ **800/336-3542** in the U.S., or 93-410-60-60. Fax 93-410-77-44. www.solmelia.com. 333 units. 220€–310€ ($286–$403) double; 350€–475€ ($455–$618) suite. AE, DC, MC, V. Parking 19€ ($25). Metro: Hospital Clinic. **Amenities:** 2 restaurants; bar; fitness center; spa; concierge; business center; room service; babysitting; laundry service; dry cleaning; nonsmoking rooms. *In room:* A/C, TV, high-speed Internet, minibar, hair dryer, safe.

INEXPENSIVE

Acropolis Guest House ★ (Moments) The quirky and slightly chaotic Acropolis, with its crumbling columns and peeling paint work, has an eccentric charm. If you're a lover of truly original (yet modest) "new experience" hotels, you shouldn't miss it. The nostalgically well-worn bohemian aura is too good to pass up. Though it's not likely you'll be traveling with your pet abroad, you may be interested to know that this is also one of the few places that welcomes them. The overgrown garden and rustic kitchen are communal, and the bedrooms are simply but comfortably decorated. Half of them have en-suite bathrooms, but the place is spotlessly clean and sharing shouldn't be a problem. The best room has its own terrace with wonderful views.

Verdi 254, Gràcia, 08024 Barcelona. ✆/fax **93-284-81-87.** acropolis@telefonica.net. 8 units. 60€ ($78) double w/bathroom; 50€ ($65) double without bathroom. No credit cards. Metro: Lesseps. **Amenities:** TV lounge; safe.

6 BARCELONETA, VILA OLÍMPICA & POBLE NOU

VERY EXPENSIVE

Grand Marina Hotel ★★★ Superbly located in the World Trade Center on the large jetty (Moll de Barcelona) opposite the Drassanes Maritim Museum, right beside the city's harbor waters, this innovative circular-shaped hotel was designed by Henry Cobb and I. M. Pei—the man behind the pyramid at the Louvre. Its bright, airy, and spacious interior is filled with a 21st-century blend of avant-garde and minimalistic artworks and sculptures that are offset by marble and glass architectural details. The bedrooms, all of which have en-suite bathrooms and Jacuzzis, are discreetly lit and sleekly designed with warm plush ochre and orange-brown decor. The Presidential Suite on the roof enjoys magnificent views across the port to the city.

World Trade Centre, Moll de Barcelona, 08039 Barcelona. (C) **93-603-90-00.** Fax 93-603-90-90. www. grandmarinahotel.com. 278 units. 250€–375€ ($325–$488) double; 400€–800€ ($520–$1,040) suite. AE, DC, MC, V. Parking 18€ ($23). Metro: Drassanes. **Amenities:** Restaurant; cafeteria; piano bar; lounge; outdoor pool; health center; Jacuzzi; sauna; business center; room service; massage service; babysitting; laundry service; dry cleaning; nonsmoking rooms. *In room:* A/C, TV, high-speed Internet, minibar, hair dryer, safe.

Hotel Arts ★★★   Managed by the Ritz-Carlton chain, this beachfront hotel occupies 33 floors in one of Barcelona's landmark skyscrapers, directly facing the sea and the Olympic Village 2.5km (1¹/₂ miles) northwest of Barcelona's historic core. The decor is contemporary and the spacious, well-equipped guest rooms have built-in furnishings; generous desk space; and large, sumptuous beds. (Four units are equipped for guests with disabilities.) Clad in pink marble, the deluxe bathrooms have fluffy robes, Belgian towels, dual basins, and phones. The hotel possesses the city's only beachside pool—overlooking Frank Gehry's bronze Peix (fish) sculpture—and its new in-house bars and restaurants, such as **Arola** (p. 162), are jump-starting nightlife into the neglected Olympic Marina. The young staff are polite and hardworking, the product of Ritz-Carlton training.

Carrer de la Marina 19–21, 08005 Barcelona. (C) **800/241-3333** in the U.S., or 93-221-10-00. Fax 93-221-10-70. www.hotelartsbarcelona.com. 482 units. 350€–800€ ($455–$1,040) double; 500€–2,000€ ($650–$2,600) suite. AE, DC, MC, V. Parking 20€ ($26). Metro: Ciutadella-Vila Olímpica. **Amenities:** 4 restaurants; cafe; 2 bars; outdoor pool; fitness center; spa; business center; hairdresser; room service; babysitting; laundry service; dry cleaning; nonsmoking rooms. *In room:* A/C, TV, high-speed Internet, minibar, hair dryer, iron, safe.

MODERATE

Hotel Front Marítim ★ (Value)   The renovated Front Marítim is the centerpiece of a major tourist development bordering the Nueva Mar Bella beach, a 10-minute walk from Port Olimpic. The guest rooms are midsize and attractively and comfortably decorated, and each has its own tiled bathroom with shower or tub. The hotel offers a range of facilities, including a lounge with large-screen TV, an a la carte restaurant, and a well-equipped fitness center. And the prices are affordable.

Poble Nou, Diagonal Mar, 08019 Barcelona. (C) **93-303-44-40.** Fax 93-303-44-41. www.hotelfront maritim.com. 177 units. 100€–120€ ($130–$156) double; 150€ ($195) superior double. AE, DC, MC, V. Parking 12€ ($16). Metro: Selva de Mar. **Amenities:** Restaurant; bar; gym; sauna; room service; laundry service; dry cleaning; nonsmoking rooms; rooms for those w/limited mobility. *In room:* A/C, TV, high-speed Internet, hair dryer.

Vincci Marítimo ★★ (Finds)   This genuine 21st-century hotel with an emphasis on interior design—lots of glass panels, polished wood, and brushed steel—is located at the quieter, lesser-known eastern beachside end of the city, close to the traditional Poble Nou suburb and a 30-minute Metro ride from the historic center. Many of the sleekly spacious bedrooms, all with en-suite light-filled bathrooms, enjoy excellent sea views. Communal facilities include a Japanese garden for relaxing breakfasts and early evening cocktails, and a smart, avant-garde restaurant. A couple of good beaches are close by, and other amenities in walking distance include the well-equipped Diagonal Shopping and Leisure Center and quaint local bars and cafes.

Bright Lights, Spa City

Barcelona has never been much of a spa town, though its meteoric rise as an international destination means that hotels are offering ever more luxurious amenities to seduce the city's visitors. First it was gourmet restaurants and movie-star cocktail bars; next came suites with clap-to-control features and rooftop swimming pools, but the latest thing to hit the Barcelona hotel circuit (and it's about time!) are spas.

It seems rather bizarre that spas should have been such a long time coming to a cosmopolitan Barcelona, but somehow, southern Europeans never seem to have embraced the whole spa therapy thing as passionately as their American neighbors (and northern Europeans). The burgeoning market does, however, have a handful of seriously stylish outfits that promise to do more than simply rest and rejuvenate travel-weary bodies.

The first on the scene was the **Royal Fitness Center** at the somewhat prim five-star Rey Juan Carlos I Hotel (p. 125), which recently upgraded its look with 21st-century fitness technologies and a new line of aphrodisiacal massages in chocolate, honey, or volcanic stone. Who says romance is dead?

For sheer fabulousness, the spa at the **Gran Hotel La Florida** (p. 125) offers a heavenly, high-class retreat in the clouds. Treatments here include beautiful mosaic-tiled Turkish steam rooms, a Finnish sauna, a bubbling hot tub, and a striking 37m-long (121-ft.) half-indoor/half-outdoor L-shaped stainless-steel infinity pool that elbows its way across the mountainside. The full range of Natura Bissé beauty treatments are on offer here, including body remolding, mud, and algae therapies that promise to shave off the years and excess pounds. Serious spa lovers can check in for a 3-night "Relaxation and Beauty" package with prices starting at 1,000€ ($1,300). Nonguests can make use of La Florida's spa facilities for 120€ ($156) a day.

The Ritz-Carlton–owned **Hotel Arts** (p. 122) has a rooftop sea-view spa that combines hip design with the latest in luxury treatments. They've teamed up with the award-winning Six Senses Spas to bring clients an exclusive range of holistic, all-natural beauty treatments in half-day, day, and weekend packages, including full-body wraps, facials, pedicures, and manicures as well as a full range of massage therapies. Water facilities include an ice shower, *hammam*, sauna, and plunge pool while the downstairs treatment rooms (eight in all) are havens of peace where infusions, fresh juices, and fruits are served in relaxation zones or on the deck. The intimate penthouse environment, with views over the sparkling Mediterranean, offers one of the most spectacular spots in Spain to pamper and preen. Treatments start at 105€ ($137) an hour.

Meanwhile, the spa at the **Hotel Omm** (p. 108) boasts a state-of-the-art design mixed with Mediterranean madness and all the comforts money can buy. Just say sp-*aah!*

If you're looking for a swim with your hotel, consider the following, which also offer beautiful views:
- **Hotel Balmes** (p. 113) for a garden oasis in the middle of the Eixample
- **Hotel Arts** (p. 122), the city's only beachside hotel
- **Hotel Omm** (p. 108) for unbeatable views of Gaudí's rooftops
- **Hotel Claris** (p. 106) for high-tech design, acres of steel, and wood decking
- **Hotel Duquesa de Cardona** (p. 95) for rooftop views over the boats and gin palaces of the Port Vell

Llull 340, Poble Nou, 08019 Barcelona. ✆ **93-356-26-00.** Fax 93-356-06-69. www.vinccihoteles.com. 144 units. 150€–200€ ($195–$260) double; 210€–250€ ($273–$325) suite. AE, DC, MC, V. Parking 16€ ($21). Metro: Poble Nou. **Amenities:** Restaurant; bar; room service; laundry service; dry cleaning; nonsmoking rooms; garden. *In room:* A/C, TV, high-speed Internet, minibar, hair dryer, safe.

INEXPENSIVE

Marina Folch ★ **Finds** This small, informal guesthouse has earned itself a loyal following among visitors who want to be close to the sea without paying the usual high prices of the now "tastefully reinvented" former fishermen's district of Barceloneta. All 10 comfortable rooms have private bathrooms with showers and are simply decorated. It's exactly what cheap, no-nonsense accommodations should be: a genuine retreat from the bustle of daily life minus the sometimes-tiring whistles and bells of more upmarket accommodations. The only drawback is that it is located above a restaurant (same management), so certain times of the day are noisy.

Mar 16, Barceloneta, 08003 Barcelona. ✆ **93-310-37-09.** Fax 93-310-53-27. 10 units. 60€–75€ ($78–$98) double. AE, DC, MC, V. Parking 20€ ($26). Metro: Barceloneta. **Amenities:** Restaurant; room service; laundry service. *In room:* A/C, TV.

Marina View B&B Just in front of the Port Vell (Old Port) and halfway between the Vía Laietana and Les Ramblas, this homey bed-and-breakfast is in a top spot for making the most of the city's prime sights and beaches. Bedrooms are fairly small but pleasantly decorated, and all have private bathrooms with shower, as well as some bonus extras like complimentary tea and coffee. Owner José María is a friendly and accommodating host, and will even provide breakfast in bed for those who want it.

Passeig de Colom s/n, Barri Gòtic, 08002 Barcelona. ✆ **60-920-64-93.** www.marinaviewbcn.com. 5 units. 115€–130€ ($150–$169) double; 175€ ($228) triple (all rates include breakfast). MC, V for down payment only. Public parking nearby 20€ ($26). Metro: Drassanes. **Amenities:** Lounge; laundry service. *In room:* A/C, TV, high-speed Internet, minibar.

7 ON THE OUTSKIRTS

VERY EXPENSIVE

Barcelona Hilton ★★ This 11-floor government-rated five-star property, located on one of the city's main arteries, is part of a huge commercial complex with an adjoining office tower. The lobby is impressively sleek with lots of velvet chairs. Public area furnishings are

Hilton-standardized, but most of the large and well-equipped rooms feature thick carpets, rich wood decor, and some of the best combination bathrooms in the city with all the extras, including dual basins and robes. Some units are nonsmoking, and others are reserved exclusively for women.

Av. Diagonal 589–591, 08014 Barcelona. © **800/445-8667** in the U.S. and Canada, or 93-495-77-77. Fax 93-495-77-00. www.hilton.com. 287 units. 320€–375€ ($416–$488) double; 350€–455€ ($455–$592) suite. AE, DC, MC, V. Parking 28€ ($36). Metro: María Cristina. **Amenities:** 3 restaurants; cafe; bar; health club; business center; room service; babysitting; laundry service; dry cleaning; nonsmoking rooms. *In room:* A/C, TV, high-speed Internet, minibar, hair dryer, iron, safe.

Gran Hotel La Florida ★★★ This former fashionable 1920s hostelry—a firm favorite with top Spaniards, from movie idols to monarchy—was transformed into a hospital during World War II before reemerging as a stylishly renovated hotel a few years ago. Filled with works of art that would not be out of place in a high-profile city gallery, it offers an array of immaculately furnished and decorated rooms and suites, all with spacious en-suite marble bathrooms with separate bath and shower. Since the hotel sits high up on Tibidabo hill, most rooms boast magnificent views. Communal amenities include a world-class restaurant, L'Orangerie; a spa and infinity pool; and terraced gardens. Service is courteous and attentive, and—a small but gracious personal touch—guests are welcomed with glasses of rose-petal water on arrival.

Carretera Vallvidrera (al Tibidabo) 83–93, 08035 Barcelona. © **93-259-30-00**. Fax 93-259-30-01. www. hotellaflorida.com. 74 units. 320€–610€ ($416–$793) double; 660€–900€ ($858–$1,170) suite. AE, DC, MC, V. Parking 18€ ($23) per day. 7km (4¹⁄₃ miles) from Barcelona. **Amenities:** Restaurant; private nightclub; indoor/outdoor pool; health club; Jacuzzi; sauna; solarium; Turkish bath; business center; room service; babysitting; laundry service; dry cleaning; nonsmoking rooms. *In room:* A/C, TV, high-speed Internet, minibar, hair dryer, iron, safe.

Rey Juan Carlos I ★★★ Named after the Spanish king who attended its opening and has visited it several times since, this government-rated five-star hotel competes effectively with other legendary top-notch hostelries such as the Ritz, Claris, and Hotel Arts. Opened just before the Olympics, it rises 17 stories at the northern end of the Diagonal in a wealthy neighborhood filled with corporate headquarters, banks, and upscale stores, a 15-minute Metro ride from Barcelona's top central attractions. Among its more striking design features is a soaring inner atrium with glass-sided elevators. The midsize to spacious guest rooms contain electronic extras, conservatively comfortable furnishings, and oversize beds. Many have views over Barcelona to the sea. Thoughtful touches include good lighting, adequate workspace, spacious closets, and blackout draperies, plus marble bathrooms with tub/shower combos.

Av. Diagonal 671, 08028 Barcelona. © **800/445-8355** in the U.S., or 93-364-40-40. Fax 93-364-42-64. www.hrjuancarlos.com. 412 units. 395€ ($514) double; 525€–1,000€ ($683–$1,300) suite. AE, DC, MC, V. Parking 15€ ($20). Metro: Zona Universitària. **Amenities:** 2 restaurants; 2 bars; indoor pool; outdoor pool; fitness center; car rental; business center; salon; room service; babysitting; laundry/ironing service; dry cleaning; nonsmoking rooms. *In room:* A/C, TV, high-speed Internet, minibar, hair dryer, safe.

MODERATE

Abba Garden Hotel This big, terra-cotta-red hilltop hotel is less than a mile from Barcelona Football Team's Camp Nou, making it a top choice for Barça *fútbol* fans and visiting sports enthusiasts. Its distance from the center (6km/3³⁄₄ miles) means that it enjoys plenty of space, with landscaped gardens, tennis courts, and a large outdoor swimming pool. It's also well located if you plan to spend your time ferrying to and from golf courses outside of Barcelona. The downside is that its slightly isolated location can mean expensive taxi rides into town. If you're eating in, there's a reasonably good on-site restaurant and bar. Bedrooms are spacious and freshly decorated with flower-print fabrics, and all have en-suite bathrooms with tub/shower combos. Twenty-nine of the rooms are nonsmoking.

Santa Rosa 33, Esplugues de Llobregat, 08950 Barcelona. ✆ **93-503-54-54.** Fax 93-503-54-55. www. abbahotels.com. 138 units. 95€–180€ ($124–$234) double. AE, DC, MC, V. Parking 15€ ($20). Metro: Zona Universitària; RENFE: Reina Elisenda. From Barcelona take Av. Diagonal out of the center to the Pedralbes area and look out for signs to Hospital S. Jean de Deu next to hotel. **Amenities:** Restaurant; cafeteria; bar; health club; sauna; solarium; tennis courts; car rental; business center; room service; babysitting; laundry service; dry cleaning; nonsmoking rooms; private garden. In room: A/C, TV, high-speed Internet, minibar, hair dryer, safe.

Hesperia Sarrià ★ (Kids)   This hotel on the northern edge of the city, a 10-minute taxi ride from the center, sits in one of Barcelona's most pleasant residential neighborhoods. Built in the late 1980s, the hotel was last renovated before the 1992 Olympics. You'll pass a Japanese rock formation to reach the stone-floored reception area with its adjacent bar. Sunlight floods the monochromatic guest rooms (all doubles—prices for singles are the same). Although most rooms are medium-size, they have enough space for an extra bed, which makes this a good choice for families. Beds have quality mattresses and fine linen, and bathrooms have tub/shower combos. The uniformed staff offer fine service.

Los Vergós 20, 08017 Barcelona. ✆ **93-204-55-51.** Fax 93-204-43-92. www.hoteles-hesperia.es. 134 units. 155€–220€ ($202–$286) double; 190€–250€ ($247–$325) suite. AE, DC, MC, V. Parking 15€ ($20). Metro: Tres Torres. **Amenities:** Restaurant; bar; business center; room service; laundry service; dry cleaning; nonsmoking rooms. In room: A/C, TV, high-speed Internet, minibar, hair dryer, safe.

Tryp Barcelona Aeropuerto   As the name suggests, the main reason for staying at this hotel is to be close to the airport. Tryp (part of the Sol Meliá group) is a reliable, four-star chain and excellent in terms of business facilities. This one has modern amenities with hardwood floors, and the comfortable spacious bedrooms all have large, marble bathrooms and tub/shower combos. A buffet breakfast is included in the room price, and there's a free 24-hour airport shuttle bus.

Parque de Negocios Mas Blau II, Prat de Llobregat 08820 Barcelona. ✆ **93-378-10-00.** Fax 93-378-10-01. www.trypbarcelonaaeropuerto.solmelia.com. 205 units. 120€–155€ ($156–$202) double; 225€ ($293) suite. AE, DC, MC, V. Valet parking 16€ ($21). 1.5km (1 mile) from airport; 10km (6¼ miles) from Barcelona. **Amenities:** Restaurant; cafeteria; bar; health center; car rental; airport shuttle service; business center; room service; laundry service; dry cleaning; nonsmoking room; safe. In room: A/C, TV, high-speed Internet, minibar, hair dryer.

8 APARTMENTS & APARTHOTELS

Aparthotel Silver ★★ (Finds)   Located in the heart of villagey Gràcia, the Silver apartments are a perfect base for those looking to remove themselves a little from the hustle and bustle of the city center. With its low-rise houses, cute sunny plazas, eclectic bars and restaurants, and bohemian vibe, Gràcia is one of Barcelona's least discovered barrios and well worth getting to know. Silver's 49 studio apartments are smartly decorated with plenty of storage space, comfortable beds, and fresh linens. They come with a kitchenette with a small electric stove and a refrigerator, and all have private bathrooms with tub/shower combos. The building also has a private garden and lawn equipped with tables and chairs and parking facilities. This place is a bargain, especially for couples seeking a little independence.

Bretón de los Herreros 26, Gràcia, 08012 Barcelona. ℂ **93-218-91-00.** Fax 93-416-14-47. www.hotel silver.com. 49 units. 80€–140€ ($104–$182) apt. AE, DC, MC, V. Metro: Fontana. Parking 12€ ($16). **Amenities:** Cafeteria; bar; Internet access; room service; laundry service; private garden. *In room:* A/C, TV, kitchenette w/refrigerator, safe.

Citadines (Kids) Modern, clean, and bright, this apartment hotel is a good choice for those who want to be right on La Rambla with the option to cook for themselves (the wonderful fresh-produce market La Boqueria is just up the street). This is especially popular with groups and families with children, providing fully equipped kitchens; optional maid service; and large, comfortable bedrooms with sofa beds in the living area. The bathrooms are clean and modern. One thing that gives the Citadines an edge over many similar self-catering places in town is the ninth-floor roof terrace offering 360-degree views over the whole city.

La Rambla 122, 08002 Barcelona. ℂ **93-270-11-11.** Fax 93-412-74-21. www.citadines.com. 115 studios; 16 apts. 190€–220€ ($247–$286) 2-person apt; 250€–270€ ($325–$351) 4-person apt. AE, DC, MC, V. Metro: Plaça de Catalunya. Parking 20€ ($26). **Amenities:** Bar; solarium; meeting rooms; maid service; laundry service. *In room:* A/C; TV; stereo; high-speed Internet; kitchenette w/microwave, dishwasher, and fridge; hair dryer; safe.

Hispanos Siete Suiza ★★★ Of all the aparthotels in Barcelona, the Suiza is far and away the most individually glamorous—a real home-away-from-home combined with the comforts of a luxury hotel. The wood-floored apartments all have two bedrooms, two bathrooms, a plush cozy living room, and a kitchen. Continental breakfast is included in the price, and the in-house restaurant, **La Cupula,** is overseen by Carles Gaig, the prestigious Michelin-starred Catalan chef. The original house was owned by the Catalan doctor Melchor Colet Torrabadella, who was also a writer, poet, and philanthropist, and was hugely interested in the arts. He was also interested in fine vintage cars (a collection of seven beautiful 1920s automobiles, from which the hotel gets its name, decorates the lobby). When his wife died of cancer, Colet set up a foundation in her memory, **Fundación Dr. Melchor Colet,** and part of the hotel's profits go to this cause.

Sicilia 255, Eixample Dreta, 08025 Barcelona. ℂ **93-208-20-51.** Fax 93-208-20-52. www.hispanos7suiza. com. 19 units. 200€ ($260) 2-bedroom apt for 2. 40€ ($52) supplement for 3 or 4 guests. AE, DC, MC, V. Metro: Sagrada Família. Parking 15€ ($20). **Amenities:** Restaurant; cocktail bar; DVD/PlayStation rental; room service; laundry service; safe; room for guests w/disabilities; shopping service. *In room:* A/C, TV, high-speed Internet, kitchen w/washing machine and dryer, minibar, safe.

6

Where to Dine

Barcelona's cuisine shot into the limelight with the media's celebration of local man Ferran Adrià as the "greatest chef in the world." But—splendid though he and his creations are—he's not the only fish in the Catalan pond. Fellow luminaries like Jordi Ruiz, Carles Abellan (owner of Comerç 24; p. 140), and Sergi Arola (who runs top eating spots in both Madrid and Barcelona) have also made their own considerable waves, aided locally by the rich supply of fresh market produce, high-quality regional wines, and an instinctive savvy in the world of eating and drinking by both purveyors and consumers. As a result, these chefs are free to experiment, mingling traditional local dishes like pigeon with, say, pears or cherries with anise, or pig's trotters with crab. The resultant hybrid *plato* is usually a delicious new taste experience.

Of course, not everyone aspires to such dizzying heights when eating out, so it's nice to see the trickle-down effect of all these top culinary concepts reaching more modest and affordable dining spots. Whether you're dining in an old-style tavern, having a late supper in one of the new cutting-edge eateries, nibbling on tapas at a bar, or launching into an alfresco paella, the quality of the food is usually high and the variety imaginative. Vegetarians can dine in an increasing number of creative spots, especially in the Old Town. There are also lots of modestly international restaurants in the earthy South American/Greek/Middle Eastern area of El Raval. And deceptively understated fast-food joints, like **Foodball** (p. 139), are also very worthwhile.

Yet for all its adventurous avant-garde culinary creations, there's always a homey quality to eating out in Barcelona. Whether it's a pricey new cutting-edge eatery like **Tapioles 53** (p. 147) or a reliable old economic standby like **Can Culleretes** (p. 134), the city's a nosher's dream.

1 FOOD FOR THOUGHT

WHAT MAKES IT CATALAN CUISINE?

Much of what these new chefs do is put an avant-garde twist on traditional Catalan cuisine. But what is that exactly? Like its language, what Catalans eat is recognizably different from the rest of Spain and varies within the region, from the Mediterranean coastline and islands to the inland villages and Pyrénées Mountains. Like Catalan culture, its cuisine looks out toward the rest of Europe (especially France) and the Mediterranean arc, rather than inward toward Castile. Writer Colman Andrews in *Catalan Cuisine,* his definitive English-language book on the subject (Grub Street, 1997), calls it "Europe's Last Great Culinary Secret." Many of the techniques and basic recipes can be traced back to medieval times, and as any Catalan is only too willing to point out, the quality of the produce proceeding from the *Països Catalans* (Catalan Countries) is some of the best available. The same goes for the locally produced wine. The D.O.s *(domaines ordinaires)* of the Penedès and Priorat regions are now as internationally renowned as La Rioja, and the local *cava* (sparkling, champagne-type wine) is consumed at celebratory tables from Melbourne to Manchester.

If there is one food item that symbolizes Catalan cuisine, it is the *pa amb tomàquet*.
Originally invented as a way of softening stale bread during the lean years of the civil war, there is barely a restaurant in Catalonia, from the most humble workman's canteen to a Michelin-starred palace, that does not have it on their menu. In its simplest form, it consists of a slice of rustic white bread that has been rubbed with the pulp of a cut tomato and drizzled with olive oil. Sometimes, especially when the bread is toasted, you are given a tomato to do this yourself and a clove of garlic to add extra flavor if that strikes your fancy. On these occasions, you top the bread with cheese, pâté, chorizo (or any other cured meat), or Iberian ham—the making of what is called a *torrada*. The idea is ingeniously simple, and like most ingeniously simple ideas, it works wonderfully, at least in Catalonia. Catalans wax lyrical about it, and after a few tries, you too will be hooked and reveling in the fact that you have kicked the high-cholesterol butter habit. But don't try this at home; the tomatoes aren't pulpy enough and the bread never absorbs the pulp (it's just one of those things).

Catalan cuisine is marked by combinations that at first seem at odds with each other; red meat and fish are cooked in the same dish, nuts are pulped for sauces, poultry is cooked with fruit, pulse (bean) dishes are never vegetarian, there is not one part of a pig that is not consumed and imported, salted cod is their favorite fish (although many others are also eaten). Vernacular concoctions that you will see popping up on menus time and time again include *zarzuela* (a rich fish stew), *botifarra amb mongetes* (pork sausage with white beans), *faves a la catalana* (broad beans with Iberian ham), *samfaina* (a sauce of eggplant, peppers, and zucchini), *esqueixada* (a salted cod salad), *fideuà* (similar to a paella, but with noodles replacing the rice), and *miel i mato* (a soft cheese with honey). It's hearty fare, and far more elaborate than the food of southern Spain. In its most traditional form, it doesn't suit light appetites, which is why many locals have only one main meal a day and that meal is normally lunch, with perhaps a light supper of a *torrada* in the evenings. Breakfast is also a light affair; a milky coffee (*café con leche* in Spanish, *café amb llet* in Catalan) with a croissant or doughnut is what most people survive on till lunchtime. Many bars do fresh orange juice.

WHEN YOU DINE IN BARCELONA

Catalans generally have lunch between 2 and 4pm and dinner after 9pm. Most kitchens stay open in the evenings till about 11pm. It is highly recommended that you make lunch your main meal and take advantage of the *menú del día* (lunch of the day) that is offered in the majority of eateries. It normally consists of three courses (wine and/or coffee and dessert included) and, at between 8€ and 12€ ($10–$16) per head, is an extremely cost-effective way of trying out some of the pricier establishments. Tipping always seems to confuse visitors, mainly because some restaurants list the 7% IVA (sales tax) separately on the bill. This is *not* a service charge; in fact, it is illegal for restaurants to charge for service. As a general rule, tips (in cash) of about 5% should be left in cheap to moderate places and 10% in more expensive ones. In bars, just leave a few coins or round your bill up to the nearest euro. If you are really unhappy with the service or food and think that it warrants following up, you are entitled to ask for an *hoja de reclamación* (complaint form) from the management. These are then perused by independent inspectors.

Vegetarian restaurants are slowly but surely on the increase. Some, like **Organic** (p. 145), even aspire to a degree of "creative cooking." Contemporary places such as **Pla** (p. 136), **Anima** (p. 144), and **Juicy Jones** (p. 137) are also fine, always with a couple of vegetarian options on offer. Apart from a tortilla, don't expect this in the traditional, old-style taverns and always double-check; the Catalan word *carn* (*carne* in Spanish) only refers to red meat. Asking for a dish "without" (*sens* in Catalan, *sin* in Spanish) does not guarantee it arrives fish- or chicken-free. Also note that nonsmoking sections in restaurants and bars are, at present, nonexistent. This is set to change in the coming years, but don't hold your breath; in most cases, it will be left up to the management if they want to implement nonsmoking sections or not. In the meantime there are plenty of outside terraces to enjoy a smoke-free (if not smog-free) meal or drink.

Below is only a small selection of the hundreds of Barcelonese restaurants, cafes, and bars. As in many other aspects of a city that is currently one of the most visited in Europe, Barcelona is a victim of its own popularity. The constant influx of tourists means that many places (especially on and around Les Ramblas) now think nothing of offering a microwaved paella or charging 10 times over the average for a coffee. But in the smaller streets of the Barri Gòtic and the blocks of the Eixample area (which has largely escaped the side effects of mass tourism), there are still plenty of value-for-money establishments that take enormous pride in introducing you to the delights of the local cuisine. Around El Raval, the city's most multicultural neighborhood, you will find dozens of cheap places run by Pakistanis, Moroccans, and South Americans should you ever get tired of the local grub. *¡Bon profit!*

2 THE BEST RESTAURANT BETS

- **Hottest Chef:** Carles Abellán has been hailed as the new wunderkind of nouvelle Catalan cuisine. His restaurant, **Comerç 24,** was conceived as a playful take on all that's hot in the tapas world. Delights such as "kinder egg surprise" (a soft-boiled egg with truffle-infused yolk) and tuna sashimi pizza await the adventurous. See p. 140.
- **Best Newcomer:** Up in the Diagonal end of the Eixample a duo of highly professional young chefs thought it would be a good idea to launch a chic low-key locale in which—*sans* drama and trumpet blowing—they would subtly produce stunningly flavored nouvelle Catalan dishes. Word soon got around and now **Hisop** is one of the most (discreetly) "in" places in town. See p. 152.
- **Best Place for a Business Lunch:** The sleek, urban decor and imaginative Spanish-Italian dishes have made **Noti**—in the heart of the power district—a hit with the city's media set and other assorted movers and shakers.
- **Best Spot for a Celebration:** You can make as much noise as you like at **Mesón David,** an old-school eatery with an interminable menu of dishes from all regions of Spain. Chances are you will be sitting next to a raucous group celebrating a birthday or engagement with waiters often joining in the revelry themselves. See p. 145.
- **Best Wine List:** You will be spoiled for choice at **La Vinya del Senyor,** a gorgeous wine bar opposite the towering Santa María del Mar church. Mull over the 300 varieties on offer while taking in its facade from the outside terrace; then order some of their delicious tapas to accompany your choice. See p. 166.
- **Best for Paella:** A paella on the beach is one of the quintessential Barcelona experiences and there is no place better to do it than **Can Majó.** Right on the seafront, this restaurant prides itself on its paellas and *fideuàs* (which replace noodles for rice) and is an established favorite among the city's well-heeled families. See p. 164.
- **Best Modern Catalan Cuisine:** With over 10 restaurants, the legendary Tragaluz group has revolutionized Barcelona's gastronomic panorama. Its flagship eatery, **Tragaluz,** defines not only the city's contemporary design aesthetic, but also its "market"

cuisine: The freshest seasonal ingredients are executed to a very
p. 154.

- **Best Traditional Catalan Cuisine: Via Veneto** exudes old-fashioned
up some of the finest Catalan cooking in the land. Some of the serving
as the sterling-silver duck press, seem to belong to another century (as
clients). See p. 167.
- **Best for Kids:** Children are welcome almost everywhere in Spanish resta   s, but
why not give them a real treat by heading for **La Paradeta?** As close as you can get to
the Catalan version of a fish and chippery, all kinds of seafood laid out on ice greet
you as you walk in. You pick what you want and a few minutes later, *bingo!* Out it
comes, hot and steaming, in a cardboard box. See p. 141.
- **Best Fusion Cuisine:** Born in Catalonia but raised in Canada, chef Jordi Artal instinc-
tively knows how to fuse old- and new-world cuisines. The five-course tasting menu
in his upscale **Cinc Sentits** is a memorable way to sample his expertise. See p. 151.
- **Best for Tapas: Taller de Tapas** was conceived to take the mystery out of tapas. Multilingual staff and menus ensure you don't get pig's cheeks when you order green leeks,
and the rest of the delectable dishes are a perfect initiation for the novice. See p. 143.
- **Best for People-Watching:** The food may not win any awards but that doesn't stop
soccer stars, models, and other assorted semi-celebs from flocking to **CDLC,** which is
right on the waterfront in the Olympic Village and decked out in fashionable faux-
Thai chic. The real fun starts with the post-dinner disco, and you're not sure whether
the breeze is rolling in off the Mediterranean or the rush of air kisses. See p. 164.
- **Best Outdoor Dining Area:** As well as being one of the best-value restaurants in the
city, the **Café de L'Academia** is blessed with one of the prettiest settings: a charming
square in the Old Town flanked by Gothic buildings and an ancient water fountain.
At night the warm glow of the table candles bounces off the stone walls, ensuring you
linger long after the last liquor. See p. 133.
- **Best View:** Dine on top of the world, or at least 75m (246 ft.) up, in **Torre d'Alta
Mar,** located in a cable-car tower. The view couldn't be more mesmerizing, allowing
you to take an almost 360-degree view of the city's skyline and the surrounding sea in
one swoop. See p. 162.
- **Best for Seafood:** Although good seafood is abundant in Barcelona, many swear that
the best catches end up in **Cal Pep,** a tiny bar near the port. Mountains of the stuff
are prepared in front of your eyes by lightning-quick staff, and your dexterity is put
to the test as you try not to elbow your neighbor while peeling your prawns. See
p. 140.
- **Best Wine Bar:** Bathed in Bordeaux red, with large arched windows looking out onto
a tranquil square, **Vinissim** has a mind-boggling array of wines from all corners of the
globe, plus a scrumptious array of tapas to soak them up. It offers a pleasing experience
for all the senses. See p. 139.
- **Best for Sunday Lunch:** The lines say it all: **7 Portes,** one of the oldest restaurants in
Barcelona, is a Sunday institution. Extended families dine on their excellent meat and
fish dishes in turn-of-the-20th-century surroundings. See p. 162.
- **Best Vegetarian Restaurant:** Though veggie newcomers are sprouting up all over
town, our favorite spot remains the established **Organic,** a barnlike place with communal wooden tables; an all-you-can-eat salad bar; and tempting rice, pasta, and tofu
dishes. See p. 145.

..st for a Sweet Tooth: Sweet but never sickly, **Espai Sucre** is perhaps the world's only restaurant that offers a menu made up entirely of desserts. Foodies rave about it and its reputation has spread far and wide as a once-in-a-lifetime gastronomic experience. Some savory dishes are available. See p. 141.

- **Best for Morning or Afternoon Tea:** The tiny street of Petritxol in the Old City is renowned for its *granjas,* cafes specializing in cakes, pastries, and hot chocolate. **Xocoa** makes its own mouthwatering chocolates and presents them in funky wrappers. See p. 225.
- **Best for Consistency: Pla** strikes that right balance between hip and highly creative without scaring you off. The menu focuses on local market produce with a touch of Asian and Arabic, and the staff is unusually friendly and helpful. See p. 136.
- **Best Snack on the Go:** Before you embark on a visit to the Museum of Contemporary Art, fuel up at **Foodball,** a new concept in fast food. Whole-grain rice balls filled with tofu, wild mushrooms, chickpeas, and the like, plus fresh juices and smoothies, are served in a quirky setting where you can also eat in. See p. 139.
- **Best Retro Interior:** For an authentic touch of the '70s, head up to **Flash-Flash Tortillería.** Bathed in dramatic red and white, the photo-murals that adorn the walls were taken by Leopoldo Pomés, one of the founders and a top fashion photographer during the city's swinging decade. See p. 159.

3 CIUTAT VELLA: BARRI GÒTIC

EXPENSIVE

Agut d'Avignon ★ CATALAN   One of my favorite restaurants in Barcelona is in a tiny alleyway near the Plaça Reial. It's still going strong after 40 years, and it has a dedicated following. Since 1983 Mercedes Giralt Salinas and her son, Javier Falagán Giralt, have run the restaurant. A small 19th-century vestibule leads to the multilevel dining area, which has two balconies and a main hall evoking a hunting lodge. You may need help translating the Catalan menu. The traditional specialties are likely to include acorn-squash soup served in its shell, fisherman's soup with garlic toast, haddock stuffed with shellfish, sole with *nyoca* (a medley of nuts), large shrimp with aioli, duck with figs, and filet beefsteak in sherry sauce.

Trinitat 3, at Carrer d'Avinyó. ℭ **93-302-60-34.** Reservations recommended. Main courses 16€–28€ ($21–$36); lunch menu 16€ ($21). AE, DC, MC, V. Daily 1–4:30pm and 9pm–12:30am. Metro: Jaume I or Liceu.

MODERATE

Agut ★ (Finds) CATALAN   In a historic building in the Barri Gòtic, 3 blocks from the harborfront, Agut epitomizes the bohemian atmosphere surrounding this gritty area. For three-quarters of a century, this has been a family-run business, with María Agut García the current reigning empress. (Don't confuse Agut with the more famous Agut d'Avignon nearby.) The aura evokes the 1940s and 1950s, and the inventive array of restaurant dishes is served at moderate prices. Begin with *mil hojas de botifarra amb zets* (layers of pastry filled with Catalan sausage and mushrooms) or the *terrine de albergines amb fortmage de cabra* (terrine of eggplant with goat cheese gratinée). One of my favorite dishes is *soufle de rape amb gambes* (soufflé of monkfish with shrimp). If you are ravenous, attempt the *chuletón de buey* (loin of ox) for two, which comes thick and juicy and

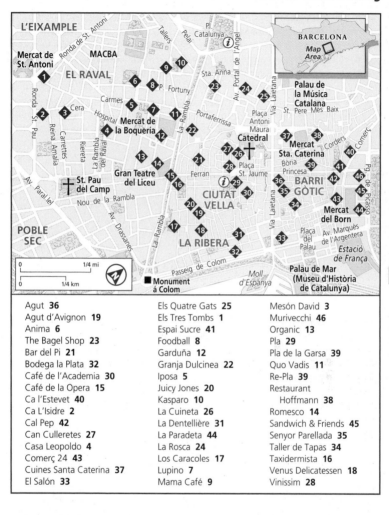

Agut **36**
Agut d'Avignon **19**
Anima **6**
The Bagel Shop **23**
Bar del Pi **21**
Bodega la Plata **32**
Café de l'Academia **30**
Café de la Opera **15**
Ca l'Estevet **40**
Ca L'Isidre **2**
Cal Pep **42**
Can Culleretes **27**
Casa Leopoldo **4**
Comerç 24 **43**
Cuines Santa Caterina **37**
El Salón **33**

Els Quatre Gats **25**
Els Tres Tombs **1**
Espai Sucre **41**
Foodball **8**
Garduña **12**
Granja Dulcinea **22**
Iposa **5**
Juicy Jones **20**
Kasparo **10**
La Cuineta **26**
La Dentellière **31**
La Paradeta **44**
La Rosca **24**
Los Caracoles **17**
Lupino **7**
Mama Café **9**

Mesón David **3**
Murivecchi **46**
Organic **13**
Pla **14**
Pla de la Garsa **39**
Quo Vadis **11**
Re-Pla **39**
Restaurant
  Hoffmann **38**
Romesco **14**
Sandwich & Friends **45**
Senyor Parellada **35**
Taller de Tapas **34**
Taxidermista **16**
Venus Delicatessen **18**
Vinissim **28**

accompanied by a mixture of fresh vegetables. For dessert, if you order *sortido,* you'll get a combination plate with an assortment of the small homemade cakes of the house.

Gignàs 16. ℭ **93-315-17-09.** Reservations required. Main courses 10€–20€ ($13–$26); fixed-price lunch menu Tues–Fri 14€ ($18). AE, DC, MC, V. Tues–Sun 1:30–4pm; Tues–Sat 9pm–midnight. Closed Aug. Metro: Jaume I.

Café de L'Acadèmia ★★ Value CATALAN/MEDITERRANEAN   In the center of the Barri Gòtic, a short walk from Plaça Sant Jaume, this 28-table restaurant looks expensive but is really one of the best and most affordable in the medieval city. The building dates from the 15th century, but the restaurant was founded only in the mid-1980s.

Dishes of this quality usually cost three times as much in Barcelona. The chef is proud of his "kitchen of the market," suggesting that only the freshest ingredients from the day's shopping are featured. Try such delights as *bacallà gratinado i musselina de carofes* (salt cod gratinée with an artichoke mousse) or *terrina d'berengeras amb fortmage de cabra* (terrine of eggplant with goat cheese). A delectable specialty sometimes available is *codorniz rellena en cebollitas tiernas y foie de pato* (partridge stuffed with tender onions and duck liver). On warm evenings, go for one of the outside, candle-lit tables on the atmospheric square dominated by a Gothic church.

Carrer Lledó 1, Plaça Sant Just. *C* **93-319-82-53.** Reservations required. Main courses 10€–18€ ($13–$23); fixed-price lunch menu 12€–14€ ($16–$18). AE, MC, V. Mon–Fri 9am–noon, 1:30–4pm, and 9–11:30pm. Closed 2–3 weeks in Aug. Metro: Jaume I.

Can Culleretes CATALAN   Founded in 1786 as a *pastelería* (pastry shop) in the Barri Gòtic, Barcelona's oldest restaurant retains many original architectural features. All three dining rooms are decorated with tile dadoes and wrought-iron chandeliers. The well-prepared food features authentic dishes of northeastern Spain, including sole Roman style, *zarzuela a la marinera* (shellfish medley), cannelloni, and paella and special game dishes, including *perdiz* (partridge). The service is old-fashioned, and sometimes it's filled more with tourists than locals, but it retains enough authentic touches to make it feel like the real McCoy. Signed photographs of celebrities, flamenco artists, and bullfighters who have visited decorate the walls.

Quintana 5. *C* **93-317-64-85.** www.culleretes.com. Reservations recommended. Main courses 10€–18€ ($13–$23); fixed-price menu Tues–Fri 17€ ($22). MC, V. Tues–Sun 1:30–4pm; Tues–Sat 9–11pm. Closed July. Metro: Liceu. Bus: 14 or 59.

Cuines Santa Caterina ★ (Finds) ASIAN/MEDITERRANEAN/ITALIAN   This spacious spot adjoining the Santa Caterina market couldn't be better located for fresh local produce, samples of which are displayed enticingly along the large front windows. Designed by top architects Enric Miralles and Benedetta Tagliabue, the CSC—as it's popularly known—features an open kitchen, subtle back lighting, and ficus trees planted in between the long olive wood tables. Lunch is a particularly good value and the place is noisily packed as locals call out their choices from the chalkboard menu. Fusion, vegetarian, and down-to-earth dishes range from fresh sushi and green asparagus to baked potato with cheese and sausage. There's also a tapas bar with a fruit and veg juice section.

Mercado de Santa Caterina, Av. Francesc Cambó 17, La Ribera. *C* **93-268-99-18.** www.grupotragaluz. com. Reservations not required. Main courses 8€–24€ ($10–$31). MC, V. Mon–Sat 1–4pm and 8–11:30pm. Metro: Jaume I.

El Salón (Moments) MEDITERRANEAN/FUSION   Dominated by a huge gilt mirror and low lighting, El Salón has long been a favorite for couples looking for a romantic dinner spot. The menu, which changes daily, pushes the definition of eclectic with Asian, Italian, and especially French influences on local market produce. It's been around long enough to have a firm and faithful following, especially among the expat community, and though the standard varies it's usually very good.

L'Hostal d'en Sol 6–8. *C* **93-315-21-59.** Reservations recommended. Main courses 10€–18€ ($13–$23); fixed-price dinner 20€ ($26). AE, DC, MC, V. Daily 9pm–midnight. Metro: Jaume I.

Els Quatre Gats ★ (Moments) CATALAN   This tastefully restored Barcelona legend has been around since 1897. The "Four Cats" (Catalan slang for "just a few people") was a favorite of Picasso, Rusiñol, and other artists, who once hung their works on its walls.

(Reproductions still adorn them.) On a narrow cobblestone street in the Barri Gòtic, the *fin-de-siècle* cafe was a base for members of the *modernista* movement that figured in the city's intellectual and bohemian life, and poetry readings by Joan Maragall and piano concerts by Isaac Albéniz and Enric Granados were regular events. It's still a popular meeting place today. The fixed-price meal is one of the better bargains in town. The homespun Catalan cooking here is called *cucina de mercat* (based on whatever looked fresh at the market) but will always include such classics as *suquet de peix* (a fish and potato hot pot) and *faves a la catalana* (baby broad beans with Serrano ham). Come at lunchtime, as it sometimes gets a bit too touristy in the evenings, with musicians playing banal 1960s Spanish pop songs.

Montsió 3. ℭ **93-302-41-40.** www.4gats.com. Reservations required. Main courses 18€–25€ ($23–$33); fixed-price lunch menu 14€ ($18). AE, DC, MC, V. Daily 1pm–1am. Cafe daily 8am–2am. Metro: Plaça de Catalunya.

Garduña CATALAN   This is the most famous restaurant in Barcelona's covered food market, La Boqueria. Originally conceived as a hotel, it has concentrated on food since the 1970s. Battered, somewhat ramshackle, and a bit claustrophobic, it's fashionable with an artistic set that might have been designated as bohemian in an earlier era. It's near the back of the market, so you'll pass endless rows of fresh produce, cheese, and meats before you reach it. You can dine downstairs, near a crowded bar, or a bit more formally upstairs. Food is ultrafresh—the chefs certainly don't have to travel far for the ingredients. You might try "hors d'oeuvres of the sea," cannelloni Rossini, grilled hake with herbs, *rape* (monkfish) *marinera,* paella, brochettes of veal, filet steak with green peppercorns, seafood rice, or a *zarzuela* (stew) of fresh fish with spices.

Jerusalem 18. ℭ **93-302-43-23.** Reservations recommended. Main courses 10€–28€ ($13–$36); fixed-price lunch 12€ ($16); fixed-price dinner 18€ ($23). DC, MC, V. Mon–Sat 1–4pm and 8pm–midnight. Metro: Liceu.

La Cuineta (Value) CATALAN   This restaurant near the Catalan government offices is a culinary highlight of the Barri Gòtic. Decorated in typical regional style, it favors local cuisine. The fixed-price menu is a good value, or you can order a la carte. The most expensive appetizer is *bellota* (acorn-fed ham), but I suggest a market-fresh Catalan dish, such as *favas* (broad beans) stewed with *botifarra,* a tasty, spicy local sausage.

Pietat 12. ℭ **93-315-01-11.** Reservations recommended. Main courses 16€–35€ ($21–$46); fixed-price menu 14€–28€ ($18–$36). AE, DC, MC, V. Daily 1–4pm and 8pm–midnight. Metro: Jaume I.

Los Caracoles (Moments) CATALAN   This restaurant must be one of the easiest to find in Barcelona. As you walk down Escudellers, one of the old quarter's most seedily atmospheric lanes, you are drawn on by the aroma of roasting chickens rotating on an outside spit over an open fire built into the side of the edifice. You enter through the main kitchen, with steaming pots and hot-under-the-collar cooks. Inside it's a labyrinth—stairways lead to even more dining rooms; private one-table nooks are hidden under stairs; and there are colorful tiles, wooden beamed ceilings, and antique fittings everywhere. The place positively oozes with character, and the cuisine is mainly Catalan comfort food: *arroz negre* (rice cooked in squid ink), grilled squid, and, of course, roast chicken. There's always a fair share of tourists and the food isn't always up to what it should be, but as an authentic slice of local culture it's definitely worth a visit.

Escudellers 14. ℭ **93-302-31-85.** Reservations recommended. Main courses 10€–28€ ($13–$36). AE, DC, MC, V. Daily 1pm–midnight. Metro: Drassanes.

Pla ★★ MEDITERRANEAN   This cool Barri Gòtic eating spot, which has adopted a totally nonsmoking policy, has been a solid hit with locals and visitors alike since its 1998 opening, thanks to its consistently high standard of *carpaccios;* wide selection of market-fresh salads exposing tasty combinations such as spinach, mushrooms, and prawns; and main dishes with Asian and Arabic touches that nearly always include a Thai curry or a Moroccan couscous dish. The candle-lit setting and cozy atmosphere are complemented by the amiable, bilingual, and informal waitstaff who take the time to talk you through your selection. (See also its more informal sister bodega-restaurant, Re-Pla, later in the chapter.)

Bellafila 5. ℂ **93-412-65-52.** www.pla-repla.com. Reservations required. Main courses 9€–18€ ($12–$23). DC, MC, V. Sun–Thurs 9pm–midnight; Fri–Sat 9pm–1am. Closed Dec 25–27. Metro: Jaume I.

Taxidermista MEDITERRANEAN   This popular restaurant, located on the bustling Plaça Reial, has high ceilings, tall narrow pillars, and attractively tiled floors. Originally, it was the 19th-century literary Gran Café Espanyol and later it became a Natural Science Museum, with a taxidermy workshop that featured stuffed beasts, from insects to lions (some of which were sold to buyers as eminent as Dali). Today it's a chic restaurant renowned for its two- or three-course set lunches, but traces of its history still exist (bears' and deer's heads decorate one wall of the salon). A la carte specialties include crayfish ravioli with shellfish sauce and a great steak tartare, and there's an extensive cellar of wines and *cavas.*

Plaça Reial 8. ℂ **93-412-45-36.** www.taxidermistarestaurant.com. Main courses 15€–20€ ($20–$26); set lunch 10€–12€ ($13–$16). AE, DC, MC, V. Tues–Sun 1:30–4pm and 8:30pm–12:30am. Closed 3 weeks in Jan. Metro: Liceu.

INEXPENSIVE

Iposa (Value) FRENCH/MEDITERRANEAN   Iposa is yet another cheap and cheerful Raval hangout with an outside leafy terrace that is coveted on sunny Saturday afternoons. The resident French chef ensures there is always something a little different on offer beyond the usual "Mediterranean Market" fare. If you're on a budget—and not too hungry—order the bargain lunchtime menu for 6€ ($7.80), but bear in mind that the portions are small and that you get just one main course, a dessert, and a drink. The food changes daily and includes things like a vegetable couscous, fresh grilled fish, or a hot "hummus" soup.

Floristes de La Rambla 14. ℂ **93-318-60-86.** Main courses 6€–10€ ($7.80–$13); fixed-price lunch 6€ ($7.80). V. Aug daily 9pm–midnight; Sept–July Mon–Sat 1:30–4pm and 9pm–midnight. Metro: Liceu.

(Finds) **Calling All Chocoholics!**

Established in 1930, **Granja Dulcinea,** Carrer de Petritxol 2 (ℂ **93-302-68-24**), is the most famous chocolate shop in Barcelona. The specialties are *melindros* (sugar-topped soft-sided biscuits), and the regulars who flock here love to dunk them into the very thick hot chocolate—so thick, in fact, that drinking it feels like eating a melted chocolate bar. A cup of hot chocolate with cream costs 3€ ($3.90), and a *ración* of *churros* (a deep-fried pastry), which also can be dipped in the hot chocolate, goes for 1.60€ ($2.10). No credit cards are accepted. Dulcinea is open daily from 9am to 1pm and 5:30 to 9pm; closed in August. Take the Metro to Liceu.

Make It Snappy

Fast-food establishments are ever on the increase, from prime-positioned McDonald's and Dunkin' Donuts to local takeouts, which are also well worth stopping for a bite if you want to eat in a hurry. **Pans & Company** and **Bocata,** for example, dispense freshly made *bocatas* (crusty rolls) filled with tasty hot and cold combinations. Also everywhere you'll see branches of **La Baguetina Catalana,** a fantastic, franchised fueling stop with mountains of carb-ridden cakes and pastries to go. A favorite with health-conscious backpackers, **Maoz** (mainly in the Old Town) churns out freshly made falafels, which you then top up yourself with as much salad as you can possibly fit into the pita bread. Along **La Rambla** (and the streets to either side) there are dozens of places for enormous *shwarmas:* giant sandwiches filled with spit-roasted chicken or lamb and salad.

Juicy Jones (Finds) VEGETARIAN A brightly colored blend of strip-cartoon and children's nursery decor greets you in this chummy Danish-run locale, where the young international waiters are friendly but sometimes give the impression they're just passing through. Hardly conventional either in style or choice of grub, it offers a very reasonably priced couscous and rice-accompanied range of inventive dishes, ranging from bean sprouts and *escalivada* (grilled onion, aubergine, and red and green peppers) to tofu and ginger salads. The marvelous selection of fresh fruit juices includes pear, mango, and grapefruit in a large (4€/$5.20) or small (3€/$3.90) glass; there are also soy milkshakes, organic wines, and beer available. You can sit at the narrow counter near the entrance or down in the secluded sunken restaurant at the back.

Cardenal Casañas 7. (C) **93-302-43-30.** Main courses 7€–10€ ($9.10–$13); lunch 9€ ($12) on weekdays. No credit cards. Open daily noon–midnight. Metro: Liceu.

La Dentellière ★ (Finds) FRENCH/INTERNATIONAL Charming, and steeped in the French aesthetic, this bistro is imbued with a modern, elegant decor. Inside, you'll find a small corner of provincial France, thanks to the dedicated effort of Evelyne Ramelot, the French writer who owns the place. After an aperitif at the sophisticated cocktail bar, you can order from an imaginative menu that includes a lasagna made from strips of salt cod, peppers, and tomato sauce, and a delectable *carpaccio* of filet of beef with pistachios, lemon juice, vinaigrette, and Parmesan cheese. The wine list is particularly imaginative, with worthy vintages mostly from France and Spain.

Ample 26. (C) **93-218-74-79.** Reservations recommended on weekends. Main courses 8€–16€ ($10–$21). MC, V. Tues–Sun 8:30pm–midnight. Metro: Drassanes.

La Rosca CATALAN/SPANISH For more than half a century, owner Don Alberto Vellve has continued to welcome customers into this little Barri Gòtic eatery, close to Plaça de Catalunya. On a short street, the place is easy to miss, except to devotees who have been coming here for decades. A mixture of Catalan and modern Spanish cuisine is served in this house, which is small and in an old rustic style with high ceilings and white walls. There are 60 unadorned tables, which diners fill quickly to take advantage of the cheap three-course lunch menu. Dig into such hearty fare as veal stew or assorted fish and grilled shellfish. Baby squid is cooked in its own ink, and one of the best dishes is white beans sautéed with ham and Catalan sausage. For a true treat, ask for the *rape a la plancha* (grilled monkfish).

Juliá Portet 6. (C) **93-302-51-73.** Main courses 10€–15€ ($13–$20); fixed-price menu 10€–14€ ($13–$18). No credit cards. Sun–Fri 9am–9:30pm. Closed Aug 20–30. Metro: Urquinaona and Plaça de Catalunya.

Romesco (Value) CATALAN/MEDITERRANEAN   Frequented by locals and travelers on a budget, Romesco is never going to win any Michelin stars, but it does offer up the sort of homemade food that is rapidly disappearing within the immediate vicinity of touristy La Rambla. The lighting is bright, the tables are laminated, and the waiters and food are both no-nonsense and generously proportioned. You will find healthy, fresh dishes like grilled tuna served with a simple salad, or hearty delights such as *arroz a la cubana* (white rice, tomato sauce, a fried egg, and a fried banana). Desserts include a creamy *crema catalana* (crème brûlée) and *arroz con leche* (rice pudding). Finish off with a strong black coffee like the locals.

Sant Pau 28. (C) **93-318-93-81.** Main courses 8€–15€ ($10–$20). No credit cards. Mon–Fri 1pm–midnight; Sat 1–6pm and 8pm–midnight. Closed Aug. Metro: Liceu.

SNACKS, TAPAS & DRINKS

The Bagel Shop CAFE   If you are craving a bagel, head for this simple cafe just off the top end of La Rambla. All the staples are here: sesame, poppyseed, blueberry, plus a few European versions such as black olive. Fillings go from honey to salmon and cream cheese, and they also have a yummy selection of cheesecakes.

Canuda 25. (C) **93-302-41-61.** Bagels 2€–6.75€ ($2.60–$8.80). No credit cards. Mon–Sat 9:30am–9:30pm; Sun 11am–4pm. Metro: Liceu.

Bar del Pi TAPAS   One of the most famous bars in the Barri Gòtic, this tiny establishment is midway between two medieval squares opening onto a Gothic church. Typical tapas, canapés, and rolls are available. Most visitors come to drink coffee, beer, or local wines, house sangrias, and *cavas*. In summer you can refresh yourself with a tiger-nut milkshake (called an *horchata*) or a slushy ice drink. You can sit inside at one of the cramped bentwood tables, or stand at the crowded bar. In warm weather, take a table beneath the single plane tree on the landmark square. The plaza usually draws an interesting group of young bohemian sorts, travelers, and musicians.

Plaça Sant Josep Oriol 1. (C) **93-302-21-23.** www.bardelpi.com. Tapas 2.75€–8€ ($3.60–$10). No credit cards. Mon–Fri 9am–11pm; Sat 9:30am–10:30pm; Sun 10am–10pm. Metro: Liceu.

Bodega la Plata ★ TAPAS   Established in the 1920s, La Plata is one of a trio of famous bodegas on this narrow medieval street. This one occupies a corner building—whose two open sides allow aromatic cooking odors to permeate the neighborhood—and contains a marble-topped bar and overcrowded tables. The culinary specialty comprises *raciones* (small plates) of deep-fried sardines—head and all. You can make a meal with two servings coupled with the house's tomato, onion, and fresh anchovy salad. The highly quaffable Penedés house wine comes in three varieties, *tinto, blanco,* and *rosado.*

Mercé 28. (C) **93-315-10-09.** Tapas/raciones 2€–4€ ($2.60–$5.20). No credit cards. Mon–Sat 1–3:45pm and 8pm–midnight. Metro: Drassanes.

Cafè de l'Opera ★ CAFE/TAPAS   This is one of the few emblematic cafes in the city that has managed to resist the ravages of modernization. The name comes from the Liceu Opera House, located directly opposite across La Rambla, and once upon a time patrons would have gathered here for a pre-performance aperitif. Although it has been renovated over the years, the interior still retains Belle Epoque details. It's a great place to pull up with a book during its quieter daytime moments, and there is also a terrace if people-watching is more your thing. Tapas are limited, but the cakes are divine. Service is brusque, exuding a jaded formality in keeping with the surroundings.

La Rambla 74. (℃ **93-302-41-80.** www.cafeoperabcn.com. Tapas from 3.50€ ($4.55); cakes from 4€ ($5.20). No credit cards. Mon–Fri 8:30am–2am; Sat–Sun 8:30am–3am. Metro: Liceu.

Foodball ★ HEALTH FOOD   Foodball is the latest concept from the shoe company **Camper** (p. 236), aiming to transport their wholesome company culture to the food industry. It's a cafe and takeout joint located near the MACBA museum, and its clientele reflects the neighborhood's neo-hippie vibe. The foodballs in question are whole-grain macrobiotic rice balls stuffed with organic mushrooms, chickpeas, tofu and alga, or chicken. You can either take them out in stylish recycled lunchboxes or choose to park yourself on the grandstand-style seating. Besides the foodballs, the only other produce available is fresh and dried fruit, juices, and purified water. If all this sounds just a bit too contrived, don't be put off; healthy fast food is scarce in Barcelona, and the foodballs are actually very, very tasty. It's a brilliant concept.

Elisabets 9. (℃ **93-270-13-63.** Foodballs 2.5€ ($3.25) each; menu 10€ ($13). Daily noon–11pm.

Venus Delicatessan CAFE   This pleasant cafe is on one of the inner-city's alternative fashion shopping streets. It's a good stopping point for tea and coffee and cakes and pastries. The "delicatessen" in the name is a bit misleading (there's not a deli counter in sight), but what it does do very well are light meals such as salads and quiches from mid-day to midnight. There is a ton of international press to thumb through and work by local artists on the wall to gaze at.

Avinyó 25. (℃ **93-301-15-85.** Main courses 7€–12€ ($9.10–$16); fixed-price lunch 12€ ($16). No credit cards. Mon–Sat noon–midnight. Metro: Jaume I.

Vinissim ★★ WINE/TAPAS   A warm burgundy and exposed-brick interior is the perfect backdrop for this cozy wine bar on a pretty square in the El Call pocket of the Barri Gòtic. Here over 50 carefully selected wines—available by glass or bottle—come from all regions of Spain. Portions range from small tapas of ham, fish, or olives to *ración*-size combos like artisan goat's cheese, sun-dried tomatoes, caramelized onions, and potato and cheese *raclette*. One of their best whites is Finca Lobeira *albariño* from Galicia (2.50€/$3.25 per glass). Rich desserts include sticky date pudding and delicious white chocolate cheesecake. All in all, this is an absolute gem of a wine bar, with grub to match.

Sant Domenec del Call 12. (℃ **93-301-45-75.** Tapas/raciones 3€–15€ ($3.90–$20); tasting menu 24€ ($31); fixed-price weekday lunch 15€ ($20). AE, DC, MC, V. Mon–Sat noon–4pm and 8pm–midnight. Metro: Liceu.

4 CIUTAT VELLA: LA RIBERA

EXPENSIVE

ABaC ★ ⓕinds INTERNATIONAL   This is the showcase of a personality chef, Xavier Pellicer, who creates a self-termed *cuisine d'auteur,* meaning a menu of completely original dishes. His minimalist restaurant has even attracted members of the Spanish royal family, eager to see what Pellicer is cooking on any given night. Some of his dishes may be too experimental for most tastes, but I've found his daring palate pleasing. He is a master in balancing flavors, and his dishes perk up the taste buds and even challenge them at times. His plates emphasize color and texture, and his sauces are perfectly balanced. You never know on any given night where his culinary inspiration has led him. Perhaps a mushroom tartare will be resting on your plate, or a velvety-smooth steamed foie gras. Roasted sea bass appears with sweet pimientos and oyster plant and Iberian suckling pig is cooked and flavored to perfection, as is his fennel ravioli with "fruits of the sea."

Tibidabo 1. (*C*) **93-319-66-00.** www.abacbarcelona.com. Reservations required. Main courses 25€–35€ ($33–$46); tasting menu 85€ ($111). AE, DC, MC, V. Tues–Sat 1:30–3:30pm; Mon–Sat 8:30–10:30pm. Closed Aug. Metro: Jaume I or Barceloneta.

Restaurant Hoffmann ★★ CATALAN/FRENCH/INTERNATIONAL This restaurant is one of the most famous in Barcelona, partly because of its creative cuisine, partly because of its close association with a respected school that trains employees for Catalonia's hotel and restaurant industry. The culinary and entrepreneurial force behind it is German/Catalan Mey Hoffmann, whose restaurant overlooks the facade of one of Barcelona's most beloved Gothic churches, Santa María del Mar. In good weather, three courtyards hold tables. Menu items change every 2 months and often include French ingredients. Examples include a superb *fine tarte* with deboned sardines, foie gras wrapped in puff pastry, baked John Dory with new potatoes and ratatouille, a ragout of crayfish with green risotto, succulent pigs' feet with eggplant, and rack of lamb with grilled baby vegetables. Especially flavorful, if you appreciate beef, is a filet steak cooked in Rioja and served with shallot confit and potato gratin. Fondant of chocolate makes a worthy dessert.

Carrer Argenteria 74–78. (*C*) **93-319-58-89.** Reservations recommended. Main courses 16€–40€ ($21–$52); tasting menu 37€ ($48). AE, DC, MC, V. Mon–Fri 1:30–3:15pm and 9–11:15pm. Closed Aug and Christmas week. Metro: Jaume I.

MODERATE

Cal Pep ★ (Finds) CATALAN Cal Pep lies just north of the Plaça de Palau, nestled beside a tiny postage-stamp square. It's generally packed, and the food is some of the tastiest in La Ribera. There's actually a Pep himself, and he's a great host, going around to see that all diners are happy with their meals. In the rear is a small dining room (book if you intend to eat here), but most patrons like to occupy one of the counter seats up front. Try the fried artichokes or the mixed medley of seafood that includes small sardines. Tiny clams come swimming in a well-seasoned broth given extra spice by a sprinkling of hot peppers. A delectable tuna dish comes with a sesame sauce, and fresh salmon is flavored with such herbs as basil—sublime.

Plaça des les Olles 8. (*C*) **93-310-79-61.** www.calpep.com. Reservations required. Main courses 14€–25€ ($18–$33). AE, DC, MC, V. Mon 8:30–11:30pm; Tues–Sat 1–4:30pm and 8:30–11:30pm. Closed Aug. Metro: Barceloneta or Jaume I.

Comerç 24 ★★ (Finds) CATALAN/INTERNATIONAL The renowned chef of this avant-garde restaurant is Carles Abellán, a disciple of the famed Ferran Adriá of El Bulli. Abellán uses fresh seasonal ingredients, balanced sauces, and bold but never outrageous combinations, and he believes in split-second timing. Samples of his most imaginative dishes include freshly diced tuna marinated in ginger and soy sauce, and fresh salmon "perfumed" with vanilla and served with yogurt. His baked eggplant with Roquefort, pine nuts, and fresh mushrooms from the countryside is another treat. Believe it or not, he serves that old-fashioned snack that Catalan children used to be offered when they came home from school, a combination of chocolate, salt, and bread flavored with olive oil. It's surprisingly good!

Carrer Comerç 24. ✆ **93-319-21-02.** www.comerc24.com. Reservations required. Main courses 12€–28€ ($16–$36); tasting menu 50€ ($65). AE, DC, MC, V. Tues–Sat 1:30–3:30pm and 8:30pm–12:30am. Closed last 3 weeks in Aug and Christmas week. Metro: Jaume I.

Espai Sucre ★★ (Finds) DESSERTS Espai Sucre (Sugar Space) is Barcelona's most unusual dining room, with a minimalist decor and seating for 30. The unique menu is entirely devoted to desserts. There is a short list of so-called salty dishes, like ginger couscous with pumpkin and grilled stingray or artichoke cream with a poached quail egg and Serrano ham. A "salad" might contain small cubes of spicy milk pudding resting on matchsticks of green apple with baby arugula leaves, peppery caramel, dabs of kafir lime and lemon curd, and a straight line of toffee. There are constant surprises. Ever had a soup of litchi, celery, apple, and eucalyptus? If not, you can try it here. If some of these concoctions frighten your palate, you'll find comfort in the more familiar—vanilla cream with coffee sorbet and caramelized banana. Every dessert comes with a recommendation for the appropriate wine to accompany it.

Princesa 53. ✆ **93-268-16-30.** www.espaisucre.com. Reservations required. Main courses 10€–18€ ($13–$23); 3-dessert platter 30€ ($39). MC, V. Tues–Sat 9–11:30pm. Closed mid-Aug and Christmas week. Metro: Arc de Triomf.

La Paradeta (Value) (Kids) SEAFOOD Most *marisco* (seafood) meals can set you back a ton in Barcelona. Not so at this busy restaurant that has more in common with a fish market than the trendy eateries of La Ribera's El Born district. This could be because of the money they save on waitstaff. The seafood—crabs, prawns, squid, and so on—is displayed in large plastic tubs. You pick out what you want at the counter, it's weighed up and heaved away, and you pick it up crisp and steaming on a platter. The same scenario goes for the drinks, which include some excellent *albariño* whites and other good, reliable local wines. It's loads of fun, but remember to order everything at once, as you often have to wait in line, especially on the weekends. There are other branches, with the same menus and opening hours, beside the Sagrada Família (Pasaje Simó 18; ✆ **93-450-01-91**) and in Sants (Carrer Riego 27; ✆ **93-431-90-59**).

Comercial 7. ✆ **93-268-19-39.** www.laparadeta.com. Fish charged per kilo (varies). Average price w/ wine 18€–28€ ($23–$36). No credit cards. Tues–Thurs 8–11:30pm; Fri 8pm–midnight; Sat 1–4pm and 8pm–midnight; Sun 1–4pm. Closed Dec 22–Jan 22. Metro: Arc de Triomf.

Senyor Parellada CATALAN/MEDITERRANEAN The glossy contemporary-looking interior of this place is in distinct contrast to the facade of a building that's at least a century old. Inside, in a pair of lemon-yellow and blue dining rooms, you'll find menu items such as Italian-style cannelloni, stuffed cabbage, cod "as it was prepared by the monks of the Poblet monastery," baked monkfish with mustard and garlic sauce, roasted duck served with figs, and roasted rack of lamb with red-wine sauce. Patrons flock faithfully to this bistro, knowing they'll be served a traditional cuisine of northeast Spain with fine local produce. The chefs know how to coax the most flavor out of the premium ingredients.

Argenteria 37. ✆ **93-310-50-94.** www.senyorparellada.com. Reservations recommended. Main courses 10€–18€ ($13–$23). AE, DC, MC, V. Daily 1–4pm and 8:30pm–midnight. Metro: Jaume I.

Murivecchi (Value) ITALIAN   If this family-run restaurant was just a few hundred meters further west in the thick of the trendy El Born neighborhood, you would probably never get a table. The un-alarming decor doesn't do it any favors either, but the food is excellent and good value for the money. There is a wood-fired oven for fans of real Neapolitan pizza, and the pasta dishes are no less delectable: *tagliatelle al funghi porcini, spaghetti vongole,* and *linguini al pesto* are just a sample. Add to this a list of *antipasti, risotti,* and *carpacci;* daily specials; and a sinful tiramisu—and you have some of the best Italian cuisine this side of Rome.

Princesa 59. (C) **93-315-22-97.** Reservations recommended on weekends. Main courses 10€–16€ ($13–$21); fixed-price lunch Mon–Fri 12€ ($16). MC, V. Daily 1–4pm and 8pm–midnight. Metro: Arc de Triomf.

Pla de la Garsa ★ (Value) MEDITERRANEAN/CATALAN   Located on the eastern side of La Ribera, this historic building is fully renovated but still retains some 19th-century fittings, such as a cast-iron spiral staircase used to reach another dining area upstairs. The ground floor is more interesting. Here you'll encounter the owner, Ignacio Sulle, an antiques collector who has filled his establishment with an intriguing collection of objets d'art. The menu boasts one of the city's best wine lists and features a daily array of favorite traditional Catalan and Mediterranean dishes. Begin with one of the pâtés, such as the goose, or a confit of duck thighs. One surprise is a terrine with black olives and anchovies. For a main course you can order a perfectly seasoned beef bourguignon or *fabetes fregides amb menta i pernil* (beans with meat and diced Serrano ham). The cheese selection is one of the finest I've found in town, especially bountiful in Catalan goat cheese, including Serrat Gros from the Pyrénées.

Assaonadors 13. (C) **93-315-24-13.** www.pladelagarsa.com. Reservations recommended on weekends. Main courses 7€–14€ ($9.10–$18). AE, DC, MC, V. Daily 8pm–1am. Metro: Jaume I.

Re-Pla ★★ CATALAN   Such was the popularity of the Pla restaurant in the Barri Gòtic that its owner opened this second branch in neighboring La Ribera, on the same street as the Picasso Museum and close to the Santa Caterina market, which provides the place with fresh produce. Unlike the intimate candlelit original restaurant, this is a brasher, down-to-earth bodega-style locale specializing in regional tapas and *raciones* like *jamón Serrano, croquetas,* and *tortillitas de champiñones* (tiny mushroom omelettes). There's a good choice of local and national wines (especially from the Penedés), and smoking is permitted here. It reopened in 2008, after undergoing renovation work, and is now one of the area's brightest and most bustling eating spots.

Montcada, 2 (La Ribera). (C) **93-268-30-03.** www.pla-repla.com. Tapas and raciones 4€–8€ ($5.20–$10); main courses 12€–15€ ($16–$20). Daily noon–11:30pm (to midnight Fri–Sat). DC, MC, V. Closed Dec 25–27. Metro: Jaume I.

SNACKS, TAPAS & DRINKS

Sandwich & Friends CAFE   Located on the main drag of the city's hippest quarter, El Born, Sandwich & Friends stands out from the rest of its fast-food rivals thanks to its huge wall mural by local but internationally famous illustrator Jordi Labanda. His portrayal of a social gathering of bright young things echoes the clientele itself, who come here to nibble on the cafe's awesome selection of over 50 sandwiches all named after "friends": *Marta* is a pork filet, tomato, and olive oil sandwich; *Daniel* is filled with frankfurter, bacon, and mustard. There is also a selection of salads if you are calorie counting, which, going by the size of the waitstaff, is pretty much the norm here. There are four other branches scattered throughout the city, one in Raval and three in L'Eixample, but this one is the coolest.

Passeig del Born 27. ✆ **93-310-07-86.** www.sandwichandfriends.com. Sandwiches and salads 4.75€–10€ ($6.20–$13). MC, V. Daily 9:30am–1am. Metro: Jaume I or Barceloneta.

Taller de Tapas ★★ TAPAS   For a foreigner, ordering tapas can be a daunting affair. Making yourself heard above the noise is one problem, and there is also the lack of written menus. The Born district's Taller de Tapas (Tapas Workshop) takes the trouble out of *tapeando.* Patrons can sit at a table and order from a trilingual menu. The tapas are prepared in an open kitchen, where there is not a microwave in sight. The owners are always on the lookout for new ingredients that will work in tapas, which means that every week there is a board of specials. The regularly featured tapas delights come from all over Spain: marinated anchovies from L'Escala on the Costa Brava, Palamós prawns with scrambled eggs, grilled duck foie, and sizzling chorizo cooked in cider. For those that like something a bit more substantial for breakfast, they do a morning tortilla menu.

L'Argentaria 51. ✆ **93-268-85-59.** www.tallerdetapas.com. Tapas 3.50€–12€ ($4.55–$16). AE, DC, MC, V. Mon–Thurs 8:45am–midnight; Fri–Sat 8:45am–12:30am; Sun noon–midnight. Metro: Jaume I. There's another location at Plaça Sant Josep Oriol 9, Barri Gòtic (✆ **93-301-80-20;** Metro: Liceu).

5 CIUTAT VELLA: EL RAVAL

EXPENSIVE

Ca L'Isidre ★ CATALAN   In spite of its seedy location in the still gritty Parel.lel district (take a cab at night!), this is perhaps the most sophisticated Catalan bistro in Barcelona. Opened in 1970, it has served King Juan Carlos and Queen Sofía, Julio Iglesias, and the famous Catalan bandleader Xavier Cugat. Isidre Gironés, helped by his wife, Montserrat, is known for his fresh cuisine, which is beautifully prepared and served. Try spider crabs and shrimp, a foie gras salad, sweetbreads with port and flap mushrooms, or carpaccio of veal. The selection of Spanish and Catalan wines is excellent.

Les Flors 12. ✆ **93-441-11-39.** www.calisidre.com. Reservations required. Main courses 18€–45€ ($23–$59). AE, DC, MC, V. Mon–Sat 1:30–4pm and 8:30–11pm. Closed Sat–Sun June–July and all Aug. Metro: Paral.lel.

Casa Leopoldo ★★ (Finds) SEAFOOD   An excursion through the earthy streets of the Barri Xino is part of the Casa Leopoldo experience. At night it's safer to come by taxi. Founded in 1939, this colorful restaurant, with its attractive tiled walls and wooden beam ceilings, serves some of the freshest seafood in town. There's a popular stand-up tapas bar in front and two dining rooms. Specialties include *rodaballo (*fresh grilled turbot), *anguila con gambas* (eel with shrimp), *percebes* (goose barnacles), *sepia* (cuttlefish), *sopa de mariscos* (seafood soup with shellfish), and *anguilas fritas* (deep-fried inch-long eels).

Sant Rafael 24. ✆ **93-441-30-14.** www.casaleopoldo.com. Reservations recommended. Main courses 25€–45€ ($33–$59); tasting menu 48€ ($62). AE, DC, MC, V. Tues–Sun 1:30–4pm; Tues–Sat 9–11pm. Closed Aug and Easter week. Metro: Liceu.

Quo Vadis ★ SPANISH/CATALAN   Elegant and impeccable, this is one of the finest restaurants in Barcelona and a favorite with the opera crowd from the Liceu Opera House next door. In a century-old building near the open stalls of the Boqueria food market, it was established in 1967 and has done a discreet but thriving business ever since. The four paneled dining rooms exude conservative charm. Culinary creations include a ragout of seasonal mushrooms, fried goose liver with prunes, filet of beef with wine sauce, and a variety of grilled or flambéed fish. There's a wide choice of desserts made with seasonal fruits imported from all over Spain.

Carme 7. ✆ **93-302-40-72.** www.restaurantquovadis.com. Reservations recommended. Main courses 18€–30€ ($23–$39); fixed-price menu 34€ ($44). AE, DC, MC, V. Mon–Sat 1:15–4pm and 8:30–11:30pm. Closed Aug. Metro: Liceu.

MODERATE

Anima MEDITERRANEAN/FUSION   Located near the MACBA, Anima is another of the new breed of Raval eateries. Inside it's all bright colors and minimalism, and a glance at the menu would lead you to think that the cuisine also skimps on the trimmings. But the food here is actually highly satisfying, especially when you eat it on their outdoor terrace in the summer. Under the plane trees, you may dine on *rape con ajillo de pistachio y granizado de algas* (monkfish in pistachio garlic and iced liquidized seaweed), mozzarella balls swimming in gazpacho, ostrich steak with caramelized cranberries, and crystalized chocolate truffles for dessert. If all this sounds a bit too risky, take a gamble with the great-value set-lunch menu before you leap in.

Angels 6. ✆ **93-342-49-12.** Reservations recommended. Main courses 10€–18€ ($13–$23); fixed-price lunch 12€ ($16). AE, DC, MC, V. Mon–Sat 1–4pm and 9pm–midnight. Dinner only in Aug. Metro: Liceu.

Lupino MEDITERRANEAN FUSION   Set in the heart of El Raval, the Lupino is renowned for its cool catwalk-like decor and an eclectically inventive cuisine that effortless blends Mediterranean, French, Creole, and North African dishes. Typical favorites are grilled entrecôte with couscous, cod with ratatouille and coconut emulsion, and pork stuffed with goat cheese with cassava chips on the side. It's all very good and the lunchtime menu is one of the best deals around. A rear terrace overlooks the back of the Boqueria market (in reality a parking lot, but oversize parasols block out the unsightly bits). Friday and Saturday are late-night cocktail nights when a DJ makes an appearance.

Carme 33. ✆ **93-412-36-97.** Reservations recommended on weekends. Main courses 14€–20€ ($18–$26); fixed-price lunch Mon–Fri 11€ ($14), Sat–Sun 13€ ($17). AE, MC, V. Mon–Thurs 1–4pm and 9pm–midnight; Sat–Sun 1:30-4:30pm and 9pm–3am. Metro: Liceu.

Mama Cafe MEDITERRANEAN FUSION   Also located in the thick of El Raval's hub of funky eateries, this is one of the more reliable bets where style doesn't give way to substance. The boho crowd is greeted by an urban-savvy staff, who churn out the dishes from a frantic open kitchen. The quality of the hamburgers here is unusually good (for Barcelona), the salads (nearly always with a fruit or goat cheese) are market fresh, and the pastas (such as salmon and capers) are more than acceptable. Mama Cafe is one of the few inner-city restaurants open on Monday (the only day when fish is not available on the menu, by the way, in case you're a seafood lover).

Doctor Dou 10. ✆ **93-301-29-40.** Reservations recommended on weekends. Main courses 10€–17€ ($13–$22); fixed-price lunch 12€ ($16). AE, MC, V. Daily 1–4pm and 9pm–midnight. Metro: Liceu.

INEXPENSIVE

Ca l'Estevet Finds CATALAN/SPANISH   This century-old eating spot is a veritable institution in El Raval, where the Estevat family has been welcoming a mixture of students, journalists, and intrepid tourists for decades. The warm homey ambience is matched by traditional Catalan dishes such as *exqueixada* (shredded salt cod salad), *botifarra negre* (black sausage), *cargols a llauna* (snails), and *conill* (rabbit). Weekday lunches are the main thing here, though it can get very crowded, so best to turn up a little earlier by Spanish standards (that is, around 1:30pm). 145

Valdonzella 46. ☏ **93-302-41-86.** Main courses 9€–16€ ($12–$21); set lunch 12€ ($16). Mon–Sat 1:30–4pm and 8–11pm. Metro: Universitat.

Mesón David ★ Ⓥⓐⓛⓤⓔ SPANISH Don't come here for a quiet evening. Mesón David is an absolute riot: Waiters scream at each other, tips are acknowledged by the ringing of a cowbell, crowds of diners sing, and somehow you have to make yourself heard. But the effort is worth it. The food is fast, furious, and excellent, and the regional specialties range from Navarran trout stuffed with Serrano ham and Galician-style broiled octopus to traditional Castilian roast suckling pork. Obviously, it isn't the place for a light meal. But it is an enormous amount of fun for a price that's unbelievably low for inner Barcelona. On busy nights you may have to wait for a table at the bar, and be shown the door on your last gulp of coffee.

Carretes 63. ☏ **93-441-59-34.** www.mesondavid.com. Reservations recommended. Main courses 7€–12€ ($9.10–$16); fixed-price lunch Tues–Fri 9€ ($12). AE, DC, MC, V. Tues–Sun 12:30–4pm and 8pm–1am. Metro: Paral.lel or Sant Antoni.

Organic Ⓥⓐⓛⓤⓔ VEGETARIAN Hip and hippie, Organic is one of the brightest vegetarian restaurants in town. At lunchtime, a happy waitstaff will show you to large communal tables and explain the system; the first course is a help-yourself soup and salad bar, all tasty and organically grown. The second (which you order from them) could be a vegetarian pizza, pasta, or perhaps a stir-fry. The self-serve desserts include apple cake, carob mousse, and fresh yogurt (smaller menus available). At night the menu is a la carte and on the weekends there is live Brazilian music. A small selection of health foods is also available, including homemade bread, and a local masseuse is there to offer her services to the lunchtime crowd.

Junta Comerç 11. ☏ **93-301-09-02.** www.antoniaorganickitchen.com. Main courses 7€–12€ ($9.10–$16); fixed-price lunch 8€–10€ ($10–$13). AE, DC, MC, V. Daily noon–midnight. Metro: Liceu.

SNACKS, TAPAS & DRINKS

Els Tres Tombs CAFE/TAPAS Els Tres Tombs is one of the most versatile bars around. Open 20 hours a day, it caters to housewives taking a break from shopping at the nearby Sant Antoni market and to young people stopping off for breakfast after a night out clubbing. The facade is pure '70s, the waiters are distinctly old-school, and the placement of the terrace ensures it receives more direct sunlight than just about any bar in Barcelona. Inside there are breakfast pastries to choose from and mounds of tapas to satisfy any daytime hunger pangs. It's a city institution.

Ronda Sant Antoni 11. ☏ **93-443-41-11.** Tapas 3€–12€ ($3.90–$16); fixed-price lunch 9€ ($12). No credit cards. Daily 6am–2am. Metro: Sant Antoni.

Kasparo CAFE/TAPAS This place has one of the all-time favorite terraces: a leafy porticoed affair just a stone's throw from the MACBA (Museum of Contemporary Art). It's so popular, in fact, that you often see people nonchalantly milling around, waiting to pounce on the next free table. A wide range of tapas—which varies from day to day—is marked up on a blackboard, and there's a good selection of tasty sandwiches. There's also a wide choice of beers and wines, and the iced melon-flavored tea is a refreshing summer

More Tapas

Traditionally, Barcelonese don't go for a tapas crawl as often as their cousins in Madrid or Andalusia. They prefer to sit down the old-fashioned way, over three courses, acres of linen, and a bucket containing a chilled bottle of white wine. But the trend of eating in small portions, and the influence of new chefs such as Carles Abellán at **Comerç 24** (p. 140), has seen heightened interest in this artful cuisine.

For classic Spanish tapas in the heart of the Old City, try **Taller de Tapas,** Calle de l'Argenteria 51 (✆ **93-268-85-59**). For a 50-strong list of snacks all freshly made on the spot, **Cal Pep,** Plaça de les Olles 8 (✆ **93-310-79-61**), comes close to godliness when you're talking spanking-fresh seafood (p. 140); or there's **Bar Celta,** Calle Mercè 16 (✆ **93-315-00-06**)—one of the oldest tapas joints in town—for purple octopus tentacles, pigs lips and ears, and delightful green peppers known as *pimientos del padrón*. On the same street you can also down rustic farmhouse ciders; flaming chorizo; and dark, deeply satisfying slivers of *cecina* (cured beef) at the smattering of *sidrerías* (Asturian tapas bars) that still exist.

In La Ribera and the Born, **Mosquito,** Calle Carders 46 (✆ **93-268-75-69**), does a well-executed range of Indian, Thai, Malaysian, and Indonesian dishes, along with *gyoza* dumplings and organic beers at unbeatable prices. More upmarket fare can be had from the ever-inventive hands of Paco Guzmán at **Santa María,** Calle Comerç 17 (✆ **93-315-12-27**). Think Spanish-Asian fusion along the lines of local fruits stuffed with Thai spiced peanuts; raw sea bass with passion fruit, tomato, and lime vinaigrettes; and suckling pig with wasabi and soy.

If you're heading up town, avoid the monster barns on the Passeig de Gràcia and opt instead for **Ciudad Condal,** Rambla de Catalunya 18 (✆ **93-318-19-97**), arguably the city's most visited tapas bar for *patatas bravas,* fried fish, and anchovies. Then, push on up the road to **Cervecería Catalana,** Carrer Majorca 236 (✆ **93-216-03-68**), for juicy slices of filet beef skewered with peppers, and giant prawn brochettes. (**Note:** These tapas are chalked up on the blackboard, not in the cool chest.)

Finish off with a pudding course courtesy of Jordi Butrón at **Espai Sucre,** Calle Princesa 53 (✆ **93-268-16-30;** p. 141). Tales of his earthy Lapsang souchong tea ice cream go before him, and for many years his was the only pudding restaurant in the world. Butrón can no longer claim that title, but this is still the ultimate end to a 21st-century tapas crawl.

alternative. If you're lucky enough to get hold of a table, you will probably find yourself lingering long after you planned to.

Plaça Vicenç Martorell 4. ✆ **93-302-20-72.** www.barcelona-on-line.es/kasparo. Tapas 4.50€–8.50€ ($5.85–$11). No credit cards. Daily 9am–midnight. Closed Dec 24–Jan 24. Metro: Plaça de Catalunya.

INEXPENSIVE

La Bella Napoli ITALIAN   Like La Bodegueta below, this Poble Sec eatery has also undergone a paring-down face-lift in recent years and now features stark brick walls, bare polished floorboards, and red-and-white gingham tablecloths. There's still plenty of original character in the food, which is authentic Italian, from the lasagna to the tiramisu. Most people, however, come for the thin-crust pizzas, which are hauled out of a wood-fired oven, perfectly crisped and ready to scarf down. Takeaway is available. Get here early, as it's amazingly popular.

Margarit 12. ℂ **93-442-50-56.** Reservations required. Main courses 12€–35€ ($16–$46). AE, DC, MC, V. Tues 8:30–11:30pm; Wed–Sun 1:30–3:30pm and 8:30–11:30pm. Closed Aug and Christmas week. Metro: Paral.lel or Poble Sec.

La Bodegueta TAPAS   This popular bodega is typical (or what was typical) of this working-class neighborhood. Even after its overhaul some years back, the period character remains, as does the original rose-petal-tiled floor. Owner Eva Amber is on hand to recommend her home cooking, which includes such favorites as lentils with chorizo and Catalan cannelloni. Meat *a al brasa* (grill-flamed) and *torrades* (toasted bread with charcuterie) are also on the agenda.

Blai 47. ℂ **93-442-08-46.** Tapas 3€–12€ ($3.90–$16). MC, V. Mon–Fri noon–4pm and 7–10:30pm; Sat noon–4pm. Closed Aug. Metro: Poble Sec.

Quimet & Quimet ★ TAPAS/CHEESE   This is a great tapas bar, especially for cheese, of which it offers the finest selection in Barcelona. Built at the turn of the 20th century, the tavern in the Poble Sec sector is still run by the fifth generation of Quimets. Their wine cellar is one of the best stocked of any tapas bar, and their cheese selection is varied. If you're not watching the calories (and cholesterol) try the prized four *quesos* (cheeses) on the same plate: *nevat* (a tangy goat cheese), *cabrales* (an intense Spanish blue cheese), *zamorano* (a hardy, nutty sheep's milk cheese), and *torta del Casar* (a soft, creamy farm cheese). You could try the *tou dels tillers,* a cheese stuffed with trout roe and truffles. Other delights include *mejillones con confit de tomate y caviar* (mussels with tomato confit and caviar), *navajas* (razor clams), and even *esturión* (sturgeon).

Poeta Cabanyes 25. ℂ **93-442-31-42.** Tapas 3€–12€ ($3.90–$16). MC, V. Mon–Fri noon–4pm and 7–10:30pm; Sat noon–4pm. Closed Aug. Metro: Paral.lel.

Tapioles 53 ★★★ ⓕⓘⓝⓓⓢ MEDITERRANEAN/ASIAN   Australian chef Sarah Stothart's restaurant has only six tables, so eating here is like being in the stylish home of a friend who also happens to be a brilliant cook. Located in a former umbrella factory, the intimate and relaxed decor is by noted designer Ricardo Feriche. Chef Stothart's menus change nightly and, in my view, are the best dining deal in town. The dishes are created from fresh ingredients gathered every morning from the Santa Caterina market. Outstanding dishes are polenta with mozzarella, fresh tomatoes and basil, stuffed baby squid, and swordfish cooked in banana leaf with rice. All dishes for that day are explained to you at your table (there's no printed menu) and prepared in the open kitchen.

Carrer Tapioles 53. ℂ **93-329-22-38.** www.tapioles53.com. Reservations required. Fixed-price menu 26€–40€ ($34–$52). MC, V. Tues–Sat 9pm–midnight. Metro: Poble Sec or Paral.lel.

7 L'EIXAMPLE

VERY EXPENSIVE

Beltxenea ★★ BASQUE/INTERNATIONAL   In a building originally designed in the late 19th century to house apartments, this restaurant celebrates Basque cuisine. Fine Basque cuisine is served here in one of the most elegantly and comfortably furnished restaurants in the city. Schedule a meal for a special night—it's worth the money. The menu might include *merluza frito en ajo o con guarnición de almejas en caldo de pescado* (hake fried with garlic or garnished with clams and served with fish broth), *cordero asado* (roast lamb), *conejo a la plancha* (grilled rabbit), and *faisan* (pheasant). There's dining outside in the formal garden during the summer.

Majorca 275. ✆ **93-215-30-24.** Reservations recommended. Main courses 22€–48€ ($29–$62); tasting menu 70€ ($91). AE, DC, MC, V. Mon–Fri 1:30–3:30pm; Mon–Sat 8:30–11:30pm. Closed Easter week, 3 weeks in Aug, and Christmas week. Metro: Passeig de Gràcia and Diagonal.

Drolma ★★★ INTERNATIONAL   In business since 1999, this is one of Barcelona's best haute-cuisine restaurants. Fermin Puig is one of Spain's most celebrated chefs, his culinary showcase found in the Hotel Majestic. Only the freshest seasonal ingredients go into his luminous and carefully balanced dishes. Highlights are pheasant-stuffed cannelloni in a velvety foie-gras sauce delicately sprinkled with the rare black truffle, *rodaballo* (wild turbot) served with fresh Catalan mushrooms, and *gambas* (prawns) with fresh asparagus tips in a virgin olive oil sauce. The *cordero* (lamb) is grilled with fresh herbs, and the bold yet delicate *chivo al horno* (baked goat) is served with potatoes and mushrooms.

In the Hotel Majestic, Passeig de Gràcia 68. ✆ **93-496-77-10.** www.hotelmajestic.es. Reservations required. Main courses 38€–120€ ($49–$156). AE, DC, MC, V. Mon–Sat 1–3:30pm and 8:30–11pm. Closed Aug. Metro: Passeig de Gràcia.

Jaume de Provença ★★★ CATALAN/FRENCH   This small, cozy restaurant is just a few steps from the Estació Central de Barcelona-Sants railway station, at the western end of L'Eixample. Named after its owner and chef, Jaume Bargués, it features modern interpretations of traditional Catalan and southern French cuisine. Examples include gratin of clams with spinach, a salad of two different species of lobster, foie gras and truffles, and pigs' trotters with plums and truffles. Or you might order crabmeat lasagna, cod with saffron sauce, sole with mushrooms in port wine sauce, or an artistic dessert specialty of orange mousse.

Provença 88. ✆ **93-430-00-29.** www.jaumeprovenza.com. Reservations recommended. Main courses 14€–38€ ($18–$49); fixed-price menu 55€ ($72); tasting menu 70€ ($91). AE, DC, MC, V. Tues–Sat 1–4pm and 9–11:15pm; Sun 1–4pm. Closed Easter week and Aug. Metro: Entença.

La Dama ★★★ CATALAN/INTERNATIONAL   This is one of the few restaurants in Barcelona that deserves, and gets, a Michelin star. In a very elegant 1918 building designed by Manuel Sayrach, this stylish and well-managed restaurant serves a clientele of local residents and civic dignitaries. You take an Art Nouveau elevator (or the sinuous stairs) up one flight to reach the dining room. Here chef Josep Bullich's specialties include salmon steak served with vinegar derived from *cava* (sparkling wine) and onions, cream of potato soup flavored with caviar, a salad of *langostinos* (crayfish) with orange-flavored vinegar, an abundant platter of autumn mushrooms, and succulent preparations that include first-rate *cordero* (lamb), *ternera* (veal), and fresh *mariscos* (shellfish).

WHERE TO DINE

6

L'EIXAMPLE

Alkimia **14**	Drolma **17**	La Bodegueta **11**
Bar Turò **1**	El Caballito	La Dama **5**
Beltxenea **15**	Blanco **10**	L'Olivé **6**
Can Ravell **21**	Gaig **23**	Moo **13**
Casa Alfonso **24**	Gorría **20**	Neichel **1**
Casa Calvet **25**	Gresca **9**	Reno **3**
Casa Tejada **2**	Hisop **18**	Rosalert **16**
Cata 1.81 **19**	Il Giardinetto **4**	TapaÇ24 **22**
Cinc Sentits **8**	Jaume de Provença **7**	Tragaluz **12**

Diagonal 423. ✆ **93-202-06-86.** www.ladama-restaurant.com. Reservations recommended. Main courses 15€–40€ ($20–$52); fixed-price menu 65€ ($85); tasting menu 85€ ($111). AE, DC, MC, V. Daily 1:30–3:30pm and 8:30–11:30pm. Metro: Provença.

EXPENSIVE

Alkimia ★★ MEDITERRANEAN   Jordi Vilà's Alkimia is the type of restaurant that attracts other chefs and fans of his singular style. Vilà is a proponent of New Catalan cuisine, the culinary wave that started with Ferran Adrià (p. 299). For starters, try the deconstructed version of the traditional *pa amb tomàquet* (a slice of white bread rubbed with tomato pulp and olive oil), in which Vilà separates the juice from the tomato before adding the oil, crumbs of toasted bread, and a little pungent *lloganissa* salami. Many of his other dishes are also an offbeat take on traditional Catalan dishes: tuna belly substitutes for Iberian ham in *faves a la catalana* (Catalan-style broad beans); truffle is daringly added to a plate of cabbage, potato, and sausage; and fried eggs and Majorcan sausage is served with preserved quinces. There's an excellent wine cellar that includes vintages from all over the country.

Industria 79. ✆ **93-207-61-15.** Reservations required. Main courses 15€–30€ ($20–$39). Tasting menu 45€ ($59) and 60€ ($78). DC, MC, V. Mon–Fri 1:30–4pm; Sat 8am–noon. Closed Easter week and Aug 8–31. Metro: Sagrada Família.

Can Ravell ★ (Finds) CATALAN   There's a good reason why Barcelona gourmets have tried—all in vain—to keep this gem to themselves. Founded in 1929 by Ignasy Ravell and discreetly tucked away on the second floor of a deli in the heart of the city, it's still only accessible via a kitchen and spiral staircase. It was and still is a food store, which is why it manages to serve up some of the city's freshest dishes. Chef Jesus Benavente, who's renowned for his divine creations, adjusts his menu according to what is best seasonally on the market. So you never know exactly what you're going to get till you arrive. A wonderful dish is *espalda de cerdo a horno con foie gras y guisantes* (braised pork shoulder with foie gras and young peas). The restaurant also has a cellar of over 10,000 bottles, including traditional *cavas* and French champagnes.

Aragó 313. ✆ **93-457-51-14.** Reservations required. Main courses 25€–50€ ($33–$65); tasting menu 44€ ($58). Tues–Wed 10am–9pm; Thurs–Fri 10am–10pm; Mon and Sat 10am–6pm. Metro: Gerona.

Casa Calvet ★★ MEDITERRANEAN   Probably the most intimate Gaudían experience you can have in Barcelona is eating at this sumptuous dining room. The Casa Calvet, one of the architect's first commissions, was built for the textile magnate Pere Calvet. Now private apartments, the building is off-limits to the public, but a restaurant occupies Calvet's former ground-floor offices. Replete with velvet drapery, florid stained glass, attractive tiles, Gaudí-designed furniture, and other memorabilia, the only thing that jolts you back to the 21st century is the contemporary twist on Miguel Alija's excellent Catalan cuisine, such as giant prawns with rosemary-infused oil or duck liver with oranges. And although the historic setting ensures a fair share of tourists, Casa Calvet is also just as popular with locals. Thankfully, the waitstaff treat everyone that walks in with equal doses of measured hospitality.

Carrer Casp 48. ✆ **93-412-40-12.** www.casacalvet.es. Reservations recommended. Main courses 20€–35€ ($26–$46); tasting menu 60€ ($78). AE, DC, MC, V. Mon–Sat 1–3:30pm and 8:30–11pm. Metro: Passeig de Gràcia.

Cata 1.81 ★★ (Finds) CATALAN/TAPAS   The dainty tapas-size dishes served here all look and taste pretty innovative till you learn that many of the recipes are based on time-tested traditional standbys. These include *Galtas de porc con nueces y higos* (pig trotters with walnuts and fresh figs) with honey ice cream, and *calamar relleno de carne de cerdo* *picada en salsa almendrada de chocolate* (squid stuffed with minced pork and served with an almond-flavored chocolate sauce). Also popular are savory rice served with fresh asparagus and black truffles, and ravioli stuffed with codfish and minced smoked ham. There is also a comprehensive and exemplary wine list.

Valencia 181. ⓒ **93-323-68-18.** www.cata181.com. Reservations required. Tasting menu 35€ ($46) for 9 dishes, 40€ ($52) for 11 dishes; tapas 4€–9€ ($5.20–$12). AE, DC, MC, V. Mon–Thurs 6pm–midnight; Fri–Sat 7pm–1am. Closed 3 weeks in Aug. Metro: Passeig de Gràcia or Hospital Clínic.

Cinc Sentits ★★ MEDITERRANEAN

This cutting-edge eatery aims to soothe the *cinc sentits* (five senses). Chef Jordi Artal offers a "Gourmet" tasting menu of eight tapas-size dishes that is diverse and delicious. You might try a crème fraîche and caviar soup or a sliver of foie with violet-petal marmalade. Artal's cuisine is a combination of Catalan culinary know-how and new-world wit. An everyday white garlic soup is graced with pan-seared lobster, a monkfish sprinkled with bacon "dust," or a soft poached egg with tomato jam. My favorite dish was the smallest: a heavenly shot glass of *cava*, egg yolk, rock salt, and maple syrup. Cinc Sentits is an example of what fusion food can be like with a combination of the finest ingredients and intelligence.

Aribau 58. ⓒ **93-323-94-90.** www.cincsentits.com. Reservations required. Main courses 14€–30€ ($18–$39); tasting menu 50€ ($65) and 60€ ($78). AE, DC, MC, V. Mon 1:30–3:30pm; Tues–Sat 1:30–3:30pm and 8:30–11pm. Closed Easter week and Aug 8–31. Metro: Passeig de Gràcia.

Gaig ★★★ MODERN CATALAN

One of the shining culinary showcases of Barcelona, Gaig was founded as an out-of-town *fonda* (small inn for travelers) in the late 19th century by the great-grandmother of present owner Carlos Gaig. Today it's a sleek deluxe downtown restaurant celebrated locally for the quality and freshness of its food. Eggs come from the chickens seen wandering about the patio, where customers often dine alfresco in the summer months. Gaig's cuisine centers on traditional Catalan recipes transformed and altered to suit lighter and more modern palates. Among the stellar choices are *arroz del delta con pichón y zetas* (rice with partridge and mushrooms), *rape asado a la catalana* (grilled monkfish with local herbs), and *els petits filet de vedella amb prunes i pinyons* (small veal filets with prunes and pine nuts). One of the tastiest dishes is marinated roast pork thigh. Desserts include *crema de Sant Joseph* (a warm flan with wild strawberries on top), homemade chocolates, and a selection of tarts.

Aragó 214. ⓒ **93-429-10-17.** www.restaurantgaig.com. Reservations recommended. Main courses 28€–45€ ($36–$59); tasting menu 80€ ($104). AE, DC, MC, V. Mon–Sat 1:30–3:30pm and 9–11pm; Sun 9–11pm. Closed Easter week and 3 weeks in Aug. Metro: Passeig de Gràcia.

Gorría ★ Finds BASQUE/NAVARRAN

This top Basque eating spot, within a stone's throw of La Sagrada Família, is run by Javier Gorría, who learned from his talented father Fermin Gorría, a master chef in his own right. Today it's Javier who pampers his regular clientele—mainly homesick expats from Navarra and the Basque country—with memories of home. No dish is finer than the herb-flavored baby lamb baked in a wood-fired oven. The classic Basque dish, hake, comes in a garlic-laced green herbal sauce with fresh mussels and perfectly cooked asparagus on the side. Braised pork also emerges from the wood-fired oven, and I could make a meal out of his *pochas* (white beans). Another favorite is a platter of artichokes stuffed with shrimp and wild mushrooms.

Diputació 421. ⓒ **93-245-11-64.** www.restaurantegorria.com. Reservations recommended. Main courses 18€–35€ ($23–$46). AE, DC, MC, V. Mon–Sat 1–3:30pm and 9–11:30pm. Closed Aug. Metro: Monumental.

Gresca ★★ (Finds) CATALAN/INTERNATIONAL Gifted Ferran Adrià disciple Rafael Peña runs this delightful little restaurant on the eastern edge of L'Eixample. A highly imaginative and inventive chef, Peña regularly entices elite noshers to road-test his more experimental dishes such as *higado de ternera con plátano y regaliz* (fresh calf's liver with plantains and licorice), *carpaccio de pulpo* (octopus carpaccio), and *butifarra negre con patatas fritas* (a very pungent black Catalan sausage served with fried potatoes—not for those on a diet!). Other pleasures include *anchoas en escabeche* (house-marinated fresh anchovies), *jamón Serrano con calamaritos fritos* (mountain ham served with fried baby squid), and *galtas de vacuno marinado en vino de Rioja* (tender beef cheeks braised in Rioja wine).

Provenza 230. ✆ **93-451-61-93.** www.gresca.net. Reservations required. Main courses 15€–30€ ($20–$39). MC, V. Daily 1:30–3:30pm; Mon–Sat 8:30–11pm. Metro: Plaça de Catalunya or Hospital Clinic.

Hisop ★ MODERN CATALAN In 2001, Guillem Pla and Oriol Ivem, two former chefs from the prestigious Neichel restaurant (see below), launched this adventurous eating spot in the upper Diagonal where the emphasis of its new Catalan cuisine is on small understated dishes with a complexity of flavors. In a coolly minimalist setting of high wooden ceilings, red and black decor, and white walls lined with thin vases—each containing a single red rose—you can enjoy such delicacies as stone bass *suquet* with *trompet,* scallops with figs and Jabugo ham, and mouthwateringly rich desserts that include peach with ginger and fennel. There's also an excellent wine list favoring top vintages from the Rioja and local Penedés vineyards.

Passatge Marimón 9. www.hisop.com. Main courses 25€–32€ ($33–$42). Tasting menu 55€ ($72). AE, DC, MC, V. Mon–Fri 1.30–4pm and 9pm–midnight. Sat 9pm–midnight. Closed Sundays and last 2 weeks in August. Metro: Hospital Clinic.

Moo ★★★ MODERN MEDITERRANEAN The famed Roca brothers first launched their exquisite cuisine at **El Cellar de Can Roca** (p. 283) a Michelin-starred eatery near Girona. Moo, their second restaurant, is located in Barcelona's applauded **Hotel Omm** (p. 108). Service is attentive and efficient, and all dishes, from the organic chicken with olives and mango to monkfish with wild mushrooms, are available at half-size portions, allowing you to create your own *menú de degustación.* You can try the set menu "Joan Roca"—five delightful dishes with wine from Moo's talented sommelier Jordi Paronella. You might start with a molded crescent of foie, followed by a lobster, rose, and licorice curry, and then a perfect filet of wild sea bass on a bed of snow peas and pine nuts. The baby goat roasted in honey and rosemary, resting on a cloud of goat's milk foam, is also hard to resist. For dessert you might choose Bvlgari, a blend of Bergamot cream, lemon sorbet, and *pensamiento* flowers, or a mouth-watering blend of chocolate cake, ginger, and 70% chocolate ice cream.

Rosselló 265. ✆ **93-445-40-00.** www.hotelomm.es. Reservations recommended. Main courses 20€–30€ ($26–$39); Menu "Joan Roca" (with wine pairing) 95€ ($124); midday menu 50€ ($65). AE, DC, MC, V. Daily 1:30–4pm and 8:30–11pm. Metro: Diagonal.

Neichel ★★★ FRENCH/MEDITERRANEAN Alsatian-born owner Jean-Louis Neichel is almost obsessively concerned with gastronomy—the savory presentation of some of the most talked-about preparations of seafood, fowl, and sweets in Spain. Your meal might include a "mosaic" of foie gras with vegetables, strips of salmon marinated in sesame and served with *escabeche* (vinaigrette) sauce, or slices of raw and smoked salmon stuffed with caviar. The prize-winning terrine of sea crab floats on a lavishly decorated bed of cold seafood sauce. Move on to *escalope* of turbot served with *coulis* (purée) of sea urchins, fricassee of Bresse chicken served with spiny lobsters, sea bass with a mousseline of truffles, Spanish milk-fed lamb served with the juice of Boletus mushrooms, or rack of lamb gratinéed in an herb-flavored pastry crust. The selection of European cheeses and the changing array of freshly made desserts are nothing short of spectacular.

Beltrán i Rózpide 1–5. ✆ **93-203-84-08.** www.neichel.es. Reservations required. Main courses 25€–40€ ($33–$52); fixed-price lunch 45€ ($59); tasting menu 60€ ($78). AE, DC, MC, V. Tues–Sat 1:30–3:30pm and 8:30–11pm. Closed Aug. Metro: Palau Reial or María Cristina.

Reno ★ CATALAN/FRENCH   One of the finest and most enduring haute-cuisine restaurants in Barcelona, Reno sits behind sidewalk-to-ceiling windows hung with fine-mesh lace to shelter diners from prying eyes on the octagonal plaza outside. The impeccably mannered staff is formal but not intimidating. Seasonal specialties might include partridge simmered in wine or port sauce, a platter of assorted fish smoked on the premises, hake with anchovy sauce, or filet of sole stuffed with foie gras and truffles or grilled with anchovy sauce. An appetizing array of pastries wheels from table to table on a cart. Dessert might also be crepes flambéed at your table.

Tuset 27. ✆ **93-200-91-29.** Reservations recommended. Main courses 15€–30€ ($20–$39); fixed-price lunch 35€ ($46); tasting menu 50€ ($65). AE, DC, MC, V. Mon–Sat 9–11:30pm; Mon–Fri 1–4pm. Closed Aug. Metro: Diagonal.

MODERATE

Il Giardinetto ★ (Moments) ITALIAN   This eatery, a perennial favorite of the uptown arts crowd, won a major design award when it was opened in 1973, and the "fantasy forest" surroundings haven't dated one iota. It's split into two levels, and the space is dominated by columns with painted branch motifs. The walls are covered with foliage cutouts and the low ceilings sport swirls of pretty pale, green leaves. After taking it all in, curl into one of the teal blue velvet banquettes and survey the menu of classic Italian dishes. You may wish to indulge in one of the heady black or white (when in season) truffle risottos or pastas, or a tuna *carpaccio*. The only slight letdown was dessert: The tiramisu was lacking in both coffee and amaretto flavors, but the sinful "fatty" vanilla ice cream with bitter chocolate sauce more than made up for this lapse. There is a resident pianist in evenings, and the service is old school but not stuffy.

La Granada del Penedès 22. ✆ **93-218-75-36.** www.ilgiardinetto.es. Reservations recommended. Main courses 15€–28€ ($20–$36); fixed-price lunch 20€ ($26). AE, DC, MC, V. Mon–Fri 1:30–4:30pm and 8:30pm–1:30am; Sat 8:30pm–2:30am. Closed Aug. Metro: Diagonal.

L'Olivé ★ CATALAN/MEDITERRANEAN   You assume that this two-floor restaurant is named after the olive that figures so prominently into its cuisine, but actually it's named for the owner, Josep Olivé. The building is designed in a modern Catalan style with walls adorned with reproductions of famous Spanish painters, such as Miró, Dalí, or Picasso. There are sections on both floors where it's possible to have some privacy, and overall the feeling is one of elegance with a touch of intimacy. It's highly unlikely you'll be disappointed by anything on the menu, especially *bacallà a la llauna* (baked salt cod) or *filet de vedella al vi negre al forn* (veal filets cooked in the oven in a red-wine sauce). Monkfish flavored with roasted garlic is a palate pleaser, and you can finish with a *crema catalana* or one of the delicious Catalan pastries.

Balmes 47. ✆ **93-452-19-90.** www.rte-olive.com. Reservations recommended. Main courses 15€– 25€ ($20–$33); *menú completo* 40€ ($52). AE, DC, MC, V. Daily 1–4pm; Mon–Sat 8.30pm–midnight. Metro: Passeig de Gràcia.

Family-Friendly Restaurants

Granja Dulcinea   This longtime favorite cafe/snack bar, at Petrixol 2 ((C) **93-302-68-24**), makes a great refueling stop any time of the day—guaranteed to satisfy any chocoholic. Lots of other sweet treats and drinks are on offer. (See also "Calling All Chocoholics," earlier in this chapter.)

Poble Espanyol (p. 196)   A good introduction to Spanish food. All the restaurants in the "Spanish Village" serve comparable food at comparable prices—let the kids choose what to eat.

La Paradeta (p. 141)   Fish and chips fun: Fish-loving kids get to choose what they want and see it being cooked.

Mesón David (p. 145)   You don't have to worry about them making a noise here; the rest of the patrons and staff are just as ear bursting.

Murivecchi (p. 142)   Friendly, family-run Italian place with plenty of pasta dishes to suit the young ones.

Rosalert ★ CATALAN/SEAFOOD   Situated at the corner of Carrer Napols close to La Sagrada Família, this restaurant has been the domain of Jordi Alert for more than 4 decades. He specializes in seafood, and his fish and crustaceans are grilled on a heated iron plate without any additives. This restaurant has Barcelona's most awesome fish tank, which has tiny octopus, succulent mussels, fat shrimp, squid, fresh oysters, and langoustines. Begin with one of the freshly made tapas, such as salt cod in vinaigrette or fava beans laced with garlic and virgin olive oil. Your best bet might be the *parrillada* (assorted fish and shellfish from the grill). A delicious no-frills choice is *rodaballo a la plancha* (turbot cooked on the grill with potatoes and fresh mushrooms).

Diagonal 301. (C) **93-207-19-48.** Reservations recommended. Main courses 12€–25€ ($16–$33); fixed-price lunch 20€ ($26); tasting menu 48€ ($62). AE, DC, MC, V. Tues–Sat noon–5pm and 8:30pm–2am. Sun noon–6pm. Closed Aug. Metro: Verdaguer or Sagrada Família.

Tragaluz ★ MEDITERRANEAN   This is the flagship restaurant of the city's most respected group of restaurateurs. It offers three very contemporary-looking dining rooms on separate floors, scattered with eclectic pieces of art and very clever lighting. Menu items are derived from fresh ingredients that vary with the season. Depending on the month of your visit, you might find terrine of duck liver, Santurce-style hake (with garlic and herbs), filet of sole stuffed with red peppers, or beef tenderloin in a Rioja wine sauce. One of the best desserts is a semi-soft slice of deliberately underbaked chocolate cake. Diners seeking low-fat dishes will find solace here, as will vegetarians. The vegetables served are the best and freshest in the market that day. Downstairs you will find Tragarapíd, a faster, more casual version of what's upstairs, and across the road is an enormously popular Japanese restaurant that is directed by the same group. The Tragaluz chefs are adept at taking local products and turning them into flavorful, carefully prepared dishes.

Passatge de la Concepció 5. (C) **93-487-06-21.** www.grupotragaluz.com. Reservations recommended. Main courses 18€–25€ ($23–$33); fixed-price lunch 25€ ($33); tasting menu 55€ ($72). AE, DC, MC, V. Sun–Wed 1:30–4pm and 8:30pm–midnight; Thurs–Sat 1:30–4pm and 8:30pm–1am. Metro: Diagonal.

El Caballito Blanco SEAFOOD/INTERNATIONAL   This Barcelona standby is famous for seafood and popular with the locals. The fluorescent-lit dining area does not offer much atmosphere, but the food is good, varied, and relatively inexpensive (unless you order lobster or other costly shellfish). The "Little White Horse," in the Passeig de Gràcia area, features a huge selection, including *lubina santurce* (sea bass), *rape* (monkfish), *mejillones marinera* (mussels marinara), and *gambas ajillo* (shrimp with garlic). If you don't want fish, try the *chuletas de cordero a la plancha* (grilled lamb cutlets). Several different pâtés and salads are offered.

Mallorca 196. ℰ **93-453-96-16.** Main courses 9€–30€ ($12–$39). AE, DC, MC, V. Tues–Sun 1–4pm; Tues–Sat 8:45–11pm. Closed Aug. Metro: Hospital Clinic or Diagonal.

SNACKS, TAPAS & DRINKS

Bar Turò TAPAS/CATALAN   Located in an affluent residential neighborhood north of the Old Town, Bar Turò serves some of the best tapas in town. In summer you can sit outside or retreat to the narrow confines of the bar. You select from about 20 kinds of tapas, including *ensalada rusa* (Russian salad), *calamares romana* (rings of fried squid), and *jamón Serrano* (mountain ham).

Tenor Viñas 1. ℰ **93-200-69-53.** Tapas 2.50€–12€ ($3.25–$16); main courses 8€–18€ ($10–$23). MC, V. Mon–Sat 8:30am–midnight; Sun 10am–4pm. Closed weekends in Aug. Metro: Hospital Clinic.

Casa Alfonso TAPAS   Spaniards love their mountain ham, which comes from many different regions. The best of the best is *jamón Jabugo,* the only one sold at this traditional establishment. Entire hams hang from steel braces. They're taken down, carved, and trimmed before you into paper-thin slices. This particular form of cured ham, generically called *jamón Serrano,* comes from pigs fed acorns in Huelva, in deepest Andalusia. Devotees of all things porcine will ascend to piggy-flavored heaven. It also serves salads and grilled meat dishes.

Roger de Llúria 6. ℰ **93-301-97-83.** Tapas 4.50€–12€ ($5.85–$16); tasting menu 18€ ($23). AE, DC, MC, V. Mon–Tues 9am–midnight; Wed–Sat 9am–1am. Metro: Urquinaona.

Casa Tejada TAPAS   Covered with rough stucco and decorated with hanging hams, Casa Tejada (established in 1964) offers some of the best tapas. Arranged behind a glass display case, they include such dishes as marinated fresh tuna, German-style potato salad, ham salad, and five preparations of squid (including one that's stuffed). For variety, quantity, and quality, this place is hard to beat.

Tenor Viñas 3. ℰ **93-200-73-41.** Tapas 3€–17€ ($3.90–$22). MC, V. Daily 7am–1:30am. Closed Aug 8–21. Metro: Hospital Clinic.

La Bodegueta TAPAS   Founded in 1940, this old wine tavern is one of the more authentic options in this ritzy boulevard. It specializes in Catalan sausage *(botifarra),* salamis, and cheeses. Wash them all down with draft *vermut* or inexpensive Spanish wines from the barrel. It's loud, no-nonsense, and a favorite with students.

Rambla de Catalunya 100. ℰ **93-215-48-94.** Tapas 2.50€–15€ ($3.25–$20). No credit cards. Mon–Sat 8am–2am; Sun 6:30pm–1am. Closed Aug 8–22. Metro: Diagonal.

TapaÇ24 ★ TAPAS   Run by adventurous new-wave chef Carles Abellán, this is one of the city's newer and more interesting tapas bars. It seems outwardly traditional, but it turns out fun and unique items like "McFoie Burgers" and *tostadas con trufas* (truffle toast), alongside delicious homemade *croquetas de jamón* (ham croquettes), *albondigas* (meatballs), *callos* (tripe), and *rabo de buey* (oxtail) tidbits. It also serves great breakfasts.

Diputació 269. (℡) **93-488-09-77.** www.carlesabellan.com/tapac24. Tapas 4€–12€ ($5.20–$16). AE, DC, MC, V. Mon–Sat 8am–midnight. Metro: Passeig de Gràcia.

---

8 GRÀCIA

EXPENSIVE

Botafumeiro ★★★ SEAFOOD Although the competition is strong, this classic *marisquería* consistently puts Barcelona's finest seafood on the table. Much of the allure comes from the attention of the white-jacketed staff. International businesspeople often rendezvous here, and the King of Spain is sometimes a patron. The establishment prides itself on its fresh- and saltwater fish, clams, mussels, lobster, crayfish, scallops, and several varieties of crustaceans—such as *percebes* (goose barnacles)—that you may have never seen before. Stored live in holding tanks or in enormous crates near the entrance, many of the creatures are flown in daily from Galicia, homeland of owner Moncho Neira. With the 100 or so fish dishes, the menu lists only four or five meat dishes, including three kinds of steak. The wine list offers a wide array of *cavas* from Catalonia and highly drinkable choices from Galicia, in particular the highly regarded *Albariño* white.

Gran de Gràcia 81. (℡) **93-218-42-30.** Reservations recommended for dining rooms. Main courses 24€–45€ ($31–$59). AE, DC, MC, V. Daily 1pm–1am. Metro: Fontana.

Coure ★★ CATALAN/INTERNATIONAL The specialty in this charming and elegant restaurant is chef/owner Albert Ventura's superb tasting menu. Be daring and try, for example, the *carpaccio de pies de cerdo,* a unique blend of pig's trotters with oysters which has captivated many visitors, or the *tuna con sabor de lima y berengena ahumado* (fresh tuna flavored with lime and served with smoked eggplant). For dessert, I recommend *helado de eucalipto* (eucalyptus ice cream).

Pasaje Marimón 20. (℡) **93-200-75-32.** Main courses 20€–30€ ($26–$39); tasting menu 45€ ($59). V. Tues–Sat 1:30–3:30pm and 9–11pm. Closed Easter Week and Aug 3–10. Metro: Hospital Clinic.

Jean Luc Figueras ★★★ CATALAN This hip Gràcia restaurant is located in a town house that was once the studio of fashion designer Balenciaga. Even if food critics narrowed the list of Barcelona restaurants down to five, the chef and owner, Jean Luc Figueras, would likely appear on the list. The setting is modern and refined, and the cookery is both traditional and innovative, as Figueras stamps every dish with his own personal touch. Figueras is a seeker of the finest raw materials on the Barcelona market, and his menu is adjusted to take advantage of the best produce in any season. The emphasis is on fresh seafood, although his meat dishes are also sublime. Fried prawn and ginger-flecked pasta in a mango and mustard sauce would make the gods weep, and sea bass with cod and blood sausage is no less brilliant. Your tastes buds will go into orbit if you're wise enough to select such nouvelle-inspired dishes as shrimp with a velvety-smooth and golden pumpkin cream sauce, or the pork with a zesty goat cheese enlivened with peach honey. The desserts are homemade and inevitably sumptuous, and I took particular delight in the seven varieties of freshly made bread.

Santa Teresa 10. (℡) **93-415-28-77.** Reservations required. Main courses 25€–50€ ($33–$65); tasting menu 90€ ($117). AE, DC, MC, V. Mon–Sat 1:30–3:30pm and 8:30–11:30pm. Metro: Diagonal.

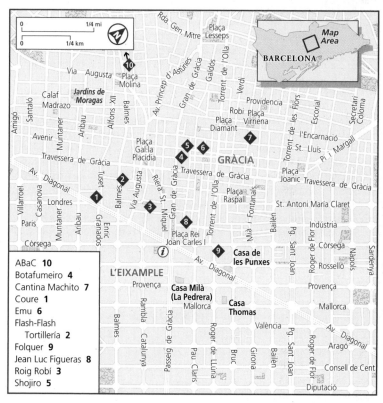

0   1/4 mi
0   1/4 km

Map Area

BARCELONA

L'EIXAMPLE

Casa Milà (La Pedrera)

Casa Thomas

Casa de les Punxes

ABaC **10**
Botafumeiro **4**
Cantina Machito **7**
Coure **1**
Emu **6**
Flash-Flash
    Tortillería **2**
Folquer **9**
Jean Luc Figueras **8**
Roig Robí **3**
Shojiro **5**

Roig Robí ★ INTERNATIONAL   This restaurant—in Catalan, the name means "ruby red" (the color of a perfectly aged Rioja)—serves excellent food from an imaginative kitchen. Although I'm not as excited about this restaurant as I once was, it still remains one of the city's most dependable choices. Order an aperitif at the L-shaped oak bar, and then head down a long corridor to a pair of flower-filled dining rooms. In warm weather, glass doors open onto a verdant walled courtyard. Seafood specialties include *bacalao a la "llauna"* (cod served with broccoli purée) and *rape y almejas con cebolla confitada* (monkfish with clams and onion confit). A mouthwatering dish is *tartare de lubina y langostinos con caviar de trucha* (sea bass and crayfish tartare with trout caviar).

Séneca 20. ✆ **93-218-92-22.** www.roigrobi.com. Reservations required. Main courses 28€–45€ ($36–$59); tasting menu 65€ ($85); fixed-price menu 48€ ($62). AE, DC, MC, V. Mon–Fri 1:30–4pm; Mon–Sat 9–11:30pm. Closed Aug 8–21. Metro: Diagonal.

Shojiro ★ ASIAN FUSION   With Japanese restaurants now the norm in Barcelona, it was only a matter of time before Nippon cuisine was fused with the local one. This quirky but deceptively brightly lit and functional-looking restaurant, led by Shojiro Ochi, a native of Japan who arrived in Barcelona in 1979, does just that. Ochi presents

Eating Alfresco

Finding a great terrace to sit out on in Barcelona is easier said than done. There are literally hundreds of sidewalk cafes where you can drink your cappuccino to the roar of passing traffic, and tourist-filled plazas lined with restaurants which serve the same old microwaved paellas. But a tucked-away garden, a tranquil terrace, or a hideaway by the sea—that's another matter altogether.

The **Café de L'Academia,** Calle Lledó 1 (℃ **93-319-82-53;** p. 133), is located on the one of the prettiest squares in Barcelona, Plaça Sant Just. Presided over by a church of the same name, it is reputedly Barcelona's oldest, and according to lore, if you believe your life to be in mortal danger you can still make a legally binding will at the altar with a friend as a witness. It was also on this square that the Romans executed the first Christians. Ghosts of the past aside, today it is one of the most peaceful and unspoiled plaças in the Old City. In the Born, the **Tèxtil Café,** Calle Montcada 12 (℃ **93-268-25-98**), is an oasis of calm enclosed within the courtyard of an 18th-century palace. Providing you're not in a hurry (service is notoriously laid-back) it's an idyllic place in the inner city to fuel up on tea, coffee, and hearty, wholesome lunches in the shade of large, white parasols or the warmth of outdoor gas fires in winter.

Barcelona's seafront has restaurant terraces aplenty, but for something a little more clandestine, continue along to the Parc del Port Olímpic, which straddles two busy highways. Here, sunk from view and traffic noise, is the gorgeous **Anfiteatro,** Av. Litoral 36 (℃ **65-969-53-45;** p. 160)—a smart restaurant serving creative Mediterranean dishes with a spacious terrace that wraps

his goodies to you in set-price four- and five-course menus. These delectable morsels include *bonito* (a type of A-grade tuna) preserved in a Catalan *escabeche,* tuna with a sherry reduction, or duck's breast with shitake mushrooms. Desserts include more unconventional delights such as a foie bonbon and ostrich *tataki.*

Ros de Olano 11. ℃ **93-415-65-48.** Fixed-price lunch 16€ ($21); fixed-price dinner 46€ ($60). AE, DC, MC, V. Mon–Sat 1:30–3:30pm; Tues–Sat 9pm–12:30am. Metro: Fontana or Joanic.

MODERATE

Emu ★ (Finds) PAN-ASIAN/THAI   Australian owners Sophie and Michael opened this Pan-Asian restaurant after deciding they couldn't find anywhere in town that provided these dishes to their satisfaction. Today, Thai food lovers flock here in increasing numbers as the word gets around. Try the spicy Thai chicken; the Malaysian *laksa,* which has red chili peppers floating in creamy coconut soup; or the Vietnamese spring rolls and Indonesian satays. Complimentary desserts include banana split with ice cream and caramel, and there's a unique selection of Aussie-only wines and beer. This is a small place with only seven tables, so be sure to reserve early.

Guilleries 17. ℃ **93-218-45-02.** Main courses 12€–16€ ($16–$21); tasting menu 32€ ($42). No credit cards. Mon–Thurs 1–4pm and 7pm–2am; Fri–Sat 1–4pm and 7pm–3am. Metro: Fontana.

around an ornamental pool. Another way to escape the crowds is to get up onto the rooftops at **La Miranda del Museu,** Museu d'Història de Catalunya, Plaça Pau Vila 3 (© **93-225-50-07**), which has fabulous views over the yachts in Port Vell. Frustratingly, the terrace is for drinks only, so go in time for an aperitif before lunch or linger over coffee afterward.

Heading a little further out and halfway up the hill to Montjuïc, **La Font del Gat,** Passeig Santa Madrona 28 (© **93-289-04-04**), is a secret garden and lunch spot chiseled out of the mountainside beneath the famed Joan Miró Foundation. The further out you go, the prettier the surroundings, and if it's real tranquillity you're seeking (not to mention exclusivity), the restaurants in the suburbs are what really shine. In Horta, **Can Travi Nou,** Jorge Manrique, Parc de la Vall d'Hebron (© **93-428-04-34**), is a converted 14th-century farmhouse with sprawling grounds, two or three ample terraces, and gardens for strolling. It's great for long Sunday lunches or evenings under the stars, and serves decent, if pricey, roast meats, fish dishes, and paella.

Finally, if you're looking to treat yourself (or somebody else), head for the Restaurant **L'Orangerie,** Gran Hotel La Florida, Carretera de Vallvidrera al Tibidabo 83–93 (© **93-259-30-00**). This fabulous eating spot is situated on the highest peak of the Collserola with stunning views over Barcelona, and its scented gardens and terraces make it one of the most spectacular dining destinations in the city.

Flash-Flash Tortillería (Moments) OMELETS/HAMBURGERS   Hamburgers, steaks, salads, and over 70 types of tortillas are served up in a pop-art setting of funky black-and-white murals and white leather banquettes. It's completely authentic; Flash-Flash was opened in 1970 and the interior hasn't been altered since. The Twiggy-like model adorning the walls was the wife of Leopoldo Pomés, a well-known fashion photographer of the time and part owner. Decor aside, the food is very good; the tortillas fly out fresh and fluffy and the bunless burgers are some of the best in town. It's a favorite with uptown business types, some of whom have been coming here since the place opened. Great news for nicotine-allergic diners: It's one of the city's few 100% nonsmoking locales!

Granada de Penedès 25. © **93-237-09–90.** Reservations recommended. Main courses 10€–25€ ($13–$33). AE, DC, MC, V. Daily 1pm–1:30am. FGC: Gràcia.

Folquer (Finds) CATALAN/SPANISH   With its bright sunny decor and animated—mainly Catalan—clientele, Folquer has an arty-bohemian feel. Rather secretively located at the southern end of Gràcia, it's a welcoming spot with inventive tasty dishes that make use of first-rate ingredients. There are two particularly good-value lunchtime menus: the standard and the "Executive." Regional dishes, meanwhile, dominate the a la carte list. Try their pungent *suquet de pop* (octopus stew).

Torrent de l'Olla 3. 🕐 **93-217-43-95.** Main courses 16€–24€ ($21–$31); set lunch 16€–25€ ($21–$33); Executive lunch 19€ ($25). AE, DC, MC, V. Mon–Sat 9–11:30pm; Mon–Fri 1–4pm. Closed Sun and last 2 weeks of Aug. Metro: Diagonal or Verdaguer.

INEXPENSIVE

Cantina Machito MEXICAN   This is generally considered to be the best Mexican restaurant in Barcelona. It's hard to get a table, especially when the cinema crowd from next door rolls in, but it's worth the wait. What they serve is far from the rudimentary Tex-Mex fare. The tacos and tortillas and a tangy guacamole are all present and correct, but so is a chicken mole and *sopa malpeña,* a warming soup of chickpeas, tomato, and chicken, plus an unusual lime and tequila mousse for dessert. The margaritas are renowned, as are their parties on Mexican national days and fiestas.

Torrijos 47. 🕐 **93-217-34-14.** Reservations recommended. Main courses 8€–15€ ($10–$20). MC, V. Daily 1–4:30pm and 7pm–1:30am. Metro: Fontana or Joanic.

9 BARCELONETA & VILA OLÍMPICA

EXPENSIVE

Anfiteatro ★ (Moments) MEDITERRANEAN   In spite of the fashionable pedigree, it's amazing how this restaurant manages to elude so many—perhaps because it's tucked away on an underground level of a boulevard in the Olympic Village. Designed by the studio of Oriol Bohigas, one of the city's leading architects who is also responsible for the Olympic Village itself, it features rationalist lines that are softened by an abundance of mosaics, and a central pond surrounded by tables. Within this unique setting of urban romanticism you can enjoy wild sea bass with grapes and a port sauce or cuttlefish and crab ravioli. If there is room for dessert, go for the mascarpone and vanilla ice cream with a mango purée.

Parc del Port Olímpic, Av. Litoral 37 (opposite Calle Rosa Sensat). 🕐 **65-969-53-45.** Reservations recommended on weekends. Main courses 16€–35€ ($21–$46); fixed-price lunch menu 35€ ($46); tasting menu 40€ ($52) and 60€ ($78). AE, MC, V. Tues–Sun 1–4pm; Tues–Sat 8:30pm–midnight. Closed Easter week. Metro: Port Olímpic.

Can Costa ★ SEAFOOD   Established in the late 1930s, Can Costa is one of the oldest seafood restaurants in this seafaring town. It has two busy dining rooms, a practiced staff, and an outdoor terrace—although a warehouse blocks the view of the harbor. Fresh seafood prepared according to traditional recipes rules the menu, which includes the best *chipirones* (baby squid) in town, sautéed in a flash so that it has a nearly grilled flavor. A long-standing chef's specialty is *fideuà de peix,* a relative of the classic Valencian shellfish paella, with noodles instead of rice. The yummy desserts are made fresh daily.

Passeig de Joan de Borbó 70. 🕐 **93-221-59-03.** www.cancosta.com. Reservations recommended. Main courses 16€–42€ ($21–$55). MC, V. Daily 12:30–4pm; Thurs–Tues 8–11:30pm. Metro: Barceloneta.

Can Solé ★ CATALAN   Located in Barceloneta's harbor area, Can Solé still honors the traditions of this former fishing village. Many of the seafood joints here are too touristy for our tastes, but this one is authentic and delivers good value. The decor is rustic and a bit raffish, with wine barrels, lots of noise, and excellent food. Begin with the sweet tiny clams or the cod cakes. *Langostinos* (king prawns) are an exquisite if expensive favorite, and everything is aromatically perfumed with fresh garlic. You might also sample one

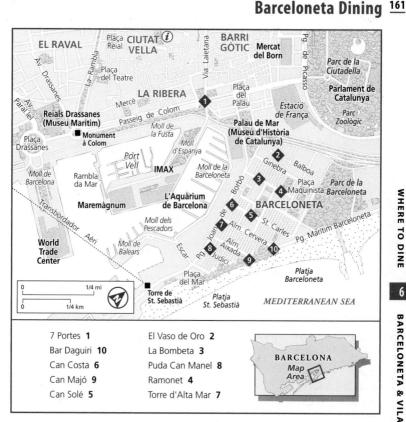

El Raval | Plaça Reial | CIUTAT (i) VELLA | BARRI GÒTIC | Mercat del Born | Parc de la Ciutadella

Plaça del Teatre — La Rambla — Av. Drassanes — Av. Paral·lel — Merce — Pg. de Picasso — LA RIBERA — Plaça del Palau — Parlament de Catalunya

Reials Drassanes (Museu Marítim) — Passeig de Colom — Moll de la Fusta — Palau de Mar (Museu d'Història de Catalunya) — Estació de França — Parc Zoològic — Monument á Colom

Plaça Drassanes — Port Vell — Moll d'Espanya — IMAX — Moll de la Barceloneta — Ginebra — Balboa — Plaça Maquinista — Parc de la Barceloneta

Moll de Barcelona — Rambla da Mar — Borbó — Plaça Maquinista — BARCELONETA

Transbordador — Maremàgnum — L'Aquàrium de Barcelona — Moll dels Pescadors — Joan de Borbó — St. Carles — Pg. Marítim Barceloneta

World Trade Center — Aeri — Moll de Balears — Escar — Alm. Cervera — Alm. Aixada — Judici

Pg. Joan de Borbó — Plaça del Mar — Torre de St. Sebastià — Platja St. Sebastià — Platja Barceloneta — MEDITERRANEAN SEA

0 — 1/4 mi — 0 — 1/4 km

WHERE TO DINE

6

BARCELONETA & VILA OLÍMPICA

7 Portes **1**
Bar Daguiri **10**
Can Costa **6**
Can Majó **9**
Can Solé **5**

El Vaso de Oro **2**
La Bombeta **3**
Puda Can Manel **8**
Ramonet **4**
Torre d'Alta Mar **7**

BARCELONA Map Area

---

of the seafood dishes such as *bacalao Serrallo* (cod with *romesco* sauce and gratinéed potatoes). Desserts are so good they're worth saving room for, especially the orange pudding or the praline ice cream.

Carrer Sant Carles 4. ℭ **93-221-50-12.** www.restaurantcansole.com. Reservations required. Main courses 10€–55€ ($13–$72). AE, DC, MC, V. Tues–Sun 1:30–4pm; Tues–Sat 8:30–11pm. Metro: Barceloneta.

Els Pescadors ★★ SEAFOOD This is generally acknowledged to be one of the best fish restaurants in Barcelona. The fact that it's located slightly out of the main drag, in the working-class beachside suburb of Poble Nou, doesn't stop foodies from making the trip. The restaurant is divided into two *ambientes:* one is old school—with marble tabletops and wooden beams—while the other is modern Mediterranean. But no one comes to gawk at the surroundings. The sole objective here is to enjoy the freshest seafood in Barcelona, cooked in classical ways with surprising touches. Local *gambas* (prawns) are served with steaming garbanzos (chickpeas), or a baked *(al horno)* fish, such as *lubina* (sea bass) or *dorada* (bream)—whatever has been trawled in that day—is served.

Plaça Prim 1. ℭ **93-225-20-18.** www.elspescadors.com. Reservations recommended on weekends. Main courses 15€–50€ ($20–$65). AE, DC, MC, V. Daily 1–3:45pm and 8:30pm–midnight. Closed Easter week. Metro: Poble Nou.

7 Portes ★ (Moments) CATALAN   Festive and elegant, 7 Portes has been around since 1836, making it one of the oldest and most prestigious restaurants in Barcelona. Pretty much anybody who is anybody has dined here over the years. While these days it's more touristy than aristocratic, there is still enough authentic charm left in the decor (and patrons) to make it well worth the visit. The white-aproned staff members are constantly on the go, which in some ways makes it feel like an upmarket canteen. There is nothing slapdash about the food, though: Regional dishes include fresh herring with onions and potatoes, different paella daily (sometimes with shellfish, for example, or with rabbit), and a wide array of fresh fish, expertly deboned and skinned at the table. You might order succulent oysters or an herb-laden stew of black beans with pork or white beans with sausage. Portions are enormous. The restaurant's name means "Seven Doors," and it really does have seven doors, underneath some charming porticoes that are typical to this portside pocket of Barcelona.

Passeig d'Isabel II 14. ℂ **93-319-30-33.** www.7portes.com. Reservations required. Main courses 18€–35€ ($23–$46). AE, DC, MC, V. Daily 1pm–1am. Metro: Barceloneta.

Torre d'Alta Mar MEDITERRANEAN   Alta Mar is sort of a mile-high gastro club. Its unique setting is the 75m-high (246-ft.) Torre de Sant Sebastián, one of the three towers that serves the port-crossing, tourist-carrying cable car (p. 197). But don't worry about rubbing shoulders with backpackers when you enter this exclusive eatery; patrons are whisked up in a private high-tech glass elevator to be greeted by a simply breathtaking 360-degree view of the city and sea. Once your jaw finally stops dropping and you are settled in the plush decor, you can dine in style from a predominantly fish menu that includes such inventions as a *merluza* (hake), porcini and artichoke stir-fry, stewed *rape* (monkfish) in *romesco* sauce, or *rodaballo* (turbot) with pumpkin ravioli.

Passeig Don Joan Borbó Comte 88. ℂ **93-221-00-07.** www.torredealtamar.com. Reservations recommended. Main courses 22€–38€ ($29–$49). Daily 1–3:30pm and 8:45–11:30pm. Metro: Barceloneta.

MODERATE

Agua ★ MEDITERRANEAN   It bustles, it's hip, and it serves well-prepared fish and shellfish in a hyper-modern setting overlooking the beach. A terrace beckons anyone who wants a close view of the sea, but if a chilly wind is blowing, you can retreat into the big-windowed blue-and-yellow dining room and, amid display cases showing the catch of the day, order heaping portions of meats and fish to be grilled over an open fire. Favorite choices include *pollo* (chicken), *pez espada* (swordfish), *gambas* (prawns), and an especially succulent version of *calamares rellenos* (stuffed squid.) Most of them are served with as little culinary fanfare and as few sauces as possible, allowing the freshness and flavor of the raw ingredients to shine through the chargrilled coatings. Risottos, some of them studded with fresh *almejas* (clams) and herbs, are usually winners, with many versions suitable for vegetarians. The only problem here is its popularity; make sure you book on the weekends.

Passeig Marítim de la Barceloneta 30 (Vila Olímpica). ℂ **93-225-12-72.** www.aguadeltragaluz.com. Reservations recommended. Main courses 12€–25€ ($16–$33). AE, DC, MC, V. Daily 1:30–4pm and 8:30pm–midnight (until 1am Fri–Sat). Metro: Ciutadella–Vila Olímpica.

Arola ★ CATALAN/SPANISH   Blessed with two Michelin stars, Catalan chef Sergi Arola is one of the rising young stars of Spain's culinary world. The setting for this, his first restaurant in Barcelona (the other, La Broche, is in Madrid), is the luxury Hotel Arts in the Olympic Village. Amid a quirky, pop-art decor of purple and lime green, Arola

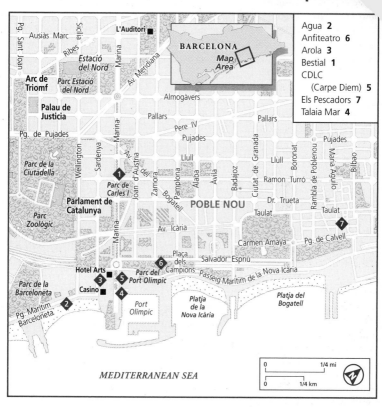

Agua **2**
Anfiteatro **6**
Arola **3**
Bestial **1**
CDLC
  (Carpe Diem) **5**
Els Pescadors **7**
Talaia Mar **4**

starts you off with hot or cold *picas* (literally, "nibbles") that may range from simple artichoke hearts with garlic and parsley or asparagus spears on a bed of romesco sauce, to *tacos de lubina* (small delicious chunks of sea bass) or *patatas bravas* cut and arranged on the plate to look like dozens of tiny female breasts. Main courses include Mediterranean standards with a touch of Arola magic: steamed *mejillones* (mussels) with citrus juice and saffron, Gorgonzola cheese croquettes, grilled *gambas* (prawns) with cold potato cream, and *lubina* (sea bass) with an emulsion of watercress, to name just a few. The dessert of goat's cheese, macadamia nuts, tomato jam, and quince cream should convince you of his talent.

Hotel Arts, Marina 19–21. ℰ **93-483-80-90.** www.arola-arts.com. Reservations required. Main courses 10€–32€ ($13–$42); tasting menu 50€ ($65). AE, DC, MC, V. Tues 8:30–11pm; Wed 1:30–3:30pm; Thurs–Fri 1:30–3:30pm and 8:30–11:30pm; Sat–Sun 2–4pm and 8:30–11pm. Closed Jan (month closed can vary each year). Metro: Ciutadella–Vila Olímpica.

Bestial MEDITERRANEAN/ITALIAN   A member of the famed Tragaluz group, this modern Mediterranean eatery brings some well-needed class to the gastronomically pedestrian Olympic Marina, and the menu has been designed as an Italian-influenced

ozens of paella restaurants in the immediate vicinity. A typical tasty
s *caprese* salad of plump red tomato slices with *buffala* mozzarella fol-
s portion of seared tuna with black-olive risotto. The outdoor setting,
zones of noise-absorbing wooden decking and oversize umbrellas, is
functional), though the interior of the dining room has the discon-
me imaginary sci-fi bus station (a hangover, presumably, from its earlier
days as Planet Hollywood).

Ramón Trias Fargas 30 (Vila Olímpica). ℰ **93-224-04-07.** www.bestialdeltragaluz.com. Main courses 9€–20€ ($12–$26). AE, DC, MC, V. Mon–Fri 1:30–4pm and 8:30pm–midnight (until 1am on Fri); Sat 1:30–5pm and 8:30pm–1am; Sun 1:30–5pm and 8:30pm–midnight. Metro: Ciutadella–Vila Olímpica.

Can Majó ★★ SEAFOOD   Set close to the harbor, this is one of the finest seafood restaurants in Barcelona. In summer a terrace table here is as desirable a place to eat as anywhere in the port. The interior decor, with its painting-lined walls, is in an inviting rustic-tavern style, and the staff is hospitable and friendly, though service is sometimes rushed. Seafood is the thing here, and the restaurant is renowned for its *veieras* (scallops), *ostras* (oysters), and wide range of Mediterranean and Atlantic fish, all delivered fresh that morning. Now into its fourth decade, the restaurant still serves as delicious a *bullabesa de mariscos* (shellfish bouillabaisse) as you'll find in the area. Also very good are the *calamares salteados* (sautéed squid) and *bacalao* (cod) served in a savory green sauce with little baby clams in their shells.

Almirall Aixada 23. ℰ **93-221-54-55.** www.canmajo.es. Reservations required. Main courses 14€–35€ ($18–$46). AE, DC, MC, V. Tues–Sun 1–4pm; Tues–Sat 8:30–11:30pm. Metro: Barceloneta.

Can Ramonet ★ SEAFOOD   Since 1763, this good but pricey restaurant has been serving a large variety of fresh seafood in a Catalan-style villa near the seaport. The front room, with stand-up tables for seafood, tapas, beer, and regional wine, is often crowded, and in the two dining rooms you can choose from a variety of marine dishes such as shrimp, hake, or monkfish. Other delights include pungent anchovies, grilled mushrooms, black rice, braised artichokes, tortilla with spinach and beans, and mussels "from the beach." A new branch, El Nou Ramonet, with similar standards of cuisine and service, has opened at nearby Calle Carbonell 5 (ℰ **93-268-33-13**).

Carrer Maquinista 17. ℰ **93-319-60-64.** www.elnouramonet.com. Reservations recommended. Main courses 12€–28€ ($16–$36). DC, MC, V. Daily noon–midnight. Metro: Barceloneta.

CDLC (Carpe Diem) MEDITERRANEAN FUSION   Before its nightly transformation into a club for *gente guapa* (beautiful people), CDLC functions as a regular quality restaurant. Rather than the food or impeccable service, the attraction here is its sea-facing terrace. Not that the cuisine, with its strong Thai and Japanese influence, is in any way unacceptable, but true foodies may be suspicious of the fact that a plate of sushi can make it to your table in just under 30 seconds. Perhaps better stick to the lunchtime fare, which includes very reasonably priced salads, sandwiches, and burgers. The wine list includes some offerings priced to impress (you could, if money were no object, treat your date to a bottle of French Cristal champagne or Saint Emilion Cheval Blanc), but usually a far more affordable Spanish Albariño white or Rioja red more than suffices.

Passeig Marítim 32. ℰ **93-224-04-70.** www.cdlcbarcelona.com. Reservations required. Main courses 12€–25€ ($16–$33); fixed-price lunch 18€ ($23). AE, DC, MC, V. Daily noon–3am. Metro: Ciutadella–Vila Olímpica.

Puda Can Manel ★ MEDITERRANEAN/SPANISH   One of the more annoying
aspects of walking down Barceloneta's main boulevard is that waiters incessantly try to
coax you into their often overpriced and ordinary outdoor restaurants. The reason none
of this goes on at Puda Can Manel is that it's both a genuine locale and a considerable
cut above the others along this touristy stretch. On Sunday afternoons you'll see locals
waiting patiently for a table while its neighbors remain empty. They are lining up for
succulent, tasty paellas and *fideuàs* (which replace rice for thin noodles), rich *arroz negre*
(rice cooked in squid ink), and *calamares* fried to perfection, all at excellent prices considering the overall standard.

Passeig Don Joan Borbó Comte 60. ✆ **93-221-50-13.** Reservations required. Main courses 10€–24€
($13–$31). AE, DC, MC, V. Tues–Sun 1–4pm and 7–11pm. Metro: Barceloneta.

Talaia Mar ★★ MEDITERRANEAN   This is the finest and most innovative restaurant at Olympic Port, thanks to the sterling efforts of chef Javier Planes. His highly savory
dishes are elegantly inventive, and his set *festival gastronómico* menu may include dishes like
tuna tartare with guacamole and salmon eggs or brochettes of lobster. Fresh fish arrives
from the market daily and two of his top seafood specialties are *merluza al vapor* (steamed
hake) in a balsamic reduction and *lubina a la plancha con gambas* (grilled sea bass with
shrimp) flavored with asparagus juice. The increasingly rare black truffle also appears in
some of his smooth and velvety risottos, and the roasted rack of lamb is excellent.

Marina 16. ✆ **93-221-90-90.** Reservations required. Main courses 19€–28€ ($25–$36); fixed-price menu
55€ ($72). AE, DC, MC, V. Tues–Sun 1–4pm and 8pm–midnight. Metro: Ciutadella–Vila Olímpica.

SNACKS, TAPAS & DRINKS

Bar Daguiri CAFE   This bar-cafe with a bohemian vibe is right on the beach, an enviable location for many a restaurateur. It serves up light meals such as salads, dips, and
sandwiches, plus coffee and drinks, to a reggae beat. The service can be irritatingly inept,
but it's all part of the laid-back beach culture in this neck of the woods. A plus is the free
Internet access—bring in your laptop and they will wire you up, and there is free live gig
(mainly jazz and Latin) music on Thursday evenings. The large selection of daily foreign
newspapers is also a welcome touch.

Grau i Torras 59. ✆ **93-221-51-09.** Snacks 8€–12€ ($10–$16). MC, V. Daily 10am–midnight. Metro: Barceloneta.

El Vaso de Oro ★ TAPAS   This is a very good Barceloneta tapas bar that also makes
its own beer. Inside, the place is ridiculously narrow, making it a challenge not to elbow
your neighbor as you raise your glass. Most people consider this part of the fun, though,
as they tuck into a juicy *solomillo* (sirloin steak) served with *pimientos del padrón* (miniature green peppers), delicately light *croquetas de jamón* (ham croquettes), or one of the
varied shellfish and seafood salads. If you are on a budget, watch what you eat, as the
portions here are quite small, and the bill tends to add up unexpectedly.

Balboa 6. ✆ **93-319-90-98.** Tapas 4.50€–15€ ($5.85–$20). MC, V. Daily 8am–midnight. Metro: Barceloneta.

La Bombeta ★ TAPAS   This place is a real slice of local life and one of the best tapas
bars in the city. It looks like a slightly modernized version of a taverna, and its house
specialty is *bombas,* deep-fried balls of fluffy mashed potato served with a spicy *brava*
sauce. Other tapas include succulent mussels, either steamed or with a marinara sauce;
giant grilled prawns; plates of paper-thin Serrano ham; and small chunks of deep-fried

> ## (Moments) A Wine Taster's Haven
>
> There are few better ways of enjoying a hedonistic afternoon of food and wine than on the street terrace of **La Vinya del Senyor,** Plaça Santa María 5 (© **93-310-33-79**), where the view is dominated by the glorious Gothic facade of Santa María del Mar. The outstanding wine list includes 13 Priorats, 31 Riojas, and more than a dozen vintages of the legendary Vega Sicilia. In all, there are more than 300 wines and selected *cavas,* sherries, and *moscatells,* and the list is constantly rotated so you can always expect some new surprise on the *carte.* If you don't want a bottle, you'll find some two dozen wines offered by the glass, including a sublime 1994 Jané Ventura Cabernet Sauvignon. To go with your wine, tantalizing tapas are served, including walnut rolls drizzled in olive oil, cured Iberian ham, and French cheese. Tapas cost from 3€ to 8€ ($3.90–$10). American Express, Diners Club, MasterCard, and Visa are accepted. Hours are Tuesday through Saturday from noon to 1:30am and Sunday from noon to midnight. Metro: Jaume I or Barceloneta.

calamari called *rabas.* Needless to say, when washed down with a jug of their excellent in-house sangria, this is a highly satisfying meal in itself.

Maquinista 3. © **93-319-94-45.** Tapas 4.50€–14€ ($5.85–$18). MC, V. Thurs–Tues 10am–midnight. Metro: Barceloneta.

10 BARRIO ALTO

MODERATE/EXPENSIVE

El Mató de Pedralbes   Mató is Catalan for cottage cheese—in this case, prepared by the nuns at the Monastery of Pedralbes (p. 200), which is just around the corner from this homey eating spot. Located in an old house in a relaxing residential corner of the city, it's high above the city's fumes and the hubbub of traffic. (An indoor terrace offers fine views.) It's the ideal spot for a relaxing traditional lunch. Sample Catalan dishes, from old standbys like *truite de patata i cebra* (Spanish omelette with potatoes and onions) to more individual offerings like *escudella barejada* (broth with chunks of veal) and *escargols a la llauna* (snails in oil, thyme, and garlic sauce).

Bisbe Català 10. © **93-204-79-62.** Main courses 15€–30€ ($20–$39). AE, DC, MC, V. Mon–Sat 1–3:45pm and 8:30–11:45pm. Closed Sun and 15 days in Aug. Metro: Reina Elisenda.

La Balsa INTERNATIONAL   Situated on the uppermost level of a circular tower built as a cistern, La Balsa offers a fine view over most of the surrounding cityscape. To reach it you climb to the structure's original rooftop, where you're likely to be greeted by owner and founder Mercedes López. Food emerges from a cramped but well-organized kitchen several floors below. (The waiters are reputedly the most athletic in Barcelona, as they have to run up the stairs carrying steaming platters.) The restaurant serves simple but exquisite dishes such as a *judías verdes* (broad beans) with strips of salmon in lemon-flavored vinaigrette, *guiso de ternera* (stewed veal) with wild mushrooms, salad of warm

lentils with anchovies, and pickled fresh salmon with chives. The restaurant is 2km (1¼
miles) north of the city's heart—you'll need a taxi—in the Tibidabo district, close to the
Science Museum (Museu de la Ciéncia). It's often booked several days in advance.

Infanta Isabel 4. ② **93-211-50-48.** www.labalsarestaurant.com. Reservations required. Main courses
12€–30€ ($16–$39). AE, DC, MC, V. Mon–Sat 9–11:30pm; Tues–Sat 2–3:30pm. Aug buffet only 9–11:30pm.
Closed Easter week. Metro: Av. Tibidabo.

Via Veneto ★★★ CATALAN   Given its consistently well-prepared cuisine and overall class, this uptown restaurant—which has been going strong for around 4 decades—
mysteriously tends to fall under the radar. Not that this in any way worries the
management, who are busy catering to regulars and visiting sports stars. The restaurant
has a reputation for serving the finest *caza* (game) and fungi around, especially in the fall.
Look out for *rovellons* and *ceps,* both wild mushrooms from the Catalan forests, cooked
to perfection in olive oil and rock salt. Other treats include *liebre* (hare) stuffed with foie
and served on a bed of baked apples, and *patito* (baby duck), which is slow roasted and
brought to the table for deboning. The wine list is dauntingly large as the cellar contains
over 10,000 bottles, so ask the sommelier to help you. Finish off with a cheese platter or
heady dessert combination such as chocolate mousse spiced with mixed peppers and
cinnamon ice cream.

Ganduxer 10. ② **93-200-72-44.** Reservations required. www.viavenetorestaurant.com. Main courses
20€–50€ ($26–$65); tasting menu 75€ ($98). AE, DC, MC, V. Mon–Sat 8:30–11:30pm; Mon–Fri 1:15–4pm.
Closed Aug 1–20. Metro: FGC La Bonanova.

11 OUT OF TOWN

VERY EXPENSIVE

Can Fabes ★★★ MEDITERRANEAN   Located in a 300-year-old building in the
provincial village of Sant Celoni, 52km (32 miles) north of the city, this gourmet citadel
is one of the greatest restaurants of Spain. Its dedicated owner, Santi Santamaría, who
founded the restaurant in the 1980s, is now regarded as one of the country's key chefs,
earning the place a Michelin three-star rating, the highest accolade of all and rare in
Spain. Each dish is inspired and carefully vetted. Two examples are hot-and-cold mack-
erel with cream of caviar and tender pigeon with duck tartare. Another heavenly concoc-
tion is spicy foie gras with Sauterne and a *coulis* (purée) of sweet red and green peppers.
Two different preparations of crayfish, each one a delight, come both raw and cooked.
Roast pigeon is prepared in ways that vary according to the seasons and the "mood of the
chef." For dessert, there's nothing finer than their "Festival de chocolate."

Sant Joan 6 (Sant Celoni). ② **93-867-28-51.** www.canfabes.com. Reservations required. Main courses
30€–60€ ($39–$78); tasting menu 140€ ($182). AE, DC, MC, V. Tues–Sun 1:30–3:30pm; Tues–Sat 8:30–
10:30pm. Closed Jan 28–Feb 11 and June 24–July 8. Take any RENFE train from the Passeig de Gràcia
station, heading for France, disembarking at Sant Celoni.

EXPENSIVE

Sant Pau ★★★ CATALAN   If Picasso (who enjoyed his seafood) were around today,
I bet he'd arrive at the doorstep of Carme Ruscalleda, Spain's leading female chef, who
owns this fashionable eating spot in the charming Maresme resort of Sant Pol de Mar, a
45-minute drive north of Barcelona. Even some of the top chefs of France are crossing

the Spanish border to sample her cuisine. Michelin grants her two stars, but I feel that she richly deserves three. Her virtuoso technique brings finesse to food and even a touch of fantasy to some of her dishes. I marvel at her ability to take the freshest of produce and add just the right spice or seasoning to maximize its flavor. Try her *raya sin cartilagos* (boneless skate) with courgettes and smoked red peppers and you'll see what all the fuss is about.

Carrer Nou 10 (Sant Pol de Mar). © **93-760-06-62.** www.ruscalleda.com. Reservations required. Main courses 35€–65€ ($46–$85). AE, DC, MC, V. Tues–Sun 1:30–3:30pm; Tues–Sat 9–11pm. From Girona, take N-I about 55km (34 miles) south.

What to See & Do

For many visitors, the city's most fascinating sights are in the Old Quarter (Ciutat Vella). In the heart of the Ciutat Vella is the monument-filled Barri Gòtic, which effortlessly whisks you back several centuries the moment you set foot in it. Above this medieval world, in a sweeping arc that stretches up to the encompassing hills, is L'Eixample (meaning "extension"), which grew when the city was forced to expand beyond its confining city walls and is, in contrast with the ultra-narrow lanes of the Ciutat Vella, a wide-open area of fine avenues and extraordinary 19th-century *moderniste* edifices.

But there's more to the city than an endless proliferation of buildings old and new. A welcome number of green belts soften the cityscape from Montjuïc and Tibidabo's high parklands to intimate hideaways like Ciutadella near the waterfront, which is in turn now a revitalized area of walkways, marinas, beaches, and top seafood eating spots. Sports from horse riding and tennis to swimming are also in easy reach.

Given the complexity of the city, getting around is surprisingly easy. An efficient system of subway and suburban trains and surface trams and buses will take you from one end to the other for the price of a coffee, and the city's ecology is conscious enough these days for bikes to be increasingly used as another means of transport.

1 CIUTAT VELLA (OLD CITY)

The Ciutat Vella (Old City) is where the top attractions are, and if you are short of precious time this is where you will want to spend most of it. The Gothic Cathedral, the Roman foundations, the earthy Raval, and the funky Ribera districts are all located within this large chunk of the city's landscape that, due to its abundance of one-way and pedestrianized streets, is best visited on foot. It seems a little daunting at first, but striking landmarks such as the city's cathedral, the MACBA (Museum of Contemporary Art), and the Plaça del Rei will help you navigate your way around the maze. To make it easier, I have divided the attractions up into three subareas: the Barri Gòtic (east of La Rambla), El Raval (west of La Rambla), and La Ribera (west of Vía Laietana). For more information on these districts, see chapter 4.

BARRI GOTIC ★★★

The old original Gothic quarter is Barcelona's greatest urban attraction. Most of it has survived intact from the Middle Ages. Spend at least 2 or 3 hours exploring its narrow streets and squares, which continue to form a vibrant, lively neighborhood. A nighttime stroll, when lanes and squares are atmospherically lit, takes on added drama. The buildings are austere and sober for the most part, the cathedral being the crowning achievement. Roman ruins and the vestiges of 3rd-century walls add further interest. This area is intricately detailed and filled with many attractions that are easy to miss. (Follow the walking tour in chapter 8, on p. 207, for a detailed rundown.)

WHAT TO SEE & DO

7

CIUTAT VELLA (OLD CITY)

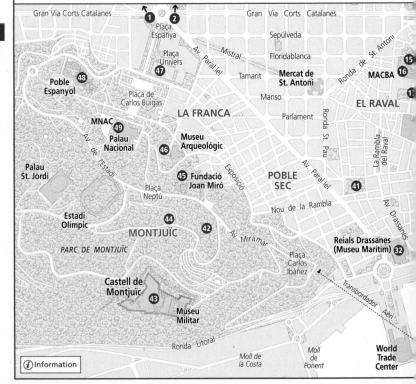

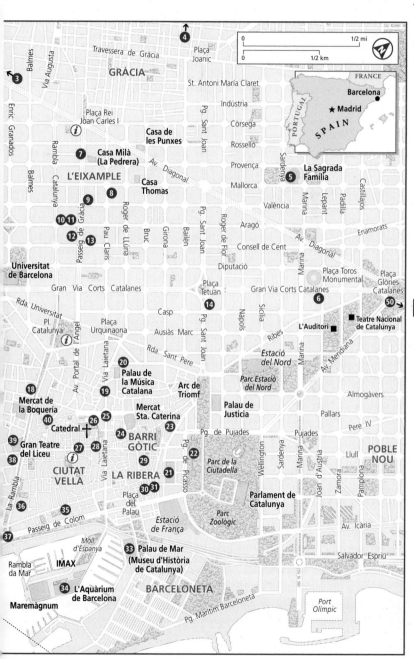

Fun Facts **How the Egg Dances**

During the feast of Corpus Christi in June, a uniquely Catalan tradition can be seen in the cathedral's cloister. *L'ou com balla* (the egg that dances) consists of an empty eggshell that is placed on top of the fountain's gushes of water and left to "dance." Its origins go back to 1637, although its significance is disputed. Some say that the egg simply represents spring and the beginning of a new life cycle, others that its form represents the Eucharist.

Catedral de Barcelona ★★★ Barcelona's cathedral is a celebrated example of Catalan Gothic architecture. Its spires can be seen from almost all over the Barri Gòtic and the large square upon which it resides, the Plaça de la Seu, is one of the neighborhood's main thoroughfares. The elevated site has always been Barcelona's center of worship: Before the present cathedral there was a Roman temple and then later a mosque. Construction on the cathedral began at the end of the 13th century, under the reign of Jaume II. (On the exterior of its southern transept, on the Plaça de Sant Lu, there is a portal commemorating the beginning of the work.) The bishops of the time ordered a wide, single nave; 28 side chapels; and an apse with an ambulatory behind a high altar. Work was finally completed in the mid–15th century (although the west facade dates from the 19th c.). The nave, cleaned and illuminated, has some splendid Gothic details. With its large bell towers, blending of medieval and Renaissance styles, high altar, side chapels, handsomely sculptured choir, and Gothic arches, it ranks as one of the most impressive cathedrals in Spain. The most interesting chapel is the Cappella de Sant Benet, behind the altar, with its magnificent 15th-century interpretation of the crucifixion by Bernat Martorell. It is the cloister, however, that enthralls most visitors. Consisting of vaulted galleries enhanced by forged iron grilles, it is filled with orange, medlar, and palm trees; features a mossy central pond and fountain; and is (inexplicably) home to a gaggle of white geese. Underneath the well-worn slabs of its stone floor, key members of the Barri Gòtic's ancient guilds are buried. The historian Cirici called this "the loveliest oasis in Barcelona." On its northern side, the cathedral's chapter house occupies the museum whose highlight is the 15th-century *La Pietat* of Bartolomé Bermejo. Another pocket of the cathedral that is worth seeking out is the alabaster sarcophagus of Santa Eulàlia, the co-patroness of the city. The martyr, allegedly a virgin daughter of a well-to-do Barcelona family, was burned at the stake by the Roman governor for refusing to renounce her Christian beliefs. You can take an elevator to the roof, where you get a wonderful view of Gothic Barcelona, but only Monday through Saturday. At noon on Sunday, you can see the *sardana*, a Catalonian folk dance, performed in front of the cathedral.

Plaça de la Seu s/n. ✆ **93-315-15-54.** www.catedralbcn.org. Free admission to cathedral; museum 1€ ($1.30). Elevator to roof 10:30am–1:30pm and 5–6pm; 2€ ($2.60). Global ticket for 1–4:30pm guided visit to museum, choir, rooftop terraces, and towers 5€ ($6.50). Cathedral daily 9am–1pm and 5–7pm; cloister museum daily 10am–1pm and 4–6:30pm. Metro: Jaume I or Liceu.

Conjunt Monumental de la Plaça del Rei (Museu d'Història de la Ciutat and Palau Reial Major) ★★★ These two museums are viewed as a double act, and both reside in Plaça del Rei, which is nestled underneath a remaining section of the old city walls. Visitors enter through the Casa Clariana Padellàs, a Gothic mansion that was originally located on the nearby Career Mercaders and was moved here when the construction of the Vía Laietana ripped though the Barri Gòtic in the early 1930s. The ground floor is dedicated to temporary exhibitions on Iberian and Mediterranean culture, with a permanent virtual-reality display on the history of the city. The highlight, however, lies underground, underneath the Plaça del Rei itself. Excavation work carried out for the relocation of the Casa Clariana Padellàs unearthed a large section of Barcino, the old Roman city. Workers unearthed a forum, streets, squares, family homes, shops, and even laundries and huge vats used for wine production. A clever network of walkways has been built over the relics, allowing you to fully appreciate the ebb and flow of daily life in old Barcino. Be on the lookout for a handful of beautiful mosaics, in situ, of what is left of family homes.

The visit continues above ground in the medieval Royal Palace. The complex dates back to the 10th century when it was the palace of the counts of Barcelona, then later became the residence of the kings of Aragón. The top step of its sweeping entrance is supposedly where King Ferdinand and Queen Isabella received Columbus after he returned from the New World. Immediately inside, the palace's chapel, the Capella de Santa Agüeda, is also used for temporary exhibitions. Adjacent to the chapel is the Saló del Tinell, a key work of the period featuring the largest stone arches to be found anywhere in Europe. Another palace highlight is the Mirador del Rei Martí (King Martin's Watchtower). Constructed in 1555, it is a later addition to the palace but in many ways one of its most interesting. King Martin was the last of the line of the city's count-kings, and this five-story tower was built to keep an eye on foreign invasions and peasant uprisings that often took place in the square below.

Plaça del Rei s/n. ℂ **93-315-11-11.** www.museuhistoria.bcn.cat. Admission 6€ ($7.80) adults, free for children 16 and under. June–Sept Tues–Sat 10am–8pm; Oct–May Tues–Sat 10am–2pm and 4–8pm; year-round Sun 10am–3pm. Metro: Liceu or Jaume I.

Barcelona's Patron Saint: Santa Eulalia

Barcelona's revered patron saint, Saint Eulalia, was a mere 13 years old when she died, a virgin, having enraged the ruling Roman authorities by throwing a fistful of sand at the altar of the Temple of Augustus after being ordered to honor it by the ruthless local ruler Dacian. This was a time when the Roman Emperor Diocletian was persecuting Christians everywhere, so such an act was almost insanely provocative. Dacian had already accused her parents, rich Sarrià merchants, of building up a fortune through the "sorcery" of their religion, so this was his chance to take revenge on their daughter. Her parents tried to protect Eulalia and themselves from Dacian's wrath by retreating to a country home, but she escaped to bravely confront him in Barcelona, berating him publicly for his cruelty to Christians. Her horrifically sadistic punishments included whippings; burnings with hot oil, lead, and braziers; burial in quick lime; and tearing of her flesh by hooks. After all these ordeals, which failed to shake her faith, she was paraded slowly around the city three times on a cart. She died on the cross at Plaça San Pedro where a monument records her martyrdom, and her remains are buried in the crypt of the cathedral.

La Mercè The church of La Mercè is dear to the heart of the people of Barcelona. Our Lady of Mercy (La Mercè) is the city's co-patron saint (the city's other patron saint is Saint Eulalia); she earned the privilege after supposedly diverting a plague of locusts in 1637. Thus, the city's main fiesta (Sept 24) is named in her honor, and many Barcelona-born females are called Mercè (among males there is an abundance of Jordis—or George—Catalonia's patron saint).

The 18th-century church itself is the only one in the city with a baroque facade. Perched on top is a statue of the lady herself, a key feature of the city's skyline. The edifice resides on an elegant square with a central fountain of Neptune.

Plaça de la Mercè 1. ✆ **93-315-27-56.** Free admission. Daily 10am–1pm and 6–8pm. Metro: Drassanes.

Mirador de Colón This monument to Christopher Columbus was erected at the Barcelona harbor on the occasion of the Universal Exhibition of 1888. It consists of three parts, the first being a circular structure raised by four stairways (6m/20 ft. wide) and eight iron heraldic lions. On the plinth are eight bronze bas-reliefs depicting Columbus's principal feats. (The originals were destroyed; these are copies.) The second part is the base of the column, consisting of an eight-sided polygon, four sides of which act as buttresses; each side contains sculptures. The third part is the 50m (164-ft.) column, which is Corinthian in style. The capital boasts representations of Europe, Asia, Africa, and America—all linked together. Finally, over a princely crown and a hemisphere recalling the newly discovered part of the globe, is a 7.5m-high (25-ft.) bronze statue of Columbus—pointing supposedly to the New World, but in reality toward the Balearic Islands—by Rafael Ataché. Inside the iron column, a tiny elevator ascends to the *mirador*. From here, a panoramic view of Barcelona and its harbor unfolds.

Portal de la Pau s/n. ✆ **93-302-52-24.** Admission 2.50€ ($3.25) adults, 1.50€ ($1.95) children 4–12, free for children 3 and under. June–Sept 9am–8:30pm; Oct–May 10am–6:30pm. Metro: Drassanes.

Museu de Cera Kids Madame Tussaud's it may not be, but Barcelona's Wax Museum still has plenty of appeal. Located in a 19th-century building that used to be a bank, the winding staircase and frescoes are a fitting setting for the array of Catalan and Spanish historical and cultural personages plus Dracula, Frankenstein, and the usual suspects. Next door, the museum's cafe, El Bosc de les Fades, is fitted out "fairy forest" style with magic mirrors, bubbling brooks, and secret doors, further adding to the fantastical experience.

Passatge de la Banca 7. ✆ **93-317-26-49.** www.museocerabcn.com. Admission 10€ ($13) adults; 6€ ($7.80) children 5–11, students, and seniors. Oct–Jun Mon–Fri 10am–1:30pm and 4–7:30pm, Sat–Sun and holidays 11am–2pm and 4:30–8:30pm; July–Sept daily 10am–10pm. Metro: Drassanes.

Museu Frederic Marès ★★ One of the biggest repositories of medieval sculpture in the region is this interesting museum, situated just behind the cathedral. Marès was a sculptor and obsessive collector, and the fruit of this passion is housed in an ancient palace with beautiful interior courtyards, chiseled stone, and soaring ceilings. He amassed a simply mind-boggling collection of religious sculpture and imagery. Downstairs, the pieces date from the 3rd and 4th centuries, then travel through to the fixating polychromatic crucifixes and statues of the Virgin Mary from the Romanesque and Gothic periods. Upstairs, the collection continues into the Baroque and Renaissance before becoming the Museu Sentimental, a collection of everyday items and paraphernalia that illustrates life in Barcelona during the past 2 centuries. The "Entertainment Room" features toys and automatons, and the "Women's Quarter" has Victorian fans, combs, and other objects deemed for "feminine use only." Outside, the **Café d'Estiu** in the courtyard is an agreeable place to rest before moving on.

Plaça de Sant Iú 5–6. ✆ **93-310-58-00**. www.museumares.bcn.es. Admission 3€ ($3.90) adults, free for children 15 and under. Tues–Sat 10am–7pm; Sun 10am–3pm. Free Wed 3–7pm. Metro: Jaume I.

Plaça Sant Jaume ★   The Plaça Sant Jaume is the political nerve center of Barcelona. Separated by a wide expanse of polished flagstones, the Casa de la Ciutat, home to the *ajuntament* (town hall), faces the Palau de la Generalitat, seat of Catalonia's autonomous government. The square itself frequently acts as a stage for protest gatherings, rowdy celebrations (such as when a local team wins a sporting event), and local traditions like the spectacular *castellers* (human towers).

The buildings themselves are only infrequently open to the public, but if they are open when you are there, they are well worth visiting, especially the **Palau de la Generalitat** ★★. Although the governing body of Catalonia has its origins in 1283, under the reign of Pere II, it wasn't until the 15th century that it was given a permanent home. The nucleus spreads out from the **Pati de Tarongers (Courtyard of Orange Trees),** an elegant interior patio with pink Renaissance columns topped with gargoyles of historical Catalan folkloric figures.

Another highlight is the **Capella de Sant Jordi (Chapel of St. George),** which is resplendent with furnishings and objects depicting the legend of Catalonia's patron saint, whose image is a recurring theme throughout the Generalitat. The walls of the Gilded Hall are covered with 17th-century Flemish tapestries.

Across the square is the late-14th-century **Casa de la Ciutat** ★, corridor of power of the *ajuntament.* Behind its neoclassical facade is a prime example of Gothic civil architecture in the Catalan Mediterranean style. The building has a splendid courtyard and staircase. Its major architectural highlights are the 15th-century Salón de Ciento (Room of the 100 Jurors) with gigantic arches supporting a beamed ceiling and the black marble Salón de las Crónicas (Room of the Chronicles). The murals here were painted in 1928 by Josep Maria Sert, the Catalan artist who went on to decorate the Rockefeller Center in New York.

Capella de Sant Jordi: Plaça de Sant Jaume s/n. ✆ **93-402-46-17.** Free admission. 2nd and last Sun of each month, Apr 25, and Sept 24 10:30am–1:30pm. Casa de la Ciutat: Plaça de Sant Jaume s/n. ✆ **93-402-70-00.** Free admission. Sun 11am–3:30pm. Metro: Jaume I or Liceu.

Santa Maria del Pi   This church takes its name from the huge pine tree outside its main entrance. The church, built over a period of nearly 200 years between the early 14th and late 16th centuries, resides on one of the most charming squares (of the same name) in the Barri Gòtic. There is always something happening on this square (which in effect merges into two other tiny plazas), whether it is an art market (Sun), a local cheese and artisan fair run by food hawkers (Thurs–Sat), street musicians strutting their stuff, or people milling around the plentiful outdoor cafes.

The church itself is a typical, if not the most complete, example of Catalan Gothic. Its wide, single nave spans nearly two-thirds of the building's length, lending the church its squat appearance. Above the main entrance is a gigantic rose window. Inside it's just as austere, although worth inspecting for the ingenious stone arch that has supported the structure's width for centuries.

Plaça del Pi 7. ✆ **93-318-47-43.** Free admission. Daily 9am–1pm and 4–9pm. Metro: Liceu.

El Call: The Jewish Quarter

Before the "Catholic Kings" Ferdinand and Isabella systematically set about persecuting all Jewish communities in Iberia in the late 15th century, Barcelona's Jews had lived harmoniously for centuries alongside Christians and enjoyed special status under the city's autonomous rule. Barcelona's Sephardic Jews flourished in the Middle Ages, reaching a population of four million people in the 13th century, 15% of the total population of the city. They were respected for their financial expertise, understanding of the law, and learned figures, including poet Ben Ruben Izahac and the astronomer Abraham Xija. The community resided in the city neighborhood El Call (pronounced "kye"), reputedly from the Hebrew word *kahal,* which means "community" or "congregation." The area was bordered by the old walls to the west and east, and its entrance was through the Plaça Sant Jaume. Today this tiny, ancient neighborhood is marked by atmospheric, narrow streets with 14th- to 16th-century buildings, some with vestiges of their former residents. The largest and most complete is the main synagogue in Calle Marlet, no. 5. Consisting of two cellar-like rooms below street level, the space was virtually unknown, serving as a warehouse until 1995 when the building with its four floors added on top was put up for sale. It was acquired by the Asociación Call de Barcelona (see below), which embarked on a meticulous process of renovation.

On the same street, in the direction of the Arc de Sant Ramón, is a wall plaque dating from 1314 bearing the inscription (in Hebrew) "Holy Foundation of Rabbi Samuel Hassardi, whose life is never ending." The remains of the female Jewish public baths can be seen nearby in the basement of the pleasant Café Caleum at the intersection of the streets Banys Nous (which means "New Baths") and Palla. The men's baths are hidden in the rear of the furniture shop S'Olivier (Banys Nous 10), although you will need to ask permission from the owner to take a peek.

Old Synagogue and Asociación Call de Barcelona: Marlet 5. ✆ **93-317-07-90.** Free admission. Hours are Tuesday through Sunday 11am to 2:30pm and 4 to 7:30pm. Metro: Jaume I or Liceu.

LA RIBERA

Smaller than the Barri Gòtic, the La Ribera district boasts two major attractions: the Picasso Museum and the soaring Gothic church of Santa María del Mar. Additional smaller treasures abound in its atmospheric streets in the form of cafes, artisan workshops, and intimate boutiques. It's a wonderful place to stroll, window-shop, and grab a bite in its many outdoor cafes, and compact enough to cover in an afternoon. At night the bars and *coctelerías* open their doors and crowds roll in.

Mercat del Born   At the end of the Passeig del Born, the pretty promenade that is the heart of the neighborhood is the Mercat del Born, the city's steel-and-glass ode to the industrial age. Inspired by Les Halles in Paris, it acted as the city's wholesale market until 1973, and its closing marked the beginning of the neighborhood's decline before its

current renaissance. Having lain abandoned for over 3 decades, [...]
2003 to turn the edifice into a library and cultural center. Wh[...]
started, the remains of entire streets and homes from Phillipe V[...]
Parc de la Ciutadella, below) were discovered underneath. Wor[...]
time and includes plans to see these significant remains undern[...]

Carrer Comerç s/n. Interior closed to public.

Museu Barbier-Mueller ★

Inaugurated in 1997, this museum is a smaller cousin
to the museum of the same name in Geneva, which is one of the most important collections of pre-Columbian art in the world. In the restored Palacio Nadal, which was built
during the Gothic period, the collection contains almost 6,000 pieces of tribal and
ancient art. Josef Mueller (1887–1977) acquired the first pieces by 1908. The pre-
Columbian cultures represented created religious, funerary, and ornamental objects of
great stylistic variety with relatively simple means. Stone sculptures and ceramic objects
are especially outstanding. For example, the Olmecs, who settled on the Gulf of Mexico
at the beginning of the 1st millennium B.C., executed notable monumental sculptures in
stone and magnificent figures in jade. Many exhibits focus on the Mayan culture, the
most homogenous and widespread of its time, dating from 1000 B.C. Mayan artisans
mastered painting, ceramics, and sculpture. Note the work by the pottery makers of the
Lower Amazon, particularly those from the island of Marajó, and the millennium-old
gold adornments from northern Peru.

Carrer de Montcada 12–14. ✆ 93-310-45-16. www.barbier-mueller.ch. Admission 3€ ($3.90) adults,
1.50€ ($1.95) students, free for children 16 and under. Tues–Sat 10am–6pm; Sun 10am–3pm. Free on 1st
Sun of the month. Metro: Jaume I.

Museu de Ciències Naturals de la Ciutadella (Geologia and Zoologia)

These
two museums, which can be viewed with the same ticket, reside inside the elegant Parc
de la Ciutadella (see below). The most crowd-pleasing is the **Museu de Zoologia ★**,
which is housed in a whimsical building designed by the *moderniste* architect Lluis
Domènech i Montaner. It was created (but not finished in time) as a cafe for the 1887–
88 World's Fair, which was largely centered around the park. Known at the time as the
Castell de Tres Dragons (Castle of the Three Dragons), it is a daring example of
medieval-inspired *modernisme* with fortress-like towers featuring ceramic heraldry, mudéjar windows, and walls of exposed brick. Inside, although extremely altered, exhibits are
displayed in Victorian-style wooden and glass cabinets. Specimens include Goliath frogs,
giant crabs, and a section on Catalan flora. Located in a colonnaded neoclassical structure, the setting for the Geological Museum is slightly less inspiring. It was, however, the
first building in the city to be constructed specifically for a museum, and it still holds the
largest geology collection in the whole country. The left wing displays various granites,
quartzes, and naturally radioactive rocks. The more interesting right wing is the area of
fossils with some nostalgic Jules Verne–type illustrations made in the 1950s, which depict
prehistoric life.

Parc de la Ciutadella, Passeig Picasso 1. ✆ 93-319-68-95 (Museu de Geologia) or 319-69-12 (Museu de
la Zoologia). Admission (for both) 3.50€ ($4.55) adults, children 16 and under free. Tues–Sat 10am–7pm;
Sun 10am–3pm. Metro: Barceloneta or Arc de Triomf.

Museu de la Xocolata ★ (Kids)

Opened in 2000 in a former convent, this museum
is an initiative from the city's chocolate and pastry makers. More like a giant, hands-on
textbook, the exhibition takes you through the discovery of the cocoa bean by New

plorers, its commercialization, and chocolate as an art form. Every Easter, the [...] is the venue for the annual *mona* competition. *Monas,* a Catalan invention, are [...]rate chocolate sculptures, often of famous buildings, people, or cartoon characters. [...]hocolate makers display them in their windows during Easter week and try to outdo each other with sheer creativity and inventiveness. Once your appetite has been whetted, you can enjoy a cup of hot chocolate or pick up some bonbons at the museum's cafe.

Antic Convent de Sant Augustí, Comerç 36. ℭ **93-268-78-78.** www.pastisseria.com. Admission 4.30€ ($5.60), seniors and students 15% discount, children 7 and under free. Mon–Sat 10am–7pm; Sun 10am–3pm. Metro: Jaume I or Arc de Triomf.

Museu d' Textil i d' Indumentària   Located in the stunning Palau dels Marquesos de Lió, a Gothic mansion adjacent to the Museu Barbier-Mueller (see above), the city's textile museum is a slightly slapdash but overall interesting permanent display of fabric and lace-making techniques and costumes. The first floor covers periods from the Gothic through the Regency, the latter consisting of crinoline skirts with bone-crushing bodices plus a wonderful selection of fans and opera glasses. Upstairs you find the 20th-century exhibits, which include ensembles from the Basque-born designer Cristóbel Balenciaga, Paco Rabanne, and Barcelona's own Pedro Rodríguez. Temporary exhibitions have ranged from Catalan jewelry to the outfits of Australian *enfant terrible* performer Leigh Bowery. There is a great cafe in the courtyard and an above-average gift shop.

Montcada 12–14. ℭ **93-319-76-03.** Admission 3.50€ ($4.55) adults, free for children 16 and under. Tues–Sat 10am–6pm; Sun 10am–3pm. Metro: Jaume I.

Museu Picasso ★★★   Five medieval mansions on this street contain this museum of the work of Pablo Picasso (1881–1973). The bulk of the art was donated by Jaume Sabartés y Gual, a lifelong friend of the artist's. Although born in Málaga, Picasso moved to the Catalan capital in 1895 after his father was awarded a teaching job at the city's Fine Arts Academy in La Llotja. The family settled in the Calle Merce, and when Picasso was a bit older, he moved to the Nou de Les Ramblas in the Barrio Chino. Although he left Spain for good at the outbreak of the Civil War—and refused to return while Franco was in power—he was particularly fond of Barcelona, where he spent his formative years painting its seedier side and hanging around with the city's Bohemians. As a sign of his love for the city, and adding to Sabartés enormous bequest, Picasso donated some 2,500 of his paintings, engravings, and drawings to the museum in 1970. All of these were executed in his youth (in fact, some of the paintings were done when he was only 9), and the collection is particularly strong on his Blue and Rose periods. Many works show the artist's debt to van Gogh, El Greco, and Rembrandt.

The highlight of the collection is undoubtedly *Las Meninas,* a series of 59 interpretations of Velázquez's masterpiece. Another key work is *The Harlequin,* a painting clearly influenced by the time the artist spent with the Ballet Russes in Paris. It was his first bequest to Barcelona. Key works aside, many visitors are transfixed by his notebooks containing dozens of sketches of Barcelona street scenes and characters, proof of his extraordinary and often overlooked drawing talents. Because the works are arranged in rough chronological order, you can get a wonderful sense of Picasso's development and watch as he discovered a trend or had a new idea, mastered it, grew bored with it, and then was off to something new. You'll learn that Picasso was a master portraitist and did many traditional representational works before his flights of fancy took off. The exhibits in the final section ("The Last Years") were donated by his widow Jacqueline and include ceramic and little-known collage work.

exhibition combined 9€ ($12) adults, 6€ ($7.80) students and those 25 and under, free for children 16 and under. Temporary exhibition only 5.80€ ($7.55) adults, 2.90€ ($3.75) students and those 25 and under. Tues–Sat 10am–8pm; Sun 10am–3pm. Metro: Jaume I, Liceu, or Arc de Triomf.

Palau de la Música Catalana ★★★   Not strictly within the borders of La Ribera but north of the Calle Princesa in the La Pere district, the Palau de la Música is, for many, the most outstanding contribution of the *moderniste* movement. Declared a UNESCO World Heritage site in 1997, it was designed by Lluis Domènech i Montaner, a contemporary of Gaudí's also responsible for the magnificent Hospital Sant Pau (p. 185).

In 1891 it was decided that the Orfeó Catalan (Catalan Coral Society) needed a permanent home. The Orfeó was a key player in La Renaixença, a heady political and cultural climate of renewed Catalan nationalism and artistic endeavor (with the two closely intertwined). The Orfeó, which still regularly performs at the Palau, had been touring Catalan rural areas, performing *catalanismo*-charged folk songs to much acclaim. The general opinion was that they deserved their own "Palace of Music." Domènech i Montaner obliged.

A riot of symbolism, the Palau de la Música Catalana, constructed between 1905 and 1908, is a feast for the senses. The facade features a rippling sculpture representing popular Catalan song and is crowned by an allegorical mosaic of the Orfeó underneath, which displays busts of composers such as Bach, Beethoven, and the period's most popular composer, Wagner. The foyer, or vestibule, is linked to the street by an arcade and features dazzling columns of mosaic. It is the first-floor auditorium, however, where the excesses of *modernisme* run wild. Using the finest craftsmen of the day, Domènech i Montaner ordered almost every surface to be embellished with the most extraordinary detail. The ceiling features a stained-glass inverted dome with the auditorium's main light source, surrounded by 40 female heads, representing a choir. On the stage's rear wall are the *Muses del Palau,* a series of dainty, instrument-bearing maidens in terra cotta and *trencadis* (broken mosaic collage). The *pièce de résistance* is the masterpiece proscenium that frames the stages. Executed by Pau Gargallo, on the left it features the Orfeó's director Josep Clavé bursting forth from the "Flowers of May," a tree representing a popular Catalan folk song. On the opposite side Beethoven peeks through a stampede of Wagner's Valkyries.

In 2003 local architect Oscar Tusquets completed his sensitive extension of El Palau, providing extra rehearsal space, a library, and another, underground auditorium. It is worth checking their program when in town; concerts range from international orchestras and soloists to jazz and sometimes world music. Tickets for local acts are often very reasonably priced. If not, there are daily tours of the building (see below). Advance purchase for these is recommended.

Career de Sant Francesc de Paula 2. ✆ **93-295-72-00** for information, or 902-442-882 to buy tickets. www.palaumusica.org. Tour 9€ ($12) adults, 7.50€ ($9.75) students. MC, V. Tickets can be bought up to 1 week in advance from the gift shop adjacent to the building. Guided tours daily, every half-hour, 10am–3:30pm. Metro: Urquinaona.

Parc de la Ciutadella ★★   Barcelona's most formal park is also the one most steeped in history. The area was formerly a loathed citadel, built by Phillip V after he won the War of the Spanish Succession (Barcelona was on the losing side). He ordered that the "traitorous" residential suburb be leveled. Between 1715 and 1718, over 60 streets and residences were torn down to make way for the structure, without any compensation to the owners (although many were relocated to the purpose-built neighborhood of Barceloneta). It never really functioned as a citadel, but was used as a political prison during subsequent uprisings and occupations. Once the decision to pull down the old city walls was made in 1858, the government decided that the citadel should go too. Work on the park began in 1872, and in 1887 and 1888 the World's Fair was held on its grounds, with the nearby Arc de Triomf acting as the event's grandiose main entrance.

Today lakes, gardens, and promenades fill most of the park, which also holds a **Zoo** (see below). Gaudí contributed to the monumental Italianate fountain in the park when he was a student; the lampposts are also his. Other highlights include the Hivernacle, an elegant, English-style hothouse with an adjacent cafe, and the unusual Umbracle, a greenhouse that contains no glass but whose facades are of bare brick with wooden louvers. Both these structures are on the Passeig de Picasso flank of the park. On the opposite side bordering Calle Wellington is the old arsenal, which now accommodates the parliament of Catalonia.

Entrances on the Passeig de Picasso and Passeig Pujades. Daily sunrise–sunset. Metro: Arc de Triomf.

Parc Zoològic ★ (Kids)   A large hunk of the Parc de la Ciutadella is taken up with the city's zoo. Until recently, the main attraction was Copito de Nieve (Snowflake), the only albino gorilla in captivity in the world. He died of skin cancer in 2003, but left behind a large family of children and grandchildren, none of whom fortunately (or unfortunately, for the scientific world) inherited his condition. Despite the zoo losing its star attraction, there are still plenty of other reasons for visiting it, not least being the pleasant (at least for humans) leafy garden setting. Many of the enclosures are barless, and the animals kept in place via a moat. This seems humane until you realize how much running space the creatures actually have at their disposal on their "islands." To be fair, Barcelona's Zoo is probably a lot more progressive than many other zoos on the continent, and unless you are of the firm belief that there is no such thing as a "good" zoo, you, and especially children, will delight at the mountain goats, llamas, lions, bears, hippos, huge primate community, and dozens of other species. There is also a dolphin show, a sizable reptile enclosure, and an exhibition on the extinction of gorillas in Snowflake's memory, from the time he was captured in Equatorial Guinea in 1966 through his rise to celebrity status as the city's mascot.

Parc de la Ciutadella. © **93-225-67-80.** www.zoobarcelona.com. Admission 15€ ($20) adults, 9.30€ ($12) students, and 8.15€ ($11) seniors 65 and over and children 3–12. Summer daily 10am–7pm; off season daily 10am–6pm; winter (Oct 26–Mar 15) daily 10am–5pm. Metro: Ciutadella or Arc de Triomf.

EL RAVAL

El Raval is a neighborhood of contrasts. Here, imaginative new buildings and urban projects are continuously being created in the streets of the city's largest inner-city neighborhood. Historically working class, the district is clearly being gentrified in many areas, while other neglected corners still retain a markedly downtrodden air. For many, El Raval symbolizes progressive 21st-century Barcelona with a new multicultural blend of Catalan, Arabic, Middle Eastern, and South American cultures evident at every turn.

Centre de Cultura Contemporània de Barcelona (CCCB) ★   Adjacent to the MACBA (see below), the CCCB is a temporary exhibition space located in what was a 19th-century poorhouse. The building has been ingeniously adapted to its current function. The extension is an impressive structure with sheer glass exterior walls supporting a large mirror that reflects the surrounding rooftops. You enter it via a pretty courtyard, and there is an exterior garden that has an outside cafeteria.

Exhibitions here tend to focus on writers and the world of literature or cultural/ political movements such as Parisian surrealism. The setting is inundated in mid-June when **Sónar,** the annual dance music festival, stages its daytime events here, and other mini-festivals such as alternative film and the plastic arts are also part of its vibrant calendar.

Montalegre 5. ✆ **93-306-41-00.** www.cccb.org. Admission: 1 exhibition 4.50€ ($5.85) adults, 3.50€ ($4.55) seniors and students; 2 exhibitions 6.50€ ($8.45) adults, 4.50€ ($5.85) seniors and students; free for children 16 and under. Tues and Thurs–Fri 11am–2pm and 4–8pm; Wed (reduced rate 3.40€/$4.45) and Sat 11am–8pm; Sun and holidays 11am–7pm. Metro: Plaça de Catalunya or Universitat.

Foment de les Arts i del Disseny (FAD)

FAD is the 100-year-old engine that drives the city's active design culture, in charge of dishing out design and architecture awards and grants and promoting its artists to Spain and the rest of the world. Its headquarters, easily identifiable by the huge steel letters spelling its name outside the main entrance, are in a converted Gothic convent opposite the MACBA, and continuous exhibitions are held in the exposed brick nave. These range from the winners of their various competitions to more didactic shows—such as pirating in the design world—to everyday, utilitarian objects from around the world. Fun stuff includes the Tallers Oberts, where artisans of the Raval throw open their workshops to the public, and *mercadillos,* where young designers sell their wares at cut prices.

Plaça dels Angels 5–6. ✆ **93-443-75-20.** www.fadweb.org. Free admission. Mon–Sat 11am–8pm. Metro: Plaça de Catalunya or Universitat.

Gran Teatre del Liceu ★★

Barcelona's opera house, El Liceu, opened to great fanfare in 1847 and again in 2000 when a new and improved version was finished after a devastating fire destroyed the original 6 years before. During its first life, El Liceu had been a symbol of the city's bourgeoisie, often provoking the wrath of the proletariat. (A telling note is that in 1893, an anarchist threw two bombs from a first-floor balcony into the audience, killing 22 people.) It was the principal venue for the Wagnerian craze that swept the city in the late 19th century. During its second life El Liceu consolidated its reputation as one of the finest opera houses in the world. The original design—based on La Scala in Milan—had a seating capacity of almost 4,000. The 1994 fire (started by sparks from the blowtorch of a stage worker) destroyed everything but the facade and members' room. The subsequent renovation saw the demolition of neighboring buildings for new rehearsal space and workrooms (much to the horror of neighborhood action groups, provoking a further backlash), and the auditorium returned to its former gilt, red velvet, and marble glory. Tickets to the concerts, at least the evening performances, are quite expensive, but as with the Palau de la Música, tours of the edifice are available.

La Rambla 51–59. ✆ **93-485-99-00,** or 90-253-33-53 for tickets. www.liceubarcelona.com. Guided tours depend on season. Information available at the Espai Liceu, the theater's bookshop and cafe in the foyer. Mon–Fri 8:30am–11:30pm; box office Mon–Fri 2–8pm, Sat–Sun 1 hr. before start of performance. AE, MC, V. Metro: Liceu.

Museu d'Art Contemporani de Barcelona (MACBA) ★★

A soaring white edifice in the once-shabby but rebounding Raval district, the Museum of Contemporary Art is to Barcelona what the Pompidou Center is to Paris. Designed by the American architect Richard Meier, the building is a work of art in itself, manipulating sunlight to offer brilliant, natural interior lighting. The permanent collection, which is expanding all the time, exhibits the work of modern international luminaries such as Broodthaers, Klee, Basquiat, and many others. Most of the museum, however, has been allotted to

Catalan artistic movements, like the **Grup del Treball,** who were a bunch of reactionaries producing conceptual art criticizing Franco's dictatorship via enormous documents promoting independence for Catalonia. On a social level, photographs by Oriol Maspons and Leonardo Pómes illustrate Barcelona street life and the bohemians of the Gauche Divine (Divine Left) in the '70s. **Dau al Set,** a surrealist movement led by the brilliant "visual poet" Joan Brossa, meanwhile, provokes thought and reflection through the juxtaposition of everyday items. Catalonia's most famous contemporary artists, Tàpies and Barceló, are both represented. Temporary exhibitions highlight international artists or a monographic show on a particular city or political movement. The museum has a library, bookshop, and cafeteria. Outside, the enormous square has become a meeting place for locals and international skateboarders who make use of the MACBA's sleek ramp, presumably with the management's blessing.

Plaça dels Angels 1. ⒸⒸ **93-412-08-10.** www.macba.es. Museum and temporary exhibitions 8.50€ ($11) adults, 6€ ($7.80) students, free for children 13 and under. Temporary exhibitions 6€ ($7.80) adults, 4.50€ ($5.85) students. Wed 3€ ($3.90) for all. MC, V. Mon and Wed–Fri 11am–7:30pm; Sat 10am–8pm; Sun 10am–3pm. Metro: Plaça de Catalunya or Universitat.

Palau de la Virreina   Built in the 1770s, this building was the former home of Manuel d'Amat, a wealthy viceroy who had made his fortune in the Americas. Set slightly back from the street, this grand structure is marked by typically Spanish top-heaviness. Inside there is a patio featuring columns, and a staircase to the right leads to the interior, most of which is not open to the public, as it is home to the city's cultural events committee. On the left, a large space is lent to a changing calendar of exhibitions, predominantly on some aspect of Barcelona. One of the best, held in September, is the Fotomercé, amateur photographs of the previous year's Mercé festival. An excellent gift shop and cultural information point can be found on the ground floor.

Les Ramblas 99. Ⓒ **93-316-10-00.** www.bcn.cat/virreinacentredelaimatge. Admission 3.50€ ($4.55); seniors and students 1.75€ ($2.30); children 16 and under free. No credit cards. Tues–Sat 11am–8:30pm; Sun 11am–3pm. Metro: Plaça de Catalunya or Liceu.

Palau Güell ★★   This mansion is an important earlier work of Antoni Gaudí's. Built between 1885 and 1889, it was the first major commission the architect received from Eusebi Güell, the wealthy industrialist who went on to become Gaudí's lifelong friend and patron.

A plot was chosen just off Les Ramblas in the lower Raval district, more for its close proximity to Güell's father's residence than anything else, and Gaudí was given a carte blanche. Although much of the marble for the town house was supplied by Güell's own quarry, it is said that his accountants criticized the architect on more than one occasion for his heavy-handed spending. Sr. Güell himself, however, as much a lover of the arts as Gaudí, wished to impress his family and Barcelona's high society with an extravagant showpiece. He got his wish. Sometimes heavy-handed in detail, the work's genius lies in its layout and inspired interconnected spaces.

The facade of the building is Venetian in style and marked by two huge arched entrances protected by intricate forged iron gates and a shield of Catalonia, lending it a fortress-like appearance. The interior of the Palau Güell can only be viewed by guided tour. First you'll see the basement stables, which feature the nature-obsessed architect's signature columns with mushroom capitals; then you ascend again to view the interconnected floors. The first, the anteroom, is in fact four salons. Most of the surfaces are dark, lending the rooms a heaviness, with Moorish-style detailing predominant throughout.

Lightness comes in the form of an ingenious system that filters natural light via a constellation of perforated stars inlaid in a parabolic dome above the central hall. Also outstanding is the screened, street-facing gallery that sweeps the entire length of the facade, also letting light into all salons except the "ladies room," where female visitors did their touchups before being received by Sr. Güell. The ceilings of the first floor, in oak and bulletwood, are beautifully decorated with foliage, starting off as buds in the first room and in full bloom by the fourth. The dining room and the private apartments contain some original furniture, a sumptuous marble staircase, and a magnificent fireplace designed by architect Camil Oliveras, a regular collaborator with Gaudí. But visitors are usually most impressed by the roof, with its army of centurion-like, *trencadís*-covered chimneys. These chimneys, along with the rest of the building, were given an overhaul in the mid-1990s, and their tilework was restored; see if you can spot the one bearing a fragment of the Olympic mascot Cobi.

Note: The Palace was still under renovation at press time, but the basement and grounds are open to the public from 10am to 2:30pm and entrance is free. The palace is scheduled for a full reopening early in 2009.

Nou de la Rambla 3–5. (C) **93-317-39-74.** Admission to basement and ground floor free until full reopening. Mon–Sat 10am–6:15pm. Metro: Drassanes.

Sant Pau del Camp ★★   Architecture from the Romanesque period is rich in rural Catalonia, which only makes the presence of this church in an inner-city street even more surprising. Its name ("Saint Paul of the countryside") stems from the fact that the church was once surrounded by green fields outside the city walls and is the oldest church in Barcelona. Given its grand old age, Sant Pau is remarkably intact. Remains of the original 9th-century structure can be seen on the capitals and bases of the portal. The church was rebuilt in the 11th and 12th centuries and is shaped in the form of a Greek cross with three apses. The western exterior door features a Latin inscription referring to Christ, Saint Peter, and Saint Paul. In the 14th-century chapter house is the tomb of Guífre Borrell, count of Barcelona in the early 10th century. The small cloister, however, is the highlight, with its Moorish arches and central fountain.

Sant Pau 99. (C) **93-441-00-01.** Admission to cloister 2.50€ ($3.25). Mon–Fri 12 noon–2pm and 5–8pm. Metro: Paral.lel.

2 L'EIXAMPLE

Barcelona's "new town," its extension beyond the old city walls, actually contains a glorious grid of 18th- and 19th-century buildings, including the most vibrant examples of the *moderniste* movement. The famous **Quadrat d'Or (Golden Triangle),** an area bordered by the streets Bruc, Aribau, Aragó, and the Diagonal, has been named the world's greatest living museum of turn-of-the-20th-century architecture. Most of the key buildings are within these hundred-odd city blocks, including Gaudí's **La Pedrera** and the ultimate *moderniste* calling card, the **Manzana de la Discordia** (see below). Many of these still serve their original use: luxury apartments for the city's 19th-century nouveau riche. Others are office buildings and even shops (the Passeig de Gràcia, the neighborhood's main boulevard, is the top shopping precinct). In case you were wondering, marine-colored, hexagonal tiles on the footpaths are reproductions of ones used by Gaudí for La Pedrera and the Casa Batlló.

La Pedrera (Casa Milà) ★★★ Commonly known as La Pedrera (The Quarry), the real name for this spectacular work of Antoni Gaudí's is the Casa Milà. The nickname stems from its stony, fortress-like appearance, much ridiculed at the time, but today it stands as the superlative example of *moderniste* architecture. The entire building was restored in 1996, the Espai Gaudí—a didactic museum—installed in the attic and one of the apartments refurbished to how it would have looked at the time of its early-20th-century residents.

The building was commissioned by Pere Mila i Camps, a rich developer who had just married an even richer widow. He wanted the most extravagant showpiece on the fashionable Passeig de Gràcia, so Gaudí, having just completed the Casa Batlló (see below), was the obvious choice.

La Pedrera occupies a corner block, and its sinuous, rippling facade is in sharp contrast to its neoclassical neighbors. In fact, it is unlike any piece of architecture anywhere in the world. La Pedrera seems to have been molded rather than built. Its massive, wavelike curtain walls are of Montjuïc limestone and the balconies' iron balustrades look like masses of seaweed. Inside, as outside, there is not one straight wall or right angle in the edifice, further adding to La Pedrera's cavelike appearance. (In a well-known anecdote, after the French president Georges Clemenceau visited the building, he reported that in Barcelona they make caves for dragons.) The apartments (many of them still private homes) are centered on two courtyards whose walls are decorated with subtle, jewel-like murals. The high point of the visit (literally!) is the spectacular rooftop. It features clusters of centurion-like chimney stacks, artfully restored and residing on an undulating surface, mirroring the arches of the attic below with outstanding views of the neighborhood, the Sagrada Família, and the port. In the summer months, jazz and flamenco concerts are held in this unique setting. The entire first floor has been handed over as an exhibition space (past shows have included artists of the caliber of Dalí and Chillida). Admission is included in the La Pedrera entry.

Provença 261–265 (on corner of Passeig de Gràcia). © **93-484-59-80** or 484-59-00. www.caixacatalunya. cat/obrasocial. Admission 8€ ($10) adults, 4.50€ ($5.85) students, free for children 12 and under. Daily 10am–7:30pm; English tours Mon–Fri 6pm. Metro: Diagonal.

La Sagrada Família ★★★ (Moments) Gaudí's incomplete masterpiece is one of the city's more idiosyncratic creations—if you have time to see only one Catalan landmark, you should make it this one. Begun in 1882 and incomplete at the architect's death in 1926, this incredible temple—the Church of the Holy Family—is a bizarre wonder. The languid, amorphous structure embodies the essence of Gaudí's style, which some have described as Art Nouveau run wild.

The Sagrada Família became Gaudí's all-encompassing obsession toward the last years of this intensely religious man's life. The commission came from the Josephines, a rightwing, highly pious faction of the Catholic Church. They were of the opinion that the decadent city needed an expiatory (atonement) temple where its inhabitants could go and do penance for their sins. Gaudí, whose view of Barcelona's supposed decadence largely coincided with that of the Josephines, by all accounts had a free hand; money was no object, nor was there a deadline to finish it. As Gaudí is known to have said, "My client [God] is in no hurry."

Literally dripping in symbolism, the Sagrada Família was conceived to be a "catechism in stone." The basic design followed that of a Gothic church, with transepts, aisles, and a central nave. Apart from the riot of stone carvings, the grandeur of the structure is owed to the elongated towers: four above each of the three facades (representing the apostles) at 100m (328 ft.) high, with four more (the evangelists) shooting up from the central section at a lofty 170m (558 ft.). The words SANCTUS, SANCTUS, SANCTUS, HOSANNA IN EXCELSIUS (Holy, Holy, Holy, Glory to God in the Highest) are written on these, further embellished with colorful geometric tilework. The last tower, being built over the apse, will be higher still and dedicated to the Virgin Mary. It is the two completed facades, however, that are the biggest crowd pleasers. The oldest, and the only one to be completed while the architect was alive, is the **Nativity Facade** on the Carrer Marina. So abundant in detail, upon first glance it seems like a wall of molten wax. As the name suggests, the work represents the birth of Jesus; its entire expanse is crammed with figurines of the Holy Family, flute-bearing angels, and an abundance of flora and fauna. Nature and its forms were Gaudí's passion; he spent hours studying its forms in the countryside of his native Reus, south of Barcelona, and much of his work is inspired by nature. On the Nativity Facade he added birds, mushrooms, even a tortoise to the rest of the religious imagery. The central piece is the "Tree of Life," a Cyprus tree scattered with nesting white doves.

On the opposite side, the **Passion Facade** is a harsh counterpart to the fluidity of the Nativity Facade. It is the work of Josep M. Subirachs, a well-known Catalan sculptor who, like Gaudí, has set up a workshop inside the church to complete his work. His highly stylized, elongated figures are of Christ's passion and death, from Last Supper to the crucifixion. The work, started in 1952, has been highly criticized. In the book *Barcelona,* art critic Robert Hughes called it "the most blatant mass of half-digested *moderniste* clichés to be plunked on a notable building within living memory."

Despite his and dozens of other voices of dissent, work plows on. In 1936 anarchists attacked the church (as they did many others in the city), destroying the plans and models Gaudí had left behind. The present architects are working from photographs of them aided by modern technology. The central nave is starting to take shape and the Glory Facade is limping along. It is estimated that the whole thing will be completed by 2026 (the centenary of Gaudí's death), funded entirely by visitors and private donations. Another step toward its completion will be the installation of a roof in 2010.

Admission includes a 12-minute video on Gaudí's religious and secular works and entrance to the museum where fascinating reconstructions of Gaudí's original models are on show.

Mallorca 401. ⏰ **93-207-30-31.** www.sagradafamilia.org. Admission 10€ ($13), groups of 20 or more 8€ ($10) per person, guide/audio guide 3€ ($3.90), elevator to the top (about 60m/197 ft.) 2.50€ ($3.25). Nov–Mar daily 9am–6pm; Apr–Sept daily 9am–8pm. Metro: Verdaguer or Sagrada Família.

L'Hospital de la Santa Creu i Sant Pau ★★★

The elegant pedestrianized boulevard, the Avenida Gaudí, stretches northward from the Sagrada Família, and at the opposite end sits another key work of the *moderniste* movement, almost equal in vitality to that of Gaudí's. The Hospital Sant Pau (as it's more commonly known) is a remarkable work by the architect Domènech i Montaner. He is often quoted as being the second most important *moderniste* architect after Gaudí, and his magnificent Palau de la Música Catalana (p. 179) is one of the movement's most emblematic pieces.

The Hospital Sant Pau was commissioned by Pau Gil i Serra, a rich Catalan banker who wished to create a hospital based on the "garden city" model. While patients languished in turn-of-the-20th-century prisonlike edifices, Gil i Serra had the then-revolutionary idea of making their surroundings as agreeable as possible. He conceived a series of colored pavilions, each (like a hospital ward) serving a specific purpose, scattered

(Moments) **Gaudí's Resting Place**

Before you leave the Sagrada Família, make sure you pay a visit to the crypt, Gaudí's resting place. The architect spent the last days of his life on the site, living a hermitlike existence in a workroom and dedicating all of his time to the project. Funds had finally dried up, and the *modernisme* movement had fallen out of fashion. In general, the Sagrada Família was starting to be viewed as a monumental white elephant.

In 1926 on his way to vespers, the old man did not see the no. 30 tram hurtling down the Gran Vía. He was taken to a hospital for the poor (in his disheveled state no one recognized the great architect), where he lay in agony for 3 days before dying and was laid to rest under a simple tombstone in the Sagrada Família's crypt.

In contrast to the rest of the Sagrada Família, the crypt is built in neo-Gothic style. The first part of the building to be completed, it is the work of Francesc de Villar, the architect who was originally commissioned for the project until Gaudí took over (Villar quit for unknown reasons). During 1936's "Tragic Week," when anarchists went on an anti-clerical rampage in the city, the crypt was ransacked. The only thing left intact was Gaudí's tomb.

among parkland. He only achieved half his vision. Although the first stone was laid in 1902, by 1911 funds ran out and only eight of the 48 projected pavilions were completed. Domènech died in 1930. After work subsequently carried out by his son, and economic intervention from another city medical institution, the Hospital Sant Pau was opened.

It's an inspiring place to visit (guided tours only—see below). The interiors of the pavilions are off-limits, but their gorgeous Byzantine- and Moorish-inspired facades and decoration, from gargoyles and angels to fauna and blossoming flora, greet you at every turn. The largest, the **Administrative Pavilion,** is also part of the tour. Its facade glows with mosaic murals telling the history of hospital care, and inside the building there are beautiful columns with floral capitals and a luxurious, dusty pink tiled ceiling.

Sant Antoni María Claret 167–171. (C) 93-488-20-78. www.santpau.es. Admission 5€ ($6.50) adults, 3€ ($3.90) students, children 15 and under free. Guided tours daily in English 10:15am and 12:15pm. Metro: Hospital San Pau.

L'EIXAMPLE ESQUERRA

Casa Amatller ★★   Constructed in a cubical design with a Dutch gable, this building was created by Puig i Cadafalch in 1900 and was the first building on the Manzana de la Discordia. It stands in sharp contrast to its neighbor, the Gaudí-designed Casa Batlló (see below). The architecture of the Casa Amatller, imposed on an older structure, is a vision of ceramic, wrought iron, and sculptures. The structure combines grace notes of Flemish Gothic—especially on the finish of the facade—with elements of Catalan architecture. The gable outside is in the Flemish style. Look out for the sculptures of animals blowing glass and taking photos, both hobbies of the architect. They were executed by Eusebi Arnau, an artist much in demand by the *modernistas*.

Casa Batlló ★★★   Next door to the Casa Amatller, Casa Batlló was designed by Gaudí in 1905 and is hands-down the superior of the three works in the *manzana*. Using sensuous curves in iron and stone and glittering, luminous *trencadis* (collage of broken tiles and ceramic) on the facade, the Casa Batlló is widely thought to represent the legend of Saint George (the patron saint of Catalonia) and his dragon. The balconies are protected by imposing skull-like formations and supported by vertebrae-like columns representing the dragon's victims, while the spectacular roof is the dragon's humped and glossy scaled back. Saint George can be seen in the turret, his lance crowned by a cross. Though the admission price may seem steep compared to many other Gaudí attractions, the interior of the building is just as extravagantly spectacular as the exterior with sinuous staircases, flowing wood paneling, and a stained-glass gallery supported by yet more bone-like columns. Custom-made Gaudí-designed furniture is scattered throughout.

Passeig de Gràcia 43. ℂ **93-488-06-66.** www.casabatllo.cat. Admission 17€ ($22) adults, 14€ ($18) children and students, free for children of 7 and under. Mon–Sun 9am–8pm. Metro: Passeig de Gràcia.

Casa Lleó Morera ★★   The last building of the trio, on the corner of Carrer del Consell de Cent, stands the Casa Lleó Morera. This florid work, completed by Doménech i Montaner in 1906, is perhaps the least challenging of the three, as it represents a more international style of Art Nouveau. One of its quirkier features is the tiered wedding cake-type turret and abundance of ornamentation: Comb the facade for a light bulb and telephone (both inventions of the period) and a lion and mulberry bush (after the owner's name: In Catalan, lion is *lleó*, and mulberry is *morera*). Tragically, the ground floor has been mutilated by its tenant, who stripped the lower facade of its detail and installed plate glass. The shop's interior, which fared no better, is the only part of the building open to the public.

Passeig de Gràcia 35. www.gaudiallgaudi.com/EA101.htm. Metro: Passeig de Gràcia.

Fundació Antoni Tàpies ★   This is the third most popular Barcelona museum, after Miró and Picasso, to be devoted to the work of a single, prolific artist. In 1984 the Catalan artist Antoni Tàpies set up a foundation bearing his name, and the city of Barcelona donated an ideal site: the old Montaner i Simon publishing house. One of the city's landmark buildings, the brick-and-iron structure was built between 1881 and 1884 by that important exponent of Catalan *moderniste* architecture, Lluis Doménech i Montaner,

La Manzana De La Discordia

The superlative showcase of the *moderniste* architecture is the **Manzana de la Discordia (Illa de la Discordia).** The "Block of Discord," which is on the Passeig de Gràcia between Consell de Cent and Aragó, consists of three works by the three master architects of the movement: Josep Puig i Cadafalch, Lluis Domènech i Montaner, and Antoni Gaudí. Although they are all quite different in style, they offer a coherent insight into the stylistic language of the period. The Casa Amatller houses the Centre del Modernismo, an information point on the *modernistas* and the movement.

Tips   Doing the Moderniste Walk

As most of Barcelona's *moderniste* legacy is in the Eixample neighborhood, it makes sense to see it on foot. The **Centre del Modernisme** at the Casa Amatller, Passeig de Gràcia 41 (*C* **93-488-01-39;** Mon–Sat 10am–7pm, Sun 10am–2pm; Metro: Gràcia), is a one-stop information point on the movement. They have devised the "modernism route," a tour of the city's 100 most emblematic Art Nouveau buildings. You can either pick up a free map or buy a well-produced, explanatory book (12€/$16), which includes a book of coupons offering discounts of between 15% and 50% on attractions that charge admission, such as Gaudí's Casa Batlló and La Pedrera.

If you wish to explore *modernisme* beyond the boundaries of Barcelona, the center can also supply you with information on towns such as Reus (Gaudí's birthplace) and Terrassa, which has an important collection of *moderniste* industrial buildings. Tours are also offered. (See our recommended Walking Tour no. 4 in chapter 8, "Strolling Around Barcelona," p. 217.)

The Centre del Modernisme also has branches at the Hospital Sant Pau and the Finca Güell in Pedralbes.

also perpetrator of the Casa Lleó Morera around the corner (see above). The core of the museum is a collection of works by Tàpies (mostly contributed by the artist) covering stages of his career as it evolved into abstract expressionism. Here, you can see the entire spectrum of media in which he worked: painting, assemblage, sculpture, drawing, and ceramics. His associations with Picasso and Miró are apparent. The largest of the works is on top of the building: a controversial gigantic sculpture, *Cloud and Chair,* made from 2,700m (8,858 ft.) of metal wiring and tubing. The lower floor is used for temporary exhibitions, nearly always on contemporary art and photography, and the upper floor has a library with an extremely impressive section on oriental art, one of the artist's inspirations.

Note: At press time, the museum was closed for renovation, but it is due to reopen in 2009.

Aragó 255. *C* **93-487-03-15.** www.fundaciotapies.org. Admission 4.50€ ($5.85) adults, 2.50€ ($3.25) students, free for children 16 and under. Tues–Sun 10am–8pm. Metro: Passeig de Gràcia.

Fundación Francisco Godia (Finds)   In 2008, the museum moved to this new location in the heart of L'Eixample. This intriguing museum showcases the famous art collection of Francisco Godia Sales, the Catalan art lover and entrepreneur. It's one of the greatest displays in the country. Godia (1921–90) combined a desire for art with a head for business and a passion for motor racing. When he wasn't driving fast ("the most wonderful thing in the world"), he was amassing his collection. In gathering these treasures he showed exquisite taste and great sensitivity.

He collected a splendid array of medieval sculptures and ceramics but showed a keener instinct for purchasing great paintings. Godia acquired works by some of the most important artists of the 20th century, including Julio González, María Blanchard, Joan Ponç, Antoni Tàpies, and Manolo Hugué, the latter a great friend of Picasso. From its earliest stages, Godia realized the artistic importance of Catalan *modernisme* and collected works by sculptors like Josep Llimona and celebrated *moderniste* painters Santiago Rusiñol and Ramon Casas. Godia also dipped deeper into the past, acquiring works, for example, of two of the most important artists of the 17th century: Jacob van Ruysdael and Luca Giordano.

Diputació 250. ✆ **93-272-31-80.** www.fundacionfgodia.org. Admission 4.50€ ($5.85) adults, 2.50€ ($3.25) students and seniors, free for children 5 and under. Wed–Mon 10am–8pm. Metro: Passeig de Gràcia.

Museu Egipci de Barcelona   Spain's only museum dedicated to Egyptology contains more than 250 pieces from the personal collection of founder Jordi Clos (owner of the Hotel Claris). On display are sarcophagi, jewelry, hieroglyphics, sculptures, and artwork. Exhibits focus on ancient Egyptians' everyday life, including education, social customs, religion, and food. The museum has its own lab for restorations. A library with more than 3,000 works is open to the public.

Valencia 284. ✆ **93-488-01-88.** www.fundclos.com. Admission 7€ ($9.10) adults, 5€ ($6.50) students, children 5 and under free. Mon–Sat 10am–8pm; Sun 10am–2pm. Guided tours Sat. Metro: Passeig de Gràcia.

3 GRÀCIA

Located above the Diagonal and L'Eixample Esquerra, Gràcia is a large neighborhood that has a unique character, a product from when it was a separate town altogether. Although notable attractions here are not abundant, Gràcia is well worth visiting for a taste of authentic *barri* life. Shopping and cafe society are particularly good around the Calle Verdi and Plaça del Sol, and nocturnal activity here is lively, particularly in the summer at the famous **Fiestas de Gràcia.** Gràcia boasts a unique mixture of proud locals that have lived there all their lives and young, progressive urbanites. This melting pot is reflected in its street life.

Casa Vicens ★★   Although this early work of Gaudí's can only be viewed from the exterior, the exuberance of its facade and form makes the trip well worth it. The architect accepted the commission for a summer residence from the tile manufacturer Manuel Vicens i Montaner in 1883, making the Casa Vicens not only one of the first architectonic examples of Art Nouveau in Barcelona but the whole of Europe.

Since the home was designed to be an exponent of Sr. Vicens's business, the entire facade is covered with florid, vividly colored tiles. At the time, Gaudí was deeply influenced by North African and Middle Eastern architecture, and this can be seen in the home's form. Its overall opulence and exoticism, with minarets and corbels, is reminiscent of the Indian Raj style. Inside Ottoman, Koranic, and Andalusian influences can also be seen in eccentric touches such as the Turkish-style smoking room. The residence, on a narrow Gràcian street, is owned by descendants of Sr. Vicens and still a private home (although they seem to have no objections to camera-flashing tourists). The interior, however, has been well photographed and is always featured in books on the architect.

Carrer de les Carolines 18–24. www.gaudiallgaudi.com/EA004.htm. Metro: Fontana.

Parc Güell ★★★   After the abundant religious symbolism of the Sagrada Família and the heavy-handedness of the Palau Güell, Gaudí's whimsical Parc Güell often seems like light relief and is for many his best-loved and most accessible work. Although it's now

WHAT TO SEE & DO

7

GRÀCIA

> ## Fun Facts   Gaudí's Patron
>
> **Eusebi Güell i Bacigalupi,** the man who launched Gaudí's career and went on to become a lifelong friend, was a product of the city's new, wealthy elite. He studied art, poetry, and theology in Paris and London and upon returning to Barcelona, put his acute business sense into practice in the shipping, banking, railroad, and textile sectors—all the industries that drove Catalonia's industrial revolution in the late 1800s.
>
> Enormously well respected, Güell was high-minded and took civic duty extremely seriously. He felt bound to improve the lives of his city's inhabitants (of all classes) through art and better working conditions. It seems Güell's first meeting with Gaudí was in a carpentry workshop Gaudí had designed as a showcase for a Barcelona glove shop, and shortly afterward Güell saw the work displayed at the 1878 International Exhibition in Paris. The fruit of the relationship materialized in such marvels as the Parc Güell, the Palau Güell, and the church for the ambitious Colònia Güell in outer Barcelona. Just before his death in 1918, Güell was made a count by King Alfonso XIII.

officially a public park, in 1900 the Parc Güell began as a real estate venture for a friend, the well-known Catalan industrialist Count Eusebi Güell (see box below), who planned to make this a model garden city community of 60 dwellings with its own market and church. It was never completed, and the city took over the property in 1926.

Spread over several acres of woodland high above central Barcelona, with wonderful views at every turn, the Parc Güell is one of the most unusual man-made landscapes on the planet. It is abundant with the architect's unique vision and expertise at finding creative solutions posed by the demands of the project.

Arriving at the main entrance in the Carrer d'Olot, you are greeted by two gingerbread-style gatehouses. At the time they were built, Gaudí was working on some set designs for the opera *Hansel and Gretel* at the Liceu Opera House, so it is presumed that the inspiration for these whimsical structures came from that. Both shimmer with broken mosaic collage and are topped with chimneys in the shape of wild and toxic mushrooms. Much has been made of the Parc Güell's symbolism, and it has even been suggested that these toadstool-chimneys reflect Gaudí's penchant for hallucinogenic substances. The fact is that mushroom gathering is a national pastime, and the work, as in most of Gaudí's cache, reflects a deep-rooted nationalism and respect for nature and Catalonia's history.

The main steps to the **Sala Hipóstila (marketplace)** feature a spectacular tiled lizard, the park's centerpiece. The covered would-be market supports a large platform above with 86 Doric columns connected by shallow vaults. This pagan-looking space is largely thought to be inspired by Barcelona's Roman foundations. The roof is embellished with four sun-shaped disks representing the seasons. Above in the elevated square, a sinuous bench, said to be the longest in the world, snakes its way around the perimeter. The decoration on this elaborate piece was carried out by architect and craftsman Josep Marià Jujol. The story goes that all the workers on the park were ordered to bring Jujol all the shards of broken crockery and glass they could lay their hands on, which accounts for the work's extraordinary mixture of colors and textures. Palm trees and vistas of the skyline add to the moment.

Three kilometers (2 miles) of more rustic-inspired paths and porticoes using material taken from the land itself weave through the rest of the park, which is filled with Mediterranean vegetation. In typical Gaudí style, sculptures and figurines pop up in the most surprising places. Worth hunting out is the **Closed Chapel** at the highest point of the park, in reality an archaic six-lobed structure crowned by a cross that seems to have taken inspiration from the ancient stone watchtowers or druid temples not uncommon in the Balearic Islands.

Only two homes were ever built in the colony, and neither of them by Gaudí. One of them, designed by the architect Ramón Berenguer, became Gaudí's residence in the latter part of his life. It is now the **Casa Museu Gaudí,** Carrer del Carmel 28 (✆ **93-219-38-11**), and contains furniture designed by the architect, drawings, and other personal effects, many of them arranged the same way as when the architect lived his reclusive life there.

Carrer d'Olot, Carretera del Carmel. ✆ **93-413-24-00.** www.gaudiallgaudi.com/AA010.htm. Admission park free; open to public daily Nov–Feb 10am–6pm, Mar and Oct 10am–7pm, Apr and Sept 10am–8pm, May–Aug 10am–9pm. Admission Casa Museu 4€ ($5.20), concessions 3€ ($3.90); open Oct–Mar 10am–5:45pm; Apr–Sept 10am–7:45pm. Metro: Lesseps (then a 15-min. walk). Bus: 24 or 25.

---

4 MONTJUÏC

For many visitors, and certainly those who arrive by sea, the mountain of Montjuïc is their first glimpse of Barcelona. Jutting out over the port on one side and facing the monumental Plaça Espanya on the other, Montjuïc is strategically placed as a pleasure ground, and a fortunate lack of a constant water source has deterred residential development. Instead it became the focal point of two of the city's key international events: first the World Fair of 1929, of which many structures still remain, and second the 1992 Olympic Games.

The largest "green zone" in the city, Montjuïc's forests and parks have always been popular with joggers, cyclists, and strollers. In recent years the city's council embarked on a project to spruce these up, install walkways and connecting escalators, and reclaim some forgotten gems in the process. One of these is the **Font del Gat,** Passeig Santa Madrona 28 (✆ **93-289-04-04**), a once-fashionable cafe built by *moderniste* architect Josep Puig i Cadafalch that now acts as a Montjuïc information point and restaurant. Top-flight hillside museums such as the Miró Foundation and the Museu Nacional d'Art de Catalunya (MNAC) are further good reasons to leave the bustle of the city behind and take the rewarding climb up here.

CaixaForum ★★   This is one of the city's more exciting contemporary art spaces, both in terms of its setting and what's inside. Opened in 2002 in the Casaramona, an old *modernista* textile factory designed by Puig i Cadalfach that was used as police barracks in the '30s, the vibrant edifice features a red brick facade and singular turret, to which the Japanese architect Arata Isozaki added a daring walkway, courtyard, and entrance. (Isozaki is the designer responsible for the Palau St. Jordi, a major music and meeting venue, further up the hill of Montjuïc.) Inside, after passing the huge abstract mural by Sol Lewitt, the elevator whisks you up to three exhibition spaces, connected by exterior halls. These are changing constantly, meaning that three normally very diverse shows can be viewed at the same time. Traditional past exhibitions have ranged from Rodin's sculptures to Turner's Venice, and a 2008 standout was a photographic exhibition by the innovative Hannah Collins. Cuban artist Jorge Pardo created the baroque setting for minimalist pieces from the CaixaForum's permanent collection. The foundation puts on a lively calendar of related events and performances, the latter focusing on world music and modern dance. There is an excellent bookshop in the foyer which opens daily from 10am to 8:30pm (10pm on Sat).

Av. Marquès de Comillas 6–8. ℂ **93-476-86-00.** www.obrasocial.lacaixa.es/centros/caixaforumbcn_es.html. Free admission. Tues–Sun 10am–8pm. Metro: Espanya. FGC: Espanya.

Fundació Joan Miró ★★★ Born in 1893, Joan Miró was one of Spain's greatest artists and, along with Tàpies, the undisputed master of contemporary Catalan art. His work is known for its whimsical abstract forms, brilliant colors, and surrealism. Some 10,000 works, including paintings, graphics, and sculptures, are collected here. Constructed in the early 1970s, the building was designed by Catalan architect Josep Lluis Sert, a close friend of Miró's (he also designed the artist's workroom in Majorca). Set in the parkland of Montjuïc, the museum consists of a series of white rationalist-style galleries with terra-cotta floors. *Claraboias* (skylights) ensure that the space is bathed in natural light. Its hilltop setting affords some wonderful views of Barcelona, especially from the rooftop terrace that also serves as a sculpture garden.

The collection, donated by the artist himself, is so huge that only a portion of it can be shown at any one time. There is also a gallery put aside for temporary exhibitions, usually focusing on an aspect of Miró's work or a contemporary artist or movement. Concerts are held in the gardens in the summer months.

The first gallery holds two of the collection's treasures: the magnificent 1979 **Foundation Tapestry,** which Miró executed especially for the space, and the extraordinary **Mercury Fountain,** a work by his friend, the American sculptor Alexander Calder. In contrast to Miró's painting, which was nearly always carried out in a primary-color palette, there is a huge collection of drawings from his days as a student. Even as a young man, you can see his deep sense of national identity and Catalanism, which (logically) later led to an extreme horror at the civil war. The key work representing this sentiment is the powerful *Man and Woman in Front of a Pile of Excrement* (1935) in the Pilar Juncosa Gallery, one of the "Wild Paintings." Much of Miró's work, though, is dreamlike and uplifting, with the sun, moon, and other celestial bodies represented again and again. Note the poetic *The Gold of the Azure* (1967) in the same gallery, a transfixing blue cloud on a golden background with dots and strokes for the planets and stars.

Even if you are already familiar with Miró's work, the excellent commentary provided via the audio guide (available at the ticket office) will supply you with special insight into this fascinating artist.

Parc de Montjuïc s/n. ℂ **93-443-94-70.** www.fundaciomiro-bcn.org Admission all exhibitions 7.50€ ($9.75) adults, 5€ ($6.50) students, free for children 14 and under; temporary exhibitions 4€ ($5.20) adults, 3€ ($3.90) students. July–Sept Tues–Wed and Fri–Sat 10am–8pm; Oct–June Tues–Wed and Fri–Sat 10am–7pm; year-round Thurs 10am–9:30pm and Sun 10am–2:30pm. Bus: 50 at Plaça Espanya or 55; Funicular de Montjuïc.

Jardí Botànic ★ Just behind the Castell de Montjuïc, the city's Botanical Garden opened in 1999 and has steadily gathered international praise for its cutting-edge landscaping and concept. The foliage focuses on species of plants, flowers, and trees that flourish in a Mediterranean-type climate (all are clearly labeled in Latin, Catalan, Spanish, and English), and come from such differing far-flung destinations as Australia and California. The park is divided up into sections representing each of these regions. The sci-fi telecommunications aerial you see a short distance away was designed by the

Valencia-born architect Santiago Calatrava for the Olympic Games. This ingenie structure has a base decorated with broken tiles (a homage to Gaudí, one of the architect's main influences), and its position, leaning at the same angle as the hill's inclination, means that it also acts as a sundial.

Doctor Font i Quer s/n, Parque de Montjuïc. (℃) **93-426-49-35.** www.jardibotanic.bcn.cat. Admission 3.50€ ($4.55) adults, 1.70€ ($2.20) students 25 and under, children 15 and under free. Open Nov–Jan 10am–5pm daily; Feb–Mar and Oct 10am–6pm daily; Apr–May and Sept 10am–7pm daily; Jun–Aug 10am–8pm daily. Transbordador Aeri (cable car; see box below) from Barceloneta to Montjuïc, then an uphill walk. Bus: PM (Parc Montjuïc) departs from Plaça Espanya 8am–9:20pm Sat–Sun and public holidays. Metro: Paral.lel, then funicular (tram) to top 9am–8pm (until 10pm July–Sept).

Museu d'Arqueologia de Catalunya ★

The Museu d'Arqueologia occupies the former Palace of Graphic Arts built for the 1929 World's Fair. It has been attractively restored, with some rooms retaining their Art Deco flavor. The artifacts, which are arranged chronologically, reflect the long history of this Mediterranean port city and surrounding province, beginning with prehistoric Iberian artifacts. The collection includes articles from the Greek, Roman, and Carthaginian periods. Some of the more interesting relics were excavated in the ancient Greco-Roman city of L'Empúries in Northern Catalonia. The Greeks in particular developed a strategic trading post here with other Mediterranean peoples, and the vessels, urns, and other everyday implements they left behind make fascinating viewing.

But undoubtedly the high point of the collection is the Roman artifacts. The Roman Empire (using Empúries as their entry point) began their conquest of Iberia in 218 B.C., and the glassware, lamps, grooming aids, and utensils here are truly outstanding. The mosaics, many of them amazingly intact, have been laid into the floor, and visitors are invited to tread on them.

Passeig de Santa Madrona 39–41, Parc de Montjuïc. (℃) **93-424-65-77.** www.mac.cat. Admission 3€ ($3.90) adults, 2.10€ ($2.75) students, free for children 16 and under. Tues–Sat 9:30am–7pm; Sun 10am–2:30pm. Metro: Espanya.

Museu Militar de Montjuïc ★

Although the collection at the city's museum is interesting enough, most people head up here for the views. Perched on the sea-facing side of Montjuïc, this fortress (Castell de Montjuïc) dates back to 1640 and was rebuilt and extended during the mid-1800s. Its gloomy cells served as a military prison during the Civil War, earning it an indifferent, if not hostile, reputation among the people of Barcelona. While there have been noises from the local government about changing the focus of the museum to a more peaceful and reflective tone, it remains pretty much the same as when it was opened, shortly after the army moved out in 1960.

The collection itself contains the usual assortment of paintings marking military events and dozens of rooms of armor, uniforms, weapons, and the instruments of war. One of the more entertaining exhibits (Room 8) contains thousands of miniatures forming a Spanish division, which first went on show during the 1929 World's Fair.

The terraces and highest points of the star-shaped fortress-castle, and the walkways that surround it, offer some breathtaking views of the Barcelona skyline and Mediterranean. The parkland around the castle is currently being dug up to make it more accessible and easier to walk around. If you don't mind an uphill stroll, note that the most spectacular way to get here is via the port-crossing cable car (see below). On the walk from the drop-off point, you will pass the famous statue of La Sardana, the traditional Catalan dance, which is featured on many postcards of the city. Otherwise, grab the funicular from Paral.lel Metro station, which drops you off pretty much at the door.

s/n. (C) **93-329-86-13.** Admission museum and castle 3€ ($3.90), castle and grounds
for children 7 and under. Nov to mid-Mar Tues–Sun 9:30am–5:30pm; mid-Mar to Oct
–8pm. Transbordador Aeri (cable car; p. 197) from Barceloneta to Montjuïc, then uphill
rc Montjuïc); departs from Plaça Espanya 8am–9:20pm Sat–Sun and public holidays.
then funicular (tram) to top 9am–8pm (until 10pm July–Sept).

Museu Nacional d'Art de Catalunya (MNAC) ★★★ This museum, which
recently underwent massive renovations and expansion, is the major depository of Catalan art. Although its mammoth collection also covers the Gothic period and 19th and
20th centuries, the MNAC is perhaps the most important center for Romanesque art in
the world. The majority of the sculptures, icons, and frescoes were taken from dilapidated churches in the Pyrénées, restored, and mounted as they would have appeared in
the churches in expertly reproduced domes and apses. Larger works are shown with a
photograph of the church and a map pointing out its location, drawing you further into
this fascinating and largely underexposed 11th- to 13th-century movement. Simplistic
yet mesmerizing, Romanesque art is marked by elongated forms, vivid colors, and expressiveness. Most outstanding is the **Apse of Santa María de Taüll** (in Ambit [Gallery] V)
with a serene, doe-eyed Christ surrounded by the apostles. Lapis lazuli was used to create
the intense blue in the piece. Also look out for a series of ceiling paintings from an Aragonese chapter house. In a more subtle color scheme, they echo Tudor miniature painting
(Ambit XI). The entire collection is in sequential order, giving the viewer a tour of
Romanesque art from its beginnings to the more advanced late Romanesque and early
Gothic eras.

Sensory overload withstanding, the next section you visit deals with the Gothic period,
made up of pieces from the 13th to 15th centuries. All styles that were adopted in Catalonia are represented: Italianate Gothic, Flemish Gothic, and a more linear, local Gothic
style. Look out for *retablos* by Jaume Huguet (Ambit XIII). The primary artist in the
Catalan school, Huguet mixed Flemish and Italian influences with local Romanesque
conventions. The Gothic collection also holds some Barcelonese Gothic quarter artifacts
such as giant object-signs (made for an illiterate population) that used to hang outside
workshops (shoes, scissors, and such) and other decorative pieces. The Gothic section
finishes with the Cambó collection. A bequest from a local businessman, the selection of
14th- to 19th-century paintings includes works by Rubens, El Greco, and Goya.

Thanks to the MNAC's most recent acquisitions—pieces of 19th- and 20th-century
decorative art and painting, most stemming from the city's all-important *moderniste*
movement—the collection now spans a millennium. While *moderniste* architecture in the
city is abundant, most buildings' interiors have been stripped bare of their mirrors, chandeliers, sculptures, and furnishings, many designed by the architects themselves, such as
Gaudí. Until mid-2004 they were on display at the Museu d'Art Modern in the Parc de
la Ciutadella. At the MNAC, they have a stunning new home.

Highlights of this collection, which spans the neoclassical, Art Nouveau (or *moderniste*), and subsequent *nou-centista* (or *fin-de-siècle*) movements, are too numerous to mention. Look out for the marquetry pieces by Gaspar Homar (a master *moderniste* carpenter)
and the Rodin-influenced sculptor Josep Clara. The superb private oratory by Joan Busquets will leave you breathless at the Art Nouveau movement's excesses and craftsmanship. There are also many pieces taken from the interiors of homes of the Manzana de la
Discordia (earlier in this chapter).

A whole floor is also now devoted to the Thyssen-Bornemisza works previously kept
in the Pedralbes Monastery.

A Bicycle Built for Two

One of the star pieces of the MNAC's *moderniste* collection is a self-portrait of Ramón Casas and fellow painter Pere Romeu riding a tandem. This iconic work was originally done for **Els Quatre Gats** (p. 134), essentially a tavern that served as a fraternity house for *moderniste* movers and shakers, bohemians, intellectuals, and poets. A young Picasso designed the menu (and held his first-ever exhibition there), and various other works donated to the owners still adorn the walls, although now most, such as Casas's peddling portrait, are reproductions of the originals. The colorful Casas, who had spent many years in the artistic circles of Montmartre, was a perpetrator of the city's newfound modernity and a notable artist in his own right. His interpretations of *fin-de-siècle* Barcelona provide valuable insight to this heady time.

Palau Nacional, Parc de Montjuïc. (C) **93-622-03-60.** www.mnac.cat. Admission for combined permanent and temporary exhibits 8.50€ ($11; valid for 2 days) adults, 6€ ($7.80) students and youths 7–21, free for children 7 and under. Tues–Sat 10am–7pm; Sun 10am–2:30pm. Metro: Espanya.

Museu Olimpic i de l'Esport One of the few museums in Europe devoted entirely to sports, the Museu Olimpic opened in 2007 opposite the Stadium. In addition to displaying the photos, costumes, and memorabilia contained in the former Galeria Olímpica in celebration of the 1992 games, the museum has added ceremonial costumes and more personal memorabilia, such as soccer player Ronaldinho's boots. There are also conference facilities, an auditorium, video recordings of athletic events, and archives. Most fun is pitting your (imaginary) skills against those of top athletes in the hands-on interactive displays.

Av. Estadi. (C) **93-292-53-79.** www.museuolimpicbcn.cat. Admission 4€ ($5.20) adults, children 14 and under and seniors 65 and over free. Apr–Sept Tues–Sat 10am–8pm, Sun 10am–2:30pm; Oct–Mar Tues–Sat 10am–6pm, Sun 10am–2:30pm. Metro: Espanya, then 15-min walk, or take bus nos. 50, 55, or 61 from Plaça Espanya.

Pavelló Mies van der Rohe ★★ Directly across the road from the CaixaForum, this serene building stands in welcome contrast to the *moderniste* style of the Casaramona and the faux traditionalism of the Poble Espanyol. Designed by German architect Mies van der Rohe, it was originally built as the German Pavilion for the 1929 World's Fair and was the last of the architect's works before he emigrated to the United States. It is considered a key work of both his and the "International Style" movement for which van der Rohe, and others, like Frank Lloyd Wright, became famous. The simple, horizontal structure contains his trademarks: precision, fluidity of space, and abundance of "pure" materials, in this case different kinds of marble and glass. The structure is built around a shallow pool featuring a statue by Georg Kolbe, the German sculptor known for his female nudes. Inside is the original **Barcelona Chair** designed by van der Rohe and seen (mainly in reproduction form) throughout the city in reception areas. Although the pavilion now stands on its original location, this wasn't always the case. After the World's Fair, it was banished to an outer suburb, only to be rescued and reconstructed in 1985 thanks to an initiative by a group of the city's prominent architects.

Av. Marquès de Comillas s/n. ☎ **93-423-40-16.** www.miesbcn.com. Admission 3.50€ ($4.55), adults, free for children 18 and under. Daily 10am–8pm. Metro: Espanya. FGC: Espanya.

Poble Espanyol ★★ (Kids)   This re-created Spanish village, built for the 1929 World's Fair, provokes mixed feelings: Purists see it as the height of kitsch, while others delight in its open spaces and Disneyland-type feel. But the question remains: Where else would you find over 100 styles of Spanish vernacular architecture crammed into one very pleasant spot? From the Levante to Galicia, from Castilian high Gothic to the humble whitewashed dwellings of the south and to colorful Basque homes, it's all here. At the entrance, for starters, stands a facsimile of the gateway to the grand walled city of Avila. This leads you to the center of the village with an outdoor cafe where you can sit and have drinks, and there are various other venues throughout, including the excellent flamenco taverna the **Tablao de Carmen** (p. 246) and a couple of other trendy nightspots. The big names of July's El Grec festival also play here, in the main plaza just inside the gates. As was originally intended, numerous shops still sell provincial crafts and souvenir items, and in some of them you can see artists at work, printing fabric, making pottery, and blowing glass. If you are lucky, your visit may coincide with a wedding at the faux Sant Miquel monastery, one of the most popular places in the city to get married. A few years back, the Poble Espanyol added the **Fundació Fran Daural** (daily 10am–7pm), a collection of contemporary Catalan art with works by Dalí, Picasso, Barceló, and Tàpies. Many families delight in the faux-Spanish atmosphere, but the more discriminating find it a bit of a tourist trap.

Av. Marquès de Comillas s/n, Parc de Montjuïc. ☎ **93-508-63-00.** www.poble-espanyol.com. Admission 8€ ($10) adults, 5€ ($6.50) children 4–12, free for children 4 and under; 20€ ($26) family ticket; 2€ ($2.60) guided tours. Mon 9am–8pm; Tues–Thurs 9am–2am; Fri–Sat 9am–5am; Sun 9am–11pm. Metro: Espanya, then 10-min. walk uphill, or take bus no. 13 or 50 from Plaça Espanya.

(Moments)   **The Magic Fountain**

Without a doubt, the most popular attraction for young and old alike in the Montjuïc area is the **Font Màgica (Magic Fountain).** During the day, the grandiose fountain at the base of the staircase to the MNAC seems like any other, but at night it takes on a different personality. At regular intervals, the fountain puts on a spectacular show. Music, ranging from pop ballads to pop classics, belts out from loudspeakers, and different colored lights are beamed from inside the fountain itself. The gushes of water, controlled externally, "dance" to the mixture of light and sound. Supposedly the only one of its kind in the world, the fountain was designed by the visionary engineer Carles Buïgas for the 1929 World's Fair, predating similar Vegas-type attractions by decades. It's free and never fails to enthrall. Grab a seat at one of the nearby outdoor cafes and enjoy. It's at Plaça Carles Buïgas 1 (Metro: Espanya). The sound and light shows run from May to early October, Thursday through Sunday at 9:30, 10, 10:30, 11, and 11:30pm. The rest of the year, they are held on Friday and Saturday at 7, 7:30, 8, and 8:30pm.

> **Tips** **Swinging over the Port**
>
> Unless you suffer from vertigo, the most spectacular way t...
> Montjuïc and the other attractions on the sea-face of the ...
> via a cable car that crosses the port. The **Transbordador /**...
> Sant Sebastiá at the very end of the Passeig de Joan de B...
> (bus: 17, 64, or 39), stops at the World Trade Center on th...
> the ascent to the peak of Montjuïc. The cable car runs every 15 minutes daily
> from 10am to 8pm June 19 to September 14, 10am to 6pm October 20 to Febru-
> ary 29, and 10:45am to 7pm during the rest of the year. Cost is 9€ ($12) one-way,
> 13€ ($17) round-trip. Call (℃ **93-430-47-16** or 441-50-71 for more information.
>
> If you're afraid of heights, you can take the **Teleféric de Montjuïc** (℃ **93-441-
> 48-20;** www.tmb.net/en_US/turistes/busturistic/teleferic.jsp), a funicular-style
> land-based service which climbs the hillside from Paral.lel Metro station in Poble
> Sec, and makes a final stop immediately below the castle at the top of Montjuïc.
> It costs 5.70€ ($7.40) adults, 4.50€ ($5.85) children 4 to 12 one-way, and 7.90€
> ($10) adults, 6€ ($7.80) children 4 to 12 round-trip.

5 THE HARBORFRONT

For a city that for centuries "lived with its back to the sea," Barcelona now sports a spectacular harborfront, the busiest leisure port in the Mediterranean, and kilometers of
urban beaches. The relocation of the commercial port and coastal freeway, and the demolition of industrial buildings and eyesores that blocked the view of the sea, were pushed
ahead for the 1992 Olympic Games. Without a doubt, the reclaiming of the city's coast
has been the most life-enhancing change Barcelona has seen in the last century. Starting
at the Columbus Monument, you can follow the city's coastal stretch via boardwalks and
esplanades to the Olympic Village and beyond. Along the way you will pass through the
modern marina, the Port Vell, the old fisherman's district of La Barceloneta, and end at
Frank Gehry's famous fish sculpture at the Olympic Port.

L'Aquarium de Barcelona ★★   One of the most impressive testimonials to sea life
anywhere opened in 1996 in Barcelona's Port Vell, a 10-minute walk from the bottom of
La Rambla. The largest aquarium in Europe, it contains 21 glass tanks positioned along
either side of a wide curving corridor. Each tank depicts a different marine habitat, with
emphasis on everything from multicolored fish and corals to seagoing worms to sharks.
The highlight is a huge "oceanarium" representative of the Mediterranean as a self-sus-
taining ecosystem. You view it from the inside of a glass-roofed, glass-sided tunnel that
runs along its entire length, making fish, eels, and sharks appear to swim around you.
Kids can let off some steam in the **Explora** section, a collection of touchy-feely educa-
tional exhibits on Catalonia's Costa Brava and Ebro Delta.

Moll d'Espanya-Port Vell. (℃ **93-221-74-74.** www.aquariumbcn.com. Admission 17€ ($22) adults, 13€
($17) seniors 60 and over, 12€ ($16) children 4–12, free for children 3 and under. July–Aug daily 9:30am–
11pm; Sept–June Mon–Fri 9:30am–9pm, Sat–Sun 9:30am–9:30pm. Metro: Drassanes or Barceloneta.

The Catalan History Museum is located in the Mar, a huge warehouse dating from the late 19th century. Many similar build- _ood alongside it before this flank of the port was redeveloped for the 1992 Olym-Games, creating the marina and recreational area that now surrounds it.

The museum, divided into eight sections, aims to provide a stroll through history, and that pretty much sums up what it does. It's a sometimes exhausting, highly didactic tour of the country. **"Roots," "Birth of a Nation,"** and **"Our Sea"** look at Catalonia's ancient ancestors, the flourishing Romanesque period, and the Catalan-Aragonese sea trade. **"On the Periphery of an Empire," "Bases of the Revolution,"** and **"Steam and Nation"** study Catalonia's decline under the Hapsburg rule and subsequent economic and cultural recovery in the industrial age. Finally, **"The Electric Years"** (which is, by far, one of the more entertaining parts of the exhibit) and **"Defeat and Recovery"** deal with the 20th century, the Civil War, Catalonia during Franco's dictatorship, and the first democratic elections after his death.

It's a lot of area to cover and the museum uses a mixture of multimedia, re-creations, models, and other interactive devices as their medium, most of the time with effective results. As all of the accompanying explanations are in Catalan, you are provided with a translation (in book form) at the entrance.

The temporary exhibitions on the ground floor are less heavy and have included some excellent shows on the Mediterranean cultures, and the relationship between the famed poet Federico García Lorca and Salvador Dalí.

After all this you may need a break. The museum's **cafe** offers great food and an excellent view of the port; also on the port side are a handful of outdoor seafood restaurants.

Plaça de la Pau Vila 3. ℰ **93-225-47-00.** www.mhcat.net. Admission 4€ ($5.20) adults; 3€ ($3.90) children 7–18, students, and seniors 65 and over. Free 1st Sun of each month. Tues–Sat 10am–7pm (until 8pm Wed); Sun 10am–2:30pm. Metro: Barceloneta.

Museu Marítim ★★★ (Kids) In the former Royal Shipyards (Drassanes Reials), the city's Maritime Museum is the finest of its kind in Spain and possibly the world. The seafaring cities of Venice, Genoa, and Valencia all had impressive arsenals, but only vestiges remain. In contrast, Barcelona's shipyards with their majestic arches, columns, and gigantic vaults are a preciously intact example of medieval civic architecture. This complex, which before the coastline receded sat right on the water's edge, was used to dry-dock, construct, and repair ships for the Catalan-Aragonese rulers. During the 18th century, the place went into decline, mainly due to the dissolution of naval construction. Right up until the Civil War, it served as an army barracks until it opened as a museum in the 1970s.

Its collection titled **The Great Adventure of the Sea** is homage to Catalonia's maritime history. The most outstanding exhibit occupies an entire bay. It is a reconstruction of La Galería Real of Don Juan of Austria, a lavish royal galley. In 1971, following extensive documentation, this model was built in celebration of the vessel's most glorious achievement 400 years earlier. The ship headed an alliance of Spanish, Venetian, Maltese, and Vatican vessels in a bloody battle against a Turkish squadron. The "Holy League" won, effectively ending Ottoman rule in the Mediterranean. There is an excellent film re-creating the battle that you watch onboard, and you can view the galley's elaborate hull, hold, and deck, where each of its 59 oars were manned by the sailors.

Other exhibits chart the traditional fishing techniques and sailing as sport through neat little caravels and draggers, snipes, and sloops. The art of wooden shipbuilding, the charting of the oceans, and the launch into the steam age are also covered. Particularly fine is the collection of late-19th-century mastheads, navigational instruments, and models of the Compañía Trasmediterránea's fleet (this local company still operates the Barcelona–Balearic Islands route). The collection also boasts a small model of *Ictíneo,* one of the world's first submarines, designed by the Catalan visionary Narcís Monturiol.

Av. de les Drassanes s/n. ✆ **93-342-99-20.** www.museumaritimbarcelona.com. Admission 6.50€ ($8.45) adults, 5.20€ ($6.75) youths 11–25 and seniors 65 and over, 3.25€ ($4.25) children 6–10. Daily 10am–8pm. Metro: Drassanes.

6 OUTER BARCELONA

Barcelona's outer suburbs are largely residential. Once they were considered to be country areas, annexed over the years by the city's continuing sprawl. Thus there are a handful of notable buildings that once stood in a village or country estate. The *barri* of Sarrià, easily reached by the FGC station of the same name, has retained a particularly authentic villagey feel. Located at the foot of Tibidabo, it's a pleasant place to wander around and take in some clean air.

Colònia Güell ★★   For many, Gaudí's most prolific work lies not within Barcelona, but outside. He designed the church for the Colònia Güell, an ambitious plan of Eusebi Güell's that lies 20 minutes by train inland from the city. Güell was a progressive man and wished to set up a colony for the workers of his textile mill, which was being transferred here from central Barcelona. The colony would contain a hospital, library, residences, theater, and church. Only the crypt was completed before Güell's death.

The haunting grotto-like structure stands on an elevated part of the *colònia* surrounded by a pine forest. Its cavernous dimensions and stone-forest interior are due to an ingenious method that the architect employed in the planning stages, one that is on display in both the Sagrada Família and La Pedrera. Gaudí devised the models for his work using lengths of string attached to weights, with the weights taking the tension, photographed the pieces, and then inverted the photos. What was concave became convex, as in an arch. Thus he was able to measure the angles, build the scaffolding and envisage the forms, and predate three-dimensional computer drawing by a hundred years. The work is one of Gaudí's most organic: Walls bend and curve at impossible angles, and windows open out like beetles' wings.

It's also worth taking a walk around the rest of the colony. The red-brick *moderniste* buildings were designed by architects Francesc Berenguer and Joan Rubió Bellver. Most of these are now private residences. Many of the other buildings, the factory and warehouses, have been abandoned, which gives the place a ghost town-like ambience.

Claudi Güell s/n, Santa Coloma de Cervelló. ✆ **93-630-58-07.** www.gaudiallgaudi.com/EA007.htm. Admission Colònia Güell and Crypt 8€ ($10) adults, 5.60€ ($7.30) seniors. Guided tour of crypt 5€ ($6.50), non-guided visit of crypt 4€ ($5.20), free for children 10 and under. Mon–Sat 10am–2pm and 3–7pm; Sun 10am–3pm (Mass at 11am and 1pm). FGC: Colònia Güell. Lines S33, S34, S8, or S7 (all leave from Plaça Espanya).

CosmoCaixa (Museu de la Ciència) ★★★ (Kids)   This spectacular Science Museum is an enlarged, much-improved version of the 1980 original. Funded by a major bank (La Caixa), the Museu de la Ciència closed in 1998 and embarked on a 6-year overhaul. The result is the best, most high-tech, and certainly most hands-on science museum in Europe.

Like the original, El Museu de la Ciència occupies a *moderniste* building (originally a poorhouse) at the foot of Tibidabo, but with a daring underground extension and renovation of the original edifice, effectively quadrupling its exhibition space to 3,700 sq. m (39,826 sq. ft.).

As well as the additional new bioresearch center, the permanent collection has been completely overhauled and, through an imaginative combination of original material and multimedia, takes the novice on a comprehensive tour of the scientific principles. The collection is divided into four categories: **"Inert Materials"** deals with the big-bang theory up to the first signs of life, **"Living Materials"** focuses on the birth of mankind, **"Intelligent Materials"** looks at the development of human intelligence, and **"Civilized Materials"** explores history and science from pioneers to the computer age.

The biggest crowd pleaser is **"The Flooded Forest,"** a living, breathing Amazonian rainforest *inside* the museum with over 100 species of animal and plant life. Kids come into close contact with animal life in the *Toca Toca* section, which has rats, frogs, spiders, and other natives from diverse ecosystems, some of which can be picked up and touched. There is a 3-D planetarium and the extraordinary "Geological Wall" that explains, through an interactive route, the history of the world from a geological perspective. All in all, the new Science Museum is a unique and highly entertaining window to the world of science.

Teodor Roviralta 47. (C) **93-212-60-50.** www.obrasocial.lacaixa.es. Admission 3€ ($3.90) adults, 2€ ($2.60) students and seniors 65 and over, free for children 2 and under; planetarium 2€ ($2.60); Toca Toca (children come into contact with animals) 2€ ($2.60). Tues–Sun 10am–8pm. FGC: Avinguda Tibidabo (then 10-min. walk). Bus: 17, 22, 58, or 73.

Finca Güell ★ The Finca Güell, or country estate of Eusebi Güell, features three works by Antoni Gaudí, the industrialist's favorite architect. Still on a private estate, they can only be viewed from the street, but that doesn't detract from the impact they have upon the viewer. Eusebi Güell asked Gaudí to create an entrance gate, a gatehouse, and stables. The first is probably one of the most stunning pieces of wrought-iron work in the world. Locally known as the Drac de Pedralbes (the Dragon of Pedralbes), a huge reptile literally jumps out at you, his tongue extended and ready to attack. The dwellings are no less powerful. Like the **Casa Vicens** (p. 189), they were designed early in Gaudí's career when he was influenced by Islamic architecture and feature turrets and white walls contrasted with brightly colored tiles. The pavilion on the right houses a library and Gaudían research center.

Gaudí took inspiration for the *finca* from the Greek myth of Hesperides. The ominous dragon is a metaphor for the beast that Hercules battled, and although they are a tad run-down, the gardens behind the gate used to be lush and full of citrus trees—the legendary gardens of Hesperides themselves.

Av. Pedralbes 7. Metro: Palau Reial.

Monestir de Pedralbes ★★ The oldest building in Pedralbes (the city's wealthiest residential area) is this monastery founded in 1326 by Elisenda de Montcada, queen of Jaume II. It housed the nuns of the Order of Saint Clare (who are now taking up residence in a much smaller adjacent building), and after the king's death Queen Elisenda took up residence in the convent. She is buried in the Gothic church next door (where the nuns still sing their vespers) in a beautiful tomb surrounded by angels.

After passing over the threshold, you come to the serene cloister with a central fountain, well, herb gardens, and other greenery. There are nearly two dozen elegant arches

Mes Que un Club (More than a Club)!

Next to the Picasso, the most visited museum in the city is the **Museu FC Barcelona,** or the museum of the city's beloved football team, Barça. It's inside their home ground Camp Nou, the largest stadium in Europe, with a capacity of 120,000. Despite its size, tickets to matches are scarce as hens' teeth. Most of the seats are taken by *socis* (members) of the richest soccer club in the world. As their slogan goes, Barça is *Mes que un club* ("More than a club"). Membership, which is often handed down through the generations, is a mark of Catalanismo (Catalan identity). During the dictatorship, the war was played out on the football field with the capital's team seen as representative of the loathed central government. Madrid is still Barça's archenemy (old grudges die hard in soccer) and when the two meet at Camp Nou, the whole city stops.

Along with the museum, you can choose to see the (empty) stadium, the chapel where players say a prayer before a big match, the club and pressrooms, and the tunnel via which players enter the field. The collection consists of photos, trophies, documents, kits, and other paraphernalia telling the dramatic and emotive history of the club from its beginnings in 1899 to the present. It's fun, makes for some light relief from other heady cultural offerings, and is not just for die-hard soccer fans.

Camp Nou stadium, access door nos. 7 and 9. Arístides Maillol s/n. ✆ **93-496-36-00.** www.fcbarcelona.cat. Admission museum and stadium: Guided tour 13€ ($17) adults, 10€ ($13) children 6 to 13; museum only 8.50€ ($11) adults, 6.80€ ($8.85) children 12 and under. April 14 to October 12 Monday to Saturday 10am to 8pm, Sunday 10am to 2:30pm; rest of year Monday to Saturday 10am to 6:30pm, Sunday 10am to 2:30pm. Metro: Collblanc.

on each side, rising three stories high. Immediately to your right is a small chapel containing the chief treasure of the monastery, the incredibly intact Chapel of St. Michael. Inside, it is decorated with murals by Ferrer Bassa, a major artist of Catalonia in the 1300s, depicting the Passion of Christ.

The original nuns' residence houses an exhibition re-creating the monastic life of the 14th century: what they ate, how they dressed, the hours of prayer, and their general comings and goings. Some of the day chambers contain original artifacts of the *monestir,* although the most evocative rooms are the kitchen and refectory and the communal dining room where the Mother Superior broke her vow of silence with mealtime Bible readings from the wooden pulpit.

Baixada del Monestir 9. ✆ **93-203-92-82.** www.museuhistoria.bcn.es. Admission 5€ ($6.50) adults, 3.50€ ($4.55) students and seniors, free for children 12 and under. Tues–Sun 10am–2pm. Free 1st Sun of month. FGC: Reina Elisenda. Bus: 75.

Museu de les Arts Decoratives/Museu de Ceràmica ★ The city's museums of decorative arts and ceramics occupy the Palau de Pedralbes and can be seen together. The palace is set in an elegant garden that once belonged to the Finca Güell, the country estate of Gaudí's patron and friend Eusebi Güell.

Tips Small but Good: Other Barcelona Museums

There are dozens of small private museums in Barcelona, some the fruit of a collector's obsessive passion, others that display an ancient guild's craft. Many are free; others charge a minimal entrance fee or ask for a donation. The charming **Museu de Calçat,** Plaça Sant Felip Neri 5 (✆ **93-301-45-33;** 2.50€/$3.25; Tues–Sun 11am–2pm; Metro: Liceu), is housed in the ancient headquarters of the city's shoemaker guild. The collection spans from Roman sandals to the boots of the famous Catalan cellist Pau Casals. The **Museu de Carrosses Fúnebres (Museum of Funeral Carriages),** Sancho d' Avilla 2 (✆ **93-484-17-00;** free admission; Mon–Fri 10am–1pm and 4–6pm, Sat–Sun 10am–1pm; Metro: Marina), also has an unusual location: the basement of the city's morgue.

Although bullfighting is not popular in Catalonia except among a handful of die-hard *aficionados,* La Monumental, Barcelona's bullring, is an exotic structure that also houses the **Museu Tauri,** Gran Vía 749 (✆ **93-245-58-03;** 5€/$6.50 adults, 4€/$5.20 children; Apr–Sept Tues–Sat 10:30am–2pm and 4–7pm, Sun 10am–1pm; Metro: Monumental), a small museum of memorabilia, costumes, and other bull-ish items. The taboo and the most sacred of cultures around the world are explored in the **Museu Etnològic,** Passeig de Santa Madrona s/n (✆ **93-424-64-02;** www.museuetnologic.bcn.es; 3€/$3.90, free for children 16 and under and seniors 65 and over; Tues–Sun 10am–2pm; Metro: Espanya). In a similar vein, ethnographic pieces collected by Capuchin nuns in the Amazon region can be viewed in their convent at the **Museu Etnogràfic Andino-Amazónic,** Cardenal Vives i Tutó 2–16 (✆ **93-204-34-58;** by appointment only; Metro: María Cristina). In 1982 the prominent Barcelonese doctor Melcior Colet donated his home, a *moderniste* dwelling designed by Puig i Cadafalch, and amassed sporting memorabilia to the city. The result, the **Museu de L'Esport Dr. Melcior Colet,** Buenos Aires 56–58 (✆ **93-419-22-32;** Mon–Fri 10am–2pm and 4–8pm; bus: 7, 15, 33, 34, or 59), is a collection of objects relating to Catalan sporting achievements.

In an outer Barcelona park, an extraordinary collection of period carriages, adornments, and uniforms worn by coachmen is at the **Museu de Carruatges,** Plaça Josep Pallach 8 (✆ **93-427-58-13;** Mon–Fri 10am–1pm; Metro: Mundet). One of the prettiest of all the city's private museums is at the rear of a perfume shop. The **Museu del Perfum,** Passeig de Gràcia 39 (✆ **93-216-01-21;** www.museudelperfum.com; 5€/$6.50 adults, 3€/$3.90 students and seniors; Mon–Fri 10:30am–1pm and 5–8pm, Sat 11am–1:30pm; Metro: Passeig de Gràcia), holds over 5,000 examples of perfume bottles, vials, and paraphernalia from Egyptian times to the present day. Watch out for the Dalí-designed Le Roi de Soleil.

The neoclassical residence was taken over by King Alfonso XIII (who hardly ever used it) in 1920, then 10 years later handed over to the local government, who turned it into an exhibition space for the decorative arts. During the dictatorship, General Franco made it his Barcelona abode, before it finally regained its status as a museum again in 1960.

Inside, the lavish halls with their gilt, marble, and frescoes make a picturesque back-drop for both these collections. By far the superior of the two is the Ceramic Museum, whose collection, arranged regionally, spans from the 11th century to the present day. Particularly striking are the mudéjar and metallic inlay work from the south and the baroque and Renaissance pieces from Castile. One extraordinary exhibit from Catalonia is an enormous plaque from the 18th century depicting a chocolate feast in the country-side.

Compared with the collection of decorative arts at the MNAC (p. 194), the small exhibition here is a slight letdown. The name is somewhat deceiving, as the focus here, at least in the latter part of the collection, is really on design, as opposed to decorative objects that may or may not be functional. That said, Catalonia's design heritage is an important one, and there are many pieces here from the city's design boom of the '80s and early '90s, featuring top names such as Javier Mariscal and Oscar Tusquets. In the future, this collection may form part of the projected Design Museum.

Av. Diagonal 686. ℂ **93-280-16-21.** www.museuceramica.bcn.cat. www.museuartsdecoratives.bcn.es. Admission (for both) 5€ ($6.50) adults, 3€ ($3.90) students, free for children 16 and under. Tues–Sat 10am–6pm; Sun 10am–3pm. Free 1st Sun of month. Metro: Palau Reial.

Parc d'Atraccions Tibidabo ★★ (Kids) The mountain of Tibidabo has been a popular retreat for Barcelonese since 1868 when a road was built connecting it to the city. You arrive there on the creaky old funicular—or, less dramatically, by bus—to find your-self confronted by an amusement park that combines tradition with modernity. In sum-mer, the place takes on a carnival-like atmosphere, and most of the credit for this can go to a wealthy pill manufacturer by the name of Dr. Andreu, who believed (quite sensibly) that fresh mountain air was good for your health. He created the Sociedad Anónima de Tibidabo, which promoted the slopes as a public garden and was instrumental in install-ing both the blue tram and aforementioned funicular which gets you there (p. 48). Some of the attractions in the park date back from Andreu's time. **L'Avio,** for example, is a quaint replica of the first plane that served the Barcelona-Madrid route. In the Tibidabo version, you are treated to a whisk over the summit in a toy-like craft suspended from a central axis. Another dated attraction designed to scare you out of your wits is **Aer-omàgic,** an exhilarating mountain ride that is greatly enhanced by the elevated position of the park itself. On a more relaxed level you can also visit a charming museum of period automatons.

The church next door to the amusement park is **Temple de Sagrat Cor,** an ugly and highly kitschy building dating from 1902 that was meant to provide Barcelona with its own Sacré Coeur. Its distinctive mountaintop silhouette can be seen from all over the city.

Plaça Tibidabo 3. ℂ **93-211-79-42.** www.tibidabo.es. 24€ ($31) for unlimited rides, 11€ ($14) students, 9€ ($12) seniors 60 and over, 7€ ($9.10) children 1.2m (4 ft.) and under, free for children 3 and under. Summer daily noon–10pm; off season Sat–Sun noon–7pm. Bus: 58 to Avinguda Tibidabo Metro, then take the Tramvía Blau, which drops you at the funicular. Round-trip 3.10€ ($4.05).

7 PARKS & GARDENS

Museums aren't Barcelona's only attractions, and contrary to first impressions, it is not solely a city of concrete squares and stone streets. In a fine Mediterranean climate, life takes place outside, in unique parks and gardens, many of which were designed by the city's top architects for the Olympic renewal frenzy. The most popular ones are the leafy and formal **Parc de la Ciutadella** (p. 179), Gaudí's visionary **Parc Güell** (p. 189), and the mountain of **Montjuïc** (p. 191). But there are plenty more parks, gardens, wide-open spaces, and leafy hideaways for a bit of solitude or one-on-one with nature. Most parks are open 9am to sunset.

Not strictly a park but a large open square, one of the city's most famous "hard plazas," the **Parc de Joan Miró,** Aragó 1 (Metro: Espanya), occupies an entire L'Eixample block, once the city's slaughterhouse. Its main features are an esplanade and a pond from which a towering sculpture by Miró, *Woman and Bird,* rises. Palm, pine, and eucalyptus trees, as well as playgrounds and pergolas, complete the picture. Nearby, the enormous Parc de l'Espanya Industrial, next to the Sants train station (near the Plaça dels Països Catalans entrance to that metro station), is a surrealist landscape of amphitheater-type seating, watchtowers, and postmodern sculpture juxtaposed with a more vegetated parkland at the rear. On the opposite side of L'Eixample, the **Parc de L' Estació del Nord,** Nápoles 70 (Metro: Arc de Triomf or Marina), is a whimsical piece of landscape gardening featuring sculptures and land art by the U.S. artist Beverly Pepper.

Another daring urban space is the **Parc de la Crueta del Coll** near the Parc Güell, Castellterçol 24 (Metro: Penitents). Located in a former quarry, this urban playground features a man-made pool and an enormous oxidized metal sculpture, the *Elogia del Agua* by Basque sculptor Eduardo Chillida. Looking somewhat like a huge claw, it is theatrically suspended from a cliff face. Even further north is **Collserola,** a natural parkland of nearly 1,800 hectares (4,448 acres). Urbanites come up here in droves on the weekend to cycle, stroll, or have a picnic. The best way to get here is to take the FGC from Plaça de Catalunya to either Baixador de Vallvidrera (which has an information office on the park) or Les Planes.

For those who like their parks more traditional, the romantic **Parc del Laberint** (Passeig de Castanyers s/n; Metro: Mundet) in the outer suburb of Horta is the oldest, and therefore most established, in the city. As the name suggests, there is a central maze of Cyprus trees, and the rest of the site is laid out over terraces with Italianate-style statues and balustrades.

One of the more recent parks to appear, opening in 2008, is the **Parc Central de Poble Nou,** designed by the controversial French architect Jean Nouvel. The park is designed in a spartan futuristic style that's more a modern art creation—with its cratered moonscape and sporadic high plants, all enclosed by flowered covered walls—than a place to relax and enjoy a picnic.

8 OUTDOOR & SPORTING PURSUITS

GOLF

One of the city's best courses, **Club de Golf Vallromanes,** Afueras s/n, Vallromanes, Barcelona (✆ **93-572-90-64;** www.clubdegolfvallromanes.com), is 20 minutes north of the city center by car. Nonmembers who reserve tee times in advance are welcome to play. The greens fee is 98€ ($127) on weekdays, 160€ ($208) on weekends. The club is open Wednesday through Monday from 9am to 9pm. Established in 1972, it is the site of Spain's most important golf tournament.

Reial Club de Golf El Prat, El Prat de Llobregat (✆ **93-379-02-78**), is a prestigious club that allows nonmembers to play under two conditions: They must have a handicap

(Kids) Happy, Happy, Joy, Joy!

Happy Parc (www.happyparc.com) is the perfect solutio[...] let off a little steam. It's a huge covered labyrinth-type s[...] touchy, feely, jumpy, rubbery contraptions for the little[...] on. Monitors are on hand and there is a special enclos[...] are two in Barcelona: one at Comtes de Bell-lloc 74–78 ([...] Sants) and the other at Pau Claris 97 (📞 **93-317-86-60**; Metro: Urquina[...]a). bou[...] are open Monday to Friday 5 to 9pm and weekends 11am to 9pm. Cost i[...]4€ ($5.20) per hour for children, free for adults.

issued by the governing golf body in their home country, and they must prove mem[...] ship in a golf club at home. The club has two 18-hole par-72 courses. Greens fees [...] 114€ ($148) Monday through Friday. Weekends are for members only. From Barcelo[...] follow Avinguda Once de Septiembre past the airport to Barrio de San Cosme. Fr[...] there follow the signs along Carrer Prat to the golf course. For more information [...] golfing around Barcelona, see p. 305.

SWIMMING

Swim where some Olympic events took place, at **Piscina Bernardo Picornell,** Av. [...] Estadí 30–40, on Montjuïc (📞 **93-423-40-41**). Adjacent to the Olympic Stadium,[...] incorporates two of the best swimming pools in Spain (one indoor, one outdoor). C[...] tom-built for the Olympics, they're open to the public Monday through Friday fro[...] 7am to midnight, Saturday from 7am to 9pm, and Sunday from 7am to 4pm. Entran[...] costs 8€ ($10) for adults and 4€ ($5.20) for children and allows full use throughout th[...] day plus the gymnasium, the sauna, and the whirlpools. Bus no. 61 makes frequent ru[...] from the Plaça Espanya.

TENNIS

The **Centre Municipal de Tennis,** Passeig Vall d'Hebron 178 (📞 **93-427-65-0[...]** Metro: Montbau), has been the training ground for some of the country's top players. [...] has 17 clay and seven grass courts set over beautiful grounds, but you will need to supp[...] your own racket and balls. Court hire is 10€ ($13) an hour for clay courts and 13€ ($1[...] an hour for grass courts.

HORSEBACK RIDING

Set high above the city on the mountain of Montjuïc, this is a top setting for a ridin[...] school. The **Escola Municipa d' Hípica,** Av. Muntayans 14–16 (📞 **93-426-10-66** Metro: Espanya), imparts classes to all ages from 16€ ($21) per hour.

SURFING & WINDSURFING

When the wind blows, Barcelona's beaches offer good conditions for wind and kite surf[...] ing and regular surfing, and the latter is really taking off. **Wind 220°,** on the corner o[...] Passeig Marítim and Pontevedra (📞 **93-221-47-02**; Metro: Barceloneta), right on th[...] beach at Barceloneta, has all the equipment you need for rent, plus storage facilities, [...] cafe, information, and courses.

ALLOW BOATS

ndrinas (Swallow Boats; ℰ 93-442-31-06; www.lasgolondrinas.com) are ttle double-deckers that take you on a leisurely cruise of the city's port, or port northern coast combined. Boats depart from the port side of the Plaça Portal de la au, directly in front of the Columbus statue. The port-only tour leaves every hour (weekends only) between 11:45am and 6pm, and the port and coast excursion daily at 11am and 1220, 1:15, and 3:30pm. Prices for adults are 5.50€ ($7.15) for port-only and 11€ ($14) for port and coast as far as the Forum; children 4 to 14 pay 2.50€ ($3.25) and 5€ ($6.50) or these respective tours.

Strolling Around Barcelona

Spain's second-largest city is also its most cosmopolitan and avant-garde, a rich repository of landmark buildings and world-class cultural centers that range from its famed *moderniste* Sagrada Família and great medieval Gothic cathedral to the MNAC's Romanesque treasures and Picasso Museum's cubist masterpieces. Cutting through the heart of its emblematic Old Quarter is the tree-lined promenade of La Rambla, a former riverbed that today is a vibrant, colorful thoroughfare perennially packed with visitors of all nations. Three of our walking tours take you on strolls through the medieval labyrinths on either side of this emblematic *paseo*. The fourth leads you out into the spacious L'Eixample to explore its long, wide boulevards and surreal 19th-century edifices.

WALKING TOUR 1	BARRI GOTIC (THE GOTHIC QUARTER)

START:	Plaça Nova (Metro: Jaume I)
FINISH:	Same point at Plaça Nova or the Vía Laietana opposite Port Vell (Metro: Barceloneta)
TIME:	2 to 3 hours
BEST TIMES:	Any sunny day or early evening

This walk will take you through the core of medieval Barcelona, through narrow lanes, across tiny plazas, and past some of the city's oldest and most imposing palaces and religious centers.

Begin at the:

❶ Plaça Nova

Set within the shadow of the cathedral, this is the largest open-air space in the Gothic Quarter. Behind you, the facade of the **Collegi de Architects,** the city's architecture school, features a frieze designed (but not executed by) Picasso. From Plaça Nova, climb the incline of the narrow asphalt-covered street (Carrer del Bisbe).

At the approach of the first street on the right, the Carrer de Montjuïc del Bisbe de Santa Llúcia, turn right and follow this winding street to the:

❷ Plaça de Sant Felip Neri

This small square is often cited as the most charming in the Barri Gòtic. Although none of the buildings are in fact Gothic (and some have been moved from other parts of the city), the central fountain, majestic trees, and overall tranquillity more than qualify it for the status of "urban oasis." The holes you see in the stonework of the lower facade of the 17th-century church (which unfortunately lost many of its baroque features in the late 18th c.) were caused by a bomb dropped by Fascist troops that killed 20 children from the adjoining school. On the opposite side, the oldest building is Renaissance in style and serves as the headquarters of the shoemakers guild with a Shoe Museum inside.

Walk back to the Carrer del Bisbe. Backtrack left, then take the immediate right, Carrer de Santa Llúcia. This will lead you to:

❸ Casa de L'Ardiaca (Archdeacon's House)

Constructed in the 15th century as a residence for Archdeacon Despla, the Gothic building has sculptural reliefs with Renaissance and early-20th-century motifs. In its cloister-like courtyard are a fountain and a palm tree. Notice the mail slot, designed by the *modernista* architect Domènech i Montaner, where five swallows and a turtle carved into stone await the arrival of important messages. This beautiful setting now holds the city's archives, but you are free to inspect the courtyard and exterior.

As you exit the Archdeacon's House, continue in the same direction several steps until you reach the:

❹ Plaça de la Seu

This square is in front of the main entrance to the **Catedral de Barcelona** (p. 172). If you are here in the first couple of weeks of December, you will be lucky enough to coincide with the lively Mercat de Santa Llúcia, an outdoor market selling Christmas trees, decorations, and figurines such as the pooping Catalan, the *caganer* (p. 39).

After touring the cathedral, exit from the door you entered and turn right onto Carrer dels Comtes, admiring the gargoyles along the way. After about 100 paces on the left, you'll approach the:

❺ Museu Frederic Marès

This wonderful museum holds an extraordinary collection of Romanesque and Gothic religious artifacts (p. 174). Even if you don't go in, the courtyard of this 13th-century former bishop's palace is well worth a peek. The outdoor cafe is a relaxing spot to take a coffee break.

Exit through the same door you entered and continue your promenade in the same direction. You'll pass the portal of the cathedral's right side, where the heads of two rather abstract angels flank the throne of a seated female saint. A few paces farther, on the left, notice the stone facade of the:

❻ Arxiu de la Carona d'Aragó

The Arxiu is the former archives center of the crown of Aragon and Catalunya. Formerly called **Palau del Lloctinent (Deputy's Palace),** this Gothic building was the work of Antonio Carbonell. It is not open to the public, but you can get a glimpse of its patios and upper arcades, admiring the century-old grapevines.

As you exit from the courtyard, you'll find yourself back on Carrer dels Comtes. Take the street in front of you, the Carrer de la Pietat, which follows the rear facade of the cathedral, and then the first street on your left, the Carrer del Paradis. At no. 10 is one of the Barri Gòtic's best-kept secrets, the:

❼ Temple d'Augustus

Inside the courtyard of this medieval building, these four majestic Corinthian columns are all that remain of Roman Barcelona's main temple. Most historians believe that it was dedicated to the emperor Caesar Augustus, hence its name. What is certain is that on the highest point of the city, known as Mons Taber, it was once the prominent feature of the Roman Forum. June through September, the temple is open Tuesday to Saturday from 10am to 8pm, Sunday from 10am to 2pm; the rest of the year, it's open Tuesday to Saturday from 10am to 2pm and 4 to 8pm, Sunday from 10am to 2pm.

Retrace your steps back along the Carrer de la Pietat to the Palau del Lloctinent. Continue in the same direction on the same street and it will bring you to the most famous squares of the Gothic Quarter:

❽ Plaça del Rei

The Great Royal Palace, an enlarged building of what was originally the residence of the counts of Barcelona, dominates this square. Here you can visit both the **Palau Reial** and the **Museu d'Història de la Ciutat** (p. 175). On the right side of the square stands the **Palatine Chapel of Santa Agata,** a 14th-century Gothic temple that is part of the Palau Reial. In this chapel is preserved the altarpiece of the Lord High Constable, a 15th-century work by Jaume Huguet.

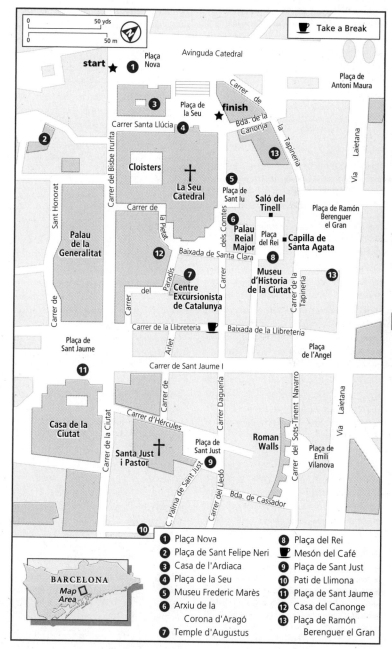

0 50 yds
0 50 m

Take a Break

Plaça Nova

start ❶

Avinguda Catedral

Plaça de Antoni Maura

❷

Carrer del Bisbe Irurita

❸ Plaça de la Seu

finish

Carrer de

Carrer Santa Llúcia

❹

Bda. de la Canonja

la Tapineria

Via Laietana

Sant Honorat

Cloisters

La Seu Catedral

✝

❺ Plaça de Sant Iu

Saló del Tinell

Plaça de Ramón Berenguer el Gran

Carrer de

la Pietat

❻ **Palau Reial Major**

Plaça del Rei

❽ ■ **Capilla de Santa Agata**

Palau de la Generalitat

❶❷

Baixada de Santa Clara

Carrer dels Comtes

Paradís

❼ **Centre Excursionista de Catalunya**

Museu d'Historia de la Ciutat

Carrer de la Tapineria

❶❸

Carrer

del

Carrer

Carrer de la Llibreteria ☕

Baixada de la Llibreteria

Plaça de Sant Jaume

Arlet

Plaça de l'Angel

❶❶

Carrer de Sant Jaume I

Casa de la Ciutat

Carrer de la Ciutat

Carrer d'Hércules

Carrer de

Carrer Dagueria

Plaça de Sant Just

Roman Walls

Carrer del Sots-Tinent Navarro

Via Laietana

Santa Just i Pastor

✝

❾

Carrer del Lledó

Plaça de Emili Vilanova

C. Palma de Sant Just

Carrer de Sant Just

Bda. de Cassador

❶❶

BARCELONA
Map Area

❶ Plaça Nova
❷ Plaça de Sant Felipe Neri
❸ Casa de l'Ardiaca
❹ Plaça de la Seu
❺ Museu Frederic Marès
❻ Arxiu de la
    Corona d'Aragó
❼ Temple d'Augustus

❽ Plaça del Rei
☕ Mesón del Café
❾ Plaça de Sant Just
❶❶ Pati de Llimona
❶❶ Plaça de Sant Jaume
❶❷ Casa del Canonge
❶❸ Plaça de Ramón
    Berenguer el Gran

STROLLING AROUND BARCELONA

8

BARRI GOTIC (THE GOTHIC QUARTER)

TAKE A BREAK
Mesón del Café, Librería 16
(© **93-315-07-54**), founded in
1909, specializes in coffee and cappuccino. It is one of the oldest coffeehouses
in the neighborhood, sometimes crowd-
ing 50 people into its tiny precincts. Some
regulars perch on stools at the bar and
order breakfast. Coffee costs .80€ ($1.05),
and a cappuccino goes for 1.75€ ($2.30).
The cafe is open Monday to Saturday
from 7am to 9:30pm.

Exit the Plaça del Rei on its southern side. Turn left
into the steep Baixada de Llibretería. At no. 7 you
will see the beautiful candle shop, the Cereria Subirà,
the oldest continuous retail establishment in Barcelona. A few paces on turn left, crossing over the busy
Carrer Ferran. Continue along the Carrer de la Dagueria. This will lead you to:

⑨ Plaça de Sant Just

The square is dominated by the entrance to
the **Església dels Sants Just i Pastor.** Above
the entrance portal, an enthroned virgin is
flanked by a pair of protective angels. The
Latin inscription hails her as VIRGO NIGRA
ET PULCHRA, NOSTRA PATRONA PIA (Black
and Beautiful Virgin, Our Holy Patroness).
This church dates from the 14th century,
although work continued into the 16th.
Some authorities claim that the church, in
an earlier, 4th-century manifestation of the
present structure, is the oldest in Barcelona.
You'll find that its doors are usually closed
except during Sunday Mass.

Opposite the church, at Plaça de Sant
Just 4, is the 18th-century **Palau Moixó,** an
aristocratic town house covered with faded
but still elegant frescoes of angels cavorting
among garlands. At its base is a public well,
the oldest water source in the city.

Continue walking in the same direction down the
Carrer de la Dagueria, which changes its name to the
Carrer de Lledó. If you like, take a detour to the
street parallel to you on your left, the Carrer del
Sorts-Tinent Navarro; here you will see the remains
of the old Roman walls. If not, take the second street
on your right, the Carrer Cometa (so named for a
sighting of a comet here in 1834). Turn right again
onto the Carrer del Regomir. At no. 3 is the:

⑩ Pati de Llimona

This lively community center, named after
its interior patio and lemon tree, has a
beautiful 15th-century gallery and vestiges
of the old Roman sewer system displayed
underneath glass in the floor. Next door,
the tiny 16th-century open **chapel of Saint
Christopher** is protected from the street by
an iron gate. It's worth checking out what
exhibitions are on in the center, normally
by local artists and photographers.

Continue walking up the Carrer Regomir (which
changes its name to the Carrer de la Ciutat) until you
reach the:

⑪ Plaça de Sant Jaume

In many ways, this plaza is the political
heart of Catalan culture. Across this
square, constructed at what was once a
major junction for two Roman streets,
rush politicians and bureaucrats intent on
Catalonian government affairs. On Sunday evenings you can witness the *sardana*,
the national dance of Catalonia. Many
bars and restaurants stand on side streets
leading from this square.

Standing in the square, with your back
to the street just left (Carrer de la Ciutat),
you'll see, immediately on your right, the
Doric portico of the **Palau de la Generalitat,** the parliament of Catalonia. Construction of this exquisite work, with its
large courtyard and open-air stairway,
along with twin-arched galleries in the
Catalonian Gothic style, began in the era
of Jaume I. A special feature of the building is the Chapel of St. George, constructed in flamboyant Gothic style
between 1432 and 1435 and enlarged in
1620 with the addition of vaulting and a
cupola with hanging capitals. The back of
the building encloses an orange tree courtyard begun in 1532. In the Gilded Hall,
the Proclamation of the Republic was
signed. Across the square are the Ionic
columns of the **Casa de la Ciutat/Ayun-
tamiento,** the Town Hall of Barcelona.
Both these buildings are only periodically
open to the public (p. 175).

With your back to the Casa de la Ciutat, cross the square to the right and turn left, once again into the Carrer del Bisbe. On your immediate right is the:

⓬ Casa del Canonge (House of the Canon)

This series of buildings, once a group of canons' houses, dates from the 14th century and was restored in 1925; escutcheons from the 15th and 16th centuries remain. Notice the heraldic symbols of medieval Barcelona on the building's stone plaques—twin towers supported by winged goats with lion's feet. On the same facade, also notice the depiction of twin angels. The building today is used as the town residence of the President of the Generalitat.

Connecting it to the Palau de la Generalitat across the road is a charming **bridge** carved into lacy patterns of stonework, also dating from the 1920s.

Continue walking along Carrer del Bisbe until you reach your starting place, the Plaça Nova. If you wish to continue your walk, cross the square to the right to the busy Vía Laietana. Here you will see:

⓭ Plaça de Ramón Berenguer el Gran

An equestrian statue dedicated to this hero (1096–1131) is ringed with the gravel of a semicircular park, whose backdrop is formed by the walls of the ancient Roman fort and, nearby, a Gothic tower. Keep walking down the Vía Laietana toward the port and you will see more of these. Known as Las Murallas in Spanish, they were constructed between A.D. 270 and 310. The walls followed a rectangular course and were built so that their fortified sections would face the sea. By the 11th and 12th centuries, Barcelona had long outgrown its confines. Jaume I ordered the opening of the Roman Walls, and the burgeoning growth that ensued virtually destroyed them, except for the foundations you see today.

WALKING TOUR 2	LA RIBERA (EL BORN & SANT PERE)

START:	Plaça de l'Angel (Metro: Jaume I)
FINISH:	Arc de Triomf at northern end of Parc de la Ciutadella (Metro: Arc de Triomf)
TIME:	2 to 3 hours
BEST TIMES:	Any day or early evening

This tour continues your exploration of the Old Quarter, concentrating on the eastern corner, formerly an area of tradesmen and artisans, but today filled with top museums and trendy cafes.

Begin at the:

❶ Plaça de l'Angel

Known in medieval times as the "Square of Wheat" (Plaça del Blat) since all grain sales were made here, this small atmospheric square stands at the busy junction of Jaume 1 and Laietana on the eastern edge of the Barri Gòtic.

From the Plaça de l'Angel take Carrer Boria east; then turn north into Carrer Mercaderes and immediately east again to Plaça Santa Caterina and the:

❷ Mercat de Santa Caterina

This is the oldest working market in the area. It occupies the original site where the medieval convent of Santa Caterina once stood and provides the usual rich cornucopia of Mediterranean produce. In 2005, after a protracted period of renovation, the market was reopened with a stunning new *moderniste* design (by the late Enric Miralles), whose colorful waved roof owes more than a little to Gaudí.

From the south-facing side of the market take Carrer Sant Jacint, turn east into Carrer Corders, and then south into the Placeta d'en Marcus.

❸ Capella d'en Marcus

Well worth a peek is this diminutive 12th-century chapel nestling in the tiny Placeta d'en Marcus, near the junction of calles Montcada and Carders (Woolcomber's St.). Originally conceived by one Bernat Marcus as a sanctuary for luckless travelers who reached the city after the gates had been closed, it's also said to have been the headquarters of the country's very first postal service.

Continue south across Carrer Princesa to reach:

❹ Carrer Montcada

Named after a powerful merchant, Guillem de Montcada, who in 1153 built a long-since-disappeared palace here, this charming medieval street would be interesting enough to stroll along even if it didn't contain three of the city's most interesting museums (to which, alas, you won't be able to do justice if you're to finish this walk the same day). The elegant buildings lining the street are reminders of the time it was a wealthy trading center, where huge fortunes were made by adroit and ambitious merchants.

❺ Museu Picasso

Located in no fewer than five former palaces in Carrer Montcada, the Picasso is generally rated the most popular museum in town. In essence it covers the artist as a young man, and even the older works on display were created when the Malagueño was a mere twenty-something. Exhibits range from notes and rough sketches to lithographs, ceramics, and oil canvases. Highlights are "Las Meninas" (his take on Velázquez's painting of the same name) and the "Harlequin," and though time will be short, keep an eye open for "La Ciencia y la Caridad" (Science and Charity), a masterpiece created when the artist was still at school.

❻ Museu Textil i Indumentaria

Over a thousand years of fashion fill the salons of this extraordinary museum, which spreads throughout a fine period house, the Palau dels Marquesos de Llio, and features the original medieval ceilings. The oldest exhibits date from early Egypt, but it's the flamboyant baroque, Regency, and 20th-century styles that really catch the eye.

TAKE A BREAK
Textil Café, Carrer Montcada (📞 **93-268-25-98**), is a convenient spot for a break between museums. This chic little cafe is tucked away in a secluded cobbled courtyard on the grounds of the Museu Textil itself. Ideal for relaxing over a café llet (café con leche) and Danish pastry.

❼ Museu Barbier Muller d'Art Precolumbi

Atmospherically housed in the 15th-century Palau Nadal, close to the above two museums, this branch of the great Geneva museum offers one of the best displays of pre-Columbian art and has been drawing in the crowds ever since it opened in 1997. Among its highlights is a dazzling selection of gold, jewelry, and masks.

Continue down Carrer Montcada to the Passeig del Born. Turn west (right) onto Carrer de Santa María.

❽ Església de Santa María del Mar

Built in the 14th century during a period of just over 50 years (quick for the time), this grandiose high-vaulted basilica, honoring the patron saint of sailors, used to stand on the city's shore when the sea reached further inland. As the welfare of sailors mainly depended on the clemency and protection of "Our Lady of the Sea," in those days large numbers of penniless people helped without pay on its construction. Bronze figures of two porters on the door commemorate this while the west portal is flanked by statues of Peter and Paul.

Today it's one of Barcelona's most imposing Gothic structures, noted for its soaring columns and uncluttered aura of space. Look out for the superb stained-glass windows, particularly the 15th-century rose-shaped one above the main entrance. (A

St. Pere Més Baix

BARCELONA
Map Area

Av. Catedral
Plaça Antoni Maura
Av. F. Cambó
Mercat Santa Caterina ②

† St. Felip Neri
† Catedral

Generalitat

Carders
Comerç

Museu Zoologia

Bòria ③
Princesa

Ferran
Plaça St. Jaume ⓘ Hercules ①

BARRI GÒTIC ④ ⑤

Passeig de Picasso

Museu Geologia

Ajuntament
† Sants Just i Pastor

Argenteria
Plassaders
Montcada
⑥ ⑦

Fusina

Mercat del Born ⑩

Comercial

CIUTAT VELLA

Via Laietana

⑧ Santa María del Mar

⑨

Ribera

Parc de la Ciutadella
⑪

LA RIBERA
Correus (Post Office)

Ample
Mercè

Llotja de Mar
Plaça del Palau

Av. Marquès de l'Argentera
Ocata

Zoo de Barcelona

† La Mercè
Passeig de Colom

Estació de França

Pg. de Circunvalació

Parc Zoològic

Take a Break

0   1/8 mi
0   1/8 km

❶ Plaça de l'Angel
❷ Mercat de Santa Caterina
❸ Capella d'en Marcus
❹ Carrer Montcada
❺ Museu Picasso
❻ Museu Tèxtil i d'Indumentària
☕ Tèxtil Cafè
❼ Museu Barbier Muller d'Art Precolumbi
❽ Església Santa María del Mar
❾ Passeig del Born
❿ Antic Merçat del Born
⓫ Parc de la Ciutadella

belated 1997 addition is, in contrast, jarringly unimpressive.) You'll want to return here for an evening concert—particularly a performance of Handel. In such a timeless setting it's an unforgettable experience.

Go back east again to the:

❾ Passeig del Born

This short wide *paseo,* or avenue, was once a center for tournaments and jousting events. (The name "Born" in Catalan means, among other things, the point of a jousting lance.) In medieval times, when Catalonia was a major naval power, the *paseo*'s fame was such that the saying "Roda el món i torna al Born" (Go around the world and return to the Born) became widespread. It was the spiritual heart of the city from the 13th century right up to the 18th century, when La Rambla took over the number-one spot. Today the

Born's revelry assumes a more modern nocturnal form, centered mainly around the countless bars and cafes that fill the bustling side streets.

At the end of the avenue is the:

⑩ Antic Merçat del Born

This massive building, with its wrought-iron roof, was formerly one of the city's biggest wholesale markets. Closed since the 1970s, it's scheduled to reopen in 2009 as a museum and cultural center, as it stands above a whole zone of 18th-century excavations, which can be viewed through glass flooring.

Cross the Passeig de Picasso just past the eastern end of the market and you enter:

⑪ Parc de la Ciutadella

Built on the site of a much-hated 18th-century Bourbon citadel, which was destroyed by General Prim in 1878 (see his statue), this 30-hectare (75-acre) oasis of relaxing greenery came about in the late 1890s just after serving as the site for the Universal Exhibition. Its many highlights include statues, fountains (one designed by a young Gaudí), a boating lake, a waterfall (La Cascada) with a giant hairy mammoth sculpture, the Domènech i Muntaner–designed Castell dels Tres Dragons (Castle of Three Dragons) which houses the zoological museum, two arboretums, and a small botanical garden. There's also a science museum and—last, but not least—the Catalan parliament, which is located in the former citadel's arsenal and can be visited by appointment. Stroll to the northern end of the park to view the *moderniste*-cum-neo-mudéjar–style Arc de Triomf, which served as the entrance to the Universal Exhibition.

WALKING TOUR 3   **EL RAVAL**

START:	Monumento de Colom (Metro: Drassanes)
FINISH:	Universidat (Metro: Universitat)
TIME:	2 to 3 hours
BEST TIMES:	Any sunny day or early evening

This tour takes you through El Raval, a once run-down and deprived corner of Old Barcelona that has reinvented itself as an earthy cosmopolitan quarter with international eating spots and cutting-edge cultural centers.

Walk north up the main La Rambla *paseo* and then turn left onto the Carrer Nou de la Rambla. Almost immediately on your left is:

❶ Palau Güell

Gaudí's first architectural creation—in reality an extension of his parents' old house, which has since been turned into a hotel—was this citadel-like *moderniste* building located just a stone's throw from La Rambla. Partial renovation work has been completed, but the whole place won't be totally renovated until 2010. In the meantime you can enjoy free entrance to the ground floor and admire its Venetian facade, entrance archways, and rooftop array of bizarre chimneys from the street.

Continue along Carrer Nou de la Rambla. When you reach the wide busy Avinguda del Paral.lel turn right onto Carrer de l'Abat Safont and then right again onto Carrer de Sant Pau. On your immediate right is:

❷ Església de Sant Pau de Camp

This rare urban example of Romanesque architecture (officially declared a national monument) is in fact Barcelona's granddaddy of all churches, filled with fascinating small sculptures and grotesque figures. When it was originally built by monks in the 9th century, the surrounding area consisted of fields and woodlands (hence its name, "Saint Paul of the Countryside"). Today's rather squat building is a delightfully intact blend of 11th- to 14th-century

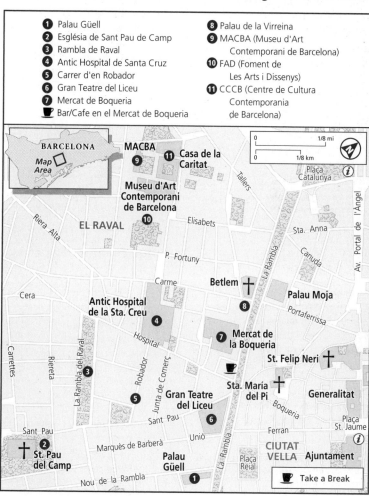

1. Palau Güell
2. Església de Sant Pau de Camp
3. Rambla de Raval
4. Antic Hospital de Santa Cruz
5. Carrer d'en Robador
6. Gran Teatre del Liceu
7. Mercat de Boqueria
☕ Bar/Cafe en el Mercat de Boqueria
8. Palau de la Virreina
9. MACBA (Museu d'Art Contemporani de Barcelona)
10. FAD (Foment de Les Arts i Dissenys)
11. CCCB (Centre de Cultura Contemporania de Barcelona)

styles, including some Visigothic decor and highlighted by a beautiful tiny cloister with Moorish archways and a stone fountain.

Continue along Carrer de Sant Pau to the:

3 Rambla de Raval

This is one of the city's newest *paseos,* created in 2000 when a large quadrangle of congested alleyways and unsalubrious tenements were removed as part of a commendable and necessary "Raval open to the heavens" plan. Today it's a sunny pedestrianized area where children play and locals can relax under the slightly uneasy-looking palm trees. Surrounded by a new blend of nifty hotels and eating spots—including various kebab locales owned by Pakistani and Turkish immigrants—it exudes a more international environment, though some of the earlier grittiness remains. Similar changes are continuing to take place as the area becomes increasingly gentrified and cosmopolitan. Look for the huge black "Gat" (cat) statue at the southern end.

At the northern end of the Rambla de Raval turn right into Carrer de l'Hospital. After 200 yards on your left is the:

❹ Antic Hospital de Santa Cruz

The name is misleading, as the famed former hospital—one of Spain's biggest in the Middle Ages—ceased to cater to the bodily sick and needy over 80 years ago, when one of its last patients was the dying Gaudí. Today, instead, it provides sustenance for the mind. Its blend of Gothic, baroque, and neoclassical styles is spread throughout several buildings, which were converted in 2001, after substantial renovation work, into a variety of cultural institutions including the main Catalan library located in the Massana Arts School.

On the right of the Antic Hospital is the:

❺ Carrer d'en Robador

This narrow winding sunless street in the heart of the old "Barrio Chino" (or Barri Xino, as it's known today) was once the notorious focus not of robbers (robadors), but of posturing frieze-like prostitutes of all shapes and sizes who filled every doorway and lined every corner. Today it's more low-key, though not entirely tart-free, a mildly risqué corner of unadorned medieval Barcelona.

At the end of Carrer d'en Robador turn right onto Sant Pau continue to the end where you meet La Rambla and the:

❻ Gran Teatre del Liceu

Tragically destroyed over a decade ago by fire, this magnificent, traditional opera house overlooking La Rambla has resurged phoenix-like from the ashes and today once more hosts some of the best classical performances in the world. Its new facade belies the opulent interior of rich, dark colors and intricate carvings where a 19th-century setting has been revived alongside various modern accoutrements.

Carry on left up La Rambla to the:

❼ Mercat de Boqueria

In a class all its own, this ever-colorful, ever-dynamic food market is among the biggest and best in Europe. Under its high wrought-iron ceilings, countless stalls sell a kaleidoscopic mix of Atlantic and Mediterranean seafood, Castilian meat, Valencian fruit, and local vegetables. The picture-postcard stalls at the front tend to be more expensive, so take an admiring look and then head further back for the better-value stuff.

 TAKE A BREAK
Inside the market you'll also find several good-value **bars and cafes** where locals come for early breakfasts or a snifter, or where chefs from top restaurants pause for a *cafe solo* between making their purchases. The bars may not look like much, but they serve some of the best coffee in the city.

Almost adjoining the Boqueria is the:

❽ Palau de la Virreina

Built in 1770, this classical baroque palace is named after the widow of a viceroy who returned a wealthy man after a successful period of duty in Peru. Today it's a cultural-events center, mainly private but with occasional public exhibitions dedicated to Barcelona history and traditions. The downstairs photographic displays are usually worth a look. You can also buy souvenirs here and consult the information desk for up-to-date cultural events.

Turn west away from La Rambla along Carrer Carmé and take the fourth left onto Carrer del Angel to arrive at the Plaça dels Angels (not to be confused with Plaça de l'Angel in the La Ribera walk). Here you'll see the following trio of avant-garde arts centers. Straight in front of you across the square is the:

❾ MACBA (Museu d'Art Contemporanea de Barcelona)

Opened in 1995 with a rather tentative display, this American-designed glass-walled emporium—with its bright white walls, intricately planned ramps, and triple atrium—illuminates its now more adventurous collection of modern art masterpieces with natural light. Alongside international favorites, like Klee, there's a strong presence of Catalan artists, reflecting various reactionary movements both in paintings and photography. Displays are constantly changing and temporary exhibitions feature new creative works (p. 181).

To your left is the:

⑩ FAD (Foment de les Arts i Dissenys)

Located in the old Convent dels Angels, opposite the MACBA, this essentially administrative body promoting talented artists and awarding grants to promising newcomers organizes many exhibitions of its own. Workshops and "art markets" also give burgeoning artists a chance to sell their own offerings.

Behind the MACBA, reached by Carrer Montealegre, is the:

⑪ CCCB (Centre de Cultura Contemporanea de Barcelona)

Built on the site of a spacious former Casa de Caritat (Alms House), this is Spain's biggest cultural center. Its design—by Viaplana and Piñon, who also created the Maremagnum commercial center by the port—is mainly a modern conglomeration of steel and glass, though the patio and facade of the former building remain. It offers an eclectic blend of movie and video shows, art exhibitions, conferences and courses, music and dance performances, and even organized walks around offbeat areas of the city. There's also a well-stocked bookshop and a bar/restaurant.

Turn right onto Carrer Valldoncella and then left along Carrer dels Tallers past Plaça de Castella for University Square and Metro stop.

WALKING TOUR 4	*MODERNISTE* ROUTE (L'EIXAMPLE)

START:	Plaça Urquinaona (Metro: Urquinaona)
FINISH:	Plaça de Catalunya (Metro: Plaça de Catalunya)
TIME:	2 to 3 hours
BEST TIMES:	Any sunny day or early evening

This stroll explores the wide-laned 19th-century-inspired L'Eixample (or "extension") of the city, where fine *moderniste* buildings stand alongside some of the city's most elegant shops and cafes.

Start at Plaça Urquinaona and head down to Carrer Sant Francesc de Paula to the:

❶ Palau de la Música Catalana

This haven for Barcelona music lovers, designed by Domenech i Muntaner and tucked away just above La Ribera, is well worth a slight detour before you begin your meander up into L'Eixample. Ornately extravagant, its highlights include busts of Palestrina, Bach, and Beethoven; multicolored mosaics and columns; and a large allegorical frieze of the Orfeu Català by Lluis Bru. The thing to do, of course, is to come

back one evening to enjoy a concert in the even more magnificent interior (p. 179).

Return to Urquinaona and walk east along Carrer Ausias March to no. 31 where you'll find:

❷ Farmacia Nordbeck

Built in 1905, this is one of the best examples of pharmacies built in a complete *moderniste* style, with stained-glass windows and dark mellow wood. Throughout L'Eixample you'll notice similarly exotic chemists—such as the Argelaguet in Carrer Roger de Llúria—emphasizing this balm-like link between curing the body and satisfying the soul.

And three buildings down the street (on the same side), you'll see:

❸ Cases Tomàs Roger

This duo of houses at nos. 37 and 39, designed by Enric Sagnier at the end of the 19th century, is noted for its fine archways and well-restored *sgraffito*.

Return to Plaça Urquinaona and head north up Carrer Roger de Llúria. At no. 85 you'll find:

❹ Queviures Murrià

Run by the same family for more than 1½ centuries, this marvelous grocery store is also an impressive work of art. The array of goodies inside is complemented by this lavish exterior by the *moderniste* painter Ramón Casas.

☕ TAKE A BREAK
Café Baume, Roger de Llúria 124
(© 93-459-05-66), is a traditional cafe where you can put your feet up on one of the old-fashioned well-worn leather chairs and enjoy a morning coffee or tea between the exhausting business of checking out the area's artistic attractions. The place is particularly popular on Sundays with locals who come to relax and browse the latest scandals and spats with Madrid in *La Vanguardia*.

Continue up Roger de Llúria to Carrer de Mallorca. Turn right and proceed to no. 291 to find:

❺ Bd Ediciones de Diseño

One of the classiest interior-design shops you'll find anywhere, this stylish building—known as Casa Tomas—was designed not by one but by several key *moderniste* architects, including the great Domènech i Muntaner. Browse through the (highly expensive) selection of chic reproductions and furnishings by the likes of Dalí and Gaudí.

Continue further up Roger de Llúria and then turn right onto the wide Avinguda Diagonal. On the opposite (north) side of the road at nos. 416 to 420 is the:

❻ Casa de los Punxes (Casa Terrados)

Known locally as the "House of Spikes" because of its sharply pointed turrets, this neo-Gothic castle-like eccentricity built by

Puig i Cadafalch in 1905 has four towers and a trio of separate entrances (one for each of the family's daughters). Its ceramic panels have patriotic motifs. Controversial in the past (a then-prominent politician, Alejandro Lerroux, called it "a crime against the nation"), it's regarded today as one of *modernisme*'s great landmarks.

Further along the Avinguda Diagonal at no. 442 is:

❼ Casa Comalat

Designed by the Gaudí-influenced architect Salvador Valeri i Popurull, this unusual house has two facades, formal at the front, more playful at the back. The former has a dozen curvy stone balconies with wrought-iron railing; the latter, which opens onto Carrer Corsèga, features polychrome, ceramic work, and wooden galleries. Though not open to the public, it's well worth a look from the outside.

Now walk west along the avenue to:

❽ Palau de Baró de Cuadras

Built in 1904 to a design by the ubiquitous Puig i Cadafalch, this mansion features a unique double facade that combines Plateresque and Gothic styles on the Diagonal-facing side; the more staid rear facade reflects the fact that the building was essentially a mere block of apartments overlooking Carrer Rosselló. Inside, the decor is predominantly Arabic with a wealth of mosaics, *sgraffito*, and polychrome woodwork. It houses the **Casa Asia** exhibition (www.casaasia.es), which aims to foster both cultural and economic relations between Asia and Europe.

Continue to Passeig de Gràcia and turn left to reach:

❾ La Pedrera (Casa Milá)

Created between 1905 and 1910, this building is, after La Sagrada Família, Gaudí's most extraordinary work. **Casa Milá**—the building's original name—may baldly be a block of apartments, but it's like no other on earth. The highly sculpted undulating limestone facade earned the place its nickname, **La Pedrera** (stone quarry), while its stunning wrought-iron balconies, parabolic arches,

1. Palau de la Musica Catalana
2. Farmacia Nordbeck
3. Cases Tomàs Roger
4. Queviures Murrià
☕ Café Baume
5. Bd. Ediciones de Diseño
6. Casa de les Punxes
   (Casa Terrados)
7. Casa Comalat
8. Palau de Baró de Cuadras
9. La Pedrera (Casa Mila)
10. Manzana de la Discordia

0 ___ 1/8 mi
0 ___ 1/8 km

Rosselló

Casa Milà
(La Pedrera)

Provença

Casa de
les Punxes

Av. Diagonal

Casa Thomas

Mallorca

València

Aragó

Aragó

Consell de Cent

Consell de Cent

Diputació

Universitat
de Barcelona

Gran Via Corts Catalanes

Gran Via Corts Catalanes

Rambla Catalunya

Ronda Universitat

Bergara

Pelai

Tallers

Plaça
Catalunya

Casp

Ausiàs Marc

Pau Claris

Roger de Llúria

Bruc

Girona

Fontanella

Plaça
Urquinaona

Ronda Sant Pere

Trafalgar

Ortigosa

Comtal

Montsió

Via Laietana

Palau de
la Música
Catalana

BARCELONA

Map
Area

☕ Take a Break

Passeig de Gràcia

Passeig de Gràcia

Balmes

Balmes

Av. Portal de l'Àngel

La Rambla

STROLLING AROUND BARCELONA

8

MODERNISTE ROUTE (L' EIXAMPLE)

and gnarled fairy-tale chimneys evoke a fantasy. The rooftop is spellbinding, even more so than the views it affords, and concerts are held here on summer weekends.

The fourth floor comprises an entire *moderniste* apartment, the Pis de Pedrera—*pis* means "apartment" in Catalan—whose rooms are laden with wondrous knickknacks and antiques. In the attic you can see the **Espai Gaudí** (Gaudí Space), which comprehensively summarizes Gaudí's style of working.

Continue a few blocks south on Passeig de Gràcia to:
❿ Manzana de la Discordia

This small zone of the Eixample is the highlight of any *moderniste* enthusiast's visit. Here you have, almost on top of each other, works by not just one great architect but three. (*Manzana,* incidentally, means both "plot of land" and "apple" in Spanish, so its double meaning intriguingly hints at the Greek myth in which Paris has to choose which beauty will win the coveted Apple of Discord.)

If there is a single victor here it's generally acknowledged to be Gaudí's exotically curvaceous **Casa Battló** (no. 43), which has only been allowing visitors in since 2002. Permanently illuminated at night, it's known affectionately by Catalans as the *casa dels ossos* (house of bones)—and sometimes alternatively the *casa del drach* (house of the dragon)—and it features an irregular blend of mauve, green, and blue fragmented tiles topped by a bizarre azure chimney-filled roof, which in 2004 was also opened to a grateful public.

Next comes Puig i Cadalfach's cubical-style **Casa Ametller** (no. 41), with its gleaming ceramic facade, Flemish Gothic pediments, and small bizarre Eusebio Arnau–sculpted statues of precociously talented animals (one of them blowing glass). Finally, there is Doménech i Muntaner's **Casa Lleó Morera** (no. 35), whose dominant turret resembles a melting (pale blue) wedding cake atop a sea of esoteric ornamentation that includes models of a lion *(lleo)* and mulberry bush *(morera).*

9

Shopping

The shopping scene in Barcelona— long a trader's haven thanks to its richly varied shipping imports, wealth of local products, and innate commercial savvy— is wide enough to satisfy the most demanding consumer.

The city has an impressive ability to move with the times, and Barcelona today offers a fascinating blend of centuries-old shops and dynamic *última moda* stores run by *fashionistas* who have a tendency to look outward for trend inspiration, rather than toward the rest of Spain. Keen shoppers have at their disposal a time-straddling gamut of traditional *colmados* (small grocery shops), family-run *tiendas,* polished specialty stores, colorful covered markets replete with Mediterranean fare, pristine modern malls, and cutting-edge designer showcases and top-name boutiques. Some of the leading global fashion names (Zara and Camper, to name a couple) are in fact Spanish, and stock a larger range of their offerings at more competitive prices.

Travelers not *au fait* with Barcelona's scene tend to blow their credit cards in London or Paris and then kick themselves for not waiting to arrive in the city where, in addition to the world-class shopping now available to them, the euro goes a lot further. So if you have been sensible enough to set aside some reserve funds, you could find yourself spending more time shopping than gallery-hopping— not, of course, that there's any reason to feel guilty about that!

1 THE SHOPPING SCENE

L'Eixample's elegant Passeig de Gràcia contains some of the most expensive retail space in Spain. Here the big guns of fashion have set up shop in gorgeous 19th- and 20th-century buildings; Chanel, Max Mara, and Loewe jostle for your attention alongside Benetton, Zara, and Diesel. All along the avenue there are dozens of outdoor cafes to rest up, enjoy a tapa or two, and examine your booty. The Rambla de Catalunya, which runs parallel to the Passeig de Gràcia, has lesser internationally known—but equally glitzy—establishments with more of a focus on housewares, books, and beauty. Don't bypass the cross streets that run between the two, as they are also scattered with some of the city's top shopping, particularly Valencia, Provença, and Consell de Cent, the latter of which is renowned for its expensive antiques shops and art galleries. The top end of the Passeig de Gràcia intersects El Diagonal, one of the city's main arteries. Here you will find the housewares giant Habitat, the megamall L'Illa, and various other boutiques in between. The Metro only sparsely services this part of town and the shops are spread out, but don't despair: The *tombus* is a comfortable minibus that does the "shopping line" along the Diagonal; hop on at any regular bus stop.

The older, more traditional shops and one-of-a-kind retailers are mostly to be found in the Ciutat Vella (El Raval, El Born, and the Barri Gòtic). Here, in the Old Quarter, you will also find intimate boutiques and galleries. One promising new hub is around the MACBA, the city's museum of contemporary art in El Raval. Smaller galleries come (and go) here at various intervals, and there are fashion and design shops springing up all the time. In the direction of the port, shops on the streets running off La Rambla (particularly Carme and Hospital) reflect the melting-pot nature of the neighborhood: Wine shops sit side by side with halal butchers and traditional Catalan bakers; others seem to have survived for centuries selling scissors. This is where you see the dusty, old emporiums of yesteryear, ones that have sadly disappeared from cities like London and New York.

Even though the Barri Gòtic is home to many traditional stores, there's no shortage of trendy spots at the top end of the area. Here, throngs hit the Portal d'Angel and Portaferrisa on Friday evenings and Saturdays, seeking out new arrivals in fashion from the top high-street names such as H&M, Levi's, Benetton, and other global fashion labels. With the major department store El Corte Inglés in the immediate vicinity, these two streets (which cross each other) make up another of the city's convenient and central shopping hubs.

Catalonia has resisted the lure of Sunday trading, mainly at the insistence of the trade unions. The good news is that most shops in the center stay open through the lunch hour and generally don't close until 9pm, even on Saturdays, with department stores extending this to 10pm. As a general rule of thumb, smaller shops are open Monday through Saturday 9:30 or 10am to 1:30 or 2pm, and then open again in the afternoon from 4:30 or 5pm to 8:30pm. You will always find exceptions to this, especially as the tourist trade fans out over the city. You may come across some that frustratingly take Monday morning off, or decide to take a long siesta, but even that adds to the unique experience of Barcelona being a modern city that has retained its quaint retro feel.

Credit cards are accepted nearly everywhere, even for smallish purchases. Note, however, that you (along with everyone else) must show a form of photo ID (passport or driver's license) when making a purchase with your credit card. Don't be offended when the assistant asks for this; it is an effective guard against fraudulent credit card use.

Sales tax is called IVA; for food items it is generally charged at 7%, rising to 16% for most other goods. Cash register receipts will show this as a separate charge (if not, ask). If you see a "Tax-Free Shopping" sticker displayed in a shop and are a non-E.U. resident, you can request a tax-free check on purchases of over 90€ ($117). Present this to the Cash Refund counter at the airport (Terminal A) when you depart the E.U. and you will be issued a cash refund. Refunds can also be made to your credit card or by check. For more information see www.globalrefund.com.

Sales (*rebajas* or *rebaixes*) start early July and early January, slightly later than northern Europe, as the Christmas gift-giving day is the Día de los Reyes on January 6. Discounts at the sales are extraordinary, often starting at 50%, but surprisingly you never see the mad rushes that fill the news programs in other countries. On the whole, shopping in Barcelona is a genteel affair; small business and trading has historically been a major backbone of its economy, and many establishments here, in terms of both service and presentation, still feel like a piece of living history.

WHAT TO BUY

Stylish clothing and shoes and leatherwear are the items to go for in Barcelona. Leather shoes, belts, jackets, and coats are particularly good buys; whether you want a high-end branch such as Loewe or succumb to the leather hawkers on La Rambla, the quality and value of leather goods is superb. Barcelona has always been renowned for its expertise in design and has a vibrant design culture supported by the local government. Decorative objects and housewares here are original and well made and can be found in the shops around the MACBA and the Picasso Museum. Artisan pieces, such as ceramic tiles and gifts and earthenware bowls and plates, are cheap and plentiful. Cookware, crockery, wine glasses, and utensils in general are a great buy; a poke around a humble hardware store can unearth some great finds, too.

What follows is only a limited selection of some of the hundreds of shops in Barcelona.

2 SHOPPING A TO Z

ANTIQUES

Serious collectors should check out the maze of streets around the Calle Palla near the Plaça de Pi in the Barri Gòtic; while there are few bargains to be had you will find everything from bric-a-brac to old posters and lace. Consell de Cent in the Eixample houses a range of shops selling fine antiques and antiquities. Every Thursday, many of these traders set up stalls outside the cathedral, transferring to Port Vell (the port end of La Rambla) at the weekend.

Angel Batlle ★★ (Finds)   This shop has an unbeatable collection of old posters from travel to advertising and music to sport, postcards, engravings, maps, prayer cards—really, anything that's printed. Some of them make a wonderful souvenir or memento; consider taking home a 1950s sherry poster rather than a Picasso or Miró print. Palla 23. (C) **93-301-58-84.** Metro: Liceu.

Artur Ramón Art ★★   One of the finest antiques and art dealers in Barcelona can be found at this three-level emporium. Set on a narrow flagstone-covered street near Plaça del Pi (the center of the antiques district), it stands opposite a tiny square, the Placeta al Carrer de la Palla. The store, which has been operated by four generations of men named Artur Ramón, also operates branches nearby and is known for its 19th- and 20th-century paintings, sculptures, drawings, and engravings, and 18th- and 19th-century decorative arts and objets d'art along with rare ceramics, porcelain, and glassware. Prices are high, as you'd expect, but the items are of high quality and lasting value. Palla 23. (C) **93-302-59-70.** www.arturamon.com. Metro: Jaume I.

Bulevard dels Antiquaris   This 70-unit indoor market just off one of the town's most aristocratic avenues has a huge collection of art, antiques, bric-a-brac, and just plain junk assembled in a series of stands and small shops. It's great for browsing, although the erratic opening hours (stall owners set their own hours) may drive you mad. Passeig de Gràcia 55. (C) **93-215-44-19.** www.bulevarddelsantiquaris.com. Metro: Passeig de Gràcia.

L'Arca de l'Avia ★★ (Moments)   This gorgeous shop sells lace and linen bedspreads and curtains, petticoats and handkerchiefs, and other assorted textiles from the 18th to early 20th centuries. Some of the sequined numbers worn by Kate Winslet in the film *Titanic* were snapped up here from their exquisite collection of period clothing. Prices aren't cheap, but the quality of their collection is unsurpassable. Banys Nous 20. (C) **93-302-15-98.** www.larcadelavia.com. Metro: Liceu.

Urbana (Finds)   Urbana sells an array of architectural remnants (usually from torndown mansions), antique furniture, and reproductions of brass hardware. There are antique and reproduction marble mantelpieces, wrought-iron gates, and garden seats, even carved wood fireplaces with the *modernisme* look. It's an impressive, albeit costly, array of merchandise. Còrsega 258. (C) **93-218-70-36.** Metro: Hospital Sant Pau.

Altaïr   This excellent up-to-date travel shop has its main branch here and another in the Palau Robert. Staff is friendly and helpful and the wide selection of books—mainly in Spanish but also some in English—covers nature, anthropology, history, and global travel. There's a good choice of material on Barcelona, of course, as well as kids' books, comics, CDs, and DVDs. Gran Vía de las Cortes Catalanes 616. ✆ 93-342-71-71. www.altair.es. Metro: Universitat.

BCN Books   Though the main content of this English-language bookshop is language-learning material that includes basic grammar and phrasebooks and a wide range of dictionaries, there's also a good selection of travel books, contemporary fiction, and classical novels. Roger de Llúria 118. ✆ 93-457-76-92. www.bcnbooks.com. Metro: Passeig de Gràcia. Other branches at Rosselló 24, ✆ 93-476-33-43; and Amigó 81, ✆ 93-200-79-53.

Buffet y Ambigú (Finds)   In among the deli stalls at the back of the Boqueria market is a unique book outlet. The stall sells cookbooks catering to most tastes, from the best tapas recipes to manuals for chefs and special editions such as El Bulli's encyclopedia explaining techniques of the Catalan super-chef Ferran Adriá. Many of the books are in English. Mercat de la Boqueria, Parada 435. ✆ 93-243-01-78. Metro: Liceu.

Casa del Llibre (Value)   This huge book barn covers all the genres, from novels to self-help, travel to technical. There are sections of foreign-language books, including English, and cover prices here tend to be the same as you would pay back home. Passeig de Gràcia 62. ✆ 93-272-34-80. Metro: Passeig de Gràcia.

Cooperativa d'Arquitectes Jordi Capell   For books on Spain's architects and interior designers, head to the basement of the city's architecture school. This bookshop has a huge range of technical books for architects as well as monographs and photographic books of the work of leading architects, from Gaudí to Gehry. Plaça Nova 5. ✆ 90-299-89-93. www.eupalinos.com. Metro: Liceu.

FNAC (Value)   The Plaça de Catalunya branch of this music and entertainment megastore has a solid section of English-language books. Most of the novels are bestsellers (or recent bestsellers), and a large range of the current travel guides to Barcelona and the rest of Spain are available. If you are here to learn Spanish, there is also a bilingual dictionary and language textbook section. El Triangle, Plaça de Catalunya 4. ✆ 93-301-99-02. www.fnac.es. Metro: Plaça de Catalunya.

Hibernian Books   This friendly secondhand English-language bookshop, a mainstay of the international literary Gràcia scene, is a favorite with residents and visitors alike. The books cover topics ranging from health to hobbies, and exchanges and generous discounts are available. The shop also gives you the lowdown on Anglo-Irish social and theatrical goings-on in the city. A kids' corner and tea and coffee service add to the homey atmosphere, and there are armchairs where you can sit and browse before you buy. Carrer Montseny. ✆ 93-217-46-96. www.hibernian-books.com. Metro: Fontana.

Laie ★★   A good selection of English-language books, including contemporary literature, travel maps, and guides, is at Laie. The bookshop has an upstairs cafe with international newspapers and a terrace. It serves breakfast, lunch (salad bar), and dinner. The cafe is open Monday through Saturday from 9am to 1am. The shop also schedules cultural events, including art exhibits and literary presentations. Pau Claris 85. ✆ 93-318-17-39. www.laie.es. Metro: Plaça de Catalunya or Urquinaona.

CHOCOLATES & CAKES

Cacao Sampaka ★★   If there were such a thing as *haute chocolat,* this establishment would be the Christian Dior. Using only the finest cacao available, a mind-boggling selection of sweetmeats is categorized into "collections": "flowers and herbs," "liquors and digestives," "gastronomic innovations," and "spices of the Americas," to name just a few. The sleek packaging turns them into true objects of desire, and there is a bar-cafe where you can enjoy a cup of creamy hot chocolate, pastries, and high-cholesterol sandwiches, all made of the highest-quality ingredients at prices not dissimilar to more pedestrian places. Consell de Cent 292. © 93-272-08-33. www.cacaosampaka.com. Metro: Passeig de Gràcia.

Escribà ★ Finds   You may have already seen the glittering facade of this beautiful Art Nouveau shop on postcards. But far from a curious relic, it sells the goods of one of the city's finest families of chocolate and cake makers. You can pop in for a coffee and croissant (outside tables in the summer) or pick up a box of bonbons or a bottle of dessert wine to take home. At Easter, the windows display *monas,* elaborate chocolate sculptures decorated with jewels and feathers. Though founder Antoni Escribá died in 2004, his legacy lives on. La Rambla 83. © 93-301-60-27. www.escriba.es. Metro: Liceu. Other branches at Gran Vía 546, © 93-454-75-35; and Ronda Litoral 42, © 93-221-07-29.

Xocoa ★   Brothers Marc and Miguel Escurell have managed to thoroughly modernize their century-old family business by employing top graphic artists to design their packaging and unveiling some novel ideas such as chocolate candles, incense, and even a CD for chocolate lovers. Try the house specialty, the *Ventall,* a scrumptious cake of almond pastry and chocolate truffle. Petritxol 11. © 93-301-11-97. www.xocoa-bcn.com. Metro: Liceu. Other branches at Roger de Llúria, © 87 93 487 24 99; and Casp 33, © 93-304-03-00. Metro: Girona for both.

DEPARTMENT STORES

El Corte Inglés   The main Barcelona branch of Spain's largest department store chain—which now has a few serious competitors—sells a wide variety of merchandise, ranging from traditional handicrafts to high-fashion items, and from Spanish records to food. The store has a restaurant and cafe and offers consumer-related services, such as a travel agent. It also has a department that will mail your purchase. Not only that, but you can have shoes re-heeled, receive hair and beauty treatments, or eat and drink in the rooftop cafe. The basement supermarket (Plaça de Catalunya branch only) is the best place to pick up wines and other foodstuffs to take back home. Open Monday through Saturday from 10am to 10pm. Plaça de Catalunya 14. © 93-306-38-00. www.elcorteingles.es. Other branches at Av. Diagonal 617–619, © 93-366-71-00, Metro: María Cristina; and Av. Diagonal 471, © 93-493-48-00, Metro: Hospital Clinic.

DESIGNER HOMEWARES

Bd Ediciones de Diseño ★★★   Started by a group of prominent Catalan architects, this gorgeous gallery-shop, housed in a sumptuous *moderniste* edifice, offers only the best contemporary pieces alongside reproductions by the likes of Gaudí, Dalí, and Mackintosh. Items by Oscar Tusquets, one of the shop's founders and a leading Catalan designer, should also be sought out. Goodies range from furniture, fittings, and rugs to smaller, easily packed items such as kitchenware and decorative objects. Sleek and serious, BD is Barcelona's bastion of design culture. Casa Tomás, Mallorca 291. © 93-458-69-09. www.bdbarcelona.com. Metro: Passeig de Gràcia.

Gotham (Finds) Although the fad for retro design pieces has been well and truly established in Spain, this shop was a pioneer. Furniture from the '50s through '60s is here, as are ceramics, crockery, vases, lights, and other items hailing from the same epoch. Prices aren't cheap, but most objects have either been restored or are in faultless condition. Cervantes 7. © **93-412-46-47**. www.gotham-bcn.com. Metro: Jaume I.

Ici et Là ★ Craftsmanship and quirky design characterize the pieces on display in this corner shop in the heart of the El Born shopping strip. Most pieces are limited editions by local artists, but they also receive regular shipments of, say, Nepalese chairs, African baskets, or Indian textiles. Glass is also featured strongly, from candleholders to delicately embossed wine glasses. Nearly everything in this shop could be described as a "conversation piece." Plaça Santa Maria 2. © **93-268-11-67**. www.icietla.com. Metro: Jaume I or Barceloneta.

Vinçon ★★ Fernando Amat's Vinçon is the best design emporium in the city, with 10,000 products—everything from household items to the best in Spanish contemporary furnishings. Its mission is to purvey good design, period. Housed in the former home of artist Ramón Casas—a contemporary of Picasso's during his Barcelona stint—the showroom is filled with the best Spain has. The always-creative window displays alone are worth the trek: Expect *anything*. Passeig de Gràcia 96. © **93-215-60-50**. www.vincon.com. Metro: Diagonal.

Vitra ★★ The famed Swiss contemporary design company has a formidable, two-story showcase in Barcelona, featuring unique pieces by Charles and Ray Eames and Phillipe Starck, Alväro Siza, and Frank Gehry, to name but a few. The prices may be restrictive and the size of most of their items means they will not fit into your hand luggage, but it's okay to dream, isn't it? Plaça Comercial 5. © **93-268-72-19**. www.vitra.com. Metro: Jaume I or Arc de Triomf.

FABRICS, TEXTILES & TRIMMINGS

Antiga Pasamaneria J. Soler (Finds) If fringes, ribbons, braids, tassels, and cords are your thing, then look no further. This place has been selling them since 1898 and has a wall-to-wall display of everything from dainty French grosgrain ribbons to thick tapestry braids and borders. Plaça del Pi 2. © **93-318-64-93**. Metro: Liceu.

Coses de Casa ★ Appealing fabrics and weavings are displayed in this 19th-century store, called simply "Household Items." Many are hand-woven in Majorca, their boldly geometric patterns inspired by Arab motifs of centuries ago. The fabric, for the most part, is 50% cotton, 50% linen; much of it would make excellent upholstery material. Cushions, spreads, and throws can be made to order. Plaça de Sant Josep Oriol 5. © **93-302-73-28**. www.cosesdecasa.com. Metro: Jaume I or Liceu.

Gastón y Daniela ★★ This century-old company originally hails from Bilbao, although these days, its name is synonymous with fine fabrics for upholstery and drapery all over Spain. Every one of their damasks, polished cottons, brocades, and tapestries is extremely lush, more suited to a time when children's fingerprints and cat hair was not an issue. It's great to browse in, even if it's just for an end-piece or a new cushion cover. Pau Claris 171. © **93-235-32-17**. www.gastonydaniela.com. Metro: Diagonal.

FASHION

Adolfo Domínguez ★ This shop, one of many outlets across Spain and Europe, displays fashion that has earned the store the appellation of the "Spanish Armani." There's one big difference: Domínguez's suits for both women and men, unlike Armani's, are designed for those with hips and limited budgets. And they cover all ages at their stores, including the youth market. As one fashion critic said of their offerings, "They are austere but not strict, forgivingly cut in urbane earth tones." Passeig de Gràcia 32. © 93-487-41-70. www.adolfodominguez.com. Metro: Passeig de Gràcia. Several other branches throughout the city.

Antonio Miró ★   This shop is devoted exclusively to the clothing design of Miró. It carries fashionable men's and women's clothing. Consell de Cent 349. © 93-487-06-70. Metro: Passeig de Gràcia.

Comité (Finds   This store is typical of the inventive fashion shops that have sprouted up in the streets around the MACBA. Inside is a charmingly naive decor of pastel colors and meters of white curtains, and much of the clothing is made of recycled items: An embroidered sheet or tablecloth is transformed into a wrap skirt or dress, or a striped men's shirt is retouched and tucked into a blouse. Notariat 8. © 93-317-68-883. www.comite barcelona.com. Metro: Plaça de Catalunya or Liceu.

Commercial Woman ★   This French-owned boutique stocks beautifully detailed and highly feminine clothing for day and evening by the likes of Cacharel, Paul & Joe, Comme des Garçons, and Spain's own Jocomomola. There is also a selection of artisan Parisian perfumes and accessories by the bijoux jewelry brand Scooter. A menswear outlet is located across the street. Calle Rec 52. © 93-319-34-63. Metro: Jaume I or Barceloneta.

Custo-Barcelona ★   First it was Hollywood, with the likes of Julia Roberts and Drew Barrymore seen sporting Custo T-shirts. Now they have taken over the world, with stores from Chicago to Perugia to Shanghai. As the name suggests, however, these tops and shirts, skirts, and pants in mad mixes of fabrics and emblazoned with '60s retro motifs are a homegrown product and have become a symbol of "Cool Barcelona." Plaça de les Olles 7. © 93-268-78-93. www.custo-barcelona.com. Metro Jaume I or Liceu. Other location at Calle Ferran 36. © 93-342-66-98. Metro: Jaume I or Barceloneta.

El Mercadillo   This is Barcelona's temple to alternative culture, with in-house DJs, piercing salons, and dozens of stalls selling urban and club wear, leather and suede jackets, records, and secondhand clothes. The kids love it, but you may have a hard time of it if you have a post-30 or post-teenage body size. Portaferrisa 17. © 93-301-89-13. Metro: Liceu.

Giménez & Zuazo ★   Quirky, colorful, and very Barcelonese, designer duo Giménez & Zuazo's creations are characterized by daring prints and unusual fabrics. Their skirts may have the silhouette of a svelte female splashed across the front, or a shirt collar may be bordered in contrasting cross-stitch. Their BoBa T-shirts, with hand-painted imagery, have become something of a cult item. Elisabets 20. © 93-412-33-81. www.boba.es. Metro: Plaça de Catalunya or Liceu. Other location at Rec 42. © 93-310-67-43. Metro: Jaume I or Barceloneta.

Jean-Pierre Bua ★★   Another pioneer, this boutique was the first to import big-name Parisian fashion houses to Barcelona. There is a large stock of Gaultier (the French *enfant terrible* and Bua are personal friends); Comme des Garçons; Spain's most international designer, Sybilla; and Brussels is represented with Dries van Noten. Despite the price tags, the staff is laid-back and no one seems to mind if you spend time simply looking. Diagonal 469. © 93-439-71-00. www.jeanpierrebua.com. Metro: Hospital Clinic.

Josep Font ★★   With a masterful eye for fabrics and attention to detail that recalls vintage St. Laurent, Catalan designer Josep Font is in a class of his own. His sumptuous shop has retained many of its original Art Nouveau features customized with Font's inherent quirkiness. Bold yet feminine, with only a slight nod to the current trends, his designs remain timeless. Provença 304. © 93-487-21-10. www.josepfont.com. Metro: Passeig de Gràcia.

The Zaravolución

Many visitors to Spain are already familiar with the **Zara** clothing label. Now with over 600 (1,900, counting the Zara offshoot brands) outlets in 49 countries, including megastores in the fashion capitals of Milan, Paris, London, and New York, Zara is hard to ignore. But many are not aware, and probably surprised to know, that Zara is Spanish-owned.

Zara was started back in the early '70s by an industrious young Galician by the name of Amancio Ortega, now the richest man in Spain. He saw a necessity for stylish housecoats for the women in his rural village, and out of that an empire grew. Today, Zara is one of the few fashion empires in the world that vertically controls the entire process, from textile manufacture to design to retail. Using a global network of buyers and trend-spotters, they interpret (many within the industry use the word "plagiarize") hot-off-the-catwalk pieces for men, women, and children at astoundingly affordable prices. They appeal to the full cross-generational demographic gamut, from urban tribes to executives. Zara's calendar doesn't just consist of four seasons; they produce and distribute clothing all year round in their behemoth headquarters in Ortega's native Galicia and Zaragoza. New, never-to-be-repeated models arrive every day, meaning converts return again and again and again . . .

A revolution needs a charismatic leader and Ortega is no exception. Until he took the company public in 2001, the press possessed only one photo of a man estimated to be worth $10.3 billion. He imposes a strict "no-press" policy to his staff and never gives interviews. He never accepts any of the dozens of accolades awarded to him in person. What he has done is, in less than a generation, democratized fashion and made it possible to dress like a film star for a song. ¡Viva la revolución!

Located at Pelayo 58 (📞 **93-301-09-78;** www.zara.com; Metro: Plaça de Catalunya), Passeig de Gràcia 16 (📞 **93-318-76-75;** Metro: Passeig de Gràcia), and all over the city.

La Boutique del Hotel   In the lobby of Hotel Axel, Barcelona's "Gay Hotel" (p. 113), the Boutique stocks (as one would perhaps expect) the best and brightest names in menswear: John Richmond, Helmut Lang, and Rykiel Homme, to name just a few. In a city that is somewhat lacking in cutting-edge menswear stores, this one is frequented by homo-, hetero-, and metrosexuals alike. Aribau 33. 📞 **93-323-93-98.** www.axelhotels.com. Metro: Passeig de Gràcia.

Loft Avignon   This emporium was largely responsible for converting this shabby Barri Gòtic street into the fashion hub that it is today. The clothes for men and women feature labels such as Vivienne Westwood, Gaultier, and Bikkembergs. Be warned, however, that the staff members are merciless, and you may find yourself handing over your credit card for a micromini you never intended to purchase. Avinyó 22. 📞 **93-301-24-20.** Metro: Jaume I or Liceu.

Mango ⒱alue   Apart from Zara (see below), Spain's other main fashion export is Mango, which in foreign countries often goes under the name MNG. Young, trendy, and midpriced is the deal here, and although the range isn't quite as extensive as their main competitors (nor do they do men's or children's wear), it's a sad day in Retail Land when you won't find at least something to pop on for that special evening out. If your visit coincides with the winter season, their suede and leather coats and jackets are definitely worth considering. There are branches all over Barcelona, including the one at Passeig de Gràcia 65 (© **93-215-75-30;** Metro: Passeig de Gràcia). Portal de l'Angel 7. © **93-317-69-85.** www.mango.es. Metro: Plaça de Catalunya.

On Land Ⓥalue   Although On Land is surrounded by hyper-trendy boutiques, the men's and women's clothing here is highly wearable; it's cross-generational without forfeiting a cutting edge. Their own label produces some well-cut trousers and jackets, and when complemented by one of Monte Ibáñez's hand-painted T-shirts, you have a distinctive outfit. Prices are good and sizes (mercifully) generous. Princesa 25. © **93-310-02-11.** www.on-land.com. Metro: Jaume I.

Textil i d'Indumentaria   Operated as a showcase for Catalonian design and ingenuity by Barcelona's Museum of Textile and Fashion, and set on a medieval street across from the Picasso Museum, this shop proudly displays and sells clothing and accessories for men, women, and children, all of which is either designed or at least manufactured within the region. Inventories include shoes, men's and women's sportswear and formalwear, jewelry, teddy bears, suitcases and handbags, umbrellas, and towels, each shaped and cut by up-and-coming Catalans. Two of the most famous designers include menswear specialist Antonio Miró (no relation to the 1950s and 1960s artist Joan Miró) and women's clothing designer Lydia Delgado. Montcada 12. © **93-310-74-04.** www.museutextil. bcn.cat. Metro: Jaume I.

FINE FOOD & WINE

Caelum Ⓕinds   Everything in this shop has been produced in monasteries and nunneries throughout Spain: jams and preserved fruit, marzipan and liquors, and quality cakes and biscuits. (Try the delicious holy honey cake.) The ornate packaging makes them great gifts, and there is a cafe downstairs where you can sample before you buy. Palla 8. © **93-302-69-93.** Metro: Liceu.

Casa Gispert   If you have trouble finding this shop behind the Santa María del Mar church, then simply follow your nose. Coffee and nuts are roasted here daily (go for the almonds straight out of the oven) and are sold alongside dried and candied fruit of all descriptions: Turkish figs, apricots, currants, and raisins, and even French *marron glacé*. Sometimes the lines spill out onto the street; such is the quality of everything this century-old shop sells. Sombrerers 23. © **93-319-75-35.** www.casagispert.com. Metro: Jaume I.

La Botifarreria de Santa María ★   If you haven't already noticed that when faced with a rib-eye filet and a *botifarra* (sausage), Catalans will opt for the latter, then visit the shop opposite the Gothic Santa María del Mar church. As well as making their own *botifarras* (reputed to be the finest in the land) on the premises, they sell the richest *jamón Jabugo* (acorn-fed ham), rare cheeses, sweet *fuet* (a thin salami) from central Catalonia, and other meaty delicacies. They will vacuum-pack your edibles for traveling (check if you can bring it back to your home country), or take some of their produce to the nearby Parc de la Ciutadella for a picnic. Santa María 4. © **93-319-91-23.** Metro: Jaume I or Barceloneta.

Lavinia ★★   Sort of like a wine megastore, Lavinia makes selection easy, as all their products are displayed according to country of origin, from Germany to Uruguay, Australia to California. As expected, the Spanish section is the most numerous, bulging with

La Boqueria: One of the World's Finest Food Markets

The **Boqueria market,** La Rambla 91–101 (✆ 93-318-20-17; www.boqueria. info; Mon–Sat 8am–8pm; Metro: Liceu), is the largest market in Europe (and probably the greatest in the world) and a must-see in the Catalan capital. It's located right in the middle of any visitor's top destination: the famous boulevard La Rambla. While many markets have little to offer a visitor in terms of practical shopping, the Boqueria boasts some of the best bars and cafes in the city, and a chance to rub shoulders with the people who are helping put the city at the forefront of Mediterranean cuisine.

Its central location is owed to a historical twist of fate. In the mid-1800s, the demolition of the city's medieval walls began. *Pageses* (Catalan peasants) had been touting their bounty roughly on the spot of the present market (originally one of the city's gates) and around the perimeter of the neighboring Convent de Sant Josep for centuries, and the authorities saw no reason to move them when the work began. When the convent burned to the ground in 1835, the market expanded, and 30 years later, the engineer Miquel de Bergue finished his plans for a grandiose, wrought-iron market of five wings supported by metal columns, a project that wasn't finished until 1914. The official name of the market is Mercat de Sant Josep (a reference to the Capuchin nuns' old dwelling), although the term *boqueria* (meaning *abattoir,* or butcher shop, in Catalan) has stuck since the 13th century, when the site was a slaughterhouse.

The Boqueria's 330 stalls are a living testament to the fertility of the peninsula (Spain produces the widest variety of farm produce in all of Europe) and its

Riojas, Priorats, *cavas,* albariños, and sherries. There is a pack-and-send service, which is handy, as most bottles come cheaper by the dozen (check your country's laws about what/ how much you can send back). Diagonal 605. ✆ 93-363-44-45. www.lavinia.es. Metro: María Cristina.

Origens 99.9% ★ Purveyors of fine, exclusively Catalan foodstuffs (.1% being the margin of error, presumably), this shop sells olive oils from Lleida, *mató* (a fresh, ricotta-like cheese) from the mountains, and wines from the Penedès and Priorat regions. There is a cafe next door where you can try before you buy. This is a good place to pick up presents for foodies back home. (Check regulations on what you can legally bring back to your country!) There's also an adjoining restaurant in this and other branches throughout the city. Muntaner 409. ✆ 93-201-45-79. www.origen99.com. Metro: Jaume I or Barceloneta.

Vila Viniteca ★★ This awesome wine shop in the heart of the El Born neighborhood supplies most of the restaurants in the area. The selection here can be frightening for the non-vinicultured among us, but those in the know rave about it. There are 4,500 different wines, sherries, *cavas,* liquors, and spirits from all over Spain, many of which are exclusive to the shop. Check out the bargain basket at the counter, where the last in the crates are sold for a song. Agullers 7–9. ✆ 90-232-77-77 or 93-310-19-56. www.vilaviniteca.es. Metro: Jaume I or Barceloneta.

surrounding seas. What lies inside is a gastronomic cornucopia that changes its palette from season to season. Early autumn sees the hues of burnt yellow, orange, and brown in the cluster of stalls selling the dozens of varieties of bolets, wild mushrooms from the hills and forests of Catalonia. In spring, the candy colors of fresh strawberries and plump peaches, and in early summer the greens of a dozen different lettuces, from curly bunches of escarole to pert little heads of endives and cogollos (lettuce hearts), make an appearance. The fish and seafood section takes prime place in a central roundabout known as the Isla del Pescado (Island of Fish), a pretty marble and shiny steel affair that was given priority in the Boqueria's recent overhaul. The variety here is awesome—from giant carcasses of tuna that send Japanese tourists into a camera-flashing frenzy to the ugly but tasty scorpionfish, prawns the size of bananas, live crayfish making a dash across their frozen beds, octopi, bug-eyed grouper, and countless other species. Other stalls range from game and delicatessens to bewildering businesses that survive by specializing in one product, whether it is lettuces, potatoes, or smoked salmon.

If you are up early enough, the best time to visit the Boqueria is the early morning as it is being hurled into life. Able-bodied men drag cartloads of produce to the stalls, while women arrange it into patterns and combinations that border on food art. Have breakfast at **Pinotxo** on the immediate right of the main entrance. Here you will rub shoulders with the city's main chefs before they embark on their daily sourcing spree. If you wish to do a bit of shopping yourself, avoid the stalls at the front unless you want to pay "tourist" prices.

GALLERIES

Despite producing some of the world's great artists, small galleries have a notoriously hard time surviving in Barcelona. This could be due to the fickleness of the scene. At the moment, gallery hubs include the streets around the Picasso Museum, the MACBA, and Calle Petritxol in the Barri Gòtic.

Art Picasso   Here you can get good lithographic reproductions of works by Picasso, Miró, and Dalí, as well as T-shirts emblazoned with the masters' designs. Tiles often carry their provocatively painted scenes. Tapinería 10. ☎ **93-310-49-57.** Metro: Jaume I.

Iguapop (Finds)   The Iguapop company is one of the leading promoters of contemporary music in Barcelona. Hardly surprising, then, that the emphasis is firmly on youth culture in their first gallery. Graffiti, video art, magazine design, and contemporary photography by young people from both Spain and abroad can be seen in their airy, white space located near the Ciutadella Park. There is an adjoining shop that sells cult streetwear and accessories. Comerç 15. ☎ **93-310-07-35.** www.iguapop.net. Metro: Jaume I.

Sala Parés ★★   Established in 1840, this is a Barcelona institution. The Maragall family recognizes and promotes the work of Spanish and Catalan painters and sculptors, many of whom have gone on to acclaim. Paintings are displayed in a two-story amphitheater, with high-tech steel balconies supported by a quartet of steel columns evocative of Gaudí. Exhibitions of the most avant-garde art in Barcelona change about every 3 weeks. Petritxol 5. ✆ **93-318-70-20.** www.salapares.com. Metro: Plaça de Catalunya.

HATS

Sombrería Obach (Finds) This reassuringly old-fashioned hat shop in the Call (old Jewish quarter) district stocks the largest color range of berets on earth, as well as Panamas, Kangol flat caps, straw sun hats, and a host of other headgear for men and women. Check out the classic Spanish sombrero: wide-brimmed, black, and very stylish. Carrer del Call 2. ✆ **93-318-40-94.** Metro: Jaume I or Liceu.

HERBS & HEALTH FOODS

Comme-Bio Comme-Bio is one-stop shopping for organic fruit and vegetables, health foods, tofu and other meat substitutes, and natural cosmetics. Don't get a shock at the prices; demand here for whole foods is just starting to take off, so expect to pay more than in the U.K. or U.S. Next to the supermarket is a juice bar and restaurant open for lunch and dinner, although the food here is a bit pedestrian. Vía Laietana 28. ✆ **93-319-89-68.** Metro: Jaume I.

Manantial de Salud This period shop has dried medicinal herbs, aromatic pills and potions, and its own range of natural beauty products all displayed in pretty pale green glass cabinets or large ceramic urns. Many locals pop in here for a natural cure to what ails them. The staff are extremely knowledgeable and used to dealing with foreigners, although you should look up a few key words in your dictionary beforehand. Xucla 23. ✆ **93-301-14-44.** www.manantialdesalud.com. Metro: Liceu.

JEWELRY

Forvm Ferlandina ★★ Contemporary jewelry and accessories from over 50 designers are on display here in tiny cubist cases that give this tiny shop just opposite the MACBA the feel of a contemporary gallery. Silversmithing, enamel work, beading, and most of the disciplines are featured. Particularly lovely are felt flower-bouquet brooches, rings, and hair ornaments which are produced in the rear workroom. Ferlandina 31. ✆ **93-441-80-18.** Metro: Liceu or Plaça de Catalunya.

Platamundi (Value) The string of Platamundi stores offers highly affordable, high-quality pieces in silver, both imported and by local designers such as Ricardo Domingo, head of the jewelry wing of FAD, the city's design council. Seek out the pieces that combine silver with enamel work in Mediterranean shades. Hospital 37. ✆ **93-410-00-48.** Metro: Liceu. Other branches at Montcada 11 (Metro: Jaume I), Plaça Santa María 7 (Metro: Jaume I), and Portaferrisa 22 (Metro: Liceu).

Tous Depending on your point of view, the jewelry and objects made by this Catalan family are either must-have or too twee to contemplate. Tous's leitmotif is the teddy bear, and the little fellow features in everything from earrings to key rings to belts and bracelets. They are adored by the city's VIP set, and their popularity has grown to such an extent that you now see pirated versions. Everything in Tous is produced to a very high standard in precious metals and semiprecious stones. Passeig de Gràcia 75. ✆ **93-488-15-58.** www.tous.es. Metro: Passeig de Gràcia.

LEATHER

Acosta ★ Started in the 1950s, this chain of stylish Spanish leather belts and bags now has 37 shops all over Spain and one in both Lisbon and Brussels. It's still a family-run affair, which is perhaps why everything sold has the air of being lovingly and meticulously produced. Prices are excellent, given the overall quality. Diagonal 602. ℂ **93-414-32-78.** Bus: 5, 7, 15, 33, or 34.

Loewe ★★★   Barcelona's biggest branch of this prestigious Spanish leather-goods chain is in one of the best-known *moderniste* buildings in the city. Everything is top-notch, from the elegant showroom to the expensive merchandise to the helpful salespeople. The company exports its goods to branches throughout Asia, Europe, and North America. With designer José Enrique Ona Selfa now at the helm, their clothing line is looking better than ever. Passeig de Gràcia 35. ℂ **93-216-04-00.** www.loewe.com. Metro: Passeig de Gràcia.

Lupo ★★   The current name in deluxe leather goods is Lupo. Trading from a minimalist silver-and-white shop in L'Eixample, their bags and belts stretch the limits of the craft by molding and folding leather into incredible shapes and using new dyeing techniques to create the most vivid colors. The world is taking notice, and the company is now exporting to the U.S., the rest of Europe, and Japan. Majorca 257, bajos. ℂ **93-487-80-50.** www.lupo.es. Metro: Passeig de Gràcia.

LINEN & TOWELS

El Indio (Finds)   Established in 1870 and easily recognizable from the florid facade and arched windows, this emporium sells all sorts of textile goods, from sheets to tea towels to tablecloths. The service and wood-lined surroundings are charmingly old school and the range mind-boggling, from cheap polyester sheets to the finest linen napkins. If they don't have it, it probably doesn't exist. Carme 24. ℂ **93-317-54-42.** Metro: Liceu.

Ràfols ★   Beautiful, made-to-order, and hand-embroidered bed linens, towels, tablecloths, and other items for your trousseau. The nimble-fingered staff will whip up any design you like, and the pure cottons and linens used are heavenly. Bori i Fontestà 4. ℂ **93-200-93-52.** Metro: Diagonal.

LINGERIE

Le Boudoir (Finds)   This may look like an upmarket sex shop (and in many ways it is), but in reality, the scarlet-red walls house a gorgeous collection of silk and lace lingerie and racy bedroom accessories, from furry handcuffs to music CDs designed to "get you in the mood" and other objects for intimate moments. In summer, they bring in an exclusive range of swimwear. Naughty, but very, very nice. Canuda 21. ℂ **93-302-52-81.** www.leboudoir.net. Metro: Plaça de Catalunya.

Women's Secret (Value)   This chain of lingerie, underwear, and sleepwear stores will make you wish you had one in your hometown. The prints are hip and colorful, the designs funky, and the prices highly palatable. Even their basics range from pure cotton bras and nighties to striped PJs and panty sets with matching slippers and toiletry bags; this is concept retailing at its cleverest. There are several shops in the center; the biggest are at Portaferrisa 7–9 (ℂ **93-318-92-42;** www.womensecret.com; Metro: Liceu), Puerta de l'Angel 38 (ℂ **93-301-07-00;** Metro: Plaça de Catalunya), Diagonal 399 (ℂ **93-237-86-14;** Metro: Diagonal), and Fontanella 16 (ℂ **93-317-93-69;** Metro: Urquinaona).

MAPS

Llibreria Quera (Finds)   This establishment was started in 1916 by the legendary adventurer Josep Quera, who pretty much covered every square inch of Catalonia and Andorra in his lifetime. Whether you are going hiking in the Pyrénées, motoring along the coast, or rock-climbing in the interior, you can plan your trip here with their selection of specialized books and maps. Petritxol 2. © **93-318-07-43**. www.llibreriaquera.com. Metro: Liceu.

MUSIC

Casa Beethoven (Finds)   Established in 1920, this store carries the most complete collection of sheet music in town. The collection naturally focuses on the works of Spanish and Catalan composers. Music lovers might make some rare discoveries. La Rambla 97. © **93-301-48-26**. www.casabeethoven.com. Metro: Liceu.

Discos Castelló   With six shops over Barcelona, Castelló pretty much has the CD market sewn up. Half of them are located in the Calle Tallers, a street of door-to-door music and vinyl shops. Opened in 1934, their flagship store at no. 7 is mainly pop rock. Next door, "Overstocks" has more of the same plus sections on jazz, world, Spanish, and country music. Classical music is sold at no. 3. Calle Tallers. © **93-412-17-69**. www.discos castello.com. Metro: Plaça de Catalunya.

FNAC (Value)   If you don't want anything too out of the mainstream, the best place to pick up music is the FNAC megastore. The second floor has CDs of all kinds—rock, pop, jazz, classical, and a tempting selection that consists of mostly not-quite-current

To Market, to Market . . .

There are a variety of outdoor markets held around the streets of Barcelona. Practice your bartering skills before heading for **El Encants flea market,** held every Monday, Wednesday, Friday, and Saturday in Plaça de les Glòries Catalanes (Metro: Glòries). Go anytime during the day to survey the selection of new and used clothing, period furniture, and out-and-out junk (although the traders will try to convince you otherwise). **Coins** and **postage stamps** are traded and sold in Plaça Reial on Sunday from 10am to 8pm. It's off the southern flank of La Rambla (Metro: Drassanes). A **book** (mainly Spanish language) and **coin market** is held at the Ronda Sant Antoni every Sunday from 10am to 2pm (Metro: Universitat) with a brisk trade in pirated software and DVDs taking place around the periphery. All types of fine-quality **antiquarian** items can be found at the **Mercat Gòtic** every Thursday 9am to 8pm, on the Plaça Nova outside the city's main cathedral (Metro: Liceu), but don't expect any bargains. More like a large **car-boot sale** is the **Encants del Gòtic,** Plaça George Orwell, Saturdays 11am to 4pm (Metro: Drassanes). The wide promenade, the Rambla del Raval, (Metro: San Antoni) is taken over by hippie-type traders all day every Saturday, hawking **handmade clothing, jewelry,** and other objects. Nearby, the **vintage and retro clothing traders** of the Riera Baixa (Metro: San Antoni) drag their goods on the street (some real bargains are to be found here). Over 50 painters set up shop every weekend in the pretty Plaça del Pi (Metro: Liceu) in a **Mostra d' Art** that is of a surprisingly high standard. If food is more your thing, over a dozen purveyors of artisan cheese, honey, biscuits, olives, chocolate, and other **Catalan delicacies** can also be found in the Plaça del Pi, on the first and third weekend of every month from 10am to 10pm.

releases of current artists at rock-bottom prices. You can ask to listen before buying, which is handy for making purchases of Spanish music and flamenco. It's open 10am to 10pm Monday through Saturday. Plaça de Catalunya 4. $\textcircled{C}$ **93-344-18-00.** www.fnac.es. Metro: Plaça de Catalunya.

OUTLETS & SECONDS

Contribución y Moda (Finds) This large split-level store sells men's and women's designer clothing from last season and beyond. It's the sort of place where you may pick up a pair of Vivienne Westwood woolen trousers for as little as 80€ ($104). That said, you can normally find at least one item to your taste and budget (especially at the beginning of the season), although the different size ranges can make you want to scream. Riera de Sant Miquel 30. $\textcircled{C}$ **93-218-71-40.** Metro: Diagonal.

La Roca Village Only true bargain hunters will perhaps be bothered to make the trip to this outer Barcelona "outlet village." But those that do will be rewarded with up to 60% off over 50 brands, including high-fashion labels such as Roberto Verino, Versace, and Carolina Herrera, shoes from Camper, luxury leatherware from Loewe and Mandarina Duck, and even sportswear from the likes of Billabong and Timberland. The setting is actually quite pleasant with a playground for the kids, cafes, and the like, and the savings here are legendary. Open daily from 11am to 9pm. Santa Agnés de Malanyanes, La Roca del Vallès. $\textcircled{C}$ **93-842-39-00.** www.larocavillage.com. By car: Take the AP-7 to Exit 12, head to Cardedeu, and then to the Centre Comercial. By train: Take the train from Sants Station to Granollers Center (trains leave every half-hour; trip time: 35 min.). From the station, a bus leaves for La Roca Village every hour at 23 min. past; a taxi will cost you 12€ ($16). By bus: Sagalés ($\textcircled{C}$ **93-870-78-60)** runs buses directly to La Roca Village from the Fabra i Puig Bus Terminal (Passeig Fabra i Puig, next to the Metro entrance). Buses (4.50€/$5.85 round-trip) leave Mon–Fri at 9am, noon, and 4 and 8pm (trip time: 50 min.).

MNG Outlet (Value) MNG is Mango, one of the biggest chains in Spain for young fashion. Their outlet store has items with *taras* (faults—of varying dimensions) and last season's stock at the silliest of prices. It's not unusual to pick up a pair of jeans here for 12€ ($16) or a T-shirt for as low as 6€ ($7.80). There is also a good selection of shoes and bags at rock-bottom prices. It gets frustratingly busy Saturdays. A few other outlet stores are located in the immediate vicinity. Girona 37. No phone. Metro: Tetuan or Urquinaona.

112 People with a foot fetish will love this Barrio Alto shop selling last year's shoes, boots, and bags at 50% off. Marc Jacobs, Givenchy, Emma Hope, Emilio Pucci, Robert Clergerie, and Rossi are just some of the names. Laforja 105. $\textcircled{C}$ **93-414-55-13.** FGC: Gràcia.

PERFUME & COSMETICS

La Galería de Santa María Novella (Finds) This is the Barcelona outlet of the famed Officina Profumo–Farmaceutica di Santa Maria Novella in Florence, the oldest and possibly most luxurious apothecary in the world. The perfumes and colognes are unadulterated scents of flowers, spices, and fruits; the soaps handmade; and the packaging seemingly unchanged since the 18th century. Prices are high. Espasería 4–8. $\textcircled{C}$ **93-268-02-37.** www.lagaleriadesantamarianovella.com. Metro: Jaume I or Barceloneta.

Regia ★ This high-end perfume and cosmetics shop has a secret: Wander through the racks stacked with Dior and Chanel and you reach a small door that leads to a unique museum (free admission). There are over 5,000 examples of perfume bottles and flasks from Grecian times to the present day. The star of the collection is the dramatic "Le Rei Soleil" by Salvador Dalí. Passeig de Gràcia 39. $\textcircled{C}$ **93-216-01-21.** www.regia.es. Metro: Passeig de Gràcia.

Sephora Cosmetics addicts may be forgiven for thinking they have died and gone to heaven when they enter this beauty megastore. All the desired brands are here: Clarins, Dior, Arden, Chanel, and so on—plus hard-to-finds such as Urban Decay and Phytomer. The house brand's range of makeup is a great value and Sephora claims not to be knowingly undersold. El Triangle, Pelai 13–37. © **93-306-39-00.** www.sephora.es. Metro: Plaça de Catalunya.

PORCELAIN

Kastoria This large store near the cathedral is an authorized Lladró dealer and stocks a big selection of the famous porcelain. It also carries many kinds of leather goods, including purses, suitcases, coats, and jackets. Av. Catedral 6–8. © **93-310-04-11.** www.kastoria. com. Metro: Plaça de Catalunya.

POTTERY

Artesana i Coses If you are in the vicinity of the Picasso Museum, pop into this jumble sale of a shop selling pottery and porcelain from every major region of Spain. Most of the pieces are heavy and thick-sided, and you can pick up a coffee mug for as little as a couple of euros. Placeta de Montcada 2. © **93-319-54-13.** Metro: Jaume I.

Art Escudellers This is one-stop shopping, unashamedly aimed at the tourist market, but in reality it contains a great range of pottery and ceramics from all over Spain. You'll see everything from the colorful, hand-painted pieces of the south to the earthy, brown and green ceramics of the north, everyday utilitarian objects, and more spectacular conversation pieces. It has a shipping service and hundreds of Spanish wines to taste and buy. Escudellers 23–25. © **93-412-68-01.** Metro: Drassanes.

Baraka Baraka's owner regularly raids the *souks* of Morocco and brings back the booty to this small shop in the trendy Born area. There is a lovely range of brightly colored and patterned pottery and ceramics, plus traditional *dhurries* (woven rugs), *bubucha* slippers, earthenware *tagines,* lamps, and other North African paraphernalia. Canvis Vells 2. © **93-268-42-20.** Metro: Jaume I.

Itaca (Finds) Here you'll find a wide array of handmade pottery from Catalonia and other parts of Spain, plus Portugal, Mexico, and Morocco. The merchandise has been selected for its basic purity, integrity, and simplicity. There is a wide range of Gaudí-esque objects, inspired by trademark *trencadis* (broken tile) work. Ferran 26. © **93-301-30-44.** Metro: Liceu.

SCARVES, SHAWLS & ACCESSORIES

Rafa Teja Atelier ★★ This shop has a sublime collection of wool, cotton, and silk scarves and shawls from India, Asia, and Spain, all neatly hung on wooden rails or folded into glorious, multicolored stacks. Whether it's a pashmina wrap, a mohair collar, or an extravagant shawl to match an evening dress, you are bound to unearth it here. They also do their own limited range of clothing, such as evening coats in Chinese brocades or sarong-style skirts in Indonesian batiks. Santa María 18. © **93-310-27-85.** Metro: Jaume I or Barceloneta.

SHOES

Camper ★★ Made on the island of Majorca, Camper shoes have now conquered the world. Their distinctive molded shapes in unusual colors are seen treading the streets of New York and Sydney, but Barcelona has the biggest range at better prices. The shop

Specialty Stores in the Barri Gòtic

The streets around the Barri Gòtic are packed with traditional establishments specializing in everything from dried cod to dancing shoes, some of them remnants from when mercantile activity and trading was Barcelona's lifeblood. If you see a shop window that entices, don't be shy; most of the shopkeepers welcome curious tourists, and a brief exchange with one of them just may be one of those fleeting traveler's experiences you cherish long after it's over.

Dating from 1761, the **Cereria Subira,** Baixada de Llibreteria 7 (© **93-315-26-06**), has the distinction of being the oldest continuous shop in Barcelona. It specializes in candles, from long and elegant white ones used at Mass to more fanciful creations. Magicians and illusionists love the **Rey de la Magia,** Princesa 11 (© **93-319-39-20;** www.elreydelamagia.com), a joke and magic shop dating from 1881. Behind the ornate Art Nouveau facade of **Alonso,** Santa Ana 27 (© **93-317-60-85**), lie dozens of gloves, from dainty calfskin to more rugged driving gloves, plus pretty fans and lace *mantillas* (Spanish shawls). More traditional Spanish garb is to be found at **Flora Albaicín,** Valllirana 71–73 (© **93-418-23-09**), which specializes in flamenco dancing shoes and spotty, swirly skirts and dresses. The **Herboristeria del Rei,** del Vidre 1 (© **93-318-05-12**), is another shop steeped in history; it has been supplying herbs, natural remedies, and cosmetics and teas since 1823. **Casa Colomina,** Cucurulla 2 (© **93-317-46-81**), makes its own *turrones,* slabs of nougat and marzipan that are a traditional Christmas treat. Nimble fingers will love the **L'Antiga Casa Sala,** Call 8 (© **93-318-45-87;** www.antigacasasala.com), which has an enormous range of beads and trinkets just begging to be turned into an original accessory. In the old Born food hub, **Angel Jobal,** Princesa 38 (© **93-319-78-02**), is the city's most famed spice merchant, selling everything from Spanish saffron to Indian pepper and oregano from Chile. **Ganiveteria Roca,** Plaça del Pi 3 (© **93-302-12-41**), has an enormous range of knives, blades, scissors, and all sorts of special-task cutting instruments. **Xancó Camiseria,** La Rambla 78–80 (© **93-318-09-89**), is one of the few period shops remaining on La Rambla; they have been making classic men's shirts in cottons, wools, and linens since 1820. If you get caught in the rain, head to **Paraguas Rambla de Las Flores,** La Rambla 104 (© **93-412-72-58**), which stocks all manner of umbrellas and walking sticks. And finally, you never know when you may need a chicken feather; the **Casa Morelli,** Banys Nous 13 (© **93-302-52-94**), has sacks of them, for simple stuffing or decorating a party outfit.

interiors, often done by the quirky Catalan designer Martí Guixe, reflect the brand's wholesome yet hip culture. There are several locations throughout the city. Valencia 249. © **93-215-63-90.** www.camper.es. Metro: Passeig de Gràcia.

Casas ★★ If you are serious about footwear, then this is the only name you need to know. With three shops in central Barcelona, Casas is a one-stop shoe shop for the most prominent Spanish brands (Camper, Vialis, Dorotea, and so on) and coveted imports from Clergerie, Rodolfo Zengarini, and Mare, plus sports and walking shoes. Three locations: La Rambla 125 (*☎* **93-302-45-98**), Portaferrisa 25 (*☎* **93-302-11-32**), and Portal de l'Angel 40 (*☎* **93-302-11-12**). Metro: Plaça de Catalunya or Liceu.

Czar If sports shoes and trainers are your thing, then look no further than Czar. They have everything from Converse, Le Coq Sportif, and Adidas classics to more bizarre creations by Diesel, W&LT, Asics, and other cult labels. Passeig del Born 20. *☎* **93-310-72-22**. Metro: Jaume I or Barceloneta.

La Manual Alpargatera (**Finds** The good people at this Old Town shop have been making espadrilles on the premises for nearly a century. As well as the classic slip-on variety, you will find the Catalan *espadenya,* which has ribbon ankle-ties, wedge-heeled versions in fashion colors, toasty lamb's wool slippers, and other "natural" footwear. Clients have included Michael Douglas and the Pope. Avinyó 7. *☎* **93-301-01-72**. www. lamanual.net. Metro: Jaume I or Liceu.

Lotusse These Majorcan cobblers are revered for their extraordinary quality. The brogues, loafers, T-bars, and other classic styles for men and women actually look and feel handmade. They won't make you stand out in a crowd, but are liable to last you a lifetime. Lotusse also sells bags, wallets, and belts. Rambla de Catalunya 103. *☎* **93-215-89-11**. Metro: Passeig de Gràcia.

Muxart ★★ Hermenegildo Muxart knows how to make heels that appeal, offering sexy, cutting-edge shoes and handbags from his L'Eixample shop. A pair of black stilettos may feature a red disc on the toe, for example, or metallic silver and electric-blue leather plaited together with straw to form an intricate tapestry. While this may sound a bit faddy, Muxart knows when to draw in the reins, making a pair of his shoes an investment buy rather than an expensive whim. Rosselló 230. *☎* **93-488-10-64**. www.muxart.com. Metro: Diagonal. Other location at Rambla de Catalunya 47. *☎* **93-467-74-23**. Metro: Passeig de Gràcia.

SHOPPING CENTERS & MALLS

Shopping malls are a bit of a contentious topic in Catalonia. Many small traders feel they are squeezing them out of the market. The local government has reacted by limiting their construction, especially in central Barcelona. But there are still enough in existence to appease any mall fan.

Centre Comercial Glòries Built in 1995, part of a huge project to rejuvenate a downtrodden part of town, this is a three-story emporium that has more than 230 shops, a few posh and others far from it. Most people head here for the Carrefour department stores, the cheaper cousin of El Corte Inglés that mainly sells electrical and home goods. Although there's a typical shopping-mall anonymity to this place, it's great for kids, with lots of open spaces and bouncy things to jump on. Open Monday through Saturday from 10am to 10pm. Av. Diagonal 208. *☎* **93-486-04-04**. www.lesglories.com. Metro: Glòries.

Diagonal Mar This is one of the city's largest modern malls, part of an urban project that has breathed residential and commercial life into the city's northern coastline. Reflecting the surrounding property prices, shops here tend to be mid- to high-end. All the fashion staples are here, plus a branch of the music and entertainment megastore FNAC, and even a movie theater. Open Monday to Saturday from 10am to 10pm. Av. Diagonal 3. *☎* **93-567-76-30** or 90-253-03-00. www.diagonalmar.com. Metro: Maresme/Forum, Selva de Mar, or Besós-Mar.

L'illa Diagonal Located in an expensive part of town, shopping here is mainly high- end. Thus, this two-story mall has stores mainly devoted to fashion products: Lacoste, Diesel, Custo Barcelona, Miss Sixty, as well as a scattering of home, gift, and toy boutiques. The first level has a huge supermarket and food hall selling everything from handmade chocolates to dried cod. Open Monday through Saturday 10am to 9:30pm. Av. Diagonal 557. ⓒ **93-444-00-00.** www.lilla.com. Metro: María Cristina.

Pedralbes Centre This two-story arcade focuses mainly on fashion. Check out the street and club wear from E4G and ZasTwo, froufrou party frocks by Puente Aereo, and the brightly colored quirky cloths of Agata Ruiz de la Prada. Other highlights include a Lavinia wine store and a branch of the Corte Inglés. Diagonal 609–615. ⓒ **93-410-68-21.** Metro: María Cristina.

SPORTING GOODS

Decathlon ⓥ**alue** If in Barcelona you plan to do some physical activity beyond a stroll down La Rambla, Decathlon is really the only name you need to know. Every single sport is covered in this French-owned megastore, from football and tennis to *ja-kai* (Basque handball) and Ping-Pong. There is swimwear, clothing for jogging, aerobics, cycling hats (and bicycles), ski gear, hiking boots, and wet suits. Their prices are pretty much unbeatable, especially on their house items. Canuda 20. ⓒ **93-342-61-61.** www.decathlon.es. Metro: Plaça de Catalunya or L'illa. Other location at Diagonal 557. ⓒ **93-444-01-65.** Metro: María Cristina.

10

Barcelona After Dark

Barcelona is a great nighttime city, and the array of after-dark diversions is staggering. There is something to interest almost everyone and to fit most pocketbooks. Fashionable **bars** and **clubs** operate in nearly every major district of the city, and where one closes, another will open within weeks.

Locals sometimes opt for an evening in the *tascas* (taverns), or perhaps settling in for a bottle of wine at a cafe, an easy and inexpensive way to spend an evening people-watching. The legal age for drinking is 18, but is rarely enforced with much vigor.

With the passing of a law in January 2006, all bars of over 100 sq. m (1,076 sq. ft.) must have a nonsmoking area. The reality, however, is that though these zones do now exist, there's not much you can do about the smoke wafting into the nonsmoking section from the far larger smoker's zone. So, as before, you usually have to air out your clothes when you get back from a night out.

If the weather is good (which is most of the time) the city's outdoor squares are at least half-filled with as many tables and chairs as can reasonably fit. Beware where two tables are squeezed next to each other: The occupants of each will be fiercely protective of its chairs and won't like it if you drag a chair from one place to make an extra seat at another table. Alfresco drinking has become so popular that the local government has been forced by complaining neighbors to restrict its hours in some areas—around midnight, it's usual to be asked to finish your drinks or to go inside. Particularly good places to sit and see the world go by are **Plaça del Sol** in Gràcia and **Passeig del Born**, **Plaça del Pi**, and **Plaça Reial** in the Old Town. The squares are also popular drinking haunts for groups of teenagers, but their tipple tends to be more of the supermarket-bought variety. The old Spanish tradition of the *botellón,* whereby groups of young people sit around on the cement swilling beer or wine, is treated as a nuisance by the local government and noise-sensitive neighbors. Despite cracking down on the practice, it persists, especially in the summer.

People-watching of a more flesh-exposed nature can be done down at the beach in the summer. Between May and October, a line of *chiringuitos* (beach bars) opens for nighttime frivolity in the sands along Barcelona's urban beaches (Barceloneta to Poble Nou). Each one has its own flavor—some play chill-out music; others have live DJs or bands. Owners, names, and styles change from year to year, but generally they open at lunchtime (or late breakfast) and stay open until 2 or 3am.

Also down near the sands, there are plenty of bars and restaurants around the Olympic marina and port. This, as well as Maremagnum, the entertainment and leisure complex, and the port end of La Rambla offer more foreigner-focused spots for those looking for strong drinks and fellow English speakers.

Other areas filled with bars include the **Carrer Avinyó** in the Barri Gòtic, the **Rambla del Raval** in El Raval, and the in streets of **El Born** in La Ribera—just walk around and see where the noise is coming from. There are plenty of local secrets to uncover, if you just follow the crowd for a while.

JOINING IN BARCELONA NIGHTLIFE

Nightlife will begin for many Barcelonese with a **promenade** *(paseo)* from about 8 to 9pm. Then things quiet down a bit until a second surge of energy brings out the post-dinner crowds from 11pm to midnight. Serious drinking in the city's pubs and bars usually begins by midnight. For the most fashionable places, Barcelonese will delay their entrances until at least 1am—meeting friends for the first drink of the evening after midnight certainly takes some getting used to. If you want to go on to a club, you should be prepared to delay things even longer—most clubs don't open until around 2am, and they will be mostly empty for the first half-hour or so, until the bars close at 3am. Many clubs stay open to as late as 6am. Most of them will have free entrance or discount flyers available in bars or given out on the streets, saving yourself between 5€ and 10€ ($6.50–$13), which is the normal club entrance price, if there is one; this will largely depend on the night, the DJ, and what the doorman thinks you look like. The price of a mixed drink (such as a *cuba libre,* which is a rum and coke) hovers between 6€ and 12€ ($7.80–$16). This may seem pricey, but drinks here are *strong.* If you are charged an admission, ask if its *amb consumició* (drink included). If so, take your ticket to the bar to get the first drink free.

Barcelona is a trendy town and the clubbing scene is notoriously fickle. New things come up and others disappear. Although I've recommended places that have been around for a while, don't be too surprised if names and styles of the places have changed from what is printed here when you roll up.

A lot of famous international names, from the Rolling Stones to Anastasia, include Barcelona in their tours. The biggest concerts take place at the **Palau Sant Jordi** on Montjuïc, a flexible and cavernous space that's also used to house the city's basketball games. In a city where the cult of the DJ reigns, Barcelona is short of small and midsize exclusively live music venues (although some clubs do both, with a concert taking place before the club kids roll in).

One of the best places to see people playing instruments (as opposed to spinning records) is the street. In the summer you'll see plenty of free entertainment—everything from opera to Romanian gypsy music—by walking around the Barri Gòtic. Festivals such as **El Grec** (July–Aug) and **La Mercè** (late Sept) are when the biggest musical offering tends to take place.

If you want to find out what's going on in the city, the best source of local information is a little magazine called ***Guía del Ocio,***

Keep It Down

Though Spain is one of the last countries on earth you'd think of as being allergic to noise, mumblings are growing over the decibels surging from the pleasure spots of city centers where—unlike in some countries—many people still live. Placards and banners pleading for more consideration hang across the narrow lanes and squares of Barcelona's Ciutat Vella with disconcerting signs like "Estem farts" (which means "we're fed up" in Catalan). One result has been a tentative crackdown on culprits making the loudest sounds, from top disco La Terrrazza in the Poble Espanyol to the veteran Bar Pastis in Poble Sec. La Terrrazza was actually closed for just over a year, so the gesture has been made and steps apparently taken to diffuse the din in both these establishments, as well as in other spots where similar problematic situations have arisen. Whether or not the noise has abated sufficiently for locals to get a decent night's sleep in those offending areas is, however, debatable.

which previews "La Semana de Barcelona" (This Week in Barcelona). It's in Spanish, but most of its listings will be comprehensible. Every news kiosk along La Rambla carries it. If you have Internet access, **Le Cool** magazine (www.lecool.com) also carries an English summary of some of the more alternative options each week.

If you've been scared off by press reports about La Rambla between the Plaça de Catalunya and the Columbus Monument, know that the area's been cleaned up in the past decade. Still, you will feel safer along the Rambla de Catalunya, in the Eixample,

north of the Plaça de Catalunya. This street and its offshoots are lively at night, with many cafes and bars.

The main area where things feel a little uneasy is in El Raval, or the Barrio Chino—that is, the lower half of the right-hand side as you go toward the port. But despite (or because of?) this, a lot of the new trendy bars are appearing there (such as Bar Pastis; p. 253). There are some great bars and strange venues down there, but do use caution if you go there, especially when withdrawing money from a cash machine (although more and more of these are locked at night anyway).

1 BEST BARS AND PUBS

- **Best Champagne Bar:** Sparkling wine in Spain is called *cava,* and often there is very little difference between the local version and what you get north of the border in France. **El Xampanyet,** Montcada 22 (② 93-319-70-73), a tiny, ceramic-lined *cava* bar opposite the Picasso Museum, has been serving up its house variety for generations and is one of the more atmospheric places to down a bottle or two. See p. 258.
- **Best Bar View:** The trek up to the peak of Tibidabo is worth it for **Mirablau,** Plaça Doctor Andreu s/n (② 93-418-58-79), a chic bar that provides an unparalleled panoramic view of the city from its floor-to-ceiling glass windows. See p. 257.
- **Best Bar for Predinner Drinks:** Strategically located just off the top end of La Rambla, **Boadas,** Tallers 1 (② 93-318-88-26), is another historic watering hole, this time with its roots in Havana, Cuba. Predictably, *mojitos* and daiquiris are a specialty, and it's relaxed enough to wander in casually dressed. See p. 248.
- **Best Irish Pub:** While Barcelona abounds with good Celtic-style pubs, their wood-lined interiors and leather seating are not altogether congenial on a summer night. **The Fastnet,** Passeig Juan de Borbón 22 (② 93-295-30-05), has an outdoor terrace that looks out onto the port and is a favorite hangout of visiting yachties and beach-loving expats. See p. 253.

2 THE PERFORMING ARTS

Culture is deeply ingrained in the Catalan soul, and the performing arts are strong. Long a city of the arts, Barcelona experienced a cultural decline during the Franco years, but now it is filled once again with the best opera, symphonic, and choral music. At the venues listed here, unless otherwise specified, ticket prices depend on the event. Tickets can be bought at the venues, but it's often more convenient and easier to use one of the special ticket services. The bank Caixa Catalunya sells *entradas* for many events, and it also has the wondrous **ServiCaixa**—an automated machine that dispenses theater and cinema tickets—in many of its branches. *Tel-entrada* (② 90-233-22-11) lets you buy over the phone with your credit card.

Gran Teatre del Liceu ★★★ This monument to Belle Epoque extravagance is one of the grandest opera houses in the world. It was designed by the Catalan architect Josep Oriol Mestes. In 1994, a disastrous fire gutted the opera house, but it was quickly rebuilt, and today it stands as a beloved citadel of the Catalan classical musical scene. The 2,300-seat theater boasts re-created ornate classical carvings, along with additional modern touches including international subtitles on the chair backs. Other new amenities include a quiet cafe and an extensive shop in the basement, open during the day. Each show offers a couple of reduced-rate performances, where ticket prices are half-price (or close to it). It's very easy to find, as it's halfway down La Rambla; guided tours of the edifice (lasting about an hour) are also available daily 10am to 6pm. Rambla dels Caputxins 51–59. *©* **93-485-99-13.** www.liceubarcelona.com. Metro: Liceu.

La Casa dels Músics Pianist Luis de Arquer has established a small chamber company in his 19th-century Gràcia home. They now call it the smallest opera house in the world, and they're probably not wrong since the performers are almost sitting on your lap as they perform small-scale productions of *opera buffa* and *bel canto*. Shows usually begin at 9pm, but you must call to confirm. For the true music lover, this could be your most charming evening in Barcelona. Encarnació 25. *©* **93-284-99-20.** www.lacasadelsmusics. com. Tickets 25€ ($33). Metro: Fontana.

L'Auditori ★★ This is the newest of the city's classical music bastions, designed as a permanent home for the Orfeó Català choral society and the OBC (Barcelona's symphony orchestra), although top-flight international names perform here as well. The edifice was designed by the award-winning Spanish architect Rafael Moneo, and its amazing state-of-the-art acoustics are among the best in town. Lepant 150. *©* **93-247-93-00.** www.auditori.org. Metro: Glòries.

Palau de la Música Catalana ★★★ In a city chock-full of architectural highlights, this one stands out. In 1908 Lluis Doménech i Montaner, a Catalan architect, designed this structure as a home for the choral society the Orfeó Català, using stained glass, ceramics, statuary, and ornate lamps, among other elements. It stands today as the most lush example of *modernisme*. Concerts (mainly classical but also jazz, folk, and other genres) and leading recitals take place here, as do daily guided tours of the buildings. But they say you only really appreciate it when enjoying a concert. A new extension called Petit Palau, including a luxury restaurant, recently opened. Open daily from 10am to 3:30pm; box office open Monday through Saturday from 10am to 9pm. Sant Francesc de Paula 2. *©* **93-295-72-00.** www.palaumusica.org. Metro: Urquinaona.

CINEMA

In Barcelona there's a good choice of cinemas showing original-language *(versió original)* movies—mostly in English—with Spanish subtitles. Some offer Monday and Wednesday discounts. Weekends are very popular (and crowded), with most movie houses also featuring late-night shows that start at 1am. Check the *Guía del Ocio* and local papers such as *El País* and *La Vanguardia* for information on showings and times.

Casablanca-Kaplan This modern multiplex shows a variety of up-to-date mainstream and art releases. Some find its minimalist-style seats distractingly hard, especially if the film you're watching doesn't keep you hooked. Passeig de Gràcia 115 (L'Eixample). *©* **93-218-43-45.** Tickets: 7.40€ ($9.60). 4 showings a day. Metro: Diagonal.

Cinemes Méliès   Two screens here provide a blend of art-house and standard commercial releases. Anything from classics to contemporary works is shown, sometimes with special seasons focusing on particular directors or stars. The program is constantly changing, so it's well worth keeping an eye on this place if you're in town for a while. Carrer de Villaroel 10 (L'Eixample). ☎ 93-451-00-51. www.cinesmelies.net. Tickets Mon 2.70€ ($3.50), Tues–Sun 4€ ($5.20). No credit cards. 8 programs a week. Metro: Urgell.

Filmoteca Aquitania   Funded by the Catalan government, this *cineaste*'s haven shows classics and lesser-known esoteric works. It offers special seasons devoted to famous and not-so-famous directors, and you can buy bargain block-purchasing booklets of 20 or more tickets, which bring the already low entry price down even further. Occasional children's shows are another attraction. All in all, a bargain. Cinema Aquitania, Av. Sarria 31–33. ☎ 93-410-75-90. Tickets 3€ ($3.90). Metro: Hospital Clinic.

Icária Yelmo Cineplex   Located in a large mall down in the Port Olimpic area, this large 15-screen multiplex features popular mainstream releases as well as the occasional offbeat European movie. Seats are numbered at the weekend when crowds flock in, so it's a safer bet to book your seat on their website. Salvador Espriu 61, Vila Olímpica. ☎ 93-221-75-85. www.yelmocineplex.es. Tickets Tues–Sun 7.40€ ($9.60), Mon 5€ ($6.50). Late shows Fri and Sat. Metro: Ciutadella-Vila Olimpica.

Renoir Floridablanca   One of the city's most centrally located cinemas, the Renoir Floridablanca features conventional—but totally up-to-date—releases on a quartet of small screens. Usually there's a choice of eight different films on any given day. Its sister movie house, the Renoir Les Corts, offers a similar program. Floridablanca: Floridablanca 135 (L'Eixample). ☎ 93-228-93-93. www.cinesrenoir.com. Les Corts: Eugenie d'Ors 12 (Les Corts). ☎ 93-490-55-10. For both: Tickets Tues–Sun 7.40€ ($9.60), Mon 4.50€ ($5.85). Late shows Fri–Sat. MC, V. Metro: Sant Antoni.

Verdi   Cozily situated in the heart of Gràcia, this five-screen movie house—the very first in town to feature original-version movies—is a recognized institution in Barcelona. Films shown tend to be more adventurous and radical than the norm, and its popularity is demonstrated by long weekend lines. Get there early, then, or book before. Its four-screen annex, Verdi Park, is close by. Verdi 32 and Verdi Park Torrijos 49 (both in Gràcia). ☎ 93-238-79-90. Tickets: 7€ ($9.10). Late shows Fri–Sat. Metro: Fontana.

THEATER

The majority of theater in Barcelona is presented in the Catalan language by Spanish production companies. Avant-garde theater and comedy is particularly strong; La Fura dels Baus is an internationally renowned troupe, El Comedients and La Cubana draw on local folklore and popular culture to make us laugh, and El Tricicle is a well-loved trio of comedians whose medium is mime. The Catalan director Calixto Bieito is one of the world's leading directors, renowned for his contemporary and often violent versions of Shakespeare's work.

Institut del Teatre ★★★   This grand new theatrical complex is where the city's theater and dance schools are located. There are three auditoriums of varying capacities, and performances range from student showcases to cutting-edge international companies to 24-hour circus "marathons." Plaça Margarida Xirgú s/n. ☎ 93-227-39-00. www.institutdel teatre.org. Metro: Espanya.

L'Antic Teatre (Finds) This is a real avant-garde small theater near the Palau Música Catalana, which hosts both touring companies and locals. You never know what to expect, so it's worth reading through the schedules on the door, if you can understand them—one night it's Belgian mime, the next South American circus skills, the next a Jamaican documentary. Tickets are always an excellent value, whatever you end up seeing. Verdaguer I Callis 12. (© **93-315-23-54.** www.lanticteatre.com. Metro: Urquinaona.

Mercat de Les Flors ★★ Housed in a building constructed for the 1929 International Exhibition at Montjuïc, this is the other major Catalan theater. Peter Brook first used it as a theater for a 1983 presentation of *Carmen*. The theater focuses on innovators in drama, dance, and music, as well as European modern-dance companies. It also often features avant-garde art festivals. The 999-seat house has a restaurant overlooking the city rooftops. Lleida 59. (© **93-426-18-75.** www.mercatflors.org. Metro: Espanya.

Teatre Nacional de Catalunya Josep Maria Flotats heads this major company in a modern, mock-Roman building a little out of the center near L'Auditori (see above). The actor/director trained in the tradition of theater repertory, working in Paris at Théâtre de la Villa and the Comédie Française. His company presents both classic and contemporary plays. Plaça de les Arts 1. (© **93-306-57-00.** www.tnc.cat. Metro: Plaça de les Glorias.

Teatre Victoria Situated in the west of the city, this unpretentious large-capacity theater hosts big-scale productions, usually musical spectaculars or comedies. Paral.lel 65. (© **93-329-91-89.** www.teatrevictoria.com. Metro: Paral.lel.

(Moments)   I Could Have Danced All Weekend

Although the city caters to music lovers of most tastes, the really big thing here is electronic dance music. DJs are the new rock heroes, and the Woodstock of this generation is called **Sónar** (www.sonar.es). The festival began in 1996 in a small, outside venue, as a way of showcasing some of the more unusual experimental music coming out of different parts of Europe. Now it takes over a significant part of the city for a long weekend in mid-June, drawing in people from far and wide. It's now really two festivals, held in two separate locations. During the day, it's held at a number of stages around the MACBA and CCCB in El Raval. At night, it moves to a huge congress and trade-fair hall outside the center, with a special bus shuffling punters in between. For the day and night gigs, tickets are sold separately, although you can buy a pass to the whole thing. Recent Sónar nighttime headliners have included Massive Attack and Björk, but the daytime music is much more open and eclectic, often accompanied by strange visuals. Of course, this being Barcelona, there's also a string of unofficial festivals running at the same time, all of which are much cheaper (or sometimes free) and can be read about on walls and from fliers in bars. This, claim the purists, is where you find the true experimental music, Sónar having sold out to the big sponsors years ago. The best thing is probably to enjoy both—but if you want to go to the official Sónar festival, you should buy your tickets (and book your accommodations) well beforehand.

Flamenco isn't the rage here that it is in Seville and Madrid, but it still has its devotees. It's not a Catalan tradition, but Barcelona has an active Andalusian population and dancers with as much verve and color as any you'd find further south.

El Tablao de Carmen ★★★   This club presents a highly rated flamenco cabaret in the re-created imitation "typical Spanish artisan village" of Poble Espanyol on the side of the Montjuïc hill. You can go early and explore the village, and even have dinner there as the sun sets. This place has long been a tourist favorite. The club is open Tuesday through Sunday from 8pm to past midnight—around 1am on weeknights, often until 2 or 3am on weekends, depending on business. The first show is always at 9:30pm; the second show is at 11:30pm on Tuesday, Wednesday, Thursday, and Sunday, and midnight on Friday and Saturday. Reservations are recommended. Av. Marqués de Comillas, Poble Espanyol de Montjuïc. ✆ 93-325-68-95. www.tablaodecarmen.com. Dinner and show 65€–80€ ($85–$104); drink and show 35€ ($46). Metro: Espanya.

Los Tarantos ★★   Established in 1963, this is the oldest flamenco club in Barcelona, with a rigid allegiance to the tenets of Andalusian flamenco. Its roster of artists changes regularly. Performers often come from Seville or Córdoba, stamping out their well-rehearsed passions in ways that make the audience appreciate the arcane nuances of Spain's most intensely controlled dance idiom; other nights it could be a lesser-known local artist or a percussion show. No food is served. The place resembles a cabaret theater, where up to 120 people at a time can drink, talk quietly, and savor the nuances of a dance that combines elements from medieval Christian and Muslim traditions. Shows are sporadic, so check before you roll up. Plaça Reial 17. ✆ 93-318-30-67. www.masimas.com/tarantos. Cover (includes 1 drink) normally around 20€ ($26). Metro: Liceu.

Tablao Flamenco Cordobés ★   At the southern end of La Rambla, a short walk from the harborfront, you'll hear the strum of the guitar, the sound of hands clapping rhythmically, and the haunting sound of the flamenco, a tradition here since 1968. Head upstairs to an Andalusian-style room where performances take place with the traditional *cuadro flamenco*—singers, dancers, and guitarist. Cordobés is said to be the city's best flamenco showcase. Three shows are offered nightly with dinner, at 7, 8:30, and 10pm. Reservations are required. La Rambla 35. ✆ 93-317-57-11. www.tablaocordobes.com. Dinner and show 50€–60€ ($65–$78); 1 drink and show 30€–35€ ($39–46). Metro: Drassanes.

Tirititran   A flamenco restaurant run by genuine *gitanos,* the background music, the pictures on the wall, and the menu all sing of the same passionate musical tradition. In the basement they have a small stage and music, and late on weekends, groups of Andalusians often come by to strum a guitar and drink some hard liquor. The atmosphere is friendly, and although you won't see many beautifully dressed dancers or roses between the teeth, they know their flamenco as good as anyone. Buenos Aires 28. ✆ 93-363-05-91. Admission 6€ ($7.80). Metro: Urgell.

CABARET, JAZZ & MORE

Espai Barroc ★★★   One of Barcelona's most culture-conscious (and slightly pretentious) nightspots occupies some of the showplace rooms of the Palau Dalmases, a stately gothic mansion in La Ribera. In a room lined with grand art objects, flowers, and large platters of fruit, you can listen to recorded opera arias and sip glasses of beer or wine. The most appealing night is Thursday—beginning at 11pm, 10 singers perform a roster of arias from assorted operas, one of which is invariably *Carmen*. Almost everyone around the bar apparently has at least heard of the world's greatest operas, and some can even discuss them more or less brilliantly. Montcada 20. ☎ **93-310-06-73.** Metro: Jaume I.

Harlem Jazz Club ★★ On a quiet street in the Ciutat Vella, this is one of Barcelona's oldest and finest jazz clubs. It's also one of the smallest, with just a handful of tables that get cleared away when the set ends so that people can dance. No matter how many times you've heard "Black Orpheus" or "The Girl from Ipanema," they always sound new again here. Music is viewed with a certain reverence; no one talks when the performers are on. Live jazz, blues, tango, Brazilian funk, Romanian gypsy music, African rhythms—the sounds are always fresh. Most gigs start around 10pm, slightly later on the weekends. Comtessa de Sobradiel 8. ☎ **93-310-07-55.** www.harlemjazzclub.es. Free admission Mon–Thurs, 8€ ($10) Fri–Sat. 1-drink minimum. Closed first 2 weeks in Aug. Metro: Jaume I.

Jamboree ★★ Among the boisterous revelry of the Plaça Reial just off La Rambla, this has long been one of the city's premier locations for good blues and jazz, although it doesn't feature jazz every night. Sometimes a world-class performer will appear here, but most likely it'll be a younger group. The crowd knows its stuff and demands only the best talent. On my last visit, I was entertained by an evening of Chicago blues, but you might also find a Latin dance band performing. As it gets late, the music changes and the place opens up as a nightclub for a young crowd, with hip-hop featuring downstairs and a more world music vibe upstairs. Most shows begin about 10pm to midnight. Plaça Reial 17. ☎ **93-301-75-64.** www.masimas.com/jamboree. Admission (includes 1 drink) 8€ ($10); shows 9€–12€ ($12–$16). Metro: Liceu.

Luz de Gas ★★ This theater is renowned for Latino jazz. The place itself is a turn-of-the-20th-century delight, with colored glass lamps, red drapery, and other details, but it's also a world-class live-music venue. It was once a theater, and its original seating has been turned into different areas, each with its own bar. The lower two levels open onto the dance floor and stage. If you'd like to talk, head for the top tier, which has a glass enclosure. Call to see what the lineup is on any given night: jazz, pop, soul, rhythm and blues, salsa, bolero, whatever. Be warned that the management can be somewhat snooty, so go with attitude. Montaner 246. ☎ **93-209-77-11.** www.luzdegas.com. Cover (includes 1 drink) usually 20€–25€ ($26–$33). Bus: 6, 27, 32, or 34.

3 BARS, CAFES, PUBS & CLUBS

CIUTAT VELLA
Bars, Cafes & Pubs
Almirall ★ Quiet and dimly lit, this bar might help you imagine what a late-19th-century Barcelona bohemian artists' hangout might have looked like. A huge Art Nouveau mirror behind the bar completes the picture. The crowd is still bohemian and it's a good place to pop in for a pre-club drink. Joaquín Costa 33 (El Raval). ☎ **92-412-15-35.** Metro: Sant Antoni or Universitat.

Barcelona Rouge (Finds Hidden in the gritty but increasingly inventive Poble Sec, this tiny scarlet-red bar serves unique cocktails (including some with absinthe) and has an overstuffed collection of furniture to cozy up in, making the overall look one of a turn-of-the-20th-century bordello. There are sporadic performances (of the legal nature) of anything from Argentine tango to acrobats. The music is more of the old-school variety, and regulars tend to shimmy up and ask you to dance. Poeta Cabanas 21 (Poble Sec). ⓒ **93-442-49-85.** Free admission. Metro: Poble Sec.

The Black Horse   This is where many of the neighborhood expats hang out. It has a traditional old pub feel and offers classic British beers on draft. It also shows all the major soccer games and even has a bilingual pub quiz on Sundays. A good place to hear what the situation in the city is from those who've been living here for years. Allada Vermell 16 (La Ribera). ⓒ **93-268-33-38.** Metro: Jaume I.

Borneo   The name is a pun on the area it's in, known as El Born, but the only concession to the historical theme is a slide show straight from the pages of *National Geographic*. Otherwise what you have is a spacious, relaxed bar with an upstairs area for those who want to escape for a while. Rec 49 (La Ribera). ⓒ **93-268-23-89.** www.barborneo.com. Metro: Jaume I.

Café Bar Padam   One of the new breed of chic bars in a down-at-heel part of town, the clientele and decor here are modern and hip. The only color in the black-and-white rooms comes from fresh flowers and modern paintings. French music is sometimes featured as well as art expositions. Rauric 9 (El Raval). ⓒ **93-302-50-62.** Metro: Liceu.

Café Zurich ⟨Overrated⟩   At the top of La Rambla overlooking Plaça de Catalunya, this is a traditional meeting point in Barcelona, and it's also great for the passing parade around Catalonia's most fabled boulevard. If the weather is fair, opt for an outdoor table, enjoying a cold beer and the gaiety, which often includes live music. Launched in the early 1920s, the cafe was moved out as they built the Triangle shopping center, and then swiftly moved back in the late 1990s after a renovation. Despite the high-ish prices, grumpy waiters, and rudimentary tapas, it's been going strong ever since. Location says it all. Plaça de Catalunya 1. ⓒ **93-317-91-53.** Metro: Plaça de Catalunya.

Cocktail Bar Boadas ★   This intimate, conservative bar is usually filled with regulars. Established in 1933, it is the city's oldest cocktail bar. It's located at the top end of La Rambla, and many visitors stop in for a pre-dinner drink and snack before wandering to one of the areas' many restaurants. It stocks a wide array of Caribbean rums, Russian vodkas, and English gins, and the skilled bartenders know how to mix them all. You won't regret trying a daiquiri. Tallers 1 (El Raval). ⓒ **93-318-95-92.** Metro: Plaça de Catalunya.

El Born   Facing a rustic-looking square, this former fish store has been cleverly converted. There are a few tables near the front, but our preferred spot is the inner room decorated with rattan furniture and modern paintings. The music might be anything from Louis Armstrong to classic rock 'n' roll. The upstairs buffet serves dinner. The room is somewhat cramped, but you'll find a simple, tasty collection of fish, meat, and

---

Is It a Bar, Cafe, Pub, or Club?

In Barcelona, it's not unusual for places to have several personalities. During the day, that peaceful cafe is the perfect place to sit and read a book or enjoy a fresh croissant. Then, as night falls, the staff changes, the music is turned up, and suddenly you might look up from your book and find yourself in a cool bar surrounded by a loud group of trendy young things. If you wait longer, you might find yourself moved from your table as the furniture is stored away so that the DJ can turn it up louder and people can dance.

vegetable dishes, all carefully laid out. Passeig del Born 26 (La Ribera). ℰ **93-319-53-33**. Metro: Jaume I or Barceloneta.

El Bosc de les Fades (Finds)   This is the most bizarre bar/cafe in Barcelona, evoking a fairy-tale forest, or at the least trying to. It's brought to you by the same people who created Museu de Cera (Wax Museum), which is next door. Expect "unreal trees" and the whispering sound of waterfalls, plus a "gnome" or two—and a magic mirror that merits 30 seconds' closer inspection. At night the place attracts essentially a young crowd who enjoys the faux woodland dell, the loud background music, and the drinks. Pasaje de la Banca 7 (Barri Gòtic). ℰ **93-317-26-49**. www.museocerabcn.com. Metro: Drassanes.

El Café Que Pone Muebles Navarro (Finds)   This strange little bar has genial aspi-rations to trendiness. Its name, which means "The Bar Where They Put Navarro Furni-ture," stems from the days when it was an old furniture storeroom, and it does feel a little like you're sitting in an old-fashioned IKEA as you sip your *fino seco* or gin and tonic. Good music, though. Riera Alta 4–6 (El Raval). ℰ **60-718-80-96**. Metro: San Antoni.

Fonfone   This is a great example of a bar that fits as many in as it can when the music gets them dancing. The colorful, lighting-based decor is particularly original, and the dance music is always of high quality for those that like modern, accessible electronica. This isn't a place to stand and talk, but rather a good place to fill in those awkward hours when you're ready to go out but it's still too early to hit the clubs. The location is perfect for finding your way anywhere in the Old Town later on. Escudellers 24 (Barri Gòtic). ℰ **93-317-14-24**. Metro: Drassanes.

Ginger ★★   This is a stylish, split-level cocktail, wine, and tapas bar on a pretty Barri Gòtic square. The well-mixed cocktails (including a rarity—a traditional Pimms) make it worth hunting out, as do the tasty snacks which include imaginative morsels such as sausages flamed-cooked in *orujo* and grilled foie. It's the sort of place you pop in for 1 hour and stay for 3. Palma de Sant Just 1 (Barri Gòtic). ℰ **93-310-53-09**. Metro: Jaume I.

Hivernacle (Finds)   This is an airy bar/cafe luring a young, hip crowd to a setting of towering palms in a 19th-century greenhouse. The location is just inside the gates of the Ciutadella Park, but it stays open after the park is closed (entrance is down one side, on Passeig Picasso). A fashionable crowd likes to come here to "graze" upon the tapas. A restaurant adjoins and there is live music during the summer months. Passeig Picasso s/n (La Ribera). ℰ **93-295-40-17**. Metro: Arc de Triomf.

La Concha (Finds)   There aren't many bars that have that Moroccan gay-kitsch feeling, but this place does, and it's also great fun to go there and hang out while staring at the walls filled with color-treated photos of Spain's starlet from the 1960s, Sara Montiel. One part of the bar becomes a tiny dance floor at weekends. This bar is a Barrio Chino insti-tution and it's still a bit hairy, but perfect to experience an authentic slice of bohemia. Guàrdia 14 (El Raval). ℰ **93-302-41-18**. Metro: Drassanes.

La Fianna   With its Moroccan feel, this is a perfect spot to lie back and relax if it's raining or when you don't want a night that's too wild. The place is international and is a real find. It houses a restaurant at the back and some normal tables and barstools, but the best thing is to come early and secure one of the cushion-filled platforms—the cozi-est place to curl up with a few drinks and a friend or three. They also do big American-style Sunday brunches. Banys Vells 15 (La Ribera). ℰ **93-315-18-10**. www.lafianna.com. Metro: Jaume I.

La Ovella Negra (Value) An Old City classic, "the black sheep" is like a hidden beer hall. The crowd is young—it's a student favorite—and the drinks are a great value. Noisy, friendly, with a beer-stained pool table and a remarkable cave-like setting, this is a fun place for young people to order some jugs of cheap sangria and meet some people. There will almost certainly be a queue at the football game table, so that's not a bad place to start. Sitges 5 (El Raval). ℰ 93-317-10-87. www.ovellanegra.com. Metro: Plaça de Catalunya.

L'Ascensor ★ "The Elevator" has an entrance just like you'd think—you pass through (rather than go up or down in) an old European sliding-door-style elevator to get into this very local bar so well known for its *mojitos* (Cuban rum cocktails) that it has a line of mint-and-sugared glasses waiting to be filled on order. Bellafila 3 (Barri Gòtic). ℰ 93-318-53-47. Metro: Jaume I.

Margarita Blue ★ They may try to cram in a few too many tables in the Mexican restaurant part, but if you can find a corner to stand in, then the bar is well worth visiting. The music's good, the crowd is lively, and the cocktails are very good, especially the eponymous Blue Margarita. Josep Anselm Clavé 6 (Barri Gòtic). ℰ 93-412-54-89. www.margarita blue.com. Metro: Drassanes. They also have a sister club called Rita Blue, Plaça Sant Agustí 3 (Barri Gòtic). ℰ 93-342-40-86. Metro: Liceu.

Molly's Fair City The hangout of expats, plus visiting Brits and Irishmen, this beer hall is incredibly popular. The sound of English voices is heard throughout the pub, growing louder as the evening wears on—and that can be very late. Expect blaring music, loud voices, and beer flowing like a river. Plus, if there's a major soccer game, a lot of friendly shouting. Ferran 7 (Barri Gòtic). ℰ 93-342-40-26. Metro: Liceu.

Nao Colón ★ Located opposite the Estacion de Francia at the southern end of the Born district, the Nao Colón is a chic designer restaurant for the first half of the week. Then from Thursdays to Sundays it gestates into a club playing funk, soul, and house. If you dine there on a Thursday, they also provide live jazz from 10pm with the meal. Marquès de l'Argentera 19 (La Ribera). ℰ 93-268-76-33. Metro: Barceloneta.

Pitin Bar Easy to spot thanks to the lit-up stars over the door, this is a great place to sit with friends. The bar downstairs may not look anything special, and the patio, though nice, is fairly standard . . . but if you can brave the small spiral staircase, upstairs is a cozy beamed Old-Town room with some funky little decorations. It's a great place to sit and talk while watching people through the windows—but tall people may have trouble with the low roof. Passeig del Born 34 (La Ribera). ℰ 93-319-50-87. Metro: Jaume I.

So-Da ★ If just the thought of shopping makes you thirsty, this bar has the perfect concept. At the back of a trendy clothes store is a cute little bar where you can have a drink and look enviously at the outfits. If you're not careful, you might find yourself agreeing to return the next day, when the shop section is open, to try some of it on. Music is of the electronic variety. Avinyó 24 (Barri Gòtic). ℰ 93-412-27-76. Metro: Liceu or Jaume I.

Travel Bar The place for the solo backpacker to start. This friendly English-speaking place's main aim is to help introduce the city to those who are passing through. Nothing particularly Spanish about the atmosphere. It's simply an easygoing, unpretentious, and convenient bar where you can get a sandwich or a beer, find out what you need to know—or hook up with others for a night of exploring. If you need some guidance in where to go, the bar also runs its own nightly bar crawls around local haunts. Boqueria 27 (Barri Gòtic). ℰ 93-342-52-52. Metro: Liceu.

Dancing with the Green Fairy

If you're feeling adventurous, there's good reason to go to **Ba**...
Pau 65 (𝄂 **93-442-72-63;** Metro: Liceu), and that's its sp...
(absenta). Picasso and Dalí are reputed to have been regulars ... ...
like they haven't dusted the bottles since. The bar's said to be Barcelona's oldest
and has been around since 1820, serving the homemade drink that's made the
place famous. Absinthe is an impossibly strong aniseed-tasting drink (the bane
of Vincent Van Gogh, among others) made, in part, with the herb wormwood.
Some countries still ban it for its alleged hallucinogenic qualities, which led to
it being called "the green fairy." Here they serve it the traditional way: with a
fork, a small bottle of water, and a sugar cube. You place the sugar on the fork
prongs up, and balance it over the rim of your glass. Then slowly drip a little of
the water (not too much!) over the sugar so that it slowly dissolves into the
drink. Wait for it to sink in, and then keep adding drips of water so that the
sugar has nearly all dripped into your glass. Then mix the last of the sugar into
your glass with the fork, and then drink. One glass won't do you much harm,
but you can see those around the bar who've had at least a few by their glassy
expressions and loose jaws.

Clubs

Apolo ★★ This is a genuine multifaceted venue located in a turn-of-the-20th-century ballroom—Tuesdays it's an alternative cinema, Thursdays it's a funk club, sometimes they have rock concerts, Sundays they have a hugely popular gay night, and on Fridays and Saturdays it's a dance club called Nitsa. Check out listings to find out what's going on when you're in town. Nou de la Rambla 113 (Poble Sec). 𝄂 **93-318-99-17.** www.sala-apolo. com. Metro: Poble Sec.

Café Royale ★★ Right next to Plaça Reial, this trendy bar is a place for beautiful people—grungy students may have problems getting past the bouncer. But if you can, it's worth it for the subtle gold lighting, the in-house DJs, and the comfortable seating all around the small dance floor. A classic central location for local trendies and models. Nou de Zurbano 3 (Barri Gòtic). 𝄂 **93-412-14-33.** Metro: Drassanes.

Club 13 ★★ This club is a favorite of the trendy set. The meeting point for those who like to see and be seen in the heart of Plaça Reial, it gets few tourists, so the majority of those striking a pose are local. Don't be fooled by how small it looks upstairs—all the real action, and the very loud music, happens in the basement where two rooms— one small, one large—house the dancing masses and the cool cats until late. The music is usually electronic dance. Plaça Reial 13 (Barri Gòtic). 𝄂 **93-317-23-52.** Metro: Drassanes.

Dot Anyone who's both a hard-core dance music fan and a Star Trek geek will love this small bar/club. The music is loud and rhythmical, but by far the best thing about the place is the transporter-style doorway between bar and dance floor. Beam me up. Nou de Sant Francesc 7 (Barri Gòtic). 𝄂 **93-302-70-26.** Metro: Drassanes.

...d-Time Dancing

Plenty of nightclubs claim to be "classics," but none can beat **La Paloma,** Tigre 27
(📞 **93-301-68-97;** Metro: Universitat)—more than 105 years young and still
going strong. The name means "the pigeon" and it opened as a ballroom in 1903,
with its famous murals and chandelier added in 1919. It's a part of Barcelona's
history—Pablo Picasso met one of his long-term girlfriends here, and Dalí used
to sit in a box by the long balcony and sketch the people who came in. During
the religiously strict time of Franco, someone called "El Moral" was employed to
make sure that couples didn't get too close to each other. But there's none of
that now. During the early evening, it opens as before for lovers of the fox trot,
tango, bolero, and so forth, accompanied by live orchestras. But, late at night
from Thursday to Sunday, the place undergoes a transformation and becomes a
hip and happening nightclub from 2:30 to 5am. From its incredible decor to the
mimes that stand outside trying to keep people quiet, this place is a true original.
Admission is 8€ ($10)—more on special nights.

La Luz de Luna ★ For lovers of music a little more Latin, La Luz de Luna ("the light
of the moon") is a friendly place that specializes in salsa. Don't worry about making a fool
of yourself on the dance floor if you don't know the moves—but if you do, you'll find no
end of partners who also really know where to put their feet and at what point to twirl you
around. Comerç 21 (La Ribera). 📞 **93-310-75-42.** Admission after 2am 5€ ($6.50). Metro: Jaume I.

Magic Make devil horns with your hands and rock your sweaty mullet at this hard-
rock/metal club. It's all harmless fun, though, and tourists are more than welcome, as
long as they can mosh with the best of them. Passeig Picasso 40 (La Ribera). 📞 **93-310-72-67.**
Metro: Barceloneta.

Moog ★ This is where lovers of techno music and hard pumping beats gather to crash
heads. The music is heavy but the people are friendly. Upstairs is a much smaller space
where, strangely, 1980s disco (including a wide selection of Abba) is played and the
flamboyant DJ himself is part of the experience. Arc del Teatre 3 (El Raval). 📞 **93-301-72-82.**
www.masimas.com/moog. Metro: Drassanes.

New York Talk about late, late nightlife in Barcelona. The gang of 20-something
patrons who like this club don't show up until 3am. It's a former strip joint, and the red
lights and black walls still evoke its heyday when the women bared all. Recorded music—
mainly hip-hop and soul/funk—is heard in the background. Carrer Escudellers 5 (Barri
Gòtic). 📞 **93-318-87-30.** Admission 5€ ($6.50), cover after 2am (includes 1 drink) 10€ ($13).
Metro: Drassanes.

Sidecar Upstairs is an international restaurant and bar, but when it gets late, they
open downstairs—a lively and fun dance club with an indie feel in a brick-lined sizable
basement. Sometimes there's live music too. Plaça Reial 7 (Barri Gòtic). 📞 **93-302-15-86.** www.
sidecarfactoryclub.com. Admission 6€ ($7.80). Metro: Drassanes.

Beach Clubs, Port Clubs & Beach Bars

Baja Beach Club If you want to dance to classic disco tracks, there's no place quite
like Baja. It can feel a bit like a meat market and it's as far from the sophisticated trendy

(Moments)   Piaf, Drag Queens & a Walk on the Wild Side

Do you long to check out the seedy part of Barcelona that writers such as Jean Genet brought so vividly to life in their books? Much of it is gone forever, but *la Vida* nostalgically lives on in pockets like the **Bar Pastis,** Carrer Santa Mónica 4 (© **93-318-79-80;** Metro: Drassanes).

Valencianos Carme Pericás and Quime Ballester opened this tiny bar just off the southern end of Les Ramblas in 1947. They made it a shrine to Edith Piaf, and her songs still play on an old phonograph in back of the bar. The decor consists mostly of paintings by Ballester, who had a dark, rather morbid vision of the world. The house special, naturally, is the French aniseed-flavored drink pastis (to be drunk straight or with a mixer) and you can order four kinds of pastis in this dimly lit "corner of Montmartre"—the district of Paris that contains the famous Sacre Coeur church.

Outside the window, check out the view—often a parade of transvestite hookers. The bar crowd is likely to include almost anyone, especially people who used to be called bohemians. The bar also features live music of the French, tango, and folk variety, squeezed into one corner.

Note: In 2008, some people rallied to shut down Pastis due to its noisiness, but the management has toned down the din, objections dwindled, and El Pastis lives to fight on. It celebrated its 61st anniversary in October 2008 in suitably exuberant style, but on that particular occasion nobody seemed to mind it too much.

club or upmarket cocktail bar as you can possibly go, but if you don't mind topless waiters and bikini-clad waitresses, and want a night dancing to cheesy songs you can sing along to from the '80s and '90s, then this is probably the place to head. You probably won't find many other places where the entrance is a giant beach ball and the DJ is standing in a speedboat on the dance floor! It's located right on the beach and also does reasonably priced food during the day. Paseo Marítimo 34. © **93-225-91-00.** www.bajabeach.es. Metro: Vila Olímpica/Ciutadella.

Carpe Diem Lounge Club ★★   People on a budget should avoid the dress-code-conscious CDLC. Prices are high and so is the snob factor at this achingly cool bar on the edge of the beach. The VIP section is a favorite of famous soccer players, but if you want to join them on the comfortable-looking white chill-out beds, you'll have to buy a 120€ ($156) bottle of liquor. It has a fairly large outside terrace for passersby to gawk at the beautiful people. The new trendy night is Sunday, when chill-out music plays early (around 11pm) for those cool enough to not have to wake up first thing on Monday. Paseo Marítimo 32. © **93-224-04-70.** www.cdlcbarcelona.com. Metro: Vila Olímpica/Ciutadella.

The Fastnet Bar ★★   Out of the dozens of Irish pubs and bars in the city, this is the only one that seems to have realized that it is situated in Mediterranean climes and not wet and windy Dublin. Located on a boulevard overlooking the marina, the bar has an ample outside terrace, which fills up on days when soccer or rugby games are being shown on the large-screen TV that is turned out to face the street. The rest of the time it is frequented by Anglo-Saxon yachters, who pop in for a Guinness and hearty bacon-and-egg breakfast. Passeig Juan de Borbón 22. © **93-295-30-05.** Metro: Barceloneta.

The Village People

During the day it's dedicated to small artisan shops, market stalls, and street theater (see "Montjuïc" in chapter 7), but at night **Poble Espanyol,** Av. Marquès de Comillas s/n (© **93-508-63-00;** www.poble-espanyol.com; Metro: Espanya), turns into a party town. Built as a "typical Spanish village" for the Universal Exhibition in 1929, it may look old, but the whole place—right down to the huge fortified towers that dominate the entrance—is fake. At night, that makes it the perfect location to party, as no one actually lives inside and the gates can be strictly guarded. You have a couple of options: One is to buy a 3€ ($3.90) ticket and enter the village to pass the night in three or four small bars which offer drinks, Spanish pop music, and outside tables to watch the partygoers pass by, and leave it at that. The other, more expensive option is to pay for a ticket (20€–24€/$26–$31) *outside* to one of the clubs that lie *inside* the walls (entrance to the village is included in your ticket price). The main venue is **La Terrrazza** (www.laterrrazza.com), rated by many as the liveliest summertime nightspot in Barcelona. It's an outdoor-only club that's open from May to October—again, trendy dance music and a great place to dance the night away until the sun comes up (but not so much when it's raining). If you stay the distance (until 6am on a weekend), look for fliers, and sometimes even buses, to take you to "after parties," situated a little out of town and open until noon.

Le Kasbah ★ Situated next to the Olympic port in the old Palau del Mar building now occupied by the Museu de Catalunya, this cool little bar/dance floor plays projections on the wall, has cushions on the benches, and offers good dance music both inside and outside on the terrace. Great place to head to on a hot evening. Plaça Pau Vila 1. © 93-238-07-22. Metro: Barceloneta.

Shôko ★ This Asian restaurant-cum-club has an annoying faux spiritual decor that doesn't sit well with its high drink prices and fashionable clientele, many of whom spill over from the neighboring über-trendy nightspot CDLC. That said, it's a nice place to boogie with the bright young things, and the VIP lounge is open to anyone willing to splash out on champagne. Passeig Marítim 36. © 93-225-92-00. www.shoko.biz. Metro: Vila Olímpica/Ciutadella.

L'EIXAMPLE

The bars and clubs of L'Eixample tend to attract a slightly more mixed age group than those of the Old City, and more of a classic nature. They are also more spread out, so you may find yourself hopping in and out of cabs if you plan to barhop.

Antilla BCN Latin Club ★★★ Catering to Barcelona's sizable Latin American and Caribbean community, this is the city's biggest salsa club. Some of the biggest names in salsa, merengue, mambo, rumba, son, and all their derivatives have passed through, and when there's not live music, the recorded variety is just as stomping. If you are unsure of how to shake your booty, the club runs a dance school on Monday and Wednesday to classes are free when you've paid your entrance fee. Open late at weekends. Aragó 141. 🕿 93-451-45-64 or 451-21-51. www.antillasalsa.com. Cover (includes 1 drink) 10€ ($13). Metro: Urgell.

City Hall ★   This dark, busy club has a small, cool VIP room upstairs and a reasonably sized dance floor downstairs. The music is usually the standard electronic dance music fare, but there's also a small, urban chill-out garden with a bar outside at the back. If you get one of the comfortable seats out there, it can be difficult to get up. The other big advantage of this place is that it's situated very close to Plaça de Catalunya—very convenient for taxis and many hotels. Discount fliers can be found in many bars. Rambla Catalunya 2–4. 🕿 93-317-21-77 or 238-07-22. www.grupo-ottozutz.com. Cover (includes 1 drink) 10€ ($13). Metro: Plaça de Catalunya.

Costa Breve ★   Sitting uptown, this is a decent disco playing a mixture of Spanish and European commercial music, with the odd surprise thrown in such as a stripper or live gig. Hugely popular with office workers in the area, and young *picos* (yuppies), the vibe is different from the Old Town clubs but its tourist-free clientele makes for a nice change. Aribau 230. 🕿 93-414-27-78 or 414-71-95. www.grupocostabreve.com. Cover 10€ ($13). FGC: Gràcia.

Nick Havanna ★★   Started in 1987, this was one of the first of the city's "designer bars"—that is, postmodern drinking palaces that spent more on decor than practicalities (such as plumbing). It's still very stylish, although in a more retro sort of way with projections, a dome over the dance floor, uncomfortable metal seating, and some of the most highly designed toilets in the city. Rosselló 208. 🕿 93-215-65-91. www.nickhavanna.com. Metro: Diagonal.

Toscano Antico ★   A noisy Italian cocktail bar that's a million miles away from the slickness you might expect. They serve all the cocktails in the same style of glass, the music is loud, and the decor very rough. But the drinks are excellent and they even offer free Italian food on the bar before 10:30pm. The place is all staffed and owned by Italians (the name means "Old Tuscany") and is so Italian that it even has its own ice cream shop a few blocks down that stays open until 1am on summer weekends. For directions, ask at the bar for the *cremería*. Aribau 167. 🕿 93-532-15-89. Metro: Diagonal.

Ⓣips   **Finding Munchies!**

After a long night out, the one thing you need is food—and the greasier the better. If you're out of the center, you might come across a traveling *churros* stand, selling fresh potato chips, long strips of greasy fried donut dough, and sometimes cups of hot chocolate to dip them into. Some tapas bars are open late or very early, such as **El Reloj** (Vía Laietana 47). If it's any early morning but Sunday, the markets usually have bars open too—the local favorite is **Bar Pinotxo** (🕿 **93-317-17-31**) in the Boqueria Market on La Rambla. Also open very early is the real local secret: the croissant factory hidden on the small Carrer Lancaster on the Raval side of La Rambla near the corner of Nou de la Rambla. It opens at about 5am and, for 2.50€ ($3.25), you can buy a box of greasy, chocolate cream-filled doughy croissants that you'll be hard-pressed to finish.

Though the area is filled with small squares and hidden corners, the center of the Gràcia world is Plaça del Sol. In the summer, it's the best place to head to meet young Catalans and to watch people on their way to party. Just as many take their own cans of beer as buy from the bars around the square—the atmosphere is noisy and fun and drives the neighbors mad.

Alfa A great club if you like indie and rock music. The walls are filled with framed covers of classic albums from bands like U2 and the Smiths, which gives you a good idea of the music. It's as local as you can get (its location in a quiet, shop-filled street means there aren't many passing tourists) and the enormous candles dripping wax onto the bar just add to the atmosphere. It's not a big place, nor a particularly clean one, but it does what it does just fine. Mayor de Gràcia 36. ☎ **93-415-18-24.** Metro: Fontana.

Café del Sol The center of the young Catalan scene, this bar is filled with bohemians, pro-independence Catalan youth, and just people who go to enjoy the tapas and the view over the plaza and its people from the large collection of outside tables. Plaça del Sol 16. ☎ **93-415-56-63.** Metro: Fontana.

KGB If the dance music is getting you down, KGB is the place where independent pop acts (metal, reggae, hip-hop) come to find people of their own kind—and to play at them, very loudly. Gigs are normally Thursday through Saturday. The rest of the time, it's a more standard club. Alegre de Dalt 55. ☎ **93-210-59-06.** www.salakgb.net. Cover 10€ ($13). Metro: Lesseps.

BARRIO ALTO

Barrio Alto is sometimes seen as a world of its own. Here is where all the rich families live, in houses no less (something unheard of down in the city), and many of them never leave the Alto enclave. The same applies to going out—rich kids aplenty, alongside some more normal types, throughout the area. The main bars and clubs are concentrated around a street called Marie Cubí, near the María Cristina Metro stop. They're all very quiet during the week, though. *Note:* The Metro system doesn't serve this part of town.

Bikini ★★★ A classic of the Barcelona nightlife scene, this place opened first as an outdoor bar and minigolf place in the 1950s, then reopened in the mid-1990s. It is now a venue both for live music and for lively dancing. One room is Latin rhythms, another disco/punk/rock/whatever's going, plus a chill-out cocktail bar tucked away as well. It's also one of the better places to hear live music; when the gig's over, the walls roll back and disco rules. Deu i Mata 105. ☎ **93-322-08-00.** www.bikinibcn.com. Cover (if no concert) 15€ ($20) including 1 drink. Metro: Les Corts.

Gimlet ★★★ In this stylish uptown cocktail bar, the lights are low, the music is jazz, and the measures are generous. Sit at the tables or head for the bar at the back and chat with the waitstaff as they shake and mix the drinks, pour them into retro glasses, and place them on the cute little coasters. There's nothing they can't whip up, and everything they do, they do with admirable style. There's another branch at Rec 24. Santaló 46 (La Ribera). ☎ **93-201-53-06.**

Otto Zutz ★★★ If you're anyone who's anyone in Barcelona, you'll have one of the gold VIP cards to Otto Zutz, which allows you access to the bar/small dance floor on the top floor, where you can watch all of the trendy wannabes down below strutting their stuff and, if the whim takes you, go down and invite one of them up to join you at the balcony. For mere mortals and those from out of town, the dance floor is a good size and the small stage often features club dancers who pose and pout almost as much as those upstairs. There's no shortage of discount cards in bars all over town, but its location means that it can be hard to get back home afterward if you're staying in the Old Town. Lincoln 15. ✆ **93-238-07-22.** www.ottozutz.es. Cover 15€ ($20). Train: FGC Gràcia.

Up and Down ★　The chic atmosphere here attracts elite Barcelonans of all ages. The more mature patrons, specifically the black-tie, post-theater crowd, head upstairs, leaving the downstairs section to loud music and flaming youth. Up and Down is the most cosmopolitan disco in Barcelona, with impeccable service, sassy waiters, and a welcoming atmosphere. Technically, this is a private club—you can be turned away at the door. Numància 179. ✆ **93-205-51-94.** Cover (includes 1 drink) 12€–18€ ($16–$23). Metro: María Cristina.

OUTER BARCELONA

Mirablau　It's all about the location at Mirablau. Although there are worse disco/bars in the city, there are certainly better ones too. But you don't go for the music, the bar prices, or the crowd—you go for the view, as Mirablau is situated right next to the funicular near the top of Tibidabo hill and has a huge window overlooking the twinkling lights of the entire city from the hill to the sea. It's open during the day for coffee, but the view at night is something else entirely. If it's pretty enough to help tune out the music, all the better. Plaça Doctor Andreu 2. ✆ **93-418-58-79.** Train: FGC Tibidabo, then Tramvía Blau.

Razzmatazz　Five clubs in one, each with its own style of music. The venue is an enormous multilevel warehouse, and it's not unusual to have a big-name DJ playing the main stage while upstairs, oblivious, a group of goths and rock chicks mosh themselves into a frenzy. If you can't find music you like here, you probably don't like music very much. The crowd can be dominated by students, but it depends very much on the night. One ticket gets you entry to all the venues, so intrepid dancers can spend the night trying them all. Pamplona 88. ✆ **93-320-82-00.** www.salarazzmatazz.com. Cover (except for special concerts) 12€ ($16). Metro: Bogatell.

CHAMPAGNE BARS

The Catalans call their own version of sparkling wine *cava* and it comes from the nearby Penedès region (p. 277). In Catalan, champagne bars are called *xampanyerias*. With more than 50 Catalan companies producing *cava,* and each bottling up to a dozen grades of wine, the best way to learn about Catalan "champagne" is to sample the products at a *xampanyeria.*

Champagne bars usually open at 7pm and stay open until midnight or later. They serve a small range of tapas, from caviar to smoked fish to frozen chocolate truffles. The traditional local time to go is on a Sunday afternoon, when entire families will have a pre-lunch sip. Most establishments sell only a limited array of house *cavas* by the glass, and more esoteric varieties by the bottle. You'll be offered a choice of *brut* (slightly sweeter), *brut nature,* or *rosat* (rosé, or pink champagne).

Can Paixano　Ⓥ**alue**　If you want to sample the cheapest *cava* in town alongside a bewildering selection of sandwiches, this is the best place to go. It's a rowdy *cava* bar where a *copa* is about 1€ ($1.30) and the most expensive Can Paixano bottle is a little over 6€ ($7.80). There are no seats, though. If you go at lunchtime, you'll be able to find some space to enjoy your drink—but if you go at night, expect the place to be crammed full. It's a good way to get tipsy early, but don't say I didn't warn you about the evenings—anytime after 7pm will start to get very, very full. It's compulsory to order two mini-sandwiches with the first bottle you buy. Open 10:30am to 10pm. Closed August 17 to September 7. Reina Cristina 7. (✆ 93-310-08-39. www.canpaixano.com. Metro: Barceloneta.

El Xampanyet ★★★ This little champagne bar, my favorite in Barcelona, has been operated by the same family since the 1930s. When the Picasso Museum opened nearby, its popularity was assured. On this ancient street, the tavern is adorned with colored tiles, antique curios, marble tables, and barrels. With your sparkling wine, you can order fresh anchovies in vinegar, impressively fat green olives, or other tapas. If you don't want the *cava,* you can order fresh cider at the old-fashioned zinc bar. Closed in August. Montcada 22. (✆ 93-319-70-03. Metro: Jaume I.

Xampanyeria Casablanca Someone had to fashion a champagne bar after the Bogart-Bergman film, and this is it. There's decor based on the evergreen 1940s hit and the joint serves four kinds of house *cava* by the glass, plus a good selection of tapas, especially pâtés. Bonavista 6. (✆ 93-237-63-99. Metro: Passeig de Gràcia.

Xampú Xampany At the corner of the Plaça de Tetuan, this *xampanyeria* offers a variety of hors d'oeuvres in addition to wine. Abstract paintings, touches of high tech, and bouquets of flowers break up the pastel color scheme. Gran Vía de les Corts Catalanes 702. (✆ 93-265-04-83. Metro: Girona.

GAY & LESBIAN BARS

The city has a vibrant, active gay nightlife, with bars and clubs to suit all tastes. The best thing to do is to walk around the area known locally as "Gayxample"—a part of the left side of the Eixample area, more or less between Carrer Sepulveda and Carrer Aragon, and Carrer Casanova and Plaça Urquinaona. By no means is every bar there a gay bar, but many are—and all of the trendy-looking ones almost certainly will be. Most bars welcome people of any persuasion—but hetero couples should be prepared to be discreet.

Aire Lesbians aren't so well served by the city, but this is the classic club of note for everyone, from fashionable young things to older women. It's a large venue with a big dance floor and a buzzing bar. Carrer Valencia 236. (✆ 93-451-58-12. www.arenadisco.com. Metro: Passeig de Gràcia.

Café Dietrich As if you didn't already know by its namesake, this cafe stages the best drag strip shows in town, a combination of local and foreign divas "falling in love again" like the great Marlene herself. It remains Barcelona's most popular gay haunt. The scantily clad bartenders are hot, and the overly posh decor lives up to its reputation as a "divinely glam musical bar/disco." Many of the drag queens like to fraternize with the handsomest of the patrons, to whom they offer deep kisses on the mouth. So be warned. Consell de Cent 255. (✆ 93-451-77-07. Metro: Gràcia or Universitat.

Medusa This minimalist-decorated bar draws a trendy young crowd, mainly of cute boys. "The cuter you are, the better your chances of getting in if we get crowded as the night wears on," I was assured by one of the staff members. A super-trendy place, Medusa draws the fashionistas. Its DJs are among the best in town. The place gets very cruisy after 1am. Casanova 75. (✆ 93-454-53-63. Metro: Urgell.

Metro Still one of the most popular gay discos in Barcelona, Metro attracts a diverse crowd—from young fashion victims to more rough-and-ready macho types. One dance floor plays contemporary house and dance music, and the other traditional Spanish music mixed with Spanish pop. This is a good opportunity to watch men of all ages dance the *sevillanas* together in pairs with a surprising degree of grace. The gay press in Barcelona quite accurately dubs the backroom here as a "notorious, lascivious labyrinth of lust." One interesting feature appears in the bathrooms, where videos have been installed in quite unexpected places. Sepulveda 185. ℭ **93-323-52-27.** Cover 10€ ($13). Metro: Universitat.

New Chaps   Gay Barcelonese refer to this saloon-style watering hole as Catalonia's premier leather-and-denim bar. In fact, the dress code usually is leather of a different stripe: more boots and jeans than leather and chains. Behind a pair of swinging doors evocative of the old American West, New Chaps contains two different bar areas. Some of Barcelona's horniest guys flock to the downstairs darkroom in the wee hours. Diagonal 365. ℭ **93-215-53-65.** www.newchaps.com. Metro: Diagonal.

Punto BCN   Barcelona's largest gay bar attracts a mixed crowd of young "hotties" and foreigners. Always crowded, it's a good base to start out your evening. There is a very popular happy hour on Wednesday from 6 to 9pm. Free passes to other Arena bars are available from the bar. Muntaner 63–65. ℭ **93-453-61-23.** www.arenadisco.com. Metro: Eixample.

Salvation   This leading gay dance club has been going strong since 1999. It's still the flashiest dive on the see-and-be-seen circuit, and a good place to wear your see-through clothing, especially as the hour grows late. There are two rooms devoted to a different type of music, the first with house music and DJs and the other with more commercial and "soapy" themes. The waiters are probably the most sensual, handsome, and muscular in town. Look your most gorgeous if you want to get past the notoriously selective doorman. Ronda de Sant Pere 19–21. ℭ **93-318-06-86.** Metro: Urquinaona.

Side Trips in Catalonia

About six million people live in Catalonia, and twice that many visit every year, flocking to the beaches along the Catalan *costas* (coasts), the area of Spain that practically invented package tourism. Though some areas—such as Lloret de Mar—have become overdeveloped, there are many unspoiled little seaside spots still to be found.

Three of the most attractive resorts are on the **Costa Brava (Rocky Coast),** 100km (62 miles) north of Barcelona: the southerly town of **Tossa de Mar,** with its walled Ciutat Vella; the idyllic coastal village of **Calella de Palafrugell;** and the northerly whitewashed fishing village of **Cadaqués,** up near the French border.

Inland from the latter lies the low-key capital of the Alt Empordà, **Figueres,** birthplace of the father of surrealism, Salvador Dalí, and home to his eccentric museum, which enthralls everyone from art lovers to the downright curious. The capital of this whole region is **Girona,** an ancient town steeped in history with a magnificent Old Quarter and cathedral.

South of Barcelona, along the **Costa Daurada (Golden Coast)** the beaches are wider and sandier. **Sitges,** a fine resort town that has a huge gay following, and **Tarragona,** the UNESCO-classified capital of the region, are the two destinations to visit here, the latter for its concentration of Roman vestiges and architecture.

Away from the coast amid attractive wooded hills and fertile valleys at the meeting point of Tarragona and Lleida provinces is a fine trio of smaller but not-to-be-missed Cistercian monasteries—**Poblet, Santes Creus,** and **Vallbona de les Monges**—all dating from the 12th century.

These are eclipsed, however, by the greatest monastery of them all: **Montserrat,** a hugely popular day excursion to the northwest of Barcelona. The serrated outline made by the sierra's steep cliffs led the Catalonians to call it *montserrat* (sawtoothed mountain). Today this Benedictine sanctuary remains the religious center of Catalonia, and thousands of pilgrims annually visit the monastery-complex to see its Black Virgin.

Due northeast of Barcelona, the atmospheric Romanesque towns of **Vich, Ripoll,** and **Camprodón**—each one more charmingly compact as you approach the Pyrénées—are well worth an off-the-beaten-track tour.

1 MONTSERRAT ★★

56km (35 miles) NW of Barcelona, 592km (368 miles) E of Madrid

The monastery at **Montserrat,** which sits atop a 1,200m-high (3,937-ft.) mountain, 11km (7 miles) long and 5.5km (3½ miles) wide, is one of the most important pilgrimage spots in Spain. It ranks alongside Zaragoza and Santiago de Compostela in Galicia, at the end of the pilgrimage route of Saint James. Thousands travel here every year to see and touch the medieval statue of La Moreneta (The Black Virgin), the most important religious icon in Catalonia. Many newly married couples flock here for her blessing.

Avoid visiting on Sunday, especially if the weather is nice, as thousands of locals pour in. At all times, remember to take along warm sweaters or jackets, since it can get cold.

Avoid visiting on Sunday, especially if the weather is nice, as thousands of locals pour in. At all times, remember to take along warm sweaters or jackets, since it can get cold.

ESSENTIALS

GETTING THERE   The best and most exciting way to go is via the Catalan railway. **Ferrocarrils de la Generalitat de Catalunya** to Montserrat-Aeri leaves every hour from the Plaça Espanya in Barcelona. The train connects with a high-tech funicular (Aeri de Montserrat), which leaves every 15 minutes.

The train, with its funicular tie-in, has taken over as the preferred and cheapest means of transport. However, long-distance **bus** service is also provided by **Autocares Julià** in Barcelona (℗ **93-490-40-00** or 90-240-00-80; www.autocaresjulia.es). Daily service from Barcelona to Montserrat is generally available, with departures near the Estació de Sants on the Plaça de Països Catalans. Buses leave at 9:15am, returning at 5pm and at 6pm in July and August; the round-trip ticket costs 10€ ($13) on weekdays and 12€ ($16) on weekends.

To drive here, exit via the Avinguda Diagonal, then take the A-2 (exit Matorell). The signposts and exit to Montserrat will be on your right. From the main road, it's 15km (9¹/₃ miles) up to the monastery through eerie rock formations and dramatic scenery.

VISITOR INFORMATION   The **tourist office** is at the Plaça de la Creu (℗ **93-877-77-77**), open daily from 8:50am to 7:30pm. This office can provide you with various maps for walks around the mountain.

EXPLORING MONTSERRAT

Among the monastery's noted attractions is the 50-member **Escolanía ★★**, one of the oldest and most renowned boys' choirs in Europe, dating from the 13th century. At 1pm daily (noon on Sun) you can hear them singing "Salve Regina" and the "Virolai" (hymn of Montserrat) in the basilica. The basilica is open Monday to Friday from 7:30am to 7:30pm and Saturday to Sunday from 7:30pm to 8:30pm. Admission is free. To view the Black Virgin, a statue from the 12th or 13th century, enter the church through a side door to the right. She was found in one of the mountain caves in the 12th century (see below) and is said to have been carved by the hands of Saint Luke himself.

At the Plaça de Santa María you can also visit the **Museu de Montserrat** (℗ **93-877-77-77**), known for its collection of ecclesiastical paintings, including works by Caravaggio and El Greco. Modern Spanish and Catalan artists are also represented (see Picasso's early *El Viejo Pescador,* 1895). Works by Dalí and such French Impressionists as Monet, Sisley, and Degas are shown. The collection of ancient artifacts is quite interesting. Be sure to look for the crocodile mummy, which is at least 2,000 years old. The museum is open Monday through Friday from 10am to 6pm, and Saturday and Sunday from 9:30am to 6:30pm, charging 5€ ($6.50) for adults and 3.50€ ($4.55) for children and students.

The 9-minute **funicular ride** (Aeri de Montserrat; ℗ **93-237-71-56;** www.acride montserrat.com) to the 1,236m-high (4,055-ft.) peak, Sant Joan, makes for a panoramic trip. The funicular operates about every 20 minutes daily from 9:25am to 1:45pm and 2:20 to 6:45pm March through October, and 10:10am to 1:45pm and 2:20 to 5:45pm (or 6:45pm on public holidays) November through February. The cost is 8€ ($10) round-trip, 5€ ($6.50) one-way. From the top on a clear day you'll see not only most of Catalonia but also the Pyrénées and—if you're very lucky—the islands of Majorca and Ibiza.

Route of the Cistercian Monasteries

Near the medieval town of **Montblanc,** 113 kilometers (70 miles) west of Barcelona in the heart of Tarragona province, is a lesser-known trio of smaller but exquisite monasteries, all founded in the 12th century by Benedictine monks from Citeaux, or Cistercium in Burgundy, France, with the purpose of returning to a simple lifestyle of austerity and unworldliness detached from material concerns.

The oldest and largest of them, **Santa María de Poblet** (Oficina Comarcal de Turismo, Monasterio de Poblet; ℭ **97-787-00-89;** www.poblet.cat; Mon–Fri 10am–12:30pm and 3–6pm, closes at 5:30pm in winter; 5€/$6.50 adults, 3€/$3.90 seniors, students, and children 18 and under), nestles on the wooded slopes of the Prades Mountains. (Its name derives from the Latin *populetum* meaning white poplars.) Founded in 1151, yet continuously expanded and reconstructed over the centuries, its styles range from Romanesque (13th-c. St. Catherine's chapel) to the Gothic (15th-c. St. George's chapel) and baroque. In its great high-vaulted chapter house the kings of Cataluña and Aragón are laid to rest in (restored) tombs. The present active community of monks originates from 1945 when the Poblet Brotherhood was created.

The nearby smaller **Monestir de Santes Creues** (ℭ **97-763-83-29;** Mar 16–Sept 15 10am–1:30pm and 3–7pm, Sept 16–Jan 15 10am–1:30pm and 3–5:30pm, Jan 16–March 15 10am–1:30pm and 3–6pm; 4€/$5.20) is set in a secluded wooded valley beside the River Gaia. Founded 7 years later than Poblet, it also underwent transitional work as recently as the 18th century. Among its highlights are the ancient Trinitat chapel and 14th-century Gothic cloister with its striking Romanesque octagonal pavilion.

The convent of **Santa María de Vallbona de les Monges** (ℭ **97-333-02-66;** Tues–Sat 10am–1:30pm and 4:30–6:45pm, Sun and holidays noon–1:30pm and 4:30–6:45pm, closed Mon; 3€/$3.90) lies just inside neighboring Lleida province in a fertile valley noted for its excellent olive oil. Founded by the Cister's feminine branch in the 12th century, it originally housed daughters of noble families from the House of Aragón. Today it still has a resident community of some 30 nuns as well as an active cultural and spiritual center. Romanesque styles predominate, especially in the north transcept doors, south and east wings of the superb cloister, and the 14th-century bell tower.

Montblanc itself is atmospheric enough to warrant an overnight stay. It was once the center of a thriving Jewish community, as the scenic Carrer Jeues (Street of Jews) testifies. Two-thirds of the surrounding 13th-century walls are still intact and the Royal Palace (Palau Reial) is a standout. Book a room at the two-star **Fonda Cal Blasi,** which is located in a converted 19-century house in the town center at Carrer Alenyá 11 (ℭ **97-786-13-36;** www.fondacalblasi.com); a double goes for 90€ to 115€ ($117–$150).

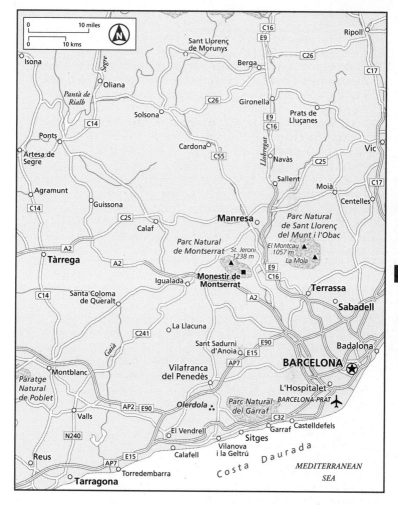

You can also make an excursion to **Santa Cova (Holy Grotto),** the alleged site of the discovery of the Black Virgin. The grotto dates from the 17th century and was built in the shape of a cross. You go halfway by funicular but must complete the trip on foot. The grotto is open year round daily from 10am to 1pm and 2 to 5:45pm. The funicular operates every 20 minutes daily from 11am to 6pm at a cost of 2.70€ ($3.50) adults, 1.50€ ($1.95) children round-trip. For more information, visit www.cremallerademontserrat.com.

A Romanesque Route to the Pyrénées

Barcelona's Museu Nacional d'Art de Catalunya (MNAC; p. 194) houses one of the finest Romanesque collections in Europe, with many of its sculptures and icons transferred from churches or monasteries high in the Pyrénées. Yet those mountains and their foothills still contain a countless host of Romanesque treasures, and a most enjoyable way of seeing some of them in their natural setting is to explore a trio of towns that lies to the northeast of the Ciudad Condal. You can do this reasonably effectively by public transportation, though this is one occasion where renting a car would help you to do the area full justice.

Vic   The first stop is **Vic**, a fascinating town that's surprisingly little known to outside visitors. Its arcaded **Plaça Mayor**, whose fine *moderniste* building, **Casa Comella,** features a four-seasons *sgrafitti* by Gaità Buigas, designer of Barcelona's Columbus statue, is also the setting for an impressive Saturday market. The neoclassical **Cathedral of Sant Pere,** founded in the 9th century and "renovated" from 1781 onward, boasts a magnificent Lombardian seven-story bell tower, and together with the **Museu Episcopal** contains fine examples of Romanesque works. Stay at the central three-star **Hotel J. Balmes Vic,** Francesc Pla el Vigatá 6 (✆ **93-889-12-72;** double 90€/$117), or out of town at the deluxe four-star **Parador de Turismo de Vic,** Carretera de Roda de Ter 14 (✆ **93-812-23-23;** double 160€–180€/$208–$234). The top local choice for a meal is the traditional **Cardona 7,** Cardona 7 (✆ **93-883-28-45**); the local sausages *(salchichones)* are legendary here.

Vic is about 65km (40 miles) from Barcelona on the C17 Puigcerda road. You can travel there by bus with Empresa Sagales service from the Fabra i Puig bus station in Barcelona (✆ **93-231-27-56**), by RENFE train service from Sants main railway station (www.renfe.es), or by car. For more information on Vic, contact the **Oficina de Turismo de Vic,** Carrer Ciutat 4 (✆ **93-886-20-91;** www.victurisme.cat).

Ripoll   Continue on to **Ripoll,** a small town with narrow medieval streets that is virtually in the foothills of the Pyrénées. Few towns of its size—even in Catalonia—can boast such a wealth of history. Dominating everything is the astounding Benedictine monastery of **Santa María de Ripoll,** founded in the

WHERE TO STAY & DINE

Few people spend the night here, but most visitors want at least one meal. There is only one restaurant on Montserrat and it is expensive (see below). Consider bringing a picnic lunch from Barcelona instead.

Abat Cisneros   This modern hotel on the main square of Montserrat offers few pretensions and a history of family management from 1958. The small rooms are simple and clean, each with a comfortable bed, and the bathrooms come with tub/shower combos. Rudimentary regional dishes are served in the in-house restaurant. The hotel's name is derived from a title given to the head of any Benedictine monastery during the Middle Ages.

Plaça de Montserrat s/n, 08199 Montserrat. ✆ **93-877-77-01.** Fax 93-877-77-24. interhotel.com/spain/es/hoteles/1829.html. 82 units. 60€–105€ ($78–$137) double. Rates include breakfast. AE, DC, MC, V.

9th century by the formidable Wilfred the Hairy, whose remains are entombed here. Like Vic cathedral, it has a seven-story bell tower, but this and its evocative cloisters and Lombardian apses are eclipsed by the incomparable exterior and interior Romanesque carvings and sculptures, the finest outside those on display in the MNAC. The nearby monastery of **Sant Joan de les Abadesses,** with its splendid Gothic bridge, was also founded by Wilfred the Hairy and is well worth the 10km (6¼-mile) detour. Stay at the **Pensió Trobada,** Passeig Honorat Vilamanya 4 (℃ **97-270-23-53;** double 70€/$91). Eat out at the traditional **Hostal del Ripollès,** Plaça Nova 11 (℃ **97-270-02-15;** www.hostaldel ripolles.com).

Ripoll is 104km (65 miles) from Barcelona on the C17 Puigcerda road. You can travel there by bus with TEISA service from the corner of Carrer Pau Claris and Carrer Consell de Cent in Barcelona (℃ **97-220-48-68**), by train from Sants or Plaça de Catalunya stations, or by car. Journey time is approximately 2 hours. For more information on Ripoll, contact the **Oficina de Turismo de Ripoll,** Plaça Abat OLiva 1 (℃ **97-270-23-51**).

Camprodón Higher up in the heart of the Pyrénées is the charming township of **Camprodón,** birthplace of Catalan composer Isaac Albeñiz, whose Alpine-style birthplace you can view from outside (but can't visit). Its **Sant Pere** church, built in the shape of a Latin cross, is the sole remaining part of the original 9th-century Cistercian monastery. The most remarkable intact structure today is the 14th-century Romanesque **Pont Nou,** which straddles the fast-flowing river Ter as it cascades down from the surrounding mountains. Stay at the **Hotel Güell,** Plaça Espanya 8 (℃ **97-274-00-11;** double 70€/$91). Dine out at the **Nuria Restaurant,** Plaça 11 (℃ **97-274-00-24**).

To visit Camprodón, follow the route to Ripoll above and then take the C26 via Sant Joan de les Abadesses. You can travel there by bus with TEISA service from the corner of Carrer Pau Claris and Carrer Consell de Cent in Barcelona (℃ **97-220-48-68**) or by car. Journey time is approximately 2½ hours. For more information, contact the **Oficina de Turismo de Camprodón,** Plaça Espanya 1 (℃ **97-274-00-10**).

Parking 8€ ($10). Bus: Autocares Julià from Plaça Espanya in Barcelona. Train: Montserrat line from Estació Sants and then Ferrocarril. **Amenities:** Restaurant; bar; lounge; laundry service. *In room:* TV, safe.

2 TARRAGONA ★★

97km (60 miles) S of Barcelona, 554km (344 miles) E of Madrid

The ancient Roman port city of **Tarragona,** on a rocky bluff above the Mediterranean, is one of the grandest but most unfairly neglected sightseeing centers in Spain. Honoring its abundance of Roman and medieval remains, UNESCO named Tarragona a World Heritage city in 2000.

The Romans captured Tarragona *(Tarraco)* in 218 B.C., and during their rule the city sheltered one million people behind 64km-long (40-mile) city walls. One of the four capitals of Catalonia when it was an ancient principality and once the home of Julius Caesar, Tarragona today consists of an Old Quarter filled with interesting buildings, particularly the houses with connecting balconies. The upper walled town is mainly medieval; the town below is newer.

In the new town, walk along the **Rambla Nova,** a fashionable wide boulevard that's the city's main artery. Running parallel with Rambla Nova to the east is the **Rambla Vella,** which marks the beginning of the Old Town. The city has a bullring, good hotels, and even some beaches, particularly the Platjes del Miracle and del Cossis.

After seeing the attractions listed below, cap off your day with a stroll along the **Balcó del Mediterráni (Balcony of the Mediterranean),** where the vistas are especially beautiful at sunset.

ESSENTIALS

GETTING THERE   Daily, there are **trains** every 15 to 45 minutes making the 1-hour trip to and from the Barcelona-Sants station. Fare is 5.80€ ($7.55) one-way. In Tarragona, the RENFE office is in the train station, the Plaça Pedrera s/n (✆ **90-224-02-02**).

From Barcelona, there are eight **buses** per day from Monday to Saturday and two on Sunday and bank holidays to Tarragona (1¹/₂ hr.) run by the company Plana (✆ **97-721-44-75**). Another company, Hispania, also operates a service which continues to Reus. All buses leave from outside the María Cristina Metro station and cost 8.95€ ($12) one-way.

To **drive,** take the A-2 southwest from Barcelona to the A-7, via Vilafranca. The route to Tarragona is well marked.

VISITOR INFORMATION   The **tourist office** is at Carrer Major 39 (✆ **97-725-07-95**). It's open July to the end of September Monday to Friday from 9am to 9pm, Saturday 9am to 2pm and 4 to 9pm, and Sunday 10am to 2pm. The rest of the year, it's open Monday to Saturday 10am to 2pm and 4 to 7pm, and Sunday 10am to 2pm.

EXPLORING THE TOWN

Amfiteatre Romà ★   At the foot of Miracle Park and dramatically carved from a cliff that rises from the beach, this Roman amphitheater recalls the days in the 2nd century when thousands gathered here to be entertained by games and gladiator fights.

Parc del Milagro s/n. ✆ **97-724-25-79.** Admission 2.10€ ($2.75) adults, 1€ ($1.30) students and seniors. Mar–Sept Tues–Sat 9am–9pm, Sun 9am–3pm; Oct–Feb Tues–Sat 9am–5pm, Sun 10am–3pm. Closed Dec 25, Jan 1, and Jan 6. Bus: 2.

Catedral ★★   At the highest point of Tarragona is this 12th-century cathedral, whose architecture represents the transition from Romanesque to Gothic. It has an enormous vaulted entrance, fine stained-glass windows, Romanesque cloisters, and an open choir. In the main apse, observe the altarpiece of Santa Tecla, the patron of Tarragona, carved by Pere Joan in 1430. Two flamboyant doors open into the chevet. The east gallery is the **Museu Diocesà,** with a collection of Catalan art.

Plaça de la Seu s/n. ✆ **97-723-72-69.** Admission to cathedral and museum 2.40€ ($3.10) adults, 1.50€ ($1.95) students and seniors, free for children 16 and under. Mar–May daily 10am–1pm and 4–7pm; June–Sept daily 10am–7pm; Oct–Feb daily 10am–2pm. Bus: 1.

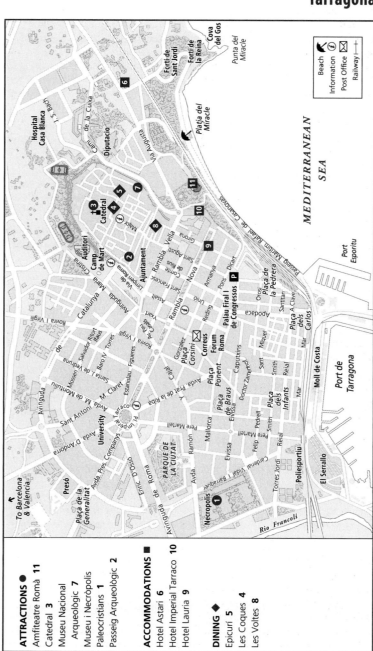

MEDITERRANEAN SEA

Cova del Gos

Punta del Miracle

Fortí de la Reina

Fortí de Sant Jordi

Platja del Miracle

Hospital Casa Blanca

Diputació

Camp de la Cuixa

J. S. Bach

6

7

5

3 Catedral

4

11

10

8

9

Auditori

Camp de Mart

Cristina

Catalunya

Rovira i Virgili

Avinguda Maria

Via de Imperi Roma

Ajuntament

Assalt

Sant Francesc

Comte de rius

Sant Agustí

Rambla Vella

Girona

Nova

Unió

Rambla Nova

Reding

Apodaca

Orosi

Santitan

Plaça de la Pedrera

Plaça A. Clave

Mar

dels Carlos

Armanya

Ports

Dicart

P

Palau Firal I de Congressos

Forum Romà

Correus

Plaça Corsini

González

Miquel

Sant

Caputxins

Capdevila

Doctor Zamenhof

Plaça Ponent

Avda. Prat de la Riba

Plaça de Braus

Plaça dels Infants

Eivissa

Elvissa

Mallorca

Ramón

Pere Martell

Pere Martell

Felip

Pedrell

Reial

Smith

Reial

Smith

Mar

Moll de Costa

Port de Tarragona

Port Esportiu

Passeig Marítim Rafael de Casanova

El Serrallo

Poliesportiu

Torres Jordi

Barberà

Cardenal Vidal i

Avda. Ramón

PARQUE DE LA CIUTAT

University

Sant Antoni

Avda. M. de Montjuïc

Avda. M. Claret

Estanislau Figueres

M. Claret

Mossèn Salvador Ritort Faus

Baró IV Torres

Santa J. de Vedruna

Avda. D'Andorra

Avinguda

de

Pl. Imperial Tarraco

Avda. Pres. Companys

Entic D'Ossó

Avinguda de Roma

Plaça de la Generalitat

Presó

1 Necropolis

Rio Francolí

To Barcelona & València

Beach

Information

Post Office

Railway

ATTRACTIONS ●
Amfiteatre Romà **11**
Catedral **3**
Museu Nacional Arqueològic **7**
Museu i Necròpolis Paleocristians **1**
Passeig Arqueologic **2**

ACCOMMODATIONS ■
Hotel Astari **6**
Hotel Imperial Tarraco **10**
Hotel Lauria **9**

DINING ◆
Epicurí **5**
Les Coques **4**
Les Voltes **8**

Museu i Necròpolis Paleocristians ★   This is one of the most important burial grounds in Spain, used by the Christians from the 3rd to the 5th century. It stands outside town next to a tobacco factory whose construction led to its discovery in 1923. While on the grounds, visit the **Museu Paleocristià,** which contains a number of sarcophagi and other objects discovered during the excavations.

Av. de Ramón y Cajal 80. (℃) **97-723-62-09.** Admission to museum, necropolis, and Museu Arqueològic 2.50€ ($3.25) adults, 1.25€ ($1.65) students, free for seniors and children 18 and under. June–Sept Tues–Sat 10am–1:30pm and 4–7pm, Sun and holidays 10am–2pm; Oct–May Tues–Sat 10am–1:30pm and 3–5:30pm, Sun and holidays 10am–2pm. Bus: 4.

Museu Nacional Arqueològic ★   Overlooking the sea, the Archaeology Museum houses a collection of Roman relics—mosaics, ceramics, coins, silver, sculpture, and more. The outstanding attraction here is the mosaic **_Head of Medusa_** ★★, with its penetrating stare.

Plaça del Rei 5. (℃) **97-723-62-09.** www.mnat.es. Admission for museum and Museu i Necròpolis Paleocristians 2.50€ ($3.25) adults, 1.25€ ($1.65) students, free for seniors and children 18 and under. June–Sept Tues–Sat 10am–8pm, Sun 10am–2pm; Oct–May Tues–Sat 10am–1:30pm and 4–7pm, Sun 10am–2pm. Bus: 8.

Passeig Arqueològic ★★   At the far end of the Plaça del Pallol, an archway leads to this .8km (¹/₂-mile) walkway along the ancient ramparts, built by the Romans on top of

Catalonia Remembers Pablo Casals

Fleeing from Franco and the fascist regime, the world's greatest cellist, Pablo Casals, left his homeland in 1939. Today his body has been returned to El Vendrell, 72km (45 miles) south of Barcelona, where he is remembered with a museum in his honor. The museum is installed in the renovated house where he lived until he went into self-imposed exile.

Seventeen rooms are filled with Casals memorabilia, including his first cello, photographs and films of his performances, the Peace Medal awarded by the United Nations in 1971, and photographs of the artist with such famous men as John F. Kennedy, who awarded him the Medal of Freedom.

Casals died in Puerto Rico in 1973 at the age of 96, and he was finally returned to his beloved Catalonia in 1979, where he is buried at the El Vendrell graveyard.

Museu Pau Casals lies at Av. Palfuriana 59–61, in Sant Salvador-El Vendrell (℃ **97-768-42-76;** www.paucasals.org). From September 16 to June 14 it is open Tuesday through Friday from 10am to 2pm and 4 to 6pm, Saturday from 10am to 2pm and 4 to 7pm, and Sunday from 10am to 2pm. From June 15 to September 15 it's open Tuesday through Saturday from 10am to 2pm and 5 to 9pm, and Sunday from 10am to 2pm. Admission is 6€ ($7.80) for adults; 3€ ($3.90) for children, students, and seniors; and free for children 8 and under. Allow 1 hour.

To reach El Vendrell from Barcelona, head south along C-32 until you come to the El Vendrell exit just past Calafell.

gigantic boulders. The ramparts have been much altered over th[e medi]eval times and in the 1600s. There are scenic views from many

El Portal del Roser s/n. ℂ **97-724-57-96.** Admission 2.10€ ($2.75) adults, free for children 16 and under. Oct–Mar Tues–Sat 9am–7pm, Sun and Tues–Sat 9am–9pm, Sun and holidays 9am–3pm. Bus: 2.

THEME PARK THRILLS

A 10-minute ride from the heart of Barcelona, the **PortAve**[ntura] (ℂ **97-777-90-90;** www.portaventura.es), is Spain's biggest theme park. Universal Stu-dios has acquired a prime stake in it and has plans to make it even larger. On a vast 809 hectares (1,999 acres), it'll be expanded to become Europe's largest entertainment center. Since its inauguration in 1995, it has already become one of the Mediterranean's favorite family destinations.

The park is a microcosm of five distinct worlds, with full-scale re-creations of classic villages ranging from Polynesia to Mexico, from China to the old American West. It also offers a thrilling variety of roller-coaster and white-water rides, all centered on a lake you can travel to via the deck of a Chinese junk.

The park is open daily March 18 to June 19 from 10am to 8pm, June 20 to September 13 from 10am to midnight, September 14 to January 8 from 10am to 8pm. It's closed January 9 to March 17. A 1-day pass costs 42€ ($55) adults, 34€ ($44) children, 21€ ($27) visitors with disabilities; a 2-day pass costs 63€ ($82) adults, 51€ ($66) children, 32€ ($42) visitors with disabilities. Nighttime admission, available only in summer months, is 27€ ($35) adults, 22€ ($29) children, 15€ ($20) visitors with disabilities. The fee includes all shows and rides.

WHERE TO STAY
Expensive

Hotel HUSA Imperial Tarraco ★★   About .4km (¹/₄ mile) south of the cathedral, atop an oceanfront cliff whose panoramas include a sweeping view of both the sea and the Roman ruins, this hotel is the finest in town. It was designed in the form of a crescent and has guest rooms that may angle out to sea and almost always include small balconies. The accommodations, all with bathrooms containing tub/shower combos, contain plain modern furniture. The public rooms display lots of polished white marble, Oriental carpets, and leather furniture. The staff respond well to the demands of both traveling businesspeople and art lovers on sightseeing excursions.

Passeig Palmeras s/n, 43003 Tarragona. ℂ **97-723-30-40.** Fax 97-721-65-66. www.hotelhusaimperial tarraco.com. 170 units. 100€–150€ ($130–$195) double; 175€–220€ ($228–$286) suite. AE, DC, MC, V. Free parking on street; Mon–Fri parking lot 15€ ($20) per day. Bus: 1. **Amenities:** Snack bar; outdoor pool; tennis court; limited room service; babysitting; laundry service; dry cleaning. *In room:* A/C, TV, minibar, hair dryer, safe.

Moderate/Inexpensive

Hotel Astari (Value   Travelers in search of peace and quiet on the Mediterranean come to the Astari, which opened in 1959. This resort hotel on the Barcelona road offers fresh and airy, though rather plain, accommodations. Most rooms are small, but each comes with a good bed and a bathroom with a tub/shower combo. The Astari has long balconies and terraces, one favorite spot being the outer flagstone terrace with its umbrella-shaded tables set among willows, orange trees, and geranium bushes. This is the only hotel in Tarragona with garage space for each guest's car.

, 43003 Tarragona. ☎ **97-723-69-00**. Fax 97-723-69-11. www.hotelastari.com. 81
104) double; 95€ ($124) business suite. AE, DC, MC, V. Parking 8€ ($10). Bus: 9. **Ameni-**
aurant; bar; pool; room service; laundry service; dry cleaning. *In room:* A/C, TV, minibar, hair
safe.

Hotel Lauria ★   Less than half a block north of the town's popular seaside promenade
(Passeig de les Palmeres), beside the tree-lined Rambla, this government-rated three-star
hotel offers unpretentious clean rooms, each of which has been recently modernized.
Rooms range from small to medium, and each bathroom is equipped with a tub/shower
combo. The rooms in back open onto a view of the sea.

Rambla Nova 20, 43004 Tarragona. ☎ **97-723-67-12**. Fax 97-723-67-00. www.hlauria.es. 72 units. 85€
($111) double. AE, DC, MC, V. Parking 10€ ($13). Bus: 1. **Amenities:** Bar; outdoor pool; business center;
room service; laundry service; dry cleaning. *In room:* A/C, TV, hair dryer, safe.

WHERE TO DINE

Epicurí ★★ ⓥ**alue** CATALAN/CONTINENTAL   In 2002 this long-established
restaurant was bought by chef Javier Andrieu, who poured years of experience into a site
in the heart of town, a very short walk from the archaeological treasures of medieval Tarragona. Within a cozy dining room whose decor falls midway between the organic
modernisme of Gaudí and the Art Nouveau opulence of turn-of-the-20th-century Paris,
you'll be presented with a choice of two set menus, the more lavish version featuring an
aperitif plus six courses. Cuisine is based on securing the best market-fresh ingredients in
town. The most intriguing dishes include half-cooked foie gras served with grapes, a succulent entrecôte of veal with artichokes, steamed veal cutlets with lemon or Madeira
sauce, maigret of duckling with tiny Catalan mushrooms known as *moixernons,* and a
heaven-sent filet of turbot with an almond-flavored saffron sauce. If the ingredients are
available in the market, you might find other such dishes as a ragout of squid cooked in
black beer.

Mare de Deú de la Mercè s/n. ☎ **97-724-44-04.** Reservations required. Main courses 10€–18€ ($13–$23);
set dinner menu 25€–36€ ($33–$47). AE, DC, MC, V. Mon–Sat 8pm–12:30am. Closed Dec 25–Jan 2.

Les Coques ★ ⓕ**inds** MEDITERRANEAN   A real discovery in the historic core of
the Old Town, this sophisticated eating spot specializes in quality fare from both land
and sea. For example, they prepare the best grilled octopus (the miniature variety) in
town. I tasted virgin olive oil and garlic, but the chef prefers to keep his other flavors
"secret." They also offer marvelously tender and succulent lamb chops flavored with rich
burgundy sauce. The specialties depend on whatever is good in any season. Their selection of wild mushrooms *(seta)* can be prepared in almost any style without losing their
marvelously woodsy taste.

Sant Lorenc 15. ☎ **97-722-83-00.** www.les-coques.com. Reservations required. Main courses 18€–25€
($23–$33). AE, DC, MC, V. Mon–Sat 1–3:45pm and 9–10:45pm. Closed 1 week in Feb and July 24–Aug 14.

Les Voltes ★ ⓕ**inds** MEDITERRANEAN   This excellent restaurant lies within the
vaults of the Roman Circus Maximus. Chiseled stone from 2,300 years ago abides harmoniously with thick plate glass and polished steel surfaces. A large 250-seat restaurant,
Les Voltes offers a kitchen of skilled chefs turning out a flavorful and well-seasoned
Mediterranean cuisine. The menu features time-tested favorites such as a succulent baked
lamb from the neighboring hills. *Rape,* or monkfish, deserves special billing, served with

The Beaches of the Costa Daurada

Running along the entire coastline of the province of Tarragona, for some 211km (131 miles) from Cunit as far as Les Cases d'Alcanar, is a series of excellent beaches and impressive cliffs, along with beautiful pine-covered headlands. In the city of Tarragona itself is **El Milagre** beach, and a little farther north are the beaches of **L'Arrabassade, Savinosa, dels Capellans,** and the **Llarga.** At the end of the latter stands **La Punta de la Mora,** which has a 16th-century watchtower. The small towns of **Altafulla** and **Torredembarra,** both complete with castles, stand next to these beaches and are the location of many hotels and urban developments.

Farther north again are the two magnificent beaches of **Comarruga** and **Sant Salvador.** The first is particularly cosmopolitan; the second is more secluded. Last come the beaches of **Calafell, Segur,** and **Cunit,** all with modern tourist complexes. You'll also find the small towns of **Creixell, Sant Vicenç de Calders,** and **Clarà,** which have wooded hills in the background.

South of Tarragona, the coastline forms a wide arc that stretches for miles and includes **La Piñeda** beach. **El Recó** beach fronts the Cape of Salou where, in among its coves, hills, and hidden-away corners, many hotels and residential centers are located. The natural port of **Salou** is nowadays a center for international, family-oriented package tourism but is pleasant enough if you don't mind the crowds and noisy night scene.

Continuing south toward Valencia, you next come to **Cambrils,** a maritime town with an excellent beach and an important fishing port. In the background stand the impressive Colldejou and Llaberia mountains. Farther south are the beaches of **Montroig** and **L'Hospitalet,** as well as the small town of **L'Ametlla de Mar** with its small fishing port.

After passing the Balaguer massif, you eventually reach the delta of the River Ebro, a wide lowland area covering more than 483km (300 miles), opening like a fan into the sea. This is an area of rice fields crisscrossed by branches of the Ebro and by an enormous number of irrigation channels. There are also some lagoons that, because of their immense size, are ideal as hunting and fishing grounds. Moreover, there are some beaches over several miles in length and others in small hidden estuaries. Two important towns in the region are **Amposta,** on the Ebro itself, and **Sant Carles de la Ràpita,** a 19th-century port town favored by King Carlos III.

The Costa Daurada extends to its most southwesterly point at the plain of **Alcanar,** a large area given over to the cultivation of oranges and other similar crops. Its beaches, along with the small hamlet of **Les Cases d'Alcanar,** mark the end of the Tarragona section of the Costa Daurada.

roasted garlic in a cockle and mussel sauce. Showing sure-handed spicing, the loin of veal is peppery and served with broiled eggplant.

Carrer Trinquet Vell 12. ☎ **97-723-06-51.** Reservations recommended. Main courses 9€–24€ ($12–$31). DC, MC, V. Tues–Sun 1–4pm; Tues–Sat 8:30–11:30pm. Closed Dec 25–Jan 2.

3 SITGES ★★

40km (25 miles) S of Barcelona, 596km (370 miles) E of Madrid

Sitges is one of the most popular resorts of southern Europe and the brightest spot on the Costa Daurada. It's especially crowded in summer, mostly with affluent young northern Europeans, many of them gay. Throughout the 19th century, the resort largely drew prosperous middle-class industrialists and traders (known as *indios* since they made their fortunes in the Americas) and many of their stately homes still stand along the sea-facing promenade, the Passeig Marítim. Today, Sitges easily accommodates a mixed crowd of affluent residents, vacationing families and couples, and swarms of day-trippers from Barcelona.

Sitges has long been known as a city of culture, thanks in part to resident artist, playwright, and bohemian dandy Santiago Rusiñol. The 19th-century *modernisme* movement was nurtured in Sitges, and the town remained the scene of artistic encounters and demonstrations long after the movement waned. Sitges continued as a resort of artists, attracting such giants as Salvador Dalí and poet Federico García Lorca. The Spanish Civil War (1936–39) erased what has come to be called the "golden age" of Sitges. Although other artists and writers arrived in the decades to follow, none had the impact of those who had gone before.

ESSENTIALS

GETTING THERE RENFE runs **trains** from Barcelona-Sants and Passeig de Gràcia to Sitges, a 30- to 40-minute trip. Call ✆ **90-224-02-02** or visit www.renfe.com for information about schedules. If you plan to stay late, check what time the last train leaves once in Sitges, as they vary.

Where the Boys Are

Along with Ibiza and Mikonos, Sitges has established itself firmly on the "A" list of gay resorts. It's a perfect destination for those who want a ready-made combination of beach and bars, all within a few minutes' walk of each other. It works well as a temporary, calmer alternative to Barcelona, which is about 30 minutes away by train, and so is great for a day trip or a few days out of the city. In the off season, it's pretty quiet on the gay front apart from the Carnaval in February, when hordes of gays and lesbians descend from Barcelona and the party really begins.

Summer, however, is pure hedonistic playtime, and the town draws males in from all over Europe. Sitges is never going to tax the intellect, but it might well exhaust the body. There's a gay beach crammed with the usual overload of muscles and summer accessories in the middle of the town in front of the Passeig Marítim. The other beach is nudist and farther out of town, between Sitges and Vilanova. The best directions are to go as far as the L'Atlántida disco and then follow the train track to the farther of the two beaches. The woods next to it are unsurprisingly packed with playful wildlife sporting short hair and deep tans.

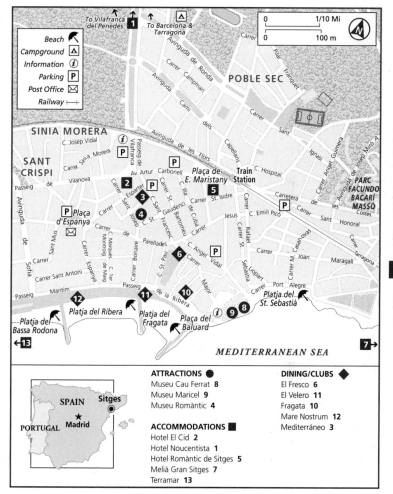

ATTRACTIONS ●
Museu Cau Ferrat **8**
Museu Maricel **9**
Museu Romàntic **4**

ACCOMMODATIONS ■
Hotel El Cid **2**
Hotel Noucentista **1**
Hotel Romàntic de Sitges **5**
Meliá Gran Sitges **7**
Terramar **13**

DINING/CLUBS ◆
El Fresco **6**
El Velero **11**
Fragata **10**
Mare Nostrum **12**
Mediterráneo **3**

Sitges is a 45-minute **drive** from Barcelona along the C-246, a coastal road. There is also an express highway, the A-7, which passes through the Garraf Tunnels. The coastal road is more scenic, but it can be extremely slow on weekends because of the heavy traffic, as all of Barcelona seemingly heads for the beaches.

VISITOR INFORMATION The **tourist office** is at Carrer Sínea Morera 1 (℃ **93-894-42-51;** www.sitges.org). From June to September 15, it's open daily from 9am to 9pm; from September 16 to May, hours are Monday through Friday from 9am to 2pm and 4 to 6:30pm, and Saturday from 10am to 1pm.

SPECIAL EVENTS The **Carnaval** at Sitges is one of the outstanding events on the Catalan calendar and frankly makes all other Carnaval celebrations in the region look lame. For more than a century, the town has celebrated the days before the beginning of Lent. Fancy dress, floats, feathered outfits, and sequins all make this an exciting event. The party begins on the Thursday before Lent with the arrival of the king of the Carnestoltes and ends with the burial of a sardine on Ash Wednesday. Activities reach their flamboyant best on Sant Bonaventura, where gay people hold their own celebrations. During the week of Corpus Christi in June blankets of flowers are laid in the streets of the Old Town, and on the night of June 23, the feast of Sant Joan, the beach lights up with fireworks and bonfires.

FUN ON & OFF THE BEACH

The old part of Sitges used to be a fortified medieval enclosure. The castle is now the seat of the town government. The local parish church, called **La Punta (The Point)** and built next to the sea on top of a promontory, presides over an extensive maritime esplanade, where people parade in the early evening. Behind the side of the church are the Museu Cau Ferrat and the Museu Maricel (see "Museums," below).

Most people are here to hit the beach. The beaches have showers, bathing cabins, and stalls; kiosks rent motorboats, watersports equipment, beach umbrellas, and sun-beds. Beaches on the eastern end and those inside the town center are the most peaceful—for example, **Aiguadolç** and **Els Balomins. Playa San Sebastián, Fragata Beach,** and the **"Beach of the Boats"** (below the church and next to the yacht club) are the area's family beaches. A young, happening crowd heads for the **Playa de la Ribera** to the west.

All along the coast, women can and certainly do go topless. Farther west are the most solitary beaches, where the scene grows racier, especially along the **Playas del Muerto,** where two tiny nude beaches lie between Sitges and Vilanova i la Geltrú. A shuttle bus runs between the church and the Hotel Terramar. From here, go along the road to the club L'Atlántida, then walk along the railway. The first beach draws nudists of every sexual persuasion, and the second is almost solely gay. Be advised that lots of action takes place in the woods in back of these beaches.

MUSEUMS

Beaches aside, Sitges has some choice museums, which really shouldn't be missed.

Museu Cau Ferrat ★★ (Moments) The Catalan artist Santiago Rusiñol combined two charming 16th-century cottages to make this house, where he lived and worked; upon his death in 1931 he willed it to Sitges along with his art collection. More than anyone else, Rusiñol made Sitges a popular resort. The museum's immense and cluttered collection includes two paintings by El Greco and several small Picassos, including *The Bullfight.* A number of Rusiñol's works are on display, along with his prolific collection of wrought-iron objects and a dazzling display of Mediterranean tilework. The edifice, with its dramatic sea views from tiny windows, is worth the visit alone.

Carrer Fonollar s/n. ⓒ **93-894-03-64.** www.mnac.es/museus/mus_ferrat.jsp?lan=003. Admission 3.50€ ($4.55) adults, 1.75€ ($2.30) students, free for children 12 and under. June 15–Sept Tues–Sun 10am–2pm and 5–9pm; Oct–June 14 Tues–Fri 10am–1:30pm and 3–6:30pm, Sat 10am–7pm, Sun 10am–3pm.

Museu Maricel ★ Opened by the king and queen of Spain, the Museu Maricel contains art donated by Dr. Jesús Pérez Rosales. The palace, owned by American Charles Deering when it was built right after World War I, is made up of two parts connected by a small bridge. The museum has a good collection of Gothic and Romantic paintings and sculptures, as well as many fine Catalan ceramics. There are three noteworthy works by Santiago Rebull and an allegorical painting of World War I by José María Sert.

Carrer del Fonollar s/n. ✆ **93-894-03-64.** Admission 3.50€ ($4.55) adults, 1.75€ ($2.30) students, free for children 12 and under. Same hours as Museu Cau Ferrat, above.

Museu Romàntic ("Can Llopis")   This museum re-creates the daily life of a Sitges land-owning family in the 18th and 19th centuries. The family rooms, furniture, and household objects are interesting. Upstairs, you'll find wine cellars and an important collection of antique dolls.

Sant Gaudenci 1. ✆ **93-894-29-69.** Admission (including guided tour) 3.50€ ($4.55) adults, 1.75€ ($2.30) students, free for children 12 and under. Same hours as Museu Cau Ferrat, above.

WHERE TO STAY

In spite of a building spree, Sitges just can't handle the large numbers of tourists who flock here in July and August. By mid-October just about everything—including hotels, restaurants, and bars—slows down considerably or closes altogether.

Expensive

Hotel Romàntic de Sitges ★ (Finds)   Made up of three beautifully restored 19th-century villas, this hotel is only a short walk from the beach and the train station. The romantic bar is an international rendezvous, and the public rooms are filled with artworks. You can have breakfast in the dining room or in a garden filled with mulberry trees. The rooms, reached by stairs, range from small to medium and are well maintained, with good beds and bathrooms with shower stalls. Overflow guests are housed in a nearby annex, the Hotel de la Renaixença.

Sant Isidre 33, 08870 Sitges. ✆ **93-894-83-75.** Fax 93-894-81-67. www.hotelromantic.com. 60 units. 80€–110€ ($104–$143) double without bathroom; 90€–125€ ($117–$163) double w/shower/bathroom. Rates include breakfast. AE, MC, V. Closed Nov–Mar 15. **Amenities:** Bar; babysitting. *In room:* Hair dryer, safe.

Meliá Gran Sitges ★   Designed with steeply sloping sides reminiscent of a pair of interconnected Aztec pyramids, this hotel was originally built to house spectators and participants in the 1992 Barcelona Olympics. Its marble lobby boasts what feels like the largest window in Spain, overlooking a view of the mountains. Each of the midsize rooms comes with a large furnished veranda for sunbathing, and each bathroom has a tub/shower combo. Many guests are here to participate in the conferences and conventions held frequently in the battery of high-tech convention facilities. It's about a 15-minute walk east of the center of Sitges, near the access roads leading to Barcelona.

Joan Salvat Papasseit 38, Puerto de Aiguadolç, 08870 Sitges. ✆ **800/336-3542** in the U.S., or 93-811-08-11 (hotel) or 90-214-44-44 (reservations). Fax 93-894-90-34. www.solmelia.com. 307 units. 90€–250€ ($117–$325) double; 280€ ($364) suite. Some rates include breakfast. AE, DC, MC, V. Parking 10€ ($13). **Amenities:** Restaurant; bar; indoor pool; outdoor pool; health club; sauna; business center; room service; babysitting; laundry service; dry cleaning. *In room:* A/C, TV, minibar, hair dryer, safe.

Terramar ★★ (Finds)   Facing the beach in a residential area of Sitges, about half a mile from the center, this resort hotel, one of the first "grand hotels" along this coast, is a Sitges landmark. Its balconied facade evokes a multi-decked yacht and the interior, renovated in the 1970s, is a near-perfect example of retro design. The foyer has a quirky marine theme, the floors and wall panels are lined with different marbles, and the ladies' restroom is hot pink. The spacious and comfortable guest rooms contain the same sort of eccentric detailing.

Passeig Marítim 80, 08870 Sitges. ✆ **93-894-00-50.** Fax 93-894-56-04. www.hotelterramar.com. 209 units. 120€–175€ ($156–$228) double; 160€–180€ ($208–$234) suite. Rates include breakfast buffet. AE, DC, MC, V. Closed Nov–Mar. **Amenities:** 2 restaurants; 2 bars; outdoor pool; 2 outdoor tennis courts;

children's center; business center; room service; babysitting; laundry service; dry cleaning. *In room:* A/C, TV, minibar, hair dryer, safe.

Moderate

Hotel Noucentista ★ (Value)   Owned by the same family that owns the popular Hotel El Xalet across the street, this is a winning choice. The name, Noucentista, means 1900, the year of the building's original construction. The interior is quite stunning, a statement of *modernisme* with much use of antiques. The small to midsize bedrooms are stylishly and comfortably furnished with ample closet space and bathrooms, each with a shower. Some of the accommodations open onto small private balconies. The inn is a 10-minute walk from the beach. The hotel is also graced with a small courtyard garden, and guests have access to Xalet's swimming pool and restaurant.

Illa de Cuba 21, 08870 Sitges. ℭ **93-811-00-70.** Fax 93-894-55-79. www.elxalet.com. 12 units. 65€–100€ ($85–$130) double; 90€–140€ ($117–$182) suite. AE, DC, MC, V. *In room:* A/C, TV, minibar, hair dryer, safe.

Inexpensive

Hotel El Cid ★   El Cid's exterior evokes Castile, and inside, appropriately enough, you'll find beamed ceilings, natural stone walls, heavy wrought-iron chandeliers, and leather chairs. The same theme is carried out in the rear dining room and in the pleasantly furnished rooms, which, though small, are still quite comfortable, with fine beds and bathrooms containing shower stalls. Breakfast is the only meal served. El Cid is off the Passeig de Vilanova in the center of town.

Sant Josep 39B, 08870 Sitges. ℭ **93-894-18-42.** Fax 93-894-63-35. 77 units. 55€–80€ ($72–$104) double. Rates include continental breakfast. MC, V. Closed Oct–Apr. **Amenities:** Bar; outdoor pool; babysitting. *In room:* No phone.

WHERE TO DINE

Expensive

El Velero ★ SEAFOOD   This is one of Sitges's leading restaurants, positioned along the beachside promenade. The most desirable tables are found on the glass greenhouse terrace, opening onto the esplanade, though there's a more glamorous restaurant inside. Try a soup, such as clam and truffle or whitefish, followed by a main dish such as paella marinara (with seafood) or suprême of salmon in pine-nut sauce.

Passeig de la Ribera 38. ℭ **93-894-20-51.** www.restaurantevelero.com. Reservations required. Main courses 18€–38€ ($23–$49); tasting menu 38€ ($49); gastronomic menu 50€ ($65). AE, DC, MC, V. Tues–Sun 1:30–4pm and 8:30–11:30pm. Closed Dec 22–Jan 6.

Moderate

El Fresco ★★ (Finds) FUSION   Many people, especially the gay community, reckon this is the best bet in Sitges; perhaps it is because it is more like an eatery you would encounter in Sydney. Owned by an Australian couple, the eclectic menu draws heavily on Asian influences. Upstairs there is a cheaper cafe, an enormously popular breakfast spot; here, you can feed your hangover on such un-Spanish fare as blueberry pancakes, fresh muesli, and muffins, or choose from a selection of salads such as Thai beef or Caesar for lunch.

Pau Barrabeig 4. ℭ **93-894-06-00.** Reservations recommended. Main courses 9€–25€ ($12–$33). MC, V. May–Sept Tues–Sun 8:30am–midnight; Oct–Apr Wed–Sun 8:30am–midnight. Closed Dec 20–Jan 20.

Fragata ★ SEAFOOD   Though its simple interior offers little more than well-scrubbed floors, tables with crisp linens, and air-conditioning, some of the most delectable seafood specialties in town are served here, and hundreds of loyal customers come

Cava Country

The Penedès region is Catalonia's wine country, the place where the crisp whites, hearty reds, and sparkling *cava* that you've tried in Barcelona's restaurants are produced. After years of being thought of solely as an agrarian region, wine tourism is starting to take off in the villages and rolling vineyards of this delightful destination.

The capital is Vilafranca del Penedés, a bustling provincial town that has a fine outdoor market on Saturday mornings and is famous for its local *castellers* (human towers) team. The **Vinseum,** Plaça Jaume I 1 (© **93-817-00-36;** www. vinseum.cat), has a collection of viniculture equipment and memorabilia considered to be the best of its kind in Europe. If you are curious to know more, the Museu de Vilafranca, located next door, has a collection of works by artists on wine-related themes and a gorgeous collection of Spanish and Catalan ceramic work from the 15th century onward. If you have time, the Basílica de Santa María (also located in the Plaça Sant Jaume) is a Gothic church dating from the 15th century. Ascend the 52m (171-ft.) bell tower for a panoramic view of the town and surrounding area.

Nothing, however, beats the hands-on experience of seeing the process of winemaking from start to finish. A handful of bodegas (wineries) are open to the public, the best being the estate of **Codorníu** (© **93-818-32-32;** www. codorniu.es), the top *cava* maker in Catalonia. Their magnificent winery is located 10km (6¼ miles) from Vilafranca in the village of Sant Sadorni d'Anoia. Designed at the end of the 19th century by Josep María Puig i Cadafalch (a master architect of the *modernisme* movement), his beautiful project reflects the luxurious product made within; the complex is replete with Art Nouveau touches and details and 15km (9⅓ miles) of sinuous underground tunnels where the product is aged. Another highlight is a museum containing gorgeous past advertising posters of the product, many by renowned artists of the period. Codorníu is open to the public Monday through Friday 9am to 5pm and Saturday 9am to 1pm. A mini train whisks you around the estate, including the vineyards, and a *cava* tasting nicely rounds out your visit.

Another sumptuous *moderniste* wine palace is that of **Freixenet,** Av. Casetas Mir s/n (© **93-891-70-25**), Codorníu's main competition. Freixenet's landmark bodega, located right beside the train station of Sant Sadorni d'Anoia, also gives tours of its headquarters (by previous appointment) on Saturday from 10am to 1pm. Its colorful, florid facade is one of the area's landmarks.

The **tourist office** in Vilafranca del Penedès is located at Carrer de la Cort 14 (© **93-892-03-58;** www.turismevilafranca.com). It's open Tuesday to Friday from 9am to 1pm and 4:30 to 7pm, and Saturday 10am to 1pm. **RENFE** (© **90-224-02-02;** www.renfe.es) runs dozens of trains a day (trip time: 55 min.) from Barcelona to Vilafranca del Penedès and Sant Sadorni d'Anoia, leaving from Plaça de Catalunya station. If you're driving, head west out of the city via the A-7. Follow the signs to Sant Sadorni d'Anoia and then stay on the same highway to Vilafranca.

to appreciate the authentic cuisine. Specialties include seafood soup, a mixed grill of fresh fish, cod salad, mussels marinara, several preparations of squid and octopus, plus some flavorful meat dishes, such as grilled lamb cutlets.

Passeig de la Ribera 1. © **93-894-10-86.** www.restaurantefragata.com. Reservations recommended. Main dishes 12€–25€ ($16–$33). AE, DC, MC, V. Daily 1–4:30pm and 8:30–11:30pm.

Mare Nostrum ★★ SEAFOOD   This landmark dates from 1950, when it opened in what had been a private home in the 1890s. The dining room has a waterfront view, and in warm weather tables are placed outside. The menu includes a full range of seafood dishes, among them grilled fish specialties and steamed hake with champagne. The fish soup is particularly delectable. Next door, the restaurant's cafe serves ice cream, milkshakes, sandwiches, tapas, and three varieties of sangria, including one with champagne and fruit.

Passeig de la Ribera 60. © **93-894-33-93.** Reservations required. Main courses 10€–24€ ($13–$31). AE, DC, MC, V. Thurs–Tues 1–4pm and 8–11pm. Closed Dec 15–Feb 1.

SITGES AFTER DARK

One of the best ways to pass an evening in Sitges is to walk the waterfront esplanade, have a leisurely dinner, then retire at about 11pm to one of the dozens of open-air cafes for a nightcap and some serious people-watching.

If you're straight, you may have to hunt to find a late-night bar that isn't predominantly gay in the center of town. For the locations of Sitges's gay bars, look for a pocket-size map that's distributed in most of the gay bars—you can pick it up in the Parrot's Pub (in the Plaça de la Industria) or it can be downloaded on **www.gaymap.info**. Nine of these bars are concentrated on **Carrer Sant Bonaventura,** a 5-minute walk from the beach (near the Museu Romàntic). If you grow bored with the action in one place, you just have to walk down the street to find another. Drink prices run about the same in all the clubs.

Mediterráneo, Sant Bonaventura 6 (no phone), is the largest gay disco/bar. It sports a formal Iberian garden and sleek modern styling. And upstairs in this restored 1690s house just east of the Plaça Espanya are pool tables and a covered terrace. On summer nights, the place is filled to overflowing.

4 GIRONA ★★

97km (60 miles) NE of Barcelona, 90km (56 miles) S of the French City of Perpignan

Founded by the Romans, **Girona** is one of the top 10 important historical sites in Spain. Later, it became a Moorish stronghold and later still, it reputedly withstood three invasions by Napoleon's troops in the early 1800s. For that and other past aggressions, Girona is often called the "City of a Thousand Sieges." These days, residents go about their daily business smug in the knowledge that their city is constantly rated the best in the country in terms of quality of life.

Split by the Onyar River, this bustling, provincial city often only gets a nod from the crowds of tourists who use its airport as a springboard for the resorts and beaches of the nearby Costa Brava. When you arrive, make your way to the narrow lanes and hidden staircases of the Old City and the Call, the remains of the sizable Jewish community, via the ancient stone footbridge across the Onyar. From here, you'll have the finest view of ochre-colored town houses flanking each side, instantly recalling Venice. Bring good

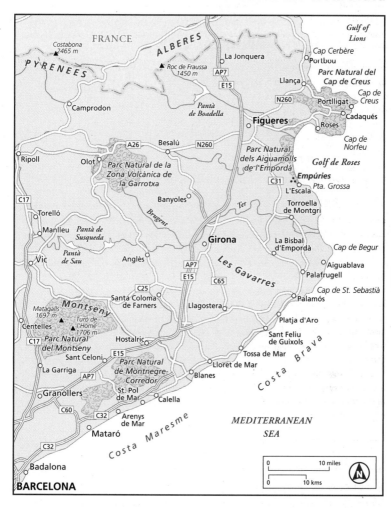

walking shoes, as you will want to circumnavigate the old city walls to fully take in the splendid stone edifices and lush countryside of its surrounds. Much of Girona can be appreciated from the outside, but it does contain some important attractions you'll want to see on the inside.

ESSENTIALS

GETTING THERE More than 26 **trains** per day run between Girona and Barcelona-Sants or Passeig de Gràcia stations. Trip time is 1 to 1¹/₂ hours, and one-way fare is 5.90€ to 6.70€ ($7.65–$8.70), depending on the train. Trains arrive in Girona at the Plaça Espanya (© **97-220-70-93;** www.renfe.com).

By **car** from Barcelona, take the A-7 at Ronda Litoral and head north via the A-7.

VISITOR INFORMATION   The **tourist office** at Rambla de la Libertat 1 (ⓒ 97-222-65-75; www.ajuntament.gi) is open Monday through Friday from 8am to 8pm, Saturday from 8am to 2pm and 4 to 8pm, and Sunday from 9am to 2pm.

EXPLORING THE MEDIEVAL CITY

Banys Arabs ★   These 12th-century Arab baths, an example of Romanesque civic architecture, are in the Old Quarter of the city. Visit the **caldarium (hot bath),** with its paved floor, and the **frigidarium (cold bath),** with its central octagonal pool surrounded by pillars that support a prismlike structure in the overhead window. Although the Moorish baths were heavily restored in 1929, they'll give you an idea of what the ancient ones were like.

Carrer Ferran el Catolic s/n. ⓒ **97-221-32-62.** Admission 2€ ($2.60) adults, 1€ ($1.30) students, free for seniors and children 16 and under. Apr–Sept Mon–Sat 10am–7pm, Sun 10am–2pm; Oct–Mar Tues–Sun 10am–2pm. Closed Jan 1, Jan 6, Easter, and Dec 25–26.

Catedral ★★★   Girona's major attraction is its magnificent cathedral, reached by climbing a 17th-century baroque staircase of 90 steep steps. The 14th-century cathedral represents many architectural styles, including Gothic and Romanesque, but it's most notably Catalan baroque. The facade you see as you climb those long stairs dates from the 17th and 18th centuries; from a cornice on top rises a bell tower crowned by a dome with a bronze angel weather vane. Enter the main door of the cathedral and go into the nave, which, at 23m (75 ft.), is the broadest example of Gothic architecture in the world.

The cathedral contains many works of art, displayed for the most part in its museum. Its prize exhibit is a **tapestry of the Creation,** a unique piece of 11th- or 12th-century Romanesque embroidery depicting humans and animals in the Garden of Eden. The other major work displayed is one of the world's rarest manuscripts—the 10th-century *Códex del Beatus,* which contains an illustrated commentary on the Revelation. From the cathedral's **Chapel of Hope,** a door leads to a **Romanesque cloister** from the 12th and 13th centuries, with an unusual trapezoidal layout. The cloister gallery, with a double colonnade, has a series of biblical scenes that are the prize jewel of Catalan Romanesque art. From the cloister you can view the 12th-century **Torre de Carlemany (Charlemagne's Tower).**

Plaça de la Catedral s/n. ⓒ **97-221-44-26.** Free admission to cathedral; nave, cloister, and museum 4€ ($5.20), students and seniors 3€ ($3.90); all free on Sun. Cathedral daily 9am–1pm and during cloister and museum visiting hours. Cloister and museum July–Sept Tues–Sat 10am–8pm, Sun 10am–2pm; Oct–Feb Tues–Sat 10am–2pm and 4–6pm, Sun 10am–2pm; Mar–June Tues–Sat 10am–2pm and 4–7pm, Sun 10am–2pm.

Església de Sant Feliu ★   This 14th- to 17th-century church was built over what may have been the tomb of Feliu of Africa, martyred during Diocletian's persecution at the beginning of the 4th century. Important in the architectural history of Catalonia, the church has pillars and arches in the Romanesque style and a Gothic central nave. The **bell tower**—one of the Girona skyline's most characteristic features—has eight pinnacles and one central tower, each supported on a solid octagonal base. The main facade of the church is baroque. The interior contains some exceptional works, including a 16th-century **altarpiece** and a 14th-century alabaster *Reclining Christo.* Notice the eight pagan and Christian **sarcophagi** set in the walls of the presbytery, the two oldest of which are from the 2nd century A.D. One shows Pluto carrying Persephone off to the depths of the earth.

Pujada de Sant Feliu s/n. ⓒ **97-220-14-07.** Free admission. Daily 8am–7:45pm.

Museu Arqueològic ★   Housed in a Romanesque church and cloister from the 11th and 12th centuries, this museum illustrates the history of the region from the Paleolithic to the Visigothic periods, using artifacts discovered in nearby excavations. The monastery itself ranks as one of the best examples of Catalan Romanesque architecture. In the cloister, note some Hebrew inscriptions from gravestones of the old Jewish cemetery.

Sant Pere de Galligants, Santa Llúcia 1. ℂ **97-220-26-32.** Admission 2€ ($2.60) adults, 1.50€ ($1.95) students, free for seniors and children 16 and under. Oct–May Tues–Sat 10am–2pm and 4–6pm, Sun 10am–2pm; June–Sept Tues–Sat 10am–1:30pm and 4–7pm, Sun 10am–2pm.

Museu d'Art ★   In a former Romanesque and Gothic Episcopal palace (Palau Episcopal) next to the cathedral, this museum displays artworks spanning 10 centuries (once housed in the old Diocesan and Provincial museums). Stop in the throne room to view the **altarpiece of Sant Pere of Púbol** by Bernat Martorell and the **altarpiece of Sant Miguel de Crüilles** by Luis Borrassa. Both of these works, from the 15th century, are exemplary pieces of Catalan Gothic painting. The museum is also proud of its **altar stone** of Sant Pere de Roda, from the 10th and 11th centuries; this work in wood and stone, depicting figures and legends, was once covered in embossed silver. The 12th-century *Crüilles Timber* is a unique piece of Romanesque polychrome wood. *Our Lady of Besalù,* from the 15th century, is one of the most accomplished depictions of the Virgin carved in alabaster.

Pujada de la Catedral 12. ℂ **97-220-38-34.** Admission 2€ ($2.60) adults, 1.50€ ($1.95) students, free for seniors and children. Mar–Sept Tues–Sat 10am–7pm, Sun 10am–2pm; Oct–Feb Tues–Sat 10am–6pm, Sun 10am–2pm. Closed Jan 1, Jan 6, Easter, and Dec 25–26.

Museu de Cinema ★★   Film buffs flock to this film museum, the only one of its kind in Spain. It houses the Tomàs Mallol collection of some 25,000 cinema artifacts, going all the way up to films shot as late as 1970. Many objects are from the "pre-cinema" era, plus other exhibits from the early days of film. The museum even owns the original

El Call

The Jewish diaspora made an indelible mark on the city of Girona. A sizable chunk of the Old Town is taken up with the remains of **El Call,** once Spain's most sizable Jewish ghetto. From 20-odd families who arrived at the end of the 9th century, the community grew to nearly 2,000, with three synagogues, butchers, bakers, and other mercantile activity taking place in the neighborhood's cobbled streets. In 1492, along with other Jewish communities on the Peninsula (including Barcelona and Majorca), they were blamed for the spread of the plague and unceremoniously ousted by Catholic powers. The **Centre Bonastruc Ca Portal,** Calle La Force 8 (ℂ **97-221-67-61**), in the heart of El Call, contains exhibitions on medieval Jewish life and customs, with an emphasis on the cohabitation of Jews and Christians, as well as exhibitions by contemporary Jewish artists. It also conducts special-interest tours of the area and courses on Jewish culture and history. It's open Monday to Saturday 10am to 8pm, Sunday 10am to 3pm. Admission 2€ ($2.60).

camera of the pioneering Lumière brothers. Fixed images such as photographs, posters, engravings, drawings, and paintings are exhibited along with some 800 films of various styles and periods. There's even a library with film-related publications.

Sèquia 1. ✆ **97-241-27-77.** Admission 3€ ($3.90) adults, 1.50€ ($1.95) students and seniors, free for children 16 and under. May–Sept Tues–Sun 10am–8pm; Oct–Apr Tues–Fri 10am–6pm, Sat 10am–8pm, Sun 11am–3pm. Closed Jan 1, Jan 6, and Dec 25–26.

WHERE TO STAY
Moderate
Hotel Carlemany ★   In a commercial area only 10 minutes from the historic core, this 1995 hotel is often cited as the best in town. A favorite of business travelers, the facilities are top class. Overall, it's contemporary with a modern (though slightly lacking in character) design. That said, the midsize to spacious rooms are soundproof and airy, and the bathrooms contain tub/shower combos.

Plaça Miquel Santaló s/n, 17002 Girona. ✆ **97-221-12-12.** Fax 97-221-49-94. www.carlemany.es. 90 units. 125€ ($163) double; 180€ ($234) suite. AE, DC, MC, V. Parking 12€ ($16). **Amenities:** Restaurant; 2 bars; room service; laundry service; nonsmoking rooms. *In room:* A/C, TV, hair dryer, safe.

Hotel Ciutat de Girona ★   This hip and high-tech four-star hotel is located right in the town center and is a good choice for people who prefer mod cons to rustic charm. Opened in 2003, all the rooms are decked out in *diseño catalán* style in tones of taupe and cream with dramatic swaths of red, and all have Internet connections (you can even get your own PC upon request). The classy cocktail bar in the foyer clinches the stylish deal.

Nord 2, 17001 Girona. ✆ **97-248-30-38.** Fax 97-248-30-26. www.hotel-ciutatdegirona.com. 44 units. 125€–150€ ($163–$195) double; 135€–200€ ($176–$260) triple. AE, DC, MC, V. Parking 14€ ($18). **Amenities:** Restaurant; bar; Wi-Fi; room service; laundry service. *In room:* A/C, TV, free minibar, hair dryer.

Hotel Ultonia   This small hotel lies a short walk from the Plaça de la Independencia. Since the late 1950s it has been a favorite with business travelers, but today it attracts more visitors, as it's close to the historical district. The rooms are compact and furnished in a modern style, with comfortable beds and bathrooms, most of which have tub/shower combos. Double-glazed windows keep out the noise. Some of the rooms opening onto the avenue have tiny balconies. In just 8 to 12 minutes, you can cross the Onyar into the medieval quarter. Guests can enjoy a breakfast buffet (not included in the rates quoted below), but no other meals are served.

Av. Jaume I 22, 17001 Girona. ✆ **97-220-38-50.** Fax 97-220-33-34. www.hotelhusaultonia.com. 45 units. 80€–120€ ($104–$156) double. AE, DC, MC, V. Parking 10€ ($13) nearby. **Amenities:** Laundry service. *In room:* A/C, TV, minibar.

Inexpensive
Bellmirall ★★ (Moments)   Across the Onyar River, this little discovery lies in the heart of the old Jewish ghetto. It's one of the best values in the Old Town. The building itself, much restored and altered over the years, dates originally from the 14th century. Bedrooms are small to midsize and are decorated in part with antiques set against brick walls. Some of these walls are adorned with paintings; others come with carefully selected ceramics. Each room comes with a small bathroom with shower. In summer, it's possible to order breakfast outside in the courtyard.

Carrer Bellmirall 3, 17004 Girona. ✆ **97-220-40-09.** 7 units. 65€–75€ ($85–$98) double; 90€ ($117) triple. Rates include breakfast. No credit cards. Free parking (hotel provides permit). Closed Jan–Feb. *In room:* No phone.

Hotel Peninsular ★ Devoid of any significant architectural character, this modest hotel provides clean but unremarkable accommodations near the cathedral and the river. The small rooms are scattered over five floors. All units contain neatly kept bathrooms with showers. The hotel is better for short-term stopovers than for prolonged stays. Breakfast is the only meal served (and is not included in the rates quoted below).

Nou 3, 17001 Girona. ✆ **97-220-38-00.** Fax 97-221-04-92. www.novarahotels.com. 47 units. 75€ ($98) double. AE, DC, MC, V. Parking 10€ ($13) nearby. **Amenities:** Breakfast bar; laundry service. *In room:* TV, hair dryer, safe.

WHERE TO DINE

Bronsoms ★ CATALAN In the heart of the Old Town, within an 1890s building that was once a private home, this restaurant is one of the most consistently reliable in Girona. Praised by newspapers as far away as Madrid, it has been under its present management since 1982. It's perfected the art of serving a Catalan-based *cocina del mercado*— that is, cooking with whatever market-fresh ingredients are available. The house specialties include fish paella, *arroz negro* (black rice, tinted with squid ink and studded with shellfish), white beans, and several preparations of Iberian ham.

Sant Francesc 7. ✆ **97-221-24-93.** Reservations recommended. Main courses 8€–20€ ($10–$26); fixed-price menu 10€ ($13). AE, MC, V. Mon–Sun 1–4pm; Mon–Sat 8–11:30pm.

Cal Ros CATALAN In the oldest part of Girona, near the Plaça de Catalunya, this restaurant thrives as a culinary staple and has done so since the 1920s. It was named after a long-ago light-haired owner, although exactly who that was, no one today seems to remember. You'll be seated in one of four rustic dining rooms, each with heavy ceiling beams, exposed stone and plaster, and a sense of old Catalonia. Menu items include savory *escudilla*, made with veal, pork, and local herbs and vegetables; at least four kinds of local fish, usually braised with potatoes and tomatoes; tender fried filets of veal with mushrooms; and flaky homemade pastries, some of them flavored with anise-flavored cream. Kosher and halal dishes are also prepared.

Cort Reial 9. ✆ **97-221-91-76.** www.calros-restaurant.com. Reservations recommended. Main courses 8€–28€ ($10–$36). AE, DC, MC, V. Tues–Sun 1–4pm, Tues–Sat 8–11pm. Closed Sun evenings and Mondays.

El Celler de Can Roca ★★★ CATALAN Just 2km (1¼ miles) from the center of Girona, El Cellar de Can Roca is the best of the new spate of Catalonian restaurants and represents the success of the campaign to transform Girona into one of the more fashionable cities in Spain. Run by three young brothers (one of whom now heads the achingly fashionable Moo Restaurant in Barcelona), the restaurant is intimate, with only 12 tables. The cuisine is an interesting combination of traditional Catalan dishes creatively transformed into contemporary Mediterranean fare. Start with an avocado purée, and for dessert you can't pass up the mandarin orange sorbet with pumpkin compote.

Can Sunyer 48. ✆ **97-222-21-57.** www.cellercanroca.com. Reservations recommended. Main courses 16€–38€ ($21–$49); fixed-price menu 60€ ($78). AE, DC, MC, V. Tues–Sat 1–4pm and 9–11pm. Closed Dec 22–Jan 6 and June 23–July 14. Bus: 5.

SHOPPING

There are some interesting shops to be found around El Call and the Old Town. Look out for little specialty shops selling local wares such as beige- and yellow-colored ceramic cookware and more upmarket designer joints. The famous Barcelonese design and furniture emporium **BD** has a branch here at Calle La Força 20 (✆ **97-222-43-39;** www.bdgirona.com), one of a handful of design and object stores on the same medieval street in El Call. There are also a couple of open-air artisan markets on Saturdays, the first at the Pont de Pedra (stone bridge) and the second in the Plaça Miquel Santaló and Plaça de les Castanyes.

GIRONA AFTER DARK

Central Girona has a good number of tapas bars and cafes. Many of them are scattered along **Les Ramblas,** around the edges of the keynote **Plaça de Independencia,** and within the antique boundaries of the **Plaça Ferran el Católic.** Moving at a leisurely pace from one to another is considered something of an art form. Some animated tapas bars in the city center are **Bar de Tapes,** Carrer Barcelona 13 (© **97-241-01-64**), near the rail station, and **Tapa't,** Plaça de l'Oli s/n (no phone), which is noteworthy for its old-fashioned charm. Also appealing for its crowded conviviality and its impressive roster of shellfish and seafood tapas is **Bar Boira,** Plaça de Independencia 17 (© **97-220-30-96**). In a street that is the hub of Girona's bar culture, **Zanpanzar,** Cort Real 10–12 (© **97-221-28-43**), pulls in the crowds for its mouthwatering Basque-style *pintxos.* **La Sala del Cel,** Pedret 118 (© **97-221-46-64**), Girona's "palace of techno," is located in an old convent with outdoor gardens. The DJs, both local and international, are top class. Be prepared for lines and a *very* late night out. Slightly more subdued is the **Sala de Ball,** Carretera de la Deversa 21 (© **97-220-14-39**), an elegant, old-style dance hall that aims to please most tastes, from hip-hop to house and salsa, depending on the night.

5 LLORET DE MAR

100km (62 miles) S of the French border, 68km (42 miles) N of Barcelona

Although it has a good half-moon-shaped sandy beach, **Lloret de Mar** is neither chic nor sophisticated, and most people who come here are Europeans on inexpensive package tours. The competition for cheap rooms is fierce.

Lloret de Mar has grown at a phenomenal rate from a small fishing village with just a few hotels to a bustling resort with more hotels than anyone can count. And more keep opening, though there never seem to be enough in July and August. The accommodations are typical of those in other Costa Brava towns, running the gamut from impersonal modern box-type structures to vintage flowerpot-adorned whitewashed buildings on the narrow streets of the Old Town. There are even a few pockets of posh. The area has rich vegetation, attractive scenery, and a mild climate.

ESSENTIALS

GETTING THERE   From Barcelona, take a **train** to Blanes station (4.10€/$5.35 one-way); then from there take the quarter-hourly **bus** 8km/5 miles (2€/$2.60) to Lloret. If you **drive,** head north from Barcelona along the A-19.

VISITOR INFORMATION   The **tourist office** at Plaça de la Vila 1 (© **97-236-47-35;** www.lloret.org) is open Monday to Friday 9am to 1pm and 4 to 7pm, Saturday 10am to 1pm.

WHERE TO STAY

Many of the hotels—particularly the government-rated three-star places—are booked solid by tour groups. Here are some possibilities if you reserve in advance.

Garden of Sea and Myrtle

The **Jardí Botànic Marimurtra,** with its meandering paths and white clifftop pergolas, towers beside the fishing town of Blanes at the southern extremity of the Costa Brava. You'll be hard-pressed to find a more lovely evocation of nature in the whole Mediterranean than this 16-hectare (40-acre) Garden of Eden with its 200,000 species of plants and shrubs from the five continents. Long declared an Area of National Cultural Interest, it was founded by biologist Karl Faust at the beginning of the 20th century as a research center for universal flora. Allow an hour for a full stroll, longer if you feel like soaking up the atmosphere and meditating in some quiet corner like the tiny Plaça de Goethe. Jardí Botànic Marimurtra is at Passeig de Carles Faust 9, Blanes (© **97-233-08-26;** www.jbotanicmarimurtra.org). Admission is 4€ ($5.20), and hours are Apr–Oct daily 9am to 6pm (until 8pm in midsummer), Nov–March 10am to 5pm. Weekends and holidays 10am to 2pm year round.

Expensive

Guitart Gran Hotel Monterrey ★★   Ranked just beneath the Husa Roger de Flor (see below), this government-rated four-star hotel is similar to a deluxe country club in a large park. It's a short walk from the casino, town center, and beaches. The hotel opened in the 1940s and has been partly renovated almost every year since. It's well known as a retreat for those who want to recharge their batteries. The interior areas have big windows with expansive views. The guest rooms are spacious and luxuriously decorated; most have balconies or lounge areas. Bathrooms contain tub/shower combinations.

Carretera de Tossa, 17310 Lloret de Mar. © 97-236-40-50. Fax 97-236-35-12. www.ghmonterrey.com. 225 units. 120€–190€ ($156–$247) double; 140€–195€ ($182–$254) suite. AE, DC, MC, V. Free parking. Closed Oct–Mar. **Amenities:** Restaurant; 2 bars; 2 pools (1 indoor); 3 tennis courts; health club; beauty spa; whirlpool; sauna; children's play area; room service; massage; babysitting; laundry service; dry cleaning. *In room:* A/C, TV, hair dryer, safe.

Hotel Santa Marta ★★ Finds   This tranquil hotel, a short walk above a crescent-shaped bay favored by swimmers, is nestled in a sun-flooded grove of pines. Both public and guest rooms are attractively paneled and traditionally furnished. The spacious guest rooms offer private balconies overlooking the sea or a pleasant garden, and all contain bathrooms with tub/shower combos. The neighborhood is quiet but desirable, about 2km (1¼ miles) west of the commercial center of town.

Playa de Santa Cristina, 17310 Lloret de Mar. © 97-236-49-04. Fax 97-236-92-80. www.hstamarta.com. 78 units. 150€–275€ ($195–$358) double; 250€–390€ ($325–$507) suite. AE, DC, MC, V. Free parking. Closed Dec 23–Jan 31. **Amenities:** 2 restaurants; 2 bars; outdoor pool; sauna; solarium; car rental; room service; babysitting; laundry service; dry cleaning; room for those w/limited mobility. *In room:* A/C, TV, minibar, hair dryer, safe.

Husa Roger de Flor ★★★   This much-enlarged older hotel, some of which is reminiscent of a private villa, is a pleasant diversion from the aging slabs of concrete filling other sections of the resort. Set at the eastern edge of town, it offers the most pleasant and panoramic views of any hotel. Potted geraniums, climbing bougainvillea, and evenly spaced rows of palms add elegance to the combination of new and old architecture. The midsize rooms are high-ceilinged, modern, and excellently furnished. Well-maintained bathrooms have tub/shower combos. The public rooms contain plenty of exposed wood and spill onto a partially covered terrace.

Turó de l'Estelat s/n, 17310 Lloret de Mar. ⓒ **97-236-48-00.** Fax 97-237-16-37. www.husarogerdeflor. com. 100 units. 120€–200€ ($156–$260) double; 175€–250€ ($228–$325) suite. Rates include breakfast. AE, DC, MC, V. Free parking. **Amenities:** Restaurant; 2 bars; saltwater pool; 2 tennis courts; fitness center; Ping-Pong table; car rental; limited room service; babysitting; laundry service; dry cleaning. *In room:* TV, minibar, hair dryer, safe.

Moderate

Hotel Vila del Mar   This century-old hotel is a short walk from the beach, close to the heart of town near the bus station. The mundane but well-maintained interior has a nautical feel. The soundproof guest rooms are pleasantly decorated and well equipped, and the bathrooms come with hydromassage and tub/shower combos.

Calle de La Vila 55, 17310 Lloret de Mar. ⓒ **97-234-92-92.** Fax 97-237-11-68. www.hotelviladelmar.com. 36 units. 80€–160€ ($104–$208) double. AE, DC, MC, V. Parking 12€ ($16). **Amenities:** Restaurant; bar; outdoor pool; health club; sauna; babysitting; laundry service; dry cleaning; nonsmoking rooms; room for those w/limited mobility. *In room:* A/C, TV, high-speed Internet, minibar, hair dryer, safe.

Inexpensive

Hotel Excelsior   This hotel attracts a beach-oriented clientele from Spain and northern Europe. The Excelsior sits almost directly on the beach, rising six floors above the esplanade. All but a handful of the rooms offer either frontal or lateral views of the sea. The furniture is modern but uninspiring. Most of the bathrooms contain tub/shower combos. During midsummer, half-board is obligatory. Even though the hotel is modest, one of the Costa Brava's greatest restaurants, Les Petxines, is located here (see below).

Passeig Mossèn Jacinto Verdaguer 16, 17310 Lloret de Mar. ⓒ **97-236-41-37.** Fax 97-237-16-54. www. bestwesternhotelexcelsior.com. 45 units. July–Sept 80€ ($104) per person double; Oct–June (including breakfast) 60€ ($78) per person double. AE, DC, V. Parking 10€ ($13). Closed Nov 1–Mar 21. **Amenities:** 2 restaurants; bar; babysitting; laundry service. *In room:* A/C, TV, safe.

WHERE TO DINE

El Trull SEAFOOD   Food lovers from all over come to this prestigious eating spot to enjoy both the food and spectacular views. Set 3km (2 miles) north of the center in the modern suburb of Urbanización Playa Canyelles, El Trull positions its tables within view of a well-kept garden and a (sometimes crowded) pool. The food is some of the best in the neighborhood. Menu items focus on seafood and include fish soup; fish stew heavily laced with lobster; many variations of hake, monkfish, and clams; and an omelet "surprise." (The waiter will tell you the ingredients if you ask.)

Cala Canyelles s/n. ⓒ **97-236-49-28.** Main courses 40€–80€ ($52–$104); fixed-price menu 14€ ($18), 38€ ($49), and 60€ ($78). AE, DC, MC, V. Daily 1–4pm and 8–11pm.

Les Petxines ★★★ MEDITERRANEAN   The resort's most carefully orchestrated food is served within the Franco-era (ca. 1954) dining room of the Hotel Excelsior, a simple 45-room seafront hotel. Thirty diners at a time sit in relative intimacy within a big-windowed dining room. The cuisine varies with the season, the inspiration of the chef, and the availability of ingredients in local markets, but you can always expect superlatively fresh fish and shellfish (*petxines* in Catalan, hence the restaurant's name). The best examples include several versions of fish soup, some of them with a confit of lemons and shrimp-stuffed ravioli; and an extremely succulent ragout of fish and shell-fish. Meat eaters can occasionally appreciate flavorful versions of pigeon, one of them stuffed with foie gras.

In the Hotel Excelsior, Passeig Mossèn J. Verdaguer 16. ✆ **97-236-41-37.** Reservations required. Main courses 20€–35€ ($26–$46); fixed-price menu 30€ ($39); 6-course "surprise menu" 70€ ($91). AE, DC, MC, V. Tues–Sun 1:15–3:35pm; Tues–Sat 8:30–11pm. Open Sun nights July–Aug.

Restaurante Santa Marta ★ INTERNATIONAL/CATALAN   Set in the hotel of the same name about 2km (1¼ miles) west of the commercial center of town (see "Where to Stay," above), this pleasantly sunny enclave offers well-prepared food and a sweeping view of the beaches and the sea. Menu specialties vary with the seasons but might include pâté of wild mushrooms in a special sauce, smoked salmon with hollandaise on toast, medallions of monkfish with a mousseline of garlic, ragout of giant shrimp with broad beans, filet of beef Stroganoff, and a regionally inspired cassoulet of chicken prepared with cloves.

In the Hotel Santa Marta, Playa de Santa Cristina. ✆ **97-236-49-04.** Reservations recommended. Main courses 20€–45€ ($26–$59); fixed-price menu 44€ ($57). AE, DC, MC, V. Daily 1:30–3:30pm and 8:30–10:30pm. Closed Dec 15–Jan 31.

LLORET DE MAR AFTER DARK

At the **Casino Lloret de Mar,** Carrer Esports 1 (✆ **97-236-61-16**), games of chance include French and American roulette, blackjack, and chemin de fer. There's a restaurant, buffet dining room, bar-boîte, and dance club, along with a pool. The casino is southwest of Lloret de Mar, beside the coastal road leading to Blanes and Barcelona. Drive or take a taxi at night and bring your passport for entry. Hours are Sunday through Thursday from 5pm to 3am, Friday and Saturday from 5pm to 4am. (The casino closes 30 min. later in summer.) Admission is 4.50€ ($5.85).

The dance club **Hollywood,** Carretera de Tossa (✆ **97-236-74-63**), at the edge of town, is the place to see and be seen. Look for it on the corner of Carrer Girona. It's open nightly 10pm to 5am.

6 TOSSA DE MAR ★★

90km (56 miles) N of Barcelona, 12km (7½ miles) NE of Lloret de Mar

The gleaming white town of **Tossa de Mar,** with its 12th-century walls, labyrinthine Old Quarter, fishing boats, and fairly good sand beaches, is perhaps the most attractive base for a Costa Brava vacation. Its character and *joie de vivre* come midway between the devil-may-care excesses of Lloret and laid-back aplomb of Sant Feliu de Guíxols just up the coast (see below). The battlements and towers of Tossa were featured in the 1951 Ava Gardner and James Mason movie *Pandora and the Flying Dutchman,* sometimes still seen on TV. A life-size bronze statue of the screen goddess herself in evening dress, built in 1998 and facing a stone inscription of an Omar Khayam quote from the movie, overlooks the bay from a high vantage point in the Ciutat Vella.

In the 18th and 19th centuries, Tossa survived as a port center, growing rich on the cork industry. But that declined in the 20th century, and many of its citizens emigrated to America. In the 1950s, thanks in part to the Ava Gardner movie, tourists began to discover the charms of Tossa, and a new industry was born.

To experience these charms, walk through the 12th-century walled town, known as **Vila Vella,** built on the site of a Roman villa from the 1st century A.D. Enter through the Torre de les Hores.

Tossa was once a secret haunt for artists and writers—Marc Chagall called it a "blue paradise." It has two main beaches, **Mar Gran** and **La Bauma.** The coast near Tossa, north and south, offers even more possibilities.

As one of the few resorts that have withstood exploitation and retain most of their allure, Tossa enjoys a broad base of international visitors—so many, in fact, that it can no longer shelter them all. In spring and fall, finding a room may be a snap, but in summer it's next to impossible unless reservations are made far in advance.

ESSENTIALS

GETTING THERE   Direct **bus** service is offered from Blanes and Lloret. Tossa de Mar is also on the main Barcelona-Palafrugell route. Service with SARFA (© **90-230-20-25;** www.sarfa.com) from Barcelona is daily from 8:15am to 8:15pm, taking 1¹/₂ hours; one-way fare 8.95€ ($12). For information call © **90-226-06-06** or 93-265-65-08. **Drive** north from Barcelona along the A-19.

VISITOR INFORMATION   The **tourist office** is at Av. El Pelegrí 25 (© **97-234-01-08;** www.infotossa.com). April, May, and October, it's open Monday to Saturday 10am to 2pm and 4 to 8pm, Sunday 10:30am to 1:30pm; November to March it's open Monday to Saturday 10am to 1pm and 4 to 7pm; June to September it's open Monday to Saturday 9am to 9pm, Sunday 10am to 2pm and 5 to 8pm.

WHERE TO STAY
Very Expensive
Grand Hotel Reymar ★   A triumph of engineering a 10-minute walk southeast of the historic walls—the hotel occupies a position on a jagged rock above the sea edge— this graceful building was constructed in the 1960s. The Reymar has several levels of expansive terraces ideal for sunbathing away from the crowds below. Each good-size room has a mix of modern wood-grained and painted furniture, a bathroom with a tub/ shower combo, a balcony, and a sea view.

Platja de Mar Menuda, 17320 Tossa de Mar. © **97-234-03-12.** Fax 97-234-15-04. www.bestwestern ghreymar.com. 148 units. 140€–290€ ($182–$377) double; 330€–395€ ($429–$514) suite. Rates include breakfast. AE, DC, MC, V. Parking 8€ ($10). Closed Nov–Apr 17. **Amenities:** 4 restaurants; 3 bars; disco; outdoor pool; health club; whirlpool; sauna; solarium; car rental; room service; babysitting; laundry service; dry cleaning. *In room:* A/C, TV, minibar, hair dryer, safe.

Moderate
Best Western Hotel Mar Menuda ★★ (Finds)   This hotel is a gem, a real Costa Brava hideaway surviving amid tawdry tourist traps and fast-food joints. Its terrace is the area's most panoramic, overlooking the sea and the architectural highlights of the town. The guest rooms range from midsize to spacious, each tastefully furnished and containing a good-size bathroom with tub/shower. The staff are helpful in arranging many watersports, such as scuba diving, windsurfing, and sailing. The cuisine served here is first class.

Platja de Mar Menuda, 17320 Tossa de Mar. © **800/528-1234** in the U.S., or 97-234-10-04. Fax 97-234-00-87. www.hotelmarmenuda.com. 50 units. 160€–190€ ($208–$247) double w/breakfast; 210€ ($273) suite. AE, DC, MC, V. Free parking. Closed Nov–Dec. **Amenities:** Restaurant; bar; tennis courts; children's playground; limited room service; babysitting; laundry service; dry cleaning; nonsmoking rooms. *In room:* A/C, TV, hair dryer, safe.

Inequexpensive

Canaima (Kids) Lacking the charm of Hotel Diana, this little inn is the resort's bargain. It lies in a tranquil zone in a residential area 150m (492 ft.) from the beach. The palm trees in this sector of Tossa evoke a real Mediterranean setting. Most of the midsize guest rooms, each with a tiled bathroom with shower and tub, have a balcony opening onto a view. Since some of the accommodations have three beds, the Canaima is also a family favorite. In lieu of its lack of amenities, it has a public phone, a bar with a TV, and a hotel safe.

Av. La Palma 24, 17320 Tossa de Mar. ©/fax **97-234-09-95.** www.hotelcanaima.com. 17 units. 60€–80€ ($78–$104) double. Rates include continental breakfast. AE, MC, V. Parking 5€ ($6.50). **Amenities:** Terrace bar. *In room:* Safe, no phone.

Hotel Cap d'Or ★ (Finds) Perched on the waterfront on a quiet edge of town, this 1790s building nestles against the stone walls and towers of the village castle. Built of rugged stone itself, the Cap d'Or is a combination of old country inn and seaside hotel. The guest rooms come in different shapes and sizes but are decently maintained, each with a good bed and a small bathroom with a shower stall. Although the hotel is a bed-and-breakfast, it does have a terrace on the promenade offering a quick meal.

Passeig de Vila Vella 1, 17320 Tossa de Mar. ©/fax **97-234-00-81.** www.hotelcapdor.com. 11 units. 80€–95€ ($104–$124) double. Rates include breakfast. MC, V. Closed Nov–Mar. **Amenities:** Restaurant; bar; laundry service; dry cleaning. *In room:* TV.

Hotel Diana ★ Set back from the esplanade, this government-rated two-star hotel is a former villa designed in part by students of Gaudí. It boasts the most elegant fireplace on the Costa Brava. An inner patio—with towering palms, vines, flowers, and fountains—is almost as popular with guests as the sandy front-yard beach. The spacious rooms contain fine traditional furnishings and bathrooms with shower stalls; many open onto private balconies.

Plaça Espanya 6, 17320 Tossa de Mar. © **97-234-18-86.** Fax 97-234-18-86. www.diana-hotel.com. 21 units. 80€–140€ ($104–$182) double; 120€–180€ ($156–$234) suite. Rates include breakfast. AE, DC, MC, V. Closed Nov–Apr. **Amenities:** Restaurant; bar; room service (breakfast). *In room:* A/C, TV, minibar, hair dryer.

Hotel Neptuno The popular Neptuno sits on a quiet residential hillside northwest of Vila Vella, somewhat removed from the seaside promenade and the bustle of Tossa de Mar's inner core. Built in the 1960s, the hotel was renovated and enlarged in the late 1980s. Inside, antiques are mixed with modern furniture. The beamed-ceiling dining room is charming. The guest rooms are tastefully lighthearted and modern, each with a good bed and a small bathroom with shower. This place is a longtime favorite with northern Europeans, who often book it solid during July and August.

La Guardia 52, 17320 Tossa de Mar. © **97-234-01-43.** Fax 97-234-19-33. www.ghthotels.com. 124 units. June–Sept 60€–120€ ($78–$156) per person double; off season 50€ ($65) per person double. Rates include breakfast. AE, DC, MC, V. Free parking. Closed Nov–Mar. **Amenities:** Restaurant; bar; outdoor pool; laundry service; dry cleaning. *In room:* A/C, TV, hair dryer, safe.

Hotel Tonet Opened in the early 1960s, in the earliest days of the region's tourist boom, this simple family-run pension is one of the resort's oldest. Renovated since then, it's on a central plaza surrounded by narrow streets and maintains the ambience of a country inn, with upper-floor terraces where you can relax amid potted vines and other plants. The small guest rooms are rustic, with wooden headboards, simple furniture, and bathrooms equipped with shower stalls. The Tonet maintains its own brand of Iberian charm.

Plaça de l'Església 1, 17320 Tossa de Mar. ℂ **97-234-02-37.** Fax 97-234-30-96. www.hoteltonet.com. 36 units. 70€ ($91) double; 95€ ($124) triple. Rates include breakfast. AE, DC, MC, V. Parking 10€ ($13) nearby. **Amenities:** Bar. *In room:* TV.

WHERE TO DINE

Bahía ★ CATALAN   Adjacent to the sea, Bahía is well known for a much-awarded chef and a history of feeding hungry vacationers since 1953. Menu favorites are for the most part based on time-honored Catalan traditions and include *simitomba* (a grilled platter of fish), *brandade* of cod, baked monkfish, and an array of grilled fish—including *salmonete* (red mullet), *dorada* (gilthead sea bream), and *calamares* (squid)—depending on what's available.

Passeig del Mar 29. ℂ **97-234-03-22.** Reservations recommended. Main courses 12€–36€ ($16–$47); *menú del día* 16€–32€ ($21–$42). AE, DC, MC, V. Daily 1–4:30pm and 7:30–11:30pm.

La Cuina de Can Simon ★★★ CATALAN   Some of the most sought-after dining tables in Tossa de Mar are within this charming, cozy, and intimate establishment containing only 18 seats. The antique, elegantly rustic stone-sided dining room was originally built in 1741. Its small size allows the hardworking staff to prepare some extremely esoteric courses. During the colder months, a fire might be burning in the stately-looking fireplace. Most diners select the *menu gastronómico,* consisting of six small courses that together make a memorable meal. Courses might include oven-roasted duckling with a sweet-and-sour sauce, crayfish-stuffed ravioli with Beluga caviar and truffle oil, or a monkfish suprême with scalloped potatoes and golden-fried sweet onions. One of the desserts we particularly fancied was an artfully arranged platter of ice cream, pastries, sauces, and tarts, each of which factored seasonal red fruits (strawberries, whortleberries, and currants) into its composition.

Portal 24. ℂ **97-234-12-69.** Reservations required. Main courses 18€–50€ ($23–$65); price-fixed menus 50€–70€ ($65–$91). AE, DC, MC, V. Wed–Mon 1–4pm and 8–11pm.

TOSSA DE MAR AFTER DARK

In Tossa de Mar's fast-changing nightlife, there's little stability or reliability. However, one place that's been in business for a while is the **Ely Club,** Carrer Bernat 2 (ℂ **97-234-00-09**). Fans from all over the Costa Brava come here to dance to up-to-date music. Daily hours are from 10pm to 5am between April 1 and October 15 only. In July and August, there's a one-drink minimum. The Ely Club is in the center of town between the two local cinemas.

7 SANT FELIU DE GUÍXOLS

110km (68 miles) N of Barcelona, 35km (22 miles) SE of Girona

Sant Feliu de Guíxols has a quiet dignity that befits its role as the official capital of the Costa Brava. Trade with Italy in past centuries may have given it what the late Catalan scribe Josep Pla described as an Italianite look, though—as he pointed out—it lacks the brighter colors of its Ligurian coastal counterparts. The once lucrative local activities of sardine fishing and cork production (with the natural product taken straight from the cork trees of the inland Gavarres forests) have waned, but it still gives the rare impression of a town that has a life of its own outside tourism. High-rise buildings have been kept to a commendable minimum and the elegant wide *Passeig Maritim* facing its enclosed sandy bay is lined with a blend of stylish cafes and impressive *moderniste* buildings. Three kilometers (2 miles) to the north, the crescent sandy area of Sant Pol adjoins the exclusive hotel resort area of S'Agaró and marvelous coastal path (Cami de Ronda) that leads past Sa Conca (another gem of a beach) to over-developed Platja d'Aro and then on as far as the sprawling port-resort of Palamós.

ESSENTIALS

GETTING THERE   The bus company SARFA (📞 **90-230-20-25;** www.sarfa.com) runs services from Plaça Urquinaona and the Estación Nort in Barcelona starting at 8am. Traveling time is 1 hour and 35 minutes and the one-way fare is 13€ ($17). From June to September coastal *cruceros* (pleasure cruisers) take the scenic sea route here from Blanes, Lloret, and Tossa. If you're renting a car and fancy an adrenaline-charging drive, try the clifftop coastal route from Tossa; it's 20km (12 miles) of twists and turns through pine-wooded headlands past dozens of tiny hidden coves. Movie buffs should check out *Pandora and the Flying Dutchman* (see "Tossa de Mar," above) and a lesser-known black-and-white 1950s thriller, *Chase a Crooked Shadow,* starring Anne Baxter and Richard Todd, for an idea of the thrill and spills involved.

VISITOR INFORMATION   The **Tourist Office** is in the Plaça del Merçat 28 (📞 **97-282-00-51**). It's open Monday through Saturday 10 am to 1pm and 4 to 7pm, Sunday 10am to 2pm.

WHAT TO SEE   The historic highlight is the 10th-century **Benedictine Monastery** (reconstructed 1723) at the southern end of the town, whose **Porta Ferrada** has three archways. The **Cultural Center** and **History Museum** exhibitions recall Sant Feliu's prosperous 19th-century cork and sardine days. Outside town, just off the Tossa road, the charming 19th-century **Chapel of Sant Elm** offers splendid panoramic coastal views.

WHERE TO STAY

Curhotel Hipócrates ★   Located halfway between Sant Feliu and S'Agaró and enjoying easy access to coastal walks, this large hotel prides itself on superb facilities, which range from steam baths to a well-equipped "aquagym." With over 2 decades of experience in the field of health treatments and therapies, it's an ideal place to relax and get in shape. Service is friendly and attentive and the comfortable rooms, each with en-suite bathroom with tub and shower, all have sea or mountain views.

Carretera Sant Pol 229, Sant Feliu de Guíxols (Girona). 📞 **97-232-06-62.** www.hipocratescurhotel.com. 92 units (88 doubles plus 4 suites). 140€–220€ ($182–$286) double; 230€–400€ ($299–$520) suite. AE, DC, MC, V. Free parking. **Amenities:** Restaurant; health food bar; outdoor pool; indoor pool; gym; fitness program; personalized therapies and diets; solarium; gardens; room service; laundry service. *In room:* A/C, TV, safe.

Hostal de la Gavina ★★★   This very chic Costa Brava hostelry is the grandest address in the northeast corridor of Spain. Since it opened in the early 1980s, the Hostal de la Gavina has attracted the rich and glamorous, including King Juan Carlos, Elizabeth Taylor, and a host of celebrities from northern Europe. It's on a peninsula jutting seaward from the center of S'Agaró, within a thick-walled Iberian villa built as the home of the Ansesa family (the hotel's owners) in 1932. Most of the accommodations are in the resort's main building, which has been enlarged and modified. The spacious guest rooms are the most sumptuous in the area, with elegant appointments and deluxe fabrics. Bathrooms contain plush towels, toiletries, and tub/shower combos.

Plaça de la Rosaleda, 17248 S'Agaró (Girona). 📞 **97-232-11-00.** Fax 97-232-15-73. www.lagavina.com. 74 units. 250€–375€ ($325–$488) double w/balcony; 300€–850€ ($390–$1,105) suite. AE, DC, MC, V. Free parking outside, garage 20€ ($26). Closed Nov–Apr. **Amenities:** 2 restaurants; 2 bars; pool; tennis courts; health club; whirlpool; sauna; room service; massage; babysitting; laundry service; dry cleaning. *In room:* A/C, TV, minibar, hair dryer, safe.

WHERE TO DINE

Casa Buxó ⓕⁱⁿᵈˢ CATALAN   Open to a grateful public since 1931, this welcoming family-run establishment in the center of Sant Feliu is now under its third generation of ownership. The kitchen is famed for its traditional Catalan starters such as *torrada amb escalivada i anxovies* (anchovy and pepper salad on toast) and first-rate main-course paella and *bacallà* (cod) dishes, all best accompanied by the house white Penedès wine.

Carrer Mayor 18, Sant Feliu de Guíxols (Girona). ⓒ **97-232-01-87.** Main courses 10€–24€ ($13–$31).

8 PALAFRUGELL & ITS BEACHES

124km (77 miles) N of Barcelona, 36km (22 miles) E of Girona

The prosperous but laid-back junction town of **Palafrugell** is noted for two things. First, it's the birthplace of Catalonia's most famous 20th-century regional chronicler, Josep Pla. Second, and of more interest to most hedonistically minded visitors, it's just a few kilometers away from three of the coast's most exquisite beach resorts, where the clear waters are a paradise for snorklers. **Calella de Palafrugell** (not to be confused with the characterless popular resort of Calella de la Costa further south on the *Maresme* coast between Blanes and Barcelona) is a white former fishing town with many attractive summer villas located just north of the charming **Cap Roig** gardens. From beneath the 19th-century archways of its diminutive Ses Voltes *paseo,* you look out past a series of sandy inlets and jutting rocks to the tiny offshore **Illes Formigues.** A 15-minute coastal walk north around the headland brings you to the sister resort of **Llafranch** with its single beach and yachting marina nestled below the clifftop lighthouse of San Sebastian. A couple of kilometers further north, isolated from these twin resorts, is one of Pla's favorite spots, **Tamariu,** a small sandy cove backed by delectable seafood restaurants.

ESSENTIALS

GETTING THERE   The bus company **SARFA** (ⓒ 90-230-20-25; www.sarfa.com) runs services from Plaça Urquinaona and the Estación Nort in Barcelona starting at 8:15am. Travel time is 2 hours and 15 minutes and the one-way fare is 15€ ($20). From Palafrugell bus station, there are half a dozen daily buses that run to Calella and Llafranch. A separate service runs three times a day to Tamariu. Each costs 1.20€ ($1.55) one-way and takes 10 to 15 minutes.

VISITOR INFORMATION   There's a tourism office at Carrilet 2 (ⓒ **97-230-02-28;** www.turismepalafrugell.org). It's open daily from 10am to 1pm and 4 to 7pm.

WHAT TO SEE   In **Palafrugell** the Sunday open **market** is one of the best on the coast, and if you want to check out the rather esoteric Josep Pla literary route, visit the **Fundación Josep Pla,** Carrer Nou 49–51 (ⓒ **97-230-55-77**).

WHERE TO STAY

El Far de Sant Sebastià ★   This highly individual little hotel stands next to a restored medieval watchtower and an 18th-century hermitage on a promontory overlooking both Calella de Palafrugell and Llafranc. Named after the lighthouse that towers amid the wooded hills on the cliff edge above, the hotel is an ideal spot for relaxing and enjoying the best of Costa Brava coastal scenery. It's open year round and has a fine restaurant where you can sample typical Empordà cuisine, ranging from fresh seafood to hearty stews.

Platja de Llafran s/n, Llafranc (Girona). ✆ **97-230-43-28.** 10 units (9 doubles and 1 suite). 160€–200€ ($208–$260) double; 260€ ($338) suite. AE, DC, MC, V. **Amenities:** Restaurant; lounge; gardens; terrace overlooking sea. *In room:* A/C, TV, minibar, hair dryer, safe.

Mas de Torrent ★★★ Just a few minutes' drive inland from **Palafrugell,** this member of Relais & Châteaux was elegantly created from a 1751 farmstead *(masía).* In the hamlet of Torrent, Mas de Torrent is one of the most artful and best hotels in Spain. Try for one of the 10 rooms in the original farmhouse, with its massive beams and spacious

A Room with a View

Radiating out around the hilltop town of **Begur,** just 6km (3¾ miles) to the north of Palafrugell, is a series of idyllic sandy coves that epitomize the very best the "Rugged Coast" has to offer: pines, rocks, secluded inlets with hidden caves that can only even now be reached by boat, and tiny resorts with evocative names like **Sa Tuna, Aigua Xelida,** and **Aigua Blava** that vie with the Palafrugell resorts for the title of most beautiful spot on the coast. Access is difficult unless you have a car, with only occasional buses running from Bagur. Should you decide to stay overnight, don't miss the chance to stay at one of the most dramatically located hotels in Spain: the clifftop **Parador Hotel de Aiguablava** (✆ **97-262-21-62;** www.parapromotions-spain.com/parador/spain/aiguablava.html), where a double will cost from 175€ to 280€ ($228–$364), and the Mediterranean vistas through the surrounding pines are out of this world. Book well ahead.

Nature on the Costa Brava

The **Illes Medes,** located a mile offshore from the small fishing port-turned-pop resort of **Estartit,** are a miniature limestone archipelago of seven islets and one lighthouse whose surrounding waters are a protected ecosystem. Here, divers can search for coral and rich aquatic life that includes lobsters and octopus. In summer you can take trips by glass-bottom boat from Estartit. For more information, contact the **Estartit-Medes Islands Water Sports Station** at ✆ **97-275-06-99** or visit www.enestartit.com.

Further north on the Costa Brava, above the ancient Roman town of Empúries, is another wildlife sanctuary: the 4,800-hectare (11,861-acre) nature reserve of **Aiguamolls de l'Empordà** natural park (✆ **97-245-42-22;** www.parcsdecatalunya.net), located near the town of **Sant Pere Pescador.** Amateur ornithologists should note that it's the best area in Catalonia for bird-watching. The watery areas also shelter turtles and otters.

Greeks & Romans in Empúries

Close to the fishing port of **L'Escala,** a 20-minute stroll along the shore of the wide Bay of Rosas, is **Empúries,** evocative site of the best Greco-Roman remains in Spain. It dates back to 600 B.C., when it was founded by Phoenicians, shortly to be followed by the Greeks, who built a town they called Neapolis (replacing their initial settlement of Paleopolis, which is now covered by the sea). The township flourished until the Romans arrived in A.D. 2, but as Barcino (Barcelona) and Tarraco (Tarragona) assumed more importance, its decline began. Today you can clearly see traces of the shoreside Greek agora harbor and fish salting area, and the impressive Roman walls, amphitheater, forum, and Paleochristian basilica. You may even feel nostalgia for a past you never knew as you wander among its crumbling pillars, fading mosaics, and paved walkways, enjoying the timeless environment of land, sea, and sky. Modern amenities include a museum and small cafe, plus an information booth beside the parking lot where you can get an audio guide to the site. For more information, visit www.cbrava.com/empuries/empuries.uk.htm.

bathrooms with deep tubs and power showers. The rooms in the more modern, bungalow-style annex are just as comfortable but lack the mellow old atmosphere. From the rooms' stone balconies, visitors can enjoy vistas of the countryside, with Catalonian vineyards in the distance. In the restaurant, the chef focuses mainly on the classic dishes of Catalonia, including monkfish in saffron or fine noodles simmered in fish consommé and served with fresh shellfish.

Afueras de Torrent, Torrent 17123 (Girona). ✆ **97-230-32-92.** Fax 97-230-32-93. www.mastorrent.com. 39 units. 295€–395€ ($384–$514) double; 475€–600€ ($618–$780) suite. Rates include breakfast. AE, DC, MC, V. Free parking. 37km (23 miles) east of Girona. **Amenities:** 2 restaurants; 2 bars; pool; tennis court; room service; babysitting; laundry; room for those w/limited mobility. *In room:* A/C, TV, minibar, hair dryer, safe.

WHERE TO DINE

La Casona   This well-regarded restaurant is situated in the heart of the town and is a favorite with visitors and locals alike. The setting is homey and the service first-rate. Main dishes include regional specialties like *suquet de peix* (seafood stew) and *pollastre pagès amb sepia i escarlamans* (country-style chicken with squid and langoustines).

Paratge de la Seulada 4, Palafrugell (Girona). ✆ **97-230-36-61.** Main courses 22€–30€ ($29–$39). Lunch only on Sun. Closed Mon.

9 FIGUERES

36km (24 miles) N of Girona, 136km (102 miles) N of Barcelona

The sleepy, laid-back capital of the northerly Alt Empordá region of Catalonia, **Figueres** once played a role in Spanish history. Philip V wed María Luisa of Savoy here in 1701 in the church of San Pedro, thereby paving the way for the War of the Spanish Succession. But that historical fact is nearly forgotten today: The town is better known as the birthplace of surrealist artist Salvador Dalí in 1904. In view of the lack of other worthy sights in the town, most people stay only a day in Figueres, using Girona, Cadaqués, or any of the other towns along the Costa Brava as a base.

ESSENTIALS

GETTING THERE   RENFE, the national railway of Spain, has an hourly **train** service between Barcelona and Figueres, stopping off at Girona along the way. All trains between Barcelona and France stop here as well.

Figueres is a $1^1/_2$- to 2-hour **drive** from Barcelona. Take the excellent north-south A-7 and exit at the major turnoff to Figueres.

VISITOR INFORMATION   The **tourist office** is at the Plaça del Sol s/n (© **97-250-31-55;** www.figueresciutat.com). From November until Easter, hours are Monday through Friday, 8:30am to 3pm. From Easter to the end of June and October, the office is open Monday through Friday from 8:30am to 3pm and 4:30 to 8pm, Saturday 9:30am to 1:30pm and 3:30 to 6:30pm. From July to August, it's open Monday to Friday 8:30am to 9pm, Saturday 9am to 9pm and Sunday 9am to 3pm. In September, it's open Monday to Friday 8:30am to 8pm and Saturday 9am to 8pm.

VISITING DALI

Casa-Museu Castell Gala Dalí ★★ (Finds)   For additional insights into the often bizarre aesthetic sensibilities of Spain's most famous surrealist, consider a 40km (25-mile) trek from Figueres eastward along highway C-252, following the signs to Parlava. In the village of Púbol, whose permanent population almost never exceeds 200, you'll find the Castell de Púbol. Dating from A.D. 1000, the rustic stone castle was partially in ruin when bought by Dalí as a residence for his estranged wife, Gala, in 1970, on the condition that he'd come only when she invited him. (She almost never did.) After her death in 1982, Dalí moved in for 2 years, moving on to other residences in 1984 after his bedroom mysteriously caught fire one night. Quieter, more serious, and much less surrealistically flamboyant than the other Dalí buildings in Port Lligat and Figueres, the castle is noteworthy for its severe Gothic and Romanesque dignity and for furniture and decor that follow the tastes of the surrealist master. Don't expect a lot of paintings—that's the specialty of the museum at Figueres—but do expect a fascinating insight into one of the most famous muses of the 20th century.

Carrer Gala Salvador Dalí s/n. © **97-248-86-55.** www.salvador-dali.org/museus. Admission 7€ ($9.10) adults, 5€ ($6.50) students, free for children 9 and under. June 15–Sept 15 Tues–Sun 10:30am–8pm; Mar 13–June 14 and Sept 16–Nov 1 Tues–Sun 10:30am–6pm; Nov 2–Dec 31 Tues–Sun 10am–5pm. Closed Jan 1–Mar 12.

Teatre-Museu Dalí ★★★   The internationally known artist Dalí was as famous for his surrealist and often erotic imagery as he was for his flamboyance and exhibitionism. At the Figueres museum, in the center of town beside the Rambla, you'll find his paintings, watercolors, gouaches, charcoals, and pastels, along with graphics and sculptures, many rendered with seductive and meticulously detailed imagery. His wide-ranging subject matter encompassed such repulsive issues as putrefaction and castration. You'll see, for instance, *The Happy Horse,* a grotesque and lurid purple beast the artist painted during one of his long exiles at Port Lligat. A tour of the museum is an experience. When a catalog was prepared, Dalí said with a perfectly straight face, "It is necessary that all of the people who come out of the museum have false information."

Plaça de Gala Dalí 5. © **97-267-75-00.** Admission 11€ ($14) adults, 8€ ($10) students and seniors, free for children 9 and under. July 1–Sept 30 daily 9am–8pm; Oct 1–Oct 30 and Mar 1–Jun 30 Tues–Sun 9:30am–6pm; Nov 1–Feb 28 Tues–Sun 10:30am–6pm. Closed Jan 1 and Dec 25.

The Mad, Mad World of Salvador Dalí

Salvador Dalí (1904–89) became one of the leading exponents of surrealism, depicting irrational imagery of dreams and delirium in a unique, meticulously detailed style. Famous for his eccentricity, he was called "outrageous, talented, relentlessly self-promoting, and unfailingly quotable." At his death at age 84, he was the last survivor of the three famous *enfants terribles* of Spain (the poet García Lorca and the filmmaker Luis Buñuel were the other two).

For all his international renown, Dalí was born in Figueres and died in Figueres. Most of his works are in the eponymous theater-museum there, built by the artist himself around the former theater where his first exhibition was held. Dalí was also buried in the theater-museum, next door to the church that witnessed both his christening and his funeral—the first and last acts of a perfectly planned scenario.

Salvador Felipe Jacinto Dalí i Domènech, the son of a highly respected notary, was born on May 11, 1904, in a house on Carrer Monturiol in Figueres. In 1922 he registered at the School of Fine Arts in Madrid and went to live at the prestigious Residencia de Estudiantes. There, his friendship with García Lorca and Buñuel had a more enduring effect on his artistic future than his studies at the school. As a result of his undisciplined behavior and the attitude of his father, who clashed with the Primo de Rivera dictatorship over a matter related to elections, the young Dalí spent a month in prison.

In the summer of 1929, the artist René Magritte, along with the poet Paul Eluard and his wife, Gala, came to stay at Cadaqués, and their visit caused sweeping changes in Dalí's life. The young painter became enamored of Eluard's wife; Dalí left his family and fled with Gala to Paris, where he became an enthusiastic member of the surrealist movement. Some of his most famous paintings—*The Great Masturbator, Lugubrious Game,* and *Portrait of Paul*

10 CADAQUÉS ★★

196km (122 miles) N of Barcelona, 31km (19 miles) E of Figueres

Cadaqués is still unspoiled and remote, despite the publicity it received when Salvador Dalí lived in the next-door village of Port Lligat in a split-level house surmounted by a giant egg. The last resort on the Costa Brava before the French border, Cadaqués is reached by a small winding road, twisting over the mountains from Rosas, the nearest major center. When you get to Cadaqués, you really feel you're off the beaten path and miles from anywhere. The village winds around half a dozen small coves, with a narrow street running along the water's edge.

Scenically, Cadaqués is a knockout: crystal-blue water, fishing boats on the sandy beaches, old whitewashed houses, narrow twisting streets, and a 16th-century parish up on a hill.

ESSENTIALS
GETTING THERE   There are three **buses** per day that run from Figueres to Cadaqués (11am, 1pm, and 7:15pm). Trip time is 1¼ hours. The service is operated by SARFA

Eluard—date from his life at Port Lligat, the small Costa Brava town where he lived and worked off and on during the 1930s.

Following Dalí's break with the tenets of the surrealist movement, his work underwent a radical change, with a return to classicism and what he called his mystical and nuclear phase. He became one of the most fashionable painters in the United States and seemed so intent on self-promotion that the surrealist poet André Breton baptized him with the anagram "Avida Dollars." Dalí wrote a partly fictitious autobiography titled *The Secret Life of Salvador Dalí* and *Hidden Faces*, a novel containing autobiographical elements. These two short literary digressions earned him still greater prestige and wealth, as did his collaborations in the world of cinema (such as the dream set for Alfred Hitchcock's *Spellbound,* 1945) and in those of theater, opera, and ballet.

On August 8, 1958, Dalí and Gala were married according to the rites of the Catholic Church in a ceremony performed in the strictest secrecy at the shrine of Els Angels, just a few miles from Girona.

During the 1960s, Dalí painted some very large works, such as *The Battle of Tetuán.* Another important work painted at this period is *Railway Station at Perpignan,* a painting that relates this center of Dalí's mythological universe to his obsession with painter Jean-François Millet's *The Angelus.*

In 1979 Dalí's health began to decline, and he retired to Port Lligat in a state of depression. When Gala died, he moved to Púbol, where, obsessed by the theory of catastrophes, he painted his last works, until he suffered severe burns in a fire that nearly cost him his life. Upon recovery, he moved to the Torre Galatea, a building he had bought as an extension to the museum in Figueres. Here he lived for 5 more years, hardly ever leaving his room, until his death in 1989.

(© **97-225-87-13;** www.sarfa.com), which also runs a twice-daily service directly from Barcelona which takes 2¹/₄ hours along the inland highway.

VISITOR INFORMATION   The **tourist office,** Cotxe 2A (© **97-225-83-15**), is open Monday through Saturday from 10:30am to 1pm and 4:30 to 7:30pm.

SEEING THE SIGHTS

Casa-Museu Salvador Dalí Portlligat ★★ (Moments)   This fascinating private

home-turned-museum completes (along with the Teatre-Museu Dalí and the Casa-Museu Castell Gala Dalí) the touted "Dalían Triangle" of northern Catalonia. The structure, home to the Dalís for over 40 years, lies in the tiny fishing port of Port Lligat and is surrounded by the eerie rock and coastal formations that feature heavily in his work. If walking from the town center, 15 minutes away, your first glimpse of the museum will be of the oversize white eggs that adorn the roof. Inside, the home has been pretty much left as it was when it was inhabited, with the expected eclectic collections of Dalían objects, art, and icons thrown together in surrealist fashion. The swimming pool and terrace, where Dalí threw many of his legendary parties in the '70s, is the highlight. The museum doesn't have a proper address, but you can't miss it.

(C) **97-225-10-15.** www.salvador-dali.org./museus. Admission 10€ ($13) adults, 8€ ($10) students and seniors, free for children 9 and under. Mid-Mar to mid-June and mid-Sep to Jan 6 Tues–Sun 10:30am–6pm; mid-June to mid-Sept daily 9:30am–9pm. Closed Jan 7 to mid-Mar.

WHERE TO STAY

Hotel Playa Sol ★   In a relatively quiet section of the port along the bay, this 1950s hotel offers a great view of the stone church that has become the town's symbol; it's located at the distant edge of the harbor and overlooks the bay of Cadaqués. Many of the rooms have balconies looking right onto the bay (specify when booking) and the smallish rooms are comfortably furnished. Most of the bathrooms have tub/shower combos. The hotel doesn't have an official restaurant, but it does offer lunch from June 15 to September 15 and breakfast all year round. The swimming pool is a definite plus.

Platja Planch 3, 17488 Cadaqués. (C) 97-225-81-00. Fax 97-225-80-54. www.playasol.com. 50 units. 110€–190€ ($143–$247) double. AE, DC, MC, V. Parking 8€ ($10). Closed Jan–Feb. **Amenities:** Bar; outdoor pool; outdoor tennis court; bike rental; limited room service. *In room:* A/C, TV.

Llane Petit ★★ (Value)   This is a little inn of considerable charm lying below the better-known Hotel Rocamar opening right onto the beach. A hospitable place, it offers decent-size and well-maintained bathrooms with both tubs and showers. All accommodations open onto a little terrace. The owners keep the hotel under constant renovation during the slow months so it's always fresh again when the summer hordes descend. Try to patronize the hotel's little dinner-only restaurant, as the cuisine is well prepared and most affordable.

Platja Llane Petit s/n, 17488 Cadaqués. (C) **97-225-10-20.** Fax 97-225-87-78. www.llanepetit.com. 37 units. 75€–135€ ($98–$176). AE, DC, MC, V. Rates include breakfast in off season. Free parking. Closed Jan 9–Feb 21. **Amenities:** Restaurant; bar; limited room service; laundry service; dry cleaning. *In room:* A/C, TV, safe.

Rocamar ★★   On the beach, this government-rated three-star hotel is one of the better choices in town, attracting a fun-loving crowd of young northern Europeans in the summer. All the accommodations are well furnished, with rustic yet comfortable pieces, along with small and neatly kept bathrooms with both tubs and showers. The rooms in front have balconies opening onto the sea; those in back have balconies with views of the mountains and beyond. The hotel is known for its good food served at affordable prices.

Doctor Bartomeus s/n, 17488 Cadaqués. (C) **97-225-81-50.** Fax 97-225-86-50. www.rocamar.com. 71 units. 100€–185€ ($130–$241) double; 200€–275€ ($260–$358) suite. Rates include breakfast. DC, MC, V. Free parking. **Amenities:** Restaurant; bar; indoor pool; outdoor pool; tennis court; sauna; morning room service; massage; babysitting; laundry service; dry cleaning. *In room:* A/C, TV, safe.

WHERE TO DINE

Es Trull (Value) SEAFOOD   On the harborside street in the center of town, this cedar-shingled cafeteria is named for the ancient olive press dominating the interior. A filling fixed-price meal is served. According to the chef, if it comes from the sea and can be eaten, he'll prepare it with that special Catalan flair. You might try mussels in marinara sauce, grilled hake, or natural baby clams. Rice dishes are a specialty—not only paella but also black rice colored with squid ink and rice with calamari and shrimp.

Port Ditxos s/n. (C) **97-225-81-96.** Reservations recommended in high season. Main courses 10€–32€ ($13–$42). AE, DC, MC, V. Daily 12:30–4pm and 7–11pm. Closed Nov–Easter.

The Most Famous Chef in the World

Ferran Adrià has been hailed not just as the most exciting chef in Spain, but also in the entire world. The press has dubbed him the "Salvador Dalí of the kitchen" because of his creative, wholly high-tech approach to cookery that challenges the concept of food as we know it. He operates his luxe **El Bulli,** Cala Montjoi (© **97-215-04-57;** www.elbulli.com), out of an old farmhouse in the little hamlet of Roses near Cadaqués, but that doesn't stop hoards of discerning international palates from seeking him out, having waited perhaps a year for the privilege. Michelin grants it three stars, an accolade most often reserved for the top restaurants of Paris.

Your only option is to order the 30-course set menu, which changes each season. You never know what's going to appear, but anticipate the most delightful surprises, based on what's the finest produce in any given month. Adrià is an alchemist in the kitchen. Originally hailed for his array of savory "foams," an idea that has now been pirated by top restaurants from Miami to Melbourne, he is constantly experimenting with the composition of food; thus, a pea soup is made into tiny, solid droplets through a process using calcium chloride and basil, pulped into an edible "paper," and served with calamari "seeds" and a mandarin concentrate. You anticipate you're in for a delightful evening at the beginning when you're given addictive little dishes of polenta chips and caramelized sunflower seeds. Your *amuse-bouche* might be a "cappuccino" of guacamole. One dish alone should give Adrià culinary immortality: his lasagna of calamari.

The *menú de degustación* is 150€ ($195) per person. American Express, MasterCard, and Visa are accepted. The restaurant is open from Easter to the end of September. To get there from Girona, take N-1 north to Figueres, then Route 260 east to Roses, for a total of 56km (35 miles).

La Galiota ★★ CATALAN/FRENCH Dozens of surrealist paintings, including some by Dalí, adorn the walls of this award-winning restaurant, the finest in town. On a sloping street below the cathedral, the place has a downstairs sitting room and a dining room converted from what was a private house. Dalí himself was a patron (his favorite meal was cheese soufflé and chicken roasted with apples) and the chef's secret is in selecting only the freshest of ingredients and preparing them in a way that enhances their natural flavors. The roast leg of lamb, flavored with garlic, is a specialty. The marinated salmon is also excellent, as are the sea bass and the sole with orange sauce.

Carrer Narciso Monturiol 9. © **97-225-81-87.** Reservations required. Main courses 18€–30€ ($23–$39). AE, DC, MC, V. Daily 1:30–3:30pm and 8:30–10:30pm. Closed Oct to mid-June.

A Side Trip to Majorca

Majorca (pronounced "mah-yohr-kah") is the most popular of Spain's beautiful quartet of Balearic Islands, which also include Minorca, Ibiza, and Formentera. One of the Mediterranean's great tourist success stories, this island annually attracts millions of visitors who come to enjoy its fine climate and multitude of holiday attractions. But some visitors also come to savor its unexpectedly unspoiled and peaceful areas. The mountainous northwest is covered with untouched olive groves, and the fertile central flatlands, which are dotted with windmills, boast millions of almond trees that burst into a sea of white blossoms in early spring.

About 209km (130 miles) from Barcelona and 145km (90 miles) from Valencia, Majorca has a coastline 500km (311 miles) long. Palma is the charming monument-filled capital, flanked by the Bay of Palma. The golden sands of Majorca are famous, with highly overbuilt pleasure beaches such as El Arenal and Magaluf spreading out in separate bays on either side of Palma. These tend to be chock-full of sun worshippers on package tours, while more isolated inlets, such as Cala de San Vincente, a pine-shrouded cove overlooked by high precipices 6.5km (4 miles) from Port of Pollença, offer almost total seclusion.

ISLAND ESSENTIALS

GETTING THERE At certain times of the year, the trip by boat or plane can be pleasant, but in August these routes to Palma must surely qualify as the major bottleneck in Europe. Don't travel without advance reservations, and be sure you have a return plane ticket if you come in August—otherwise you may not get off the island until September!

Iberia (© **90-240-05-00;** www.iberia.com) flies to Palma's Aeroport Son San Joan (© **97-178-90-00**) from Barcelona, Valencia, and Madrid. There are daily planes from Madrid and Barcelona year round, with increased numbers in summer. **Spanair** (© **90-213-14-15;** www.spanair.com) flies into Palma from Barcelona and from Madrid, Bilbao, Minorca, Santiago de Compostela, Málaga, and Tenerife. **Air Europa** (© 90-240-15-01; www.aireuropa.com) also flies to Palma from Barcelona up to twice a day during peak season. There are also flights to the island from Madrid, Minorca, Ibiza, and Seville.

Countless charter flights also make the run. Bookings are very tight in August, and delays of at least 24 hours, sometimes more, are common. If you're flying—say, Iberia—on a transatlantic flight from New York to Madrid or Barcelona, you should have Majorca written into your ticket before your departure if you plan to visit the Balearics as part of your Spanish itinerary.

(Tips) Not an Island for All Seasons

July and August are high season for Majorca; don't even think of coming then without a reservation. It's possible to swim comfortably from June to October; after that it's prohibitively cold.

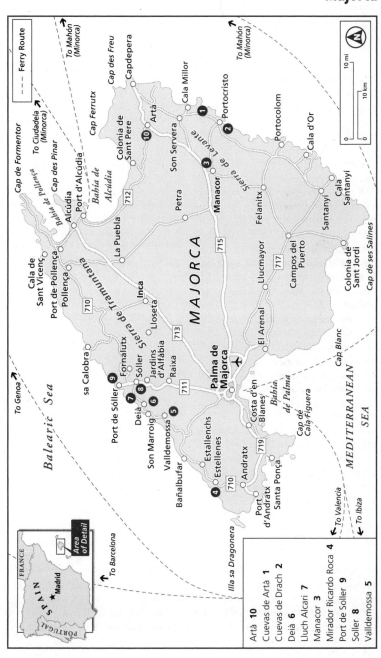

Ferry Route

To Mahón (Minorca)

To Ciudadela (Minorca)

To Mahón (Minorca)

Cap de Formentor

Cap des Pinar

Cap de Freu

Capdepera

Cap Ferrutx

Portocristo

Artà

Cala Millor

Son Servera

Colonia de Sant Pere

Portocolom

Cala d'Or

Cap des Salines

Sierra de Levante

Manacor

Felanitx

Santanyí

Cala Santanyí

Colonia de Sant Jordi

Cap de Formentor

Cala de Sant Vicenç

Port de Pollença

Pollença

Alcúdia

Port d'Alcúdia

Babia de Alcúdia

La Puebla

Petra

Campos del Puerto

MAJORCA

Inca

Lloseta

Llucmajor

El Arenal

Sierra de Tramuntana

sa Calobra

Fornalutx

Sóller

Port de Sóller

Jardins d'Alfàbia

Raixa

Palma de Majorca

Babia de Palma

Cap Blanc

MEDITERRANEAN SEA

To Genoa

Balearic Sea

Deià

Son Marroig

Valldemossa

Estallenchs

Estellenes

Bañalbufar

Andratx

Port d'Andratx

Santa Ponça

Costa d'en Blanes

Cap de Cala-Figuera

To Valencia

To Ibiza

Illa sa Dragonera

To Barcelona

Area of Detail

FRANCE

SPAIN

Madrid

PORTUGAL

To Barcelona

10 mi

10 km

Artà 10
Cuevas de Artà 1
Cuevas de Drach 2
Deià 6
Lluch Alcari 7
Manacor 3
Mirador Ricardo Roca 4
Port de Sóller 9
Sóller 8
Valldemossa 5

From Palma de Majorca–Son San Joan airport, bus no. 1 takes you to Plaça Espanya in the center of Palma from 5:30am to 2:15pm daily; the trip takes about 30 minutes and costs 2.50€ ($3.25). A metered cab charges from 25€ ($33) for the 25-minute drive into the city.

Trasmediterránea, Estació Marítim in Palma (© **90-245-46-45;** www. trasmediterranea.es), operates a daily **ferry** from Barcelona, taking 8 hours and costing from 60€ ($78) one-way. Tickets can be booked at the Trasmediterránea office at Estació Marítim in Barcelona (© **90-245-46-45**). Any travel agent in Spain can also book you a seat. Schedules and departure times (subject to change) should always be checked and double-checked.

GETTING AROUND At the tourist office in Palma, you can pick up a **bus** schedule that explains island routes. Or contact **Empresa Municipal de Transports** (© 97-175-22-45 or 90-250-78-50; www. emtpalma.es), a company that runs city buses from its main terminal, Estació Central D'Autobus, Plaça Espanya. The standard one-way fare is 1.20€ ($1.55) within Palma; at the station you can buy a booklet good for 10 rides, costing 7€ ($9.10). For buses covering the whole island, contact **TIB** (Transport de les Illes Balears; © 97-117-77-77; tib.caib.es). Buses leave the d'Eusebi Estada station for towns all over the island, including Manacor and Porto Cristo (for the Caves of Drach) in the east,

to Deya (45 min.), Valldemossa (30 min.), Sóller, and Pollença (1 hr. each) in the north and northwest. Fares range from 3€ to 6€ ($3.90–$7.80) one-way, depending on the distance.

Ferrocarril de Sóller, Carrer Eusebio Estada 1 (© **97-175-20-51;** www. trendesoller.com), off Plaça Espanya, is a **train** service operating between Palma and Sóller that makes for an unforgettable journey passing through majestic mountain scenery. Trains run from 8am to 7pm, and a ticket costs 9€ ($12) one-way or 14€ ($18) round-trip.

Another train runs to Inca; it's often called the "Leather Express" because most passengers are onboard to buy inexpensive leather goods in the Inca shops. **Servicios Ferroviarios de Mallorca** leaves from Plaça Espanya (© 97-175-22-45 for more information and schedules). The train ride is only 40 minutes, with 40 departures per day Monday through Saturday and 32 per day on Sunday. A one-way fare costs 3€ ($3.90). For a **taxi,** call © 97-175-54-40.

If you plan to stay in Palma, you don't need a car. The city is extremely traffic-clogged, and parking is scarce. However, if you do choose to drive, you can rent cars at such companies as **Europa Car Rental,** at the airport terminal (© 95-615-01-38), where rentals range from 57€ to 100€ ($74–$130) per day. Both **Atesa** and **Avis** maintain offices at the airport. Reservations should always be made in advance.

1 PALMA DE MAJORCA ★★

Palma, on the southern tip of the island, is the seat of the autonomous government of the Balearic Islands, as well as the center for most of Majorca's hotels, restaurants, and nightclubs. Founded by the Romans in 123 B.C., the Moors later constructed Palma in the style of a Casbah, or walled city. Its foundations are still visible, although obscured by the high-rise hotels that line the Paseo Maritimo.

Old Palma is characterized by the area immediately surrounding the cathedral. Mazes of narrow alleys and cobblestone streets recall the era when Palma was one of the chief ports in the Mediterranean.

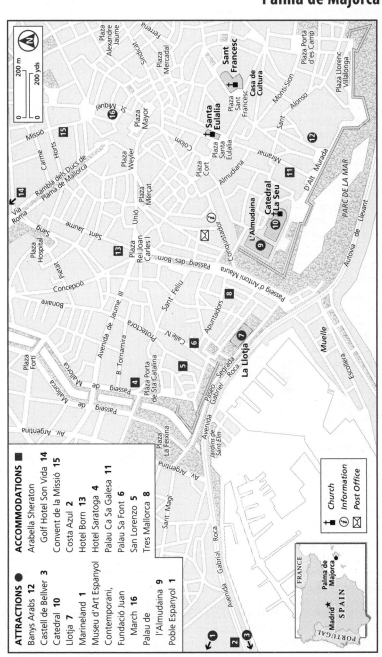

ATTRACTIONS ●

Banys Arabs **12**
Castell de Bellver **3**
Catedral **10**
Llotja **7**
Marineland **1**
Museu d'Art Espanyol
Contemporani,
Fundació Juan
March **16**
Palau de
l'Almudaina **9**
Poble Espanyol **1**

ACCOMMODATIONS ■

Arabella Sheraton
Golf Hotel Son Vida **14**
Convent de la Missió **15**
Costa Azul **2**
Hotel Born **13**
Hotel Saratoga **4**
Palau Ca Sa Galesa **11**
Palau Sa Font **6**
San Lorenzo **5**
Tres Mallorca **8**

Church
Information
Post Office

Today the Majorcan capital is a bustling city whose massive tourist industry has more than made up for its decline as a major seaport. It's estimated that nearly half the island's population lives in Palma, which has miraculously managed to retain much of its original charm and character. The islanders call Palma simply "Ciutat" (City), and as the largest of the Balearic ports, its bay is often clogged with yachts. Arrival by sea is the most impressive, with the skyline dominated by the turrets of Bellver Castle and the cathedral's Gothic bulk.

ESSENTIALS

VISITOR INFORMATION The **National Tourist Office** is in Palma at Plaça Reyna 2 (© **97-171-22-16**). It's open Monday to Friday 9am to 8pm, and Saturday 9am to 2pm.

GETTING AROUND In Palma, you can get around the Old Town and the *paseo* on foot. Otherwise, you can make limited use of taxis, or take one of the buses that cut across the city. Out on the island, you'll have to depend mainly on buses or rented cars.

FAST FACTS The **U.S. Consulate,** Edificio Reina Constanza, Porto Pi, B, 9D (© **97-140-37-07**), is open from 10:30am to 1:30pm Monday to Friday. The **British Consulate,** Plaça Mayor 3D (© **97-171-24-45**), is open from 9am to 2pm Monday to Friday.

In case of an **emergency,** dial © **112.** If you fall ill, head to **Clínica Rotger,** Calle Santiago Rusiñol 9 (© **97-171-66-00**), or **Clínica Juaneda,** Calle Son Espanyolet 55 (© **97-173-16-47**). Both clinics are open 24 hours.

For **Internet access,** go to **Babaloo,** Calle Verja 2 (© **97-195-77-25;** www.babaloo internet.com), just off Calle Sant Magi. It charges 2.50€ ($3.25) per hour and is open Monday to Saturday 10am to 10pm and Sunday 3 to 10pm.

Majorca observes the same **holidays** as the rest of Spain but also celebrates June 29, the Feast of Saint Peter, the patron saint of all fishers.

The central **post office** is at Constitución 6 (© **97-172-70-54** or 90-219-71-97). Hours are Monday to Friday 8:30am to 8:30pm, and Saturday 9:30am to 2pm.

FUN ON & OFF THE BEACH

There is a beach fairly close to the cathedral in Palma, but some readers have been discouraged from swimming here because of the pollution nearby. The closest public beach is **Playa Nova,** a 35-minute bus ride from downtown Palma. Some hotels, however, have private beaches. If you head east, you reach the excellent beaches of **Ca'n Pastilla** and **El Arenal;** both are very well equipped with tourist facilities. Going to the southwest, you find good but often crowded beaches at **Cala Mayor** and **Sant Agustí.**

You can swim from late June to October; don't believe the promoters who try to sell you on mild Majorcan winters in January and February—it can get downright cold. Spring and fall can be heaven sent, and in summer the coastal areas are pleasantly cooled by sea breezes.

ⓘ Tips Where to Get Those Phone Cards

Local newsstands and tobacco shops sell phone cards valued between 3€ and 15€ ($3.90–$20). They can be used in any public telephone booth, and they allow you to make both domestic and international calls.

GOLF Majorca is a golfer's dream. The best course is Son Vida Club de Golf, Urbanización Son Vida, about 13km (8 miles) east of Palma along the Andrade Highway. This 18-hole course is shared by the guests of the island's two best hotels, Arabella Golf Hotel and Son Vida. However, the course is open to all players who call for reservations (© **97-179-12-10;** www.sonvidagolf.com). Greens fees range from 65€ to 80€ ($85–$104) for hotel guests and 90€ ($117) for nonguests for 18 holes. Golf-cart rentals are also available for 45€ ($59).

There are many golf courses on the island. For information about them, contact **Federación Balear de Golf,** Av. Jaime III no. 17, Palma (© **97-172-27-53;** www.fbgolf.com).

HIKING Because of the hilly terrain in Majorca, this sport is better pursued here than on Ibiza or Minorca. The mountains of the northwest, the Serra de Tramuntana, are best for exploring. The tourist office (see above) will provide you with a free booklet called *20 Hiking Excursions on the Island of Majorca.* For hiking information, contact **Grup Excursionista de Mallorca,** the Majorcan Hiking Association, at Carrer Andreu Feliu 20 in Palma (© **87-194-79-00;** www.gemweb.org).

TENNIS If your hotel doesn't have a court, head for the **Club de Tenis,** Carrer Sil s/n (© **97-169-22-61**).

WATERSPORTS Most beaches have outfitters who will rent you windsurfers and dinghies. The best outfitter is **Escola d'Esports Nàutics,** Paseo Playa d'en Repic, at Port de Sóller (© **97-163-30-01;** www.nauticsoller.com).

SHOPPING

Stores in Palma offer handicrafts, elegant leather goods, Majorcan pearls, and fine needlework. The best shopping is on the following streets: San Miguel, Carrer Sindicato, Jaume II, Jaume III, Carrer Platería, Vía Roman, and Passeig des Borne, plus the streets radiating from the Borne all the way to Plaça Cort, where the city hall stands. Most shops close on Saturday afternoon and Sunday.

The famous **Casa Bonet ★★★**, Plaça Federico Chopin 2 (© **97-172-21-17**), founded in 1860, sells finely textured needlework. The sheets, tablecloths, napkins, and pillowcases are made in Majorca from fine linen or cotton (or less expensive acrylic). Many are hand-embroidered, using ancient designs and floral motifs popularized by this establishment.

Loewe, Av. Jaume III no. 1 (© **97-171-52-75**), offers fine leather, elegant accessories for men and women, luggage, and chic apparel for women.

Perlas Majorica, Av. Jaume III no. 1 (© **97-171-21-59**), is the authorized agency for the authentic Majorcan pearl. The pearl producers offer a decade-long guarantee for their products. Pearls come in varied sizes and settings. Palma's leading department store, **El Corte Inglés 3,** Av. Jaume III no. 15 (© **97-177-01-77;** www.elcorteingles.es), stocks an exceptional collection of Majorcan handicrafts.

SEEING THE SIGHTS

Most visitors don't spend much time exploring the historic sights in Palma, but there are a number of places to see if you've had too much sun.

Viajes Sidetours, Passeig Marítim 19 (© **97-128-39-00;** www.sidetours.com), offers numerous full- and half-day excursions throughout Palma and the surrounding countryside. The full-day excursion to Valldemossa and Sóller takes visitors through the monastery where former island residents Chopin and his lover, George Sand, spent their scandalous winter. After leaving the monastery, the tour explores the peaks of the Sierra Mallorquina, and then makes its way to the seaside town of Sóller. Call ahead for ticket prices. Tours are reserved for groups with a minimum of 37 people.

Another full-day tour of the mountainous western side of the island is conducted by train and boat, including a ride on one of Europe's oldest railways to the town of Sóller and the Monasterio de Lluch, as well as a boat ride between the port of Sóller and La Calobra. The eastern coast of Majorca is explored in the Caves of Drach and Hams tour. A concert on the world's largest underground lake (Lake Martel), tours through the caves, a stop at an olive-wood works, and a visit to the Majorica Pearl Factory are all covered. Times of departure may vary.

Balearic Discovery, Calle Jaime Solivellas 11, Selva (ⓒ **97-187-53-95;** www.balearic discovery.com), offers tailor-made tours around Majorca. The company can arrange everything from art tours to windsurfing excursions.

Banys Arabs   These authentic Moorish baths date from the 10th century. They are the only complete remaining Moorish-constructed buildings in Palma. One room contains a dome supported by 12 columns.

Carrer Serra 7. ⓒ **97-172-15-49.** Admission 1.60€ ($2.10). Apr–Sept daily 9am–7pm; Oct–Mar daily 9am–6pm. Bus: 15.

Castell de Bellver ★   Erected in 1309, this hilltop round castle was once the summer palace of the kings of Majorca—during the short period when there were kings of Majorca. The castle, which was a fortress with a double moat, is well preserved and now houses the Museu Municipal, which is devoted to archaeological objects and old coins. It's really the view from here, however, that is the chief attraction. In fact, the name, Bellver, means "beautiful view."

Btw. Palma and Son Armadams. ⓒ **97-173-06-57.** Admission 1.90€ ($2.45) adults; 1€ ($1.30) children 14–18, students, and seniors; free for children 14 and under. Apr–Sept Mon–Sat 8am–8:30pm, Sun 10am–5pm; Oct–Mar Mon–Sat 8am–7:15pm, Sun 10am–5pm. Museum closed Sun. Bus: 3 or 15.

Catedral (La Seu) ★★   This Catalonian Gothic cathedral, called La Seu, stands in the Old Town overlooking the seaside. It was begun during the reign of Jaume II (1276–1311) and completed in 1601. Its central vault is 43m (141 ft.) high, and its columns rise 20m (66 ft.). There is a wrought-iron *baldachin* (canopy) by Gaudí over the main altar. The treasury contains supposed pieces of the True Cross and relics of San Sebastián, patron saint of Palma. Museum and cathedral hours often change; call ahead to make sure they're accepting visitors before you go.

Carrer Palau Reial. ⓒ **97-172-31-30.** Free admission to cathedral; museum and treasury 3.75€ ($4.90). Apr–May and Oct Mon–Fri 10am–5:15pm; Nov–Mar Mon–Fri 10am–3:15pm; June–Sept Mon–Fri 10am–6:15pm; year round Sat 10am–2:15pm. Bus: 15.

Fundación Pilar i Joan Miró a Mallorca ★   The great artist Joan Miró and his wife, Pilar Juncosa, donated four workshops in which the artist carried out his creative work on the island from 1956 until his death in 1983. At Miró's former estate, rotating exhibitions devoted to his life and work are presented along with a permanent collection of his art and sculptures. You can also see his studio as it was at the time of his death.

Carrer Joan de Saridakis 29. ⓒ **97-170-14-20.** http://miro.palmademallorca.es. Admission 5€ ($6.50) adults, 2.80€ ($3.65) children and seniors. Mid-May to mid-Sept Tues–Sat 10am–7pm; off season Tues–Sat 10am–6pm; year round Sun 10am–3pm. Bus: 3 or 6.

Llotja ★   This 15th-century Gothic structure is a leftover from the wealthy mercantile days of Majorca. La Lonja (its Spanish name) was, roughly, an exchange or guild. Exhibitions here are announced in local newspapers.

Plaça de la Llotja. ☎ **97-171-17-05.** Free admission. Tues–Sun 11am–2pm; Tues–Sat 5–9pm. Bus: 15.

Marineland Ⓚ   Eighteen kilometers (11 miles) west of Palma, just off the coast road en route to Palma Nova, this attraction offers a variety of amusements—dolphin, sea lion, and parrot shows. The daily dolphin shows are at 11:45am and 3:15pm; the parrot shows daily at 10:30am, 12:30pm, and 4:30pm. There's a Polynesian pearl-diving demonstration and a small zoo. You'll find a cafeteria, picnic area, and children's playground, as well as beach facilities.

Costa d'en Blanes. ☎ **97-167-51-25.** www.marineland.es. Admission 21€ ($27) adults, 15€ ($20) children 3–12, free for children 2 and under. Mar 17–Nov 30 daily 9:30am–6pm. Direct bus, marked MARINELAND, from Palma rail station.

Museu d'Art Espanyol Contemporani, Fundació Juan March ★   The Juan March Foundation's Museum of Spanish Contemporary Art houses a collection of art that represents one of the most fertile periods of 20th-century art, with canvases by Picasso, Miró, Dalí, and Juan Gris, as well as Antoni Tàpies, Carlos Saura, Miquel Barceló, Lluis Gordillo, Susana Solano, and Jordi Teixidor. There is a room devoted to temporary exhibits; one series, for example, featured 100 Picasso engravings from the 1930s. The oldest and best-known work in the museum is Picasso's *Head of a Woman,* from his cycle of paintings known as *Les Demoiselles d'Avignon.* These works form part of the collection that the Juan March Foundation began to amass in 1973.

Carrer Sant Miquel 11. ☎ **97-171-35-15.** Free admission. Mon–Fri 10am–6:30pm; Sat 10:30am–2pm.

Palau de l'Almudaina   Long ago, Muslim rulers erected this splendid fortress surrounded by Moorish-style gardens and fountains opposite the cathedral. During the short-lived reign of the kings of Majorca, it was converted into a royal residence that evokes the Alcázar at Málaga. Now it houses a museum displaying antiques, artwork, suits of armor, and Gobelin tapestries. Panoramic views of Palma's harbor can be seen from here.

Carrer Palau Reial. ☎ **97-121-41-34.** Admission 3.50€ ($4.55) adults, 2.50€ ($3.25) children, free for all Wed. Mon–Fri 10am–2pm and 4–6:30pm; Sat 10am–1:15pm. Closed holidays. Bus: 15.

Poble Espanyol ★   This is a touristy collection of buildings evoking Spain in miniature and is similar to the Poble Espanyol in Barcelona. Bullfights are held in its *corrida* on summer Sundays. There are mock representations of such famous structures as the Alhambra in Granada, Torre de Oro in Seville, and El Greco's House in Toledo.

Carrer Pueblo Español s/n. ☎ **97-173-70-75.** Admission 8€ ($10) adults, 5€ ($6.50) students, 6€ ($7.80) children 7–12. Mon 9am–8pm; Tues–Thurs 9am–2pm; Fri 9am–4pm; Sun 9am–midnight. Bus: 5.

WHERE TO STAY

If you go in high season, reserve well in advance—Majorca's staggering number of hotels is still not enough to hold the August crowds. Some of our hotel recommendations in Palma are in the El Terreno section, the heart of the local nightlife; don't book into one of these hotels unless you like plenty of action, continuing until late at night.

Palma's suburbs, notably Cala Mayor, about 4km (2½ miles) from the center, and San Agustín, about 5km (3 miles) from town, continue to sprawl. In El Arenal, part of Playas de Palma, there is a huge concentration of hotels. The beaches at El Arenal are quite good but have a Coney Island atmosphere.

ArabellaSheraton Golf Hotel Son Vida ★★★ (Kids) The natural environment of the area surrounding this hotel has been fiercely protected. Don't come here expecting raucous good times on the beach; the resort is elegant and rather staid. There's no health club and no shuttle to the beach; many visitors drive to the several nearby beaches. But it does boast one of the only hotel bullrings in Spain.

The low-rise complex is intensely landscaped and offers views over the lush green grounds (not of the sea) from many of its good-size rooms. Accommodations have white walls, dark-stained furnishings, carpeting, bathrooms with tub/shower combos, and, in the more expensive accommodations, balconies or verandas.

Carrer de la Vinagrella, 07013 Palma de Majorca. © 800/325-3535 in the U.S. or 97-178-71-00. Fax 97-178-72-00. www.mallorca-resort.com/golfhotel. 93 units. 350€–450€ ($455–$585) double; 1,200€–1,500€ ($1,560–$1,950) suite. Rates include breakfast. AE, DC, MC, V. Free parking. Bus: 7. **Amenities:** 2 restaurants; bar; 2 pools (1 indoor); golf course; 3 tennis courts; fitness center; sauna; children's programs; salon; room service; babysitting; laundry service; dry cleaning; nonsmoking rooms; rooms for those w/limited mobility. *In room:* A/C, TV, minibar, hair dryer, safe.

Palacio Ca Sa Galesa ★★ (Finds) This place is a delight and far more personal than the bigger chains. For generations this 15th-century town house languished as a decaying apartment building facing the side of the cathedral. Back in 1993, an entrepreneurial couple from Cardiff, Wales, began restoring the place, salvaging the original marble floors and stained-glass windows, sheathing the walls of the public areas with silk, and adding modern amenities. Today, the place is the most alluring in all of Palma, loaded with English and Spanish antiques and paintings. Most rooms overlook an enclosed courtyard draped with potted plants and climbing vines. The guest rooms are quite opulent, with antiques and Persian rugs. Neatly kept bathrooms come with tub/shower combos. There's no restaurant, but a hearty buffet is served each morning (for an extra charge).

Carrer de Miramar 8, 07001 Palma de Majorca. © 97-171-54-00. Fax 97-172-15-79. www.palaciocasa galesa.com. 12 units. 320€ ($416) double; 375€–450€ ($488–$585) suite. AE, MC, V. Parking 15€ ($20). **Amenities:** 2 lounges; whirlpool; sauna; room service; massage; babysitting; laundry service; dry cleaning; nonsmoking rooms; rooms for those w/limited mobility. *In room:* A/C, TV, minibar, beverage maker, hair dryer, safe.

Expensive

Convent de la Missió ★★ (Finds) This magnificent 17th-century convent is hidden away in the Ciutat Vella amid narrow streets and plant-filled patios and adjoining a church of the same name. Missionaries are no longer taught here, for the building has been massively restored and turned into a hotel with many amenities, including a solarium and a whirlpool. The guest rooms, which range from small to spacious, are comfortably furnished and smartly minimalist in style, with white and sand the predominant colors. Suites are equipped with Jacuzzis, while standard doubles come with combo tub/shower or just shower.

Carrer de la Missió, 07003 Palma de Majorca. © 97-122-73-47. Fax 97-122-73-48. www.conventdelamissio.com. 4 units. 250€ ($325) double; 290€ ($377) junior suite; 350€ ($455) suite. Rates include buffet breakfast. AE, DC, MC, V. Parking 12€ ($16). **Amenities:** Restaurant; bar; sauna; solarium; room service; babysitting; laundry service. *In room:* A/C, TV, minibar, hair dryer, safe.

Palau Sa Font ★ (Finds) This 16th-century palace was successfully converted into one of Majorca's most charming boutique hotels. It's located a 3-minute walk from the harbor, and a 15-minute walk from the cathedral. The atmosphere is a bit funky unless you like jelly-bean colors. Distressed iron and island stone add more traditional notes. Especially popular with English visitors, this has been called the hippest and most atmospheric place to stay in the Old Town by some London tabloids. Designers transformed the guest rooms into a blend of modern and traditional, each with a shiny bathroom with tub or shower. Plump comforters, linen curtains, rustic iron furnishings, and plain walls lend style and grace. The breakfast is one of the reasons to stay here, featuring such delights as smoked salmon, Serrano ham, tortillas, and fresh fruit.

Carrer Apuntadores 38, Barrio Antiguo, 07017 Palma de Majorca. ☏ **97-171-22-77.** Fax 97-171-26-18. www.palausafont.com. 19 units. 160€–215€ ($208–$280) double; 245€ ($319) junior suite. Rates include buffet breakfast. AE, DC, MC, V. No parking. Closed Jan. **Amenities:** Breakfast lounge; bar; outdoor pool; babysitting; laundry service; nonsmoking rooms. *In room:* A/C, TV, minibar, hair dryer.

Hotel Tres ★★ (**Finds**) Located right in the heart of the Old Town, this one-of-a-kind character hotel is a tasteful blend of two well-preserved old palaces. Here guests enjoy an infinity splash pool, as well as sweeping vistas of Palma and its port, and walk across a linking bridge from one roof terrace to another. The midsize bedrooms are minimalist in decor but comfortably and attractively furnished, with wood floors, lots of glass and white surfaces, fresh cotton sheets, plush sofas in flamboyant colors, and superb bathrooms with tub or shower. A suite boasts its own private terrace and Jacuzzi. A romantic stone courtyard, with a towering palm tree, is an idyllic place for either breakfast or a glass of wine before dinner.

Calle Apuntadores 3, 07012 Palma de Mallorca. ☏ **97-171-73-33.** Fax 97-171-73-72. www.hoteltres.com. 41 units. 220€–275€ ($286–$358) double; 320€ ($416) junior suite; 550€ ($715) suite. Rates include breakfast. AE, DC, MC, V. No parking. **Amenities:** Restaurant; bar; outdoor pool; business center; room service; laundry service; nonsmoking rooms; rooms for those w/limited mobility. *In room:* A/C, TV, Wi-Fi (in some), minibar, hair dryer, safe.

Moderate

Hotel Saratoga ★ Under an arcade beside the Old City's medieval moat is the entrance to the Hotel Saratoga. The hotel features bright, well-furnished guest rooms, many with balconies or terraces with views of the bay and city of Palma. The mostly midsize guest rooms include well-maintained, tiled bathrooms, most with tub/shower combos. One of the hotel's most attractive features is a cafe-bar on the seventh floor enjoying Mediterranean vistas.

Passeig Majorca 6, 07012 Palma de Majorca. ☏ **97-172-72-40.** Fax 97-172-73-12. www.hotelsaratoga.es. 187 units. 150€–160€ ($195–$208) double; 200€–225€ ($260–$293) suite. Rates include breakfast. AE, DC, MC, V. Parking 10€ ($13). Bus: 3, 7, or 15. **Amenities:** Restaurant; cafe/bar; 2 outdoor pools; fitness center; sauna; salon; room service; laundry service; dry cleaning. *In room:* A/C, TV, Wi-Fi, minibar, hair dryer, iron, safe.

San Lorenzo ★★ This antique hotel and romantic oasis occupies the center of the maze of winding streets that form Palma's Old City. The building is 18th century, and the decor is a pleasant mix of modern and traditional Majorcan styles. (The fixtures in its Art Deco bar once decorated a saloon in Paris.) All guest rooms are comfortable, airy and gleaming white, with beamed ceilings. While some have balconies, the more luxurious rooms offer fireplaces and private terraces. All bathrooms have tub/shower combos. This hotel is perfect for relaxing after a day of sightseeing or shopping.

San Lorenzo 14, 07012 Palma de Majorca. ☏ **97-172-82-00.** Fax 97-171-19-01. www.hotelsanlorenzo. com. 6 units. 135€–190€ ($176–$247) double; 240€ ($312) suite. AE, DC, MC, V. No parking. **Amenities:** Bar; outdoor pool; room service; babysitting; laundry service. *In room:* A/C, TV, minibar, hair dryer, safe.

Costa Azul (Value)   This established waterfront hotel, located right beside Palma Bay, not only offers reasonable rates, but also superb views of the yachts in the harbor. In short, if location is your top priority, it's a bargain. The bright sunny rooms are neatly if modestly furnished and spotlessly clean. Each has a bathroom equipped with a tub/shower combo. It's a short stroll into town along the *paseo* or up the hill behind the hotel to the bars and clubs of Plaça Gomila in El Terreno.

Av. Gabriel Roca (Passeig Marítim) 7, 07014 Palma de Majorca. © **97-173-19-40.** Fax 97-173-19-71. www. esperanzahoteles.com. 126 units. 95€–120€ ($124–$156) double. AE, DC, MC, V. Parking 12€ ($16). Bus: 1, 3, or 21. **Amenities:** Restaurant; bar; outdoor pool; sauna; room service; laundry service; dry cleaning; rooms for those w/limited mobility. *In room:* A/C, TV, safe.

Hotel Born ★ (Value)   If you'd like to stay within the city of Palma itself, there is no better bargain than this government-rated two-star hotel in the city's exact center. A 16th-century palace, it once belonged to the marquis of Ferrandell. It was vastly altered and extended in the 18th century with the addition of a Majorcan courtyard shaded by a giant palm tree. Today it's a small, cozy inn with all the modern amenities, and it still retains many of its original architectural features, such as Romanesque arches. Guest rooms are mostly spacious and well equipped, with neatly tiled bathrooms with shower. Off Plaça Rei Juan Carlos, the hotel opens onto a tranquil side street.

Carrer Sant Jaume 3, 07012 Palma de Mallorca. © **97-171-29-42.** Fax 97-171-86-18. www.hotelborn. com. 30 units. 80€–110€ ($104–$143) double; 125€ ($163) suite. Rates include breakfast. AE, DC, MC, V. No parking. **Amenities:** Bar; bike rentals; nonsmoking rooms. *In room:* A/C, TV.

At Illetas

This built-up resort-suburb of Palma lies 8km (5 miles) west of the center, beside a series of intimate coves.

Hotel Bonsol ★ (Kids)   Set across from the beach, this government-rated four-star hotel was built in 1953 and renovated frequently since then. It charges less than hotels with similar amenities, and the on-site swimming facilities make it quite popular with vacationing families, who dine within the airy, somewhat spartan dining room. The core is a four-story, white-sided masonry tower; some of the suites are clustered into simple, outlying villas. The hotel overlooks a garden, adjacent to the sea. The midsize rooms are larger than you might expect, efficient but comfortable and well suited to beachfront vacations.

Paseo de Illetas 30, 07181 Illetas. © **97-140-21-11.** Fax 97-140-21-11. www.bonsol.es. 147 units. 100€–150€ ($130–$195) double. Rates include breakfast. AE, DC, MC, V. Free parking. Closed Nov 20–Dec 20. **Amenities:** 2 restaurants; lounge; outdoor pool; 2 tennis courts; fitness center; Jacuzzi; sauna; room service; babysitting; laundry service; dry cleaning; nonsmoking rooms. *In room:* A/C, TV, minibar, hair dryer, safe.

Meliá de Mar ★★   Originally built in 1964, Meliá de Mar is one of the most comfortable (albeit expensive) hotels in Palma. This seven-story hotel is close to the beach and sports a large garden. The marble-floored lobby and light, summery furniture offer a cool refuge from the hot sun. The calm, deliberately uneventful setting is evocative of spa hotels in central Europe. Guest rooms, mainly midsize, have many fine features, including original art, terra-cotta-tiled balconies, marble or wrought-iron furnishings, and excellent beds. Marble-clad bathrooms come with deluxe toiletries, tub/shower combos, and dual basins.

Paseo de Illetas 7, 07015 Calvia. ☎ **97-140-25-11.** Fax 97-140-58-52. www.solmelia.com. 144 units. 190€–325€ ($247–$423) double; from 350€ ($455) suite. AE, DC, MC, V. Free parking. **Amenities:** 3 restaurants; bar; 2 pools (1 indoor); tennis court; salon; room service; massage; babysitting; laundry service; dry cleaning; nonsmoking rooms. *In room:* A/C, TV, minibar, coffeemaker, hair dryer, iron, safe.

At Costa d'en Blanes

Located at the western end of Palma Bay, 9km (5²/₃ miles) from the capital, this hotel enjoys a privileged position in the sheltered resort of Costa d'en Blanes. Count on a 10-minute drive from the center of Palma.

H10 Punta Negra Resort ★★   In an exclusive area, this two-story hotel is surrounded by two Mediterranean beaches and an array of golf courses. Elegant and posh, it's constructed in classic Majorcan style with white walls, antique furnishings, carpeted floors, and panoramic views of either the sea or pine forests. The hotel is only 1.5km (1 mile) from the yachting port of Puerto Portals. Spacious and beautifully furnished rooms are equipped with elegant bathrooms containing tub/shower combos.

Carretera Andaitz Km 12, Costa d'en Blanes, 07181 Majorca. ☎ **97-168-07-62.** Fax 97-168-39-19. www. h10.es. 137 units. 100€–150€ ($130–$195) double; 175€–200€ ($228–$260) suite. Rates include continental breakfast. AE, DC, MC, V. Free parking. **Amenities:** 2 restaurants; bar; 3 pools (1 indoor); nearby 18-hole golf course; tennis courts; Turkish bath; sauna; salon; room service; babysitting; laundry service; dry cleaning; nonsmoking rooms; rooms for those w/limited mobility; casino. *In room:* A/C, TV, minibar, hair dryer, iron, safe.

WHERE TO DINE

Majorca's most typical main dish is *lomo,* or pork loin, the specialty in any restaurant offering Majorcan cuisine. *Lomo con col* is a method of preparation wherein the loin is enveloped in cabbage leaves and served with a sauce made with tomatoes, grapes, pine nuts, and bay leaf.

A local sausage, *sobrasada,* is made with pure pork and red peppers. Paprika gives it its characteristic bright red color. *Sopa mallorquina* can mean almost anything, but basically it is mixed greens in a soup flavored with olive oil and thickened with bread. When garbanzos (chickpeas) and meat are added, it becomes a meal in itself.

The best-known vegetable dish is *el tumbet,* a kind of cake with a layer of potato and another of lightly sautéed eggplant. Everything is covered with a tomato sauce and peppers, then boiled for a while. Eggplant, often served stuffed with meat or fish, is one of the island's vegetable mainstays. *Frito mallorquín* is basically a traditional country dish of fried onions and potatoes, mixed with red peppers, diced lamb liver, "lights" (lungs), and fennel. It's hearty, unsophisticated, and quite filling.

ⓕ Finds   A Special Treat

Dating from 1700, **Can Joan de S'aigo,** Carrer can Sanç 10 (☎ **97-171-07-59**), is the oldest ice-cream parlor on the island. Correspondingly elegant and Old World, it serves its homemade ice creams (try the almond), pastries, cakes, *ensaimadas* (light-textured and airy specialty cakes of Palma), fine coffee, and several kinds of hot chocolate in a setting of marble-top tables, beautiful tiled floors, and an indoor garden with a fountain.

In the Balearic Islands, only Majorca produces wine, but this wine isn't exported except in small quantities to major Spanish cities like Barcelona and Madrid. The red wine bottled around Felanitx and Binissalem tends to be the best, and you should add Franja Roja and Viña Paumina to your wine list. Most of the wine, however, comes from mainland Spain. *Café carajillo*—coffee with cognac—is a Spanish specialty particularly enjoyed by Majorcans.

Expensive

Mediterráneo 1930 ★ MEDITERRANEAN   Named after the Art Deco, 1930s-era styling that fills its interior, this is a well-managed, artfully hip restaurant adjacent to Hotel Meliá Victoria. One of Palma's top eating spots, with a sense of chic defined by its cosmopolitan owners Juan and Mary Martí, it has a beige-and-white decor accented by verdant plants and Art Deco sculptures. The menu relies heavily on seafood, with special emphasis on fish slowly baked in a salt crust, a process that adds a light-textured flakiness to even the most aromatic fish. Another specialty is beefsteak cooked on a hot stone carried directly to your table and served with such sauces as béarnaise, pepper, or port.

Av. Gabriel Roca (Passeig Marítim) 33. ℂ **97-173-03-77.** www.mediterraneo1930.com. Reservations recommended. Main courses 18€–35€ ($23–$46); fixed-price lunch 28€ ($36); fixed-price dinner 35€ ($46). AE, DC, MC, V. Daily 1–4pm and 8–11:30pm. Bus: 1.

Porto Pí ★ MODERN MEDITERRANEAN   This restaurant, a favorite of King Juan Carlos, occupies an elegant 19th-century mansion above the yacht harbor at the western end of Palma. Contemporary paintings complement the decor, and there is an outdoor terrace. The food has a creative Mediterranean influence. Specialties change with the season but might be house-style fish *en papillote,* angelfish with shellfish sauce, or quail stuffed with foie gras cooked in a wine sauce. Game is a specialty in winter.

Joan Miró 174. ℂ **97-140-00-87.** Reservations required. Main courses 20€–30€ ($26–$39). AE, DC, MC, V. Mon–Fri 1–3:30pm; daily 7:30–11:30pm. Bus: Palma-Illetas or 3.

Refectori ★★★ INTERNATIONAL   Jaime Oliver—no relation to *The Naked Chef*—is one of the island's most celebrated chefs, and his superb kitchen on the ground floor of the Convent de la Missió (see "Where to Stay," above) offers the island's most creative cuisine. Book well ahead to enjoy it, especially if you're aiming for an open-air terrace table. First-rate seasonal produce and a wide-ranging wine list await diners, who can also sit in the main room decorated with black-and-white photographs of Majorcan salt mounds. Oliver's delectable dishes range from the deceptively simple poached eggs and mushrooms with crème and soy emulsion to the exquisite lamb in a crust of basil and goat cheese. For something more challenging try the candied-style squid, stuffed with shrimp and pine-nut praline. The menu changes frequently and the desserts are among the most sumptuous on the island.

Carrer de la Missió. ℂ **97-122-73-47.** www.conventdelamissio.com. Reservations required way in advance. Main courses 25€–30€ ($33–$39). AE, DC, MC, V. Mon–Fri 1–3:30pm; Mon–Sat 8–11pm.

Tristán ★★★ NOUVELLE CUISINE   Several miles southwest of Palma, Tristán overlooks the marina of Port Portals. This is the finest restaurant in the Balearics, winning a coveted two stars from Michelin, a designation previously unheard of in the archipelago. The sophisticated menu varies, depending on what's best in the market each day. Selections may be pigeon in rice paper, a medley of Mediterranean vegetables, or the catch of the day, usually prepared Majorcan style. But this recitation doesn't prepare you for the exceptional bursts of flavor you'll sample in the chef's creations.

Port Portals 1, Portals Nous. (✆ 97-167-55-47. www.grupotristan.com. Reservations required. Main courses 34€–60€ ($44–$78); special menus 120€–140€ ($156–$182); gourmet tapas menu 145€ ($189). V. Daily 1–3:30pm and 8:30–11:30pm. Closed Jan 7–Feb 28.

Moderate

Arrocería Sa Cranca SEAFOOD   This sophisticated restaurant, which specializes in seafood dishes (in many cases, mixed with rice), has an ideal setting overlooking the port. The best way to appreciate its somewhat offbeat charm is to begin your meal with grilled baby sardines or a well-seasoned version of *buñuelos de bacalau* (minced and herb-laden cod patties). Either of these might be followed by a *parrillada*—an array of grilled fish and shellfish—or a rice casserole. Two of the best are black rice with squid and squid ink, and a particularly succulent one with spider crabs, clams, and mussels. Other variations include vegetables, roasted goat, or hake with tomatoes and garlic.

Passeig Marítim 13. (✆ 97-173-74-47. Reservations recommended. Main courses 16€–36€ ($21–$47). AE, DC, MC, V. Tues–Sun 1–4pm; Tues–Sat 8pm–midnight. Bus: 1.

Lonja del Pescado (Ca'n Eduardo) ★★ SEAFOOD   Thriving since the 1930s, this no-frills restaurant serves the catch of the day, taken directly from the boat to the kitchen. Specialties include seafood paella and *zarzuela* (fish stew). It's also possible to get fresh lobster. The rest of the menu consists of various types of fish, most prepared in the Majorcan style. Situated in the very heart of the harbor alongside the fishing boats that bring in their daily catch, this is far and away the most atmospheric restaurant in town to sample seafood.

Industria Pesquera 4, Es Mollet. (✆ 97-172-11-82. Reservations required. Main courses 14€–32€ ($18–$42). AE, MC, V. Tues–Sat 1–3:30pm and 8–11pm; Sun 1–3pm. Bus: 1 or 4.

Inexpensive

La Bóveda SPANISH   Set in the oldest part of Palma, a few steps from the cathedral, this rustic-looking restaurant maintains a busy tapas bar near the entrance, and no more than 14 tables set near the bar or in the basement. The menu lists predictable Spanish staples, each well prepared, including roasted or fried veal, pork, chicken, and fish, served with fresh greens, potatoes, or rice. Any of the roster of tapas from the bar (fava beans with strips of ham, spinach tortillas, grilled or deep-fried calamari, and shrimp with garlic sauce) can be served while you're at your table, along with bottles of full-bodied red or more delicate white wines. A worthy and particularly refreshing dessert consists of freshly made sorbet, sometimes garnished with a shot of vodka or bourbon, depending on the flavor of the sorbet.

Calle Botería 3. (✆ 97-171-48-63. Reservations recommended for a table in the restaurant, not necessary for the tapas bar. Main courses 12€–25€ ($16–$33). AE, MC, V. Mon–Sat 1:30–4pm and 8:30pm–midnight. Bus: 7 or 13.

Sa Caseta ★ (Finds) MAJORCAN   For some of the best-tasting regional cuisine, I like to head directly west of the city to the satellite village of Gènova. Here, in the attractive dining rooms of an hacienda, you can enjoy typical local cuisine served by a helpful staff. *Sopa mallorquina* (the island's famed vegetable soup) begins many a meal here. The chef obviously loves *bacalao* (cod), and he cooks it superbly in at least 10 different preparations. If you're traveling with friends, you might want to order some of the best suckling pig or roast baby lamb in

Majorca. On hotter days, you may prefer one of the local fish dishes, including (our favorite) *rape* (monkfish) in a shellfish sauce. Paella is served with dried salt cod and vegetables, an unusual variation on this classic dish. A series of homemade desserts, including ice cream, is a special feature. Most dishes are priced at the lower end of the scale.

Carrer Alférez Martínez Vaquer 1, Gènova. ℂ **97-140-26-40.** www.sacaseta.com. Reservations recommended. Main courses 12€–30€ ($16–$39); tasting menu 40€ ($52). AE, DC, MC, V. Daily 1pm–midnight.

PALMA AFTER DARK

Palma is packed with bars and dance clubs. Sure, there are some fun hangouts along the island's northern tier, but for a rocking, laser- and strobe-lit club, you'll have to boogie in Palma.

Set directly on the beach, close to a dense concentration of hotels, **Tito's,** Passeig Marítim (ℂ **97-173-00-17;** www.titosmallorca.com), charges a cover of 15€ to 18€ ($20–$23), including the first drink. A truly international crowd mingles on a terrace overlooking the Mediterranean. This club is the most popular, panoramic, and appealing disco on Majorca. If you visit only one nightclub during your time on the island, this should be it. Between June and September, it's open every night of the week from 11pm to at least 6am. The rest of the year, it's open Thursday to Sunday 11pm to 6am.

Bar Barcelona, Carrer Apuntadores 5 (ℂ **97-171-35-57**), a popular jazz club, evokes its namesake city with its spiral staircase and atmospheric, subdued lighting. Despite its location in the heart of Palma's busiest nightlife area, it attracts a predominantly local crowd that comes to enjoy live jazz every night from 11pm to 3am. There is no cover, and drinks are reasonably priced, making this one of Palma's best values for a night out. It's open Sunday to Thursday 8:30pm to 1am, Friday and Saturday 8:30pm to 3am.

B.C.M. Planet Dance, Av. Olivera s/n, Magalluf (ℂ **97-113-26-09;** www.bcm-planetdance.com), is the busiest and most cosmopolitan disco in Majorca. Boasting high-tech strobe lights and lasers, this sprawling, three-story venue offers a different sound system on each floor, giving you a wide variety of musical styles. If you're young, eager to mingle, and like to dance, this place is for you. The cover charge of 12€ ($16) includes your first drink and entitles you to party until 7am.

Come and enjoy a Caribbean cocktail with one of Palma's more charismatic bar owners, Pasqual, who just might invite you to dance a bit of salsa at **Bodeguita del Medio,** Carrer Vallseca 18 (ℂ **97-171-78-32**). The music is Latin-inspired and the crowd is a mix of locals and visitors from almost everywhere. Try their delicious *mojito* cocktail, more potent than it tastes, costing 5€ ($6.50). Inside is rustic in tone; outside is more intimate and romantic, with Chinese lanterns illuminating a garden that overlooks the sea. The bar is open Sunday to Thursday 8pm to 1am, Friday and Saturday 8pm to 3am.

ABACO, Carrer Sant Joan 1 (ℂ **97-171-49-39**), just might be the most opulently decorated nightclub in Spain—a cross between a harem and a czarist Russian church. The bar is decorated with a trove of European decorative arts. The place is always packed, with many customers congregating in a beautiful courtyard, which contains exotic caged birds, fountains, more sculpture than the eye can absorb, extravagant bouquets, and hundreds of flickering candles. All this exoticism is enhanced by the lushly romantic music (Ravel's *Boléro,* at our last visit) piped in through the sound system. Whether you view this as a bar, a museum, or a sociological survey, be sure to go. The bar is open Sunday to Thursday 8pm to 1am, Friday and Saturday 8pm to 3am, from February to December only. Wandering around is free; however, drinks cost 6€ to 12€ ($7.80–$16).

Gran Casino Mallorca lies on the harborfront promenade at Av. Gabriel Roca 4 (© 97-113-00-00; www.casinodemallorca.com). It's the place to go in search of Lady Luck. You'll need a passport—plus a shirt and tie—to enter, and must pay a 5€ ($6.50) cover charge. Inside, you can play American or French roulette, blackjack, or dice, or simply pull the lever on one of the many slot machines. The casino is open daily 5pm to 5am.

Although Majorca is generally a permissive place, it doesn't have the gay scene that Ibiza does.

---

2 VALLDEMOSSA & DEIA (DEYA)

Valldemossa is the site of the **Cartoixa Reial** ★, Plaça de las Cartujas s/n (© 97-161-21-06), where George Sand and the tubercular Frédéric Chopin wintered in 1838 and 1839. The monastery was founded in the 14th century, but the present buildings are from the 17th and 18th centuries. After monks abandoned the dwelling, the cells were rented to guests, which led to the appearance of Sand and Chopin, who managed to shock the conservative locals. They occupied cell nos. 2 and 4. The only belongings left are a small painting and a French piano. The peasants, fearing they'd catch Chopin's tuberculosis, burned most of the rest after the couple returned to the mainland. The cells may be visited November to February, Monday to Saturday 9:30am to 4:30pm, Sunday 10am to 1:30pm, and March to October, Monday to Saturday 9:30am to 6pm. Admission is 8.50€ ($11) adults, free for children 10 and under.

From Valldemossa, continue through the mountains, following the signposts for 11km (6³/₄ miles) to Deià. Before the village, consider a stopover at **Son Marroig** (© 97-163-91-58; www.sonmarroig.com), at Km 26 on the highway. Now a museum, this was once the estate of Archduke Luis Salvador. Born in 1847, the archduke tired of court life in his early 20s and found refuge here with his young bride in 1870. A tower on the estate is from the 1500s. Many of the archduke's personal furnishings and mementos, such as photographs and his ceramic collection, are still here. The estate is surrounded by lovely gardens leading to the cliff edge, and the property has many panoramic views including one of the striking Na Foradada rock with its keyhole gap in the middle. It is open Monday to Saturday 9:30am to 6:30pm (to 5:30pm in winter). Admission is 3€ ($3.90).

There are more tributes to the Austrian archduke at **Costa Nord,** Av. Palma 6 (© 97-161-24-25), a cultural center opened by actor Michael Douglas, who has a home in the area. A life-size reproduction of the archduke's yacht is on exhibit and a 15-minute film, narrated by Douglas, covers the history and geography of this corner of the island. Classical music and flamenco shows are performed in the auditorium during summer on Friday and Saturday nights. Admission is 7.50€ ($9.75) for adults, 6€ ($7.80) for seniors and students, 4.50€ ($5.85) for ages 7 to 12, and free for ages 6 and under. Summer hours are daily 10am to 6pm; off-season visits are possible daily 9am to 5pm.

Bus Nort Balear (© 97-149-06-80) operates a bus service to Valldemossa 13 times daily for a one-way fare of 2€ ($2.60). Buses leave Palma at Plaça Espanya (Calle Eusebio Estrada).

Set against the backdrop of olive-green mountains, **Deià (Deyá)** is a peaceful and serene village, with its stone houses and creeping bougainvillea. It has long had a special meaning for artists. Robert Graves, the English poet and novelist (*I, Claudius* and *Claudius the God*), lived in Deià, and died here in 1985. He is buried in the local cemetery.

His house, **Ca N'Alluny** ★, Carretera de Sóller Km 1 (☎ **97-163-61-85**), a 5-minute stroll from the village center, has been restored the way it was when Graves returned to the island in 1946, containing the original furnishings, even the electrical fittings. Visitors can explore the studies of both Robert Graves and his wife Paura and visit the kitchen and dining room.

To reach Deià by public transportation from Palma, 27km (17 miles) away, just stay on the bus that stops in Valldemossa. If you're driving from Palma, take the Carretera Valldemossa–Deià to Valldemossa; from there, you can continue to Deià. Those with cars might want to consider one of the idyllic and tasteful accommodations offered in this little Majorcan village, which has very few tourist facilities outside the hotels.

WHERE TO STAY

Deià offers some of the most tranquil and stunning retreats on Majorca—La Residencia and Es Molí—but it has a number of inexpensive little boardinghouses as well.

Hotel Es Molí ★★   One of the best recommended and most spectacular hotels on Majorca originated in the 1880s as a severely dignified manor house in the rocky highlands above Deià, home of the landowners who controlled access to the town's freshwater springs. In 1966 the manor house was augmented by two annexes, transforming it into this luxurious four-star hotel. Guest rooms are beautifully furnished and impeccably maintained, often with access to a private veranda overlooking the gardens or the faraway village. All units have neatly kept bathrooms with tub/shower combos. Some hardy souls make it a point to hike for 30 minutes to the public beach at Deià Bay; others wait for the shuttle bus to take them to the hotel's private beach, 6km (3³/₄ miles) away.

Carretera Valldemossa s/n, 07179 Deià. ☎ **97-163-90-00**. Fax 97-163-93-33. www.esmoli.com. 87 units. 106€–119€ ($138–$155) double; 158€–175€ ($205–$228) junior suite; 188€–208€ ($244–$270) suite. Rates include breakfast; half-board 21€ ($27) extra per person per day. AE, DC, MC, V. Free parking. Closed early Nov to late Apr. **Amenities:** Restaurant; bar; lounge; outdoor pool; tennis court; room service; babysitting; laundry service; dry cleaning. *In room:* A/C, TV, minibar, hair dryer, safe.

La Residencia ★★★   Launched by Virgin Airlines owner Richard Branson, this stylish and expensive hilltop property is something of an elitist celebrity haven. Guests have included everyone from Queen Sofia to the emperor of Japan to America's rock 'n' roll elite. Surrounded by 12 hectares (30 acres) of rocky Mediterranean gardens, the hotel's two sprawling stone 16th- and 17th-century mansions offer guests every conceivable luxury. Spacious rooms are outfitted with rustic antiques, terra-cotta floors, romantic four-poster beds, and, in some cases, beamed ceilings, all with luxurious appointments, including bathrooms with tub/shower combos. Open hearths, deep leather sofas, wrought-iron candelabras, and a supremely accommodating staff make this hotel internationally famous. Although it's technically defined as a four-star resort and a member of Relais & Châteaux, only the lack of certain luxuries prevents it from reaching government-rated five-star status.

Camino Son Canals s/n, 07179 Deià. ☎ **97-163-90-11**. Fax 97-163-93-70. www.hotel-laresidencia.com. 59 units. 295€–505€ ($384–$657) double; 455€–755€ ($592–$982) junior suite; 615€–995€ ($800–$1,294) suite; 1,200€–2,500€ ($1,560–$3,250) suite w/private pool. Rates include breakfast. AE, DC, MC, V. Free parking. **Amenities:** 2 restaurants; 2 bars; 3 pools (1 indoor); 2 tennis courts; fitness center; spa; sauna; salon; room service; babysitting; laundry service; dry cleaning; rooms for those w/limited mobility. *In room:* A/C, TV, hair dryer, safe.

Ca'n Quet ★ INTERNATIONAL   This restaurant, belonging to the Hotel Es Molí
(see above), is one of the most sought-after dining spots on the island. Set on a series of
terraces above a winding road leading out of town, the building is modern and stylish,
with an undeniably romantic air. Cascades of pink geraniums adorn its terraces, and if
you wander along the sloping pathways you'll find groves of orange and lemon trees,
roses, and a swimming pool ringed with neoclassical balustrades.

There's a spacious and sunny bar, an elegant indoor dining room with a blazing fire in
winter, and alfresco dining on the upper terrace under an arbor. The food is well prepared
and the portions generous. Meals can include a salad of marinated fish, terrine of fresh
vegetables, fish crepes, shellfish stew, duck with sherry sauce, and an ever-changing selection of fresh fish.

Carretera Valldemossa–Sóller. ✆ **97-163-91-96.** www.esmoli.com. Reservations required. Main courses
20€–40€ ($26–$52); tasting menus 60€–65€ ($78–$85). AE, MC, V. Tues–Sun 1–4pm and 8–11pm. Closed
Nov–Mar.

El Olivo ★★ INTERNATIONAL/MEDITERRANEAN   A 30- to 40-minute drive
north of Palma, this is one of the island's most elegant and upscale restaurants, visited by pop stars and royalty from Sting and Bruce Springsteen to the emperor of
Japan and king and queen of Spain. It's set inside a thick-walled centuries-old olive
press in the gardens of the La Residencia Hotel. Much of the illumination comes
from theatrical-looking candelabras placed on every table, whose flickering light
throws shadows against thick ceiling beams, antique accessories, and very formal
table settings. The cuisine is modern and subtly flavored. The chefs know how to
take classic dishes and add inventive taste-bud-stimulating touches. Menu items
include a salad of red mullet with julienne of vegetables and vinaigrette, roasted rack
of lamb with tomato and herb sauce, baked hake with a seafood risotto, and a dessert
specialty of almond soufflé.

In La Residencia Hotel, San Canals. ✆ **97-163-93-92.** www.hotel-laresidencia.com. Reservations recommended. Main courses 34€–80€ ($44–$104); fixed-price menu 85€ ($111). AE, DC, MC, V. Summer daily
1–3pm and 8–11pm; winter daily 1–3pm and 7:30–9:30pm.

3 PORT DE POLLENÇA/FORMENTOR

Beside a sheltered bay and between Cape Formentor to the north and Cape del Pinar to
the south is Port de Pollença, 65km (40 miles) north of Palma. The inland market town
of Pollença is located 4km (2¹/₂ miles) inland from the port and overlooked by two hills:
Calvary to the west and **Puig** to the east. A cypress-lined stone stairway leads to the
chapel that tops the former, while the longer pathway to the latter winds though pine
woods to reach a monastery, the Santuari del Puig de María, which provides ultra-cheap
dormitory accommodations. Both hills enjoy splendid views of the northern coastline
and surrounding countryside.

The port's low-rise hotels, private homes, restaurants, and snack bars line the very
attractive beach, which is somewhat narrow at its northwestern end but has some of the
island's finest, whitest sand and warmest, clearest water; the area also has excellent water-
skiing and sailing facilities. For several miles along the bay there is a pleasant pedestrian
promenade. There is only one luxury hotel in the area, however, and that is out on the
Formentor Peninsula.

Tons of fine white sand were imported to the beach at the southeastern end of Pollença Bay to create a broad ribbon of sunbathing space that stretches for several miles along the bay. Windsurfing, water-skiing, and scuba diving are among the watersports offered in the area.

Cabo de Formentor ★, "the devil's tail," can be reached from Port de Pollença via a spectacular road, twisting along to the lighthouse at the cape's end. Formentor is Majorca's fjord country—a dramatic landscape of mountains, pine trees, rocks, and sea, plus some of the best beaches in Majorca. In Cape Formentor, you'll see *miradores,* or lookout windows, which provide panoramic views.

ESSENTIALS

GETTING THERE   Five **buses** a day leave the Plaça Espanya in Palma, pass through Inca, and continue on to Port de Pollença; a one-way fare costs 5.25€ ($6.85). You can continue on from Deià (see above) along C-710, or from Inca on C-713, all the way to Pollença.

VISITOR INFORMATION   The **tourist information office,** on Carrer Monges (© **97-186-54-67**), is open Monday to Saturday 8am to 3pm and 5 to 7pm.

WHERE TO STAY

Barceló Formentor ★★★   This famous cliffside hotel on the northern tier of the island has hosted a wealth of famous guests, from Sir Winston Churchill to Charlie Chaplin. Seen from afar as a gleaming white rectangular gash amid the greenery of the surrounding pines, it nestles in splendid seclusion above one of the island's most idyllic beaches. The place was opened in 1929, shortly before the Spanish Civil War and the dark days of World War II, and it wasn't until 2 decades later that it began to prosper, attracting royalty, politicians, musicians, writers, and painters. Though it is now owned by the prestigious Barceló company, the hotel still retains its uniquely original character. Unlike many other hotels this side of the island, the Formentor is a year-round destination, and its guest rooms are attractively styled, traditionally furnished, and immaculately maintained, coming in a variety of sizes and shapes. Its chefs deserve high praise for their combination of international and Mediterranean cuisine.

Playa Formentor, 07470 Port de Pollença. © **97-189-91-01.** Fax 97-186-51-55. www.barceloformentor. com. 131 units. 210€–490€ ($273–$637) double; 550€–750€ ($715–$975) junior suite. Rates include breakfast. AE, DC, MC, V. Free parking. **Amenities:** 3 restaurants; 3 bars; 2 outdoor pools; 5 tennis courts; gym; horseback riding; windsurfing; boating; room service; babysitting; laundry service; dry cleaning. *In room:* A/C, TV, minibar, hair dryer, safe.

Hotel Illa d'Or ★   Originally built in the same year as the Formentor, and enlarged and improved several times since then, this four-story hotel sits on the seashore at the northwestern edge of Port de Pollença, enjoying fabulous views across the bay to Alcudia. Decorated in a mixture of colonial Spanish and English reproductions, it offers a seafront terrace with a view of the mountains and airy, simply furnished spaces. Guest rooms are midsize to spacious, each with comfortable furnishings, including good beds and bathrooms with tub/shower combos. The beach is just a few steps away.

Passeig Colón 265, 07470 Port de Pollença. © **97-186-51-00.** Fax 97-186-42-13. www.hotelillador.com. 120 units. 120€–225€ ($156–$293) double; 280€–500€ ($364–$650) suite. Rates include breakfast. DC, V. Free parking. Closed Dec–Jan 9. **Amenities:** Restaurant; 2 bars; 2 pools (1 indoor); fitness center; sauna; room service; laundry service; dry cleaning. *In room:* A/C, TV, minibar, hair dryer, safe.

WHERE TO DINE

Restaurant Clivia ★ MALLORQUINA/SPANISH   The best and most appealing restaurant in Pollença, the Clivia attracts a large clientele. The restaurant, in a century-old house in the heart of town, is composed of two dining rooms scattered with antique furniture, and an outdoor patio. Its tactful, well-organized staff produce a limited list of meats (veal, chicken, pork, and beef) and a more appealing roster of seafood prepared with skill and finesse. Specialties depend on the availability of fish, such as cod, monk-fish, dorado, eel, squid, and whitefish, either baked in a salt crust or prepared as part of a succulent *parrillada* (platter) of shellfish that's among the freshest anywhere. Begin with a spicy fish soup and accompany it with fresh vegetables, such as asparagus or spinach. The restaurant's name derives from the variety of bright red flowers *(las clivias)* planted profusely beside the patio that bloom throughout the summer.

Av. Pollentia 7, 07460 Pollença. ✆ **97-153-46-16.** Reservations recommended. Main courses 14€–25€ ($18–$33). AE, DC, MC, V. Year round daily 1–3pm and 7–11pm (closed Mon and Wed afternoons May–Oct). Closed Nov 15–Dec 15.

Appendix A: Fast Facts, Toll-Free Numbers & Websites

1 FAST FACTS: BARCELONA

AMERICAN EXPRESS There are two American Express offices in Barcelona: one at Passeig de Gràcia 101 (© **93-415-23-71**), and the other at La Rambla 74 (© **93-301-11-66**).

AREA CODES The area code for Barcelona is **93.**

ATM NETWORKS Maestro, Cirrus, and Visa cards are readily accepted at all ATMs. See also "Money & Costs" in chapter 3, "Planning Your Trip to Barcelona," p. 49.

BABYSITTERS Most major hotels can arrange for babysitters, called *canguros* (literally, kangaroos) or *niñeras*. Rates vary considerably but are usually reasonable.

BUSINESS HOURS Banks are open Monday through Friday from 8:30am to 2pm. Most offices are open Monday through Friday from 9am to 6 or 7pm. In July this changes from 8pm to 3pm for many businesses, especially those in the public sector. In August, businesses are on skeleton staff if they are not closed altogether. In restaurants, lunch is usually from 2 to 4pm and dinner from 9 to 11:30pm or midnight. There are no set rules for the opening of bars and taverns. Many open at 8am, others at noon, and most stay open until midnight or later. Major stores are open Monday through Saturday from 9:30 or 10am to 8pm; smaller establishments, however, often take a siesta, doing business from 9:30am to 2pm and 4:30 to 8 or 8:30pm. Hours can vary from store to store.

CAR RENTALS See "Toll-Free Numbers & Websites," p. 326.

DRINKING LAWS The legal age for drinking is 18. Alcoholic drinks are available in practically every bar, hotel, and restaurant in the city, and by law cannot be served to minors under 18. Opening hours of bars and establishments selling liquors vary widely. They can open as early as 6am and close as late as 2am. Nightclubs, late-night bars, and after-hours establishments fill the remaining hours up to and after dawn. Generally, you can purchase alcoholic beverages in almost any market; supermarkets sell alcoholic drinks from 9 or 10am until closing time around 9 or 10pm.

Breathalyzers are now used more frequently than in the past and drivers may be subjected to spot checks whether or not they've just had an accident or broken the law. The official permitted limit for drinking is the equivalent to two glasses of wine, two *cañas* (small glasses) of beer, or two glasses of spirits (given the size of Spanish measures, one glass here would suffice if you're thinking of driving yourself).

DRIVING RULES See "Getting There & Getting Around," in chapter 3, "Planning Your Trip to Barcelona."

ELECTRICITY Most hotels have 220 volts AC (50 cycles). Some older places have 110 or 125 volts AC. Carry your adapter with you, and always check at your hotel desk before plugging in any electrical appliance. It's best to travel with battery-operated equipment or just buy a new hair dryer in Spain.

EMBASSIES & CONSULATES If you lose your passport, fall seriously ill, get into legal trouble, or have some other serious problem, your embassy or consulate can help. These are the Barcelona addresses and hours:

The **United States Consulate,** Passeig de Reina Elisenda 23 (© 93-280-22-27; FGC: Reina Elisenda), is open Monday through Friday from 9am to 1pm.

The **Canadian Consulate,** Carrer de Elisenda Pinós 10 (© 93-204-27-00; FGC: Reina Elisenda), is open Monday through Friday from 10am to 1pm.

The **United Kingdom Consulate-General,** Diagonal 477 (© 93-366-62-00; Metro: Hospital Clinic), is open Monday through Friday from 9:30am to 3pm.

The **Republic of Ireland** has a small consulate at Gran Vía Carles III 94 (© 93-491-50-21; Metro: María Cristina); it's open Monday through Friday from 10am to 1pm.

In the adjacent building is the **Australian Consulate,** Gran Vía Carles III 98 (© 93-490-90-13; Metro: María Cristina). It is open Monday though Friday from 10am to noon.

Citizens of **New Zealand** have a consulate at Travesera de Gràcia 64 (© 93-209-03-99; FGC: Gràcia); it's open Monday through Friday from 9am to 4:30pm and 4 to 7pm.

EMERGENCIES For an ambulance © 061; or fire © 080.

GASOLINE/PETROL For the price of unleaded petrol (used in practically all vehicles now) see "Getting There & Getting Around," in chapter 3.

HOLIDAYS See "Barcelona Calendar of Events" in chapter 3.

HOSPITALS/CLINICS In Barcelona, the **Centre d'Urgències Perecamps,** located near Les Ramblas at Av. de las Drassanes 13–15, is a good bet. *Farmacias* (pharmacies) are everywhere, and they usually have highly trained staff and can often replace a trip to the doctor (most drugs are available over the counter). Pharmacies work on a shift basis; when one is closed they display a list of nearby 24-hour or extended-hour pharmacies on their front doors.

HOTLINES Call the city hall information service at © 010 for opening and closing times of attractions, special events, and other hard-to-find info.

INSURANCE Since Spain for most of us is far from home, and a number of things could go wrong—lost luggage, trip cancellation, a medical emergency—consider the following types of insurance.

For travel overseas, most U.S. health plans (including Medicare and Medicaid) do not provide coverage, and the ones that do often require you to pay for services upfront and reimburse you only after you return home.

As a safety net, you may want to buy travel medical insurance, particularly if you're traveling to a remote or high-risk area where emergency evacuation might be necessary. If you require additional medical insurance, try **MEDEX Assistance** (© 410/453-6300; www.medexassist.com) or **Travel Assistance International** (© 800/821-2828; www.travelassistance.com; for general information on services, call the company's **Worldwide Assistance Services, Inc.,** at © 800/777-8710).

Canadians should check with their provincial health plan offices or call **Health Canada** (℃ **866/225-0709;** www.hc-sc. gc.ca) to find out the extent of their coverage and what documentation and receipts they must take home in case they are treated overseas.

Travelers from the U.K. should carry their European Health Insurance Card (EHIC), which replaced the E111 form as proof of entitlement to free/reduced-cost medical treatment abroad (℃ **0845/606-2030;** www.ehic.org.uk). Note, however, that the EHIC only covers "necessary medical treatment," and for repatriation costs, lost money, baggage, or cancellation, travel insurance from a reputable company should always be sought (www.travel insuranceweb.com).

Travel Insurance The cost of travel insurance varies widely, depending on the destination, the cost and length of your trip, your age and health, and the type of trip you're taking, but expect to pay between 5% and 8% of the vacation itself. You can get estimates from various providers through **InsureMyTrip.com.** Enter your trip cost and dates, your age, and other information for prices from more than a dozen companies.

U.K. citizens and their families who make more than one trip abroad per year may find an annual travel insurance policy works out cheaper. Check **www.money supermarket.com,** which compares prices across a wide range of providers for single- and multitrip policies.

Most big travel agents offer their own insurance and will probably try to sell you their package when you book a holiday. Think before you sign. **Britain's Consumers' Association** recommends that you insist on seeing the policy and reading the fine print before buying travel insurance. The **Association of British Insurers** (℃ **020/7600-3333;** www.abi.org.uk) gives advice by phone and publishes Holiday Insurance, a free guide to policy provisions and prices. You might also shop around for better deals: Try **Columbus Direct** (℃ **0870/033-9988;** www.columbus direct.net).

Trip Cancellation Insurance Trip-cancellation insurance will help retrieve your money if you have to back out of a trip or depart early, or if your travel supplier goes bankrupt. Trip cancellation traditionally covers such events as sickness, natural disasters, and State Department advisories. The latest news in trip-cancellation insurance is the availability of **expanded hurricane coverage** and the **"any-reason"** cancellation coverage—which costs more but covers cancellations made for any reason. You won't get back 100% of your prepaid trip cost, but you'll be refunded a substantial portion. **TravelSafe** (℃ **888/ 885-7233;** www.travelsafe.com) offers both types of coverage. Expedia also offers any-reason cancellation coverage for its air-hotel packages. For details, contact one of the following recommended insurers: **Access America** (℃ 866/807-3982; www. accessamerica.com), **Travel Guard International** (℃ 800/826-4919; www.travel guard.com), **Travel Insured International** (℃ 800/243-3174; www.travelinsured. com), and **Travelex Insurance Services** (℃ 888/457-4602; www.travelex-insurance. com).

INTERNET ACCESS Internet access is plentiful, both in cybercafes and more and more frequently in hotels. The **Bornet Internet Café** (Barra del Ferro 3, Born; ℃ **93-268-15-07;** www.bornet-bcn.com) has 16 terminals and charges 2.60€ ($3.40) per hour.

LANGUAGE There are two official languages in Catalonia: Castilian Spanish *(Castellano)* and Catalan. After years of being outlawed during the Franco dictatorship, Catalan has returned to Barcelona and Catalonia with the language and its derivatives spoken throughout the *Països*

Catalans (Catalan Countries), namely Catalonia, Valencia, the Balearic Islands (including Majorca, even though natives there will tell you they speak *Mallorquín*), and pockets of Southern France and Aragon. Although street signs and much of media are in Catalan, no tourist is expected to speak it, although you will be met with delight if you can at least master a few phrases. Descriptions in museums are in both Catalan and Spanish with some also in English. Most restaurants have an English menu.

LAUNDROMATS   There are a few self-service and serviced laundromats in the Old Town, including **Tigre,** Carrer de Rauric 20, and **Lavamax,** Junta de Comerç 14. Some dry cleaners *(tintorerías)* also do laundry.

LEGAL AID   Should you happen to break the law and get arrested, you will be assigned an *abogado de oficio* or duty solicitor free of charge. You'll also be allowed to phone your consulate, who will alternately put you in touch with an English-speaking lawyer.

LOST & FOUND   Be sure to tell all of your credit card companies the minute you discover your wallet has been lost or stolen and file a report at the nearest police precinct. Your credit card company or insurer may require a police report number or record of the loss. Most credit card companies have an emergency toll-free number to call if your card is lost or stolen; they may be able to wire you a cash advance immediately or deliver an emergency credit card in a day or two.

Visa's emergency number in Spain is ✆ **90-099-11-24.** American Express cardholders and traveler's check holders should call ✆ **90-237-56-37** in Spain. Master-Card holders should call ✆ **90-097-12-31** in Spain.

If you need emergency cash over the weekend when all banks and American Express offices are closed, you can have money wired to you via **Western Union** (✆ **800/325-6000;** www.westernunion.com).

MAIL   The local postage system is both reliable and efficient, though services such as FedEx are available if you prefer to use them. To send an airmail letter or postcard to the United States costs .78€ ($1) for up to 20 grams. Airmail letters to Britain or other E.U. countries cost .60€ (78¢) up to 20 grams; letters within Spain cost .39€ (51¢).

Post your letters in the post office itself or in yellow post boxes called *buzones.* Buy stamps in an **Oficina de Correos** (post office) or in an *estanco* (a government-licensed tobacconist easily recognized by its brown and yellow logo). For further information, check the Spanish post office website, www.correos.es.

Postcards have the same rates as letters. Post your letters in the post office itself or in yellow post boxes called *buzones.* Allow about 8 days for delivery to North America, generally less to the United Kingdom; in some cases, letters take 2 weeks to reach North America. Rates change frequently, so check at your local hotel before mailing anything. As for surface mail to North America, forget it. Chances are you'll be home long before your letter arrives. For more information, check the Spanish post office website, www.correos.es.

If you don't want to receive your mail at your hotel or the American Express office, direct it to *Lista de Correos* at the central post office (Correu Central). To pick up mail, go to the window marked *Lista,* where you'll be asked to show your passport. Barcelona's central office is in Plaza San Antonio López, past the southern end of the Born; the nearest Metro station is Barceloneta (✆ **93-486-80-50**).

MAPS   See chapter 3, "Planning Your Trip to Barcelona," for information on where to get maps of the city, and Metro and suburban railways lines.

MEASUREMENTS See the chart on the inside front cover of this book for details on converting metric measurements to nonmetric equivalents.

NEWSPAPERS & MAGAZINES Foreign newspapers and magazines are available on the newsstands along Les Ramblas. *Catalonia Today* is a free newsletter in English published by the Catalan newspaper *El Punt.*

The Paris-based *International Herald Tribune,* which sometimes includes an English-language version of *El País* (see below), is sold at most newsstands in the tourist districts, as is *USA Today,* plus the *Financial Times, Wall Street Journal,* and European editions of *Time* and *Newsweek.* Top Catalan newspapers are *La Vanguardia* and *Avui* (the latter is in Catalan), while major national Spanish newspapers are *El País, El Mundo, ABC,* and *La Razón. Barcelona Metropolitan* is a monthly magazine in English with loads of information on events as well as features on Barcelona living. You can pick it up in bars and pubs. The *Guía del Ocio* is the most comprehensive "What's On." There is a small section at the back in English. **Free** Spanish newspapers which give you a briefer rundown on what's going on both in the city and around the world are handed out at the entrances to Metro stations. These publications include *Metro, Qué,* and *20 Minutos.*

PASSPORTS The websites listed provide downloadable passport applications as well as the current fees for processing applications. For an up-to-date, country-by-country listing of passport requirements around the world, go to the "International Travel" tab of the U.S. State Department at **http://travel.state.gov**.

For Residents of Australia You can pick up an application from your local post office or any branch of Passports Australia, but you must schedule an interview at the passport office to present your application

materials. Call the **Australian Passport Information Service** at ✆ **131-232,** or visit the government website at www.passports.gov.au.

For Residents of Canada Passport applications are available at travel agencies throughout Canada or from the central **Passport Office,** Department of Foreign Affairs and International Trade, Ottawa, ON K1A 0G3 (✆ **800/567-6868;** www.ppt.gc.ca). *Note:* Canadian children who travel must have their own passport. However, if you hold a valid Canadian passport issued before December 11, 2001, that bears the name of your child, the passport remains valid for you and your child until it expires.

For Residents of Ireland You can apply for a 10-year passport at the **Passport Office,** Setanta Centre, Molesworth Street, Dublin 2 (✆ **01/671-1633;** www.irlgov.ie/iveagh). Those under age 18 and over 65 must apply for a 3-year passport. You can also apply at 1A South Mall, Cork (✆ **21/494-4700**), or at most main post offices.

For Residents of New Zealand You can pick up a passport application at any New Zealand Passports Office or download it from their website. Contact the **Passports Office** at ✆ **0800/225-050** in New Zealand or 04/474-8100, or log on to www.passports.govt.nz.

For Residents of the United Kingdom To pick up an application for a standard 10-year passport (5-yr. passport for children under 16), visit your nearest passport office, major post office, or travel agency or contact the **United Kingdom Passport Service** at ✆ **0870/521-0410** or search its website at www.ukpa.gov.uk.

For Residents of the United States Whether you're applying in person or by mail, you can download passport applications from the U.S. State Department website at **http://travel.state.gov**.

To find your regional passport office, either check the U.S. State Department website or call the **National Passport Information Center** toll-free number (© 877/487-2778) for automated information.

POLICE In an emergency, dial © **112.**

SMOKING New smoking restrictions came into effect on Jan 1, 2006, regarding the workplace, and bars and cafes were given the "to smoke or not to smoke" choice with scarcely any real change. Officially bars and restaurants of over 100 square meters (1,076 sq. ft.) should have a small no-smoking area. Smoking is not allowed in airports, banks, post offices, and other "public" buildings. Most good hotels have nonsmoking rooms, although to date total bans on smoking, similar to those in France and Great Britain, have not been implemented.

TAXES The internal sales tax (known in Spain as IVA) ranges between 7% and 33%, depending on the commodity being sold. Food, wine, and basic necessities are taxed at 7%; most goods and services (including car rentals) at 13%; luxury items (jewelry, all tobacco, imported liquors) at 33%; and hotels at 7%.

If you are not a European Union resident and make purchases in Spain worth more than 90€ ($117), you can get a tax refund. To get this refund, you must complete three copies of a form that the store will give you, detailing the nature of your purchase and its value. Citizens of non-E.U. countries show the purchase and the form to the Spanish Customs Office. The shop is supposed to refund the amount due you. Inquire at the time of purchase how they will do so and discuss in what currency your refund will arrive.

TELEPHONES See "Staying Connected" in chapter 3.

TIME Spain is 6 hours ahead of Eastern Standard Time in the United States. **Daylight saving time** is in effect from the last Sunday in March to the last Sunday in October.

TIPPING More expensive restaurants add a 7% tax to the bill and cheaper ones incorporate it into their prices. This is *not* a service charge, and a tip of 5% to 10% is expected in these establishments. For coffees and snacks most people just leave a few coins or round up to the nearest euro.

Don't over-tip. The government requires restaurants and hotels to include their service charges—usually 15% of the bill. However, that doesn't mean you should skip out of a place without dispensing an extra euro or two. Although tipping is not mandatory for hotel staff, you should be aware that wages in the hospitality industry are extremely low, so any supplement will be more than welcome.

The following are some guidelines:

Your hotel porter should get 1€ ($1.30) per bag. Maids should be given 1€ ($1.30) per day, more if you're generous. Tip doormen 1€ ($1.30) for assisting with baggage and 1€ ($1.30) for calling a cab. In top-ranking hotels the concierge will often submit a separate bill, showing charges for newspapers and other services; if he or she has been particularly helpful, tip extra. For cab drivers, add about 10% to the fare as shown on the meter. At airports, such as Barajas in Madrid and major terminals, the porter who handles your luggage will present you with a fixed-charge bill.

In both restaurants and nightclubs, a 15% service charge is added to the bill. To that, add another 3% to 5% tip, depending on the quality of the service. Waiters in deluxe restaurants and nightclubs are accustomed to the extra 5%, which means you'll end up tipping 20%. If that seems excessive, you must remember that the initial service charge reflected in the fixed price is distributed among all the help.

Barbers and hairdressers expect a 10% to 15% tip. Tour guides expect 2€ ($2.60), although a tip is not mandatory. Theater and bullfight ushers get 0.50€ (65¢).

TOILETS There aren't many public toilets in Barcelona. Best places to find them are bus and train stations (where their conditions vary greatly) or more pleasantly in public parks like La Ciutadella and big stores like El Corte Inglés. Most bars and cafes won't mind if you ask to use their facilities. (It's polite to ask first, though.)

USEFUL PHONE NUMBERS U.S. Department of State Travel Advisory, ℭ 202/647-5225 (manned 24 hr.); **U.S. Passport Agency,** ℭ 202/647-0518; **U.S. Centers for Disease Control International Traveler's Hot Line,** ℭ 404/332-4559.

VISAS These are not required by Australian, American, British, Canadian, and New Zealand visitors. (See "Entry Requirements" in chapter 3.)

WATER Although the water in Barcelona is safe to drink, most people find the taste unpleasantly chlorinated and instead buy bottled water.

2 TOLL-FREE NUMBERS & WEBSITES

MAJOR INTERNATIONAL AIRLINES

Air France
ℭ 800/237-2747 (in U.S.)
ℭ 800/375-8723 (in U.S. and Canada)
ℭ 087/0142-4343 (in U.K.)
www.airfrance.com

Alitalia
ℭ 800/223-5730 (in U.S.)
ℭ 800/361-8336 (in Canada)
ℭ 087/0608-6003 (in U.K.)
www.alitalia.com

British Airways
ℭ 800/247-9297 (in U.S. and Canada)
ℭ 087/0850-9850 (in U.K.)
www.british-airways.com

Continental Airlines
ℭ 800/523-3273 (in U.S. and Canada)
ℭ 084/5607-6760 (in U.K.)
www.continental.com

Delta Air Lines
ℭ 800/221-1212 (in U.S. and Canada)
ℭ 084/5600-0950 (in U.K.)
www.delta.com

Iberia Airlines
ℭ 800/722-4642 (in U.S. and Canada)
ℭ 087/0609-0500 (in U.K.)
www.iberia.com

Lufthansa
ℭ 800/399-5838 (in U.S.)
ℭ 800/563-5954 (in Canada)
ℭ 087/0837-7747 (in U.K.)
www.lufthansa.com

Olympic Airlines
ℭ 800/223-1226 (in U.S.)
ℭ 514/878-9691 (in Canada)
ℭ 087/0606-0460 (in U.K.)
www.olympicairlines.com

Qantas Airways
ℭ 800/227-4500 (in U.S.)
ℭ 084/5774-7767 (in U.K. and Canada)
ℭ 13 13 13 (in Australia)
www.qantas.com

Swiss International Air Lines
ℭ 877/359-7947 (in U.S. and Canada)
ℭ 084/5601-0956 (in U.K.)
www.swiss.com

United Airlines
ℭ 800/864-8331 (in U.S. and Canada)
ℭ 084/5844-4777 (in U.K.)
www.united.com

US Airways
ℭ 800/428-4322 (in U.S. and Canada)
ℭ 084/5600-3300 (in U.K.)
www.usairways.com

Virgin Atlantic Airways
- ☎ 800/821-5438 (in U.S. and Canada)
- ☎ 087/0574-7747 (in U.K.)
- www.virgin-atlantic.com

BUDGET AIRLINES

Aer Lingus
- ☎ 800/474-7424 (in U.S. and Canada)
- ☎ 087/0876-5000 (in U.K.)
- www.aerlingus.com

Air Berlin
- ☎ 087/1500-0737 (in U.K.)
- ☎ 018/0573-7800 (in Germany)
- ☎ 180/573-7800 (all others)
- www.airberlin.com

BMI Baby
- ☎ 870/126-6726 (in U.S.)
- ☎ 087/1224-0224 (in U.K.)
- www.bmibaby.com

easyJet
- ☎ 870/600-0000 (in U.S.)
- ☎ 090/5560-7777 (in U.K.)
- www.easyjet.com

Ryanair
- ☎ 081/830-3030 (in Ireland)
- ☎ 087/1246-0000 (in U.K.)
- www.ryanair.com

CAR RENTAL AGENCIES

Advantage
- ☎ 866/661-2722 (in U.S.)
- ☎ 021/0344-4712 (outside of U.S.)
- www.advantage.com

Auto Europe
- ☎ 888/223-5555 (in U.S. and Canada)
- ☎ 0800/2235-5555 (in U.K.)
- www.autoeurope.com

Avis
- ☎ 800/331-1212 (in U.S. and Canada)
- ☎ 084/4581-8181 (in U.K.)
- www.avis.com

Budget
- ☎ 800/527-0700 (in U.S.)
- ☎ 800/268-8900 (in Canada)
- ☎ 087/0156-5656 (in U.K.)
- www.budget.com

Enterprise
- ☎ 800/261-7331 (in U.S.)
- ☎ 514/355-4028 (in Canada)
- ☎ 012/9360-9090 (in U.K.)
- www.enterprise.com

Hertz
- ☎ 800/645-3131 (for reservations in U.S. and Canada)
- ☎ 800/654-3001 (for international reservations)
- www.hertz.com

National
- ☎ 800/CAR-RENT (227-7368; for reservations in U.S. and Canada)
- ☎ 800/CAR-EUROPE (227-3876; for reservations in Europe)
- www.nationalcar.com

Thrifty
- ☎ 800/367-2277 (in U.S. and Canada)
- ☎ 918/669-2168 (international)
- www.thrifty.com

MAJOR INTERNATIONAL HOTEL & MOTEL CHAINS

Best Western International
- ☎ 800/780-7234 (in U.S. and Canada)
- ☎ 0800/393-130 (in U.K.)
- www.bestwestern.com

Four Seasons
- ☎ 800/819-5053 (in U.S. and Canada)
- ☎ 0800/6488-6488 (in U.K.)
- www.fourseasons.com

Hilton Hotels
- ☎ 800/HILTONS (445-8667; in U.S. and Canada)
- ☎ 087/0590-9090 (in U.K.)
- www.hilton.com

Holiday Inn
- ☎ 800/315-2621 (in U.S. and Canada)
- ☎ 0800/405-060 (in U.K.)
- www.holidayinn.com

Hyatt
- ☎ 888/591-1234 (in U.S. and Canada)
- ☎ 084/5888-1234 (in U.K.)
- www.hyatt.com

InterContinental Hotels & Resorts
☎ 800/424-6835 (in U.S. and Canada)
☎ 0800/1800-1800 (in U.K.)
www.ichotelsgroup.com

Marriott
☎ 877/236-2427 (in U.S. and Canada)
☎ 0800/221-222 (in U.K.)
www.marriott.com

Radisson Hotels & Resorts
☎ 888/201-1718 (in U.S. and Canada)
☎ 0800/374-411 (in U.K.)
www.radisson.com

Ramada Worldwide
☎ 888/2-RAMADA (272-6232; in U.S. and Canada)
☎ 080/8100-0783 (in U.K.)
www.ramada.com

Renaissance
☎ 888/236-2427
www.marriott.com

Sheraton Hotels & Resorts
☎ 800/325-3535 (in U.S.)
☎ 800/543-4300 (in Canada)
☎ 0800/3253-5353 (in U.K.)
www.starwoodhotels.com/sheraton

Westin Hotels & Resorts
☎ 800-937-8461 (in U.S. and Canada)
☎ 0800/3259-5959 (in U.K.)
www.starwoodhotels.com/westin

Appendix B:
Useful Terms & Phrases

Most Catalans are very patient with foreigners who try to speak their languages. For English speakers, Catalan pronunciation is a lot easier than Spanish pronunciation, so give it a go. If you know a little French or Italian, you will probably find it quite easy. If not, most good restaurants and hotels have English speakers on hand.

1 USEFUL WORDS & PHRASES

ENGLISH	SPANISH/CATALAN	PRONUNCIATION
Good day/ Good morning	Buenos días/Bon dia	*bweh*-nohs *dee*-ahs/ bohn *dee*-ah
How are you?	¿Cómo está?/Com està?	*koh*-moh es-*tah*/com ehs-*tah*
Very well	Muy bien/Molt bé	mwee byehn/mohl beh
Thank you	Gracias/Gràcies	*grah*-syahs/*grah*-syahs
You're welcome	De nada/De res	deh *nah*-dah/duh ress
Goodbye	Adiós/Adéu	ah-*dyos*/ah-*deh*-yoo
Please	Por favor/Si us plau	por fah-*vohr*/see yoos plow
Yes	Sí/Sí	see
No	No/No	noh
Excuse me	Perdóneme/Perdoni'm	pehr-*doh*-neh-meh/ per-*don*-eem
Where is . . . ?	¿Dónde está . . . ?/On és . . . ?	*dohn*-deh es-*tah*/ohn ehs
the station	la estación/la estació	lah es-tah-*syohn*/la es-tah-*cyo*
a hotel	un hotel/l'hotel	oon oh-*tehl*/ehl ho-*tehl*
the market	el mercado/el mercat	ehl mehr-*kah*-doh/ ehl mehr-*kah*
a restaurant	un restaurante/un restaurant	oon rehs-tow-*rahn*-teh/ oon rehs-tow-*rahn*
the toilet	el baño/el lavabo	ehl *bah*-nyoh/ehl lah-*vah*-boh
a doctor	un médico/un metge	oon *meh*-dee-koh/oon meht-*jah*
the road to . . .	el camino a/al cami per	ehl kah-*mee*-noh ah/ ahl kah-*mee* pehr

ENGLISH	SPANISH/CATALAN	PRONUNCIATION
To the right	A la derecha/A la dreta	ah lah deh-*reh*-chah/ ah lah *dreh*-tah
To the left	A la izquierda/A l'esquerra	ah lah ees-*kyehr*-dah /ahl ehs-kee-*ra*
I would like . . .	Quisiera/Voldría	kee-*syeh*-rah/vohl-*dree*-ah
I want . . . to eat. a room.	Quiero/Vull comer/menjar una habitación/un habitacion	*kyeh*-roh/*boo*-wee ko-*mehr*/mehn-*jahr* *oo*-nah ah-bee-tah-*syohn*/oon ah-bee-tah-*syohn*
Do you have . . . ? a book a dictionary	¿Tiene usted?/Té? un libro/un llibre un diccionario/un diccionari	tyeh-neh oo-*sted*/teh oon *lee*-broh/oon *yee*-breh oon deek-syoh-*nah*-ryoh/ oon deek-syoh-*nah*-ree
How do you say it in Catalan?	Como se dice eso en Catalan?/ Com se diu aixó en Català?	*coh*-mo say *dith*-ay *es*-so en Cah-tah-*lan*?/comm say *dee*-oh esh-*aw* en Cah-tah-*là*?
How much is it?	¿Cuánto cuesta?/Quant es?	*kwahn*-toh *kwehs*-tah/ kwahnt ehs?
When?	¿Cuándo?/Quan?	*kwahn*-doh/kwahn
What?	¿Qué?/Com?	keh/cohm
There is (Is there . . . ?)	(¿)Hay (. . . ?)/Hi ha? *or* Hi han?	aye/ee ah/ee ahn
What is there?	¿Qué hay?/Que hi ha?	keh aye/keh ee ah
Yesterday	Ayer/Ahir	ah-*yehr*/ah-*yeer*
Today	Hoy/Avui	oy/ah-*wee*
Tomorrow	Mañana/Demá	mah-*nyah*-nah/deh-*mah*
Good	Bueno/Bon	*bweh*-noh/bohn
Bad	Malo/Mal	*mah*-loh/mahl
Better (Best)	(Lo) Mejor/Millor	(loh) meh-*hohr*/mee-*yohr*
More	Más/Mes	mahs/mehss
Less	Menos/Menys	*meh*-nohs/*meh*-nyus
Hot	Caliente/Calent	cah-lee-*yen*-tay/cah-*lent*
Cold	Frío/Fred	*free*-yoh/fred
To rent	Alquilar/Lloguer	*all*-kee-lar/lyogg-*air*
Do you speak English?	¿Habla inglés?/Parla anglès?	ah-blah een-*glehs*/pahr-lah ahn-*glehs*
I speak a little Spanish/Catalan.	Hablo un poco de español/ Parlo una mica de Català	ah-bloh oon *poh*-koh deh es-pah-*nyoll*/pahr-loh *oo*-nah mee-kah *deh* kah-tah-*lahn*

ENGLISH	SPANISH/CATALAN	PRONUNCIATION
I don't understand.	**No entiendo/No comprenc**	noh ehn-*tyehn*-doh/ noh cohm-*prehnk*
What time is it?	**¿Qué hora es?/Quina hora és?**	keh *oh*-rah ehss/*kee*-nah *oh*-rah ehss
The check, please.	**La cuenta, por favor/ El compte, si us plau**	lah *kwehn*-tah pohr fah-*vohr*/ ehl *cohmp*-tah see yoos plow

2 NUMBERS

NUMBER	SPANISH	CATALAN
1	**uno** (*oo*-noh)	**un** (oon)
2	**dos** (dohs)	**dos** (dohs)
3	**tres** (trehs)	**tres** (trehs)
4	**cuatro** (*kwah*-troh)	**quatre** (*kwah*-trah)
5	**cinco** (*seen*-koh)	**cinc** (sink)
6	**seis** (says)	**sis** (sees)
7	**siete** (*syeh*-teh)	**set** (seht)
8	**ocho** (*oh*-choh)	**vuit** (vweet)
9	**nueve** (*nweh*-beh)	**nou** (noo)
10	**diez** (dyehs)	**deu** (*deh*-yoo)
11	**once** (*ohn*-seh)	**onze** (*ohn*-zah)
12	**doce** (*doh*-seh)	**dotze** (*doh*-tzah)
13	**trece** (*treh*-seh)	**tretze** (*treh*-tzah)
14	**catorce** (kah-*tohr*-seh)	**catorza** (kah-*tohr*-zah)
15	**quince** (*keen*-seh)	**quinza** (*keen*-zah)
16	**dieciséis** (dyeh-see-*says*)	**setze** (*seh*-tzah)
17	**diecisiete** (dyeh-see-*syeh*-teh)	**disset** (dee-*seht*)
18	**dieciocho** (dyeh-*syoh*-choh)	**divuit** (dee-*vweet*)
19	**diecinueve** (dyeh-see-*nweh*-beh)	**dinou** (dee-*noo*)
20	**veinte** (*bayn*-teh)	**vint** (vehnt)
30	**treinta** (*trayn*-tah)	**trenta** (*trehn*-tah)
40	**cuarenta** (kwah-*rehn*-tah)	**quaranta** (kwah-*rahn*-tah)
50	**cincuenta** (seen-*kwehn*-tah)	**cinquanta** (theen-*kwahn*-tah)
60	**sesenta** (seh-*sehn*-tah)	**seixanta** (see-*shahn*-tah)
70	**setenta** (seh-*tehn*-tah)	**setanta** (seh-*tahn*-tah)
80	**ochenta** (oh-*chehn*-tah)	**vuitanta** (vwee-*tahn*-tah)
90	**noventa** (noh-*behn*-tah)	**noranta** (noh-*rahn*-tah)
100	**cien** (*syehn*)	**cent** (sent)

INDEX

See also Accommodations and Restaurant indexes, below.